DATE DUE

THE LETTERS
OF LORD
CHESTERFIELD

VOL. FOUR

THE LETTERS OF
PHILIP DORMER STANHOPE

4TH EARL OF
CHESTERFIELD

EDITED, WITH AN INTRODUCTION, BY

BONAMY DOBRÉE

★

IN SIX VOLUMES

VOLUME FOUR

LETTERS: 1748-1751

1932

AMS PRESS · NEW YORK

Reprinted with the permission of Eyre & Spottiswoode
From the edition of 1932, London & New York
First AMS EDITION published 1968
Manufactured in the United States of America

Reprinted from a copy in the collections of the
Harvard College Library.

Library of Congress Catalogue Card Number: 68-59007

AMS PRESS, INC.
New York, N.Y. 10003

THE LETTERS OF
PHILIP DORMER STANHOPE
FOURTH EARL OF
CHESTERFIELD

Nos. 1580–1797

22nd August, 1748–15th November, 1751

IV. A

1748

(continued)

No. 1580

À Madame la Marquise de Monconseil

Ayez la bonté, je vous en conjure, Madame, de dire pour moi à Monsieur le Prince de Conti[1] tout ce qu'en ma place vous diriez vous-même; alors, avec l'esprit qu'il a il croira que j'en ai aussi beaucoup, car je prétends que vous lui souteniez, en même temps, que je vous l'ai écrit mot à mot. Je ne pense pas que vous soyez assez ladre pour me refuser ce petit présent, dont vous ne sentirez pas le besoin, et que je ne demande que de votre surabondance. Au reste, ajoutez, s'il vous plaît, que je me flatte de pouvoir en quelque temps d'ici lui envoyer des recrues de cette sort de chiens: on en avait négligé la race, depuis qu'il n'y avait plus de loups en Irlande, mais j'ai écrit à quelques-uns des mes ami de m'en faire faire.

Vos guerriers auront, du moins pour quelque temps, loisir de chasser, quoique pourtant il me semble que ce traité définitif ne finit point. Je ne sais à qui en est la faute, puisqu'il a paru assez clairement que vous voulez la paix, et qu'il est très sûr que nous la voulons aussi; et il me semble que dès que nous sommes d'accord, il faut bien que nos alliés respectifs marchent.

Sauriez-vous, Madame, qui l'on destine chez vous pour Ambassadeur ici? Nous supposons ici qu'il y a deux concurrents pour cette commission, Monsieur de Mirepoix, et Monsieur le Maréchal de Belleisle; pour moi je demande seulement qu'il soit de vos amis, et que par conséquent il pense comme moi sur votre sujet.

Je tâcherai de procurer pour Monsieur votre beau-frère les papiers qu'il souhaite, mais à présent tous ceux qui

---

[1]Louis François, Prince de Conti, born in 1717; a man of cultivated mind and literary taste.—M.

seraient en état de me les fournir sont encore en Flandres; et d'ailleurs, pour vous dire la vérité, je doute beaucoup de l'exactitude de nos militaires dans ces matières-là. Ils se battent bien, il en faut convenir; mais ils n'ont pas cette attention, et ce goût pour leur métier, qu'ont les vôtres.

Je vois bien que vous ne convenez pas de mes raisons au sujet de votre futur élève: cela n'est pas extraordinaire; mais ce qui l'est, c'est que je ne me rende point aux vôtres. Il faut en tout des gradations, et les petites villes le prépareront peu à peu pour les grandes. Paris fourmille actuellement d'Anglais, que je ne lui donnerais pas volontiers, ou pour modèles ou pour connaissances, mais qui seraient infailliblement l'un et l'autre s'il y allait présentement; au lieu que Turin achèvera de le dépayser, après quoi, n'étant plus d'aucun pays, il adoptera sûrement le vôtre. Adieu, Madame; je vous fais grâce d'une page entière, récompensez-moi en en ajoutant une à celle dont vous m'honorerez.

No. 1581

To his Son

(*Stanhope CLIX*)

London, 23 *August O.S.* 1748

DEAR BOY,

Your friend Mr. Eliot[1] has dined with me twice since I returned hither; and I can say with truth, that, while I had the Seals, I never examined or sifted a state-prisoner with so much care and curiosity as I did him. Nay, I did more; for, contrary to the laws of this country, I gave him, in some manner, the *question* ordinary and extraordinary; and I have infinite pleasure in telling you that the rack which I put him to did not extort from him one single word that was not such as I wished to hear of you. I heartily congratulate you upon such an advantageous testimony from

[1]Edward Eliot (1727-1804), for some years M.P. for St. Germans; created Lord Eliot in 1784.

so creditable a witness. *Laudari a laudato viro* is one of the greatest pleasures and honours a rational being can have; may you long continue to deserve it! Your aversion to drinking and your dislike to gaming, which Mr. Eliot assures me are both very strong, give me the greatest joy imaginable for your sake; as the former would ruin both your constitution and understanding, and the latter your fortune and character. Mr. Harte wrote me word some time ago, and Mr. Eliot confirms it now, that you employ your pin-money in a very different manner from that in which pin-money is commonly lavished; not in gewgaws and baubles, but in buying good and useful books. This is an excellent symptom, and gives me very good hopes. Go on thus, my dear boy, but for these two next years, and I ask no more. You must then make such a figure and such a fortune in the world as I wish you, and as I have taken all these pains to enable you to do. After that time, I allow you to be as idle as ever you please; because I am sure that you will not then please to be so at all. The ignorant and the weak only are idle; but those who have once acquired a good stock of knowledge always desire to increase it. Knowledge is like power in this respect, that those who have the most are most desirous of having more. It does not cloy by possession, but increases desire, which is the case of very few pleasures.

Upon receiving this congratulatory letter, and reading your own praises, I am sure that it must naturally occur to you how great a share of them you owe to Mr. Harte's care and attention; and, consequently, that your regard and affection for him must increase, if there be room for it, in proportion as you reap, which you do daily, the fruits of his labours.

I must not, however, conceal from you that there was one article in which your own witness, Mr. Eliot, faltered; for, upon my questioning him home as to your manner of speaking, he could not say that your utterance was either distinct or graceful. I have already said so much to you upon this point that I can add nothing. I will therefore only repeat

this truth, which is, That if you will not speak distinctly
and gracefully, nobody will desire to hear you.

I am glad to learn that Abbé Mably's *Droit Public de
l'Europe* makes a part of your evening amusements. It is a
very useful book, and gives a clear deduction of the affairs
of Europe, from the Treaty of Munster to this time. Pray
read it with attention, and with the proper maps, always
recurring to them for the several countries or towns yielded,
taken, or restored. Père Bougeant's third volume will give
you the best idea of the Treaty of Munster, and open to you
the several views of the belligerent and contracting parties;
and there never were greater than at that time. The House of
Austria, in the war immediately preceding that treaty, intended to make itself absolute in the Empire, and to over-
throw the rights of the respective states of it. The view of
France was, to weaken and dismember the House of Austria
to such a degree, as that it should no longer be a counterbalance to that of Bourbon. Sweden wanted possessions
upon the continent of Germany, not only to supply the
necessities of its own poor and barren country, but likewise
to hold the balance in the empire between the House of
Austria and the States. The House of Brandenburg wanted
to aggrandize itself by pilfering in the fire; changed sides
occasionally, and made a good bargain at last, for I think it
got, at the peace, nine or ten Bishops secularized. So that
we may date from the Treaty of Munster the decline of the
House of Austria, the great power of the House of Bourbon,
and the aggrandizement of that of Brandenburg; and I am
much mistaken if it stops where it is now.

Make my compliments to Lord Pulteney, to whom I
would have you be not only attentive but useful, by setting
him (in case he wants it) a good example of application and
temperance. I begin to believe that, as I shall be proud of
you, others will be proud too of imitating you. Those expectations of mine seem so well grounded, that my disappointment, and consequently my anger, will be so much

the greater if they fail; but, as things stand now, I am most affectionately and tenderly

Yours.

No. 1582

TO HIS SON

(Stanhope CLX)

London, 30 August O.S. 1748

DEAR BOY,

Your reflections upon the conduct of France, from the Treaty of Munster to this time, are very just; and I am very glad to find by them that you not only read, but that you think and reflect upon what you read. Many great readers load their memories without exercising their judgments, and make lumber-rooms of their heads, instead of furnishing them usefully: facts are heaped upon facts without order or distinction, and may justly be said to compose that

——Rudis indigestaque moles,
Quam dixere chaos.[1]

Go on, then, in the way of reading that you are in; take nothing for granted upon the bare authority of the author, but weigh and consider in your own mind the probability of the facts and the justness of the reflections. Consult different authors upon the same facts, and form your opinion upon the greater or lesser degree of probability arising from the whole, which, in my mind, is the utmost stretch of historical faith: certainty (I fear) not being to be found. When an historian pretends to give you the causes and motives of the events, compare those causes and motives with the characters and interests of the parties concerned, and judge for yourself whether they correspond or not. Consider whether you cannot assign others more pro-

[1]Adapted from Ovid, *Metam.* I. 7.

bable; and in that examination do not despise some very mean and trifling causes of the actions of great men; for so various and inconsistent is human nature, so strong and so changeable are our passions, so fluctuating are our wills, and so much are our minds influenced by the accidents of our bodies, that every man is more the man of the day than a regular and consequential character. The best have something bad, and something little; the worst have something good, and sometimes something great; for I do not believe that Velleius Paterculus (for the sake of saying a pretty thing) says of Scipio, *Qui nihil non laudandum aut fecit, aut dixit, aut sensit.* As for the reflections of historians, with which they think it necessary to interlard their histories, or at least to conclude their chapters (and which, in the French histories, are always introduced with a *tant il est vrai*, and in the English, *so true it is*), do not adopt them implicitly upon the credit of the author, but analyse them yourself, and judge whether they are true or not.

But, to return to the politics of France, from which I have digressed:—you have certainly made one farther reflection, of an advantage which France has, over and above its abilities in the cabinet, and the skill of its negotiators; which is (if I may use the expression) its *soleness*, continuity of riches and power within itself, and the nature of its government. Near twenty millions of people, and the ordinary revenue of above thirteen millions sterling a-year, are at the absolute disposal of the Crown. This is what no other Power in Europe can say; so that different Powers must now unite to make a balance against France; which union, though formed upon the principle of their common interest, can never be so intimate as to compose a machine so compact and simple as that of one great kingdom, directed by one will, and moved by one interest. The Allied Powers (as we have constantly seen) have, besides the common and declared object of their alliance, some separate and concealed view, to which they often sacrifice the general one;

which makes them, either directly or indirectly, pull different ways. Thus, the design upon Toulon failed in the year 1706, only from the secret view of the House of Austria upon Naples; which made the Court of Vienna, notwithstanding the representations of the other Allies to the contrary, send to Naples the 12,000 men that would have done the business at Toulon. In this last war, too, the same causes had the same effects: the Queen of Hungary, in secret, thought of nothing but recovering Silesia, and what she had lost in Italy; and therefore never sent half that quota, which she had promised and we paid for, into Flanders; but left that country to the Maritime Powers to defend as they could. The King of Sardinia's real object was Savona, and all the Riviera di Ponente; for which reason he concurred so lamely in the invasion of Provence: where the Queen of Hungary, likewise, did not send one-third of the force stipulated; engrossed as she was, by her oblique views upon the plunder of Genoa, and the recovery of Naples. Insomuch that the expedition into Provence, which would have distressed France to the greatest degree, and have caused a great detachment from their army in Flanders, failed, shamefully, for want of everything necessary for its success. Suppose, therefore, any four or five Powers, who, all together, shall be equal, or even a little superior, in riches and strength, to that one Power against which they are united; the advantage will still be greatly on the side of that single Power, because it is but one. The power and riches of Charles V. were, in themselves, certainly superior to those of Francis I.; and yet, upon the whole, he was not an overmatch for him. Charles V.'s dominions, great as they were, were scattered and remote from each other; their constitutions different; and, wherever he did not reside, disturbances arose: whereas the compactness of France made up the difference in the strength. This obvious reflection convinced me of the absurdity of the Treaty of Hanover, in 1725, between France and England, to which the Dutch afterwards acceded; for it was made upon the apprehensions, either real or pretended, that the marriage of Don Carlos with the eldest Archduchess, now Queen of Hungary, was settled in the Treaty of Vienna, of the same year, between Spain and the late Emperor, Charles VI.; which marriage, those consummate politicians said, would revive in Europe the exorbitant power of Charles V. I am sure I heartily wish it had; as, in that case, there had been, what there certainly is not now—one Power in Europe to counterbalance that of France; and then the Maritime Powers would, in reality, have held the balance of Europe in their hands. Even supposing that the Austrian Power would then have been an overmatch for that of France; which (by the way) is not clear; the weight of the Maritime Powers, then thrown into the scale of France, would infallibly have made the balance at least even. In which case, too, the moderate efforts of the Maritime Powers, on the side of France, would have been sufficient; whereas, now, they are obliged to exhaust and beggar themselves, and that too ineffectually, in hopes to support the shattered, beggared, and insufficient House of Austria.

This has been a long political dissertation, but I am informed that political subjects are your favourite ones; which I am glad of, considering your destination. You do well to get your materials all ready, before you begin your work. As you buy, and (I am told) read, books of this kind, I will point out two or three for your purchase and perusal; I am not sure that I have not mentioned them before; but that is no matter, if you have not got them. *Mémoires pour servir à l'Histoire du 17me Siècle* is a most useful book for you to recur to, for all the facts and chronology of that century; it is in four volumes octavo, and very correct and exact. If I do not mistake, I have formerly recommended to you *Les Mémoires du Cardinal de Retz*; however, if you have not yet read them, pray do, and with the attention they deserve. You will there find the best account of a very interesting period of the minority of Louis XIV. The characters are drawn short, but in a strong and masterly manner; and the political reflections are the only just and practical ones, that I ever saw in print; they are all well worth your transcribing. *Le Commerce des Anciens, par Monsieur Huet,*[1] *Evêque d'Avranche,* in one little volume octavo, is worth your perusal, as commerce is a very considerable part of political knowledge. I need not, I am sure, suggest to you, when you read the course of commerce, either of the ancients or of the moderns, to follow it upon your map; for there is no other way of remembering geography correctly, than by looking perpetually in the map for the places one reads of, even though one knows before, pretty nearly, where they are.

Adieu! As all the accounts which I receive of you grow better and better, so I grow more and more affectionately yours.

No. 1583. To the Duke of Newcastle

[*Endorsed*] 31 *August* [*O.S.*] 1748

To recommend Grevenkop[2] as a German translator.

(*Add. MSS.* 32,716, *f* 145)

No. 1584

To Solomon Dayrolles, Esq.

(*Mahon III. 284*)

London, 2 September O.S. 1748

DEAR DAYROLLES,

I received very safe, by Sir Matthew Decker, your long letter of the 23rd August O.S. in which you give me, what

[1] Bishop Pierre Daniel Huet (1630-1721), was tutor to the Dauphin, and edited sixty-two volumes of the Latin classics, known as the Delphine editions, and edited many theological treatises. His name is added to those of Bossuet and Fénelon as the great bishops under Louis XIV.

[2] Who had been his secretary at the Hague.

I had long desired, *l'Histoire amoureuse de la Haye*. As I am personally acquainted with most of the characters, I am convinced that all the facts are true; and I particularly foresee the ruin of one family, from the ill-conduct of the lady, which will not be endured when the honeymoon is over. I am now an unconcerned spectator of the transactions of the gallant, as well as of the busy, part of the world—the first from necessity, the latter from choice; so that I only inform myself of them for my amusement, without being any otherwise affected by them than as a citizen of the world. As such, I am glad that the horrors and devastations of war are now suspended; but as such, too, I am sorry to foresee the moment of their revival so near as I think I do; I mean the death of the King of Sweden.[1] If you will have my prophetic politics, here they are. I think that the Queen of Hungary has made all these difficulties of coming into the definite treaty, not in the expectation of succeeding in any one of them, but only with the intention of delaying the return of the Russians, and of forming a plan with Russia, and possibly *some Princes* of the Empire, for the recovery of Silesia. Upon this supposition, I expect that she will very soon come into the definitive treaty, in order to be able to employ all her force *elsewhere*. The death of the King of Sweden is, in my opinion, to be the signal for this northern war. The Czarina will not suffer the Prince-Successor to succeed. This Prince-Successor is brother-in-law to the King of Prussia, who has lately, in conjunction with France, guaranteed that succession to him. Reinforcements of Russians are marched into Finland; our Russians loiter in Germany; to me the conclusion is plain.

I am glad that my old friend Van der Duyn[2] has got a pension, but I am astonished at the size of it. A thousand pounds a year sounds like an English pension; *d'ailleurs*, he

---

[1] Which did not take place until two years later.

[2] A Lieutenant-General, brother to M. de Sgravemoer, one of the College of Nobles in the Province of Holland.—M.

has a regiment of guards and a government. This is certain, that the money will not stagnate in my General's strong box, but circulate very quickly through the Hague. *À propos* of the quick circulation of species, it is fixed that Lord Holderness is to be our Ambassador to the Republic, out of compliance to the Greffier and the Bentincks, who insisted upon it. He will, I think, do you no harm, if he does you no good; for, as business will certainly not be my Lord's pleasure, pleasure will, I presume, be my Lord's only business. This, too, without the least flattery to you, is certain, that when he shall be at the Hague, you will be *à juste titre, le beau ministre anglais.*

Adieu for this time; you shall hear from me more fully before it is long.

Yours.

No. 1585

To his Son

(Stanhope CLXI)

London, 5 *September O.S.* 1748

DEAR BOY,

I have received yours, with the inclosed German letter to Mr. Grevenkop, which he assures me is extremely well written, considering the little time that you have applied yourself to that language. As you have now got over the most difficult part, pray go on diligently, and make yourself absolutely master of the rest. Whoever does not entirely possess a language will never appear to advantage, or even equal to himself, either in speaking or writing it: his ideas are fettered, and seem imperfect or confused, if he is not master of all the words and phrases necessary to express them. I therefore desire that you will not fail writing a German letter once every fortnight to Mr. Grevenkop; which will make the writing of that language familiar to you: and, moreover, when you shall have left Germany and

1205

be arrived at Turin, I shall require you to write even to me
in German, that you may not forget with ease what you
have with difficulty learned. I likewise desire that, while
you are in Germany, you will take all opportunities of conversing in German, which is the only way of knowing that
or any language accurately. You will also desire your
German master to teach you the proper titles and super-
scriptions to be used to people of all ranks, which is a point
so material in Germany, that I have known many a letter
returned unopened because one title in twenty has been
omitted in the direction.

St. Thomas's day now draws near, when you are to leave
Saxony and go to Berlin; and I take it for granted, that if
anything is yet wanting to complete your knowledge of the
state of that Electorate, you will not fail to procure it before
you go away. I do not mean, as you will easily believe, the
number of churches, parishes, or towns; but I mean the
constitution, the revenues, the troops, and the trade of that
Electorate. A few questions sensibly asked of sensible
people will procure you the necessary informations; which
I desire you will enter in your little book. Berlin will be
entirely a new scene to you, and I look upon it in a manner
as your first step into the great world: take care that step be
not a false one, and that you do not stumble at the threshold.
You will there be in more company than you have yet been;
manners and attentions will therefore be more necessary.
Pleasing in company is the only way of being pleased in it
yourself. Sense and knowledge are the first and necessary
foundations for pleasing in company; but they will by no
means do alone, and they will never be perfectly welcome
if they are not accompanied with manners and attentions.
You will best acquire these by frequenting the companies
of people of fashion; but then you must resolve to acquire
them in those companies by proper care and observation;
for I have known people who, though they have frequented
good company all their lifetime, have done it in so inatten-

tive and unobserving a manner as to be never the better
for it, and to remain as disagreeable, as awkward, and as
vulgar, as if they had never seen any person of fashion.
When you go into good company (by good company is
meant the people of the first fashion of the place) observe
carefully their turn, their manners, their address, and conform your own to them. But this is not all, neither; go
deeper still; observe their characters, and pry, as far as you
can, into both their hearts and their heads. Seek for their
particular merit, their predominant passion, or their prevailing weakness; and you will then know what to bait your
hook with to catch them. Man is a composition of so many
and such various ingredients, that it requires both time and
care to analyse him; for, though we have all the same ingredients in our general composition, as reason, will,
passion, and appetites; yet the different proportions and
combinations of them in each individual, produce that infinite variety of characters which in some particular or other
distinguishes every individual from another. Reason ought
to direct the whole, but seldom does. And he who addresses himself singly to another man's reason, without
endeavouring to engage his heart in his interest also, is no
more likely to succeed, than a man who should apply only
to a King's nominal minister and neglect his favourite. I
will recommend to your attentive perusal, now you are going into the world, two books, which will let you as much
into the characters of men as books can do. I mean *Les
Réflexions Morales de Monsieur de la Rochefoucauld*, and *Les
Caractères de La Bruyère*: but remember at the same time
that I only recommend them to you as the best general
maps to assist you in your journey, and not as marking out
every particular turning and winding that you will meet
with. There, your own sagacity and observation must come
to their aid. La Rochefoucauld is I know blamed, but I
think without reason, for deriving all our actions from the
source of self-love. For my own part, I see a great deal of

truth and no harm at all in that opinion. It is certain that
we seek our own happiness in everything we do; and it is
as certain that we can only find it in doing well, and in con-
forming all our actions to the rule of right reason, which is
the great law of nature. It is only a mistaken self-love that
is a blameable motive, when we take the immediate and indiscriminate gratification of a passion or appetite for real happiness. But am I blameable if I do a good action, upon account
of the happiness which that honest consciousness will give me?
Surely not. On the contrary, that pleasing consciousness is
a proof of my virtue. The reflection which is the most
censured in Monsieur de la Rochefoucauld's book, as a very
ill-natured one, is this: *On trouve dans le malheur de son
meilleur ami, quelque chose qui ne déplaît pas.* And why not?
Why may I not feel a very tender and real concern for the
misfortune of my friend, and yet at the same time feel a pleasing consciousness of having discharged my duty to him, by
comforting and assisting him to the utmost of my power in
that misfortune? Give me but virtuous actions, and I will
not quibble and chicane about the motives. And I will give
anybody their choice of these two truths, which amount to
the same thing: He who loves himself best is the honestest
man; or, The honestest man loves himself best.

The characters of La Bruyère are pictures from the life;
most of them finely drawn, and highly coloured. Furnish
your mind with them first; and when you meet with their
likeness, as you will every day, they will strike you the
more. You will compare every feature with the original;
and both will reciprocally help you to discover the beauties
and the blemishes.

As women are a considerable, or at least a pretty numerous part, of company; and as their suffrages go a great way
towards establishing a man's character in the fashionable
part of the world (which is of great importance to the
fortune and figure he proposes to make in it), it is necessary
to please them. I will therefore, upon this subject, let you

into certain *arcana*, that will be very useful for you to know, but which you must, with the utmost care, conceal, and never seem to know. Women, then, are only children of a larger growth;[1] they have an entertaining tattle and some-times wit; but for solid, reasoning good-sense, I never in my life knew one that had it, or who reasoned or acted con-sequentially for four-and-twenty hours together. Some little passion or humour always breaks in upon their best resolutions. Their beauty neglected or controverted, their age increased, or their supposed understandings depreciated, instantly kindles their little passions, and overturns any system of consequential conduct, that in their most reasonable moments they might have been capable of forming. A man of sense only trifles with them, plays with them, humours and flatters them, as he does with a sprightly, forward child; but he neither consults them about, nor trusts them with, serious matters; though he often makes them believe that he does both; which is the thing in the world that they are proud of; for they love mightily to be dabbling in business (which, by the way, they always spoil); and being justly distrustful that men in general look upon them in a trifling light, they almost adore that man who talks more seriously to them, and who seems to consult and trust them; I say, who seems, for weak men really do, but wise ones only seem to do it. No flattery is either too high or too low for them. They will greedily swallow the highest, and gratefully accept of the lowest; and you may safely flatter any woman, from her understanding down to the exquisite taste of her fan. Women, who are either indisputably beau-tiful, or indisputably ugly, are best flattered upon the score of their understandings; but those who are in a state of mediocrity, are best flattered upon their beauty, or at least their graces; for every woman who is not absolutely ugly, thinks herself handsome; but, not hearing often that she is so, is the more grateful and the more obliged to the few

---

[1]'Men are but children of a larger growth.' Dryden, *All for Love*, iv. 1.

who tell her so; whereas a decided and conscious beauty looks upon every tribute paid to her beauty, only as her due; but wants to shine, and to be considered on the side of her understanding; and a woman who is ugly enough to know that she is so, knows that she has nothing left for her but her understanding, which is consequently (and probably in more senses than one) her weak side. But these are secrets which you must keep inviolably, if you would not, like Orpheus, be torn to pieces by the whole sex; on the contrary, a man who thinks of living in the great world, must be gallant, polite, and attentive to please the women. They have, from the weakness of men, more or less influence in all Courts; they absolutely stamp every man's character in the *beau monde*, and make it either current, or cry it down, and stop it in payments. It is, therefore, absolutely necessary to manage, please, and flatter them; and never to discover the least marks of contempt, which is what they never forgive; but in this they are not singular, for it is the same with men; who will much sooner forgive an injustice than an insult. Every man is not ambitious, or covetous, or passionate; but every man has pride enough in his composition to feel and resent the least slight and contempt. Remember, therefore, most carefully to conceal your contempt, however just, wherever you would not make an implacable enemy. Men are much more unwilling to have their weaknesses and their imperfections known, than their crimes; and, if you hint to a man that you think him silly, ignorant, or even ill-bred or awkward, he will hate you more, and longer, than if you tell him plainly that you think him a rogue. Never yield to that temptation, which to most young men is very strong, of exposing other people's weaknesses and infirmities, for the sake either of diverting the company, or of showing your own superiority. You may get the laugh on your side by it, for the present; but you will make enemies by it for ever; and even those who laugh with you then will, upon reflection, fear, and consequently hate you; besides that, it is ill-natured, and a good heart desires rather to conceal than expose other people's weaknesses or misfortunes. If you have wit, use it to please, and not to hurt: you may shine like the sun in the temperate zones, without scorching. Here it is wished for: under the line it is dreaded.

These are some of the hints which my long experience in the great world enables me to give you; and which, if you attend to them, may prove useful to you in your journey through it. I wish it may be a prosperous one; at least, I am sure that it must be your own fault if it is not.

Make my compliments to Mr. Harte, who, I am very sorry to hear, is not well. I hope by this time he is recovered.

Adieu!

No. 1586

À Madame la Marquise de Monconseil

(*Maty I. xxix*)

À Londres, ce 5 septembre V.S. 1748

Oui vraiment, Madame, j'ai un boudoir, mais il a un défaut, c'est qu'il est si gai et si riant, qu'on n'y pourra jamais bouder quand on y sera seul: c'est un défaut aimable pour qui aime la bouderie aussi peu que moi, mais en tout cas, il est facile de le réparer, en y recevant les gens maussades, fâcheux, et désagréables, que de temps en temps on est obligé d'essuyer. Quand on m'annoncera un animal de la sorte, je courrai d'abord à mon boudoir, comme à mon sanctuaire, l'y recevoir; là il aura moins de prise sur moi, car, de la façon que nous sommes faits, les objets extérieurs ne sont nullement indifférents par rapport à l'esprit, et tel sot qui m'accablerait dans une chambre lugubre, pourra peut-être m'amuser dans un cabinet orné et riant. De tout ceci il résulte, que la véritable étymologie de boudoir est (pour parler Latin) *a non boudare* comme *lucus* un bois *a non lucendo*, c'est-à-dire qu'on ne boude point dans l'un, et qu'on ne voit goutte dans l'autre: au reste si ce trait de profonde érudition vous embarrasse, l'Abbé Sallier, que je salue de tout mon cœur, vous l'expliquera, et vous en fera sentir toute la solidité. Voulez-vous la description, aussi bien que l'étymologie, de ce boudoir? La voici. La boisure et le plafond sont d'un beau bleu, avec beaucoup de sculptures et de dorures; les tapisseries et les chaises sont d'un ouvrage à fleurs au petit-point, d'un dessein magnifique sur un fond blanc; par-dessus la cheminée, qui est de *Giallo di Sienna*, force glaces, sculptures, dorures, et au milieu le portrait d'une très belle femme, peint par la Rosalba.[1] Je vous ferais la description du reste de la maison, mais comme le second Pline a échoué en voulant donner la description de la sienne, où l'on n'entend absolument rien, je n'ai pas pu espérer d'y pouvoir réussir, et vous savez qu'il est de la sagesse de ne pas tenter des choses au-dessus de ses forces.

Il faut que vos Cerbères de la douane soient bien plus inexorables que les nôtres, car j'ai bien instruit mon marchand de ne se pas laisser prendre les étoffes, faute d'un certain compliment, auquel ces Messieurs sont d'ordinaire très sensibles. Il faut espérer que Monsieur votre Contrôleur aura la politesse de relâcher des prisonniers qui doivent vous toucher de si près.

Dites-moi de grâce, Madame, pourquoi votre Parlement de Paris a tant sévi contre un livre que je viens de lire, intitulé *Les Mœurs*. Comme j'avais lu l'arrêt, avant que d'avoir lu le livre, je m'attendais à trouver dans ce dernier toutes sortes d'impiétés, et de relâchement; au lieu de quoi j'y ai trouvé la religion et la loi naturelle fortement établies et inculquées, une morale même rigoureuse, et tous les devoirs de l'homme bien constatés. Il est vrai que l'auteur

---

[1]This lady, a native of Venice, or as others say Vicenza, distinguished herself by her works in crayons. *Ses tableaux*, says M. Artaud, *furent recherchés dans toute l'Europe*. She died in 1757, having lost her sight two years before.—M. Philarète Chasles gives his opinion, without any of the support needed for so wild a statement, that this was a portrait of Mlle. du Bouchet, Philip's mother.

n'adopte aucune secte particulière, ni culte extérieur en matière de religion, aussi n'était-ce pas de son ressort en traitant des mœurs. Je sens bien que les ecclésiastiques de toutes les religions en seront offensés, mais est-ce une raison pour que le Parlement le soit aussi? En vérité je trouve beaucoup de bon dans ce livre, il y a du bon sens, de l'esprit et des portraits bien caractérisés; il est vrai que quelquefois les raisonnements sont plus jolis que forts, et il semble que l'auteur aime souvent mieux orner que pousser son argument. Soupçonne-t-on à Paris qui c'est? pour moi, si je voulais me livrer à des conjectures, j'en soupçonnerais l'auteur des Lettres Persanes.[1]

Monsieur le Prince de Conti, croit-il que j'ai l'esprit délicat et aimable? C'est-à-dire, Madame, vous êtes-vous acquittée fidèlement de ma commission auprès de lui? En ce cas, que les Rois seraient heureux d'être servis comme moi, puisqu'alors il n'y aurait peut-être qu'une vingtaine de ceux qui les approchent de plus près, qui sauraient qu'ils n'ont point d'esprit!

À propos, le temps est passé sans que la métamorphose que je souhaitais tant se soit faite,[2] et à présent j'en désespère, car dès que les prophéties ne s'accomplissent pas à point nommé, c'en est fait. Au moins j'ai gagné par l'imposture, et ce que vous me dites sur ce sujet vaut presque la métamorphose même, car je prends tout à la lettre, et je me donne bien garde d'approfondir cette matière. On est trop heureux d'être trompé, ou de se tromper soi-même, agréablement: je voudrais bien que vous puissiez m'avoir une pareille obligation, mais le moyen?—vous ne me tiendriez aucun compte de vérités reconnues, et pourtant on n'y peut rien ajouter; vous donnez beaucoup à penser, mais vous ne laissez rien à dire.

[1]Namely, Montesquieu. Chesterfield was mistaken in supposing he was the author, as *Les Mœurs* was written by M. Toussaint, who had to fly the country from the wrath of the clergy, and take refuge in Prussia.

[2]See the conclusion of the letter to Madame Monconseil, of 30th July.

No. 1587

To his Son

(Stanhope CLXII)

London, 13 *September O.S.* 1748

Dear Boy,

I have more than once recommended to you the Memoirs of the Cardinal de Retz, and to attend particularly to the political reflections interspersed in that excellent work. I will now preach a little upon two or three of those texts.

In the disturbances at Paris, Monsieur de Beaufort, who was a very popular, though a very weak man, was the Cardinal's tool with the populace. Proud of his popularity, he was always for assembling the people of Paris together, thinking that he made a great figure at the head of them. The Cardinal, who was factious enough, was wise enough, at the same time, to avoid gathering the people together except when there was occasion, and when he had something particular for them to do. However, he could not always check Monsieur de Beaufort, who, having assembled them once very unnecessarily, and without any determined object, they ran riot, would not be kept within bounds by their leaders, and did their cause a great deal of harm; upon which the Cardinal observes, most judiciously, *Que Monsieur de Beaufort ne savait pas, que qui assemble le peuple, l'émeut.* It is certain that great numbers of people, met together, animate each other, and will do something, either good or bad, but oftener bad; and the respective individuals, who were separately very quiet, when met together in numbers, grow tumultuous as a body, and ripe for any mischief that may be pointed out to them by the leaders; and, if their leaders have no business for them, they will find some for themselves. The demagogues, or leaders of popular factions, should, therefore, be very careful not to assemble the people unnecessarily, and without a settled and well-considered object; besides that, by making those popular assemblies too frequent, they make them likewise too familiar, and consequently, less respected by their enemies. Observe any meetings of people, and you will always find their eagerness and impetuosity rise or fall in proportion to their numbers; when the numbers are very great, all sense and reason seem to subside, and one sudden frenzy to seize on all, even the coolest of them.

Another very just observation of the Cardinal's is, That the things which happen in our own times, and which we see ourselves, do not surprise us near so much as the things which we read of in times past, though not in the least more extraordinary; and adds, that he is persuaded that, when Caligula made his horse a Consul, the people of Rome, at that time, were not greatly surprised at it, having necessarily been in some degree prepared for it, by an insensible gradation of extravagancies from the same quarter. This is so true, that we read every day, with astonishment, things which we see every day without surprise. We wonder at the intrepidity of a Leonidas, a Codrus, and a Curtius, and are not the least surprised to hear of a sea-captain who has blown up his ship, his crew, and himself, that they might not fall into the hands of the enemies of his country. I cannot help reading of Porsenna and Regulus with surprise and reverence; and yet I remember that I saw, without either, the execution of Shepherd, a boy of eighteen years old, who intended to shoot the late King, and who would have been pardoned, if he would have expressed the least sorrow for his intended crime; but, on the contrary, he declared that if he was pardoned he would attempt it again, that he thought it a duty which he owed his country, and that he died with pleasure for having endeavoured to perform it.[1] Reason equals Shepherd to Regulus; but prejudice, and the recency

[1] James Shepherd, apprentice to a coach-painter, was executed for high treason at Tyburn on 17th March, 1718, on the evidence of a clergyman named Leake, whom he had informed of his intention by letter.

of the fact, make Shepherd a common malefactor, and Regulus a hero.

Examine carefully, and re-consider all your notions of things; analyse them, and discover their component parts and see if habit and prejudice are not the principal ones; weigh the matter, upon which you are to form your opinion, in the equal and impartial scales of reason. It is not to be conceived how many people, capable of reasoning if they would, live and die in a thousand errors, from laziness; they would rather adopt the prejudices of others, than give themselves the trouble of forming opinions of their own. They say things, at first, because other people have said them, and then they persist in them, because they have said them themselves.

The last observation that I shall now mention of the Cardinal's is: That a secret is more easily kept by a good many people than one commonly imagines. By this he means a secret of importance, among people interested in the keeping of it. And it is certain that people of business know the importance of secrecy, and will observe it, where they are concerned in the event. And the Cardinal does not suppose that anybody is silly enough to tell a secret merely from the desire of telling it, to anyone that is not some way or other interested in the keeping of it, and concerned in the event. To go and tell any friend, wife, or mistress, any secret with which they have nothing to do, is discovering to them such an unretentive weakness, as must convince them that you will tell it to twenty others, and, consequently, that they may reveal it without the risk of being discovered. But a secret properly communicated, only to those who are to be concerned in the thing in question, will probably be kept by them, though they should be a good many. Little secrets are commonly told again, but great ones generally kept.

Adieu!

No. 1588

TO THE REV. DR. MADDEN

(Maty App. XIV)

London, 15 September 1748

SIR,

I am very sensibly affected with the late mark which you have given me of your remembrance and friendship. I assure you that I deserve them both, as far as the truest regard for your parts and merit can entitle me to them.

Your Poem, of which I have read the first Canto with equal pleasure and attention, has (without any compliment to you) a great deal of wit and invention in it: the characters are perfectly well preserved; and the moral, which it is easy to foresee from the first Canto, is excellent. You cannot doubt of my being proud to have such a performance addressed to me; and I should be prouder of it still, if the author's name were to appear; but as your friend, I must confess, that I think you in the right to conceal it; for, though the moral be good, yet, as the propriety of characters has obliged you to put some warm expressions in the mouths of Venus and Cupid, some silly or malicious people might lay hold of them, and quote them to your disadvantage. As to the Dedication, I must tell you very sincerely, and without the least false modesty, that I heartily wish you would lower it: the honest warmth of your friendship makes you view me in a more partial light than other people do, or, upon my word, than I do myself. The few light, trifling things that I have accidentally scribbled in my youth, in the cheerfulness of company, or sometimes (it may be) inspired by wine, do by no means entitle me to the compliments which you make me as an author; and my own vanity is so far from deceiving me upon that subject, that I repent of what I have shown, and only value myself upon what I have had the prudence to burn.

Though my cares for Ireland are ceased, you do me but justice in being convinced that my wishes for the prosperity of that country will cease but with my life. The best wish that I could form for it would be, that half its inhabitants were like you; nay, I would compound for twenty who would, like you, devote their thoughts, their time, and a proportionable share of their fortunes, to the public good. Your late considerable benefaction to Dublin College, will be a perpetual monument of your public spirit, and your love of mankind. How greatly would arts and sciences flourish in Ireland if those who are much better able than you are, would contribute but half as much as you do to their improvement! You shine, indeed, the more for it; but I know you well enough to know, that you would rather *prodesse quam conspici.* The Irish may be a rich and happy people, *bona si sua norint.* Free from the heavy load of debts and taxes under which the English groan, as fit for arts, sciences, industry and labour, as any people in the world, they might, notwithstanding some hard restraints which England, by a mistaken policy, has laid them under, push several branches of trade to great perfection and profit, and not only supply themselves with everything they want, but other nations, too, with many things. But jobs and claret engross and ruin the people of fashion, and the ordinary people (as is usual in every country) imitate them in little momentary and mistaken views of present profit, and in whisky. As to the incorporating by Charter the Dublin Society, I see many advantages that might arise from it; but I must at the same time own, that I foresee some dangers too.[1] Jobs have hitherto always accompanied Charters, however they may have been calculated to prevent them. The Dublin Society has hitherto gone on extremely well, and done infinite good: why? Because, that not being a permanent, incorporated Society, and having no employments to dispose of, and depending only for their existence

[1] A charter was obtained in 1750, which instituted it the Royal Dublin Society.

1218

on their own good behaviour, it was not a theatre for job-bers to show their skill upon; but when once established by Charter, the very advantages which are expected from, and which, I believe, will attend that Charter, I fear may prove fatal. It may then become an object of party, and Parlia-mentary views (for you know how low they stoop); in which case it will become subservient to the worst instead of the best designs. Remember the Linen Board, where the paltry dividend of a little flax-seed was become the seed of jobs, which indeed produced one hundred fold. However, I submit my fears to your hopes; and will do all that I can to promote that Charter which you, who I am sure have considered it in every light, seem so desirous of. Mr. Mac-aulay, who is now here, has brought over the rough draft of a Charter, which he and I are to meet and consider of next week. I hope your worthy fellow-labourers, and my worthy friends, the Bishop of Meath and Mr. Prior, are well. May you long be so, for the good of mankind, and for the particular satisfaction of

Your most sincere friend and faithful servant.

I hope you will send me the other Cantos by proper opportunities, for I long to see them.

No. 1589

TO ALDERMAN FAULKNER[1]

(Add MSS. Egerton 201, f 11)

London, 17 September 1748

MY GOOD FRIEND,

I am much obliged to you for the marks of your remembrance and friendship which you send me from time to time. The Sermon of Robert Hort, A.M., is certainly of

---

[1]Alderman George Faulkner (1699-1775) was a famous printer and publisher in Dublin. He was a correspondent of Swift and Berkeley, as well as of Chester-field.

a very singular nature; but as you do not give me your opinion upon it, I shall not give you mine. Possibly, indeed, we have neither of us formed one. Thus much only I will say, and that very sincerely; that if Mr. Hort is in the right, I heartily wish that you may live to see and feel, that general *Restoration* and *Perfection of all things*; as by the one you will recover your natural leg; and by the other, the letter of your Journal will be as black as ink, and the paper as white as snow, which I reckon make up the perfection of a Journal. But whatever may be the state of printing in those days, however black your letter, however white your paper, I observe with concern, that you are not likely to have Mr. Hort's custom or interest, his sermon being printed by S. Powell.[1] In the meantime, I hope business goes on well, and that you print and sell a great number of books, whether they are read or not. If they become but fashionable furniture, it will serve your purpose as well, or it may be better; for if people bought no more books than they intended to read, and no more swords than they intended to use, the two worst trades in Europe would be a bookseller's and a sword-cutler's; but, luckily for both, they are reckoned genteel ornaments.

Here has been lately published the first volume of a History of the Popes, by one Mr. Bower, who was a Jesuit at Rome. It is extremely well wrote, and I believe it would be very well worth your while to print an octavo edition of it at Dublin; for our edition here is a large quarto, and consequently, an expensive one. When finished, it will be four quartos. As yet, no lesser edition has appeared here. In this, or any other undertaking, I assure you, that nobody can wish you more sincerely well, than

Your friend and servant.

As I know you often see the Chief Baron,[2] whom I esteem and honour much, pray make him my compliments.

[1]Another Dublin printer.   [2]John Bowes.

No. 1590

TO HIS SON

(Stanhope CLXIII)

London, 20 September O.S. 1748

DEAR BOY,

I wait with impatience for your accurate history of the *Chevaliers Porte Epées,* which you promised me in your last, and which I take to be the forerunner of a larger work, that you intend to give the public, containing a general account of all the Religious and Military Orders of Europe. Seriously; you will do well to have a general notion of all those Orders, ancient and modern; both as they are frequently the subjects of conversation, and as they are more or less interwoven with the histories of those times. Witness the Teutonic Order, which, as soon as it gained strength, began its unjust depredations in Germany, and acquired such considerable possessions there; and the Order of Malta also, which continues to this day its piracies upon the infidels. Besides, one can go into no company in Germany, without running against *Monsieur le Chevalier,* or *Monsieur le Commandeur de l'Ordre Teutonique.* It is the same in all the other parts of Europe, with regard to the Order of Malta; where you never go into company without meeting two or three *Chevaliers* or *Commandeurs,* who talk of their *preuves,* their *langues,* their *caravanes,* etc., of all which things I am sure you would not willingly be ignorant. On the other hand, I do not mean that you should have a profound and minute knowledge of these matters, which are of a nature that a general knowledge of them is fully sufficient. I would not recommend to you to read Abbé Vertot's History of the Order of Malta, in four quarto volumes; that would be employing a great deal of good time very ill. But I would have you know the foundations, the objects, the *insignia,* and the short general history of them all.

As for the ancient religious military Orders, which were chiefly founded in the eleventh and twelfth centuries, such as Malta, the Teutonic, the Knights Templars, etc., the injustice and the wickedness of those establishments cannot, I am sure, have escaped your observation. Their pious object was, to take away by force other people's property; and to massacre the proprietors themselves, if they refused to give up that property, and adopt the opinion of these invaders. What right or pretence had these confederated Christians of Europe to the Holy Land? Let them produce their grant of it in the Bible. Will they say that the Saracens had possessed themselves of it by force? and that, consequently, they had the same right. Is it lawful then to steal goods, because they were stolen before? Surely not. The truth is, that the wickedness of many, and the weakness of more, in those ages of ignorance and superstition, concurred to form those flagitious conspiracies against the lives and properties of unoffending people. The Pope sanctified the villainy, and annexed the pardon of sins to the perpetration of it. This gave rise to the Croisadoes, and carried such swarms of people from Europe to the conquests of the Holy Land. Peter the Hermit, an active and ambitious priest, by his indefatigable pains was the immediate author of the first Croisade. Kings, princes, all professions and characters united, from different motives, in this great undertaking, as every sentiment, except true religion and morality invited to it. The ambitious hoped for kingdoms; the greedy and the necessitous for plunder; and some were enthusiasts enough to hope for salvation, by the destruction of a considerable number of their fellow-creatures, who had done them no injury. I cannot omit, upon this occasion, telling you that the eastern Emperors at Constantinople (who, as Christians, were obliged at least to seem to favour these expeditions), seeing the immense numbers of the *croisés*, and fearing that the Western Empire might have some mind to the Eastern Empire too, if it succeeded against the infidels, as *l'appétit vient en mangeant*; these eastern Emperors, very honestly, poisoned the waters where the *croisés* were to pass, and so destroyed infinite numbers of them.

The later Orders of knighthood—such as the Garter in England; the Elephant in Denmark; the Golden Fleece in Burgundy; the St. Esprit, St. Michael, St. Louis, and St. Lazare, in France, etc., are of a very different nature and institution. They were either the invitations to, or the rewards of brave actions in fair war; and are now rather the decorations of the favour of the prince, than the proofs of the merit of the subject. However, they are worth your inquiries to a certain degree; and conversation will give you frequent opportunities for them. Wherever you are, I would advise you to inquire into the respective Orders of that country, and to write down a short account of them. For example; while you are in Saxony, get an account of *l'Aigle Blanc*, and of what other Orders there may be, either Polish or Saxon; and, when you shall be at Berlin, inform yourself of the three Orders, *l'Aigle Noir, la Générosité, et le Vrai Mérite*, which are the only ones that I know of there. But whenever you meet with straggling ribands and stars, as you will with a thousand in Germany, do not fail to inquire what they are, and to take a minute of them in your memorandum book; for it is a sort of knowledge that costs little to acquire, and yet is of some use. Young people have frequently an incuriousness about them, arising either from laziness, or a contempt of the object, which deprives them of several such little parts of knowledge that they afterwards wish they had acquired. If you will put conversation to profit, great knowledge may be gained by it; and is it not better (since it is full as easy) to turn it upon useful than upon useless subjects? People always talk best upon what they know most; and it is both pleasing them, and improving one's self, to put them upon that subject. With people of a particular profession, or of a distinguished eminency in any branch of learning, one is not at a loss; but with those, whether men or women, who properly constitute what is called the *beau monde*, one must not choose deep subjects, nor hope to get any knowledge above that of orders, ranks, families, and court anecdotes; which are therefore the proper (and not altogether useless) subjects of that kind of conversation. Women, especially, are to be talked to, as below men, and above children. If you talk to them too deep, you only confound them, and lose your own labour; if you talk to them too frivolously, they perceive and resent the contempt. The proper tone for them is, what the French call the *entregent*, and is, in truth, the polite jargon of good company. Thus, if you are a good chemist, you may extract something out of everything.

A propos of the *beau monde*; I must again and again recommend the Graces to you. There is no doing without them in that world; and to make a good figure in that world is a great step towards making one in the world of business, particularly that part of it for which you are destined. An ungraceful manner of speaking, awkward motions, and a disagreeable address, are great clogs to the ablest man of business; as the opposite qualifications are of infinite advantage to him. I am therefore very glad that you learn to dance, since I am told there is a very good dancing-master at Leipsig. I would have you dance a minuet very well— not so much for the sake of the minuet itself (though that, if danced at all, ought to be danced well), as that it will give you an habitual genteel carriage, and manner of presenting yourself.

Since I am upon little things, I must mention another, which, though little enough in itself, yet, as it occurs at least once in every day, deserves some attention: I mean carving. Do you use yourself to carve *adroitly* and genteely, without hacking half an hour across a bone, without bespattering the company with the sauce, and without overturning the glasses into your neighbours' pockets? These awkwardnesses are extremely disagreeable, and, if often repeated, bring ridicule. They are very easily avoided by a little attention and use.

How trifling soever these things may seem, or really be, in themselves, they are no longer so when above half the world thinks them otherwise; and, as I would have you *omnibus ornatum—excellere rebus*, I think nothing above or below my pointing out to you, or your excelling in. You have the means of doing it, and time before you to make use of them. Take my word for it, I ask nothing now but what you will, twenty years hence, most heartily wish that you had done. Attention to all these things for the next two or three years will save you infinite trouble and endless regrets hereafter. May you, in the whole course of your life, have no reason for any one just regret! Adieu!

Your Dresden china is arrived, and I have sent it to your Mamma.

No. 1591

Á MADAME LA MARQUISE DE MONCONSEIL

(Maty I. xxx)

À Londres, ce 22 septembre V.S. 1748

C'est que je ne sais plus comment m'y prendre avec vous, Madame, vous rejettez les vérités les plus simples parcequ'elles vous sont avantageuses. Pour les compliments, nous les avions déjà bannis de notre commerce depuis long-temps; et si vous voulez seulement entendre parler de vos défauts, il faut vous adresser à quelqu'un qui vous en connaisse. Il est vrai qu'on s'entend dire plus volontiers les choses qu'on voudrait mériter, ou que, par illusion, on croit mériter, que celles qu'on mérite réellement. Un ancien,[1] je ne sais plus lequel, disait à Trajan; *la flatterie est épuisée depuis longtemps envers vos prédécesseurs; tout ce qui*

---

[1]Pliny, the younger:—'Simul cum jampridem novitas omnis adulatione consumpta sit, non alius erga te novus honor superest, quam si aliquando de te tacere audeamus.'—*Panegyr.* lv. 3.

nous reste donc à votre égard, c'est d'oser nous taire. Voilà donc le parti que je prends.

Que je languis pour vos bras, Madame! L'expression paraît vive et tendre; il faut l'expliquer, en cas qu'on ouvre la lettre. Je languis donc pour ces bras de porcelaine, que vous avez la bonté de m'envoyer par le retour de mon marchand, qui, depuis qu'il est au monde, n'a jamais été attendu avec une impatience égale à la mienne. Je m'en fie bien à votre goût, et je ne m'embarrasse pas de la couleur; j'ai déjà toutes les couleurs du monde dans ce boudoir, de façon que vos bras n'y peuvent pas être déplacés, de quelque couleur qu'ils soient. Je vous en remercierai donc, Madame, de tout mon cœur, et tout simplement. Voiture n'aurait pas sitôt quitté un si beau sujet pour son esprit, ni le Chevalier d'Her———[1] pour ses épigrammes.

Votre homme à feu est employé dans le grand feu d'artifice qu'on doit tirer ici au sujet de la conclusion de la paix; je crains seulement que sa poudre ne se moisisse, et que ses préparatifs ne se gâtent, avant que le traité définitif qui ne finit point ne se finisse. Je serais charmé de rendre service à votre artiste, mais vous me pardonnerez, j'en suis sûr, si en entrant d'abord dans ma nouvelle maison, je ne lui donne pas l'occasion de la faire sauter ou brûler, ou d'en enfumer même les meubles; suites ordinaires du voisinage d'un feu d'artifice. Pour votre compositeur Adolphati, je vous dirai naturellement que je n'augure rien d'avantageux pour lui dans ce pays; l'opéra, que nous devons avoir cet hiver, étant entièrement sous la direction d'un seul *impresario* qui vient d'Italie, et qui mène avec lui, et sa troupe, et son compositeur, de sorte que de ce côté là il n'y a pas d'ouverture pour notre *virtuoso*.[2] Du côté des oratorios, des motets, et de cette sorte de musique, il y en a encore moins; Handel, qui sans contredit est le plus grand compositeur de l'Europe,

---

[1] The *Lettres du Chevalier d'Her——* were written by Fontenelle in early youth, but never owned by him.—See Lord Chesterfield's Letters to his Son, of 24th December 1750.—M.

[2] See the letter of 1st May, 1749.

en ayant tant donné qu'on en est las, qu'on n'y va plus. Il suffit qu'il me vienne de votre part pour que je fasse tous mes efforts pour le servir; mais franchement je crains que ce ne soit inutilement.

Bon soir, Madame; aussi la longueur de cette lettre pourra bien y contribuer.

No. 1592

To Solomon Dayrolles, Esq.

(Mahon III. 295)

London, 23 *September O.S.* 1748

Dear Dayrolles,

I thank you for your promise of a second tome of your *Histoire Amoureuse*, when an occasion shall present itself; for, upon my word, Petronius[1] nor Bussy[2] could not write a better than your first. The winter, which will assemble everybody at the Hague, will probably furnish you materials.

Your towns and provinces seem to be running a race to the goal of slavery; and they put me in mind of the nobles and commons in Denmark, who, in the last century, strove which should get first rid of their liberties. Your Stadtholder must have great self-denial, or great timidity, if he is not very soon as absolute over the Seven Provinces as Louis XV. is in France. For my own part, not being a Dutchman, and having no thoughts of living in Holland, I have no objection to this new-erected despotism; which, for aught I know, may make the Seven Provinces a better barrier for us against France than they were before, as an absolute government is more military, and generally in a better state of defence, than a free one. And upon this principle, were I to cut and carve out Europe to my mind, I would add the other ten provinces to the present seven, and so revive the

[1]In the *Satyricon.*

[2]Roger de Rabutin, Comte de Bussy (1618-1693) who wrote a satire upon the gallantries of the Court of Louis XIV, *Histoire Amoureuse des Gaules.* It ruined him.

Duchy of Burgundy[1]; which, I am sure, would make a better barrier against France, than ever those ten provinces, in the hands of the House of Austria, will prove. *A propos* of Austria, the conjectures which I have formed these four months, and which I lately hinted to you, begin, I think to be verified. The Russians stay in Germany, which is the first point; they will certainly somehow or other be juggled out of our pay and service, which is the second point; and then the third is pretty plain. *Ce n'est pas mon affaire.* Let the northern bears worry each other as much as they please, the gazettes will be but the more entertaining, and amuse me the more, *dans mon petit boudoir;* which (by the way) will be the prettiest thing you ever saw. Nothing in the world so gay. *Il sera impossible d'y bouder; d'ailleurs, comme vous savez, je n'y suis pas naturellement trop porté.*

I have spoken to Mr. Pelham about your pay; which I believe, will be ordered very soon. However, *bride en main;* do not run out, *et n'y mettez point du vôtre. Vous n'en seriez pas plus gras d'un côté, mais vous en seriez bien plus maigre d'un autre.*

The town is now so empty, that I have no tittle-tattle to send you. The house of Kildare[2] comes here from Ireland next month; and then, I presume, that your friend, who by this time has got the full ascendant over her husband, will open her campaign with *éclat*, though these are very bad times for the female quality and gentry, it being the great fashion for our young fellows, not only to deal with, but to marry, common whores. So that the unmarried ladies can get no husbands; and the married ones none but their husbands!

Things go to the full as well as I could wish, and much better than I expected, at Leipsig;[3] we are absolutely masters

---

[1] As was actually done in 1815 by the creation of the kingdom of the Netherlands, thus making a powerful border kingdom, as Burgundy had been under Philip the Good.

[2] Lady Emily Lennox, born in 1731, and married in 1747 to James, then Earl of Kildare, and afterwards Duke of Leinster.—M.

[3] Where his son was.

of Latin, Greek, French, and German, the last of which we write currently. We have *le droit public de l'Empire*, history and geography very ready; so that, in truth, now we only want rubbing and cleaning. We begin for that purpose with Berlin at Christmas next; Vienna at Lady-day; and the Academy at Turin, at Midsummer; for a whole year. Then to Paris, *et si cela ne nous décrotte pas, il faut que le diable s'en mêle.* If at any of these places it should fall in your way, by letter or verbal recommendation, to help us, I am very sure that you will; for I never doubt of any marks of your friendship to the most faithful of your friends.

No. 1593

To his Son

(Stanhope CLXIV)

London, 27 September O.S. 1748

Dear Boy,

I have received your Latin lecture upon War, which, though it is not exactly the same Latin that Cæsar, Cicero, Horace, Virgil, and Ovid spoke, is, however, as good Latin as the *erudite Germans* speak or write. I have always observed, that the most learned people—that is, those who have read the most Latin—write the worst; and this distinguishes the Latin of a gentleman scholar from that of a pedant. A gentleman has, probably, read no other Latin than that of the Augustan age, and therefore can write no other; whereas the pedant has read much more bad Latin than good, and consequently writes so too. He looks upon the best classical books as books for schoolboys, and consequently below him; but pores over fragments of obscure authors, treasures up the obsolete words which he meets with there, and uses them, upon all occasions, to show his reading, at the expense of his judgment. Plautus is his favourite author, not for the sake of the wit and the *vis comica* of his comedies, but upon account of the many obsolete words and the cant of low characters, which are to be met with nowhere else. He will rather use *olli* than *illi*, *optume* than *optime*, and any bad word, rather than any good one, provided he can but prove that, strictly speaking, it is Latin—that is, that it was written by a Roman. By this rule, I might now write to you in the language of Chaucer or Spenser, and assert that I wrote English, because it was English in their days; but I should be a most affected puppy if I did so, and you would not understand three words of my letter. All these, and such-like affected peculiarities, are the characteristics of learned coxcombs and pedants, and are carefully avoided by all men of sense.

I dipped, accidentally, the other day, into Pitiscus's[1] preface to his Lexicon, where I found a word that puzzled me, and which I did not remember ever to have met before; it is the adverb *præfiscine*, which means, *in a good hour*— an expression which, by the superstition of it, appears to be low and vulgar. I looked for it, and at last I found that it is once or twice made use of in Plautus; upon the strength of which, this learned pedant thrusts it into his preface. Whenever you write Latin, remember that every word or phrase which you make use of, but cannot find in Cæsar, Cicero, Livy, Horace, Virgil, and Ovid, is bad, illiberal Latin, though it may have been written by a Roman.

I must now say something as to the matter of the lecture; in which, I confess, there is one doctrine laid down that surprises me; it is this: *Quum vero hostis sit lenta citave morte omnia dira nobis minitans quocunque bellantibus negotium est, parum sane interfuerit quo modo eum obruere et interficere satagamus, si ferociam exuere cunctetur. Ergo veneno quoque uti fas est, etc.*, whereas I cannot conceive that the use of poison can, upon any account, come within the lawful means of self-defence. Force may, without doubt, be justly repelled by force, but not by treachery and fraud;

[1] Samuel Pitiscus (1637-1727), a well-known classic and famous teacher.

1230

for I do not call the stratagems of war, such as ambuscades, masked batteries, false attacks, etc., frauds or treachery; they are mutually to be expected and guarded against; but poisoned arrows, poisoned waters, or poison administered to your enemy (which can only be done by treachery), I have always heard, read, and thought to be unlawful and infamous means of defence, be your danger ever so great.[1] But, *si ferociam exuere cunctetur*; must I rather die than poison this enemy? Yes, certainly, much rather die than do a base or criminal action; nor can I be sure, beforehand, that this enemy may not, in the last moment, *ferociam exuere*. But the public lawyers now seem to me rather to warp the law, in order to authorise, than to check those unlawful proceedings of princes and states, which, by being become common, appear less criminal; though custom can never alter the nature of good and ill.

Pray let no quibbles of lawyers, no refinements of casuists, break into the plain notions of right and wrong, which every man's right reason, and plain common sense, suggest to him. To do as you would be done by, is the plain, sure, and undisputed rule of morality and justice. Stick to that; and be convinced, that whatever breaks into it, in any degree, however speciously it may be turned, and however puzzling it may be to answer it, is, notwithstanding, false in itself, unjust, and criminal. I do not know a crime in the world which is not, by the casuists among the Jesuists (especially the twenty-four collected, I think, by Escobar[2]) allowed in some, or many, cases not to be criminal. The principles first laid down by them are often specious, the reasonings plausible, but the conclusion always a lie; for it is contrary to that evident and undeniable rule of justice

[1] The opinion of Lord Chesterfield is entirely conformable to that of all great authorities upon this subject; such as Grotius, see his *Droit de la Guerre*, etc., livre iii. ch. iv. sec. 16, ed. Barbeyrac.—M.

[2] Antoine Esobar, a Spanish Jesuit (1589-1669), who wrote *Cases of Conscience*, etc.; his doctrines were opposed by Pascal in the *Lettres Provinciales*. Chesterfield is prejudiced: Escobar is not a typical casuist.

which I have mentioned above, of not doing to anyone what you would not have him do to you. But, however, these refined pieces of casuistry and sophistry, being very convenient and welcome to people's passions and appetites, they gladly accept the indulgence, without desiring to detect the fallacy of the reasoning; and, indeed, many, I might say most, people are not able to do it, which makes the publication of such quibblings and refinements the more pernicious. I am no skilful casuist, nor subtle disputant; and yet I would undertake to justify and qualify the profession of a highwayman, step by step, and so plausibly as to make many ignorant people embrace the profession, as an innocent, if not even a laudable one; and to puzzle people of some degree of knowledge to answer me point by point.

I have seen a book, entitled *Quidlibet ex Quolibet*, or, the making anything out of anything; which is not so difficult as it would seem, if once one quits certain plain truths, obvious in gross to every understanding, in order to run after the ingenious refinements of warm imaginations and speculative reasonings. Doctor Berkeley, Bishop of Cloyne, a very worthy, ingenious, and learned man, has written a book to prove that there is no such thing as matter, and that nothing exists but in idea: that you and I only fancy ourselves eating, drinking, and sleeping; you at Leipsig, and I at London; that we think we have flesh and blood, legs, arms, etc., but that we are only spirit. His arguments are, strictly speaking, unanswerable; but yet I am so far from being convinced by them, that I am determined to go on to eat and drink, and walk and ride, in order to keep that *matter*, which I so mistakenly imagine my body at present to consist of, in as good plight as possible. Common sense (which, in truth, is very uncommon) is the best sense I know of; abide by it; it will counsel you best. Read and hear, for your amusement, ingenious systems, nice questions subtilely agitated, with all the refinements that warm imaginations suggest, but consider them only as exercitations for the mind, and return always to settle with common sense.

I stumbled, the other day, at a bookseller's, upon *Comte de Gabalis*,[1] in two very little volumes, which I had formerly read. I read it over again, and with fresh astonishment. Most of the extravagancies are taken from the Jewish Rabbins, who broached those wild notions, and delivered them in the unintelligible jargon which the Cabalists and Rosicrucians deal in to this day. Their number is, I believe, much lessened, but there are still some; and I myself have known two, who studied and firmly believed in that mystical nonsense. What extravagancy is not man capable of entertaining, when once his shackled reason is led in triumph by fancy and prejudice! The ancient alchemists gave very much in to this stuff, by which they thought they should discover the philosopher's stone; and some of the most celebrated empirics employed it in the pursuit of the universal medicine. Paracelsus,[2] a bold empiric and wild cabalist, asserted that he had discovered it, and called it his *Alkahest*. Why, or wherefore, God knows; only that those madmen call nothing by an intelligible name. You may easily get this book from the Hague; read it, for it will both divert and astonish you; and, at the same time, teach you *nil admirari*; a very necessary lesson.

Your letters, except when upon a given subject, are exceedingly laconic, and neither answer my desires, nor the purpose of letters; which should be familiar conversations between absent friends. As I desire to live with you upon the footing of an intimate friend, and not of a parent, I could wish that your letters gave me more particular accounts of yourself, and of your lesser transactions. When you write to me, suppose yourself conversing freely with

[1]By the Abbé de Montfauçon de Villars, published at Paris in 1670; an English translation, entitled *The Count of Gabalis, or the Extravagant Mysteries of the Cabalists*, was published in London, 1680. It was used by Pope for the 'machinery' of *The Rape of the Lock*, and by Anatole France in *La Rôtisserie de la Reine Pédauque*.

[2]Paracelsus was born near Zurich in 1493, and died at Salzburg in 1541.

me, by the fireside. In that case, you would naturally mention the incidents of the day; as, where you had been, whom you had seen, what you thought of them, etc. Do this in your letters; acquaint me sometimes with your studies, sometimes with your diversions; tell me of any new persons and characters that you meet with in company, and add your own observations upon them; in short, let me see more of you in your letters.

How do you go on with Lord Pulteney? and how does he go on at Leipsig? Has he learning, has he parts, has he application? Is he good or ill-natured? In short, what is he? at least, what do you think him? You may tell me without reserve, for I promise you secrecy. You are now of an age, that I am desirous to begin a confidential correspondence with you; and as I shall, on my part, write you very freely my opinion upon men and things, which I should often be very unwilling that anybody but you and Mr. Harte should see; so, on your part, if you write to me without reserve, you may depend upon my inviolable secrecy.

If you have ever looked into the Letters of Madame de Sévigné to her daughter, Madame de Grignan, you must have observed the ease, freedom, and friendship of that correspondence; and yet, I hope and believe, they did not love one another better than we do. Tell me what books you are now reading, either by way of study or amusement; how you pass your evenings when at home, and where you pass them when abroad. I know that you go sometimes to Madame Valentin's assembly. What do you do there? do you play or sup? or is it only *la belle conversation?* Do you mind your dancing while your dancing-master is with you? As you will be often under the necessity of dancing a minuet, I would have you dance it very well. Remember, that the graceful motion of the arms, the giving your hand, and the putting-on and pulling-off your hat genteely, are the material parts of a gentleman's dancing. But the greatest advantage of dancing well is, that it necessarily teaches you to present yourself, to sit, stand, and walk genteely; all which are of real importance to a man of fashion.

I should wish that you were polished, before you go to Berlin; where, as you will be in a great deal of good company, I would have you have the right manners for it. It is a very considerable article to have *le ton de la bonne compagnie*, in your destination particularly. The principal business of a foreign minister is, to get into the secrets, and to know all *les allures* of the Courts at which he resides; this he can never bring about, but by such a pleasing address, such engaging manners, and such an insinuating behaviour, as may make him sought for, and in some measure domestic, in the best company and the best families of the place. He will then, indeed, be well informed of all that passes, either by the confidences made him, or by the carelessness of people in his company; who are accustomed to look upon him as one of them, and consequently not upon their guard before him. For a minister, who only goes to the Court he resides at in form, to ask an audience of the Prince or the Minister, upon his last instructions, puts them upon their guard, and will never know anything more than what they have a mind that he should know.

Here women may be put to some use. A King's mistress, or a Minister's wife or mistress, may give great and useful informations; and are very apt to do it, being proud to show they have been trusted. But then, in this case, the height of that sort of address which strikes women is requisite; I mean that easy politeness, genteel and graceful address, and that *extérieur brillant*, which they cannot withstand. There is a sort of men so like women, that they are to be taken just in the same way; I mean those who are commonly called *fine men*, who swarm at all Courts, who have little reflection and less knowledge, but who, by their good-breeding, and *train-tran* of the world, are admitted into all companies, and by the imprudence or carelessness of their superiors pick up secrets worth knowing, which are easily got out of them by proper address. Adieu!   *1235*

No. 1594

To Edward Eliot

(*MSS. of the Earl of St. Germans*)

London, 29 *September* 1748

Sir,

As this is about the time when you proposed being in Town, and as I should be very much concerned if I were not to have the pleasure of seeing you before your return to Leipsig, you will (I am sure) excuse the precaution which I now take to prevent, if possible, that disappointment.

The worse than indifferent state of my health obliges me to go to the Bath, for which place I shall set out on this day seven-night the 6th of Oct. and consequently be there on the 9th. Though I am in hopes still of seeing you in Town before I leave it, yet if I should not have that good fortune, I take the Bath to be almost in your way from Cornwall to London, or at least so little out of your road, that I will venture to propose that digression to you, if we do not meet here by the 6th. I can offer you no other inducement to it, than the pleasure which it will give to one, who knows and values your merit, who desires your friendship, and who wishes for every opportunity to prove to you the truth and esteem, with which he is

Your most faithful humble servant

Chesterfield.

No. 1595

To Solomon Dayrolles, Esq.

(*Maty II. xxxix*)

Bath, 11 *October O.S.* 1748

Dear Dayrolles,

I received your letter of the 11th N.S. just as I was setting out for this place. I had been much out of order for above a month; languors and vertigos succeeded each other, the latter attended with sickness at my stomach. I underwent the discipline of the faculty to little purpose; who, at last pronouncing that the seat and source of my disorder was my stomach, sent me here. I have already received advantage from these waters, though I have drunk them but four days; which convinces me that they will set me quite right.

I am persuaded, that your first setting out at the Hague must have put you behind-hand; but I hope that you will take care to retrieve; for the credit of living a little better will not do you so much good, as contracting a considerable debt will do you harm. If you can get leave to come here for three or four months, when Lord Holderness shall be settled at the Hague, which I should think would be no difficult matter, that suspension of your expense would, I suppose, go near to set you right. But, in the mean time, should you want money, draw upon me *sans façon*: for I will not have you run in debt to anybody else; and you and I can, I believe, trust each other.

By all I can hear now, and by all that I knew before, the Republic is so far from being settled, that I do not consider it as a government or a nation. More money is wanted than is to be found, and even the methods of collecting what is there to be found will not be easily fixed. The people will not have *pachters*.[1]; Collectors, without the powers of the *pachters*, will collect nothing, and with those powers they become *pachters* themselves, in the most odious and oppressive sense of that word. The Prince of Orange has got more power than by the constitution he ought to have; and if he does not get all the rest, he will lose what he has got. *Il n'y a point de milieu*: power must either be constitutional or unlimited. Losing gamesters will not leave off while they have anything left, and will never be quiet till they have lost all. When Cæsar had once passed the Rubicon, he well

[1]See note to letter, 24th June, 1748.

knew that he must be Cæsar or nothing. And this is now the Prince's case.

I now plainly see the prelude to the Pyrrhic dance in the north, which I have long foretold; the return of Comte Biron and the Duke of Brunswick to Petersburg announces destruction to the Holstein family. The Prince-Successor of Sweden will be the first instance of it, upon the death of that King, which I take to be very near. The next will be, setting aside the Imperial Prince of Russia, and declaring little Czar Iwan the successor. In these transactions, the King of Prussia will necessarily be implicated, which has all along been *l'intention de l'auteur*; that is of the Court of Vienna, which absolutely governs that of Petersburg, *moyennant* some pecuniary assistance from *another quarter*. But be all this as it will, my *boudoir* and my library, which are my two objects, will be never the worse for it. And I maintain that both of them will be, in their different kinds, the completest things in England, as I hope you will soon have ocular proof of.

Baron Schmitburg was not arrived when I left London. My compliments to my Baron, to whom I will write very soon. Adieu; *Je vous aime véritablement.*

No. 1596

To his Son

(Stanhope CLXV)

Bath, 12 October O.S. 1748

Dear Boy,

I came here three days ago, upon account of a disorder in my stomach, which affected my head, and gave me vertigos. I already find myself something better; and, consequently, do not doubt that a course of these waters will set me quite right. But, however, and wherever I am, your welfare, your character, your knowledge, and your morals, employ my thoughts more than anything that can happen to me, or that I can fear or hope for myself. I am going off the stage, you are coming upon it; with me, what has been, has been, and reflection now would come too late; with you, everything is to come, even, in some manner, reflection itself; so that this is the very time when my reflections, the result of experience, may be of use to you, by supplying the want of yours. As soon as you leave Leipsig, you will gradually be going into the great world; where the first impressions that you shall give of yourself will be of great importance to you; but those which you shall receive will be decisive, for they always stick. To keep good company, especially at your first setting out, is the way to receive good impressions. If you ask me what I mean by good company, I will confess to you, that it is pretty difficult to define; but I will endeavour to make you understand it as well as I can.

Good company is not what respective sets of company are pleased either to call or think themselves, but it is that company which all the people of the place call and acknowledge to be good company, notwithstanding some objections which they may form to some of the individuals who compose it. It consists chiefly (but by no means without exception) of people of considerable birth, rank, and character; for people of neither birth nor rank are frequently, and very justly, admitted into it, if distinguished by any peculiar merit, or eminency in any liberal art or science. Nay, so motley a thing is good company, that many people, without birth, rank, or merit, intrude into it by their own forwardness, and others slide into it by the protection of some considerable person; and some even of indifferent characters and morals make part of it. But, in the main, the good part preponderates, and people of infamous and blasted characters are never admitted. In this fashionable good company, the best manners and the best language of the place are most unquestionably to be learnt; for they establish and give the tone to both, which are therefore called the language and manners of good company, there being no legal tribunal to ascertain either.

A company consisting wholly of people of the first quality cannot, for that reason, be called good company, in the common acceptation of the phrase, unless they are, into the bargain, the fashionable and accredited company of the place; for people of the very first quality can be as silly, as ill-bred, and as worthless, as people of the meanest degree. On the other hand, a company consisting entirely of people of very low condition, whatever their merit or parts may be, can never be called good company, and consequently should not be much frequented, though by no means despised.

A company wholly composed of men of learning, though greatly to be valued and respected, is not meant by the words *good company*; they cannot have the easy manners and *tournure* of the world, as they do not live in it. If you can bear your part well in such a company, it is extremely right to be in it sometimes, and you will be but more esteemed in other companies for having a place in that; but then do not let it engross you, for, if you do, you will be only considered as one of the *literati* by profession, which is not the way either to shine or rise in the world.

The company of professed wits and poets is extremely inviting to most young men, who, if they have wit them-selves, are pleased with it, and, if they have none, are sillily proud of being one of it; but it should be frequented with moderation and judgment, and you should by no means give yourself up to it. A wit is a very unpopular denomina-tion, as it carries terror along with it; and people in general are as much afraid of a live wit in company as a woman is of a gun, which she thinks may go off by itself, and do her a mischief. Their acquaintance is, however, worth seeking, and their company worth frequenting; but not exclusively of others, nor to such a degree as to be considered only as one of that particular set.

But the company which of all others you should most carefully avoid, is that low company which, in every sense of the word, is low indeed—low in rank, low in parts, low in manners, and low in merit. You will, perhaps, be surprised that I should think it necessary to warn you against such company; but yet I do not think it wholly unnecessary, after the many instances which I have seen of men of sense and rank, discredited, vilified, and undone, by keeping such company. Vanity, that source of many of our follies, and of some of our crimes, has sunk many a man into company in every light infinitely below himself, for the sake of being the first man in it; there he dictates, is applauded, admired; and, for the sake of being the *Coryphæus* of that wretched chorus, disgraces and disqualifies himself soon for any better company. Depend upon it, you will sink or rise to the level of the company which you commonly keep;— people will judge of you, and not unreasonably, by that. There is good sense in the Spanish saying, 'Tell me whom you live with, and I will tell you who you are.' Make it therefore your business, wherever you are, to get into that company which everybody of the place allows to be the best company, next to their own:—which is the best definition which I can give you of good company. But here, too, one caution is very necessary, for want of which many young men have been ruined, even in good company. Good company (as I have before observed) is composed of a great variety of fashionable people, whose characters and morals are very different, though their manners are pretty much the same. When a young man, new in the world, first gets into that company, he very rightly determines to conform to and imitate it; but then he too often, and fatally, mistakes the objects of his imitation. He has often heard that absurd term of genteel and fashionable vices. He there sees some people who shine, and who in general are admired and esteemed; and observes that these people are whoremasters, drunkards, or gamesters; upon which he adopts their vices, mistaking their defects for their perfections, and thinking that they owe their fashion and their lustre to those genteel vices. Whereas it is exactly the reverse, for these people have acquired their reputation by their parts, their learning, their good-breeding, and other real accomplishments; and are only blemished and lowered, in the opinions of all reasonable people, and of their own, in time, by these genteel and fashionable vices. A whore-master in a flux, or without a nose, is a very genteel person indeed, and well worthy of imitation; a drunkard, vomiting up at night the wine of the day, and stupified by the headache all the next, is, doubtless, a fine model to copy from; and a gamester, tearing his hair and blaspheming, for having lost more than he had in the world, is surely a most amiable character. No; these are allays, and great ones too, which can never adorn any character, but will always debase the best. To prove this, suppose any man, without parts and some other good qualities, to be merely a whore-master, a drunkard, or a gamester—how will he be looked upon by all sorts of people? Why, as a most contemptible and vicious animal. Therefore it is plain that, in these mixed characters, the good part only makes people forgive, but not approve, the bad.

I will hope, and believe, that you will have no vices; but if, unfortunately, you should have any, at least I beg of you to be content with your own, and to adopt no other body's. The adoption of vice has, I am convinced, ruined ten times more young men than natural inclinations.

As I make no difficulty of confessing my past errors, where I think the confession may be of use to you, I will own that, when I first went to the university, I drank and smoked, notwithstanding the aversion I had to wine and tobacco, only because I thought it genteel, and that it made me look like a man. When I went abroad, I first went to the Hague, where gaming was much in fashion; and where I observed that many people of shining rank and character gamed too. I was then young enough, and silly enough, to believe that gaming was one of their accomplishments; and, as I aimed at perfection, I adopted gaming as a necessary step to it. Thus I acquired, by error, the habit of a vice which, far from adorning my character, has, I am conscious, been a great blemish in it.

Imitate, then, with discernment and judgment, the real perfections of the good company into which you may get; copy their politeness, their carriage, their address, and the easy and well-bred turn of their conversation; but remember, that, let them shine ever so bright, their vices, if they have any, are so many spots, which you would no more imitate than you would make an artificial wart upon your face, because some very handsome man had the misfortune to have a natural one upon his; but, on the contrary, think how much handsomer he would have been without it.

Having thus confessed some of my *égarements*, I will now show you a little of my right side. I always endeavoured to get into the best company wherever I was, and commonly succeeded. There I pleased, to some degree, by showing a desire to please. I took care never to be absent or *distrait*; but, on the contrary, attended to everything that was said, done, or even looked, in company; I never failed in the minutest attentions, and was never *journalier*. These things, and not my *égarements*, made me fashionable.

Adieu! this letter is full long enough.

No. 1597
TO EDWARD ELIOT, ESQ.
(*MSS. of the Earl of St. Germans*)

Bath, 19 *October*, 1748

SIR,

I have this moment received the favour of your letter of the 16th, in consequence of which I withdraw the instances I made you to take Bath in your way to London. For as you do not propose leaving Port Eliot till the 30th of this month, and cannot probably be in London till the 7th of the next, and as I take it for granted that you will stay in Town ten or twelve days, I hope to have the pleasure of seeing you there with much less trouble to yourself. I shall certainly be in London at latest on the 21st of next month, but possibly a week sooner, if these waters shall have done what, by that time, I expect from them. They have already done me good, but what is that good? Only an expedient which my shattered carcase is obliged from time to time to have recourse to. My fabric is too much decayed to admit of solid repairs; props and buttresses are its only refuge. Your undissipated youth will, I hope and believe, secure you from those premature inconveniences of old age. The sanity of the mind contributes to that of the body, to which, consequently, no man has a better right than yourself. It is all that you have left your friends to wish you; *de te nam caetera sumes.*

I am, etc.

No. 1598

To his Son

(*Stanhope CLXVI*)

Bath, 19 *October O.S.* 1748

DEAR BOY,

Having, in my last, pointed out what sort of company you should keep, I will now give you some rules for your conduct in it; rules which my own experience and observation enable me to lay down and communicate to you with some degree of confidence. I have often given you hints of this kind before, but then it has been by snatches; I will now be more regular and methodical. I shall say nothing with regard to your bodily carriage and address, but leave them to the care of your dancing-master, and to your own attention to the best models; remember, however, that they are of consequence.

Talk often, but never long; in that case, if you do not please, at least you are sure not to tire your hearers. Pay your own reckoning, but do not treat the whole company; this being one of the very few cases in which people do not care to be treated, every one being fully convinced that he has wherewithal to pay.

Tell stories very seldom, and absolutely never but where they are very apt, and very short. Omit every circumstance that is not material, and beware of digressions. To have frequent recourse to narrative betrays great want of imagination.

Never hold anybody by the button, or the hand, in order to be heard out; for, if people are not willing to hear you, you had much better hold your tongue than them.

Most long talkers single out some one unfortunate man in company (commonly him whom they observe to be the most silent, or their next neighbour) to whisper, or at least, in a half voice, to convey a continuity of words to. This is excessively ill-bred, and, in some degree, a fraud; conversation-stock being a joint and common property. But, on the other hand, if one of these unmerciful talkers lays hold of you, hear him with patience, and at least seeming attention, if he is worth obliging; for nothing will oblige him more than a patient hearing, as nothing would hurt him more than either to leave him in the midst of his discourse, or to discover your impatience under your affliction.

Take, rather than give, the tone of the company you are in. If you have parts, you will show them, more or less, upon every subject; and, if you have not, you had better talk sillily upon a subject of other people's than of your own choosing.

Avoid as much as you can, in mixed companies, argumentative polemical conversations; which, though they

1245

should not, yet certainly do, indispose, for a time, the contending parties towards each other; and, if the controversy grows warm and noisy, endeavour to put an end to it by some genteel levity or joke. I quieted such a conversation hubbub once, by representing to them that, though I was persuaded none there present would repeat, out of company, what passed in it, yet I could not answer for the discretion of the passengers in the street, who must necessarily hear all that was said.

Above all things, and upon all occasions, avoid speaking of yourself, if it be possible. Such is the natural pride and vanity of our hearts, that it perpetually breaks out, even in people of the best parts, in all the various modes and figures of the egotism.

Some abruptly speak advantageously of themselves, without either pretence or provocation. They are impudent. Others proceed more artfully, as they imagine, and forge accusations against themselves, complain of calumnies which they never heard, in order to justify themselves, by exhibiting a catalogue of their many virtues. 'They acknowledge it may, indeed, seem odd, that they should talk in that manner of themselves; it is what they do not like, and what they never would have done; no, no tortures should ever have forced it from them, if they had not been thus unjustly and monstrously accused. But, in these cases, justice is surely due to one's self, as well as to others; and, when our character is attacked, we may say, in our own justification, what otherwise we never would have said.' This thin veil of modesty drawn before vanity, is much too transparent to conceal it, even from very moderate discernment.

Others go more modestly and more slyly still (as they think) to work; but, in my mind, still more ridiculously. They confess themselves (not without some degree of shame and confusion) into all the cardinal virtues; by first degrading them into weaknesses, and then owning their misfortune, in being made up of those weaknesses. 'They cannot see people suffer, without sympathizing with, and endeavouring to help them. They cannot see people want, without relieving them; though, truly, their own circumstances cannot very well afford it. They cannot help speaking truth, though they know all the imprudence of it. In short, they know that, with all these weaknesses, they are not fit to live in the world, much less to thrive in it. But they are now too old to change, and must rub on as well as they can.' This sounds too ridiculous and *outré*, almost for the stage; and yet, take my word for it, you will frequently meet with it upon the common stage of the world. And here I will observe, by the bye, that you will often meet with characters in nature so extravagant, that a discreet poet would not venture to set them upon the stage in their true and high colouring.

This principle of vanity and pride is so strong in human nature, that it descends even to the lowest objects; and one often sees people angling for praise, where, admitting all they say to be true (which, by the way, it seldom is), no just praise is to be caught. One man affirms that he has rode post an hundred miles in six hours: probably it is a lie; but supposing it to be true, what then? Why, he is a very good post-boy, that is all. Another asserts, and probably not without oaths, that he has drank six or eight bottles of wine at a sitting; out of charity, I will believe him a liar; for, if I do not, I must think him a beast.

Such, and a thousand more, are the follies and extravagancies, which vanity draws people into, and which always defeat their own purpose, and, as Waller says upon another subject,—

> Make the wretch the most despised,
> Where most he wishes to be prized.[1]

[1]Adapted from Waller's *On Love.*
> Postures which render him despised,
> Where he endeavours to be prized.

He quotes the next two lines in letter of 24th May, 1750.

The only sure way of avoiding these evils is never to speak of yourself at all. But when historically you are obliged to mention yourself, take care not to drop one single word, that can directly or indirectly be construed as fishing for applause. Be your character what it will, it will be known; and nobody will take it upon your own word. Never imagine that anything you can say yourself will varnish your defects, or add lustre to your perfections; but, on the contrary, it may, and nine times in ten will, make the former more glaring, and the latter obscure. If you are silent upon your own subject, neither envy, indignation, nor ridicule will obstruct or allay the applause which you may really deserve; but if you publish your own panegyric, upon any occasion, or in any shape whatsoever, and however artfully dressed or disguised, they will all conspire against you, and you will be disappointed of the very end you aim at.

Take care never to seem dark and mysterious; which is not only a very unamiable character, but a very suspicious one too; if you seem mysterious with others, they will be really so with you, and you will know nothing. The height of abilities is, to have *volto sciolto* and *pensieri stretti*;[1] that is, a frank, open, and ingenuous exterior, with a prudent and reserved interior; to be upon your own guard, and yet, by a seeming natural openness, to put people off theirs. Depend upon it, nine in ten of every company you are in will avail themselves of every indiscreet and unguarded expression of yours, if they can turn it to their own advantage. A prudent reserve is therefore necessary as a seeming openness is prudent. Always look people in the face when you speak to them; the not doing it is thought to imply conscious guilt; besides that, you lose the advantage of observing by heir countenances what impression your discourse makes

[1]This is a favourite maxim of Chesterfield's. Sir Henry Wotton, in a letter to Milton acknowledging *Comus*, and advising him before setting out to Italy, tells him that Alberto Scipioni said to him: 'Signor Amigo mio, I pensieri stretti, ed il viso sciolto will go safely through the whole world.'

upon them. In order to know people's real sentiments, I trust much more to my eyes than to my ears; for they can say whatever they have a mind I should hear; but they can seldom help looking what they have no intention that I should know.

Neither retail nor receive scandal willingly; for though the defamation of others may for the present gratify the malignity of the pride of our hearts, cool reflection will draw very disadvantageous conclusions from such a disposition; and in the case of scandal, as in that of robbery, the receiver is always thought as bad as the thief.

Mimicry, which is the common and favourite amusement of little low minds, is in the utmost contempt with great ones. It is the lowest and most illiberal of all buffoonery. Pray, neither practise it yourself, nor applaud it in others. Besides that, the person mimicked is insulted; and, as I have often observed to you before, an insult is never forgiven.

I need not, I believe, advise you to adapt your conversation to the people you are conversing with; for I suppose you would not, without this caution, have talked upon the same subject and in the same manner to a minister of state, a bishop, a philosopher, a captain, and a woman. A man of the world must, like the chameleon, be able to take every different hue, which is by no means a criminal or abject, but a necessary complaisance, for it relates only to manners, and not to morals.

One word only as to swearing; and that I hope and believe is more than is necessary. You may sometimes hear some people in good company interlard their discourse with oaths, by way of embellishment, as they think; but you must observe, too, that those who do so are never those who contribute in any degree to give that company the denomination of good company. They are always subalterns, or people of low education; for that practice, besides that it has no one temptation to plead, is as silly and as illiberal as it is wicked.

Loud laughter is the mirth of the mob, who are only pleased with silly things; for true wit or good sense never excited a laugh since the creation of the world. A man of parts and fashion is therefore only seen to smile, but never heard to laugh.

But, to conclude this long letter; all the above-mentioned rules, however carefully you may observe them, will lose half their effect if unaccompanied by the Graces. Whatever you say, if you say it with a supercilious, cynical face, or an embarrassed countenance, or a silly, disconcerted grin, will be ill received. If, into the bargain, *you mutter it, or utter it indistinctly and ungracefully*, it will be still worse received. If your air and address are vulgar, awkward, and *gauche*, you may be esteemed indeed if you have great intrinsic value; but you will never please, and without pleasing you will rise but heavily. Venus, among the ancients, was synonymous with the Graces, who were always supposed to accompany her; and Horace tells us, that even youth, and Mercury, the god of arts and eloquence, would not do without her.

> —*Parum comis* sine te Juventas
> Mercuriusque.[1]

They are not inexorable ladies, and may be had if properly and diligently pursued. Adieu!

No. 1599

To his Son

(*Stanhope CLXVII*)

Bath, 29 October O.S. 1748

DEAR BOY,

My anxiety for your success increases in proportion as the time approaches for your taking your part upon the great stage of the world. The audience will form their

[1] *Odes*, I. 30.

opinion of you upon your first appearance (making the proper allowance for your inexperience), and so far it will be final, that, though it may vary as to the degrees, it will never totally change. This consideration excites that restless attention with which I am constantly examining how I can best contribute to the perfection of that character in which the least spot or blemish would give me more real concern than I am now capable of feeling upon any other account whatsoever.

I have long since done mentioning your great religious and moral duties, because I could not make your understanding so bad a compliment, as to suppose that you wanted or could receive any new instructions upon those two important points. Mr. Harte, I am sure, has not neglected them; besides, they are so obvious to common sense and reason, that commentators may (as they often do) perplex, but cannot make them clearer. My province, therefore, is to supply by my experience your hitherto inevitable inexperience in the ways of the world. People at your age are in a state of natural ebriety, and want rails and *gardefous* wherever they go, to hinder them from breaking their necks. This drunkenness of youth is not only tolerated, but even pleases, if kept within certain bounds of discretion and decency. Those bounds are the point which it is difficult for the drunken man himself to find out; and there it is that the experience of a friend may not only serve, but save him.

Carry with you, and welcome, into company all the gaiety and spirits, but as little of the giddiness of youth as you can. The former will charm, but the latter will often, though innocently, implacably offend. Inform yourself of the characters and situations of the company before you give way to what your imagination may prompt you to say. There are in all companies more wrong heads than right ones, and many more who deserve than who like censure. Should you therefore expatiate in the praise of some virtue, which some in company notoriously want, or declaim against any vice which others are notoriously infected with, your reflexions, however general and unapplied, will, by being applicable, be thought personal and levelled at those people. This consideration points out to you sufficiently not to be suspicious and captious yourself, nor to suppose that things, because they may be, are therefore meant at you. The manners of well-bred people secure one from those indirect and mean attacks; but if, by chance, a flippant woman or a pert coxcomb lets off anything of that kind, it is much better not to seem to understand, than to reply to it.

Cautiously avoid talking of either your own or other people's domestic affairs. Yours are nothing to them, but tedious; theirs are nothing to you. The subject is a tender one; and it is odds but you touch somebody or other's sore place; for in this case there is no trusting to specious appearances, which may be, and often are, so contrary to the real situations of things between men and their wives, parents and their children, seeming friends, etc., that, with the best intentions in the world, one often blunders disagreeably.

Remember, that the wit, humour, and jokes of most mixed companies are local. They thrive in that particular soil, but will not often bear transplanting. Every company is differently circumstanced, has its particular cant and jargon, which may give occasion to wit and mirth within that circle, but would seem flat and insipid in any other, and therefore will not bear repeating. Nothing makes a man look sillier than a pleasantry not relished or not understood; and if he meets with a profound silence when he expected a general applause, or, what is worse, if he is desired to explain the *bon mot*, his awkward and embarrassed situation is easier imagined than described. *À propos* of repeating; take great care never to repeat (I do not mean here the pleasantries) in one company what you hear in another. Things seemingly indifferent, may, by circulation, have much graver consequences than you would imagine.

Besides, there is a general tacit trust in conversation by which a man is obliged not to report anything out of it, though he is not immediately enjoined secrecy. A retailer of this kind is sure to draw himself into a thousand scrapes and discussions, and to be shyly and uncomfortably received wherever he goes.

You will find, in most good company, some people who only keep their place there by a contemptible title enough, —these are what we call *very good-natured fellows*, and the French *bons diables*. The truth is, they are people without any parts or fancy, and who, having no will of their own, readily assent to, concur in, and applaud whatever is said or done in the company; and adopt, with the same alacrity, the most virtuous or the most criminal, the wisest or the silliest scheme, that happens to be entertained by the majority of the company. This foolish, and often criminal complaisance, flows from a foolish cause—the want of any other merit. I hope you will hold your place in company by a nobler tenure, and that you will hold it (you can bear a quibble, I believe, yet) *in capite*. Have a will and an opinion of your own, and adhere to them steadily; but then do it with good-humour, good-breeding, and (if you have it) with urbanity; for you have not yet heard enough either to preach or censure.

All other kinds of complaisance are not only blameless, but necessary in good company. Not to seem to perceive the little weaknesses, and the idle but innocent affectations of the company, but even to flatter them in a certain manner, is not only very allowable, but, in truth, a sort of polite duty. They will be pleased with you, if you do; and will certainly not be reformed by you, if you do not. For instance; you will find, in every *groupe* of company, two principal figures, *viz.* the fine lady and the fine gentleman; who absolutely give the law of wit, language, fashion, and taste, to the rest of that society. There is always a strict, and often, for the time being, a tender alliance between these two figures. The lady looks upon her empire as founded upon the divine right of beauty (and full as good a divine right it is, as any king, emperor, or pope can pretend to); she requires, and commonly meets with, unlimited passive obedience. And why should she not meet with it? Her demands go no higher than to have her unquestioned preeminence in beauty, wit, and fashion, firmly established. Few sovereigns (by the way) are so reasonable. The fine gentleman's claims of right are, *mutatis mutandis*, the same; and though, indeed, he is not always a wit *de jure*, yet, as he is the wit *de facto* of that company, he is entitled to a share of your allegiance; and everybody expects, at least, as much as they are entitled to, if not something more. Prudence bids you make you court to these joint sovereigns; and no duty, that I know of, forbids it. Rebellion, here, is exceedingly dangerous, and inevitably punished by banishment, and immediate forfeiture of all your wit, manners, taste, and fashion; as, on the other hand, a cheerful submission, not without some flattery, is sure to procure you a strong recommendation, and most effectual pass, throughout all their, and probably the neighbouring dominions. With a moderate share of sagacity, you will, before you have been half an hour in their company, easily discover these two principal figures; both by the deference which you will observe the whole company pay them, and by that easy, careless, and serene air, which their consciousness of power gives them. As in this case, so in all others, aim always at the highest; get always into the highest company, and address yourself particularly to the highest in it. The search after the unattainable philosopher's stone has occasioned a thousand useful discoveries, which otherwise would never have been made.

What the French justly call *les manières nobles*, are only to be acquired in the very best companies. They are the distinguishing characteristics of men of fashion; people of low education never wear them so close but that some part or other of the original vulgarism appears. *Les manières nobles* equally forbid insolent contempt, or low envy and jealousy. Low people in good circumstances, fine clothes, and equipages, will insolently show contempt for all those who cannot afford as fine clothes, as good an equipage, and who have not (as their term is) as much money in their pockets; on the other hand, they are gnawed with envy, and cannot help discovering it, of those who surpass them in any of these articles, which are far from being sure criterions of merit. They are likewise jealous of being slighted, and, consequently, suspicious and captious; they are eager and hot about trifles, because trifles were, at first, their affairs of consequence. *Les manières nobles* imply exactly the reverse of all this. Study them early; you cannot make them too habitual and familiar to you.

Just as I had written what goes before, I received your letter of the 24th N.S. but I have not received that which you mention from Mr. Harte. Yours is of the kind that I desire, for I want to see your private picture drawn by yourself at different sittings; for though, as it is drawn by yourself, I presume you will take the most advantageous likeness, yet I think I have skill enough in that kind of painting to discover the true features, though ever so artfully coloured or thrown into skilful lights and shades.

By your account of the German play, which I do not know whether I should call tragedy or comedy, the only shining part of it (since I am in a way of quibbling) seems to have been the fox's tail. I presume, too, that the play has had the same fate as the squib, and has gone off no more. I remember a squib much better applied, when it was made the device of the colours of a French regiment of grenadiers; it was represented bursting with this motto under it,— *Peream dum luceam.*

I like the description of your *pic-nic*, where I take it for granted that your cards are only to break the formality of a circle, and your *symposion* intended more to promote conversation than drinking. Such an *amicable collision*, as Lord Shaftesbury very prettily calls it, rubs off and smooths those rough corners which mere nature has given to the smoothest of us. I hope some part, at least, of the conversation is in German. *À propos*; tell me—do you speak that language correctly, and do you write it with ease? I have no doubt of your mastering the other modern languages, which are much easier, and occur much oftener; for which reason I desire you will apply most diligently to German while you are in Germany, that you may speak and write that language most correctly.

I expect to meet Mr. Eliot in London in about three weeks; after which you will see him at Leipsig. Adieu!

No. 1600

To Solomon Dayrolles, Esq.

(Mahon III. 300)

Bath, 4 November O.S. 1748

Dear Dayrolles,

I have received yours of the 5th N.S. and am glad to find, that your landed estate pays so well as to make up the arrears of the treasury. As soon as I go to town, which will be next week, I will quicken Mr. Pelham to pay his debts; but *en tout cas*, I repeat it again, upon any emergency, draw upon me, for, upon my word, such sums as you can want will be no inconveniency to me to advance. You are besides very responsible, whether considered as a monied or as a landed man; so that, if you should be backward in payment I should forthwith seize Henley Park.[1]

À propos of money; as I believe it is much wanted by many people, even of fashion, both in Holland and Flanders, I should think it very likely that many good pictures of Rubens, Teniers, and other Flemish and Dutch Masters, may be picked up now at reasonable rates. If so, you are

[1]Dayrolles's seat, near Guildford.

likely to hear of it as a *virtuoso*; and if so, I should be glad to profit of it, as an humble *dilettante*. I have already, as you know, a most beautiful landscape by Rubens, and a pretty little piece of Teniers; but if you could meet with a large capital history, or allegorical piece, of Rubens, with the figures as big as the life, I would go pretty deep to have it, as also for a large and capital picture of Teniers. But as I would give a good deal for them if they were indisputably eminent, I would not give threepence for them unless they were so. I have pretty pictures enough already; but what I want to complete my collection, is only two or three of the most eminent Masters, of whom I have none now. I can trust entirely to your taste and skill; so that if you meet with such a thing, do not miss it for fifty pounds, more or less.

The packet of *brochures*, and flourished ruffles, which you sent me by Hop, waits for me in town. I am sure, by the former, which you sent me, I shall like these: *je m'en fie à votre bon goût.* I shall go to them in about ten days, though, I doubt, not quite restored by these waters, which have not had their usual effects upon me this season. My vertigos still chicane and tease me, though not quite so frequently as formerly, but still enough to make me fear passing a languid and uncomfortable winter. Patience: I might have more painful complaints, and I will comfort myself by the comparison.

I have some reasons to believe, that what my Baron mentioned to me of a new successor to Sweden, is by no means groundless. I am very sorry for it, as I think it can only be attended with very ill consequences for this country. Reflect upon the tenure and situation of Bremen and Verden, and upon the amicable disposition of two certain brothers[1] towards each other, and those consequences will immediately occur to you.

[1]This is said ironically, and appears to allude to the differences between the Prince of Orange and the Duke of Cumberland.—M.

I look upon your Republic as a chaos, in the situation which it is now in; some order may spring from it, but as yet God knows what. The ancient government certainly does not exist; and I see no new one established in its stead. Abject court, it is true, is made to the Prince of Orange, from fear on one hand, and hopes on the other; but still, while he has more power than he should have for the late form of government, and yet less than is necessary to carry on any other, it is no government at all. This was the great difficulty under which Cromwell, one of the ablest men in the world, laboured, and which he was sensible of, when he wanted to be declared King; for he was above minding the title. But he knew that his government wanted that form and consistency which were necessary for its effect and authority.

The peace is, upon the whole, better than could have been expected, from the circumstances and hurry in which it was made; but the article relating to the hostages,[1] and that wherein France only renounces the Pretender and his family, by reference to one in an old obsolete Treaty, shock me, as injurious and personally insulting to the King.

I fear you will not get a furlough this winter, for I do not find that Lord Holderness is yet making any preparations for his embassy. *Bon soir, aimons-nous toujours.*

No. 1601

To his Son

(Stanhope CLXVIII)

London, 18 November O.S. 1748

DEAR BOY,

Whatever I see or whatever I hear, my first consideration is, whether it can in any way be useful to you. As a

[1] At the conclusion of the peace of Aix-la-Chapelle, two British noblemen, the Earl of Sussex and Lord Cathcart, were sent to Paris as hostages for the restitution of Cape Breton.—M.

proof of this, I went accidentally the other day into a print-shop, where, among many others, I found one print from a famous design of Carlo Maratti, who died about thirty years ago,[1] and was the last eminent painter in Europe; the subject is *il Studio del Disegno*, or the School of Drawing. An old man, supposed to be the master, points to his scholars, who are variously employed, in perspective, geometry, and the observation of the statues of antiquity. With regard to perspective, of which there are some little specimens, he has wrote, *tanto che basti*, that is, *as much as is sufficient*; with regard to geometry, *tanto che basti*, again; with regard to the contemplation of the ancient statues, there is written, *non mai a bastanza,—there never can be enough*. But, in the clouds, at the top of the piece, are represented the three Graces, with this just sentence written over them, *senza di noi ogni fatica è vana*; that is, *without us all labour is vain*. This everybody allows to be true in painting; but all people do not seem to consider, as I hope you will, that this truth is full as applicable to every other art or science; indeed to everything that is said or done. I will send you the print itself by Mr. Eliot, when he returns; and I will advise you to make the same use of it that the Roman Catholics say they do of the pictures and images of their saints,—which is, only to remind them of those, for the adoration they disclaim. Nay, I will go farther, and, as the transition from popery to paganism is short and easy, I will classically and poetically advise you to invoke and sacrifice to them every day—and all the day. It must be owned that the Graces do not seem to be natives of Great Britain; and, I doubt, the best of us here have more of the rough than the polished diamond. Since barbarism drove them out of Greece and Rome, they seem to have taken refuge in France, where their temples are numerous, and their worship the established one. Examine yourself seriously why such and such

[1]Maratti (1625-1713) was born at Camerino in Italy; he became a pupil of Andrea Sacchi. Fuseli enormously admired his *Bathsheba viewed by David.*

people please and engage you more than such and such others of equal merit, and you will always find that it is because the former have the Graces and the latter not. I have known many a woman, with an exact shape and a symmetrical assemblage of beautiful features, please nobody; while others, with very moderate shapes and features, have charmed everybody. Why?—Because Venus will not charm so much without her attendant Graces as they will without her. Among men, how often have I seen the most solid merit and knowledge neglected, unwelcome, or even rejected, for want of them! While flimsy parts, little knowledge, and less merit, introduced by the Graces, have been received, cherished, and admired. Even virtue, which is moral beauty, wants some of its charms if unaccompanied by them.

If you ask me how you shall acquire what neither you nor I can define or ascertain, I can only answer—*by observation.* Form yourself, with regard to others, upon what you feel pleases you in them. I can tell you the importance—the advantage of having the Graces; but I cannot give them you; I heartily wish I could, and I certainly would; for I do not know a better present that I could make you.

To show you that a very wise, philosophical, and retired man thinks upon that subject as I do, who have always lived in the world, I send you, by Mr. Eliot, the famous Mr. Locke's book upon education,[1] in which you will find the stress that he lays upon the Graces, which he calls (and very truly) good-breeding. I have marked all the parts of that book which are worth your attention; for, as he begins with the child, almost from its birth, the parts relative to its infancy would be useless to you. Germany is still less than England the seat of the Graces; however, you had as good not say so while you are there. But the place which you are going to in a great degree is; for I have known as many

[1]John Locke (1632-1704), the famous philosopher, wrote his *Treatise on Education* in 1684 in the form of letters to Edward Clarke. They were published later.

well-bred, pretty men come from Turin as from any part of Europe. The late King Victor Amédée took great pains to form such of his subjects as were of any consideration both to business and manners. The present King, I am told, follows his example; this, however, is certain, that in all Courts and congresses where there are various foreign ministers, those of the King of Sardinia are generally the ablest, the politest, and *les plus déliés*. You will, therefore, at Turin, have very good models to form yourself upon; and remember, that with regard to the best models, as well as to the antique Greek statues in the print, *non mai a bastanȥa*. Observe every word, look, and motion of those who are allowed to be the most accomplished persons there. Observe their natural and careless, but genteel air; their unembarrassed good-breeding; their unassuming, but yet unprostituted dignity. Mind their decent mirth, their discreet frankness, and that *entregent*, which, as much above the frivolous as below the important and the secret, is the proper medium for conversation in mixed companies. I will observe, by the bye, that the talent of that light *entregent* is often of great use to a foreign minister; not only as it helps him to domesticate himself in many families, but also as it enables him to put by and parry some subjects of conversation which might possibly lay him under difficulties— both what to say and how to look.

Of all the men that ever I knew in my life (and I knew him extremely well), the late Duke of Marlborough possessed the Graces in the highest degree, not to say engrossed them; and, indeed, he got the most by them, for I will venture (contrary to the custom of profound historians, who always assign deep causes for great events) to ascribe the better half of the Duke of Marlborough's greatness and riches to those Graces. He was eminently illiterate; wrote bad English, and spelled it still worse. He had no share of what is commonly called *parts*; that is, he had no brightness, nothing shining in his genius. He had, most undoubtedly, an excellent good plain understanding, with sound judgment. But these alone would probably have raised him but something higher than they found him, which was page to King James the Second's Queen. There the Graces protected and promoted him; for, while he was an Ensign of the Guards, the Duchess of Cleveland, then favourite mistress to King Charles the Second, struck by those very Graces, gave him five thousand pounds, with which he immediately bought an annuity for his life, of five hundred pounds a-year, of my grandfather, Halifax, which was the foundation of his subsequent fortune. His figure was beautiful, but his manner was irresistible, by either man or woman. It was by this engaging, graceful manner, that he was enabled, during all his war, to connect the various and jarring powers of the Grand Alliance, and to carry them on to the main object of the war, notwithstanding their private and separate views, jealousies, and wrong-headednesses. Whatever Court he went to (and he was often obliged to go himself to some resty[1] and refractory ones), he as constantly prevailed, and brought them into his measures. The Pensionary Heinsius, a venerable old minister, grown grey in business, and who had governed the Republic of the United Provinces for more than forty years, was absolutely governed by the Duke of Marlborough, as that Republic feels to this day. He was always cool, and nobody ever observed the least variation in his countenance; he could refuse more gracefully than other people could grant; and those who went away from him the most dissatisfied as to the substance of their business, were yet personally charmed with him, and, in some degree, comforted by his manner. With all his gentleness and gracefulness, no man living was more conscious of his situation, nor maintained his dignity better.

With the share of knowledge which you have already gotten, and with the much greater which I hope you will

[1]*Resty*: stiff, stubborn. This phrase is quoted in the *N.E.D.*

soon acquire, what may you not expect to arrive at, if you join all these Graces to it! In your destination particularly, they are, in truth, half your business; for if you can once gain the affections, as well as the esteem, of the prince or minister of the Court to which you are sent, I will answer for it that will effectually do the business of the Court that sent you; otherwise it is up-hill work. Do not mistake, and think that these Graces, which I so often and so earnestly recommend to you, should only accompany important transactions, and be worn only *les jours de gala*; no, they should, if possible, accompany every the least thing that you do or say; for, if you neglect them in little things, they will leave you in great ones. I should, for instance, be extremely concerned to see you even drink a cup of coffee ungracefully, and slop yourself with it, by your awkward manner of holding it; nor should I like to see your coat buttoned, or your shoes buckled awry. But I should be outrageous if I heard you mutter your words unintelligibly, stammer in your speech, or hesitate, misplace, and mistake in your narrations: and I should run away from you with greater rapidity, if possible, than I should now run to embrace you, if I found you destitute of all those Graces, which I have set my heart upon their making you one day, *omnibus ornatum excellere rebus.*

This subject is inexhaustible, as it extends to everything that is to be said or done; but I will leave it for the present, as this letter is already pretty long. Such is my desire, my anxiety for your perfection, that I never think I have said enough, though you may possibly think I have said too much; and though, in truth, if your own good sense is not sufficient to direct you in many of these plain points, all that I or anybody else can say will be insufficient. But where you are concerned, I am the insatiable man in Horace, who covets still a little corner more, to complete the figure of his field. I dread every little corner that may deform mine, in which I would have (if possible) no one defect.

I this moment receive yours of the 17th N.S. and cannot condole with you upon the secession of your German *commensaux*; who, both by your and Mr. Harte's description, seem to be *des gens d'une aimable absence*; and, if you can replace them by any other German conversation, you will be a gainer by the bargain. I cannot conceive, if you understand German well enough to read any German book, how the writing of the German character can be so difficult and tedious to you, the twenty-four letters being very soon learned; and I do not expect that you should write yet with the utmost purity and correctness, as to the language; what I meant by your writing once a fortnight to Grevenkop, was only to make the written character familiar to you. However, I will be content with one in three weeks or so.

I believe you are not likely to see Mr. Eliot again soon, he being still in Cornwall with his father, who, I hear, is not likely to recover. Adieu!

No. 1602

À Madame la Marquise de Monconseil

(Maty I. xxxi)

À Londres, ce 21 novembre V.S 1748

Je reviens, Madame, depuis quatre jours seulement des Bains, auxquels mes vieilles indispositions m'avaient obligé d'avoir recours. Pendant mon séjour là, des vertiges et des migraines rendaient ma tête très indigne de vous dire la moindre chose, et elle n'était guère en état de vous expliquer les sentiments de mon cœur: ce qui m'en consolait, c'était que vous les connaissiez depuis longtemps. En attendant, je me trouve endetté de quatre lettres, que j'ai reçues de vous par différents canaux; c'est une dette que je ne pourrai jamais payer en espèces de même valeur, et je prétends seulement m'en acquitter par mon obéissance à vos ordres.

Il faut convenir que le théâtre français l'emporte en tout

genre sur tous les autres, et même sur les anciens, avec tout le respect que je leur dois.

Je suis charmé des honneurs, dont Monsieur de Richelieu est comblé; il les mérite, ou bien les aurait mérités à Gênes, s'il eût été question de la défendre, mais, grâce à nos bons alliés les Austro-Sardes, cette ville n'a pas seulement été assiégée. Il est vrai qu'il y avait une soi-disante armée devant la ville, mais pas plus nombreuse que la garnison même, et manquant absolument de tout ce qui était nécessaire pour faire un siège. Voila comme nous avons été soutenus partout de nos alliés; trente mille Autrichiens en ont représenté soixante, qui devaient se trouver en Flandres, et que nous payons comme complets. Heureusement la paix a mis fin à tous ces abus, et il est inutile de regarder en arrière.

Je n'ai pas encore les bras, pour lesquels je m'impatiente si fort, mais ils sont arrivés et je les attends à tous moments; c'est tout ce qui manque à présent à mon boudoir, qui d'ailleurs est fini, et charmant; j'y entre à Noël.

Adieu, Madame, pour cette fois; ma lettre se ressent de ma tête, et je vous assure que ma tête se ressent déjà de ma lettre.

No. 1603

To Edward Eliot

(*MSS. of the Earl of St. Germans*)

SIR,   *Monday morning* [21 *Nov.* 1748]

I will not trouble you with any professions of my concern for your loss of a very good Father, as the part which I dare say you believe that I take in everything that relates to you, would render such assurances unnecessary; this therefore is only to offer you most sincerely my best services, if it is in my power to do you any, and to assure you that I am with the warmest sentiments of esteem and friendship

Your most faithful humble servant, CHESTERFIELD.

I will have the pleasure of waiting upon you, when you shall let me know that I shall not be troublesome, and not till then; but in the meantime, I will venture to advise you not to take hastily any political engagements, with any person whatsoever; you will be tried by more than one upon that subject; but the previous arrangement of your own domestic affairs is a just answer to everybody.

No. 1604

To his Son

(*Stanhope CLXIX*)

London, 29 November O.S. 1748

DEAR BOY,

I delayed writing to you till I could give you some account of the motions of your friend, Mr. Eliot, for whom I know you have, and very justly, the most friendly concern. His father and he came to town together in a post-chaise, a fortnight ago, the rest of the family remaining in Cornwall. His father with difficulty survived the journey, and died last Saturday was sevennight. Both concern and decency confined your friend till two days ago, when I saw him; he has determined, and I think very prudently, to go abroad again, but how soon it is yet impossible for him to know, as he must necessarily put his own private affairs in some order first; but I conjecture he may possibly join you at Turin; sooner, to be sure, not. I am very sorry that you are likely to be so long without the company and example of so valuable a friend; and, therefore, I hope that you will make it up to yourself, as well as you can at this distance, by remembering and following his example. Imitate that application of his, which has made him know all thoroughly, and to the bottom. He does not content himself with the surface of knowledge; but works in the mine for it, knowing that it lies deep. Pope says, very truly, in his Essay upon Criticism,

> A little learning is a dangerous thing;
> Drink deep, or taste not the Pierian spring.

I shall send you by a ship that goes to Hamburg next week (and by which Hawkins sends Mr. Harte some things that he wrote for) all those which I proposed sending you by Mr. Eliot, together with a very little box, that I am desired to forward to Mr. Harte. There will be, likewise, two letters of recommendation for you to Monsieur Andrié and Comte Algarotti,[1] at Berlin, which you will take care to deliver to them, as soon as you shall be rigged and fitted out to appear there. They will introduce you into the best company, and I depend upon your own good sense for your avoiding of bad. If you fall into bad and low company there, or anywhere else, you will be irrecoverably lost; whereas, if you keep good company, and company above yourself, your character and your fortune will be immovably fixed.

I have not time to-day, upon account of the meeting of the Parliament, to make this letter of the usual length; and, indeed, after the volumes that I have written to you, all I can add must be unnecessary. However, I shall probably, *ex abundanti*, return soon to my former prolixity, and you will receive more and more last words from

Yours.

[1]Francesco Algarotti was born at Venice in 1712. In 1737 he published at Paris a popular sketch of the Newtonian system, entitled *Newtonianismo per le Dame*. Frederick the Great invited him to Berlin, and conferred on him the title of Count and the office of Chamberlain. He dedicated a work on the Opera to William Pitt; and wrote a letter to Gray complimenting him on his Odes, to which Gray replied 9th September, 1763. He died at Pisa in 1764. His epitaph, written by himself, is—

'HIC JACET FR. ALGAROTTUS, NON OMNIS.'

—M.

No. 1605

To the Rev. Dr. Madden

(*Maty App. XV*)

London, 29 *November* 1748

Sir,

A return of my old complaint of vertigos and pains in my head, which sent me to Bath, from whence I am but lately arrived here, and that with less benefit than I hoped for, delayed till now my acknowledgments for your last friendly letter, which accompanied the remainder of your poem. I read it with great pleasure, and not without some surprise, to find a work of that length continued to the end with the same spirit and fire with which it begins. Horace's great rule of *qualis ab incepto* was, I believe, never better observed. If the public receive the same pleasure from it that I have done, you will have the satisfaction of having discharged every office towards mankind that a private citizen of the world is capable of. Your example, your fortune, and your genius, will all have been devoted to the service, the improvement, and the rational pleasures, of your fellow creatures.

I make no doubt but that the Charter for the Dublin Society, when once you have formed it properly among yourselves, will be granted here; and, upon the whole, I am much for it, and will promote it to my power; not but that I foresee some danger on that side of the question too. Abuses have always hitherto crept into corporate bodies, and will probably, in time, creep into this too; but I hope that it will have such an effect, at first, as to make the future abuses of less consequence. The draught which Mr. Macauley showed me here of the Charter, seems to have all the provisions in it that human prudence can make against human iniquity.

Good health and long life attend you, my good friend,

for the sake of mankind in general, and of that country in particular which will ever have a great share of the warmest wishes of

Yours, etc.

No. 1606

To his Son

(Stanhope CLXX)

London, 6 December O.S. 1748

Dear Boy,

I am at present under very great concern for the loss of a most affectionate brother, with whom I had always lived in the closest friendship. My brother John died last Friday night, of a fit of the gout, which he had had for about a month in his hands and feet, and which fell at last upon his stomach and head. As he grew towards the last lethargic, his end was not painful to himself. At the distance which you are from hence, you need not go into mourning upon this occasion, as the time of your mourning would be near over before you could put it on.

By a ship which sails this week for Hamburg, I shall send you those things which I proposed to have sent you by Mr. Eliot—viz. a little box from your mamma, a less box for Mr. Harte, Mr. Locke's book upon education, the print of Carlo Maratti (which I mentioned to you some time ago), and two letters of recommendation, one to Monsieur Andrié, and the other to Comte Algarotti, at Berlin. Both those gentlemen will, I am sure, be as willing as they are able to introduce you into the best company, and I hope you will not (as many of your countrymen are apt to do) decline it. It is in the best companies only that you can learn the best manners, and that *tournure* and those Graces which I have so often recommended to you, as the necessary means of making a figure in the world.

I am most extremely pleased with the account which Mr. Harte gives me of your progress in Greek, and of your having read Hesiod, almost critically. Upon this subject I suggest but one thing to you, of many that I might suggest, which is, that you have now got over the difficulties of that language, and therefore it would be unpardonable not to persevere to your journey's end, now that all the rest of your way is down-hill.

I am also very well pleased to hear that you have such a knowledge of, and taste for, curious books, and scarce and valuable tracts. This is a kind of knowledge which very well becomes a man of sound and solid learning, but which only exposes a man of slight and superficial reading; therefore, pray make the substance and matter of such books your first object, and their title-pages, indexes, letter, and binding, but your second. It is the characteristic of a man of parts and good judgment to know, and give, that degree of attention that each object deserves; whereas little minds mistake little objects for great ones, and lavish away upon the former that time and attention which only the latter deserve. To such mistakes we owe the numerous and frivolous tribe of insect-mongers, shell-mongers, and pursuers and driers of butterflies, etc. The strong mind distinguishes not only between the useful and the useless, but likewise between the useful and the curious. He applies himself intensely to the former; he only amuses himself with the latter. Of this little sort of knowledge which I have just hinted at, you will find at least as much as you need wish to know, in a superficial but pretty French book entitled *Spectacle de la Nature*, which will amuse you while you read it, and give you a sufficient notion of the various parts of nature. I would advise you to read it at leisure hours; but that part of nature which Mr. Harte tells me you have begun to study, with the *Rector magnificus*, is of much greater importance, and deserves much more attention—I mean Astronomy. The vast and immense planetary system, the astonishing order and regularity of those innumerable worlds, will open a scene to you which not only deserves your attention as a matter of curiosity, or rather astonishment, but still more, as it will give you greater, and consequently juster, ideas of that eternal and omnipotent Being, who contrived, made, and still preserves that universe, than all the contemplation of this comparatively very little orb which we at present inhabit could possibly give you. Upon this subject, Monsieur Fontenelle's *Pluralité des Mondes*, which you may read in two hours' time, will both inform and please you. God bless you!

Yours.

No. 1607. To the Duke of Devonshire

Wednesday. [*December* 1748][1]

Election arrangements at Derby.[2]

(*MSS. of the Duke of Devonshire.* 338, 2)

No. 1608

To Solomon Dayrolles, Esq.

(*Mahon III. 305*)

London, 6 December O.S. 1748

Dear Dayrolles,

By the death of poor John, you have lost a true friend, and I a most affectionate brother and friend into the bargain. The gout fell upon his bowels and head, and threw him into the convulsions of which he died.

I acknowledge now your last of the 6th N.S. together with your former letters, which my brother's illness and a hurry of other affairs hindered me from answering sooner.

[1]Endorsed by the 6th Duke.

[2]Walpole to Mann, 26th December 1748. 'The families of Devonshire and Chesterfield have received a great blow at Derby, where, on the death of John Stanhope, they set up another of the name. One Mr. Rivett, the Duke's chief friend and manager, stood himself and carried it by a majority of seventy-one. Lord Chesterfield had sent down credit for ten thousand pounds.'

Mr. Pelham has faithfully promised me, that before Christmas you shall be paid up as high as any Minister in the King's service, which I hope will prevent any anticipations.

Lord Sandwich is, I know, impatient to come over, and I know that nobody is ready to go from hence; so that I cannot expect to see you for some months; and in the meantime the whole business of Holland will be in your hands, except what may be separately transacted between Bentinck there and his Grace[1] here. This, I think, is a lucky circumstance for you, as it will put you in possession of the business to a certain degree at least, and consequently strengthen the claim which you mentioned to his Grace. Though Lord Holderness is strongly insisted upon by the Bentincks, and will therefore, I suppose, be sent at last, yet I know that his distinguished incapacity for business staggers a good deal those who are to send him. *Tant mieux* if he goes, you will be of the more importance, which is my only object, for I have done with business, but not with you.

The prices of Van Huysen's flower-pieces, notwithstanding the scarcity of money in Holland, is owing only to that local frenzy which always prevails in Holland for some pretty trifling object; tulips, hyacinths, and pigeons, have all had their day, and now Van Huysen has his. But while these high-finished finical pieces bear such high prices, the bold and masterly pieces of the last and the foregoing century are slighted, and more likely to come reasonably. Do not, by any means, suffer that capital picture of Rubens, which you say is to be sold at Brussels, to slip through your hands, by the delay of sending me a drawing of it, if you can but be sure that it is an original, and not damaged. Three hundred guineas cannot be dear, and anything under that must be cheap. Wherefore, upon the two conditions of its being an undoubted original, and not damaged, buy it me

[1]Newcastle.

as soon as you can, or some other body may step in between.

Captain Irwine,[1] whom I believe you know, son to the old General, goes by the next packet-boat to Holland: he has got a furlough from his father for a year, during which time he intends to see as much as he can abroad. I think him a good pretty young fellow; and, considering that he has never been yet out of his native country, much more *presentable* than one could expect. Pray, carry him to Court, and into some companies, where I think you will not be ashamed of him, which will seldom be your case with my countrymen. I promised him that I would recommend him to you. *Adieu, mon cher infant!* I am so hurried by lawyers, appraisers, and creditors, that I can say no more now.

P.S. *À propos*, do not mention to anybody that the picture is for me, or what it may cost.

No. 1609

To his Son

(*Stanhope CLXXI*)

London, 13 *December O.S.* 1748

DEAR BOY,

The last four posts have brought me no letters, either from you or from Mr. Harte, at which I am uneasy—not as a mamma would be, but as a father should be; for I do not want your letters as bills of health: you are young, strong, and healthy, and I am, consequently, in no pain about that. Moreover, were either you or Mr. Harte ill, the other would

---

[1] Captain Irwine afterwards Sir John Irwine, K.C.B., and Commander-in-Chief in Ireland. 'He began the world as page of honour to Lionel, Duke of Dorset, by whose interest he was pushed forward in the army, and obtained a regiment. He afterwards married, and lived in a style of vain extravagance, which ended in involving him in pecuniary difficulties.' (Note to Madame du Deffand's Letters, vol. i. p. 240.) Madame du Deffand says of him: 'Il me paraît comme un assez bon homme.'—M.

See Lord Chesterfield's letter to Captain Irwine, of 4th April 1749.

doubtless write me word of it. My impatience for yours or
Mr. Harte's letters arises from a very different cause, which
is, my desire to hear frequently of the state and progress of
your mind. You are now at that critical period of life, when
every week ought to produce fruit or flowers answerable
to your culture, which I am sure has not been neglected;
and it is by your letters, and Mr. Harte's accounts of you,
that, at this distance, I can only judge of your gradations
to maturity. I desire, therefore, that one of you two will
not fail to write to me once a week. The sameness of your
present way of life, I easily conceive, would not make out a
very interesting letter to an indifferent bystander; but, so
deeply concerned as I am in the game you are playing, every
the least move is to me of importance, and helps me to
judge of the final event.

As you will be leaving Leipsig pretty soon after you
shall have received this letter, I here send you one inclosed,
to deliver to Mr. Mascow. It is to thank him for his attention and civility to you during your stay with him; and I
take it for granted that you will not fail making him the
proper compliments at parting; for the good name that we
leave behind at one place, often gets before us to another,
and is of great use. As Mr. Mascow is much known and
esteemed in the republic of letters, I think it would be of
advantage to you if you got letters of recommendation from
him to some of the learned men at Berlin. Those testi-
monials give a lustre which is not to be despised; for the
most ignorant are forced to seem, at least, to pay a regard
to learning, as the most wicked are to virtue. Such is their
intrinsic worth!

Your friend Duval dined with me the other day, and com-
plained most grievously that he had not heard from you of
above a year: I bade him abuse you for it himself, and
advised him to do it in verse, which, if he was really angry,
his indignation would enable him to do.[1] He accordingly

[1]An allusion to the line of Juvenal:
Si natura negat, facit indignatio versum.

brought me, yesterday, the enclosed reproaches and challenge, which he desired me to transmit to you. As this is
his first essay in English poetry, the inaccuracies in the
rhymes and the numbers are very excusable. He insists, as
you will find, upon being answered in verse, which I should
imagine that you and Mr. Harte together could bring about;
as the late Lady Dorchester[1] used to say, that she and Dr.
Radcliffe together could cure a fever. This is, however,
sure, that it now rests upon you; and no man can say what
methods Duval may take, if you decline his challenge. I am
sensible that you are under some disadvantages in this
proffered combat. Your climate, at this time of the year
especially, delights more in the wood fire than in the poetic
fire; and I conceive the Muses (if there are any at Leipsig)
to be rather shivering than singing. Nay, I question whether
Apollo is even known there as God of Verse, or as God of
Light; perhaps, a little, as God of Physic. These will be
fair excuses if your performance should fall something
short, though I do not apprehend it will.

While you have been at Leipsig (which is a place of study
more than of pleasure or company) you have had all opportunities of pursuing your studies uninterruptedly, and have
had, I believe, very few temptations to the contrary. But
the case will be quite different at Berlin, where the splendour
and dissipation of a Court, and the *beau monde*, will present
themselves to you in gaudy shapes, attractive enough to all
young people. Do not think, now, that, like an old fellow,
I am going to advise you to reject them, and shut yourself
up in your closet: quite the contrary. I advise you to take
your share, and enter into them with spirit and pleasure;
but then I advise you, too, to allot your time so prudently,

---

[1]Catherine Sedley, mistress to King James the Second, and by him created
Countess of Dorchester. She was the daughter of Sir Charles Sedley, courtier,
wit, poet, playwright. She died, it is said, repentant.
    'And Sedley cursed the form that pleased a king,'
Johnson remarked in *The Vanity of Human Wishes*. She had married, in 1696,
the first Earl Portmore.

as that learning may keep pace with pleasures: there is full time in the course of the day for both, if you do but manage that time right, and like a good economist. The whole morning, if diligently and attentively devoted to solid studies, will go a great way at the year's end; and the evening, spent in the pleasures of good company, will go as far in teaching you a knowledge not much less necessary than the other—I mean the knowledge of the world. Between these two necessary studies—that of books in the morning, and that of the world in the evening, you see that you will not have one minute to squander or slattern away. Nobody ever lent themselves more than I did, when I was young, to the pleasures and dissipation of good company: I even did it too much. But then I can assure you that I always found time for serious studies; and, when I could find it no other way, I took it out of my sleep; for I resolved always to rise early in the morning, however late I went to bed at night: and this resolution I have kept so sacred, that, unless when I have been confined to my bed by illness, I have not, for more than forty years, ever been in bed at nine o'clock in the morning, but commonly up before eight.

When you are in Berlin, remember to speak German as often as you can in company: for everybody there will speak French to you, unless you let them know that you can speak German, which then they will choose to speak. Adieu!

No. 1610

To his Son

(*Stanhope CLXXII*)

London, 20 December O.S. 1748

Dear Boy,

I received, last Saturday, by three mails which came in at once, two letters from Mr. Harte, and yours of the 8th N.S.

It was I who mistook your meaning with regard to your German letters, and not you who expressed it ill. I thought it was the writing of the German character that took up so much of your time, and therefore I advised you, by the frequent writing of that character, to make it easy and familiar to you. But, since it is only the propriety and purity of the German language, which make your writing it so tedious and laborious, I will tell you I shall not be nice upon that article; and did not expect you should yet be master of all the idioms, delicacies, and peculiarities of that difficult language. That can only come by use, especially frequent speaking; therefore, when you shall be at Berlin, and afterwards at Turin, where you will meet many Germans, pray take all opportunities of conversing in German, in order not only to keep what you have got of that language, but likewise to improve and perfect yourself in it. As to the characters, you form them very well, and, as you yourself own, better than your English ones; but then, let me ask you this question—Why do you not form your Roman characters better? for I maintain, that it is in every man's power to write what hand he pleases; and, consequently, that he ought to write a good one. You form, particularly, your *ll* and your *tt* in zigzag, instead of making them straight, as thus, *u*, *ll*; a fault very easily mended. You will not, I believe, be angry with this little criticism, when I tell you, that by all the accounts that I have had of late, from Mr. Harte and others, this is the only criticism that you give me occasion to make. Mr. Harte's last letter, of the 14th N.S. particularly, makes me extremely happy, by assuring me, that in every respect you do exceedingly well. I am not afraid by what I now say of making you too vain; because I do not think that a just consciousness, and an honest pride of doing well, can be called vanity; for vanity is either the silly affectation of good qualities which one has not, or the sillier pride of what does not deserve commendation in itself. By Mr. Harte's account, you are got very near the goal of Greek and Latin; and therefore I cannot suppose that, as your sense increases, your endeavours and your speed will slacken, in finishing the small remains of your course. Consider what lustre and *éclat* it will give you when you return here, to be allowed to be the best scholar of a gentleman in England; not to mention the real pleasure and solid comfort which such knowledge will give you throughout your whole life. Mr. Harte tells me another thing, which, I own, I did not expect; that is, that when you read aloud, or repeat parts of plays, you speak very properly and distinctly. This relieves me from great uneasiness, which I was under upon account of your former bad enunciation. Go on, and attend most diligently to this important article. It is, of all the Graces (and they are all necessary), the most necessary one.

Comte Pertingue, who has been here about a fortnight, far from disavowing, confirms all that Mr. Harte has said to your advantage. He thinks he shall be at Turin much about the time of your arrival there, and pleases himself with the hopes of being useful to you: though, should you get there before him, he says that Comte du Perron, with whom you are a favourite, will take that care. You see by this one instance, and, in the course of your life you will see by a million of instances, of what use a good reputation is, and how swift and advantageous a harbinger it is, wherever one goes. Upon this point, too, Mr. Harte does you justice, and tells me that you are desirous of praise from the praiseworthy: this is a right and generous ambition; and without which, I fear, few people would deserve praise.

But here let me, as an old stager upon the theatre of the world, suggest one consideration to you; which is, to extend your desire of praise a little beyond the strictly praiseworthy; or else you may be apt to discover too much contempt for at least three parts in five of the world, who will never forgive it you. In the mass of mankind, I fear, there is too great a majority of fools and knaves; who, simply from their number, must to a certain degree be respected, though they are by no means respectable. And a man who will show every knave or fool that he thinks him such, will engage in a most ruinous war against numbers much superior to those that he and his allies can bring into the field. Abhor a knave, and pity a fool in your heart; but let neither of them unnecessarily see that you do so. Some complaisance and attention to fools is prudent, and not mean: as a silent abhorrence of individual knaves is often necessary, and not criminal.

As you will now soon part with Lord Pulteney, with whom, during your stay together at Leipsig, I suppose you have formed a connection, I imagine that you will continue it by letters, which I would advise you to do. They tell me he is good-natured, and does not want parts, which are of themselves two good reasons for keeping it up; but there is also a third reason, which, in the course of the world, is not to be despised: his father cannot live long, and will leave him an immense fortune, which, in all events, will make him of some consequence, and, if he has parts into the bargain, of very great consequence; so that his friendship may be extremely well worth your cultivating, especially as it will not cost you above one letter in one month.

I do not know whether this letter will find you at Leipsig; at least, it is the last I shall direct there. My next, to either you or Mr. Harte, will be directed to Berlin; but, as I do not know to what house or street there, I suppose it will remain at the posthouse till you send for it. Upon your arrival at Berlin, you will send me your particular direction; and also, pray be minute in your accounts of your reception there by those whom I recommend you to, as well as by those to whom they present you. Remember, too, that you are going to a polite and literate Court, where the Graces will best introduce you.

Adieu! God bless you! and may you continue to deserve my love as much as you now enjoy it!

P.S.—Lady Chesterfield bids me tell you that she decides entirely in your favour, against Mr. Grevenkop, and even against herself; for she does not think that she could, at this time, write either so good a character or so good German. Pray write her a German letter upon that subject, in which you may tell her that, like the rest of the world, you approve of her judgment, because it is in your favour; and that you true Germans cannot allow Danes[1] to be competent judges of your language, etc.

No. 1611

To Solomon Dayrolles, Esq.

(Mahon III. 307)

London, 23 December O.S. 1748

Dear Dayrolles,

My former was almost an answer, beforehand, to your last letter, which I received the day after I had wrote mine; I mean, with regard to the Rubens, which I desired you not to let slip. But I am now more confirmed in that opinion, by the drawing, which you sent me, and by the assurances that you give me of the picture being a capital one, and in high preservation. Therefore, secure it as cheap as you can; but give the three hundred, rather than not buy it; the subject, as you observe, might have been a more pleasing one, but this admits of great expression.

The family-piece, which you mention by Vandyke, I would not give six shillings for, unless I had the honour of being of Sir Melchior's family. The several portraits are, I dare say, finely painted; but then where is the action, where the expression? The good man and his wife generally sit serene in a couple of easy chairs, surrounded by five or six of their children, insignificantly motionless in the presence of Papa and Mamma; and the whole family seem as insipid, and weary, as when they are really together.

[1]Grevenkop was a Dane.

Their likenesses may indeed be valuable to their own
posterity, but in my mind to nobody else. Titian has done
more skilfully in his fine picture of the Cornaro family,
which he has put in action.

The Venus and Adonis of Vandyke, of which you likewise sent me the drawing, I do not care for, as it is a subject
already *rebattu* by still greater masters, and in my mind
better, as far as I can judge by the drawing; for Adonis,
when he tears himself away from Venus, seems fierce and
angry, which I see no occasion for. He is determined, indeed, to leave her for his field sports; but should, in my
opinion, soften the rudeness by all possible complaisance in
his words and looks.

So much for *virtù*, which, when I shall have bought this
picture, I have done with, unless a very capital Teniers
should come in your way. You will draw upon me for the
money as soon as ever you please.

I am really sorry for my Baron's accumulated misfortunes; his terrors must be unspeakable; his wife, if she
died, would be a great loss to him, not indeed in a carnal,
but in a domestic sense, and his son turning out a rascal,
fills up the measure. Make my compliments to him when
you see him.

This wind which keeps the Duke still in Holland, keeps
you in breath, and Lord Sandwich in a fever, who longs to
be here, *pour s'orienter* a little at home. He and *his Grace*[1]
were lately by no means well together, and even strong
expressions in writing had passed between them. But all
that may come right again, for politicians neither love nor
hate.[2] Interest, not sentiment, directs them. If Bentinck
pouts, he may possibly carry a present point by it, from
people, who it may be, do not yet care to break openly with
him; but he will lose their favour, and even incur their
secret hatred. An able man will do whatever he does *de*

[1] A reference to the inevitable quarrel between Newcastle and his late pet.
[2] *Absalom and Achitophel*, I. l. 223.

bonne grâce quoique le diable n'y perd rien. Half anger and half confidence are the most imprudent things in the world.

Could you send me, in some of your letters, some seed of the right Cantelupe melons? I should not know what to do with more than a dozen, or at most twenty, of them; so that all the seed I shall want will neither increase the bulk nor weight of a letter. The Cantelupes are, in my opinion, the best sort of melons; at least they always succeed best here. It is for Blackheath that I want it, where you can easily judge that my melon-ground is most exceedingly small. I am obliged to keep that place for seven years, my poor brother's lease being for that time; and I doubt I could not part with it, but to a very great loss, considering the sums of money that he had laid out upon it. For otherwise I own that I like the country up, much better than down, the river.[1]

As I promised to send Captain Irwine a couple of letters to the Hague, for Paris, I must put you to the expense of inclosing them to you, and to the trouble of giving them to him, not knowing how to direct them for him.

Yours faithfully.

No. 1612

To Solomon Dayrolles, Esq.

(*Mahon III. 310*)

London, 23 December O.S. 1748

Dear Dayrolles,

I have received yours, with the inclosed drawing of the Vandyke, which must certainly be a very fine one, if the

[1]This villa at Blackheath afterwards became Lord Chesterfield's constant summer residence. He purchased a prolongation of the lease, built a handsome gallery and other additions to the house, and, with respect to the gardens and hothouses, was, as he says himself, strongly seized with the *furor hortensis*. After his death it passed in succession through several other hands, but being built on Crown-land has finally become the Ranger's Lodge, and is given with the office of Ranger of Greenwich Park. Still, however, it frequently goes by the name of Chesterfield House.—M.

execution, as doubtless it is, be answerable to the disposition: but, however, I continue my negative to it, for the reasons which I gave you before, the price, and that it is a portrait, however fine a one. The Rubens, of which I have a great notion, must and shall, for a time at least, content me, unless I strain a little for the Teniers, which you hint at, which if it be a capital one, I will; and then have done. My great room will be as full of pictures as it ought to be; and all capital ones.

I gave you by my last letter a very unnecessary trouble, which I now retract. I had forgot that you had some time ago stocked me with excellent Cantelupe melon-seed, which I have since remembered and found, and given to my gardener to sow at the proper season. I hope to give you some of them in perfection next summer; for I do not flatter myself with the hopes of seeing you here before that time.

I am really sorry for poor Kreuningen, and cannot conceive what will become of him. You gave him the best advice with regard to his son, but yet I doubt it will not do, for either a good or a bad reputation outruns and gets before people wherever they go. I do not write to the father myself, not knowing what to say to him, but pray make him my compliments, and assure him of the sincere part that I take in whatever concerns him.

Adieu, dear Dayrolles. I am hurried by a complication of most disagreeable affairs,[1] but always, Yours.

No. 1613

À Madame la Marquise de Monconseil

(*Maty I. xxxii*)

À Londres, ce 26 décembre V.S. 1748

Ils sont arrivés sains et saufs, Madame, je les ai, j'en suis charmé; le goût en est parfait; vous jugez bien qu'il est

[1]No doubt the defeat in the election at Derby.

question de vos bras, dont il n'y a pas un doigt de cassé.
Ils flatteront sûrement les yeux de tout le monde, mais à
moi, ils me flatteront encore plus le cœur. La main délicate
de l'ouvrier sera ce que j'envisagerai le moins; mais ce sera
le souvenir et l'amitié de la personne, qui me les a envoyés,
qui leur donneront leur véritable prix. Ils m'ont jeté pourtant dans un certain embarras; tirez m'en, Madame, par vos
conseils; c'est que je voudrais bien m'en servir, et en même
temps je crains de m'en servir. J'en suis glorieux comme
d'une belle maîtresse; mais j'en suis aussi jaloux; si je ne les
produis point, ma vanité en souffrira; et si je les produis,
que sait-on? Ils sont fragiles, d'autres les toucheront, les
casseront peut-être, du moins je craindrai furieusement pour
eux dans mon absence. Décidez donc ce que je dois faire.
Ils vont aux deux côtés de la cheminée de mon boudoir,
comme s'ils étaient faits exprès, je les ai mis, et je les ai ôtés,
de sorte que l'affaire est encore dans son entier, et je ne
demande pas votre conseil comme on le demande ordinairement, après avoir pris son parti.

La maladie, et ensuite la mort, d'un frère que j'aimais
tendrement, jointes à ma propre indisposition, dont je ne
suis pas encore tout-à-fait quitte, m'ont mis en arrière avec
vous en fait de lettres, mais aussi, qui ne l'est pas vis-à-vis
de vous en fait de tout? En cela mon sort est commun, mais
ne croyez pas pour cela que mes sentiments le soient aussi;
au contraire, c'est le seul point que je disputerai avec tous
vos serviteurs.

P.S. Les compliments de la nouvelle année sont sous-
entendus; aussi je crois qu'il vaut mieux les sous-entendre
que de dire ce qui s'est dit depuis six mille ans.

No. 1614

To Solomon Dayrolles, Esq.

(Mahon III. 313)

London, 27 *December O.S.* 1748

Dear Dayrolles,

I received this morning your letter of the 3rd of January N.S. with the two parcels of melon-seed, which as I told you in my last, I might have saved you the trouble of sending me, if I had but remembered how plentifully you had supplied me before; but since I have so carelessly put you to that trouble, all I can now do, is to have it sowed the latest, so that you may be sure to taste the fruits of it when you shall be here, which I do not expect will be till autumn. A new Minister will not, before that time, be well settled at the Hague; and till then you will not nor should I wish you to, leave it. I can account for a certain person's[1] having changed his opinion and desiring to remain now where he is. Things are much altered, and the prospect which a little while ago he had here is vanished; his Grace[2] speaks of him very differently from what he used to do, and their epistolary quarrels are, I believe, remembered with equal resentment on both sides. In my opinion if his Grace could get off his engagement to Lord Holderness and his friend, on your side of the water, he would be glad enough to let the present Minister remain there as long as he pleases, for he dreads his influence over his brother Grace;[3] and not without reason. Tom Villiers,[4] who has succeeded my brother in the Admiralty, goes *Ministre de Confiance* to Vienna, which commission he would not accept of without having the Admiralty in hand first.

[1]Lord Sandwich.   [2]Of Newcastle.   [3]Of Bedford.

[4]Afterwards first Earl of Clarendon, of the second creation. Horace Walpole speaks of him as 'a very silly fellow.'—To Sir H. Mann, 26th December 1748. —M.

Where this will shove Keith, I cannot guess; only I should not like his coming back to the Hague to Lord Sandwich.

As to my Rubens, for I now call it mine, you have acted with your usual prudence and economy. But if it turns out such as it is represented to you, I do not expect that you will get any considerable abatement of the first price of £300. As to the method of getting it over safe here, I refer myself to your abilities; many officers' baggage will be coming, Ligonier's especially, into which you may possibly thrust it. Draw upon me, in an amicable way I mean, how and when you please; for I do not take your finances to be in a situation to allow long and large advances.

Your Leipsig acquaintance is setting out for Berlin. He has applied himself extremely, and with great success, at Leipsig, having made himself perfect master, as I am assured by his master, of Greek, Latin, the Laws of Nations and of the Empire, and of the German language to boot; which, by the way, he writes as well as any German I ever knew. I am therefore no longer in the least pain about the learning part, of which he has now got such a stock, that he will have a pleasure, instead of a toil, in improving it. All that he wants now is *les grâces*, in pursuit of which he goes, as soon as the roads will permit, from Berlin to Turin, there to remain for at least a year. I know no Court that sends out at least *des gens plus déliés*. I do not know what those may be, whom they keep at home; but by the samples I judge well of them.

The Prince of Wales will, I believe, buy Vandyke's Sir Melchior and company. I have given him the drawing you sent me; and Mr. Laurenzy is wrote to by this post to speak to you about it.

Yours very sincerely,

No. 1615
TO HIS SON
(Stanhope CLXXIII)

London, 30 December O.S. 1748

DEAR BOY,

I direct this letter to Berlin, where, I suppose, it will either find you, or, at least, wait but a very little time for you. I cannot help being anxious for your success, at this your first appearance upon the great stage of the world; for, though the spectators are always candid enough to give great allowances, and to show great indulgence to a new actor, yet, from the first impressions which he makes upon them, they are apt to decide, in their own minds, at least, whether he will ever be a good one or not. If he seems to understand what he says, by speaking it properly; if he is attentive to his part, instead of staring negligently about; and if, upon the whole, he seems ambitious to please, they willingly pass over little awkwardnesses and inaccuracies, which they ascribe to a commendable modesty in a young and inexperienced actor. They pronounce that he will be a good one in time; and, by the encouragement which they give him, make him so the sooner. This, I hope, will be your case: you have sense enough to understand your part; a constant attention, and ambition to excel in it, with a careful observation of the best actors, will inevitably qualify you, if not for the first, at least for considerable parts.

Your dress (as insignificant a thing as dress is in itself) is now become an object worthy of some attention; for, I confess, I cannot help forming some opinion of a man's sense and character from his dress; and, I believe, most people do as well as myself. Any affectation whatsoever in dress implies, in my mind, a flaw in the understanding. Most of our young fellows here display some character or other by their dress; some affect the tremendous, and wear

a great and fiercely-cocked hat, an enormous sword, a short
waistcoat, and a black cravat; these I should be almost
tempted to swear the peace against, in my own defence, if
I were not convinced that they are but meek asses in lions'
skins. Others go in brown frocks, leather breeches, great
oaken cudgels in their hands, their hats uncocked, and their
hair unpowdered; and imitate grooms, stage-coachmen, and
country bumpkins so well in their outsides, that I do not
make the least doubt of their resembling them equally in
their insides. A man of sense carefully avoids any particular
character in his dress; he is accurately clean for his own
sake, but all the rest is for other people's. He dresses as
well, and in the same manner, as the people of sense and
fashion of the place where he is. If he dresses better, as he
thinks, that is, more than they, he is a fop; if he dresses
worse, he is unpardonably negligent: but of the two, I
would rather have a young fellow too much than too little
dressed; the excess on that side will wear off with a little
age and reflection; but if he is negligent at twenty, he will
be a sloven at forty, and stink at fifty years old. Dress
yourselves fine where others are fine, and plain where others
are plain; but take care always that your clothes are well
made, and fit you, for otherwise they will give you a very
awkward air. When you are once well dressed for the day,
think no more of it afterwards; and, without any stiffness
for fear of discomposing that dress, let all your motions be
as easy and natural as if you had no clothes on at all. So
much for dress, which I maintain to be a thing of consequence in the polite world.

As to manners, good-breeding, and the Graces, I have so
often entertained you upon these important subjects, that I
can add nothing to what I have formerly said. Your own
good sense will suggest to you the substance of them; and
observation, experience, and good company, the several
modes of them. Your great vivacity, which I hear of from
many people, will be no hindrance to your pleasing in good

company; on the contrary, will be of use to you, if tempered by good-breeding, and accompanied by the Graces. But then, I suppose your vivacity to be a vivacity of parts, and not a constitutional restlessness; for the most disagreeable composition that I know in the world, is that of strong animal spirits with a cold genius. Such a fellow is troublesomely active, frivolously busy, foolishly lively; talks much with little meaning, and laughs more with less reason: whereas, in my opinion, a warm and lively genius, with a cool constitution, is the perfection of human nature.

Do what you will at Berlin, provided you do but do something all day long. All that I desire of you is, that you will never slattern away one minute in idleness and in doing nothing. When you are not in company, learn what either books, masters, or Mr. Harte can teach you; and, when you are in company, learn (what company only can teach you) the characters and manners of mankind. I really ask your pardon for giving you this advice, because, if you are a rational creature and a thinking being, as I suppose and verily believe you are, it must be unnecessary, and to a certain degree injurious. If I did not know, by experience, that some men pass their whole time in doing nothing, I should not think it possible for any being, superior to M. Descartes's automatons, to squander away in absolute idleness one single minute of that small portion of time which is allotted us in this world.

I have lately seen one Mr. Cranmer, a very sensible merchant, who told me he had dined with you, and seen you often at Leipsig; and yesterday I saw an old footman of mine, whom I made a messenger, who told me that he had seen you last August. You will easily imagine that I was not the less glad to see them because they had seen you; and examined them both narrowly in their respective departments—the former as to your mind, the latter as to your body. Mr. Cranmer gave me great satisfaction, not only by what he told me of himself concerning you, but by what he was commissioned to tell me from Mr. Mascow. As he speaks German perfectly himself, I asked him how you spoke it, and he assured me very well for the time, and that a very little more practice would make you perfectly master of it. The messenger told me you were much grown, and, to the best of his guess, within two inches as tall as I am; that you were plump, and looked healthy and strong, which was all I could expect, or hope, from the sagacity of the person.

I send you, my dear child (and, you will not doubt, very sincerely), the wishes of the season. May you deserve a great number of happy New Years! and, if you deserve, may you have them! Many new years, indeed, you may see, but happy ones you cannot see without deserving them. These, virtue, honour, and knowledge alone can merit— alone can procure. *Dii tibi dent annos, de te nam cætera sumes*,[1] was a pretty piece of poetical flattery, where it was said; I hope that, in time, it may be no flattery when said to you. But I assure you that, whenever I cannot apply the latter part of the line to you with truth, I shall neither say, think, nor wish the former. Adieu!

[1]Ovid, *Ex Ponto*, II. i. 53:
Dii tibi dent annos! a te nam cætera sumes;
Erat modo virtuti tempora longa tuæ.

1749

London, 10 *January O.S.* 1749

Dear Boy,

I have received your letter of the 31st December N.S. Your thanks for my present, as you call it, exceed the value of the present; but the use which you assure me that you will make of it is the thanks which I desire to receive. Due attention to the inside of books, and due contempt for the outside, is the proper relation between a man of sense and his books.

Now that you are going a little more into the world, I will take this occasion to explain my intentions as to your future expenses, that you may know what you have to expect from me, and make your plan accordingly. I shall neither deny nor grudge you any money that may be necessary for either your improvement or your pleasures—I mean, the pleasures of a rational being. Under the head of improvement, I mean the best books and the best masters, cost what they will; I also mean, all the expense of lodgings, coach, dress, servants, etc., which, according to the several places where you may be, shall be respectively necessary to enable you to keep the best company. Under the head of rational pleasures, I comprehend—first, proper charities to real and compassionate objects of it; secondly, proper presents to those to whom you are obliged, or whom you desire to oblige; thirdly, a conformity of expense to that of the company which you keep—as in public spectacles, your share of little entertainments, a few pistoles at games of mere commerce, and other incidental calls of good company. The only two articles which I will never supply are—the profusion of low riot, and the idle lavishness of negligence and laziness. A fool squanders away, without credit or advantage to himself, more than a man of sense spends with both. The latter employs his money as he does his time, and never spends a shilling of the one, nor a minute of the other, but in something that is either useful or rationally pleasing to himself or others; the former buys whatever he does not want, and does not pay for what he does want. He cannot withstand the charms of a toy-shop; snuff-boxes, watches, heads of canes, etc., are his destruction. His servants and tradesmen conspire with his own indolence to cheat him; and in a very little time he is astonished, in the midst of all the ridiculous superfluities, to find himself in want of all the real comforts and necessaries of life. Without care and method, the largest fortune will not—and with them, almost the smallest will—supply all necessary expenses. As far as you can possibly, pay ready money for everything you buy, and avoid bills. Pay that money, too, yourself, and not through the hands of any servant, who always either stipulates poundage, or requires a present for his good word, as they call it. Where you must have bills (as for meat and drink, clothes, etc.), pay them regularly every month, and with your own hand. Never, from a mistaken economy, buy a thing you did not want because it is cheap, or, from a silly pride, because it is dear. Keep an account in a book of all that you receive, and of all that you pay; for no man, who knows what he receives and what he pays, ever runs out. I do not mean that you should keep an account of the shillings and half-crowns which you may spend in chair-hire, operas, etc.; they are unworthy of the time, and of the ink, that they would consume. Leave such *minuties* to dull, penny-wise fellows; but remember, in economy, as well as in every other part of life, to have the proper attention to proper objects, and the proper contempt for little ones. A strong mind sees things in their true proportions; a weak one views them through a magnifying medium, which, like the microscope, makes an elephant of a flea, magnifies all little objects, but cannot receive great ones. I have known many a man pass for a miser, by saving a penny and wrangling for twopence, who was undoing himself at the same time by living above his income, and not attending to essential articles, which were above his *portée*. The sure characteristic of a sound and strong mind is, to find in everything those certain bounds, *quo ultra citraque nequit consistere rectum*.[1] These boundaries are marked out by a very fine line, which only good sense and attention can discover: it is much too fine for vulgar eyes. In manners, this line is good-breeding; beyond it, is troublesome ceremony; short of it, is unbecoming negligence and inattention. In morals, it divides ostentatious puritanism from criminal relaxation. In religion, superstition from impiety; and, in short, every virtue from its kindred vice or weakness. I think you have sense enough to discover the line: keep it always in your eye, and learn to walk upon it; rest upon Mr. Harte, and he will poise you till you are able to go alone. By the way, there are fewer people who walk well upon that line than upon the slack rope, and therefore a good performer shines so much the more.

Your friend, Comte Pertingue, who constantly inquires after you, has written to Comte Salmour, the Governor of the Academy at Turin, to prepare a room for you there, immediately after the Ascension, and has recommended you to him in a manner which I hope you will give him no reason to repent or be ashamed of. As Comte Salmour's son, now residing at the Hague, is my particular acquaintance, I shall have regular and authentic accounts of all that you do at Turin.

[1]Horace, *Sat.* I. i. 107.

During your stay at Berlin, I expect that you should inform yourself thoroughly of the present state of the civil,
military, and ecclesiastical government of the King of
Prussia's dominions, particularly of the military, which is
upon a better footing in that country than in any other in
Europe.[1] You will attend at the reviews, see the troops
exercise, and inquire into the numbers of troops and companies in the respective regiments of horse, foot, and
dragoons; the numbers and titles of the commissioned and
non-commissioned officers in the several troops and companies; and also take care to learn the technical military
terms in the German language; for, though you are not to be
a military man, yet these military matters are so frequently
the subjects of conversation, that you will look very awkwardly if you are ignorant of them. Moreover, they are
commonly the objects of negotiation, and, as such, fall within your future profession. You must also inform yourself
of the reformation which the King of Prussia has lately made
in the law, by which he has both lessened the number and
shortened the duration of lawsuits; a great work, and worthy
of so great a prince! As he is indisputably the ablest prince
in Europe, every part of his government deserves your most
diligent inquiry, and your most serious attention. It must
be owned that you set out well as a young politician, by
beginning at Berlin, and then going to Turin, where you
will see the next ablest monarch to that of Prussia; so that,
if you are capable of making political reflections, those two
princes will furnish you with sufficient matter for them.

I would have you endeavour to get acquainted with Monsieur de Maupertuis,[2] who is so eminently distinguished by

[1] Frederick the Great, out of respect and admiration for Chesterfield, whom he
had invited to see him, paid attentions to Philip Stanhope.

[2] Pierre Louis Moreau de Maupertuis (1698-1759). In 1736 he was chief of the
Academicians in the expedition to Lapland to measure a degree of the meridian.
Voltaire, then his friend, wrote beneath his portrait—

Son sort est de fixer la figure du monde,
De lui plaire et de l'éclairer.

After a quarrel Voltaire assailed him in the *Diatribe du Docteur Akakia.* He was

all kinds of learning and merit, that one should be both
sorry and ashamed of having been even a day in the same
place with him, and not to have seen him. If you should
have no other way of being introduced to him, I will send
you a letter from hence. Monsieur Cagnoni, at Berlin, to
whom I know you are recommended, is a very able man of
business, thoroughly informed of every part of Europe; and
his acquaintance, if you deserve and improve it as you
should do, may be of great use to you.

Remember to take the best dancing-master at Berlin,
more to teach you to sit, stand, and walk gracefully, than to
dance finely. The Graces, the Graces! remember the Graces!
Adieu!

No. 1617

To Solomon Dayrolles, Esq.

(*Mahon III. 316*)

London, 20 January 1749

Dear Dayrolles,

Last post brought me yours of the 24th N.S. My old
disorder in my head, which has of late plagued me, hindered
me from acknowledging your two former letters. I am now
much better, thanks to a good blister, which I clapped upon
my head, on the part offending.

Since the Rubens is secured, I am in no haste to receive
it, for I could not hang it up yet, its place not being ready.
The way you mention of sending it by the sloop is, I think,
the best; and pray let it be directed to Mr. Hotham, one of
the Commissioners of the Customs, who will take care of
it, and pay the duty for me. You will take care to have it

invited to Berlin in 1740 by Frederick the Great to reconstruct the Academy of
Berlin, which, after the death of Leibniz in 1716, had decayed. He followed
Frederick to the field, and was taken prisoner at the battle of Molwitz; after his
release in 1746 he returned to Berlin, and was elected President of the new
Academy.

so safely packed up, that it may receive no damage *en chemin faisant*.

If Lord Sandwich did not really know (which by the way I can hardly believe) that Tom Villiers was to go to Vienna, he must be very little in the secret of affairs here, for it is very well known that Villiers refused going to Vienna, unless he had the Admiralty down first in hand. But I do believe that Lord Sandwich is not upon very good terms with *his Grace*, as my Baron calls him. He arrived here on Tuesday night. The town talks him out of the Admiralty, and the Duke of Cumberland into it; but I do not believe either. You have convinced me that you need not fear the return of Keith, who will look higher.

I am astonished at your being so much behind-hand, for I was most strongly promised that you should, before this time, be cleared off to last Michaelmas at least. I will speak to Mr. Pelham again about it; though after what I have already said to him, and he to me, upon that subject, I fear that it will be to little purpose.

I am glad that I have prevailed with my Baron to return to his old house, for the first warm weather must have suffocated him where he now is. If he escapes dying of the first fright when he goes back, all the rest will do very well, and go on just as it used to do. His *beaux sentiments pour la défunte*, I dare say, will not kill him.

I am rejoiced to hear that I shall have another *tome* of the *Histoire Amoureuse*, for now that (thank God) I have no business, that kind of reading amuses me. The *Histoire Politique* of the United Provinces would at present be but a gloomy one. I see no Government there at all; but I see power without authority, and expense without the possible means of supplies. The Prince of Orange wants a Sully instead of a Bentinck. The reduction of the troops will be a decisive point; if it is a considerable one, the Prince of Orange is nobody; and if it is not, the Republic is undone.

I have read Lord Sandwich's farewell speech, in which I

think there are some things more boldly asserted than clearly proved, for it does not by any means appear to me that the Republic was stronger last year, when the enemy was at its gates, than it was three or four years before, when the French were no nearer than Tournay; nor am I as yet sensible of the great advantages which the change of the Government in the Republic has produced with regard to England, when the former cannot in the whole Seven Provinces raise one hundred thousand ducats to pay its share of the Russians, but is obliged to borrow that trifling sum of the latter. But these reflection are entirely out of my present province, and have nothing to do with my house and garden, which employ both my thoughts and my time. I am at work about them all day, and shall take possession of them in about a month. There I shall be impatient to see you, and there I believe you will not be sorry to see

Yours.

No. 1618

To his Son

(*Stanhope CLXXV*)

London, 24 January O.S. 1749

Dear Boy,

I have received your letter of the 12th N.S. in which I was surprised to find no mention of your approaching journey to Berlin, which, according to the first plan, was to be on the 20th N.S. and upon which supposition I have for some time directed my letters to you and Mr. Harte at Berlin. I should be glad that yours were more minute with regard to your motions and transactions; and I desire that, for the future, they may contain accounts of what and whom you see and hear in your several places of residence; for I interest myself as much in the company you keep, and the pleasures you take, as in the studies you pursue, and therefore equally desire to be informed of them all. Another thing I desire, which is, that you will acknowledge my letters by their dates, that I may know which you do, and which you do not receive.

As you found your brain considerably affected by the cold, you were very prudent not to turn it to poetry in that situation, and not less judicious in declining the borrowed aid of a stove, whose fumigation, instead of inspiration, would at best have produced what Mr. Pope calls a *souter-kin* of wit. I will show your letter to Duval, by way of justification for not answering his challenge; and I think he must allow the validity of it; for a frozen brain is as unfit to answer a challenge in poetry, as a blunt sword is for single combat.

You may, if you please, and therefore I flatter myself that you will, profit considerably by your stay at Berlin, in the articles of manners and useful knowledge. Attention to what you will see and hear there, together with proper in- quiries, and a little care and method in taking notes of what is most material, will procure you much useful knowledge. Many young people are so light, so dissipated, and so in- curious, that they can hardly be said to see what they see, or hear what they hear—that is, they hear in so superficial and inattentive a manner, that they might as well not see nor hear at all. For instance; if they see a public building, as a college, an hospital, an arsenal, etc., they content themselves with the first *coup d'œil*, and neither take the time nor trouble of informing themselves of the material parts of them, which are the constitution, the rules, and the order and economy in the inside. You will, I hope, go deeper, and make your way into the substance of things. For example: should you see a regiment reviewed at Berlin or Potsdam, instead of contenting yourself with the general glitter of the collective corps, and saying, *par manière d'acquit*, that is very fine; I hope you will ask what number of troops or companies it consists of; what number of officers

of the *état major*, and what number of *subalternes*; how many
bas officiers, or non-commissioned officers, as *sergeants,
corporals, anspessades, frey corporals,* etc.; their pay, their
clothing, and by whom; whether by the colonels or cap-
tains, or commissaries appointed for that purpose; to whom
they are accountable, the method of recruiting, completing,
etc.

The same in civil matters: inform yourself of the juris-
diction of a court of justice; of the rules, and members, and
endowments of a college or an academy, and not only by
the dimensions of the respective edifices: and let your letters
to me contain these informations, in proportion as you
acquire them.

I often reflect, with the most flattering hopes, how proud
I shall be of you, if you should profit as you may, by the
opportunities which you have had, still have, and will have,
of arriving at perfection; and, on the other hand, with dread
of the grief and shame you will give me if you do not. May
the first be the case! God bless you!

No. 1619

À MADAME LA MARQUISE DE MONCONSEIL

(Maty I. xxxiii)

À Londres, ce 26 janvier V.S. 1749

Comme je respecte vos décisions, Madame, infiniment
plus que celles des Papes et des Conciles, fussent-ils même
œcuméniques, vos bras sont arborés dans mon boudoir, et
y font l'effet que vous pouvez bien croire: mais, à ne vous
rien cacher, deux autres motifs ont contribué à m'y déter-
miner; le premier, que les questions qu'on me fera à leur
sujet me donneront tous les jours occasion de parler de
vous; l'autre, que ma vanité trouvera son compte à dire que
je les tiens de vous. Croyez-vous que la vanité n'entre pour
rien dans les sentiments les plus délicats de l'amitié, et même

de l'amour? Au moins je vous avoue que je ne tiens pas contre la vanité qui me résulte des marques de votre amitié, et bien vous en prend même, qu'il n'est question que de l'amitié, car ma foi je ne répondrais pas de ma discrétion, s'il était question de quelque chose de plus. Nous ne mettons jamais les préférences marquées, de la part de certaines gens, que sur le compte de notre propre mérite; et c'est en partie sur ce principe que j'érige vos bras comme les trophées du mien.

J'ai lu avec attention la pièce[1] que vous avez eu la bonté de m'envoyer, et d'autant plus qu'elle paraît avoir votre approbation. Vous m'ordonnez de vous en dire mon sentiment; si je pouvais vous obéir à regret, ce serait dans cette occasion, dans laquelle je vois que mon sentiment est différent du vôtre. Je vous avouerai donc naturellement, Madame, que la pièce n'a pas répondu à mon attente, ni à l'idée que je m'en étais formée, tant par rapport à l'auteur, que par rapport au temps qu'il a travaillé. Je conviens qu'il y a des beaux vers, des endroits brillants, du sublime, et que le caractère de Catilina est achevé; mais après cela, la conduite de la pièce me choque. Quand une tragédie est faite sur une histoire, ou peu connue ou douteuse, comme quand il est question d'un grand Mogol, d'un Sultan, d'un Soliman, d'un Orosmane, il est très permis à un poète de l'accommoder à ses besoins, et la véritable histoire étant ignorée, le poète devient en quelque façon l'historien: mais de violenter, au point que fait Monsieur de Crébillon, une histoire si connue, si constatée, que celle de Catalina, et peut-être la seule histoire ancienne sur laquelle tous les différents auteurs sont d'accord, c'est en vérité abuser des droits du cothurne. Tullie était à la bavette quand Catilina fut tué, et Catilina n'eut garde de se tuer lui-même, pour satisfaire à l'unité du temps et du lieu de Monsieur de Crébillon,[1] mais voulut éprouver premièrement le sort d'une

---

[1]Crébillon père's tragedy, *Catilina*; Voltaire composed his *Rome Sauvée* in opposition to it.

bataille, où il fut criblé de coups à la tête de son armée. Si,
par exemple, on vous eût donné une tragédie de Monsieur
de Cinq Mars,[1] dans laquelle, pour la commodité du poète,
cet infortuné se serait tué lui-même, au lieu de mourir,
comme il le fit, sur l'échafaud, où il aurait été aimé, trahi, et
dénoncé par Madame de Combalet, et où le Cardinal de
Richelieu n'aurait paru sur la scène que pour déclarer qu'il
avait une peur horrible, et qu'il ne savait au monde que faire,
qu'en diriez-vous, Madame? et pardonneriez-vous au poète
un tel outrage fait à la vérité historique? Je ne le crois pas;
et pourtant l'histoire de Monsieur de Cinq Mars n'est pas
plus généralement connue, ni mieux constatée que celle de
Catilina. J'allais même dire qu'à peine était-elle plus
récente, puisque les livres qu'on a presque toujours à la main
la renouvellent incessamment. Cicéron, il faut l'avouer,
était naturellement irrésolu et timide; mais, malheureusement pour le poète, la seule occasion où il brilla, et où il
témoigna véritablement de la fermeté et du courage, est
justement celle où il en fait un linge mouillé; et le Consul,
qu'on admire dans l'histoire, fait seulement pitié dans la
pièce. Caton paraît sur la scène, uniquement pour gronder
et dire pis que pendre des Romains, car tout ce qu'il fait ne
mène à rien dans la pièce. Je me serais passé aussi volontiers
de la présence de son Excellence Monsieur l'Ambassadeur
Sunnon, qui ne se produit que pour donner aux Français
d'aujourd'hui le plaisir de savoir que les Gaulois, il y a dix-
sept cents ans, étaient bien les meilleures gens du monde.
Je ne puis pas démêler le caractère de Tullie; aime-t-elle
véritablement Catilina? ou en fait-elle seulement semblant,
pour mieux découvrir ses desseins, et sauver la patrie? Cela
n'est pas assez marqué. Si elle aime véritablement Catilina,
et en même temps sa patrie, et son papa, déchirée par des
sentiments si opposés, et pourtant si forts, sa situation
devrait être si violente que tout le monde y prendrait

[1]Condemned and beheaded with the younger de Thou in 1642 for a plot against
Richelieu.

intérêt, au lieu que pour moi, franchement je ne m'en inquiète point, et je la laisse faire. Pour le caractère de Catilina, il est beau, grand et soutenu jusqu'à la fin, et on l'aime en dépit de ses crimes: mais permettez-moi aussi d'ajouter, que je fais de cela même un crime au poète, qui n'aurait pas dû choisir un sujet si opposé au véritable but de la tragédie, qui est de rendre le crime haïssable et non pas aimable. Un de nos meilleurs poètes anglais[1] reproche, et pas sans raison, à Milton, que le diable est en effet le héros de son poème, puisqu'il est par tout habile, intrépide, même aimable, et qu'il vient à bout de son dessein, qui était de damner le genre humain. Il ne faut pas choisir des sujets qui entrainent nécessairement de telles suites. Voilà, Madame, ma petite critique.

Au reste, je vous en prie, gardez pour vous seule ces idées hasardées. Si elles sont justes, je ne voudrais pas qu'elles fussent connues, pour l'amour de Monsieur de Crébillon, dont je respecte le génie et le caractère; et si elles sont fausses, ce qui me paraît le plus vraisemblable, puisqu'elles ne sont pas conformes aux vôtres, je ne voudrais point qu'elles fussent sues pour l'amour de votre très humble serviteur, qui ne s'érige nullement en critique, et qui aime bien mieux trouver des beautés que chercher des défauts.

A propos de tragédies, Denys le Tyran, par Monsieur de Marmontel,[2] qu'on m'assure n'avoir pas encore vingt-trois ans, annonce un grand poète tragique; du moins son coup d'essai me paraît presque un coup de maître. Envoyez-moi, je vous en prie, Madame, la traduction de l'Anti-Lucrèce; quelque médiocre qu'elle soit, elle aura toujours du mérite, si elle conserve seulement un peu du sens de l'original.

[1]Dryden.

[2] Jean François Marmontel (1723-1799), writer of tragedies, *Contes Moraux*, etc.: elected to the Academy in 1763.

No. 1620

To Solomon Dayrolles, Esq.

(Maty II. xlvi)

London, 3 February O.S. 1749

Dear Dayrolles,

I have honoured your bill, as they call it; but properly speaking I have done better, for I have paid it. I think you have brought me off very cheaply, and so much so, that I shall not own it, when I show the picture, but intimate a much higher price; for you *virtuosos,* I know, often take the price into your consideration, in forming your judgments as to the value of a thing. I sincerely forgive you the three florins, which your curiosity costs me, and will never demand that sum of either you or your heirs, administrators, or assigns. Besides that I really think, that a gratification of three florins is by no means unreasonable for the trouble you have been at. I can tell you by the way, that when my pictures, bronzes, and marbles, shall come to be properly placed, as they will be in my new house, the collection will not appear a contemptible one. There will be nothing that is not excellent of the kind. I hope you will be here time enough to direct me in the arrangement; for Lord Holderness is now preparing in good earnest for his embassy, and talks of going soon, that is, in two or three months. He has appointed Parson Tindal, who translated Rapin,[1] and well, to be both his chaplain and his secretary; he goes first, as I hear, without Madame, who is to follow him some time afterwards. But though, as you will easily believe, I am impatient to see you, I would not advise you to ask leave to come over immediately upon his arrival, but to stay a couple of months at least after it.

[1]Paul de Rapin, Sieur de Thoyras (1661-1725), wrote an *Histoire d'Angleterre* from the invasion of the Romans to the death of Charles I. Tindal's translation appeared 1725-31. His own *Christianity as Old as the Creation* was adjudged heretical, and the second volume burnt by the Bishops.

I had a letter the other day from my Baron, by which he seems to be pretty well comforted, and to thirst again for pamphlets, of which I have sent him a fresh cargo. Pray, when you see *L'ami*,[1] make him my compliments, and assure him of my esteem and friendship. I suppose *qu'il n'est pas question de lui à la Cour*. As for your Republic, it is undone, and I think of it no more. *Conclamatum est.* Adieu.

No. 1621

To his Son

(*Stanhope CLXXVI*)

London, 7 February O.S. 1749

DEAR BOY,

You are now come to an age capable of reflection, and I hope you will do, what, however, few people at your age do, exert it, for your own sake, in the search of truth and sound knowledge. I will confess (for I am not unwilling to discover my secrets to you) that it is not many years since I have presumed to reflect for myself. Till sixteen or seventeen, I had no reflection; and, for many years after that, I made no use of what I had. I adopted the notions of the books I read, or the company I kept, without examining whether they were just or not; and I rather chose to run the risk of easy error, than to take the time and trouble of investigating truth. Thus, partly from laziness, partly from dissipation, and partly from the *mauvaise honte* of rejecting fashionable notions, I was (as I have since found) hurried away by prejudices, instead of being guided by reason; and quietly cherished error, instead of seeking for truth. But since I have taken the trouble of reasoning for myself, and have had the courage to own that I do so, you cannot imagine how much my notion of things are altered, and in

[1]See letter of 2nd June 1747 and note.

how different a light I now see them, from that in which I formerly viewed them through the deceitful medium of prejudice or authority. Nay, I may possibly still retain many errors, which from long habit, have perhaps grown into real opinions; for it is very difficult to distinguish habits, early acquired and long entertained, from the result of our reason and reflection.

My first prejudice (for I do not mention the prejudices of boys and women, such as hobgoblins, ghosts, dreams, spilling salt, etc.) was my classical enthusiasm, which I received from the books I read, and the masters who explained them to me. I was convinced there had been no common sense nor common honesty in the world for these last fifteen hundred years; but that they were totally extinguished with the ancient Greek and Roman governments. Homer and Virgil could have no faults, because they were ancients; Milton and Tasso could have no merit, because they were modern. And I could almost have said, with regard to the ancients, what Cicero, very absurdly and unbecomingly for a philosopher, says with regard to Plato, *Cum quo errare malim quam cum aliis recte sentire.*[1] Whereas now, without any extraordinary effort of genius, I have discovered that nature was the same three thousand years ago as it is at present; that men were but men then as well as now; that modes and customs vary often, but that human nature is always the same. And I can no more suppose, that men were better, braver, or wiser, fifteen hundred or three thousand years ago, than I can suppose that the animals or vegetables were better then than they are now.

I dare assert, too, in defiance of the favourers of the ancients, that Homer's hero, Achilles, was both a brute and a scoundrel, and, consequently, an improper character for the hero of an epic poem; for he had so little regard for his country, that he would not act in defence of it because he

[1] *Tuscul. Quaest.* lib. i. 17, 'Errare metercule malo cum Platone, quam tu quanti facias, scio, et quem ex tuo ore admirar, quam cum istis sentire.'

had quarrelled with Agamemnon about a whore; and then, afterwards, animated by private resentment only, he went about killing people basely, I will call it, because he knew himself invulnerable; and yet, invulnerable as he was, he wore the strongest armour in the world; which I humbly apprehend to be a blunder, for a horse-shoe clapped to his vulnerable heel would have been sufficient. On the other hand, with submission to the favourers of the moderns, I assert, with Mr. Dryden, that the Devil is in truth the Hero of Milton's poem; his plan, which he lays, pursues, and at last executes, being the subject of the poem. From all which considerations I impartially conclude, that the ancients had their excellencies and their defects, their virtues and their vices, just like the moderns; pedantry and affectation of learning decide clearly in favour of the former; vanity and ignorance, as peremptorily, in favour of the latter.

Religious prejudices kept pace with my classical ones; and there was a time when I thought it impossible for the honestest man in the world to be saved, out of the pale of the Church of England; not considering that matters of opinion do not depend upon the will; and that it is as natural, and as allowable, that another man should differ in opinion from me, as that I should differ from him; and that, if we are both sincere, we are both blameless, and should consequently have mutual indulgence for each other.

The next prejudices I adopted, were those of the *beau monde*; in which, as I was determined to shine, I took what are commonly called the genteel vices to be necessary. I had heard them reckoned so, and, without farther inquiry, I believed it; or, at least, should have been ashamed to have denied it, for fear of exposing myself to the ridicule of those whom I considered as the models of fine gentlemen. But I am now neither ashamed nor afraid to assert that those genteel vices, as they are falsely called, are only so many blemishes in the character of even a man of the world, and what is called a fine gentleman, and degrade him in the opinions of those very people to whom he hopes to recommend himself by them. Nay, this prejudice often extends so far, that I have known people pretend to vices they had not, instead of carefully concealing those they had.

Use and assert your own reason; reflect, examine, and analyse everything, in order to form a sound and mature judgment; let no οὖτος ἔφα impose upon your understanding, mislead your actions, or dictate your conversation. Be early what, if you are not, you will, when too late, wish you had been. Consult your reason betimes; I do not say that it will always prove an unerring guide, for human reason is not infallible; but it will prove the least erring guide that you can follow. Books and conversation may assist it; but adopt neither blindly and implicitly; try both by that best rule which God has given to direct us—reason. Of all the troubles, do not decline, as many people do, that of thinking. The herd of mankind can hardly be said to think; their notions are almost all adoptive; and, in general, I believe it is better that it should be so, as such common prejudices contribute more to order and quiet than their own separate reasonings would do, uncultivated and unimproved as they are. We have many of those useful prejudices in this country, which I shall be very sorry to see removed. The good Protestant conviction, that the Pope is both Antichrist and the Whore of Babylon, is a more effectual preservative in this country against Popery than all the solid and unanswerable arguments of Chillingworth. The idle story of the Pretender's having been introduced in a warming-pan into the Queen's bed, though as destitute of all probability as of all foundation, has been much more prejudicial to the cause of Jacobitism than all that Mr. Locke and others have written to show the unreasonableness and absurdity of the doctrines of indefeasible hereditary right and unlimited passive obedience. And that silly, sanguine notion, which is firmly entertained here, that one Englishman can beat three Frenchmen, encourages, and has sometimes enabled, one Englishman, in reality, to beat two.

A Frenchman ventures his life with alacrity *pour l'honneur du Roi*; were you to change the object which he has been taught to have in view, and tell him that it was *pour le bien de la Patrie*, he would very probably run away. Such gross, local prejudices prevail with the herd of mankind, and do not impose upon cultivated, informed, and reflecting minds; but then there are notions equally false, though not so glaringly absurd, which are entertained by people of superior and improved understandings, merely for want of the necessary pains to investigate, the proper attention to examine, and the penetration requisite to determine the truth. Those are the prejudices which I would have you guard against by a manly exertion and attention of your reasonable faculty. To mention one instance of a thousand that I could give you: It is a general prejudice, and has been for these sixteen hundred years, that arts and sciences cannot flourish under an absolute government; and that genius must necessarily be cramped where freedom is restrained. This sounds plausible, but is false in fact. Mechanic arts, as agriculture, manufactures, etc., will indeed be discouraged where the profits and property are, from the nature of the government, insecure. But why the despotism of a government should cramp the genius of a mathematician, an astronomer, a poet, or an orator, I confess I never could discover. It may indeed deprive the poet or the orator of the liberty of treating of certain subjects in the manner they would wish; but it leaves them subjects enough to exert genius upon, if they have it. Can an author with reason complain that he is cramped and shackled if he is not at liberty to publish blasphemy, bawdry, or sedition? all which are equally prohibited in the freest governments, if they are wise and well-regulated ones. This is the present general complaint of the French authors; but, indeed, chiefly of the bad ones. No wonder, say they, that England produces so many great geniuses; people there may think as they please, and publish what they think. Very true; but who hinders them from thinking as they please? If, indeed, they think in a manner destructive of all religion, morality, or good manners, or to the disturbance of the state, an absolute government will certainly more effectually prohibit them from, or punish them for, publishing such thoughts than a free one could do. But how does that cramp the genius of an epic, dramatic, or lyric poet? Or how does it corrupt the eloquence of an orator, in the pulpit or at the bar? The number of good French authors, such as Corneille, Racine, Molière, Boileau, and La Fontaine, who seemed to dispute it with the Augustan age, flourished under the despotism of Louis XIV; and the celebrated authors of the Augustan age did not shine till after the fetters were rivetted upon the Roman people by that cruel and worthless Emperor. The revival of letters was not owing, either, to any free government, but to the encouragement and protection of Leo X and Francis I—the one as absolute a pope, and the other as despotic a prince, as ever reigned. Do not mistake, and imagine that, while I am only exposing a prejudice, I am speaking in favour of arbitrary power, which from my soul I abhor, and look upon as a gross and criminal violation of the natural rights of mankind.

Adieu!

No. 1622

This letter has usually been dated as of 9 February, 1749. It seems, however, more properly to belong to 1743, where it has accordingly been transferred as Letter No. 738 A.

No. 1623

To Solomon Dayrolles, Esq.

(Mahon III. 326)

London, 24 February O.S. 1749

DEAR DAYROLLES,

The picture is arrived, and is, in my mind, the best I ever saw of Rubens; but as yet I have only my own opinion for it, as I have not shown it, nor will not, till it is in perfect order. A little of the varnish, in some immaterial parts, was rubbed off in the carriage, but the painting not the least damaged. I have given it to Anderson, who is a very safe man, to take off that crust of varnish, with which they are so apt to load their pictures in Flanders and Holland; and, when this picture shall be delivered of it, it will be quite another thing. The figure of the Virgin is the most graceful and beautiful that I ever saw, and not so Flemish-built as most of his women are. In short, the whole is excellent. The frame though not a fashionable is a handsome one, and shall, with the addition that I will make to it, be a fine one. I do not dislike something a little *antique* in the frame of an old picture; provided it be rich, I think it is more respectable. As soon as the supreme connoisseurs shall have sat upon it, I will let you know their verdict, not that for my own part I shall care twopence about it, for I distrust the skill of most, and the truth of all, of them. They pronounce according to the pictures that they either have or have not, or that they want to buy or sell, of the same hand. You are an excellent *commissionnaire*; and my most dutiful thanks attend you for your care and trouble.

Pray do not let your *maladie du pays* hurry you into every *étourderie*. The Ambassador's *inefficiency* may very possibly make your stay at the Hague more necessary than you are aware of, and you of more importance, which circumstance may hereafter be of great use to you. Upon his arrival at the Hague, exert yourself to get the best and freshest informations, and write them immediately, and add now and then a few reasonings of your own upon them. By these means your despatches will be the material ones from the Hague. By-the-by, your Court there is by no means well with the Court here, therefore beware of panegyric on the one hand as well as of censure on the other. Blame all unnecessary expenses, and remark that those sums would be better employed upon the Civil and Military Government, *car tel est le ton présent d'une certaine Personne*.[1] Keep, however, well with the Ambassador, but tell him nothing but what he knows before, and God knows that will be very little. When you shall thus have shown yourself to be the efficient man there, ask leave *à la bonne heure* to come over here; but then take care to establish such correspondences as may enable you to inform the Ministers here, of what shall be doing in Holland, better than the Ambassador, though upon the spot.

Pray tell my Baron, that I took particular care to send him the *Inquiry into the Conduct and Principles of the Two Brothers*;[2] so that it must necessarily have been taken out of the packet. Possibly they have no mind that it should be dispersed abroad. I will send it him again the first opportunity. Rutter is now out of town; the moment he comes, I will deliver Mr. Slingelandt's[3] message to him.

We say here, that it is quite over with the two Bentincks. Is it so? Say nothing for or against them, in your public despatches, but impartially relate matters of fact concerning them; for they are yet well *here*.

Adieu. Yours faithfully.

[1]The King. [2]Pelham and the Duke of Newcastle.
[3]Son of the late Pensionary.

No. 1624
To his Son
(Stanhope CLXXVII)

London, 28 *February O.S.* 1749

Dear Boy,

I was very much pleased with the account that you gave me of your reception at Berlin; but I was still better pleased with the account which Mr. Harte sent me of your manner of receiving that reception, for he says you behaved yourself to those crowned heads with all the respect and modesty due to them, but, at the same time, without being any more embarrassed than if you had been conversing with your equals. This easy respect is the perfection of good-breeding, which nothing but superior good-sense or a long usage of the world can produce; and as, in your case, it could not be the latter, it is a pleasing indication to me of the former.

You will now, in the course of a few months, have been rubbed at three of the considerable Courts of Europe— Berlin, Dresden, and Vienna; so that I hope you will arrive at Turin tolerably smooth, and fit for the last polish. There you may get the best, there being no Court I know of that forms more well-bred and agreeable people. Remember, now, that good-breeding, genteel carriage, address, and even dress (to a certain degree), are become serious objects, and deserve a part of your attention.

The day, if well employed, is long enough for them all; one half of it bestowed upon your studies and your exercises will finish your mind and your body; the remaining part of it, spent in good company, will form your manners and complete your character. What would I not give to have you read Demosthenes critically in the morning, and understand him better than anybody; at noon, behave yourself better than any person at Court; and, in the evenings, trifle

1312

more agreeably than anybody in mixed companies! All this
you may compass if you please; you have the means, you
have the opportunities. Employ them for God's sake, while
you may, and make yourself that all-accomplished man that
I wish to have you. It entirely depends upon these two
years; they are the decisive ones.

I send you here enclosed a letter of recommendation to
Monsieur Capello, at Venice, which you will deliver him immediately upon your arrival, accompanying it with compliments from me to him and Madame, both whom you
have seen here. He will, I am sure, be both very civil and
very useful to you there, as he will also be afterwards at
Rome, where he is appointed to go Ambassador. By the
way, wherever you are, I would advise you to frequent, as
much as you can, the Venetian ministers, who are always
better informed of the Courts they reside at than any other
minister—the strict and regular accounts which they are
obliged to give to their own government making them very
diligent and inquisitive.

You will stay at Venice as long as the Carnival lasts; for
though I am impatient to have you at Turin, yet I would
wish you to see thoroughly all that is to be seen at so
singular a place as Venice, and at so showish a time as the
Carnival. You will take also particular care to view all those
meetings of the government, which strangers are allowed
to see; as the assembly of the Senate, etc.; and likewise to
inform yourself of that peculiar and intricate form of
government. There are books that give an account of it,
among which the best is Amelot de la Houssaye;[1] this I
would advise you to read previously; it will not only give
you a general notion of that constitution, but also furnish
you with materials for proper questions and oral informations upon the place, which are always the best. There are

[1]Amelot de la Houssaye (1634-1706), Secretary to the French Embassy at
Venice. He wrote philosophic and historical works, and edited the letters of
Cardinal d'Ossat.

likewise many very valuable remains, in sculpture and paintings, of the best masters, which deserve your attention.

I suppose you will be at Vienna as soon as this letter will get thither; and I suppose, too, that I must not direct above one more to you there. After which my next shall be directed to you at Venice, the only place where a letter will be likely to find you till you are at Turin; but you may, and I desire that you will, write to me from the several places in your way from whence the post goes.

I will send you some other letters, for Venice, to Vienna, or to your banker at Venice; to whom you will, upon your arrival there, send for them; for I will take care to have you so recommended from place to place that you shall not run through them, as most of your countrymen do, without the advantage of seeing and knowing what best deserves to be seen and known; I mean the men and the manners.

God bless you, and make you answer my wishes; I will now say, my hopes! Adieu!

No. 1625

To Solomon Dayrolles, Esq.
(*Mahon III. 328*)

London, 9 March O.S. 1749

DEAR DAYROLLES,

I do not absolutely admit of all the reasonings of your last; for though I agree that Lord Holderness will from his relation to, and connexion with, the Greffier, have the best informations, yet I think he will put them very ill together, and with good materials make but scurvy letters; moreover, you may depend upon it, that he will only write what that Cabal would have him write, so that his accounts will be partial; whereas yours, as far as they go, will be fair, and give the whole. I cannot see neither why the utmost of your hopes should go no farther than the additional £300 a year, nor why you should not in time be *Monsieur l'Envoyé*, somewhere or other. Many have enjoyed, and some do enjoy, that character who in every respect deserve it less. When I see you we will talk these matters over more fully than we can write upon them. Lord Holderness has not yet kissed the King's hand, and of course will not go soon: therefore I do not expect to see you till the end of July or August. Upon my soul I long to see you for two reasons, which I have not for longing to see many people; they are, that I love you, and that I know you love me. I shall keep a little room for you at Blackheath, where I will refresh you with the best ananas[1] and melons in England.

Pray tell Monsieur Slingelandt that I have spoken to Rutter about the horse in question; and the better to know whether he was gentle enough for him, I asked him whether he was enough so for me; to which Rutter could not answer in the affirmative, so that I bid him not send him. I take it for granted that Monsieur Slingelandt, who is a civil quiet gentleman as well as myself, chooses, as I do, a horse like Père Canaye's *qualem me decet esse mansuetum*,[2] which serene kind of beast is still more necessary in Holland, in the midst of canals, and windmills, than here.

Kreuningen's son, he writes me word, is coming to England, which I am sorry for upon account of Trevor, whom it embarrasses extremely. It does not embarrass me, because I am resolved to be totally ignorant of all that has passed, and to invite him to dinner, as if nothing had happened. But Trevor cannot plead that ignorance, and Hop, I believe, will not receive him, so that I fancy his stay will not be long here. I should think that Russia would be the best, as it is the remotest, place for him, and possibly Comte Golofkin could get him into that service. Kreuningen *le Père* tells me that he has some thoughts of coming here

[1] Lord Mahon's note is here:—'The word "pine-apple" has not yet, it appears, come into common use'; but it occurs in Letter of August 1, 1754; and is found as early as Locke. Bradshaw.

[2] An allusion to the *Conversation du Marechal d'Hoquincourt avec le Père Canaye*, by St. Evremond.—Note by Dayrolles.

himself next summer; I should be glad of it for my own sake, but sorry for his; complaisance for singular characters being by no means the natural turn of this country. His oddnesses would be indulged by few, but laughed at by many; so that I think he would pass his time ill here, which would mortify him. I am now three letters in his debt, which I will pay off as soon as I can; but I am so hurried and unsettled at present, being to remove to my new house this day se'nnight, that I have hardly time to write, or table to write upon.

It is said here, that our ministers are altogether by the ears, and I believe that there is some degree of truth in the report. There is certainly no love lost between their *two Graces*. Lord Sandwich holds with, or rather governs, his Grace of Bedford; Fox is mutinous, and all the parts of the Ministerial machine disjointed. What order will at last spring out of this confusion, I neither know nor care. The new discipline which is to be established in both Fleet and Army by Act of Parliament,[1] has caused great debates and long sittings in the House of Commons, has given great dissatisfaction to those two bodies of men, and great alarm to everybody else. This measure is thought to be His Royal Highness, the Duke's; which has added so much to his former unpopularity, that the most scandalous libels imaginable are published every day upon the subject.

Bentinck may possibly have still some remaining credit at your Court, but I am sure not very much power; for I know his turn well enough to know, that if he had much power he would not suffer the Pensionary to be tolerably received there, much less consulted.

I forgot to tell you before, that I cannot for my soul explain the riddle which you sent me some time ago. The A. E. I. are to me impenetrable. Pray send me the solution. *Bon soir, mon ami.*

[1]This was a proposal for making all half-pay officers subject to martial law. It was carried as to the military, but not as to the naval service.—M.

No. 1626

À Madame la Marquise de Monconseil

(Maty I. xxxiv)

À Londres, ce 12 mars V.S. 1749

J'ai reçu, Madame, la traduction de l'Anti-Lucrèce[1] que vous avez eu la bonté de m'envoyer. Monsieur l'Abbé de la Ville, avec sa politesse ordinaire, l'a accompagnée d'une lettre très obligeante. Nous étions à la fois amis et ennemis à la Haye, et il n'a pas tenu à nous que la paix ne se soit faite il y a quatre ans; son souvenir m'a flatté, car je l'estime beaucoup. Je trouve la traduction très bonne; les beautés de l'original y sont aussi bien rendues que la prose le permet; mais un beau poème perd nécessairement beaucoup à être traduit, même en vers. Je ne puis pas m'empêcher de regretter, qu'un des plus beaux morceaux de l'original, qui selon moi est le sixième livre, tienne à une philosophie si fausse et si pitoyable que celles des automates de Monsieur Descartes, qui certainement ne l'a pas crue lui-même.

Monsieur de Mirepoix viendra-t-il ici, ou se sera-t-il rebuté de certains incidents assez déplacés à mon avis? Je n'ai pas l'honneur de le connaître personnellement, mais ce que tout le monde dit de lui me fait souhaiter qu'il vienne. Madame de Mirepoix est bien aimable; j'ai eu l'honneur de la connaître à Paris; si je pouvais leur être bon à quelque chose ici, j'en serais charmé, et je m'acquitterais de mon mieux des commissions dont ils voudraient bien me charger. Ayez la bonté, Madame, de me procurer, si vous le pouvez, l'emploi de leur commissionnaire.

Je ferai tous mes efforts pour obtenir de Milord Crawford[2] ce que souhaite Monsieur votre beau-frère; mais j'avoue que je doute un peu si je réussirai, car j'ai demandé

[1]See letter of 8th Sept. 1747 and note; the translation was by M. Bougainville, Secretary of the *Académie des Belles Lettres*: see the letter to him, June 1755.

[2]John Lindsay, eighteenth Earl of Crawford, a distinguished general officer. He died in December 1749.—M.

la même chose il y a quelque temps à un autre de nos officiers, qui me l'a refusé tout net; disant qu'il ne savait pas s'il était en droit de le faire, et qu'il pourrait peut-être lui-même donner quelque jour des mémoires de la dernière guerre: enfin, l'Anglais n'est pas naturellement communicatif.

Je suis à présent dans une situation ridiculement violente; j'entre en deux jours dans ma nouvelle maison, qui n'est pas encore à demi meublée, quoique celle où je suis soit tout-à-fait démeublée. Je ne vis que des aumônes de mes amis, et j'écris cette lettre, faute de table, sur un livre sur mes genoux. Je la finis pourtant pour l'amour de vous, mais ce n'est pas pour me tirer d'une attitude gênante, à laquelle on ne pense pas quand on s'entretient avec vous.

No. 1627

To his Son

(*Stanhope CLXXVIII*)

[*March* 1749]

DEAR BOY,

I direct this letter to your banker at Venice, the surest place for you to meet with it, though I suppose it will be there some time before you; for as your intermediate stay anywhere else will be but short, and as the post from hence, in this season of easterly winds, is uncertain, I direct no more letters to Vienna; where I hope both you and Mr. Harte will have received the two letters which I sent you respectively; with a letter of recommendation to Monsieur Capello at Venice, which was enclosed in mine to you. I will suppose, too, that the inland post on your side of the water has not done you justice; for I received but one single letter from you, and one from Mr. Harte, during your whole stay at Berlin; from whence I hoped for and expected very particular accounts.

I persuade myself that the time you stay at Venice will be properly employed in seeing all that is to be seen at that extraordinary place; and in conversing with people who can inform you, not of the raree-shows of the town, but of the constitution of the government; for which purpose I send you the enclosed letters of recommendation from Sir James Gray,[1] the King's resident at Venice, but who is now in England. These, with mine to Monsieur Capello, will carry you, if you will go, into all the best company at Venice.

But the important point and the important place is Turin; for there I propose your staying a considerable time, to pursue your studies, learn your exercises, and form your manners. I own I am not without my anxiety for the consequence of your stay there, which must be either very good or very bad. To you it will be entirely a new scene. Wherever you have hitherto been, you have conversed chiefly with people wiser and discreeter than yourself, and have been equally out of the way of bad advice or bad example; but in the Academy at Turin you will, probably, meet with both, considering the variety of young fellows of about your own age—among whom, it is to be expected that some will be dissipated and idle, others vicious and profligate. I will believe, till the contrary appears, that you have sagacity enough to distinguish the good from the bad characters, and both sense and virtue enough to shun the latter and connect yourself with the former; but, however, for greater security, and for your sake alone, I must acquaint you that I have sent positive orders to Mr. Harte to carry you off instantly to a place which I have named to him, upon the very first symptom which he shall discover in you of drinking, gaming, idleness, or disobedience to his orders; so that, whether Mr. Harte informs me or not of the particulars, I shall be able to judge of your conduct in general by the time of your stay at Turin. If it is short, I shall know why, and I promise you that you shall soon find that I do; but, if Mr. Harte lets

[1]This diplomatist was employed at Venice during several years. Lady Mary Wortley Montague writes of him: 'Sir James Gray was, as I am told, universally esteemed during his residence here; but, alas! he is gone to Naples.' (To the Countess of Bute, 3rd April 1758.)—M.

you continue there as long as I propose you should, I shall then be convinced that you make the proper use of your time, which is the only thing I have to ask of you. One year is the most that I propose you should stay at Turin; and that year, if you employ it well, perfects you. One year more of your late application with Mr. Harte will complete your classical studies. You will be, likewise, master of your exercises in that time, and will have formed yourself so well at that Court as to be fit to appear advantageously at any other. These will be the happy effects of your year's stay at Turin, if you behave and apply yourself there as you have done at Leipsig; but if either ill advice or ill example affect and seduce you, you are ruined for ever. I look upon that year as your decisive year of probation; go through it well, and you will be all accomplished, and fixed in my tenderest affection for ever; but, should the contagion of vice or idleness lay hold of you there, your character, your fortune, my hopes, and consequently my favour, are all blasted, and you are undone. The more I love you now, from the good opinion that I have of you, the greater will be my indignation, if I should have reason to change it. Hitherto you have had every possible proof of my affection, because you have deserved it; but when you cease to deserve it, you may expect every possible mark of my resentment. To leave nothing doubtful upon this important point, I will tell you fairly, beforehand, by what rule I shall judge of your conduct: by Mr. Harte's accounts. He will not, I am sure—nay, I will say more, he cannot—be in the wrong with regard to you; he can have no other view but your good; and you will I am sure allow, that he must be a better judge of it than you can possibly be at your age. While he is satisfied, I shall be so too; but, whenever he is dissatisfied with you, I shall be much more so. If he complains you must be guilty; and I shall not have the least regard for anything that you may allege in your own defence.

I will now tell you what I expect and insist upon from you

at Turin:—First, that you pursue your classical and other studies every morning with Mr. Harte, as long and in whatever manner Mr. Harte shall be pleased to require; secondly, that you learn, uninterruptedly, your exercises of riding, dancing, and fencing; thirdly, that you make yourself master of the Italian language; and lastly, that you pass your evenings in the best company. I also require a strict conformity to the hours and rules of the Academy. If you will but finish your year in this manner at Turin, I have nothing further to ask of you, and I will give you everything that you can ask of me. You shall after that be entirely your own master: I shall think you safe, shall lay aside all authority over you, and friendship shall be our mutual and only tie. Weigh this, I beg of you, deliberately in your own mind, and consider whether the application and the degree of restraint which I require but for one year more will not be amply repaid by all the advantages, and the perfect liberty, which you will receive at the end of it. Your own good-sense will, I am sure, not allow you to hesitate one moment in your choice. God bless you! Adieu!

P.S.—Sir James Gray's letters not being yet sent me, as I thought they would, I shall enclose them in my next, which, I believe, will get to Venice as soon as you.

No. 1628

To Solomon Dayrolles, Esq.

(*Mahon III. 333*)

London, 31 *March O.S.* 1749
Hôtel Chesterfield

Dear Dayrolles,

I showed your letter to Hop, to whom it gave great satisfaction, and who thinks himself much obliged to you for the part which you take in his affairs. He was uneasy before, and is not quite easy yet, for he fears that if the

Bentinck party prevails, they will send some dependent of their own here in his stead, either to mark out their credit, or to carry on their secret; and he has taken such a fancy to this country, that I do not believe he would change his destination here for any other in the world. He refused the embassy to Paris, which he was even pressed to accept.

I can tell you nothing, with any degree of certainty, of the squabbles among our Ministers. That there are some, is undoubtedly true; but then, in the reports, they are either magnified or lessened, according to the wishes or the interests of the reporters. Their two Graces are evidently very ill together, which I long ago knew, and said, could not fail. Mr. Pelham is cordially well with neither of them, though affectedly well with his brother. The Duke of Bedford, governed in general, but not in every particular, by Lord Sandwich, is pretty strong, *moyennant* the Gower family and others whom he brings into Parliament. He likewise gains ground with the Duke of Cumberland, who is, in truth, Minister as well as General, of which you will easily imagine his Grace of Newcastle is horribly jealous. These are, I believe, pretty near the outlines of the present ministerial piece. Mr. Pelham, who really means well, has the least power, and possibly for that very reason.

But, upon the whole, *que le chien mange le loup, ou le loup le chien*, I am got into my new house, from whence I shall be a most unconcerned spectator of those silly scenes. I have yet finished nothing but my *boudoir* and my library: the former is the gayest and most cheerful room in England the latter the best. My garden is now turfed, planted, and sown, and will in two months more make a scene of verdure and flowers not common in London.

Anderson has restored the Rubens perfectly well, by taking off that damned varnish with which it was loaded, and fetching out the original painting. The *connoisseurs* have sat upon it, and, what is extraordinary, are unanimous in declaring it one of the best in England. Many have guessed it at £800, none less than £500. *Je les laisse dire, et je ne dis rien.*

I do not care for the Teniers you mention, both my picture-rooms being completely filled—the great one with capital pictures, the cabinet with *bijoux.* So that I will buy no more, till I happen to meet with some very capital ones of some of the most eminent old Italian masters, such as Raphael, Guido, Correggio, etc., and in that case I will make an effort.

I will look out for a horse fit for Mr. Slingelandt, of which I think I am a better judge than a better horseman. You may tell him I shall not much regard the beauty of it, but the intrinsic merit. I desire he should be safe, for I love him, both upon his own account and his father's.

I am glad to hear for his own sake that young Kreuningen does not come here, where I find he would have been in general very ill. Hop was determined not to receive him, and Trevor not to present him anywhere.

I agree with you that my Baron, far from travelling into other countries, will never more see his own, or put on a coat. He will think that he has escaped infection so providentially now, that I am apt to think he will endeavour to trust Providence no more.

Yours, etc.

No. 1629

To Solomon Dayrolles, Esq.

(Mahon III. 335)

London, 4 April O.S. 1749

Dear Dayrolles,

Since my last to you, I have received your two letters of the 8th and 11th N.S. together with the pamphlet in Dutch, which you sent me by General Elliot,[1] who delivered

[1] A Lieutenant-General in the Dutch service.—M.

it to me very safe. It has made me rub up my almost forgotten Dutch, and I think I understand the meaning of it
perfectly. It is extremely well written, and I daresay the
facts are all as true, as the reasonings upon them are just.
It coincides with, and confirms, all the notions I had formed
of the present state of affairs in the Republic. I should be
obliged to you if you would inform me, who is either the
real, or supposed, author of it. Whoever he is, he is well
informed. I am very much obliged to you for sending it to
me. I have laid it by carefully, with my own predictions of
general bankruptcy and confusion, which I fear a little time
more will accomplish.

General Elliot *est un dégourdi, et du bon ton.* I have not
seen any Englishman more degenerated by being abroad
than he is. I met him at Hop's before I knew who he was
and I was astonished to find a man who spoke English so
well, behave himself so well.

I differ with you in opinion about the King of Prussia's
two very different letters to the two poets, for I am persuaded that they are both genuine. They are in character,
seeking at once to please and to deceive. Should the two
poets happen to compare notes, such is human vanity, and
still more such is poetical vanity, that each would be convinced that the other was the dupe, and himself his Majesty's
most favoured poet. *S'il fait bon battre les glorieux, il fait
aussi bon les tromper.* In the first case they do not complain;
in the second they do not even see.

We do not comprehend here any more than you do in
Holland why Lord Holderness has not yet kissed the King's
hand, though he talks of setting out hence in a month.
Some of his friends here are uneasy at his undertaking, in
this critical situation, a commission to which they think he
would be unequal in any, and have, I know, tried to dissuade
him from it. This is certain at least, that, considering his relations and connections in Holland, he will always be looked
upon as a party in all their domestic factions and cabals: a light

1324

in which a Foreign Minister, to serve his own country well, should never appear, however deeply engaged privately. Moreover, he will be involved in the disgrace of the Bentincks, which, notwithstanding their present favour, I will venture to prophesy is not very remote. If what I have heard be true, her Royal Highness *la leur garde bonne, quelque mine qu'elle faise à présent.*

Yours, etc.

No. 1630

To Captain Irwine (at Paris)

(*In the possession of Mrs. Reynolds-Peyton*)

London, 4 April O.S. 1749

Sir,

I send you the letter of recommendation to Mr. Villettes,[1] which you desired, by yours to Mr. Grevenkop; but I fear that he will be gone from Turin before you arrive there. But in that case you will find a young academician and his governor there, who will be very glad to do you any service, and to whom I have sent orders upon that subject. They will take the Carnival at Venice in their way, where you will likewise probably meet them, for I take it for granted that you will contrive to see that uncommon ceremony. It is worth your while. There will be a much greater ceremony next Christmas at Rome, which, at all events, I think you ought to see; that is, the Grand Jubilee, which is celebrated but once in fifty years. So that young as you are, if you do not see it then, you probably never will; and, upon so extraordinary an occasion, I cannot suppose that your father will refuse to prolong your leave of absence. For my own part, I think it so well worth seeing, that I send my young traveller there, though it very much shortens the stay which I originally intended that he should

---

[1] Arthur Villettes, envoy at Turin.

make at the Academy at Turin. I return you my sincere thanks for the favour of your letter, with the inclosed speech of Monsieur de Richelieu's, which is perfectly in character, and, I dare say, all his own. Any instance of your friendship and remembrance will always be agreeable to one, who is, with those sentiments of esteem with which I am, Sir, etc.

No. 1631

TO HIS SON

(*Stanhope CLXXIX*)

London, 12 *April O.S.* 1749

DEAR BOY,

I received by the last mail a letter from Mr. Harte, dated Prague, April the 1st N.S.; for which I desire you will return him my thanks, and assure him that I extremely approve of what he has done, and proposes eventually to do, in your way to Turin. Who would have thought you were old enough to have been so well acquainted with the heroes of the *Bellum Tricennale* as to be looking out for their great-grandsons in Bohemia, with that affection with which I am informed you seek for the Wallsteins, the Kinskis, etc.? As I cannot ascribe it to your age, I must to your consummate knowledge of history, that makes every country and every century, as it were, your own. Seriously; I am told that you are both very strong and very correct in history; of which I am extremely glad. This is useful knowledge.

Comte du Perron and Comte Lascaris are arrived here; the former gave me a letter from Sir Charles Williams, the latter brought me your orders. They are very pretty men, and have both knowledge and manners; which, though they always ought, seldom do go together. I examined them, particularly Comte Lascaris, concerning you; their report is a very favourable one, especially on the side of knowledge; the quickness of conception which they allow you I can

1326

easily credit; but the attention which they add to it pleases me the more, as, I own, I expected it less. Go on in the pursuit and the increase of knowledge; nay, I am sure you will, for you now know too much to stop; and, if Mr. Harte would let you be idle, I am convinced that you would not. But now that you have left Leipsig, and are entered into the great world, remember there is another object that must keep pace with, and accompany, knowledge; I mean, manners, politeness, and the Graces, in which Sir Charles Williams, though very much your friend, owns you are very deficient. The manners of Leipsig must be shook off; and in that respect you must put on the new man. No scrambling at your meals as at a German ordinary; no awkward overturns of glasses, plates, and salt-cellars; no horse-play. On the contrary, a gentleness of manners, a graceful carriage, and an insinuating address, must take their place. I repeat, I shall never cease repeating to you, *the Graces, the Graces*.

I desire that, as soon as ever you get to Turin, you will apply yourself diligently to the Italian language; that, before you leave that place, you may know it well enough to be able to speak tolerably when you get to Rome; where you will soon make yourself perfectly master of Italian, from the daily necessity you will be under of speaking it. In the meantime, I insist upon your not neglecting, much less for- getting, the German you already know; which you may not only continue, but improve by speaking it constantly to your Saxon boy, and as often as you can to the several Germans you will meet in your travels. You remember, no doubt, that you must never write to me from Turin but in the German language and character.

I send you the inclosed letter of recommendation to Mr. Smith, the King's Consul at Venice; who can, and I dare say will, be more useful to you there than anybody. Pray make your court and behave your best to Monsieur and Madame Capello, who will be of great use to you at Rome. Adieu! Yours, tenderly.   *1327*

No. 1632

(Maty, Appendix XVI)

To the Rev. Dr. Madden

London, 15 *April* 1749

Sir,

You are, I am sure, too well persuaded of my sincere regard and friendship for you, to impute my late silence to negligence or forgetfulness; but two concurrent causes have hindered me from acknowledging your two last letters: the one was the ill state of my health; the other was the unsettled state of my person, in my migration from my old house to my new one, where I have hardly yet got pen, ink, paper, and a table. This latter has, I believe, been attested to you by your son, who saw me unfurnished in my old house, and since unsettled in my new one. I have (as I told him that I would) executed your orders with regard to my booksellers. I have told them, more fully than I can tell you, my thoughts of the work, and have raised their impatience for some of the copies, for which they will treat with your printer. How they will sell (considering the whimsical and uncertain decision of the public in those matters) I do not know; but how they ought to sell, if the public judges right, I well know—for I never saw more wit, fancy, and imagination, upon any one single subject. Every one of your alterations are, in my opinion, for the better, excepting those which you say you have made in my favour, and in which I fear the public will too justly differ from you. Your partiality to me had carried you but too far before.

I congratulate both you and Ireland most heartily, upon the increasing fruits of your labours for the public good; for I am informed from all hands, that a spirit of industry diffuses itself through all Ireland; the linen manufacture gains ground daily in the south and south-west, and new manufactures arise in different parts of the kingdom. All which, I will venture to say, is originally owing to your judicious and indefatigable endeavours for the good of your country. You know the nature of mankind in general, and of our countrymen in particular (for I still think and call myself an Irishman), well enough to know, that the invitation by premiums would be much more effectual than laws, or remote considerations of general public good, upon which few people reason well enough to be convinced that their own solid private interest essentially depends. The Dublin Society, and in particular, my good friends the Bishop of Meath and Prior, have seconded you very well; and it is not saying too much of them to say, that they deserve better of Ireland than any one other set of men in it; I will not even except the Parliament. The premiums for flax-seed raised, instead of the former iniquitous distribution of it have, I am told, and believe, had very good consequences for the linen manufacture; and, as there was an infamous job got the better of, I am in hopes that all jobs will be hindered from creeping into that excellent establishment of the Protestant Charter-schools, which, if it be kept pure but for some years, will have a prodigious effect as to the religious and political state of Ireland; but if once Protestant [*sic* Catholic?] children slip into those schools, as was attempted in my time, the end of their institution ceases. I hope the University of Dublin, that enjoys a share of your premiums, deserves them. Our two Universities, at least, will do it no hurt, unless by their examples, for I cannot believe that their present reputations will invite people in Ireland to send their sons there. The one (Cambridge) is sunk into the lowest obscurity; and the existence of Oxford would not be known, if it were not for the treasonable spirit publicly avowed, and often exerted there. The University of Dublin has this great advantage over ours; it is one compact body, under the eye and authority of one head, who, if he is a good one, can enforce order and discipline, and establish the public exercises as he thinks proper; among which the purity and elegance of the English language ought to be particularly attended to, for there you are apt to fail in Ireland. But I trouble you too long upon subjects of which you are a much better judge than I am, and upon the spot to observe. My thoughts are only *Quæ censet amiculus*, and I give them you, *Ut si cæcus iter monstrare velit.* My wishes for the prosperity of your country are as warm and as sincere as the sentiments of regard, esteem, and friendship, with which I am,

Yours, etc.

No. 1633

To his Son

(*Stanhope CLXXX*)

London, 19 *April O.S.* 1749

Dear Boy,

This letter will, I believe, still find you at Venice, in all the dissipation of masquerades, ridottos, operas, etc.; with all my heart; they are decent evening amusements, and very properly succeed that serious application to which I am sure you devote your mornings. There are liberal and illiberal pleasures as well as liberal and illiberal arts. There are some pleasures that degrade a gentleman as much as some trades could do. Sottish drinking, indiscriminate gluttony, driving coaches, rustic sports, such as fox-chases, horse-races, etc., are, in my opinion, infinitely below the honest and industrious professions of a tailor and a shoemaker, which are said to *déroger.*

As you are now in the musical country, where singing, fiddling, and piping are not only the common topics of conversation, but almost the principal objects of attention; I cannot help cautioning you against giving into those (I will call them illiberal) pleasures (though music is commonly reckoned one of the liberal arts), to the degree that most of your countrymen do when they travel in Italy. If you love music, hear it; go to operas, concerts, and pay fiddlers to play to you; but I insist upon your neither piping nor fiddling yourself. It puts a gentleman in a very frivolous, contemptible light; brings him into a great deal of bad company; and takes up a great deal of time, which might be much better employed. Few things would mortify me more, than to see you bearing a part in a concert, with a fiddle under your chin, or a pipe in your mouth.

I have had a great deal of conversation with Comte du Perron, and Comte Lascaris, upon your subject; and I will tell you, very truly, what Comte du Perron (who is, in my opinion, a very pretty man) said of you. *Il a de l'esprit, un savoir peu commun à son âge, une grande vivacité, et quand il aura pris des manières il sera parfait; car il faut avouer qu'il sent encore le collège; mais cela viendra.* I was very glad to hear, from one whom I think so good a judge, that you wanted nothing but *des manières*; which I am convinced you will now soon acquire in the company which henceforwards you are likely to keep. But I must add, too, that, if you should not acquire them, all the rest will be of very little use to you. By *manières*, I do not mean bare common civility; everybody must have that, who would not be kicked out of company; but I mean engaging, insinuating, shining manners; a distinguished politeness, an almost irresistible address; a superior gracefulness in all you say and do. It is this alone that can give all your other talents their full lustre and value; and, consequently, it is this which should now be the principal object of your attention. Observe minutely, wherever you go, the allowed and established models of good-breeding, and form yourself upon them. Whatever pleases you most, in others, will infallibly please others, in you. I have often repeated this to you; now is your time of putting it in practice.

Pray make my compliments to Mr. Harte; and tell him I have received his letter from Vienna, of the 16th N.S., but that I shall not trouble him with an answer to it till I have received the other letter, which he promises me, upon the subject of one of my last. I long to hear from him after your settlement at Turin; the months that you are to pass there will be very decisive ones for you. The exercises of the Academy, and the manners of Courts, must be attended to and acquired, and, at the same time, your other studies continued. I am sure you will not pass, nor desire, one single idle hour there; for I do not foresee that you can, in any part of your life, put out six months to greater interest, than those next six at Turin.

We will talk hereafter about your stay at Rome, and in other parts of Italy. This only I will now recommend to you; which is, to extract the spirit of every place you go to. In those places, which are only distinguished by classical fame, and valuable remains of antiquity, have your Classics in your hand and in your head; compare the ancient geography, and descriptions, with the modern; and never fail to take notes. Rome will furnish you with business enough of that sort; but then it furnishes you with many other objects well deserving your attention, such as deep ecclesiastical craft and policy. Adieu!

No. 1634

To Solomon Dayrolles, Esq.

(*Mahon III. 341*)

London, 25 *April O.S.* 1749

Dear Dayrolles,

I am now three letters in your debt, which I would have paid more punctually, if I had any tolerable current species to have paid you in: but I have nothing but farthings to offer, and most of them, too, counterfeit; for being, thank God, no longer concerned in the coinage, I cannot answer for the weight of the coin. I hear, as everybody does, more lies than truth, and am not in a situation of knowing which is which. It is said, for example, that our great men are reconciled, and I believe that they say so themselves; but I believe at the same time *que le diable n'y perd rien.* One *Grace*[1] is too jealous not to suspect his best friend, and the other *Grace*[2] too obstinate to forgive or forget the least injury. Lord Sandwich, who governs the latter, and detests the former, who in return abhors him, takes care to keep this fire alive, so that he may blow it into a flame whenever it may serve his purpose to do so; and I am much mistaken, if he does not make it blaze often.

The Prince of Wales gains strength in Parliament in proportion as the King grows older; and Mr. Pelham loses ground there from the public conviction that he has but little power, which indeed I believe is true; the Army being entirely in the Duke of Cumberland, the Navy in Lord Sandwich, and the whole Church in the Duke of Newcastle. All other employments are scrambled for; and sometimes one Minister, and sometimes another, gets one. The situation of things little enables Mr. Pelham to satisfy the hungry and greedy rascals of the House of Commons, and consequently creates schisms and subdivisions in the Court party. The next Session will produce events.

However disjointly business may go on, pleasures, I can assure you, go roundly. To-morrow there is to be, at Ranelagh Garden, a masquerade in the Venetian manner.[3] It is to begin at three o'clock in the afternoon; the several *loges* are to be shops for toys, *limonades, glacés,* and other *rafraîchissements.* The next day come the fireworks, at which hundreds of people will certainly lose their lives or their limbs, from the tumbling of scaffolds, the fall of rockets, and other accidents inseparable from such crowds. In order to repair this loss to society, there will be a subscription masquerade

[1]Newcastle.   [2]Bedford.

[3]See a full description of this masquerade in Horace Walpole's Letters to Mann, 3rd May 1749.—M.

on the Monday following, which, upon calculation, it is thought, will be the occasion of getting about the same number of people as were destroyed at the fireworks!

I hear nothing yet of Lord Holderness going to Holland, and therefore do not ask you when I may hope to see you here; for I suppose that his arrival must be previous to your departure: moreover, I am told that you are so busy in moving from one house to another, that you could not yet move from one country to another. Where is your new dwelling at the Hague?

I am glad to hear that Madame de Berkenroodt goes Ambassadress[1] to Paris; she will pass her time well there, and she deserves it. Pray make her my compliments of congratulation, and tell her that I am strongly tempted to pay my respects to her at Paris myself; but that, if I cannot, I will at least do it by proxy this winter twelvemonth, and send her an Ambassador about forty years younger, and consequently forty times better than myself. My boy will then be at Paris; he is now at Venice, goes to Turin till November, and then to Rome till the October following, when I shall emancipate him at Paris. I hear so well of him from all quarters, that I think he will do. *Adieu; portez-vous bien, et aimez-moi toujours.*

No. 1635
To his Son
(*Stanhope CLXXXI*)

London, 27 April O.S. 1749

DEAR BOY,

I have received your letter from Vienna, of the 19th N.S., which gives me great uneasiness, upon Mr. Harte's account. You and I have reason to interest ourselves very

[1]Wife of L'Estevenou van Berkenroede, the Dutch ambassador. Luynes (March, 1753) describes her as young, pretty and fond of dancing. Walpole in his marginal notes to Maty adds: 'She was afterwards separated from her husband for her galantries at Paris.'

334

particularly in everything that relates to him. I am glad, however, that no bone is broken or dislocated; which being the case, I hope he will have been able to pursue his journey to Venice; in that supposition I direct this letter to you at Turin; where it will either find, or at least not wait very long for you; as I calculate that you will be there by the end of next month N.S. I hope you reflect how much you have to do there, and that you are determined to employ every moment of your time accordingly. You have your classical and severer studies to continue with Mr. Harte; you have your exercises to learn; the turn and manners of a Court to acquire; reserving always some time for the decent amusements and pleasures of a gentleman. You see that I am never against pleasures; I loved them myself when I was of your age, and it is as reasonable that you should love them now. But I insist upon it, that pleasures are very combinable with both business and studies, and have a much better relish from the mixture. The man who cannot join business and pleasure, is either a formal coxcomb in the one, or a sensual beast in the other. Your evenings I therefore allot for company, assemblies, balls, and such sort of amusements; as I look upon those to be the best schools for the manners of a gentleman; which nothing can give but use, observation, and experience. You have, besides, Italian to learn, to which I desire you will diligently apply; for though French is, I believe, the language of the Court at Turin, yet Italian will be very necessary for you at Rome, and in other parts of Italy; and if you are well grounded in it while you are at Turin (as you easily may, for it is a very easy language), your subsequent stay at Rome will make you perfect in it. I would also have you acquire a general notion of fortification; I mean so far as not to be ignorant of the terms, which you will often hear mentioned in company; such as *ravelin*, *bastion*, *glacis*, *contrescarpe*, etc. In order to this, I do not propose that you should make a study of fortification, as if you were to be an engineer; but a very easy way of knowing

as much as you need know of them, will be to visit often
the fortifications of Turin, in company with some old officer
or engineer, who will show and explain to you the several
works themselves; by which means you will get a clearer
notion of them, than if you were to see them only upon paper
for seven years together. Go to originals whenever you
can, and trust to copies and descriptions as little as possible.
At your idle hours while you are at Turin, pray read the
history of the House of Savoy, which has produced a great
many very great men. The late King, Victor Amedée, was
undoubtedly one, and the present King is in my opinion
another. In general, I believe that little princes are more
likely to be great men, than those whose more extensive
dominions, and superior strength, flatter them with a
security, which commonly produces negligence and indolence. A little prince in the neighbourhood of great ones,
must be alert, and look out sharp, if he would secure his
own dominions; much more still if he would enlarge them.
He must watch for conjunctures, or endeavour to make them.
No princes have ever possessed this art better than those of
the House of Savoy; who have enlarged their dominions
prodigiously within a century, by profiting of conjunctures.

I send you here enclosed a letter from Comte Lascaris,
who is a warm friend of yours; I desire that you will answer
it very soon, and very cordially; and remember to make
your compliments in it to Comte du Perron. A young man
should never be wanting in these attentions; they cost little,
and bring in a great deal, by getting you people's good word
and affection. They gain the heart, to which I have always
advised you to apply yourself particularly; it guides ten
thousand for one that reason influences.

I cannot end this letter, or, I believe, any other, without
repeating my recommendation of *the Graces*. They are to
be met with at Turin; for God's sake, sacrifice to them, and
they will be propitious. People mistake grossly, to imagine
that the least awkwardness, in either matter or manner,

1336

mind or body, is an indifferent thing, and not worthy of attention. It may possibly be a weakness in me (but in short we are all so made); I confess to you fairly, that when you shall come home, and that I first see you, if I find you ungraceful in your address, and awkward in your person and dress, it will be impossible for me to love you half so well as I should otherwise do, let your intrinsic merit and knowledge be ever so great. If that would be your case with me, as it really would, judge how much worse it might be with others, who have not the same affection and partiality for you, and to whose hearts you must make your own way.

Remember to write to me constantly, while you are in Italy, in the German language and character, till you can write to me in Italian; which will not be till you have been some time at Rome.

Adieu, my dear boy; may you turn out, what Mr. Harte and I wish you! I must add that, if you do not, it will be both your own fault and your own misfortune.

No. 1636

À Madame la Marquise de Monconseil

(Maty I. xxxv)

À Londres, ce 1 mai V.S. 1749

J'ai actuellement devant mes yeux, Madame, trois de vos lettres, dont je n'ai pas encore accusé une seule. Vous jugez bien que j'en rougis, cela est vrai; mais vous jugez bien en même temps que j'avais des raisons valables. Cela est bien vrai aussi; mais je ne vous les détaillerai point, pour ne vous ennuyer que le moins qu'il me sera possible.

Venons à présent au fait, c'est-à-dire, aux ordres dont vous m'avez chargé, auxquels je me fais gloire, et un véritable plaisir, d'obéir. J'ai arrêté donc, pour Madame de Mirepoix, la maisonnette, plutôt que la maison, qu'a eu Monsieur l'Ambassadeur de Venise l'année passée, à un mille d'ici. Le payement en commencera la semaine prochaine, qui est de trois guinées par semaine. Le propriétaire n'a pas voulu attendre plus long-temps vu que c'est à présent la saison que ces petites maisons se louent ordinairement pour les six mois d'été. Au reste, que Madame de Mirepoix ne s'attende pas à des chambres spacieuses, bien meublées, à des sophas, et à des chaises commodes; tout cela n'est pas le ton de nos petites maisons; mais pour la simple propreté, elle y est, et voilà tout.

Quand au pauvre Adolphati, je vous dirai très naturelle- ment, que je pourrais tout aussitôt débiter cinquante mille de ses *trios* que cinquante: on est excédé, accablé, assommé ici de musique; on est tout-a-fait rebuté du grand nombre de souscriptions qu'on sollicite pour des cantates, des sonates, et tout ce qu'il vous plaira, en faveur de com- positeurs très habiles, établis ici depuis quelque temps, et qui s'y sont fait même quelques amis, au lieu que notre Adolphati est absolument inconnu ici, et en Italie. Entre nous soit dit, ceux qui ont entendu sa musique ici ne l'ont nullement goûtée. J'ai prié quelques bons connoisseurs pour l'entendre chez moi, où il a joué de ses compositions, qu'on a trouvées bien ennuyeuses. Je suis bien fâché de ne pouvoir pas lui faire plaisir à cet égard, parce qu'il me parait bon enfant, et encore plus parce que vous vous y intéressez; mais en vérité la chose est impossible, et je suis persuadé que Madame de Richmond vous en dira autant.

Monsieur le Marquis de Centurioni et moi, nous nous sommes cherchés inutilement l'un l'autre jusqu'ici, nous croisant toujours. Je m'impatiente de le voir, indépendem- ment de tout le mérite qu'il peut avoir, parce qu'il me vient de vous, qu'il vous connaît, par conséquent qu'il vous honore, et qu'il me parlera beaucoup de vous.

No. 1637

To Solomon Dayrolles, Esq.

(*Mahon III. 345*)

London, 4 May O.S. 1749

DEAR DAYROLLES,

The stroke is struck, I find at last;[1] and, if I am not much mistaken, he who struck it will have reason to repent it before it be very long. It is true, that it marks out his power; but, at the same time, it makes him the mark of resentment and jealousy, especially of the jealousy of *one person,* who will not bear even the appearance of a rival. Moreover, he cannot carry on the machine himself, he has neither temper nor knowledge sufficient for it. He must call for help, and then he will be in the case of the Horse, who called the Man to his assistance. Comte Groensfeldt will, in my opinion, be that man, who will soon get astride upon that Horse. He is industrious, temperate, and able; and can work under, still better than above, ground. If he is brought into the *Corps des Nobles,* as they say he is to be, it will be, considering all circumstances, such a glaring and decided proof of his personal favour, that everybody will look up to him; and the public opinion of his power will contribute to increase it. This scramble for power, in your little Court, and in your ruined Republic, puts me in mind of Lord Rochester's image of contending Ministers. He compares them to schoolboys, who, at the hazard of their necks,

[1]This passage refers to the sudden dismissal from his office of the Pensionary Gilles. Mr. Dayrolles writes upon it as follows 'The Pensionary's fall, and the manner in which he was obliged to resign his post, seems to affect prodigiously the old Republican party, and, though they don't dare speak out, yet one may easily see by the gloominess of their countenances how it works upon them. It appears as if before this event they had never conceived a true notion of the Prince of Orange's power, which they now find to be as unlimited almost as that of the King of France. And after all I don't see any harm in its being so, and I dare say that the Stadtholder with an absolute power will be able to retrieve the affairs of this country much sooner than if his hands were tied up like those of his predecessors.'—To Lord Chesterfield, 23rd May N.S. 1749. From the original MS.—M.

climb for crabs, which, if they were upon the ground, solid pigs would disdain.[1] How the Pensionary could be ignorant of the favour intended him, as it is reported that he was when he received the message, is what I cannot conceive; for I knew it above a month ago. The manner in which he took it, and spoke the next day in the Assembly, was wise and skilful; but his accepting the pension,[2] for it is merely a pension, since he is excluded all Assemblies, is dirty, and vilifies him. If I had been he, I would sooner have lived all my life, as Van Beuningen did, by way of experiment, one year, upon six and thirty florins. Though his diet would have been but low, his character would have been high.

I have seen Laurenzi, who, I believe, must observe that diet too, unless he can get an increase of his appointments, which he is labouring for; but I much doubt of his success. He confirms the accounts I had had before from many, of *la délicatesse et le bon goût de votre table.* Marquis d'Havrincourt was worthy of it, excelling as he does, not only in the theory, but in the practical part, of the table. He dined with me once or twice, and I think I never saw a more vigorous performer. He is a very pretty man, and has *l'extrêmement bon ton de la parfaitement bonne campagnie,* which is at present the short but comprehensive *éloge d'un honnête homme.*

I am in debt, at least three, if not four, letters to my Baron, who is a most excellent correspondent. I will pay him soon in much better coin than my own letters; for I shall send him by the first opportunity a good cargo of good books and pamphlets. Pray, make him my compliments, and tell him that I will write to him soon.

I hear nothing yet of Lord Holderness's going to Holland.
Yours most faithfully.

[1] In a letter to Henry Savile, 1679. Nonesuch Edition by John Hayward, 263.
[2] 'Of 8,000 florins, about £730.'—Note by Dayrolles.

No. 1638

To Solomon Dayrolles, Esq.

(Maty II, liii)

London, 9 May O.S. 1749

Dear Dayrolles,

The person who will give you this letter, is the nephew of Monsieur Boissier, a rich, and, for all that, a very honest merchant of the City, from whom I have received many civilities. He is a Swiss, and probably you know him by name and reputation. This nephew is desirous to get into the service of the Republic; and I wish that you could be useful to him in that view. I do not mean, nor does he, that you can procure him a commission; but we think that you may be able to point out to him *le moyen d'y parvenir*, whatever that may be. If it be solicitation, you will tell him where to address it; if a private tip, you will tell him where to apply it. In short, I am sure that, from the part I take in him upon his uncle's account, you will do him what service you can.

By the way, do not apprehend from this, that I shall plague you often with recommendations of this kind, for I have refused them to several people, and shall continue to do so to nine in ten. They desire impertinent, unreasonable, or impossible things; and then desire that I will recommend them to you, because they are sure that I have great interest with you. My answer to which is, that I verily believe I have interest with you, and for that very reason will not recommend to you an impertinent or an impossible thing.

I am now assured that Lord Holderness, though he has not yet kissed the King's hand, will go in three weeks at farthest: so that in six I hope to see you here. I need not tell you how glad I shall be of it. We have not been so long asunder since we loved one another; as we still, I believe, do. Adieu!

No. 1639

To his Son

(*Stanhope CLXXXII*)

London, 15 *May O.S.* 1749

Dear Boy,

This letter will, I hope, find you settled to your serious studies, and your necessary exercises, at Turin, after the hurry and dissipation of the Carnival at Venice. I mean, that your stay at Turin should, and I flatter myself that it will, be an useful and ornamental period of your education; but, at the same time, I must tell you, that all my affection for you has never yet given me so much anxiety as that which I now feel. While you are in danger, I shall be in fear, and you are in danger at Turin. Mr. Harte will, by his care, arm you as well as he can against it; but your own good sense and resolution can alone make you invulnerable. I am informed, there are now many English at the Academy at Turin; and I fear those are just so many dangers for you to encounter. Who they are I do not know, but I well know the general ill conduct, the indecent behaviour, and the illiberal views of my young countrymen abroad; especially wherever they are in numbers together. Ill example is of itself dangerous enough, but those who give it seldom stop there; they add their infamous exhortations and invitations; and, if these fail, they have recourse to ridicule; which is harder for one of your age and inexperience to withstand, than either of the former. Be upon your guard, therefore, against these batteries, which will all be played upon you. You are not sent abroad to converse with your own countrymen; among them, in general, you will get little knowledge, no languages, and, I am sure, no manners. I desire that you will form no connections, nor (what they impudently call) friendships, with these people; which are, in truth, only combinations and conspiracies against good morals and

good manners. There is commonly in young people a
facility that makes them unwilling to refuse anything that is
asked of them; a *mauvaise honte*, that makes them ashamed to
refuse; and, at the same time, an ambition of pleasing and
shining in the company they keep; these several causes
produce the best effect in good company, but the very
worst in bad. If people had no vices but their own, few
would have so many as they have. For my own part, I
would sooner wear other people's clothes than their vices;
and they would sit upon me just as well. I hope you will
have none; but if ever you have, I beg, at least, they may be
all your own. Vices of adoption are, of all others, the most
disgraceful and unpardonable. There are degrees in vices
as well as in virtues; and I must do my countrymen the
justice to say, they generally take their vices in the lowest
degree. Their gallantry is the infamous mean debauchery
of stews, justly attended and rewarded by the loss of their
health, as well as their character. Their pleasures of the
table end in beastly drunkenness, low riot, broken windows,
and very often (as they well deserve) broken bones. They
game for the sake of the vice, not of the amusement; and
therefore carry it to excess; undo, or are undone by, their
companions. By such conduct, and in such company
abroad, they come home, the unimproved, illiberal, and ungentlemanlike creatures that one daily sees them; that is, in
the park and in the streets, for one never meets them in
good company; where they have neither manners to present
themselves, nor merit to be received. But, with the manners
of footmen and grooms, they assume their dress too; for
you must have observed them in the streets here, in dirty-
blue frocks, with oaken sticks in their hands, and their hair
greasy and unpowdered, tucked up under hats of an enormous size. Thus finished and adorned by their travels, they
become the disturbers of playhouses; they break the windows, and commonly the landlords, of the taverns where
they drink; and are at once the support, the terror, and the

victims of the bawdy-houses they frequent. These poor mistaken people think they shine, and so they do indeed; but it is as putrefaction shines in the dark.

I am not now preaching to you, like an old fellow, upon either religious or moral texts; I am persuaded you do not want the best instructions of that kind: but I am advising you as a friend, as a man of the world, as one who would not have you old while you are young, but would have you take all the pleasures that reason points out and that decency warrants. I will therefore suppose, for argument's sake (for upon no other account can it be supposed), that all the vices above mentioned were perfectly innocent in themselves; they would still degrade, vilify, and sink those who practised them; would obstruct their rising in the world, by debasing their characters; and give them a low turn of mind and manners, absolutely inconsistent with their making any figure in upper life, and great business.

What I have now said, together with your own good sense, is I hope sufficient to arm you against the seduction, the invitations, or the profligate exhortations (for I cannot call them temptations) of those unfortunate young people. On the other hand, when they would engage you in these schemes, content yourself with a decent but steady refusal; avoid controversy upon such plain points. You are too young to convert them, and I trust too wise to be converted by them. Shun them, not only in reality, but even in appearance, if you would be well received in good company; for people will always be shy of receiving a man who comes from a place where the plague rages, let him look ever so healthy. There are some expressions, both in French and English, and some characters, both in those two and in other countries, which have, I dare say, misled many young men to their ruin. *Une honnête débauche, une jolie débauche; an agreeable rake, a man of pleasure.* Do not think that this means debauchery and profligacy; nothing like it. It means at most the accidental and unfrequent irregularities of youth and vivacity, in opposition to dulness, formality, and want of spirit. A *commerce galant* insensibly formed with a woman of fashion; a glass of wine or two too much unwarily taken in the warmth and joy of good company, or some innocent frolic by which nobody is injured, are the utmost bounds of that life of pleasure which a man of sense and decency, who has a regard for his character, will allow himself, or be allowed by others. Those who transgress them in the hopes of shining, miss their aim, and become infamous, or at least contemptible.

The length or shortness of your stay at Turin will sufficiently inform me (even though Mr. Harte should not) of your conduct there; for, as I have told you before, Mr. Harte has the strictest orders to carry you away immediately from thence upon the first and least symptom of infection that he discovers about you; and I know him to be too conscientiously scrupulous, and too much your friend and mine, not to execute them exactly. Moreover, I will inform you that I shall have constant accounts of your behaviour from Comte Salmour, the governor of the Academy, whose son is now here, and my particular friend. I have also other good channels of intelligence of which I do not apprise you. But, supposing that all turns out well at Turin, yet, as I propose your being at Rome for the jubilee at Christmas, I desire that you will apply yourself diligently to your exercises of dancing, fencing, and riding, at the Academy; as well for the sake of your health and growth, as to fashion and supple you. You must not neglect your dress neither, but take care to be *bien mis*.

Pray send for the best operator for the teeth at Turin, where I suppose there is some famous one, and let him put yours in perfect order, and then take care to keep them so afterwards yourself. You had very good teeth, and I hope they are so still; but even those who have bad ones should keep them clean, for a dirty mouth is in my mind ill manners: in short, neglect nothing that can possibly please. A thousand nameless little things, which nobody can describe, but which everybody feels, conspire to form that *whole* of pleasing; as the several pieces of a mosaic work, though separately of little beauty or value, when properly joined, form those beautiful figures which please everybody. A look, a gesture, an attitude, a tone of voice, all bear their parts in the great work of pleasing. The art of pleasing is more particularly necessary in your intended profession than perhaps in any other; it is in truth the first half of your business; for, if you do not please the Court you are sent to, you will be of very little use to the Court you are sent from. Please the eyes and the ears, they will introduce you to the heart; and nine times in ten the heart governs the understanding.

Make your court particularly, and show distinguished attentions, to such men and women as are best at Court, highest in the fashion, and in the opinion of the public; speak advantageously of them behind their backs, in companies who you have reason to believe will tell them again. Express your admiration of the many great men that the House of Savoy has produced; observe, that nature, instead of being exhausted by those efforts, seems to have redoubled them in the persons of the present King and the Duke of Savoy: wonder at this rate where it will end, and conclude that it must end in the government of all Europe. Say this, likewise, where it will probably be repeated; but say it unaffectedly, and, the last especially, with a kind of *enjouement*. These little arts are very allowable, and must be made use of in the course of the world; they are pleasing to one party, useful to the other, and injurious to nobody.

What I have said with regard to my countrymen in general does not extend to them all without exception: there are some who have both merit and manners. Your friend Mr. Stevens is among the latter, and I approve of your connection with him. You may happen to meet with some others, whose friendship may be of great use to you hereafter, either from their superior talents, or their rank and fortune. Cultivate them; but then I desire that Mr. Harte should be the judge of those persons.

Adieu, my dear child! Consider seriously the importance of the two next years, to your character, your figure, and your fortune.

No. 1640

To Solomon Dayrolles, Esq.

(Mahon III. 348)

London, 16 *May O.S.* 1749

Dear Dayrolles,

Lord Holderness sets out for the Hague the beginning of next week at farthest, so that I hope to see you here before it is long. However, do not press importunately for leave to return, because that would imply that a superior Minister at the Hague rendered you unnecessary there, which I would not have thought here. I mention this here upon account of a conversation that passed lately between Mr. Pelham and myself concerning you. He asked me, whether I thought you would care to remain at the Hague after the arrival of Lord Holderness? Though I guessed immediately the meaning of that question, I seemed not to do it, and asked him whether they had a mind to employ you anywhere else. He answered, no; but that he did not know whether you would care to act a subordinate part under Lord Holderness. I told him that I was persuaded you would make no difficulty of that, for that you took your post in those very circumstances under Lord Sandwich. 'Why then,' said he, 'he must e'en stay, and it is only an unnecessary expense to the Government.' I answered, that I did not look upon the expense of a Resident at the Hague as an unnecessary one by any means—that there had almost always been one, and that I believed that a Resident was, at least, as necessary with Lord Holderness as with any other Minister that had ever been there. This he acknowledged, and added, that there were certainly no thoughts of removing you, unless of your own desire. His object, I know, was public economy, which, as he cannot practise where he pleases, he wants to do where he can. But, however, after what passed between us, I will answer for it that he will do you no harm.

On the other hand, I know that the Duke of Newcastle recommended you strongly the other day to Lord Holderness, and advised him to have the utmost confidence in you; so that you seem to be very safe. But, however, I would not have your post, especially by your own admission, pass for an absolute sinecure, and an unnecessary expense to the Government; therefore I would advise you, when you ask leave to come here for two or three months, on account of your own private affairs, to say that the several details of your post are not so many at this time of the year, and will not be so teazing to the Minister upon whom they will devolve by your absence. Lord Holderness, I must acquaint you, has the pride that all little minds have: flatter that, and you may do what you will with him. Far from a jealousy of business, I think he will be very willing that you should do it all, if you please. If I were you, I would tell him, that now he was at the Hague, all the important business would doubtless be carried on by him only, and that I looked upon myself as no longer concerned in it;—that I had, therefore, nothing now to write but the common occurrences of the Hague, but that I would constantly show his Lordship my letters, if he would give himself the trouble to read them. This offer his laziness and pleasures will never let him accept; but it will give him a confidence in you, and then you will continue to write the best accounts you can get; and, without a compliment to you, I will venture to say that your letters will be the letters of business from the Hague, excepting those particular ones which the Greffier may, upon some important and secret points, dictate to Lord Holderness. We will talk more fully upon this subject when I see you.

It is reported here that Grovestein is disgraced. Is that true? I should not wonder at it. I am called away of a sudden.

Yours faithfully.

No. 1641

To his Son

(*Stanhope CLXXXIII*)

London, 22 May O.S. 1749

DEAR BOY,

I recommended to you in my last an innocent piece of art—that of flattering people behind their backs, in presence of those who, to make their own court, much more than for your sake, will not fail to repeat, and even amplify, the praise to the party concerned. This is, of all flattery, the most pleasing, and consequently the most effectual. There are other, and many other, inoffensive arts of this kind, which are necessary in the course of the world, and which he who practises the earliest will please the most, and rise the soonest. The spirits and vivacity of youth are apt to neglect them as useless, or reject them as troublesome; but subsequent knowledge and experience of the world remind us of their importance, commonly when it is too late. The principal of these things is the mastery of one's temper, and that coolness of mind, and serenity of countenance, which hinder us from discovering, by words, actions, or even looks, those passions or sentiments by which we are inwardly moved or agitated, and the discovery of which gives cooler and abler people such infinite advantages over us, not only in great business, but in all the most common occurrences of life. A man who does not possess himself enough to hear disagreeable things without visible marks of anger and change of countenance, or agreeable ones without sudden bursts of joy and expansion of countenance, is at the mercy of every artful knave or pert coxcomb. The former will provoke or please you by design, to catch unguarded words or looks, by which he will easily decipher the secrets of your heart, of which you should keep the key yourself, and trust it with no man living. The latter will, by his absurdity, and without intending it, produce the same discoveries, of which other people will avail themselves. You will say, possibly, that this coolness must be constitutional, and consequently does not depend upon the will; and I will allow that constitution has some power over us; but I will maintain, too, that people very often, to excuse themselves, very unjustly accuse their constitutions. Care and reflection, if properly used, will get the better; and a man may as surely get a habit of letting his reason prevail over his constitution, as of letting, as most people do, the latter prevail over the former. If you find yourself subject to sudden starts of passion or madness (for I see no difference between them, but in their duration), resolve within yourself, at least, never to speak one word while you feel that emotion within you. Determine, too, to keep your countenance as unmoved and unembarrassed as possible—which steadiness you may get a habit of by constant attention. I should desire nothing better, in any negotiation, than to have to do with one of these men of warm, quick passions, which I would take care to set in motion. By artful provocations, I would extort rash and unguarded expressions; and, by hinting at all the several things that I could suspect, infallibly discover the true one, by the alteration it occasioned in the countenance of the person. *Volto sciolto con pensieri stretti* is a most useful maxim in business. It is so necessary at such games, such as *berlan, quinʒe, etc.,* that a man who had not the command of his temper and countenance would infallibly be undone by those who had, even though they played fair; whereas in business you always

1350

play with sharpers, to whom at least you should give no fair advantages. It may be objected, that I am now recommending dissimulation to you; I both own and justify it. It has been long said, *Qui nescit dissimulare nescit regnare*; I go still farther, and say, that without some dissimulation no business can be carried on at all. It is *simulation* that is false, mean, and criminal: that is the cunning which Lord Bacon calls crooked or left-handed wisdom, and which is never made use of but by those who have not true wisdom. And the same great man says, that dissimulation is only to hide our own cards; whereas simulation is put on in order to look into other people's. Lord Bolingbroke, in his *Idea of a Patriot King*,[1] which he has lately published, and which I will send you by the first opportunity, says, very justly, that simulation is a *stiletto*; not only an unjust, but an unlawful weapon, and the use of it is rarely to be excused, never justified: whereas dissimulation is a shield, as secrecy is armour; and it is no more possible to preserve secrecy in business, without some degree of dissimulation, than it is to succeed in business without secrecy. He goes on and says, that those two arts of dissimulation and secrecy are like the alloy mingled with pure ore: a little is necessary, and will not debase the coin below its proper standard; but if more than that little be employed (that is, simulation and cunning), the coin loses its currency and the coiner his credit.

Make yourself absolute master, therefore, of your temper and your countenance—so far, at least, as that no visible change do appear in either, whatever you may feel inwardly. This may be difficult, but it is by no means impossible; and, as a man of sense never attempts impossibilities on one hand, on the other he is never discouraged by difficulties; on the contrary, he redoubles his industry and his diligence. he perseveres, and infallibly prevails at last. In any point, which prudence bids you pursue, and which a manifest

[1] Published in 1749.

utility attends, let difficulties only animate your industry, not deter you from the pursuit. If one way has failed, try another; be active, persevere, and you will conquer. Some people are to be reasoned, some flattered, some intimidated, and some teased into a thing; but, in general, all are to be brought into it at last, if skilfully applied to, properly managed, and indefatigably attacked in their several weak places. The time should likewise be judiciously chosen. Every man has his *mollia tempora*, but that is far from being all day long; and you would choose your time very ill, if you applied to a man about one business, when his head was full of another, or when his heart was full of grief, anger, or any other disagreeable sentiment.

In order to judge of the inside of others, study your own; for men in general are very much alike; and though one has one prevailing passion, and another has another, yet their operations are much the same; and whatever engages or disgusts, pleases or offends you in others, will, *mutatis mutandis*, engage, disgust, please, or offend others in you. Observe, with the utmost attention, all the operations of your own mind, the nature of your own passions, and the various motives that determine your will; and you may, in a great degree, know all mankind. For instance, do you find yourself hurt and mortified, when another makes you feel his superiority, and your own inferiority, in knowledge, parts, rank, or fortune? You will certainly take great care not to make a person whose goodwill, good word, interest, esteem, or friendship, you would gain, feel that superiority in you, in case you have it. If disagreeable insinuations, sly sneers, or repeated contradictions tease and irritate you, would you use them where you wished to engage or please? Surely not; and I hope you wish to engage, and please, almost universally. The temptation of saying a smart and witty thing, or *bon mot*, and the malicious applause with which it is commonly received, has made people who can say them, and, still oftener, people who think they can, but cannot, but

1352

yet try, more enemies, and implacable ones too, than any one other thing that I know of. When such things, then, shall happen to be said at your expense (as sometimes they certainly will), reflect seriously upon the sentiments of uneasiness, anger, and resentment, which they excite in you; and consider whether it can be prudent, by the same means, to excite the same sentiments in others against you. It is a decided folly, to lose a friend for a jest; but, in my mind, it is not a much less degree of folly, to make an enemy of an indifferent and neutral person for the sake of a *bon mot*. When things of this kind happen to be said of you, the most prudent way is to seem not to suppose that they are meant at you, but to dissemble and conceal whatever degree of anger you may feel inwardly; and, should they be so plain, that you cannot be supposed ignorant of their meaning, to join in the laugh of the company against yourself; acknowledge the hit to be a fair one, and the jest a good one, and play off the whole thing in seeming good humour; but by no means reply in the same way; which only shows that you are hurt, and publishes the victory which you might have concealed. Should the thing said, indeed, injure your honour, or moral character, there is but one proper reply; which I hope you never will have occasion to make.

As the female part of the world has some influence, and often too much, over the male, your conduct, with regard to women (I mean women of fashion, for I cannot suppose you capable of conversing with any others), deserves some share in your reflections. They are a numerous and loquacious body; their hatred would be more prejudicial than their friendship can be advantageous to you. A general complaisance, and attention to that sex, is therefore established by custom, and certainly necessary. But where you would particularly please any one whose situation, interest, or connections can be of use to you, you must show particular preference. The least attentions please, the greatest charm them. The innocent, but pleasing flattery of their persons, however gross, is greedily swallowed, and kindly digested; but a seeming regard for their understandings, a seeming desire of, and deference for, their advice, together with a seeming confidence in their moral virtues, turns their heads entirely in your favour. Nothing shocks them so much as the least appearance of that contempt, which they are apt to suspect men of entertaining of their capacities; and you may be very sure of gaining their friendship, if you seem to think it worth gaining. Here dissimulation is very often necessary, and even simulation sometimes allowable; which, as it pleases them, may be useful to you, and is injurious to nobody.

This torn sheet, which I did not observe when I began upon it, as it alters the figure, shortens too the length of my letter. It may very well afford it; my anxiety for you carries me insensibly to these lengths. I am apt to flatter myself that my experience, at the latter end of my life, may be of use to you at the beginning of yours; and I do not grudge the greatest trouble if it can procure you the least advantage. I even repeat frequently the same things, the better to imprint them on your young, and, I suppose, yet giddy mind; and I shall think that part of my time the best employed, that contributes to make you employ yours well. God bless you, child!

No. 1642

To Solomon Dayrolles, Esq.

(Mahon III. 350)

Dear Dayrolles,   *London, 9 June O.S.* 1749

As I find, by your last, that your stay in Holland will now be but short, my letters will be so too. We can talk more fully as well as more freely than we can write. You have set out well with our new Minister, and I believe will go on so. He is one of those people whom a man of sense will not quarrel with, but humour; *cela ne coûte rien.*

1354

Hop showed me yesterday the print of your fireworks; they seem to be so fine and so expensive, that, considering the present necessitious condition of the Republic, they put me in mind of a good *fanfaron* motto upon a French standard, *Peream, modo luceam.* I should have told you first, that the device was a bursting grenado.

My boy, who was going to the Carnival at Venice, was suddenly seized with a violent inflammation upon his lungs, at a miserable post-house, two posts beyond Laybach, in Carniole,[1] where he remained in great danger for twelve days. He is now recovering at Laybach; and, by this time, I hope, out of all danger. However, as soon as the heats are over, that is, at the latter end of September, I intend to send him to Naples, the best place in the world for tender lungs, and his are so yet. I shall send him a letter of recommendation to Marquis Fogliani, who is the only person I know there; and, as there is no Neapolitan Minister here, that will be the only letter I can give him. Could you easily get a letter or two for him from Monsieur Finochetti? If you can, you may bring them with you here; and I can send them to him time enough from hence. You will remember to call him my nephew. I am told that the Princess Strongoli and General Mahoni's are the two best houses there.

The Parliament is to be prorogued next Tuesday, when the Ministers will have six months' leisure to quarrel, and patch up, and quarrel again. Garrick and the Violetti will likewise, about the same time, have an opportunity of doing the same thing, for they are to be married next week.[2] They are, at present, desperately in love with each other. Lady Burlington was at first outrageous, but upon cooler reflection upon what the Violetti, if provoked, might say or rather invent, she consented to the match, and superintends the writings. *Adieu; je languis de vous voir.*

[1] See Letter to his Son of 6th June 1751 and note.

[2] La Violette had been a dancer at the Austrian Court, and when in London was under the protection of Lady Burlington. She was all the rage at about this time.

No. 1643
À Madame la Marquise de Monconseil
(Maty I. xxxvi)

À Londres, ce 13 juin V.S. 1749

C'est que le ton grondeur vous va au mieux, Madame, et vous l'apprêtez d'une façon que vous lui donnez un goût flatteur. De tels reproches donnent l'exclusion à l'indifférence, et on est charmé de les recevoir, quand on est bien sûr de ne les avoir pas mérités; et je suis dans ce cas. Moi! aller à Aix-la-Chapelle sans vous faire ma cour à Paris, ou en allant, ou en revenant! c'est en vérité un soupçon aussi injurieux à mon goût qu'à mes sentiments. Je pourrais peut-être me servir du prétexte d'aller à Aix-la-Chapelle, pour satisfaire à mon envie d'aller à Paris, mais je n'ai garde d'en faire ou l'unique, ou le véritable, objet d'un trajet de mer. Non, Madame, si je fais un pélérinage, ce sera pour faire mes dévotions dans la rue de Verneuil ou à Bagatelle, et y renouveler les vœux d'une amitié respectueuse et sincère; mais pour cette année, il m'est impossible de sortir d'Angleterre. Un engagement tendre, et plusieurs affaires sérieuses m'y retiennent; l'engagement tendre est celui de ma nouvelle maison, dont je n'ai pas tout-à-fait joui encore, et c'est un grand item en fait de tendresse. Elle me refuse ses dernières faveurs, jusqu'à ce que je l'aie entièrement nippée; ce qui ne sera fait que vers l'hiver, car mes deux plus belles pièces ne sont rien moins que finies. Mes engagements nécessaires sont des arrangements de famille,[1] où par conséquent la chicane entre pour quelque chose et les délais pour beaucoup.

Votre Marquis de Centurioni a réellement de l'esprit, et de l'acquis, mais quand même il n'en aurait point eu, votre recommandation seule les lui aurait bien valu auprès de moi. Vous le reverrez bientôt, puisqu'il part d'ici cette semaine: le seul défaut que je lui trouve, c'est qu'il veut absolument

[1]Consequent on his brother's death.

être français et petit-maître; et ne l'est pas qui veut. Le petit-maître français a des grâces, avec tous ses défauts, et il plaît en dépit de la raison, qui sûrement n'autorise point sa conduite; mais cette étourderie brillante, cette pétulance aimable, se trouvent très déplacées, quand un italien, un allemand, ou un anglais veut s'en parer: il n'y a que l'original qui plaît, toutes les traductions en sont pitoyables.

À propos de traductions, je tâche de faire actuellement traduire en italien votre futur élève, votre enfant adoptif: il est en Italie, et il doit passer son hiver à Rome. J'ai une grâce à vous demander sur son sujet, c'est de vouloir bien le recommander à Monsieur le Duc de Nivernais votre Ambassadeur; j'aurai l'honneur de lui écrire moi-même, pour satisfaire au respect et à l'estime que je lui dois: cela n'est que pour les formes; mais c'est de votre recommandation que j'attends tout le solide. Je conçois bien que Monsieur de Nivernais, par la politesse qui lui est si naturelle, le prendrait à dîner ou à souper deux ou trois fois pendant son séjour à Rome, et voila où finissent les recommandations ordinaires, mais ce n'est pas là mon fait: et je souhaiterais que Monsieur de Nivernais en fit son galopin, qu'il le regardât comme un petit Français de sa suite, et qu'il fût si domestiqué dans son antichambre, qu'il eût, moyennant cela, de temps en temps des occasions d'étudier le caractère d'honnête homme, sur le meilleur modèle que je connaisse. Ce bonheur ne peut lui arriver que par votre moyen; et permettez moi de vous dire que vous êtes intéressée à le lui procurer. Plus il sera formé, avant que de vous appartenir en propre, moins il vous sera à charge; et quelques leçons à l'Hôtel de Nivernais vous épargneront bien de la peine après. Je compte qu'il sera à Rome vers le milieu de décembre; et dans une année, ou une année et demie après, il sera à Paris; ou pour mieux dire, cinq ou six heures du jour chez vous, je ne lui demande pas d'autre Paris que cela. J'y serai peut-être son avant-coureur, au moins je le souhaite, et c'est le seul souhait qui me reste. L'âge éteint tous les souhaits de l'amour; la raison et l'expérience ceux de l'ambition; ceux de l'amitié vous sont bien dus, Madame, et je vous les adresse très véritablement.

No. 1644

To his Son

(Stanhope CLXXXIV)

London, 16 June O.S. 1749

DEAR BOY,
I do not guess where this letter will find you, but I hope it will find you well: I direct it eventually to Laybach; from whence, I suppose, you have taken care to have your letters sent after you. I received no account from Mr. Harte by last post, and the mail due this day is not come in; so that my informations come down no lower than the 2nd June N.S. the date of Mr. Harte's last letter. As I am now easy about your health, I am only curious about your motions, which I hope have been either to Inspruck or Verona; for I disapprove extremely of your proposed long and troublesome journey to Switzerland. Wherever you may be, I recommend to you, to get as much Italian as you can before you go either to Rome or Naples: a little will be of great use to you upon the road; and the knowledge of the grammatical part, which you can easily acquire in two or three months, will not only facilitate your progress, but accelerate your perfection in that language, when you go to those places where it is generally spoken, as Naples, Rome, Florence, etc.

Should the state of your health not yet admit of your usual application to books, you may in a great degree, and I hope you will, repair that loss by useful and instructive conversations with Mr. Harte; you may, for example, desire him to give you in conversation the outlines, at least, of Mr. Locke's logic; a general notion of ethics, and a verbal

1358

epitome of rhetoric; of all which, Mr. Harte will give you clearer ideas in half an hour by word of mouth, than the books of most of the dull fellows who have written upon those subjects would do in a week.

I have waited so long for the post, which I hoped would come, that the post, which is just gone out, obliges me to cut this letter short. God bless you, my dear child, and restore you soon to perfect health!

My compliments to Mr. Harte, to whose care your life is the least thing that you owe.

No. 1645

To his Son

(*Stanhope CLXXXV*)

London, 22 *June O.S.* 1749

DEAR BOY,

The outside of your letter of the 7th N.S. directed by your own hand, gave me more pleasure than the inside of any other letter ever did. I received it yesterday, at the same time with one from Mr. Harte, of the 6th. They arrived at a very proper time, for they found a consultation of physicians in my room, upon account of a fever which I had for four or five days, but which has now entirely left me. As Mr. Harte says, *that your lungs, now and then, give you a little pain*; and that *your swellings come and go variably*; but, as he mentions nothing of your coughing, spitting, or sweating, the doctors take it for granted that you are entirely free from those three bad symptoms; and from thence conclude, that the pain which you sometimes feel upon the lungs, is only symptomatical of your rheumatic disorder, from the pressure of the muscles, which hinders the free play of the lungs. But, however, as the lungs are a point of the utmost importance and delicacy, they insist upon your drinking, in all events, asses' milk twice a day, and goats' whey as often as you please, the oftener the better: in your common diet they recommend an attention to pectorals, such as sago, barley, turnips, etc. These rules are equally good in rheumatic, as in consumptive cases; you will therefore, I hope, strictly observe them; for I take it for granted you are above the silly likings or dislikings, in which silly people indulge their tastes at the expense of their healths.

I approve of your going to Venice, as much as I disapprove of your going to Switzerland. I suppose that you are by this time arrived, and, in that supposition, I direct this letter there. But if you should find the heat too great, or the weather offensive at this time of the year, I would have you go immediately to Verona, and stay there till the great heats are over, before you return to Venice.

The time you will probably pass at Venice will allow you to make yourself master of that intricate and singular form of government, which few of our travellers know anything of. Read, ask, and see everything that is relative to it. There are likewise many valuable remains of the remotest antiquity, and many fine pieces of the *antico moderno*; all which deserve a different sort of attention from that which your countrymen commonly give them. They go to see them as they go to see the lions, and kings on horseback, at the Tower here; only to say that they have seen them. You will, I am sure, view them in another light; you will consider them as you would a poem, to which indeed they are akin. You will observe whether the sculptor has animated his stone, or the painter his canvas, into the just expression of those sentiments and passions which should characterise and mark their several figures. You will examine likewise whether, in their groups, there be an unity of action or proper relation; a truth of dress and manners. Sculpture and painting are very justly called liberal arts; a lively and strong imagination, together with a just observation, being absolutely necessary to excel in either; which, in my opinion, is by no means the case of music, though called a liberal art, and now

1360

in Italy placed even above the other two: a proof of the decline of that country. The Venetian school produced many great painters, such as Paul Veronese, Titian, Palma, etc., by whom you will see, as well in private houses as in churches, very fine pieces. The *Last Supper*, by Paul Veronese, in the church of St. George, is reckoned his capital performance, and deserves your attention; as also does the famous picture of the Cornaro family by Titian. A taste of sculpture and painting is in my mind as becoming as a taste of fiddling and piping is unbecoming a man of fashion. The former is connected with history and poetry, the latter with nothing that I know of but bad company.

Learn Italian as fast as ever you can, that you may be able to understand it tolerably, and speak it a little, before you go to Rome and Naples. There are many good historians in that language, and excellent translations of the ancient Greek and Latin authors, which are called the *Collana*: but the only two Italian poets that deserve your acquaintance are Ariosto and Tasso, and they undoubtedly have great merit.

Make my compliments to Mr. Harte, and tell him that I have consulted about his leg; and that, if it was only a sprain, he ought to keep a tight bandage about the part for a considerable time, and do nothing else to it. Adieu! *Jubeo te bene valere.*

No. 1646

To Solomon Dayrolles, Esq.

(*Mahon III. 354*)

London, 23 June O.S. 1749

Dear Dayrolles,

I have this instant received your letter of the 27th N.S. which I am very little able to answer, having been ill of a fever ever since Sunday last, and this being the first day that I have been allowed to go out of my bed-chamber. I am very weak, partly from the distemper itself, and partly from being starved. On Monday I shall go to Blackheath for a week, which I hope will restore me. But I would not delay making you easier than you seem to be at present, about the event of your letter to the Duke of Newcastle. I happened to meet him last Saturday at Boden's country-house, where he told me that Stone had that morning delivered him a letter from you, asking leave to come here for a very short time. I told him that I supposed you would obtain it; to which he answered: Most undoubtedly. So that your having yet had no answer to it, I am convinced, proceeds only from his Grace's usual hurry and negligence. I believe he has at present business enough upon his hands; for in order to strengthen himself against the Dukes of Cumberland and Bedford, and Lord Sandwich, he has been negotiating with Lord Granville, who in consequence of that negotiation had the Garter given to him yesterday. He has refused the Lieutenancy of Ireland, which was offered him about three weeks ago; but he wisely chose rather to remain upon the spot without a place, than to go to Ireland for one. His Grace will very soon find, that, instead of calling in an auxiliary, he has taken a master.

I thank you heartily for the letters you have procured the boy for Naples; he is now so well recovered that he is gone to Venice, where he will stay till the middle of September, and then proceed to Naples. My head will not allow me to write any more; it is my heart adds, that I am faithfully,

Yours.

No. 1647
To the Earl of Huntingdon[1]
(Steuart I)

London, 26 June O.S. 1749

My Dear Lord,

I have received, I do not say the honour (for I cannot write to you in that style) but the pleasure of your letter, and a real pleasure it was. I grew impatient to hear of your health and your motions, but knew nobody who could inform me of either, Lady Huntingdon being at Bristol; and the warm and sincere part that I take in both, had determined me to address myself to the fountain head; accordingly I was sitting down to write to you, when your letter came in, and saved me the indiscretion. A thousand thanks to you, my dear Lord, for that mark of your remembrance and friendship; believe me, mine will attend you faithfully wherever you go.

You have done very prudently in leaving Caen and going to a place where you are under a necessity of speaking and hearing only French; that necessity will teach you the language sooner than the best master. And I would advise you to continue under that necessity, till the facility of speaking French delivers you from the temptation of speaking English. The French language (by the way) is the only thing you will get from the good Cordeliers, who are in general grossly ignorant, as indeed are all the regular Popish clergy, except the Jesuits, the Benedictines and the Pères de l'Oratoire. The Professor of Divinity of a Convent of Augustans at Lisle showed me in their polyglot Bible the Greek for the Hebrew and the Hebrew for the Greek. I gently hinted my doubts that he was mistaken, but he assured me that he was not, and I submitted.

[1] Francis Hastings (1729-1789), tenth Earl. His mother, a daughter of the second Earl Ferrers, and so the sister of Lady Frances Shirley, founded a sect of Calvinistic Methodists, known as Lady Huntingdon's Connexion, of which Whitefield was a chaplain.

1363

Your Lordship will daily find more and more the utility, not to say the necessity, of modern languages and modern history. Greek, Latin and ancient history are ornamental in the opinion of the world and pleasing in one's own closet. The title, too, of a good scholar makes a figure among the other titles of a man of quality, and the more so as it is very rare; but in the common course of life, whether in pleasures or in business, modern languages and modern history, are the useful, I might say the necessary parts of knowledge.

Your observation of the undisguised vanity of the French is a very just one; it is the avowed motive of most of their actions; but, however, it produces very good effects, and wherever I reap the benefit of the effects, I will not quarrel with the causes. Moreover, I fear that if we were to inquire too strictly into the causes of most human actions, the discovery would rather be mortifying than satisfactory; it is certain that the vanity which the French have, in being reckoned the best bred, makes them in truth the most engaging people in the world, especially to strangers. You will find them still more so than anybody, as you will make their judgment co-operate with their vanity.

Permit me, my dear Lord, as a faithful friend and servant, to recommend to you a suspension of your classical and academical studies while you are abroad; you have a sufficient stock of them already to live nobly upon whenever you shall think fit. Divide your present time between reading the state of Europe from Charlemagne downwards, and learning the present world by seeing it with your own eyes. Read men and women, but read the latter *unbound* for some years at least. Wherever you go the best companies are the best books you can study.

A fever seized me the day after I received the pleasure of your letter, and hindered me from acknowledging it sooner. It has not yet quite left me, but it is so much abated that I hope to be entirely free from it in three or four days. I am still very weak, and go to-morrow to Blackheath for a week, where the air and the idleness will, I hope, restore my strength and spirits.

Let me have the pleasure of hearing from you whenever you have any idle time upon your hands, or whenever I can be of any use to you here by executing your orders. Your own health and happiness are my first care. My second will ever be to convince you of the true affection, honour, and esteem, with which I am, etc.

No. 1648

To his Son

(*Stanhope CLXXXVI*)

London, 6 July O.S. 1749

DEAR BOY,

As I am now no longer in pain about your health, which I trust is perfectly restored, and as, by the various accounts I have had of you, I need not be in pain about your learning, our correspondence may for the future turn upon less important points, comparatively, though still very important ones; I mean, the knowledge of the world, decorum, manners, address, and all those (commonly called little) accomplishments, which are absolutely necessary to give greater accomplishments their full value and lustre.

Had I the admirable ring of Gyges, which rendered the wearer invisible; and had I, at the same time, those magic powers, which were very common formerly, but are now very scarce, of transporting myself by a wish to any given place; my first expedition would be to Venice, there to *reconnoitre* you unseen myself. I would first take you in the morning at breakfast with Mr. Harte, and attend to your natural and unguarded conversation with him; from whence I think I could pretty well judge of your natural turn of mind. How I should rejoice if I overheard you asking him pertinent questions upon useful subjects, or making judicious reflections upon the studies of that morning or the occurrences of the former day! Then I would follow you into the different companies of the day, and carefully observe in what manner you presented yourself to, and behaved yourself with, men of sense and dignity: whether your address was respectful and yet easy, your air modest and yet unembarrassed: and I would at the same time penetrate into their thoughts, in order to know whether your first *abord* made that advantageous impression upon their fancies, which a certain address, air, and manners never fail doing. I would afterwards follow you to the mixed companies of the evening, such as assemblies, suppers, etc., and there watch if you trifled gracefully and genteelly; if your good-breeding and politeness made way for your parts and knowledge. With what pleasure should I hear people cry out, *Che garbato cavaliere, com' è pulito, disinvolto, spiritoso!* If all these things turned out to my mind, I would immediately assume my own shape, become visible, and embrace you: but, if the contrary happened, I would preserve my invisibility, make the best of my way home again, and sink my disappointment upon you and the world. As unfortunately these supernatural powers of genii, fairies, sylphs, and gnomes have had the fate of the oracles they succeeded, and have ceased for some time, I must content myself (till we meet naturally and in the common way) with Harte's written accounts of you, and the verbal ones which I now and then receive from people who have seen you. However, I believe it would do you no harm if you would always imagine that I was present, and saw and heard everything you did and said.

There is a certain concurrence of various little circumstances, which compose what the French call *l'aimable*, and which, now you are entering into the world, you ought to make it your particular study to acquire. Without them, your learning will be pedantry; your conversation often improper—always unpleasant; and your figure, however good

1366

in itself, awkward and unengaging. A diamond, while rough, has indeed its intrinsic value; but, till polished, is of no use, and would neither be sought for nor worn. Its great lustre, it is true, proceeds from its solidity and strong cohesion of parts; but, without the last polish, it would remain for ever a dirty rough mineral, in the cabinets of some few curious collectors. You have, I hope, that solidity and cohesion of parts; take now as much pains to get the lustre. Good company, if you make the right use of it, will cut you into shape, and give you the true brilliant polish. *À propos* of diamonds: I have sent you, by Sir James Gray, the King's minister, who will be at Venice about the middle of September, my own diamond buckles, which are fitter for your young feet than for my old ones: they will probably adorn you—they would only expose me. If Sir James finds anybody whom he can trust, and who will be at Venice before him, he will send them by that person; but if he should not, and that you should be gone from Venice before he gets there, he will in that case give them to your banker, Monsieur Cornet, to forward to you, wherever you may then be. You are now of an age at which the adorning your person is not only not ridiculous, but proper and becoming. Negligence would imply, either an indifference about pleasing, or else an insolent security of pleasing, without using those means to which others are obliged to have recourse. A thorough cleanliness in your person is as necessary for your own health, as it is not to be offensive to other people. Washing yourself, and rubbing your body and limbs frequently with a flesh-brush, will conduce as much to health as to cleanliness. A particular attention to the cleanliness of your mouth, teeth, hands, and nails, is but common decency, in order not to offend people's eyes and noses.

I send you here enclosed a letter of recommendation to the Duke of Nivernais, the French Ambassador at Rome,[1]

[1]Louis Jules Barbon Mancini Mazarini, Duc de Nivernais (1716-1798), afterwards Ambassador to England. See Letter of 7th Dec. 1762. Besides the 'manner

who is, in my opinion, one of the prettiest men I ever knew in my life. I do not know a better model for you to form yourself upon: pray observe and frequent him as much as you can. He will show you what manners and graces are. I shall, by successive posts, send you more letters, both for Rome and Naples, where it will be your own fault entirely if you do not keep the very best company.

As you will meet swarms of Germans wherever you go, I desire that you will constantly converse with them in their own language; which will improve you in that language, and be, at the same time, an agreeable piece of civility to them.

Your stay in Italy will, I do not doubt, make you critically master of Italian. I know it may, if you please; for it is a very regular, and consequently a very easy, language. Adieu! God bless you!

No. 1649
À Madame la Marquise de Monconseil
(Maty I. xxxvii)

À Babiole, ce 8 juillet V.S. 1749

Vous voulez donc absolument, Madame, que je vous croie solidement fâchée contre moi; je le veux bien, votre colère m'est trop glorieuse pour la refuser, et mon innocence fait que je n'y suis sensible que du bon côté. Une belle, qui manquerait à un rendez-vous, où d'ailleurs elle aurait souhaité de se trouver, serait bien fâchée si son amant ne l'était point. Il gronde, il s'emporte, elle se justifie, il s'appaise. Elle a prouvé sa bonne volonté, lui son empressement, et ils n'en sont que mieux après. Il en est de même dans l'amitié que dans l'amour, quoique d'ailleurs ces sentiments ne se ressemblent guère. Je soutiens que nous sommes

and graces' for which Lord Chesterfield extols him, he was remarkable for combining, like Lord Chesterfield himself, though in a much less eminent degree, literary taste with political distinction.—M. He wrote, Mr. Bradshaw adds, poetical imitations of Virgil, Horace, Ovid, Ariosto, and Milton. He suffered imprisonment in 1793 during the Revolution.

actuellement mieux ensemble que jamais, et je suis charmé que vous soyez contente des étoffes qu'à la fin vous avez reçues; elles se sont fait trop longtemps attendre: il y a un point d'attente qui pique, mais il y en a un autre qui lasse.

À propos du bagage de notre Ambassadeur,[1] je puis vous assurer que l'Ambassadeur même est très sensible à toutes vos politesses, dont il m'a entretenu une heure de suite.

Mon nom seul, sans doute, sera plus efficace que toutes vos recommandations auprès de Monsieur le Duc de Nivernais! Cela est très poli de votre part, mais Monsieur de Nivernais ne vous en aurait guère d'obligation: en tout cas, faites comme si cela n'était point, et recommandez-lui fortement votre élève, je vous en supplie, au mois de novembre prochain, puisqu'il sera à Rome au commencement de décembre. Plus il fréquentera Monsieur de Nivernais, moins vous en rougirez quand il sera sous vos soins à Paris. Il ne lui manque que les manières, car pour la lecture et le savoir, il en a à revendre. Au reste, ne croyez pas que c'est son arrivée à Paris qui décidera de la mienne; au contraire, je ne voudrais pas pour chose au monde le voir avant qu'il eût été bien formé et poli à Paris, car si je le trouvais ou allemand ou italien, et il doit naturellement être un composé de ces deux, j'en prendrais du dégoût pour le reste de mes jours: ces deux nations, quoique par des raisons très différentes, n'ayant pas l'honneur de me plaire infiniment.

Je reviens depuis quinze jours d'une fièvre chaude, dont j'ai pensé ne pas revenir du tout: c'est votre étoile, Madame, qui m'a sauvé, et qui n'a pas voulu que vous perdissiez encore un si fidèle serviteur. Procurez-moi, je vous en prie, pour quelque temps, la continuation de cette influence, car si vous le trouvez bon, je voudrais encore vivre dix ou douze ans, pour vous mieux prouver la constance de mon amitié. Je suis actuellement, pour me rétablir, à une très petite maison, que j'ai à cinq petites milles de Londres, et que j'aurais appelé *Bagatelle*, si ce n'eût été par respect pour la

[1]Lord Albemarle.

vôtre; mais que j'appelle *Babiole*, pour en marquer la sub-ordination, et pour laisser à *Bagatelle* la préférence qui lui est due. *Babiole* est située dans un des parcs du Roi, à cent pas de la Tamise, où l'on voit tous les jours une cinquantaine de gros vaisseaux marchands, et quelques vaisseaux de guerre, qui vont et qui viennent: les promenades sont les plus belles du monde, il y fait toujours sec, et l'air y est extrêmement fin. Il y a cinq cents ans qu'il n'aurait presque rien coûté à quelque fée ou magicien de nos amis, de transporter dans un moment *Babiole* au Bois de Boulogne, pour faire sa cour à *Bagatelle*, mais à présent on ne sait à qui s'adresser pour ces sortes de choses là; il est vrai, comme l'on dit, que le siècle n'en est pas digne, la foi y manque. Au moins, sans mettre votre foi à de grandes épreuves, vous me croirez bien le plus zélé et le plus attaché de vos serviteurs.

No. 1650

To his Son

(*Stanhope CLXXXVII*)

London, 20 July O.S. 1749

DEAR BOY,

I wrote to Mr. Harte last Monday, the 17th O.S. in answer to his letter of the 20th June N.S. which I had received but the day before, after an interval of eight posts, during which I did not know whether you or he existed, and indeed I began to think that you did not. By that letter, you ought at this time to be at Venice, where I hope you are arrived in perfect health, after the baths of Tieffer, in case you have made use of them. I hope they are not hot baths, if your lungs are still tender.

Your friend, the Comte d'Einsiedlen, is arrived here; he has been at my door, and I have been at his, but we have not yet met; he will dine with me some day this week. Comte Lascaris inquires after you very frequently, and with great affection. Pray answer the letter which I forwarded to you a great while ago from him. You may enclose your answer to me, and I will take care to give it him. Those attentions ought never to be omitted: they cost little, and please a great deal; but the neglect of them offends more than you can yet imagine. Great merit, or great failings, will make you respected or despised; but trifles, little attentions, mere nothings, either done or neglected, will make you either liked or disliked, in the general run of the world. Examine yourself, why you like such and such people, and dislike such and such others, and you will find that those different sentiments proceed from very slight causes. Moral virtues are the foundation of society in general, and of friendship in particular; but attentions, manners, and graces both adorn and strengthen them. My heart is so set upon your pleasing, and consequently succeeding, in the world, that possibly I have already (and probably shall again) repeat the same things over and over to you. However, to err, if I do err, on the surer side, I shall continue to communicate to you those observations upon the world which long experience has enabled me to make, and which I have generally found to hold true. Your youth and talents, armed with my experience, may go a great way; and that armour is very much at your service, if you please to wear it. I premise that it is not my imagination, but my memory, that gives you these rules. I am not writing pretty, but useful reflections.

A man of sense soon discovers, because he carefully observes, where, and how long, he is welcome, and takes care to leave the company, at least as soon as he is wished out of it. Fools never perceive where they are either ill-timed or ill-placed.

I am this moment agreeably stopped in the course of my reflections by the arrival of Mr. Harte's letter of the 13th July N.S. to Mr. Grevenkop, with one enclosed for your Mamma. I find by it, that many of his and your letters to me must have miscarried; for he says that I have had regular accounts of you. Whereas all those accounts have been only his letter of the 6th and yours of the 7th June N.S.; his of the 20th June N.S. to me; and now his of the 13th July N.S. to Mr. Grevenkop. However, since you are so well as Mr. Harte says you are, all is well. I am extremely glad you have no complaint upon your lungs, but I desire that you will think you have for three or four months to come. Keep in a course of asses' or goats' milk, for one is as good as the other, and possibly the latter is the best; and let your common food be as pectoral as you can conveniently make it. Pray tell Mr. Harte that, according to his desire, I have wrote a letter of thanks to Mr. Firmian. I hope you write to him too, from time to time. The letters of recommendation of a man of his merit and learning will, to be sure, be of great use to you among the learned world in Italy; that is, provided you take care to keep up to the character he gives you in them, otherwise they will only add to your disgrace.

Consider that you have lost a good deal of time by your illness; fetch it up now you are well. At present you should be a good economist of your moments, of which company and sights will claim a considerable share; so that those which remain for study must be not only attentively, but greedily employed. But indeed I do not suspect you of one single moment's idleness in the whole day. Idleness is only the refuge of weak minds, and the holiday of fools. I do not call good company and liberal pleasures, idleness; far from it—I recommend to you a good share of both.

I send you here enclosed a letter for Cardinal Alexander Albani,[1] which you will give him as soon as you can get to Rome, and before you deliver any others; the Purple expects that preference: go next to the Duc de Nivernais, to whom

[1] There were two Cardinal Albanis at the same time, uncle and nephew. Alexander (1692-1779) was nephew of Pope Clement XI, and became Librarian of the Vatican. In 1762 his collection of drawings and engravings, 300 volumes, was purchased by George III. John Francis was born in 1720, and created Cardinal in 1747; his property was plundered when the French entered Rome; he died in 1803.

you are recommended by several people at Paris, as well as by myself. Then you may carry your other letters occasionally.

Remember to pry narrowly into every part of the government of Venice; inform yourself of the History of that Republic, especially of its most remarkable eras; such as the *Ligue de Cambray*, in 1509, by which it had like to have been destroyed; and the conspiracy formed by the Marquis de Bedmar, the Spanish Ambassador, to subject it to the Crown of Spain. The famous disputes between that Republic and the Pope are worth your knowledge; and the writings of the celebrated and learned Frà Paolo di Sarpi, upon that occasion, worth your reading. It was once the greatest commercial power in Europe, and, in the 14th and 15th centuries, made a considerable figure; but at present its commerce is decayed, and its riches consequently decreased; and, far from meddling now with the affairs of the continent, it owes its security to its neutrality and inefficacy; and that security will last no longer than till one of the great powers in Europe engrosses the rest of Italy; an event which this century possibly may, but which the next probably will, see.

Your friend Comte d'Einsiedlen, and his Governor, have been with me this moment, and delivered me your letter from Berlin, of February the 28th N.S. I like them both so well, that I am glad you did; and still more glad to hear what they say of you. Go on, and continue to deserve the praises of those who deserve praises themselves. Adieu!

I break open this letter to acknowledge yours of the 30th June N.S. which I have but this instant received, though thirteen days antecedent in date to Mr. Harte's last. I never in my life heard of bathing four hours a day; and I am impatient to hear of your safe arrival at Venice, after so extraordinary an operation.

No. 1651

To his Son

(Stanhope CLXXXVIII)

London, 30 *July* O.S. 1749

Dear Boy,

Mr. Harte's letters and yours drop in upon me most irregularly; for I received by the last post, one from Mr. Harte, of the 9th N.S. and that which Mr. Grevenkop had received from him the post before, was of the 13th; at last, I suppose, I shall receive them all.

I am very glad that my letter, with Dr. Shaw's opinion, has lessened your bathing; for, since I was born, I never heard of bathing four hours a day, which would surely be too much, even in Medea's kettle, if you wanted (as you do not yet) new boiling.

Though, in that letter of mine, I proposed your going to Inspruck, it was only in opposition to Lausanne, which I thought much too long and painful a journey for you; but you will have found, by my subsequent letters, that I entirely approve of Venice, where I hope you have now been some time, and which is a much better place for you to reside at, till you go to Naples, than either Tieffer or Laybach. I love capitals extremely; it is in capitals that the best company is always to be found; and, consequently, the best manners to be learned. The very best provincial places have some awkwardnesses, that distinguish their manners from those of the metropolis. *A propos* of capitals; I send you here two letters of recommendation to Naples, from Monsieur Finochetti, the Neapolitan minister at the Hague; and in my next I shall send you two more, from the same person to the same place.

I have examined Count Einsiedlen so narrowly concerning you, that I have extorted from him a confession, that you do not care to speak German, unless to such as understand no other language. At this rate, you will never speak it well, which I am very desirous that you should do, and of which you would, in time, find the advantage. Whoever has not the command of a language, and does not speak it with facility, will always appear below himself, when he converses in that language; the want of words and phrases will cramp and lame his thoughts. As you now know German enough to express yourself tolerably, speaking it very often will soon make you speak it very well; and then you will appear in it whatever you are. What with your own Saxon servant, and the swarms of Germans you will meet with wherever you go, you may have opportunities of conversing in that language half the day; and I do very seriously desire that you will, or else all the pains you have already taken about it are lost. You will remember, likewise, that, till you can write in Italian, you are always to write to me in German.

Mr. Harte's conjecture concerning your distemper seems to be a very reasonable one; it agrees entirely with mine, which is the universal rule by which every man judges of another man's opinion. But, whatever may have been the cause of your rheumatic disorder, the effects are still to be attended to; and as there must be a remaining acrimony in your blood, you ought to have regard to that, in your common diet, as well as in your medicines; both which should be of a sweetening alkaline nature, and promotive of perspiration. Rheumatic complaints are very apt to return, and those returns would be very vexatious and detrimental to you, at your age, and in your course of travels.

Your time is, now particularly, inestimable; and every hour of it, at present, worth more than a year will be to you twenty years hence. You are now laying the foundation of your future character and fortune; and one single stone wanting in that foundation, is of more consequence than fifty in the superstructure, which can always be mended and embellished if the foundation is solid. To carry on the metaphor of building: I would wish you to be a Corinthian edifice, upon a Tuscan foundation; the latter having the utmost strength and solidity to support, and the former all possible ornaments to decorate. The Tuscan column is coarse, clumsy and unpleasant; nobody looks at it twice; the Corinthian fluted column is beautiful and attractive; but, without a solid foundation, can hardly be seen twice, because it must soon tumble down.

Yours affectionately.

No. 1652

To his Son

(*Stanhope CLXXXIX*)

London, 7 August O.S. 1749

Dear Boy,

By Mr. Harte's letter to me of the 18th July N.S. which I received by the last post, I am at length informed of the particulars both of your past distemper, and of your future motions. As to the former, I am now convinced, and so is Doctor Shaw, that your lungs were only symptomatically affected, and that the rheumatic tendency is what you are chiefly now to guard against, but (for greater security) with due attention still to your lungs, as if they had been, and still were, a little affected. In either case, a cooling, pectoral regimen is equally good. By cooling, I mean cooling in its consequences, not cold to the palate; for nothing is more dangerous than very cold liquors, at the very time that one longs for them the most, which is when one is very hot. Fruit, when full ripe, is very wholesome; but then it must be within certain bounds as to quantity; for I have known many of my countrymen die of bloody fluxes, by indulging in too great a quantity of fruit, in those countries where, from the goodness and ripeness of it, they thought it could do them no harm. *Ne quid nimis* is a most excellent

1376

rule in everything; but commonly the least observed, by people of your age, in anything.

As to your future motions, I am very well pleased with them, and greatly prefer your intended stay at Verona to Venice, whose almost stagnating waters must, at this time of the year, corrupt the air. Verona has a pure and clear air, and, as I am informed, a great deal of good company. Marquis Maffei[1] alone would be worth going there for. You may, I think, very well leave Verona about the middle of September, when the great heats will be quite over, and then make the best of your way to Naples, where, I own, I want to have you, by way of precaution (I hope it is rather over-caution) in case of the least remains of a pulmonic disorder. The amphitheatre at Verona is worth your attention; as are also many buildings there and at Vicenza, of the famous Andrea Palladio,[2] whose taste and style of building were truly *antique*. It would not be amiss, if you employed three or four days in learning the five Orders of Architecture, with their general proportions; and you may know all that you need know of them in that time. Palladio's own book of Architecture is the best you can make use of for that purpose, skipping over the lowest mechanical parts of it, such as the materials, the cement, etc.

Mr. Harte tells me, that your acquaintance with the classics is renewed; the suspension of which has been so short, that I dare say it has produced no coldness. I hope, and believe, you are now so much master of them, that two hours every day, uninterruptedly, for a year or two more, will make you perfectly so; and I think you cannot now allot them a greater share than that of your time, considering the many other things you have to learn and to do. You must know how to speak and write Italian perfectly; you

---

[1] The Marquis Franceso Scipione Maffei (1675-1755), author of the tragedy of *Merope Verona Illustrata*, and the *Museum Veronense*. At the age of twenty-seven he publicly sustained at Verona a thesis on love, of which ladies were the judges.

[2] Palladio was born at Vicenza in 1518, and died in 1580: his influence on English architecture through Vanbrugh was considerable.

must learn some logic, some geometry, and some astronomy, not to mention your exercises where they are to be learnt; and, above all, you must learn the world, which is not soon learnt; and only to be learnt by frequenting good and various companies.

Consider therefore how precious every moment of time is to you now. The more you apply to your business, the more you will taste your pleasures. The exercise of the mind in the morning whets the appetite for the pleasures of the evening, as much as the exercise of the body whets the appetite for dinner. Business and pleasure, rightly understood, mutually assist each other, instead of being enemies, as silly or dull people often think them. No man tastes pleasures truly who does not earn them by previous business; and few people do business well, who do nothing else. Remember, that, when I speak of pleasures, I always mean the elegant pleasures of a rational being, and not the brutal ones of a swine. I mean *la bonne chère*, short of gluttony; wine, infinitely short of drunkenness; play, without the least gaming; and gallantry, without debauchery. There is a line in all these things, which men of sense, for greater security, take care to keep a good deal on the right side of: for sickness, pain, contempt, and infamy lie immediately on the other side of it. Men of sense and merit in all other respects, may have had some of these failings; but then those few examples, instead of inviting us to imitation, should only put us the more upon our guard against such weaknesses. Whoever thinks them fashionable will not be so himself. I have often known a fashionable man have some one vice; but I never in my life knew a vicious man a fashionable man. Vice is as degrading as it is criminal. God bless you, my dear child!

No. 1653

To his Son

(*Stanhope CXC*)

Dear Boy,   *London*, 10 *August O.S.* 1749

Let us resume our reflections upon men, their characters, their manners; in a word, our reflections upon the
world. They may help you to form yourself and to know
others. A knowledge very useful at all ages, very rare at
yours; it seems as if it were nobody's business to communicate it to young men. Their masters teach them, singly,
the languages or the sciences of their several departments;
and are indeed generally incapable of teaching them the
world; their parents are often so too, or at least neglect
doing it, either from avocations, indifference, or from an
opinion that throwing them into the world (as they call it)
is the best way of teaching it them. This last notion is in a
great degree true; that is, the world can doubtless never be
well known by theory; practice is absolutely necessary; but
surely, it is of great use to a young man, before he sets out
for that country, full of mazes, windings, and turnings, to
have at least a general map of it, made by some experienced
traveller.

There is a certain dignity of manners absolutely necessary, to make even the most valuable character either
respected or respectable.

Horse-play, romping, frequent and loud fits of laughter,
jokes, waggery, and indiscriminate familiarity, will sink both
merit and knowledge into a degree of contempt. They compose at most a merry fellow; and a merry fellow was never
yet a respectable man. Indiscriminate familiarity either
offends your superiors, or else dubs you their dependant,
and led captain. It gives your inferiors just, but troublesome
and improper claims of equality. A joker is near akin to a
buffoon; and neither of them is the least related to wit.
Whoever is admitted or sought for in company, upon any

1379

other account than that of his merit and manners, is never respected there, but only made use of. We will have such-a-one, for he sings prettily; we will invite such-a-one to a ball, for he dances well; we will have such-a-one at supper, for he is always joking and laughing; we will ask another, because he plays deep at all games, or because he can drink a great deal. These are all vilifying distinctions, mortifying preferences, and exclude all ideas of esteem and regard. Whoever *is had* (as it is called) in company for the sake of any one thing singly, is singly that thing, and will never be considered in any other light; consequently never respected, let his merits be what they will.

This dignity of manners, which I recommend so much to you, is not only as different from pride, as true courage is from blustering, or true wit from joking; but is absolutely inconsistent with it; for nothing vilifies and degrades more than pride. The pretensions of the proud man are oftener treated with sneer and contempt than with indignation; as we offer ridiculously too little to a tradesman who asks ridiculously too much for his goods, but we do not haggle with one who only asks a just and reasonable price.

Abject flattery and indiscriminate assentation degrade, as much as indiscriminate contradiction and noisy debate disgust. But a modest assertion of one's own opinion, and a complaisant acquiescence in other people's, preserve dignity.

Vulgar, low expressions, awkward motions and address, vilify; as they imply, either a very low turn of mind, or low education and low company.

Frivolous curiosity about trifles, and a laborious attention to little objects, which neither require nor deserve a moment's thought, lower a man; who from thence is thought (and not unjustly) incapable of greater matters. Cardinal de Retz, very sagaciously, marked out Cardinal Chigi[1] for a little mind, from the moment that he told him he had wrote

[1]Elected Pope in April 1655, under the name of Alexander VII. He may have had a little mind, but his vigorous reforms, his patronage of letters and the arts, and his munificence to the Universities do not indicate it.

three years with the same pen, and that it was an excellent
good one still.

A certain degree of exterior seriousness in looks and
motions, gives dignity, without excluding wit and decent
cheerfulness, which are always serious themselves. A constant smirk upon the face, and a whiffling activity of the
body, are strong indications of futility. Whoever is in a
hurry, shows that the thing he is about is too big for him.
Haste and hurry are very different things.

I have only mentioned some of those things which may
and do, in the opinion of the world, lower and sink characters in other respects valuable enough; but I have taken
no notice of those that affect and sink the moral characters:
they are sufficiently obvious. A man who has patiently been
kicked may as well pretend to courage as a man blasted by
vices and crimes may to dignity of any kind. But an
exterior decency and dignity of manners will even keep
such a man longer from sinking than otherwise he would
be: of such consequence is the τὸ πρέπον, even though
affected and put on! Pray read frequently and with the utmost attention; nay, get by heart, if you can, that incomparable chapter in Cicero's Offices upon the τὸ πρέπον, or
the *Decorum*. It contains whatever is necessary for the
dignity of manners.

In my next I will send you a general map of Courts; a
region yet unexplored by you, but which you are one day
to inhabit. The ways are generally crooked and full of turnings, sometimes strewed with flowers, sometimes choked
up with briars; rotten ground and deep pits frequently lie
concealed under a smooth and pleasing surface; all the paths
are slippery, and every slip is dangerous. Sense and discretion must accompany you at your first setting out;
but notwithstanding those, till experience is your guide,
you will every now and then step out of your way or
stumble.

Lady Chesterfield has just now received your German

letter, for which she thanks you; she says the language is very correct, and I can plainly see the character is well formed, not to say better than your English character. Continue to write German frequently, that it may become quite familiar to you. Adieu!

No. 1654

To his Son

(*Stanhope CXCI*)

London, 21 *August O.S.* 1749

Dear Boy,

By the last letter that I received from Mr. Harte, of the 31st July N.S. I suppose you are now either at Venice or Verona, and perfectly recovered of your late illness, which I am daily more and more convinced had no consumptive tendency: however, for some time still, *faites comme s'il y en avait,* be regular, and live pectorally.

You will soon be at Courts, where though you will not be concerned, yet reflection and observation upon what you see and hear there may be of use to you when hereafter you may come to be concerned in Courts yourself. Nothing in Courts is exactly as it appears to be; often very different, sometimes directly contrary. Interest, which is the real spring of everything there, equally creates and dissolves friendships, produces and reconciles enmities; or rather, allows of neither real friendships nor enmities; for, as Dryden very justly observes, *Politicians neither love nor hate.*[1] This is so true, that you may think you connect yourself with two friends to-day, and be obliged to-morrow to make your option between them as enemies: observe, therefore, such a degree of reserve with your friends as not to put yourself in their power if they should become your enemies; and such a degree of moderation with your

[1] *Absalom and Achitophel,* l. 223.

enemies as not to make it impossible for them to become your friends.

Courts are unquestionably the seats of politeness and good-breeding; were they not so, they would be the seats of slaughter and desolation. Those who now smile upon and embrace, would affront and stab each other if manners did not interpose: but ambition and avarice, the two prevailing passions at Courts, found dissimulation more effectual than violence; and dissimulation introduced that habit of politeness which distinguishes the courtier from the country gentleman. In the former case the strongest body would prevail, in the latter the strongest mind.

A man of parts and efficiency need not flatter everybody at Court, but he must take great care to offend nobody personally; it being in the power of very many to hurt him, who cannot serve him. Homer supposes a chain let down from Jupiter to the earth to connect him with mortals. There is at all Courts a chain which connects the prince or the minister with the page of the back-stairs or the chambermaid. The king's wife or mistress has an influence over him; a lover has an influence over her; the chambermaid or the valet-de-chambre has an influence over both; and so *ad infinitum*. You must, therefore, not break a link of that chain by which you hope to climb up to the prince.

You must renounce Courts if you will not connive at knaves and tolerate fools; their number makes them considerable. You should as little quarrel as connect yourself with either.

Whatever you say or do at Court, you may depend upon it, will be known; the business of most of those who crowd levees and antichambers being to repeat all that they see or hear, and a great deal that they neither see nor hear, according as they are inclined to the persons concerned, or according to the wishes of those to whom they hope to make their court. Great caution is therefore necessary; and if to great caution you can join seeming frankness and openness, you will unite what *Machiavel* reckons very difficult, but very necessary to be united, *volto sciolto e pensieri stretti.*

Women are very apt to be mingled in Court intrigues; but they deserve attention better than confidence: to hold by them is a very precarious tenure.

I am agreeably interrupted in these reflections by a letter which I have this moment received from Baron Firmian. It contains your panegyric, and with the strongest protestations imaginable, that he does you only justice. I received this favourable account of you with pleasure, and I communicate it to you with as much. While you deserve praise, it is reasonable you should know that you meet with it; and I make no doubt but it will encourage you in persevering to deserve it. This is one paragraph of the Baron's letter: '*Ses mœurs dans un âge si tendre, réglées selon toutes les lois d'une morale exacte et sensée, son application* (that is what I like) *à tout ce qui s'appelle étude sérieuse, et belles-lettres, éloignée de l'ombre même d'un faste pédantesque, le rendent très digne de vos tendres soins; et j'ai l'honneur de vous assurer que chacun se louera beaucoup de son commerce aisé, et de son amitié; j'en ai profité avec plaisir ici et à Vienne, et je me crois très heureux de la permission, qu'il m'a accordée de la continuer par la voie de lettres.*'

Reputation, like health, is preserved and increased by the same means by which it is acquired. Continue to desire and deserve praise, and you will certainly find it; knowledge adorned by manners will infallibly procure it. Consider that you have but a little way farther to get to your journey's end; therefore, for God's sake, do not slacken your pace: one year and a half more of sound application, Mr. Harte assures me, will finish his work; and, when his work is finished well, your own will be very easily done afterwards. *Les manières et les grâces* are no immaterial parts of that work; and I beg that you will give as much of your attention to them as to your books. Everything depends upon them: *senza di noi ogni fatica è vana.* The various companies

1384

you now go into will procure them you, if you will carefully observe, and form yourself upon, those who have them.

Adieu! God bless you! and may you ever deserve that affection with which I am now

Yours!

No. 1655

To Lord Huntingdon

(Steuart 2)

London, 31 *August O.S.* 1749

My Dear Lord,

Though you do not yet speak French readily, which it is impossible you should do, considering the little time that you have been in France, yet I find that you judge already very correctly both of the French and their language. A happy people, always pleased, and therefore often pleasing! A language of phrases which often supply the place of wit, and sometimes conceal the want even of common sense. The late Duke of Richmond[1] (whom I well remember) was very near a wit in French, and very near a fool in English. You observe very justly that a man can never bear his own part in a conversation where he is not perfect master of the language. He must necessarily be much below himself not only where his thoughts are cramped for want of common expression, but even where they are deprived of those ornaments and graces, which purity and elegancy of diction give them. You therefore do extremely right to go to those places where the constant necessity of speaking French will the soonest make you master of that now most necessary language. That great share of classical and academical knowledge which you have already acquired will be an ornament

---

[1]Charles Duke of Richmond (1672-1723), son of Charles II and the Duchess of Portsmouth. Macky (*Characters*) says he was 'good natured to a fault, very well-bred, and has many valuable things in him; is an enemy to business; very credulous.' Swift, however, calls him 'a shallow coxcomb.' (Steuart).

to your character and an agreeable refuge for your leisure hours; but the thorough knowledge of modern languages, modern history and geography, and the manners and characters of the present times, can alone enable you to make that figure which your rank entitles, and your talents qualify you to make in the world. Let Homer, who sometimes nods, sleep soundly upon your shelf for three or four years, and let useful facts and dates from Charlemagne down to this day, take place of useless and endless metaphysical researches and jargon. That dissipation which you seem to confess as a fault I cannot in the least look upon in that light; your dissipation will I am sure never be of the frivolous and unprofitable kind; for it will be in good company, and consequently teach you the manners and characters of the age you live in which no theory or speculations can teach. As soon as you have conquered the first difficulties of the French language, I could wish that you would either return to Caen, or go to some other Academy where you might for a year take your exercises of riding, fencing and dancing, things in themselves of no great intrinsic use, but which still a man of your fashion ought to be master of to a certain degree. Pardon me, my dear Lord, for pretending to give advice to you who want it less than any man I ever knew of your age; but people of mine are inclined to prate, and your indulgence to the liberties I have formerly taken has not only encouraged but hardened me, so that I fear I shall go on, confident that you will receive as a friend, what you are very sure comes from a very faithful one. Upon that right and title singly, I will presume to tell you, that I have heard it whispered among women that you have not wrote to Lady Huntingdon above once since you left England. And you may be very sure that those who whisper blame it. Other, more rational creatures than women may possibly blame it too when they know it, if it be true; and as I would not have you do, or omit any one thing, for which any one reasonable body may with but seeming justice

1386

blame you, forgive me, my dear Lord, if I take the liberty of begging you, for your own sake, to write to her from time to time with marks of affection. I neither know nor inquire how you are together; but be that as it will, my concern is only that you may appear blameless. One must sometimes sacrifice a little to appearances. Socrates thought it right to do it, even when he was dying.

I now hesitate whether I shall send this impertinent letter to the post. Your good sense encourages me to do it. You will not, I am sure, impute to the officiousness of pretended friendship what flows only from those sincere sentiments of esteem, affection, and real friendship, with which I am, my dear Lord, most faithfully yours.

No. 1656

To his Son

(Stanhope CXCII)

London, 5 *September O.S.* 1749

Dear Boy,

I have received yours from Laybach, of the 17th of August N.S. with the enclosed for Comte Lascaris, which I have given him, and with which he is extremely pleased, as I am with your account of Carniola. I am very glad that you attend to, and inform yourself of, the political objects of the countries you go through. Trade and manufactures are very considerable, not to say the most important ones; for, though armies and navies are the shining marks of the strength of countries, they would be very ill paid, and consequently fight very ill, if manufactures and commerce did not support them. You have certainly observed in Germany the inefficiency of great powers, with great tracts of country and swarms of men, which are absolutely useless, if not paid by other powers, who have the resources of manufactures and commerce. This we have lately experienced to be

the case of the two Empresses of Germany and Russia.
England, France, and Spain must pay their respective allies,
or they may as well be without them.

I have not the least objection to your taking into the
bargain the observation of natural curiosities: they are very
welcome, provided they do not take up the room of better
things. But the forms of government, the maxims of policy,
the strength or weakness, the trade and commerce, of the
several countries you see or hear of, are the important
objects which I recommend to your most minute inquiries
and most serious attention. I thought that the republic of
Venice had by this time laid aside that silly and frivolous
piece of policy, of endeavouring to conceal their form of
government, which anybody may know, pretty nearly, by
taking the pains to read four or five books, which explain
all the great parts of it; and as for some of the little wheels
of that machine, the knowledge of them would be as little
useful to others as dangerous to themselves. Their best
policy (I can tell them) is to keep quiet, and to offend no
one great power, by joining with another. Their escape
after the *Ligue of Cambray* should prove an useful lesson to
them.

I am glad you frequent the assemblies at Venice. Have
you seen Monsieur and Madame Capello? and how did they
receive you? Let me know who are the ladies whose houses
you frequent the most. Have you seen the Comtesse
d'Orselska, Princess of Holstein? Is Comte Algarotti, who
was the *tenant* there, at Venice?

You will, in many parts of Italy, meet with numbers of
the Pretender's people (English, Scotch, and Irish fugitives),
especially at Rome, and probably the Pretender himself.
It is none of your business to declare war on these people;
as little as it is your interest, or, I hope, your inclination, to
connect yourself with them; and, therefore, I recommend to
you a perfect neutrality. Avoid them as much as you can
with decency and good manners; but, when you cannot,

avoid any political conversations or debates with them: tell them that you do not concern yourself with political matters —that you are neither a maker nor a deposer of Kings— that, when you left England, you left a King in it, and have not since heard either of his death, or of any revolution that has happened, and that you take kings and kingdoms as you find them; but enter no farther into matters with them, which can be of no use, and might bring on heat and quarrels. When you speak of the old Pretender, you will call him only the Chevalier de St. George, but mention him as seldom as possible. Should he chance to speak to you at any assembly (as, I am told, he sometimes does to the English), be sure that you seem not to know him; and answer him civilly, but always either in French or in Italian; and give him, in the former, the appellation of *Monsieur*, and in the latter of *Signore*. Should you meet with the Cardinal of York,[1] you will be under no difficulty, for he has, as Cardinal, an undoubted right to *Eminenza*. Upon the whole, see any of those people as little as possible; when you do see them, be civil to them, upon the footing of strangers; but never be drawn into any altercations with them about the imaginary right of their King as they call him.

It is to no sort of purpose to talk to those people of the natural rights of mankind, and the particular constitution of this country. Blinded by prejudices, soured by misfortunes, and tempted by their necessities, they are as incapable of reasoning rightly as they have hitherto been of acting wisely. The late Lord Pembroke never would know anything that he had not a mind to know; and, in this case, I advise you to follow his example. Never know either the father or the two sons,[2] any otherwise than as foreigners;

[1]Henry, the second son of the Pretender (James), was raised to the Purple in July 1747, with the title of Cardinal York. After the decease of Charles Edward in 1788, a medal was struck in his name as Henry the Ninth, King of England, with the motto (which he had assumed even as Cardinal), NON DESIDERIIS HOMINUM SED VOLUNTATE DEI.—M. He died at Rome in 1807, a pensionary of George III.

[2]James died in 1765; it was not till after his father's death that Charles Edward came to Rome.

and so, not knowing their pretensions, you have no occasion to dispute them.

I can never help recommending to you the utmost attention and care to acquire *les manières, la tournure, et les grâces, d'un galant homme, et d'un homme de cour.* They should appear in every look, in every action—in your address, and even in your dress, if you would either please or rise in the world. That you may do both (and both are in your power) is most ardently wished you, by

Yours.

P.S.—I made Comte Lascaris show me your letter, which I liked very well; the style was easy and natural, and the French pretty correct. There were so few faults in the orthography, that a little more observation of the best French authors will make you a correct master of that necessary language.

I will not conceal from you that I have lately had extraordinary good accounts of you, from an unsuspected and judicious person, who promises me that, with a little more of the world, your manners and address will equal your knowledge. This is the more pleasing to me, as those were the two articles of which I was the most doubtful. These commendations will not, I am persuaded, make you vain and coxcombical, but only encourage you to go on in the right way.

No. 1657

À Madame la Marquise de Monconseil

(Maty I, XXXVIII)

À Londres, ce 7 septembre V.S. 1749

C'est que j'ai battu la campagne depuis plus d'un mois, comme un juif, sans avoir de séjour fixe. Vous comprenez bien, Madame, ce que cela veut dire; d'ailleurs, qu'aurais-je pu répondre à votre dernière, qui a pensé tourner ma tête?

Je n'en ai ma foi échappé que moyennant certaines réflexions assez humiliantes, que, malgré mon amour propre, j'ai fait sur moi-même, mais que je n'ai garde de vous communiquer. Si vous êtes réellement dans l'erreur, cette erreur m'est trop flatteuse pour que je tâche de vous en désabuser; et si vous voulez seulement m'en faire accroire, vous le faites avec trop d'esprit et trop d'agréments, pour que je me prive du plaisir de me voir, pour un moment, dans le miroir trompeur que vous me présentez. Voila comme nous sommes faits, un moment d'illusion agréable nous charme, toute illusion que nous la sachions; la réflexion nous désabuse après, mais elle n'empêche pas que nous ne nous prêtions avec la même facilité à une nouvelle, ou souvent à la même illusion, dès qu'elle se présente avec les grâces et la séduction dont vous savez bien l'accompagner. Enfin il en est de l'esprit comme de tout le reste; nous vivons dans une alternative perpétuelle de péché et de pénitence.

Milord Albemarle vous a dit, plutôt ce que je souhaitais faire, que ce que je pouvais faire, quand il vous a dit que j'aurais l'honneur de vous voir cette année à Paris. La volonté au moins y était, et il n'y a que la nécessité qui puisse jamais l'emporter sur la volonté; mais cette nécessité s'y est trouvée, nécessité d'autant plus désagréable qu'elle résulte d'une infinité de détails, et d'arrangements domestiques, que je déteste, et auxquels je ne suis guère propre. À propos de notre Ambassadeur, en êtes-vous contents chez vous? Pour votre beau paladin, et votre aimable petite paladine,[1] ils font à merveille ici. C'est un grand état, une belle dépense, leurs manières marquent bien leur naissance et leur usage du grand monde; ils s'accommodent à tout, et jurent qu'ils sont charmés de tout; ils me permettent de les fréquenter, et j'en profite jusqu'à l'abus. Je cherche, et je trouve chez eux les agréments de la société, que je chercherais inutilement chez plusieurs de mes compatriotes.

[1]Charles-Pierre-Gaston-Francois de Levis-Lomagne, marquis, later duc, de Mirepoix (1699-1758), French ambassador in London, and his wife. (See p. 1539, note 2.)

J'ai reçu en dernier lieu une lettre du petit Centurioni, que j'aime beaucoup; mais l'étourdi ne m'y a pas donné son adresse. Oserais-je vous prier, Madame, de vouloir bien lui faire tenir l'incluse? Il me dit qu'il m'a fait une tracasserie avec vous, en vous découvrant mon indiscrétion au sujet de vos bras. Je conviens du fait; mais qui n'en aurait pas fait autant? L'indifférence est ordinairement la mère de la discrétion, de sorte que vous avez tout à craindre de ma part d'un sentiment contraire.

No. 1658

To his Son

(Stanhope CXCIII)

DEAR BOY,   *London*, 12 *September O.S.* 1749

It seems extraordinary, but it is very true, that my anxiety for you increases in proportion to the good accounts which I receive of you from all hands. I promise myself so much from you, that I dread the least disappointment. You are now so near the port, which I have so long wished and laboured to bring you safe into, that my concern would be doubled, should you be shipwrecked within sight of it. The object, therefore, of this letter is (laying aside all the authority of a parent) to conjure you as a friend, by the affection you have for me (and surely you have reason to have some), and by the regard you have for yourself, to go on, with assiduity and attention, to complete that work, which of late you have carried on so well, and which is now so near being finished. My wishes and my plan were to make you shine, and distinguish yourself equally in the learned and the polite world. Few have been able to do it. Deep learning is generally tainted with pedantry, or at least unadorned by manners; as, on the other hand, polite manners, and the turn of the world, are too often unsupported by knowledge, and consequently end contemptibly in the

frivolous dissipation of drawing-rooms and *ruelles*. You are
now got over the dry and difficult parts of learning; what
remains, requires much more time than trouble.

You have lost time by your illness; you must regain it
now or never. I therefore most earnestly desire, for your
own sake, that, for these next six months, at least six hours
every morning, uninterruptedly, may be inviolably sacred
to your studies with Mr. Harte. I do not know whether he
will require so much, but I know that I do, and hope you
will, and consequently prevail with him to give you that
time: I own it is a good deal; but when both you and he
consider that the work will be so much better and so much
sooner done by such an assiduous and continued application, you will neither of you think it too much, and each
will find his account in it. So much for the mornings, which,
from your own good sense, and Mr. Harte's tenderness and
care of you, will, I am sure, be thus well employed. It is
not only reasonable, but useful too, that your evenings
should be devoted to amusements and pleasures; and therefore I not only allow but recommend, that they should be
employed at assemblies, balls, *spectacles*, and in the best
companies; with this restriction only, that the consequences
of the evening's diversions may not break in upon the
mornings' studies, by breakfastings, visits, and idle parties
into the country. At your age, you need not be ashamed,
when any of these morning parties are proposed, to say
that you must beg to be excused, for you are obliged to
devote your mornings to Mr. Harte; that I will have it so;
and that you dare not do otherwise. Lay it all upon me;
though I am persuaded it will be as much your own inclination as it is mine. But those frivolous, idle people, whose
time hangs upon their own hands, and who desire to make
others lose theirs too, are not to be reasoned with; and indeed it would be doing them too much honour. The
shortest, civil answers are the best; *I cannot, I dare not*,
instead of *I will not*; for, if you were to enter with them into

the necessity of study, and the usefulness of knowledge, it would only furnish them with matter for their silly jests; which, though I would not have you mind, I would not have you invite. I will suppose you at Rome, studying six hours uninterruptedly with Mr. Harte every morning, and passing your evenings with the best company of Rome, observing their manners and forming your own; and I will suppose a number of idle, sauntering, illiterate English, as there commonly is there, living entirely with one another, supping, drinking, and sitting up late at each others' lodgings; commonly in riots and scrapes when drunk; and never in good company when sober. I will take one of these pretty fellows, and give you the dialogue between him and yourself; such as I dare say it will be on his side, and such as I hope it will be on yours.

Englishman.—Will you come and breakfast with me tomorrow? there will be four or five of our countrymen; we have provided chaises, and we will drive somewhere out of town after breakfast.

Stanhope.—I am very sorry I cannot; but I am obliged to be at home all morning.

Englishman.—Why then, we will come and breakfast with you.

Stanhope.—I can't do that neither, I am engaged.

Englishman.—Well, then, let it be the next day.

Stanhope.—To tell you the truth, it can be no day in the morning; for I neither go out, nor see anybody at home before twelve.

Englishman.—And what the devil do you do with yourself till twelve o'clock?

Stanhope.—I am not by myself, I am with Mr. Harte.

Englishman.—Then what the devil do you do with him?

Stanhope.—We study different things; we read, we converse.

Englishman.—Very pretty amusement, indeed! Are you to take orders, then?

1394

Stanhope.—Yes; my father's orders, I believe, I must take.

Englishman.—Why, hast thou no more spirit than to mind an old fellow a thousand miles off?

Stanhope.—If I don't mind his orders, he won't mind my drafts.

Englishman.—What! does the old prig threaten, then? threatened folks live long; never mind threats.

Stanhope.—No, I can't say he has ever threatened me in his life; but I believe I had best not provoke him.

Englishman.—Pooh! you would have one angry letter from the old fellow, and there would be an end of it.

Stanhope.—You mistake him mightily; he always does more than he says. He has never been angry with me yet, that I remember, in his life; but, if I were to provoke him, I am sure he would never forgive me: he would be coolly immovable, and I might beg and pray, and write my heart out, to no purpose.

Englishman.—Why, then, he is an old dog, that's all I can say; and pray, are you to obey your dry-nurse too, this same what's his name—Mr. Harte?

Stanhope.—Yes.

Englishman.—So, he stuffs you all morning with Greek, and Latin, and Logic, and all that. Egad, I have a dry-nurse too, but I never looked into a book with him in my life; I have not so much as seen the face of him this week, and don't care a louse if I never see it again.

Stanhope.—My dry-nurse never desires anything of me that is not reasonable, and for my own good; and therefore I like to be with him.

Englishman.—Very sententious and edifying, upon my word! At this rate you will be reckoned a very good young man.

Stanhope.—Why, that will do me no harm.

Englishman.—Will you be with us to-morrow in the evening, then? We shall be ten, with you; and I have got some excellent good wine, and we'll be very merry.

Stanhope.—I am very much obliged to you, but I am engaged for all the evening, to-morrow; first at Cardinal Albani's, and then to sup at the Venetian Ambassadress's.

Englishman.—How the devil can you like being always with these foreigners? I never go amongst them, with all their formalities and ceremonies. I am never easy in company with them, and I don't know why, but I am ashamed.

Stanhope.—I am neither ashamed nor afraid; I am very easy with them, they are very easy with me; I get the language, and I see their characters by conversing with them; and that is what we are sent abroad for. Is it not?

Englishman.—I hate your modest women's company—your woman of fashion as they call 'em. I don't know what to say to them, for my part.

Stanhope.—Have you ever conversed with them?

Englishman.—No, I never conversed with them, but I have been sometimes in their company, though much against my will.

Stanhope.—But at least they have done you no hurt; which is, probably, more than you can say of the women you do converse with.

Englishman.—That's true, I own; but, for all that, I would rather keep company with my surgeon half the year, than with your women of fashion the year round.

Stanhope.—Tastes are different, you know, and every man follows his own.

Englishman.—That's true; but thine's a devilish odd one, Stanhope. All morning with thy dry-nurse, all the evening in formal fine company, and all day long afraid of old daddy in England. Thou art a queer fellow, and I am afraid there's nothing to be made of thee.

Stanhope.—I am afraid so too.

Englishman.—Well, then, good night to you; you have no objection, I hope, to my being drunk to-night, which I certainly will be.

Stanhope.—Not in the least; nor to your being sick to-morrow, which you as certainly will be; and so good night too.

You will observe that I have not put into your mouth those good arguments, which upon such an occasion would, I am sure, occur to you; as, piety and affection toward me; regard and friendship for Mr. Harte; respect for your own moral character, and for all the relative duties of man, son, pupil, and citizen. Such solid arguments would be thrown away upon such shallow puppies. Leave them to their ignorance, and to their dirty, disgraceful vices. They will severely feel the effects of them, when it will be too late. Without the comfortable refuge of learning, and with all the sickness and pains of a ruined stomach and a rotten carcase, if they happen to arrive at old age, it is an uneasy and ignominious one. The ridicule which such fellows endeavour to throw upon those who are not like them, is, in the opinion of all men of sense, the most authentic panegyric. Go on, then, my dear child, in the way you are in, only for a year and a half more; and that is all I ask of you. After that I promise that you shall be your own master, and that I will pretend to no other title than that of your best and truest friend. You shall receive advice, but no orders, from me; and in truth you will want no other advice but such as youth and inexperience must necessarily require. You shall certainly want nothing that is requisite, not only for your conveniency, but also for your pleasures, which I always desire should be gratified. You will suppose that I mean the pleasures *d'un honnête homme.*

While you are learning Italian, which I hope you do with diligence, pray take care to continue your German, which you may have frequent opportunities of speaking. I would also have you keep up your knowledge of the *Jus Publicum Imperii,* by looking over, now and then, those *inestimable manuscripts,* which Sir Charles Williams, who arrived here last week, assures me you have made upon that subject. It will be of very great use to you, when you come to be concerned in foreign affairs, as you shall be (if you qualify yourself for them) younger than ever any other was; I mean, before you are twenty. Sir Charles tells me that he will answer for your learning; and that he believes you will acquire that address, and those Graces, which are so necessary to give it its full lustre and value. But he confesses that he doubts more of the latter than of the former. The justice which he does Mr. Harte, in his panegyrics of him, makes me hope that there is likewise a great deal of truth in his encomiums of you. Are you pleased with, and proud of, the reputation which you have already acquired? Surely you are, for I am sure I am. Will you do anything to lessen or forfeit it? Surely you will not. And will you not do all you can to extend and increase it? Surely you will. It is only going on for a year and a half longer, as you have gone on for the two years last past, and devoting half the day only to application, and you will be sure to make the earliest figure and fortune in the world, that ever man made. Adieu!

No. 1659

To Dr. William Warburton

(*Add. MSS. Egerton 1955, f 11*)

London, 14 *September* 1749

SIR,

I have but two livings in my gift worth anybody's taking, and they are both in Nottinghamshire.

The best is the living of Bingham, worth three hundred pounds a year, of which my father was pleased to sell the then next presentation, and the then incumbent is still alive, so that with regard to that, and to my own age, I look upon myself to be out of the question. The other is the living of Gedling, worth about one hundred pounds a year, and that I disposed of five years ago to a man not forty years old; consequently there is little probability of my disposing of

1398

it again. But should it, by great chance, be vacant in my time, I have one engagement, and but one in the world, to a clergyman of great want and merit, to whom (if at that time unprovided for) I must give it. This is the true state of my Ecclesiastical affairs, which I am very sorry gives me no better hopes of serving you. As for my interest with the administration, either in these or other matters, my situation tells you how considerable it must be. Retirement is not in the road that leads to interest at Court, and he who will enjoy the former (as I am determined to do) must renounce the latter. The political road is (by the by) not one jot cleaner than the Ecclesiastical one. I know it by long experience; for, though I endeavoured to keep as clean as I could, I found that if I did not bemire myself, I was sure to be bespattered at least by others who rode full speed either to overtake or to jostle me. I have therefore put an end to my journey, instead of drudging on to my journey's end.

Thus you see I am a very useless, though your very sincere friend and humble servant.

Pray make my compliments to the most worthy Mr. Allen.[1]

No. 1660

To his Son

(*Stanhope CXCIV*)

London, 22 September O.S. 1749

Dear Boy,

If I have faith in philtres and love potions, I should suspect that you had given Sir Charles Williams some, by the manner in which he speaks of you, not only to me, but to everybody else. I will not repeat to you what he says of the extent and correctness of your knowledge, as it might

---

[1]'This was in answer to one I wrote him to desire a living for my nephew, if ever he had one fall that way disengaged. What he says of the Eccl. and Pol. Road alludes to something I said in mine.'—Note by W. Warburton.

either make you vain, or persuade you that you had already enough of what nobody can have too much. You will easily imagine how many questions I asked, and how narrowly I sifted him upon your subject; he answered me, and I dare say with truth, just as I could have wished; till, satisfied entirely with his accounts of your character and learning, I inquired into other matters, intrinsically indeed of less consequence, but still of great consequence to every man, and of more to you than to almost any man; I mean, your address, manners, and air. To these questions, the same truth which he had observed before, obliged him to give me much less satisfactory answers. And, as he thought himself, in friendship both to you and me, obliged to tell me the disagreeable as well as the agreeable truths, upon the same principle I think myself obliged to repeat them to you.

He told me, then, that in company you were frequently most *provokingly* inattentive, absent, and *distrait*. That you came into a room, and presented yourself very awkwardly; that at table you constantly threw down knives, forks, napkins, bread, etc., and that you neglected your person and dress, to a degree unpardonable at any age, and much more so at yours.

These things, however immaterial soever they may seem to people who do not know the world and the nature of mankind, give me, who know them to be exceedingly material, very great concern. I have long distrusted you, and therefore frequently admonished you upon these articles; and I tell you plainly, that I shall not be easy till I hear a very different account of them. I know no one thing more offensive to a company, than that inattention and *distraction*. It is showing them the utmost contempt; and people never forgive contempt. No man is *distrait* with the man he fears, or the women he loves; which is a proof that every man can get the better of that *distraction* when he thinks it worth his while to do so; and, take my word for it, it is always worth his while. For my own part, I would rather be in company with a dead man than with an absent one; for if the dead man gives me no pleasure, at least he shows me no contempt; whereas the absent man, silently indeed, but very plainly, tells me that he does not think me worth his attention. Besides, can an absent man make any observations upon the characters, customs, and manners of the company? No. He may be in the best companies all his lifetime (if they will admit him, which, if I were they, I would not), and never be one jot the wiser. I never will converse with an absent man; one may as well talk to a deaf one. It is, in truth, a practical blunder, to address ourselves to a man who we see plainly neither hears, minds, nor understands us. Moreover, I aver that no man is, in any degree, fit for either business or conversation, who cannot, and does not, direct and command his attention to the present object, be that what it will. You know, by experience, that I grudge no expense in your education, but I will positively not keep you a flapper. You may read, in Dr. Swift, the description of these flappers, and the use they were to your friends the Laputans; whose minds (Gulliver says) are so taken up with intense speculations, that they neither can speak, nor attend to the discourses of others, without being roused by some external action upon the organs of speech and hearing; for which reason, those people who are able to afford it, always keep a flapper in their family, as one of their domestics, nor ever walk about, or make visits, without him. This flapper is likewise employed diligently to attend his master in his walks, and, upon occasion, to give a soft flap upon his eyes; because he is always so wrapped up in cogitation, that he is in manifest danger of falling down every precipice, and bouncing his head against every post, and, in the streets, of jostling others, or being jostled into the kennel himself. If *Christian* will undertake this province into the bargain, with all my heart; but I will not allow him any increase of wages upon that score. In short, I give you fair warning, that when we meet, if you are absent in mind,

I will soon be absent in body; for it will be impossible for me to stay in the room; and if at table you throw down your knife, plate, bread, etc., and hack the wing of a chicken for half an hour, without being able to cut off it, and your sleeve all the time in another dish, I must rise from table to escape the fever you would certainly give me. Good God! how I should be shocked if you came into my room, for the first time, with two left legs, presenting yourself with all the graces and dignity of a tailor, and your clothes hanging upon you like those in Monmouth Street, upon tenterhooks! whereas I expect, nay require, to see you present yourself with the easy and genteel air of a man of fashion who has kept good company. I expect you not only well dressed, but very well dressed; I expect a gracefulness in all your motions, and something particularly engaging in your address. All this I expect, and all this it is in your power, by care and attention, to make me find; but, to tell you the plain truth, if I do not find it, we shall not converse very much together; for I cannot stand inattention and awkwardness; it would endanger my health.

You have often seen, and I have as often made you observe, L(yttleton)'s[1] distinguished inattention and awkwardness. Wrapped up like a Laputan in intense thought, and possibly sometimes in no thought at all; which, I believe, is very often the case of absent people; he does not know his most intimate acquaintance by sight, or answers

---

[1]George, eldest son of Sir Thomas Lyttelton, in 1757 created Lord Lyttleton. His worth and his accomplishments, his extensive knowledge, and his unsullied probity, were never adorned by the Graces. Horace Walpole says of him, that he had 'the figure of a spectre, and the gesticulations of a puppet!'—(*Memoirs of George II*, vol. i. p. 175.)—M.

And Lord Hervey: 'This new favourite, Mr. Lyttelton, was, in his figure, extremely tall and thin; his face was so ugly, his person so ill made, and his carriage so awkward, that every feature was a blemish, every limb an encumbrance, and every motion a disgrace; but, as disagreeable as his figure was, his voice was still more so, and his address more disagreeable than either. He had a great flow of words, that were always uttered in a lulling monotony, and the little meaning they had to boast of was generally borrowed from the commonplace maxims and sentiments of moralists, patriots, and poets, crudely imbibed, half digested, ill put together, and confusedly refunded.' *Memoirs*. Ref. to E. & S. Edition.

them as if they were at cross purposes. He leaves his hat in
one room, his sword in another, and would leave his shoes
in a third, if his buckles, though awry, did not save them;
his legs and arms, by his awkward management of them,
seem to have undergone the *question extraordinaire*; and his
head, always hanging upon one or other of his shoulders,
seems to have received the first stroke upon a block. I
sincerely value and esteem him for his parts, learning, and
virtue; but, for the soul of me, I cannot love him in company. This will be universally the case, in common life, of
every inattentive, awkward man, let his real merit and knowledge be ever so great. When I was of your age, I desired
to shine, as far as I was able, in every part of life; and was
as attentive to my manners, my dress, and my air, in company of evenings, as to my books and my tutor in the
mornings. A young fellow should be ambitious to shine in
everything; and, of the two, always rather overdo than
underdo. These things are by no means trifles; they are of
infinite consequence to those who are to be thrown into the
great world, and who would make a figure or a fortune in
it. It is not sufficient to deserve well, one must please well
too. Awkward, disagreeable merit, will never carry anybody far. Wherever you find a good dancing-master, pray
let him put you upon your haunches; not so much for the
sake of dancing, as for coming into a room and presenting
yourself genteelly and gracefully. Women, whom you
ought to endeavour to please, cannot forgive a vulgar and
awkward air and gestures; *il leur faut du brillant*. The
generality of men are pretty like them, and are equally taken
by the same exterior graces.

I am very glad that you have received the diamond
buckles safe: all I desire in return for them is that they may
be buckled even upon your feet, and that your stockings
may not hide them. I should be sorry you were an egregi-
ous fop; but I protest that, of the two, I would rather have
you a fop than a sloven. I think negligence in my own dress,

even at my age, when certainly I expect no advantages from my dress, would be indecent with regard to others. I have done with fine clothes; but I will have my plain clothes fit me, and made like other people's. In the evenings I recommend to you the company of women of fashion, who have a right to attention, and will be paid it. Their company will smooth your manners, and give you a habit of attention and respect; of which you will find the advantage among men.

My plan for you, from the beginning, has been to make you shine, equally in the learned and in the polite world; the former part is almost completed to my wishes, and will, I am persuaded, in a little time more, be quite so. The latter part is still in your power to complete; and I flatter myself that you will do it, or else the former part will avail you very little; especially in your department, where the exterior address and graces do half the business; they must be the harbingers of your merit, or your merit will be very coldly received: all can, and do, judge of the former, few of the latter.

Mr. Harte tells me that you have grown very much since your illness; if you get up to five feet ten, or even nine inches, your figure will, probably, be a good one; and, if well dressed and genteel, will probably please; which is a much greater advantage to a man than people commonly think. Lord Bacon calls it a letter of recommendation.

I would wish you to be the *omnis homo, l'homme universel.* You are nearer it, if you please, than ever anybody was at your age; and if you will but, for the course of this next year only, exert your whole attention to your studies in the morning, and to your address, manners, air, and *tournure* in the evenings, you will be the man I wish you, and the man that is rarely seen.

Our letters go, at best, so irregularly, and so often miscarry totally, that, for greater security, I repeat the same things. So, though I acknowledged by last post Mr. Harte's letter of the 8th September N.S. I acknowledge it again by this to you. If this should find you still at Verona, let it inform you, that I wish you would set out soon for Naples; unless Mr. Harte should think it better for you to stay at Verona, or any other place on this side Rome, till you go there for the Jubilee. Nay, if he likes it better, I am very willing that you should go directly from Verona to Rome; for you cannot have too much of Rome, whether upon account of the language, the curiosities, or the company. My only reason for mentioning Naples, is for the sake of the climate, upon account of your health; but, if Mr. Harte thinks your health is now so well restored as to be above climate, he may steer your course wherever he thinks proper; and, for aught I know, your going directly to Rome, and consequently staying there so much the longer, may be as well as anything else. I think you and I cannot put our affairs into better hands than in Mr. Harte's; and I will stake his infallibility against the Pope's, with some odds on his side. *A propos* of the Pope; remember to be presented to him before you leave Rome, and go through the necessary ceremonies for it, whether of kissing his slipper or his breech; for I would never deprive myself of anything that I wanted to do or see, by refusing to comply with an established custom. When I was in Roman Catholic countries, I never declined kneeling in their churches at the elevation, nor elsewhere, when the Host went by. It is a compliance due to the custom of the place, and by no means, as some silly people have imagined, an implied approbation of their doctrine. Bodily attitudes and situations are things so very indifferent in themselves, that I would quarrel with nobody about them. It may indeed be improper for Mr. Harte to pay that tribute of complaisance, upon account of his character.

This letter is a very long, and possibly a very tedious one; but my anxiety for your perfection is so great, and particularly at this critical and decisive period of your life, that I am only afraid of omitting, but never of repeating, or

1405

dwelling too long upon anything that I think may be of the least use to you. Have the same anxiety for yourself that I have for you, and all will do well. Adieu, my dear child!

No. 1661

To his Son

(Stanhope CXCV)

London, 27 September O.S. 1749

DEAR BOY,

A vulgar, ordinary way of thinking, acting, or speaking, implies a low education, and a habit of low company. Young people contract it at school, or among servants, with whom they are too often used to converse; but, after they frequent good company, they must want attention and observation very much, if they do not lay it quite aside. And indeed, if they do not, good company will be very apt to lay them aside. The various kinds of vulgarisms are infinite; I cannot pretend to point them out to you; but I will give some samples, by which you may guess at the rest.

A vulgar man is captious and jealous; eager and impetuous about trifles. He suspects himself to be slighted, thinks everything that is said meant at him; if the company happens to laugh, he is persuaded they laugh at him; he grows angry and testy, says something very impertinent, and draws himself into a scrape, by showing what he calls a proper spirit, and asserting himself. A man of fashion does not suppose himself to be either the sole or principal object of the thoughts, looks, or words of the company; and never suspects that he is either slighted or laughed at, unless he is conscious that he deserves it. And if (which very seldom happens) the company is absurd or ill-bred enough to do either, he does not care two-pence, unless the insult be so gross and plain as to require satisfaction of another kind. As he is above trifles, he is never vehement and eager about them; and, wherever they are concerned, rather acquiesces than wrangles. A vulgar man's conversation always savours strongly of the lowness of his education and company. It turns chiefly upon his domestic affairs, his servants, the excellent order he keeps in his own family, and the little anecdotes of the neighbourhood; all which he relates with emphasis, as interesting matters. He is a man gossip.

Vulgarism in language is the next, and distinguishing characteristic of bad company and a bad education. A man of fashion avoids nothing with more care than that. Proverbial expressions and trite sayings are the flowers of the rhetoric of a vulgar man. Would he say that men differ in their tastes; he both supports and adorns that opinion, by the good old saying, as he respectfully calls it, that *what is one man's meat is another man's poison*. If anybody attempts being *smart*, as he calls it, upon him, he gives them *tit for tat*, ay, that he does. He has always some favourite word for the time being; which, for the sake of using often, he commonly abuses: such as *vastly* angry, *vastly* kind, *vastly* handsome, and *vastly* ugly.[1] Even his pronunciation of proper words carries the mark of the beast along with it. He calls the earth, *yearth*; he is *obleiged*, not *obliged*, to you. He goes *to wards*, and not *towards*, such a place. He sometimes affects hard words by way of ornament, which he always mangles, like a learned woman. A man of fashion never has recourse to proverbs and vulgar aphorisms; uses neither favourite words nor hard words; but takes great care to speak very correctly and grammatically, and to pronounce properly; that is, according to the usage of the best companies.

An awkward address, ungraceful attitudes and actions, and a certain left-handedness (if I may use that word) loudly proclaim low education and low company; for it is impossible to suppose that a man can have frequented good com-

[1]Chesterfield amusingly castigates this abuse of language in *The World*, 5th Dec. 1754, No. 101.

pany, without having catched something, at least, of their air and motions. A new-raised man is distinguished in a regiment by his awkwardness; but he must be impenetrably dull, if, in a month or two's time, he cannot perform at least the common manual exercise, and look like a soldier. The very accoutrements of a man of fashion are grievous incumbrances to a vulgar man. He is at a loss what to do with his hat, when it is not upon his head; his cane (if unfortunately he wears one) is at perpetual war with every cup of tea or coffee he drinks; destroys them first, and then accompanies them in their fall. His sword is formidable only to his own legs, which would possibly carry him fast enough out of the way of any sword but his own. His clothes fit him so ill, and constrain him so much, that he seems rather their prisoner than their proprietor. He presents himself in company, like a criminal in a court of justice; his very air condemns him; and people of fashion will no more connect themselves with the one, than people of character will with the other. This repulse drives and sinks him into low company; a gulf from whence no man, after a certain age, ever emerged.

Les manières nobles et aisées, la tournure d'un homme de condition, le ton de la bonne compagnie, les grâces, le je ne sais quoi qui plaît, are as necessary to adorn and introduce your intrinsic merit and knowledge as the polish is to the diamond; which, without that polish, would never be worn, whatever it might weigh. Do not imagine that these accomplishments are only useful with women; they are much more so with men. In a public assembly, what an advantage has a graceful speaker, with genteel motions, a handsome figure, and a liberal air, over one who shall speak full as much good-sense, but destitute of these ornaments! In business, how prevalent are the Graces, how detrimental is the want of them! By the help of these I have known some men refuse favours less offensively than others granted them. The utility of them in Courts and negotiations is inconceivable.

1408

You gain the hearts, and consequently the secrets, of nine in ten that you have to do with, in spite even of their prudence; which will, nine times in ten, be the dupe of their hearts and of their senses. Consider the importance of these things as they deserve, and you will not lose one moment in the pursuit of them.

You are travelling now in a country once so famous both for arts and arms, that (however degenerated at present) it still deserves your attention and reflection. View it, therefore, with care, compare its former with its present state, and examine into the causes of its rise and its decay. Consider it classically and politically, and do not run through it, as too many of your young countrymen do, musically, and (to use a ridiculous word) *knick-knackically*. No piping nor fiddling, I beseech you; no days lost in poring upon almost imperceptible *intaglios* and *cameos*; and do not become a virtuoso of small wares. Form a taste of painting, sculpture, and architecture, if you please, by a careful examination of the works of the best ancient and modern artists; those are liberal arts, and a real taste and knowledge of them become a man of fashion very well. But, beyond certain bounds, the man of taste ends, and the frivolous virtuoso begins.

Your friend Mendes, the good Samaritan, dined with me yesterday. He has more good nature and generosity than parts. However, I will show him all the civilities that his kindness to you so justly deserves; he tells me that you are taller than I am, which I am very glad of. I desire you may excel me in everything else too; and, far from repining, I shall rejoice at your superiority. He commends your friend Mr. Stevens extremely; of whom, too, I have heard so good a character from other people, that I am very glad of your connection with him. It may prove of use to you hereafter. When you meet with such sort of Englishmen abroad, who, either from their parts or their rank, are likely to make a figure at home, I would advise you to cultivate them, and get their favourable testimony of you here, especially those who are to return to England before you. Sir Charles Williams has puffed you (as the mob call it) here extremely. If three or four more people of parts do the same, before you come back, your first appearance in London will be to great advantage. Many people do, and indeed ought to, take things upon trust; many more do, who need not; and few dare dissent from an established opinion. Adieu!

No. 1662

À Madame la Marquise de Monconseil

(*Maty I. xxxix*)

À Londres, ce 28 septembre V.S. 1749

Je suis bien aise, Madame, de n'avoir appris la maladie de Mademoiselle votre fille qu'en même temps avec sa convalescence. J'aurais pris part à vos alarmes, comme j'en prends actuellement à votre joie, et comme j'en prendrai éternellement à tout ce qui vous touche. Je conçois bien que votre sang et vos soins doivent nécessairement avoir formé une fille digne de vos plus tendres inquiétudes. Cette occasion lui en aura fait sentir toute l'étendue et la délicatesse, et vous vous serez réciproquement plus chères, l'une à l'autre, par le danger où vous avez été toutes deux d'une séparation, dont peut-être ni l'une ni l'autre n'avait encore senti toute la rigueur. Nous ne connaissons jamais tout le prix d'un bien, que quand nous nous voyons au moment de la perdre. Puissiez vous longtemps, Madame, jouir d'un bien si cher que vous venez de sauver! Je ne compte pas non plus pour rien la conservation de sa beauté: les dévots et les philosophes ont beau parler sentences contre la beauté, je soutiens qu'elle est un avantage réel, puisqu'elle orne, et qu'elle recommande même l'esprit le plus juste, et le mérite le plus solide; je m'en rapporte à vous, vous devez bien savoir si j'ai raison ou non.

Je ne sais pas par quelle fatalité cela ne va pas si bien que je l'aurais cru, entre Milord Albemarle et vos gens. Je le trouve très aimable, et poli; il aime les plaisirs et la volupté, c'est là aussi le ton chez vous, et pourtant cela ne s'agence point. Notre Ambassadeur a un avantage sur le vôtre, il vous a trouvée à Paris, et j'ose assurer Monsieur de Mirepoix qu'il ne vous trouvera pas à Londres.

Votre garçon sera à Rome en deux mois, de façon que vous n'avez qu'à écrire à Monsieur de Nivernais aussitôt que vous n'aurez rien autre chose à faire; mais ayez la bonté de le prévenir sur un article, qui est, qu'il doit s'attendre à voir un jeune homme, qui n'a ni tournure ni manières, mais qui est encore incrusté de la crotte anglaise, épaissie même de celle de l'université de Leipsig. Il est si fort appliqué à ses études, qu'il ne s'est pas donné le temps, quand même il en aurait eu les occasions, de prendre l'air et les manières d'un honnête homme: j'espère que l'air de l'hôtel de Nivernais lui sera favorable.

No. 1663

To his Son

(*Stanhope CXCVI*)

London, 2 October O.S. 1749

DEAR BOY,

I received by the last post your letter of the 22nd September N.S. but I have not received that from Mr. Harte to which you refer, and which you say contained your reasons for leaving Verona and returning to Venice, so that I am entirely ignorant of them. Indeed, the irregularity and negligence of the post provoke me, as they break the thread of the accounts I want to receive from you, and of the instructions and orders which I send you almost every post. Of these last twenty posts, I am sure that I have wrote eighteen, either to you or to Mr. Harte; and it does not

appear by your letter that all, or even any, of my letters
have been received. I desire, for the future, that both you
and Mr. Harte will constantly, in your letters, mention the
dates of mine. Had it not been for their miscarriage, you
would not have been in the uncertainty you seem to be in
at present with regard to your future motions. Had you
received my letters, you would have been by this time at
Naples; but we must now take things where they are.

Upon the receipt then of this letter, you will, as soon as
conveniently you can, set out for Rome, where you will
not arrive too long before the Jubilee, considering the difficulties of getting lodgings and other accommodations there
at this time. I leave the choice of the *route* to you, but I do
by no means intend that you should leave Rome after the
Jubilee, as you seem to hint in your letter; on the contrary,
I will have Rome your head-quarters for six months at least,
till you shall have, in a manner, acquired the *jus civitatis*
there. More things are to be seen and learned there than in
any other town in Europe; there are the best masters to
instruct, and the best companies to polish you. In the spring
you may make (if you please) frequent excursions to Naples;
but Rome must still be your head-quarters, till the heats of
June drive you from thence to some other place in Italy,
which we shall think of by that time. As to the expense,
which you mention, I do not regard it in the least; from your
infancy to this day, I never grudged any expense in your
education, and still less do it now, that it is become more
important and decisive. I attend to the objects of your
expenses, but not to the sums. I will certainly not pay one
shilling for your losing your nose, your money, or your
reason; that is, I will not contribute to women, gaming, and
drinking; but I will most cheerfully supply, not only every
necessary, but every decent expense you can make. I do
not care what the best masters cost. I would have you as
well dressed, lodged, and attended, as any reasonable man
of fashion is in his travels. I would have you have that

1412

pocket-money that should enable you to make the proper expense, *d'un honnête homme.* In short, I bar no expense that has neither vice nor folly for its object; and, under those two reasonable restrictions, draw, and welcome.

As for Turin, you may go there hereafter, as a traveller, for a month or two; but you cannot conveniently reside there as an academician, for reasons which I have formerly communicated to Mr. Harte, and which Mr. Villettes, since his return here, has shown me in a still stronger light than he had done by his letters from Turin, of which I sent copies to Mr. Harte, though probably he never received them.

After you have left Rome, Florence is one of the places with which you should be thoroughly acquainted. I know that there is a great deal of gaming there; but at the same time there are, in every place, some people whose fortunes are either too small, or whose understandings are too good, to allow them to play for anything above trifles; and with those people you will associate yourself, if you have not (as I am assured you have not, in the least) the spirit of gaming in you. Moreover, at suspected places, such as Florence, Turin, and Paris, I shall be more attentive to your drafts, and such as exceed a proper and handsome expense will not be answered, for I can easily know whether you game or not without being told.

Mr. Harte will determine your *route* to Rome, as he shall think best; whether along the coast of the Adriatic, or that of the Mediterranean, it is equal to me; but you will observe to come back a different way from that you went.

Since your health is so well restored, I am not sorry that you are returned to Venice, for I love capitals. Everything is best at capitals—the best masters, the best companies, and the best manners. Many other places are worth seeing, but capitals only are worth residing at. I am very glad that Madame Capello received you so well; Monsieur, I was sure, would. Pray assure them both of my respects, and of my sensibility of their kindness to you. Their house will be a very good one for you at Rome, and I would advise you to be domestic in it if you can; but Madame, I can tell you, requires great attentions. Madame Micheli has written a very favourable account of you to my friend the Abbé Grossa Testa, in a letter which he showed me, and in which there are so many civil things to myself, that I would wish to tell her how much I think myself obliged to her. I approve very much of the allotment of your time at Venice. Pray go on so, for a twelvemonth at least, wherever you are. You will find your own account in it.

I like your last letter, which gives me an account of yourself and your own transactions; for, though I do not recommend the *egotism* to you with regard to anybody else, I desire that you will use it with me, and with me only. I interest myself in all that you do, and as yet (excepting Mr. Harte) nobody else does. He must, of course, know all, and I desire to know a great deal.

I am glad you have received, and that you like, the diamond buckles. I am very willing that you should make, but very unwilling that you should *cut*, a figure with them at the Jubilee: the *cutting a figure* being the very lowest vulgarism in the English language, and equal in elegancy to "Yes, my Lady," and "No, my Lady." The words *vast* and *vastly*, you will have found by my former letter that I had proscribed out of the diction of a gentleman, unless in their proper signification of *size* and *bulk*. Not only in language, but in everything else, take great care that the first impressions you give of yourself may be not only favourable, but pleasing, engaging, nay, seducing. They are often decisive; I confess they are a good deal so with me; and I cannot wish for farther acquaintance with a man whose first *abord* and address displease me.

So many of my letters have miscarried, and I know so little which, that I am forced to repeat the same thing over and over again eventually. This is one. I have wrote twice to Mr. Harte to have your picture drawn in miniature, while you were at Venice, and to send it me in a letter: it is all one to me, whether in enamel or in water-colours, provided it is but very like you. I would have you drawn exactly as you are, and in no whimsical dress. I lay more stress upon the likeness of the picture than upon the taste and skill of the painter. If this be not already done, I desire that you will have it done forthwith, before you leave Venice, and enclose it in a letter to me: which letter, for greater security, I would have you desire Sir James Gray to enclose in his packet to the office, as I, for the same reason, send this under his cover. If the picture be done upon vellum, it will be the most portable. Send me, at the same time, a thread or silk of your own length, exactly. I am solicitous about your figure; convinced, by a thousand instances, that a good one is a real advantage. *Mens sana in corpore sano,* is the first and greatest blessing; I would add, *et pulchro,* to complete it. May you have that and every other! Adieu!

Have you received my letters of recommendation to Cardinal Albani and the Duke de Nivernais, at Rome?

No. 1664

To his Son

(Stanhope CXCVII)

London, 9 *October O.S.* 1749

Dear Boy,

If this letter finds you at all, of which I am very doubtful, it will find you at Venice, preparing for your journey to Rome; which, by my last letter to Mr. Harte, I advised you to make along the coast of the Adriatic through Rimini, Loretto, Ancona, etc., places that are all worth seeing, but not worth staying at; and such I reckon all places where the eyes only are employed. Remains of antiquity, public buildings, paintings, sculptures, etc., ought to be seen, and that with a proper degree of attention; but this is soon done, for they are only outsides. It is not so with more important objects, the insides of which must be seen; and they require and deserve much more attention. The characters, the heads, and the hearts of men are the useful science of which I would have you perfect master: that science is best taught and best learnt in capitals, where every human passion has its object, and exerts all its force or all its art in the pursuit. I believe there is no place in the world where every passion is busier, appears in more shapes, and is conducted with more art, than at Rome. Therefore, when you are there, do not imagine that the Capitol, the Vatican, and the Pantheon are the principal objects of your curiosity. But, for one minute that you bestow upon those, employ ten days in informing yourself of the nature of that government, the rise and decay of the Papal power, the politics of that Court, the *brigues* of the Cardinals, the tricks of the Conclaves; and, in general, everything that relates to the interior of that extraordinary government; founded originally upon the ignorance and superstition of mankind; extended by the weakness of some princes and the ambition of others; declining of late in proportion as knowledge has increased; and owing its present precarious security, not to the religion, the affection, or the fear of the temporal powers, but to the jealousy of each other. The Pope's excommunications are no longer dreaded; his indulgences little solicited, and sell very cheap; and his territories, formidable to no power, are coveted by many, and will, most undoubtedly, within a century, be scantled out among the great powers who have now a footing in Italy, whenever they can agree upon the division of the bear's skin. Pray inform yourself thoroughly of the history of the Popes and of the Popedom; which, for many centuries, is interwoven with the history of all Europe. Read the best authors who treat of these matters, and especially Fra Paolo, *de Beneficiis,*[1] a short but very

---

[1]Pietro Sarpi (1552-1623), whose name in religion was Paul. His *Tractatus de Beneficiis* was included in the edition of his complete works in 1750.

material book. You will find at Rome some of all the religious orders in the Christian world; inform yourself carefully of their origin, their founders, their rules, their reforms, and even their dresses: get acquainted with some of all of them, but particularly with the Jesuits, whose Society I look upon to be the most able and best governed society in the world. Get acquainted, if you can, with their General, who always resides at Rome; and who, though he has no seeming power out of his own society, has (it may be) more real influence over the whole world than any temporal prince in it. They have almost engrossed the education of youth. They are, in general, confessors to most of the princes of Europe; and they are the principal missionaries out of it; which three articles give them a most extensive influence, and solid advantages; witness their settlement in Paraguay. Roman Catholics in general declaim against that society, and yet are all governed by individuals of it. They have, by turns, been banished, and with infamy, almost every country in Europe; and have always found means to be restored even with triumph. In short, I know no government in the world that is carried on upon such deep principles of policy, I will not add morality. Converse with them, frequent them, court them; but know them.

Inform yourself too of that infernal court, the Inquisition; which, though not so considerable at Rome[1] as in Spain and Portugal, will however be a good sample to you of what the villainy of some men can contrive, the folly of others receive, and both together establish, in spite of the first natural principles of reason, justice, and equity.

These are the proper and useful objects of the attention of a man of sense, when he travels; and these are the objects for which I have sent you abroad; and I hope you will return thoroughly informed of them.

[1]The Roman Inquisition, presided over by the Pope, was founded in 1543 and abolished by Napoleon in 1808.

I receive, this very moment, Mr. Harte's letter of the 1st October N.S. but I have never received his former, to which he refers in this, and you refer in your last; in which he gave me the reasons for your leaving Verona so soon; nor have I ever received that letter in which your case was stated by your physicians. Letters to and from me have worse luck than other people's; for you have written to me, and I to you, for these last three months, by way of Germany, with as little success as before.

I am edified with your morning applications, and your evening gallantries, at Venice, of which Mr. Harte gives me an account. Pray go on with both, there, and afterwards at Rome; where, provided you arrive in the beginning of December, you may stay at Venice as much longer as you please.

Make my compliments to Sir James Gray and Mr. Smith, with my acknowledgments for the great civilities they show you.

I wrote to Mr. Harte by the last post, October the 6th O.S. and will write to him in a post or two, upon the contents of his last. Adieu! *Point de distractions*; and remember the *Graces*.

No. 1665

To his Son

(*Stanhope CXCVIII*)

London, 17th October O.S. 1749

DEAR BOY,

I have, at last, received Mr. Harte's letter, of the 19th September N.S. from Verona. Your reasons for leaving that place were very good ones; and, as you stayed there long enough to see what was to be seen, Venice (as a capital) is, in my opinion, a much better place for your residence. Capitals are always the seats of Arts and Sciences, and the

1418

best companies. I have stuck to them all my lifetime; and I advise you to do so too.

You will have received, in my three or four last letters, my directions for your furthei motions to another capital; where I propose that your stay shall be pretty considerable. The expense, I am well aware, will be so too; but that, as I told you before, will have no weight, when your improvement and advantage are in the other scale. I do not care a groat what it is, if neither vice nor folly are the objects of it, and if Mr. Harte gives his sanction.

I am very pleased with your account of Carniola; those are the kind of objects worthy of your inquiries and knowledge. The produce, the taxes, the trade, the manufactures, the strength, the weakness, the government, of the several countries which a man of sense travels through, are the material points to which he attends; and leaves the steeples, the market-places, and the signs, to the laborious and curious researches of Dutch and German travellers.

Mr. Harte tells me, that he intends to give you, by means of Signor Vicentini, a general notion of civil and military architecture; with which I am very well pleased. They are frequent subjects of conversation; and it is very right that you should have some idea of the latter, and a good taste of the former; and you may very soon learn as much as you need know of either. If you read about one-third of Palladio's Book of Architecture with some skilful person, and then, with that person, examine the best buildings by those rules, you will know the different proportions of the different orders; the several diameters of their columns; their inter-columniations, their several uses, etc. The Corinthian order is chiefly used in magnificent buildings, where ornament and decoration are the principal objects; the Doric is calculated for strength; and the Ionic partakes of the Doric strength and of the Corinthian ornaments. The Composite and the Tuscan orders are more modern, and were unknown to the Greeks: the one is too light, the other too clumsy. You may soon be acquainted with the considerable parts of civil architecture; and for the minute and mechanical parts of it, leave them to masons, bricklayers, and Lord Burlington;[1] who has, to a certain degree, lessened himself, by knowing them too well. Observe the same method as to military architecture; understand the terms; know the general rules, and then see them in execution with some skilful person. Go with some engineer or old officer, and view with care the real fortifications of some strong place; and you will get a clearer idea of bastions, half-moons, horn-works, ravelins, glacis, etc., than all the masters in the world could give you upon paper. And thus much I would by all means have you know of both civil and military architecture.

I would also have you acquire a liberal taste of the two liberal arts of painting and sculpture; but without descending into those *minuties*, which our modern virtuosi most affectedly dwell upon. Observe the great parts attentively; see if nature be truly represented; if the passions are strongly expressed; if the characters are preserved; and leave the trifling parts, with their little jargon, to affected puppies. I would advise you, also, to read the history of the painters and sculptors; and I know none better than Félibien's.[2] There are many in Italian; you will inform yourself which are the best. It is a part of history, very entertaining, curious enough, and not quite useless. All these sorts of things I would have you know, to a certain degree; but remember, that they must only be the amusements, and not the business, of a man of parts.

Since writing to me in German would take up so much of your time, of which I would not now have one moment

---

[1] Richard Boyle (1695-1753), third Earl of Burlington, to whom Pope inscribed his *Epistle on the Use of Riches*, an enthusiastic amateur in architecture, with a considerable influence on it in England. Horace Walpole says of him, that he 'had every quality of a genius and artist, except envy.'

[2] Jean Francis Félibien (died 1733) wrote *Entretiens sur les Vies et sur les Ouvrages des plus excellents Peintres, anciens et modernes*; London 1705.

wasted, I will accept of your composition, and content myself with a moderate German letter, once a fortnight, to Lady Chesterfield, or Mr. Grevenkop. My meaning was only, that you should not forget what you had already learned of the German language and character; but, on the contrary, that, by frequent use, it should grow more easy and familiar. Provided you take care of that, I do not care by what means; but I do desire that you will, every day of your life, speak German to somebody or other (for you will meet with Germans enough), and write a line or two of it every day, to keep your hand in. Why should you not, for instance, write your own little memorandums and accounts in that language and character? by which, too, you would have this advantage into the bargain, that, if mislaid, few but yourself could read them.

I am extremely glad to hear that you like the assemblies at Venice well enough to sacrifice some suppers to them; for I hear that you do not dislike your suppers neither. It is therefore plain, that there is somebody or something at those assemblies which you like better than your meat. And as I know there is none but good company at those assemblies, I am very glad to find that you like good company so well. I already imagine you a little smoothed by it; and that you have either reasoned yourself, or that they have laughed you out of your absences and *distractions*; for I cannot suppose that you go there to insult them. I likewise imagine that you wish to be welcome where you wish to go; and, consequently, that you both present and behave yourself there, *en galant homme, et pas en bourgeois.*

If you have vowed to anybody there one of those eternal passions, which I have sometimes known, by great accident, last three months; I can tell you, that without great attention, infinite politeness, and engaging air and manners, the omens will be sinister, and the goddess unpropitious. Pray tell me what are the amusements of those assemblies? Are they little commercial play, are they music, are they *la belle conversation,* or are they all three? *Y file-t-on le parfait amour? Y débite-t-on les beaux sentiments? Ou est-ce qu'on y parle épigramme?* And pray which is your department? *Tutis depone in auribus.* Whichever it is, endeavour to shine and excel in it. Aim, at least, at the perfection of everything that is worth doing at all, and you will come nearer it than you would imagine; but those always crawl infinitely short of it, whose aim is only mediocrity. Adieu!

P.S.—By an uncommon diligence of the post I have this moment received yours of the 9th N.S.

No. 1666

À MADAME LA MARQUISE DE MONCONSEIL

(Maty I. xl)

À Londres, ce 23 octobre V.S. 1749

Vous défendez les gentillesses, Madame; ayez donc la bonté de les définir, afin que je n'en dise pas sans y penser. J'ai insinué qu'il était possible que Mademoiselle votre fille pût être jolie, vous soutenez qu'elle ne l'est point. Voici une question de fait, et j'en veux la décision, mais le moyen, direz-vous? le voici, et je crois, ce qui n'arrive guère, que nous en serons tous deux contents. Je m'en rapporte à Mademoiselle elle-même; sa bouche décidera en votre faveur, son cœur en la mienne. À vous, Madame, à cette heure. Je ne vous ai vu, dites-vous, que changée et dépérie, et par conséquent je dois croire que vous avez toujours été fort désagréable. *Nego,* Madame, comme dit élégamment Thomas Diafoirus;[1] je vous intente procès là-dessus, et je vous laisserai même le choix de vos juges; j'aurai le triomphe, et vous aurez le plaisir, de vous voir condamnée avec frais et dépens.

Je suis fâché que notre ami[2] qui pourrait plaire s'il le

[1] In Molière's *Malade Imaginaire.*   [2] Lord Albemarle.

voulait, ne le veuille point; j'ai su depuis longtemps son attachement pour la Sultane[1] à laquelle il sacrifie ses soirées, c'est-à-dire sa vie, à Paris; mais j'espérais qu'il lui ferait ses sacrifices le matin: c'était au moins autrefois la belle heure des sacrifices.

Je ne vous dis rien, ni à Monsieur de Nevers non plus, au sujet des lettres que vous avez écrites à Monsieur de Nivernais en faveur de votre élève. Chez vous deux, les politesses et les amitiés coulent de source, on s'y attend toujours, on ne s'y trompe jamais, et elles paraissent si fort dans l'ordre, qu'il faut quelque réflexion pour vous en avoir de l'obligation. On ne sait presque pas gré à une bonne pendule pendant qu'elle va juste, et on n'y fait attention que quand elle manque, parcequ'alors on est surpris. Ce devrait pourtant être tout le contraire; l'un est très difficile, et il n'y a rien au monde de si facile que l'autre.

Je voudrais bien que votre élève eût fini ses affaires en Italie, afin que j'en fusse quitte, et que je le visse dans des meilleures mains que les miennes; car sachez que du moment qu'il arrive à Paris, je n'ai plus rien à faire avec lui, il vous appartiendra en propre, et vous me répondrez de ses manières, de sa politesse, et même de ses sentiments. Gentillesse à part, je sais que vous en pourrez faire tout ce que vous voudrez. Il vous sera livré par la poste à Paris , du mois de mai en un an.

No. 1667

TO HIS SON

(*Stanhope CXCIX*)

DEAR BOY,   *London, 24 October O.S.* 1749

By my last I only acknowledged, by this I answer, your letter of the 9th October N.S.

I am very glad that you approved of my letter of September the 12th O.S. because it is upon that footing that

---

[1]Mademoiselle Gauchet, his 'old Columbine.'—See Walpole's Letter to Mann, 19th May 1750.

I always propose living with you. I will advise you seriously, as a friend of some experience; and I will converse with you cheerfully, as a companion: the authority of a parent shall for ever be laid aside; for, wherever it is exerted, it is useless; since, if you have neither sense nor sentiments enough to follow my advice as a friend, your unwilling obedience to my orders, as a father, will be a very awkward and unavailing one, both to yourself and me. Tacitus, speaking of an army that awkwardly and unwillingly obeyed its generals, only from the fear of punishment, says, they obeyed indeed, *sed ut qui mallent jussa Imperatorum interpretari, quam exequi.* For my own part, I disclaim such obedience.

You think, I find, that you do not understand Italian; but I can tell you, that, like the *Bourgeois Gentilhomme*, who spoke prose without knowing it, you understand a great deal, though you do not know that you do; for, whoever understands French and Latin so well as you do, understands at least half the Italian language, and has very little occasion for a dictionary. And for the idioms, the phrases, and the delicacies of it, conversation and a little attention will teach them you, and that soon. Therefore, pray speak it in company, right or wrong, *à tort ou à travers*, as soon as ever you have got words enough to ask a common question, or give a common answer. If you can only say *buon giorno*, say it, instead of saying *bon jour*, I mean to every Italian; the answer to it will teach you more words, and, insensibly, you will be very soon master of that easy language. You are quite right in not neglecting your German for it, and in thinking that it will be of more use to you; it certainly will, in the course of your business: but Italian has its use too, and is an ornament into the bargain; there being many very polite and good authors in that language. The reason you assign for having hitherto met with none of my 'swarms of Germans' in Italy, is a very solid one; and I can easily conceive that the expense necessary for a traveller must amount to a number of *thalers, groschen,* and *kreutzers,* tremendous to a German fortune. However, you will find several at Rome, either Ecclesiastics, or in the *suite* of the Imperial Minister; and more when you come into the Milanese, among the Queen of Hungary's officers. Besides, you have a Saxon servant, to whom I hope you speak nothing but German.

I have had the most obliging letter in the world from Monsieur Capello, in which he speaks very advantageously of you, and promises you his protection at Rome. I have wrote him an answer by which I hope I have domesticated you at his *hôtel* there, which I advise you to frequent as much as you can. *Il est vrai qu'il ne paye pas beaucoup de sa figure;* but he has sense and knowledge at bottom, with a great experience of business, having been already Ambassador at Madrid, Vienna, and London. And I am very sure that he will be willing to give you any informations in that way that he can.

Madame was a capricious, whimsical fine lady, till the smallpox, which she got there, by lessening her beauty, lessened her humours too; but, as I presume it did not change her sex, I trust to that for her having such a share of them left as may contribute to smooth and polish you. She doubtless still thinks that she has beauty enough remaining to entitle her to the attentions always paid to beauty; and she has certainly rank enough to require respect. Those are the sort of women who polish a young man the most, and who give him that habit of complaisance, and that flexibility and versatility of manners, which prove of great use to him with men, and in the course of business.

You must always expect to hear more or less from me upon that important subject of manners, graces, address, and that undefinable *je ne sais quoi* that ever pleases. I have reason to believe that you want nothing else; but I have reason to fear, too, that you want these; and that want will keep you poor, in the midst of all the plenty of knowledge which you may have treasured up. Adieu!   *1425*

No. 1668

To Captain Irwine (at Dublin)

(*In the possession of Mrs. Reynolds-Peyton*)

London, 26 October 1749

Sir,

You judged very right in believing that I take a part in what concerns Ireland; I do, and always shall, though an unavailing one. You judged as right too in thinking that no accounts of that country could come to me from a more welcome hand than yours. Nothing can be better or more clearly stated than your account of the present *important* transactions relative to Charles Lucas,[1] apothecary at Dublin, who, I believe, is the first apothecary that ever was voted an enemy to his country. That apothecary's stuff, of which till now only the recipes were printed, will hence-forwards be universally taken, and make a part of the Dublin Dispensatory. In the Book of Holy Martyrs there are many Charles Lucases, whose names would hardly have been known in their own times, but certainly never transmitted down to ours, if they had not been broiled a little. And the obscure Dr. Sacheverell's fortune was made by a Parliamentary prosecution, much about the same time that the French prophets[2] were totally extinguished by a puppet-show. Great souls are sometimes desirous to purchase fame at the expense of their bodies. If Charles Lucas, apothecary, is one of those, one should congratulate him upon this occasion; but if his views were, as from his profession I

---

[1] 'The discontented in Ireland had been headed by one Lucas (1713-1771), an apothecary, who was soon after banished from that kingdom, and turned physician in London, where he wrote controversy in his own profession.' (Horace Walpole's *Memoirs*, vol. i. p. 244.) He founded the *Freeman's Journal*, 1763.

[2] 'Ces Prophètes (du Languedoc) allèrent ensuite en Angleterre. . . . Ils offrirent de ressusciter un mort, et même tel mort que l'on voudrait choisir. . . . La scène finit par mettre au pilori les Prophètes.'—*Siècle de Louis XIV*, ch. xxxii.—M. See Letter of 26th January 1766. Sacheverell made his fame in 1710 by attacking the Whig oligarchy, especially Godolphin. His trial by the Lords was the success of the season.

should be very apt to think they were, of a much *lower nature*, one ought to condole with him upon the suspension of them at least for some time. In this uncertainty, I withhold my compliments of either kind to Charles Lucas, apothecary.

But let us come to a better subject. Pray are you Major, or only Captain still? For greater security, I direct this to you by the latter title; but if, in so doing, I injure you, I will publish my recantation upon the back of my next. But, in either case, I hope you have not laid aside the thoughts of going abroad again. You have travelled a little with great profit; travel again, and it will be with still greater. The knowledge of the manners, the language, and the governments of the several countries of Europe, is well worth two years' delay of military promotion, supposing that should be the case. I am, with great truth, etc.

No. 1669

To his Son

(*Stanhope CC*)

London, 3 November O.S. 1749

DEAR BOY,

From the time that you have had life, it has been the principal and favourite object of mine to make you as perfect as the imperfections of human nature will allow; in this view I have grudged no pains nor expense in your education; convinced that education, more than nature, is the cause of that great difference which we see in the characters of men. While you were a child, I endeavoured to form your heart habitually to virtue and honour, before your understanding was capable of showing you their beauty and utility. Those principles which you then got, like your grammar rules, only by rote, are now, I am persuaded, fixed and confirmed by reason. And indeed they are so plain and clear, that they require but a very moderate degree of understanding, either to comprehend or practise them. Lord Shaftesbury says, very prettily, that he would be virtuous for his own sake, though nobody were to know it; as he would be clean for his own sake, though nobody were to see him.[1] I have therefore, since you have had the use of your reason, never written to you upon those subjects; they speak best for themselves; and I should now just as soon think of warning you gravely not to fall into the dirt or the fire, as into dishonour or vice. This view of mine I consider as fully attained. My next object was sound and useful learning. My own care first, Mr. Harte's afterwards, and *of late* (I will own it to your praise) your own application, have more than answered my expectations in that particular, and, I have reason to believe, will answer even my wishes. All that remains for me then to wish, to recommend, to inculcate, to order, and to insist upon, is good-breeding; without which all your other qualifications will be lame, unadorned, and, to a certain degree, unavailing. And here I fear, and have too much reason to believe, that you are greatly deficient. The remainder of this letter, therefore, shall be (and it will not be the last by a great many) upon that subject.

A friend of yours and mine has very justly defined good-breeding to be, *the result of much good-sense, some good-nature, and a little self-denial for the sake of others, and with a view to obtain the same indulgence from them.* Taking this for granted (as I think it cannot be disputed), it is astonishing to me that anybody who has good-sense and good-nature (and I believe you have both) can essentially fail in good-breeding. As to the modes of it, indeed, they vary according to persons, places, and circumstances, and are only to be acquired by observation and experience; but the substance of it is everywhere and eternally the same. Good

---

[1]This is implicit throughout the *Characteristics*; it may well be a reference to a passage in *An Essay on the Freedom of Wit and Humour*, Part iii. § 4.

manners are, to particular societies, what good morals are to society in general; their cement and their security. And as laws are enacted to enforce good morals, or at least to prevent the ill effects of bad ones, so there are certain rules of civility, universally implied and received, to enforce good manners, and punish bad ones. And indeed there seems to me to be less difference, both between the crimes and punishments, than at first one would imagine. The immoral man, who invades another's property, is justly hanged for it; and the ill-bred man, who by his ill manners invades and disturbs the quiet and comforts of private life, is by common consent as justly banished society. Mutual complaisances, attentions, and sacrifices of little conveniences, are as natural an implied compact between civilised people, as protection and obedience are between kings and subjects; whoever in either case violates that compact, justly forfeits all advantages arising from it. For my own part, I really think, that, next to the consciousness of doing a good action, that of doing a civil one is the most pleasing; and the epithet which I should covet the most, next to that of Aristides, would be that of well-bred. Thus much for goodbreeding in general; I will now consider some of the various modes and degrees of it.

Very few, scarcely any, are wanting in the respect which they should show to those whom they acknowledge to be infinitely their superiors; such as crowned heads, princes, and public persons of distinguished and eminent posts. It is the manner of showing that respect which is different. The man of fashion, and of the world, expresses it in its fullest extent; but naturally, easily, and without concern; whereas a man who is not used to keep good company, expresses it awkwardly; one sees that he is not used to it, and that it costs him a great deal; but I never saw the worst bred man living guilty of lolling, whistling, scratching his head, and such little indecencies, in company that he respected. In such companies, therefore, the only point to be attended to is, to show that respect, which everybody means to show, in an easy, unembarrassed, and graceful manner. This is what observation and experience must teach you.

In mixed companies, whoever is admitted to make part of them, is, for the time at least, supposed to be upon a footing of equality with the rest; and, consequently, as there is no principal object of awe and respect, people are apt to take a greater latitude in their behaviour, and to be less upon their guard; and so they may, provided it be within certain bounds, which are upon no occasion to be transgressed. But, upon these occasions, though no one is entitled to distinguished marks of respect, every one claims and very justly, every mark of civility and good-breeding. Ease is allowed, but carelessness and negligence are strictly forbidden. If a man accosts you, and talks to you ever so dully or frivolously, it is worse than rudeness, it is brutality, to show him, by a manifest inattention to what he says, that you think him a fool or a blockhead, and not worth hearing. It is much more so with regard to women, who, of whatever rank they are, are entitled, in consideration of their sex, not only to an attentive, but an officious good-breeding from men. Their little wants, likings, dislikes, preferences, antipathies, fancies, whims, and even impertinences, must be officiously attended to, flattered, and, if possible, guessed at and anticipated by a well-bred man. You must never usurp to yourself those conveniences and *agréments* which are of common right—such as the best places, the best dishes, etc.; but, on the contrary, always decline them yourself, and offer them to others, who, in their turns, will offer them to you; so that, upon the whole, you will in your turn enjoy your share of the common right. It would be useless for me to enumerate all the particular instances in which a well-bred man shows his good-breeding in good company; and it would be injurious to you to suppose that your own good-sense will not point them out to you; and then your

1430

own good-nature will recommend, and your self-interest enforce, the practice.

There is a third sort of good-breeding, in which people are the most apt to fail, from a very mistaken notion that they cannot fail at all; I mean, with regard to one's most familiar friends and acquaintances, or those who really are our inferiors; and there, undoubtedly, a greater degree of ease is not only allowed, but proper, and contributes much to the comforts of a private, social life. But that ease and freedom have their bounds too, which must by no means be violated. A certain degree of negligence and carelessness becomes injurious and insulting, from the real or supposed inferiority of the persons; and that delightful liberty of conversation among a few friends is soon destroyed, as liberty often has been, by being carried to licentiousness.[1] But example explains things best, and I will put a pretty strong case.

Suppose you and me alone together, I believe you will allow that I have as good a right to unlimited freedom in your company, as either you or I can possibly have in any other; and I am apt to believe, too, that you would indulge me in that freedom as far as anybody would. But, notwithstanding this, do you imagine that I should think there were no bounds to that freedom? I assure you, I should not think so ; and I take myself to be as much tied down by a certain degree of good manners to you, as by other degrees of them to other people. Were I to show you, by a manifest inattention to what you said to me, that I was thinking of something else the whole time, were I to yawn extremely or snore in your company, I should think that I behaved myself to you like a beast, and should not expect that you would care to frequent me. No. The most familiar and intimate habitudes, connections, and friendships, require a degree of good-breeding, both to preserve and cement them. If ever

---

[1]'Friendship cannot live with ceremony, nor without civility.'—Halifax *Maxims*.

a man and his wife, who pass nights as well as days together, absolutely lay aside all good-breeding, their intimacy would soon degenerate into a coarse familiarity, infallibly productive of contempt or disgust. The best of us have our bad sides; and it is as imprudent as it is ill-bred to exhibit them. I shall certainly not use ceremony with you; it would be misplaced between us; but I shall certainly observe that degree of good-breeding with you, which is, in the first place, decent, and which, I am sure, is absolutely necessary to make us like one another's company long.

I will say no more now upon this important subject of good-breeding, upon which I have already dwelt too long, it may be, for one letter, and upon which I shall frequently refresh your memory hereafter; but I will conclude with these axioms:—

That the deepest learning, without good-breeding, is unwelcome and tiresome pedantry, and of use nowhere but in a man's own closet—and, consequently, of little or no use at all.

That a man who is not perfectly well-bred, is unfit for good company, and unwelcome in it; will consequently dislike it, soon afterwards renounce it; and be reduced to solitude, or (what is worse) low and bad company.

That a man who is not well-bred, is full as unfit for business as for company.

Make then, my dear child, I conjure you, good-breeding the great object of your thoughts and actions, at least, half the day. Observe carefully the behaviour and manners of those who are distinguished by their good-breeding; imitate, nay, endeavour to excel, that you may at least reach them; and be convinced that good-breeding is, to all worldly qualifications, what charity is to all Christian virtues. Observe how it adorns merit, and how often it covers the want of it. May you wear it to adorn, and not to cover you! Adieu!

No. 1670

To his Son

(*Stanhope CCI*)

DEAR BOY,   *London,* 14 *November O.S.* 1749

There is a natural good-breeding which occurs to every man of common sense, and is practised by every man of common good-nature. This good-breeding is general, independent of modes, and consists in endeavours to please and oblige our fellow-creatures by all good offices short of moral duties. This will be practised by a good-natured American savage as essentially as by the best-bred European. But, then, I do not take it to extend to the sacrifice of our own conveniences for the sake of other people's. Utility introduced this sort of good-breeding as it introduced commerce, and established a truck of the little *agréments* and pleasures of life. I sacrifice such a conveniency to you, you sacrifice another to me; this commerce circulates, and every individual finds his account in it upon the whole. The third sort of good-breeding is local, and is variously modified, in not only different countries, but in different towns of the same country. But it must be founded upon the two former sorts: they are the matter to which, in this case, fashion and custom only give the different shapes and impressions. Whoever has the two first sorts will easily acquire this third sort of good-breeding, which depends singly upon attention and observation. It is, properly, the polish, the lustre, the last finishing strokes of good-breeding. It is to be found only in capitals, and even there it varies; the good-breeding of Rome differing in some things from that of Paris; that of Paris, in others, from that of Madrid; and that of Madrid, in many things from that of London. A man of sense, therefore, carefully attends to the local manners of the respective places where he is, and takes for his models those persons whom he observes to be at the head of the fashion and good-breeding. He watches how they address themselves to their superiors, how they accost their equals, and how they treat their inferiors; and lets none of these little niceties escape him; which are to good-breeding what the last delicate and masterly touches are to a good picture; and of which the vulgar have no notion, but by which good judges distinguish the master. He attends even to their air, dress, and motions, and imitates them liberally, and not servilely; he copies, but does not mimic. These personal graces are of very great consequence: they anticipate the sentiments before merit can engage the understanding; they captivate the heart, and give rise, I believe, to the extravagant notions of charms and philtres. Their effects were so surprising that they were reckoned supernatural. The most graceful and best bred men, and the handsomest and genteelest women, give the most philtres; and, as I verily believe, without the least assistance of the devil. Pray be not only well-dressed, but shining in your dress; let it have *du brillant*; I do not mean by a clumsy load of gold and silver, but by the taste and fashion of it. Women like and require it; they think it an attention due to them; but, on the other hand, if your motions and carriage are not graceful, genteel, and natural, your fine clothes will only display your awkwardness the more. But I am unwilling to suppose you still awkward; for surely by this time you must have catched a good air in good company. When you went from hence you were not naturally awkward; but your awkwardness was adventitious and Westmonasterial. Leipzig, I apprehend, is not the seat of the Graces; and I presume you acquired none there. But now, if you will be pleased to observe what people of the first fashion do with their legs and arms, heads and bodies, you will reduce yours to certain decent laws of motion. You danced pretty well here, and ought to dance very well before you come home; for what one is obliged to do sometimes one ought to be able to do well. Besides, *la belle danse donne du brillant à un jeune homme*. And you should endeavour to shine. A calm serenity, negative merit and graces, do not become your age. You should be *alerte, adroit, vif;* be wanted, talked of, impatiently expected, and unwillingly parted with in company. I should be glad to hear half a dozen women of fashion say, *Où est donc le petit Stanhope? Que ne vient-il? Il faut avouer qu'il est aimable.* All this I do not mean singly with regard to women as the principal object; but with regard to men, and with a view of your making yourself considerable. For, with very small variations, the same things that please women please men; and a man whose manners are softened and polished by women of fashion, and who is formed by them to an habitual attention and complaisance, will please, engage, and connect men much easier and more than he would otherwise. You must be sensible that you cannot rise in the world without forming connections and engaging different characters to conspire in your point. You must make them your dependents without their knowing it, and dictate to them while you seem to be directed by them. Those necessary connections can never be formed or preserved but by an uninterrupted series of complaisance, attentions, politeness, and some constraint. You must engage their hearts if you would have their support; you must watch the *mollia tempora*, and captivate them by the *agréments*, and charms of conversation. People will not be called out to your service only when you want them; and, if you expect to receive strength from them, they must receive either pleasure or advantage from you.

I received in this instant a letter from Mr. Harte, of the 2nd N.S. which I will answer soon; in the meantime I return him my thanks for it, through you. The constant good accounts which he gives me of you will make me suspect him of partiality, and think him *le médicin tant mieux*. Consider, therefore, what weight any future deposition of his against you must necessarily have with me; as, in that case, he will be a very unwilling, he must consequently be a very important witness. Adieu!

1435

No. 1671

To his Son

(*Stanhope CCII*)

[*November* 1749]

Dear Boy,

My last was upon the subject of good-breeding; but,
I think, it rather set before you the unfitness and disadvantages of ill-breeding, than the utility and necessity of good;
it was rather negative than positive. This, therefore, shall
go further, and explain to you the necessity, which you, of
all people living, lie under, not only of being positively
actively well-bred, but of shining and distinguishing yourself by your good-breeding. Consider your own situation
in every particular, and judge whether it is not essentially
your interest, by your own good-breeding to others, to
secure theirs to you; and that, let me assure you, is the only
way of doing it; for people will repay, and with interest too,
inattention with inattention, neglect with neglect, and ill
manners with worse; which may engage you in very disagreeable affairs. In the next place, your profession requires,
more than any other, the nicest and most distinguished
good-breeding. You will negotiate with very little success,
if you do not, previously, by your manners, conciliate and
engage the affections of those with whom you are to
negotiate. Can you ever get into the confidence and the
secrets of the Courts where you may happen to reside, if
you have not those pleasing, insinuating manners which
alone can procure them? Upon my word, I do not say too
much when I say, that superior good-breeding, insinuating
manners, and genteel address, are half your business. Your
knowledge will have but little influence upon the mind, if
your manners prejudice the heart against you; but, on the
other hand, how easily will you dupe the understanding
where you have first engaged the heart! and hearts are by
no means to be gained by that mere common civility which

everybody practises. Bowing again to those who bow to you, answering drily those who speak to you, and saying nothing offensive to anybody, is such negative good-breeding, that it is only not being a brute; as it would be but a very poor commendation of any man's cleanliness to say that he did not stink. It is an active, cheerful, officious, seducing good-breeding that must gain you the good-will and first sentiments of the men, and the affections of the women. You must carefully watch and attend to their passions, their tastes, their little humours and weaknesses, and *aller au devant*. You must do it, at the same time, with alacrity and *empressement*, and not as if you graciously condescended to humour their weaknesses.

For instance, suppose you invited anybody to dine or sup with you, you ought to recollect if you had observed that they had any favourite dish, and take care to provide it for them: and, when it came, you should say, *You seemed to me, at such and such a place, to give this dish a preference, and therefore I ordered it. This is the wine that I observed you liked, and therefore I procured some.* The more trifling these things are, the more they prove your attention for the person, and are consequently the more engaging. Consult your own breast, and recollect how these little attentions, when shown you by others, flatter that degree of self-love and vanity, from which no man living is free. Reflect how they incline and attract you to that person, and how you are propitiated afterwards to all which that person says or does. The same causes will have the same effects in your favour. Women, in a great degree, establish or destroy every man's reputation of good-breeding; you must, therefore, in a manner, overwhelm them with these attentions; they are used to them, they expect them; and, to do them justice, they commonly requite them. You must be sedulous, and rather over-officious than under, in procuring them their coaches, their chairs, their conveniences in public places; not see what you should not see; and rather assist

where you cannot help seeing. Opportunities of showing
these attentions present themselves perpetually; but, if they
do not, make them. As Ovid advises his lover, when he
sits in the *circus* near his mistress, to wipe the dust off her
neck, even if there be none: *Si nullus, tamen excute nullum.*[1]
Your conversation with women should always be respectful; but, at the same time, *enjoué*, and always addressed to
their vanity. Everything you say or do, should convince
them of the regard you have (whether you have it or not)
for their beauty, their wit, or their merit. Men have possibly
as much vanity as women, though of another kind; and both
art and good-breeding require, that instead of mortifying
you should please and flatter it, by words and looks of
approbation. Suppose (which is by no means improbable)
that, at your return to England, I should place you near
the person of some one of the Royal Family; in that
situation, good-breeding, engaging address, adorned with
all the graces that dwell at Courts, would very probably
make you a favourite, and, from a favourite, a minister; but
all the knowledge and learning in the world, without them,
never would. The penetration of princes seldom goes
deeper than the surface. It is the exterior that always
engages their hearts; and I would never advise you to give
yourself much trouble about their understandings. Princes
in general (I mean those *Porphyrogenets*[2] who are born and
bred in purple) are about the pitch of women; bred up like
them, and are to be addressed and gained in the same
manner. They always see, they seldom weigh. Your lustre,
not your solidity, must take them; your inside will after-

---

[1] *De Arte Amandi*, lib. i. l. 112.

[2] 'In the Greek language *purple* and *porphyry* are the same word; and as the
colours of nature are invariable, we may learn that a dark, deep red was the
Tyrian dye which stained the purple of the ancients. An apartment of the Byzan-
tine palace was lined with porphyry; it was reserved for the use of the pregnant
empresses, and the royal birth of their children was expressed by the appellation
of *Porphyrogenite*, or Born in the Purple. Several of the Roman princes had been
blessed with an heir; but this peculiar surname was first applied to Constantine
the Seventh ' (A.D. 911).—Gibbon's *Decline and Fall*, ch. xlviii. Bradshaw.

wards support and secure what your outside has acquired. With weak people (and they undoubtedly are three parts in four of mankind), good-breeding, address, and manners are everything; they can go no deeper; but let me assure you, that they are a great deal even with people of the best under-standings. Where the eyes are not pleased, and the heart is not flattered, the mind will be apt to stand out. Be this right or wrong, I confess I am so made myself. Awkward-ness and ill-breeding shock me to that degree, that, where I meet with them, I cannot find in my heart to inquire into the intrinsic merit of that person; I hastily decide in myself, that he can have none; and am not sure, I should not even be sorry to know that he had any. I often paint you in my imagination in your present *lontananʒa*; and, while I view you in the light of ancient and modern learning, useful and ornamental knowledge, I am charmed with the prospect; but when I view you in another light, and represent you awkward, ungraceful, ill-bred, with vulgar air and manners, shambling towards me with inattention and *distractions*, I shall not pretend to describe to you what I feel; but will do as a skilful painter did formerly, draw a veil before the countenance of the father.

I dare say you know already enough of architecture to know that the Tuscan is the strongest and most solid of all the orders; but, at the same time, it is the coarsest and clumsiest of them. Its solidity does extremely well for the foundation and base floor of a great edifice; but if the whole building be Tuscan; it will attract no eyes, it will stop no passengers; it will invite no interior examination; people will take it for granted, that the finishing and furnishing cannot be worth seeing, where the front is so unadorned and clumsy. But if, upon the solid Tuscan foundation, the Doric, the Ionic, and the Corinthian orders rise gradually with all their beauty, proportions, and ornaments, the fabric seizes the most incurious eye, and stops the most careless passenger, who solicits admission as a favour, nay, often purchases it. Just so will it fare with your little fabric, which, at present, I fear, has more of the Tuscan than of the Corinthian order. You must absolutely change the whole front, or nobody will knock at the door. The several parts, which must compose this new front, are elegant, easy, natural, superior good-breeding; an engaging address; genteel motions; an insinuating softness in your looks, words, and actions; a spruce, lively air; fashionable dress; and all the glitter that a young fellow should have.

I am sure you would do a great deal for my sake; and therefore consider, at your return here, what a disappointment and concern it would be to me, if I could not safely depute you to do the honours of my house and table; and if I should be ashamed to present you to those who frequent both. Should you be awkward, inattentive, and *distrait*, and happen to meet Mr. Lyttleton at my table, the consequences of that meeting must be fatal; you would run your heads against each other, cut each other's fingers, instead of your meat, or die by the precipitate infusion of scalding soup.

This is really so copious a subject, that there is no end of being either serious or ludicrous upon it. It is impossible, too, to enumerate or state to you the various cases in good-breeding; they are infinite; there is no situation or relation in the world, so remote or so intimate, that does not require a degree of it. Your own good-sense must point it out to you; your own good-nature must incline, and your interest prompt you to practise it; and observation and experience must give you the manner, the air, and the graces, which complete the whole.

This letter will hardly overtake you till you are at or near Rome. I expect a great deal, in every way, from your six months' stay there. My morning hopes are justly placed in Mr. Harte, and the masters he will give you; my evening ones, in the Roman ladies; pray be attentive to both. But I must hint to you, that the Roman ladies are not *les femmes*

1440

savantes, et ne vous embrasseront point pour l'amour du grec.[1]
They must have *il garbato, il leggiadro, il disinvolto, il lusin-
ghiero, quel non sò che, che piace, che alletta, che incanta.*

I have often asserted, that the profoundest learning, and
the politest manners, were by no means incompatible,
though so seldom found united in the same person; and I
have engaged myself to exhibit you as a proof of the truth
of this assertion. Should you, instead of that, happen to
disprove me, the concern indeed will be mine, but the loss
will be yours. Lord Bolingbroke is a strong instance on my
side of the question; he joins, to the deepest erudition, the
most elegant politeness and good-breeding that ever any
courtier and man of the world was adorned with. And Pope
very justly called him 'all-accomplished St. John,' with
regard to his knowledge and his manners. He had, it is
true, his faults; which proceeded from unbounded ambition,
and impetuous passions; but they have now subsided by
age and experience; and I can wish you nothing better than
to be what he is now, without what he has been formerly.
His address pre-engages, his eloquence persuades, and his
knowledge informs all who approach him. Upon the whole,
I do desire, and insist, that, from after dinner till you go to
bed, you make good-breeding, address, and manners, your
serious object and your only care. Without them, you will
be nobody; with them, you may be anything.

Adieu, my dear child! My compliments to Mr. Harte.

[1]*Les Femmes Savantes* of Molière, iii. 5:
   'PHILAMINTE. Quoi! Monsieur sait du grec! Ah, permettez, de grace,
          Que pour l'amour du grec, Monsieur, on vous embrasse.'
  But HENRIETTE says to Vadius, *qui veut aussi l'embrasser,*
      'Excusez-moi, Monsieur, je n'entends pas le grec!'

No. 1672
To his Son
(*Stanhope CCIII*)

DEAR BOY,   *London,* 24 *November O.S.* 1749

Every rational being (I take it for granted) proposes to himself some object more important than mere respiration and obscure animal existence. He desires to distinguish himself among his fellow-creatures; and, *alicui negotio intentus, præclari facinoris, aut artis bonæ, famam quærit.* Cæsar,[1] when embarking in a storm, said, that it was not necessary he should live; but that it was absolutely necessary he should get to the place to which he was going. And Pliny leaves mankind this only alternative; either of doing what deserves to be written, or of writing what deserves to be read. As for those who do neither, *eorum vitam mortemque juxta æstumo; quoniam de utraque siletur.* You have, I am convinced, one or both of these objects in view; but you must know, and use the necessary means, or your pursuit will be vain and frivolous. In either case, *sapere est principium et fons*; but it is by no means all. That knowledge may be adorned, it must have lustre as well as weight, or it will be oftener taken for lead than for gold. Knowledge you have, and will have; I am easy upon that article. But my business, as your friend, is not to compliment you upon what you have, but to tell you with freedom what you want; and I must tell you plainly, that I fear you want everything but knowledge.

I have written to you so often of late upon good-breeding, address, *les manières liantes*, the Graces, etc., that I shall confine this letter to another subject, pretty near akin to them, and which, I am sure, you are full as deficient in—I mean style.

Style is the dress of thoughts; and let them be ever so just, if your style is homely, coarse, and vulgar, they will

1442   [1]Plutarch tells the story of Pompey.

appear to as much disadvantage, and be as ill received as your person, though ever so well proportioned, would, if dressed in rags, dirt, and tatters. It is not every understanding that can judge of matter, but every ear can and does judge, more or less, of style; and were I either to speak or write to the public, I should prefer moderate matter, adorned with all the beauties and elegances of style, to the strongest matter in the world, ill-worded and ill-delivered. Your business is negotiation abroad, and oratory in the House of Commons at home. What figure can you make in either case, if your style be inelegant, I do not say bad? Imagine yourself writing an office-letter to a Secretary of State, which letter is to be read by the whole Cabinet Council, and very possibly afterwards laid before Parliament; any one barbarism, solecism, or vulgarism in it would, in a very few days, circulate through the whole kingdom, to your disgrace and ridicule. For instance; I will suppose you had written the following letter from the Hague, to the Secretary of State at London; and leave you to suppose the consequences of it.

My Lord,

I *had*, last night, the honour of your Lordship's letter of the 24th; and will *set about doing* the orders contained *therein*; and *if so be* that I can get that affair done by the next post, I will not fail *for to* give your Lordship an account of it by *next post*. I have told the French Minister, *as how*, *that if* that affair be not soon concluded, your Lordship would think it *all long of him*; and that he must have neglected *for to* have wrote to his Court about it. I must beg leave to put your Lordship in mind, *as how*, that I am now full three quarters in arrear; and if *so be* that I do not very soon receive at least one half year, I shall *cut a very bad figure*; for *this here* place is very dear. I shall be *vastly beholden* to your Lordship for *that there* mark of your favour; and so I *rest*, or *remain*, Your, etc.

1443

You will tell me, possibly, that this is a *caricatura* of an illiberal and inelegant style; I will admit it; but assure you, at the same time, that a despatch with less than half these faults would blow you up for ever. It is by no means sufficient to be free from faults in speaking and writing; you must do both correctly and elegantly. In faults of this kind, it is not *ille optimus qui minimis urgetur*; but he is unpardonable who has any at all, because it is his own fault; he need only attend to, observe, and imitate the best authors.

It is a very true saying, that a man must be born a poet, but that he may make himself an orator; and the very first principle of an orator is, to speak his own language particularly, with the utmost purity and elegancy. A man will be forgiven, even great errors, in a foreign language; but in his own, even the least slips are justly laid hold of and ridiculed.

A person of the House of Commons, speaking two years ago upon naval affairs, asserted, that we had then the finest navy *upon the face of the yearth*. This happy mixture of blunder and vulgarism, you may easily imagine, was matter of immediate ridicule; but I can assure you, that it continues so still, and will be remembered as long as he lives and speaks. Another, speaking in defence of a gentleman, upon whom a censure was moved, happily said, that he thought that gentleman was more *liable* to be thanked and rewarded, than censured. You know, I presume, that *liable* can never be used in a good sense.

You have with you three or four of the best English authors, Dryden, Atterbury, and Swift: read them with the utmost care, and with a particular view to their language; and they may possibly correct that *curious infelicity of diction* which you acquired at Westminster. Mr. Harte excepted, I will admit that you have met with very few English abroad, who could improve your style; and with many, I dare say, who speak as ill as yourself, and it may be worse; you must, therefore, take the more pains, and consult your authors, and Mr. Harte, the more. I need not tell you how attentive the Romans and Greeks, particularly the Athenians, were to this object. It is also a study among the Italians and the French; witness their respective academies and dictionaries, for improving and fixing their languages. To our shame be it spoken, it is less attended to here than in any polite country; but that is no reason why you should not attend to it; on the contrary, it will distinguish you the more. Cicero says, very truly, that it is glorious to excel other men in that very article, in which men excel brutes; *speech.*

Constant experience has shown me, that great purity and elegance of style, with a graceful elocution, cover a multitude of faults, in either a speaker or a writer. For my own part, I confess (and I believe most people are of my mind) that if a speaker should ungracefully mutter or stammer out to me the sense of an angel, deformed by barbarisms and solecisms, or larded with vulgarisms, he should never speak to me a second time, if I could help it. Gain the heart, or you gain nothing; the eyes and the ears are the only roads to the heart. Merit and knowledge will not gain hearts, though they will secure them when gained. Pray have that truth ever in your mind. Engage the eyes by your address, air, and motions; soothe the ears by the elegancy and harmony of your diction; the heart will certainly follow; and the whole man, or woman, will as certainly follow the heart. I must repeat it to you, over and over again, that, with all the knowledge which you may have at present, or hereafter acquire, and with all the merit that ever man had, if you have not a graceful address, liberal and engaging manners, a prepossessing air, and a good degree of eloquence in speaking and writing, you will be nobody; but will have the daily mortification of seeing people, with not one-tenth of your merit or knowledge, get the start of you, and disgrace you both in company and in business.

You have read Quintilian; the best book in the world to form an orator: pray read Cicero, *de Oratore*; the best book in the world to finish one. Translate and retranslate, from

and to Latin, Greek, and English; make yourself a pure and
elegant English style; it requires nothing but application. I
do not find that God has made you a poet; and I am very
glad that he has not; therefore, for God's sake, make yourself an orator, which you may do. Though I still call you
boy, I consider you no longer as such; and when I reflect
upon the prodigious quantity of manure that has been laid
upon you, I expect you should produce more at eighteen,
than uncultivated soils do at eight-and-twenty.

Pray tell Mr. Harte I have received his letter of the 13th
N.S. Mr. Smith was much in the right, not to let you go, at
this time of the year, by sea; in the summer you may
navigate as much as you please: as for example; from
Leghorn to Genoa, etc. Adieu!

No. 1673

To his Son

(Stanhope CCIV)

London, 26 November O.S. 1749

DEAR BOY,

While the Roman Republic flourished, while glory was
pursued and virtue practised, and while even little irregularities and indecencies, not cognizable by law, were, however, not thought below the public care, Censors were
established, discretionally to supply, in particular cases, the
inevitable defects of the law, which must and can only be
general. This employment I assume to myself, with regard
to your little republic, leaving the legislative power entirely
to Mr. Harte. I hope and believe that he will seldom, or
rather never, have occasion to exert his supreme authority;
and I do by no means suspect you of any faults that may
require that interposition. But, to tell you the plain truth,
I am of opinion that my censorial power will not be useless
to you, nor a *sinecure* to me. The sooner you make it both,

1446

the better for us both. I can now exercise this employment
only upon hearsay, or, at most, written evidence, and therefore shall exercise it with great lenity and some diffidence;
but when we meet, and that I can form my judgment upon
ocular and auricular evidence, I shall no more let the least
impropriety, indecorum, or irregularity pass uncensured,
than my predecessor Cato did. I shall read you with the
attention of a critic, not with the partiality of an author;
different in this respect, indeed, from most critics, that I
shall seek for faults only to correct, and not to expose them.

I have often thought, and still think, that there are few
things which people in general know less, than how to love
and how to hate. They hurt those they love, by a mistaken
indulgence; by a blindness, nay, often a partiality to their
faults. Where they hate, they hurt themselves, by ill-timed
passion and rage. Fortunately for you, I never loved you
in that mistaken manner; from your infancy I made you the
object of my most serious attention, and not my plaything;
I consulted your real good, not your humours or fancies;
and I shall continue to do so while you want it, which will
probably be the case during our joint lives; for, considering
the difference of our ages, in the course of nature, you will
hardly have acquired experience enough of your own while
I shall be in a condition of lending you any of mine. People
in general will much better bear being told of their vices or
crimes than of their little failings and weaknesses. They,
in some degree, justify or excuse (as they think) the former,
by strong passions, seduction, and artifices of others; but
to be told of, or to confess, their little failings and weaknesses, implies an inferiority of parts too mortifying to that
self-love and vanity which are inseparable from our natures.
I have been intimate enough with several people to tell them
that they had said or done a very criminal thing; but I never
was intimate enough with any man to tell him, very seriously, that he had said or done a very foolish one. Nothing
less than the relation between you and me can possibly

authorise that freedom; but, fortunately for you, my parental rights, joined to my censorial powers, give it me in its fullest extent, and my concern for you will make me exert it. Rejoice, therefore, that there is one person in the world who can and will tell you what will be very useful to you to know, and yet what no other man living could or would tell you. Whatever I shall tell you of this kind, you are very sure, can have no other motive than your interest. I can neither be jealous nor envious of your reputation or your fortune, which I must be both desirous and proud to establish and promote: I cannot be your rival, either in love or in business; on the contrary, I want the rays of your rising to reflect new lustre upon my setting light. In order to this, I shall analyse you minutely, and censure you freely, that you may not (if possible) have one single spot when in your meridian.

There is nothing that a young fellow, at his first appearance in the world, has more reason to dread, and, consequently, should take more pains to avoid, than having any ridicule fixed upon him. It degrades him with the most reasonable part of mankind, but it ruins him with the rest; and I have known many a man undone by acquiring a ridiculous nick-name; I would not, for all the riches in the world, that you should acquire one when you return to England. Vices and crimes excite hatred and reproach; failings, weaknesses, and awkwardnesses excite ridicule; they are laid hold of by mimics, who, though very contemptible wretches themselves, often, by their buffoonery, fix ridicule upon their betters. The little defects in manners, elocution, address, and air (and even of figure, though very unjustly), are the objects of ridicule, and the causes of nick-names. You cannot imagine the grief it would give me, and the prejudice it would do you, if by way of distinguishing you from others of your name, you should happen to be called Muttering Stanhope, Absent Stanhope, Ill-bred Stanhope, or Awkward, Left-legged Stanhope; therefore, take great care to put it out of the power of Ridicule itself to give you any of these ridiculous epithets; for, if you get one, it will stick to you like the envenomed shirt.[1] The very first day that I see you I shall be able to tell you, and certainly shall tell you, what degree of danger you are in; and I hope that my admonitions, as censor, may prevent the censures of the public. Admonitions are always useful; is this one, or not? You are the best judge. It is your own picture which I send you, drawn at my request by a lady at Venice; pray let me know how far, in your conscience, you think it like, for there are some parts of it which I wish may, and others which I should be sorry were. I send you, literally, the copy of that part of her letter to her friend here which relates to you.

Tell Mr. Harte that I have this moment received his letter of the 22nd N.S. and that I approve extremely of the long stay you have made at Venice. I love long residences at capitals; running post through different places is a most unprofitable way of travelling, and admits of no application.
Adieu!

'Selon vos ordres, j'ai soigneusement examiné le jeune Stanhope; et je crois l'avoir approfondi. En voici le portrait que je crois très fidèle. Il a le visage joli, l'air spirituel, et le regard fin. Sa figure est à present trop carrée, mais s'il grandit, comme il en a encore et le temps et l'étoffe, elle sera bonne. Il a certainement beaucoup d'acquit, et on m'assure qu'il sait à fond les langues savantes. Pour le français, je sais qu'il le parle parfaitement bien; et l'on dit qu'il en est de même de l'allemand. Les questions qu'il fait sont judicieuses, et marquent qu'il cherche à s'instruire. Je ne vous dirai pas qu'il cherche autant à plaire; puisqu'il paraît négliger les attentions et les grâces. Il se présente mal, et n'a rien moins que l'air et la tournure aisée et noble qu'il lui faudrait. Il est vrai qu'il est encore jeune et neuf, de sorte

---

[1]Of Deianira.

qu'on a lieu d'espérer que ses exercices, qu'il n'a pas encore faits, et la bonne compagnie où il est encore novice, le décrotteront, et lui donneront tout ce qui lui manque à present. Un arrangement avec quelque femme de condition et qui a du monde, quelque Madame de Lursay,[1] est précisément ce qu'il lui faut. Enfin j'ose vous assurer qu'il a tout ce que Monsieur de Chesterfield pourrait lui souhaiter, à l'exception des manières, des grâces, et du ton de la bonne compagnie, qu'il prendra sûrement avec le temps, et l'usage du grand monde. Ce serait bien dommage au moins qu'il ne les prit point, puisqu'il mérite tant de les avoir. Et vous savez bien de quelle importance elles sont. Monsieur son père le sait aussi, les possédant lui-même comme il fait. Bref, si le petit Stanhope acquiert les grâces, il ira loin, je vous en réponds; si non, il s'arrêtera court dans une belle carrière, qu'il pourrait autrement fournir.'

You see, by this extract, of what consequence other people think these things; therefore, I hope you will no longer look upon them as trifles. It is the character of an able man to despise little things in great business; but then he knows what things are little, and what not. He does not suppose things little because they are commonly called so; but by the consequences that may or may not attend them. If gaining people's affections, and interesting their hearts in your favour, be of consequence, as it undoubtedly is, he knows very well that a happy concurrence of all these, commonly called little things, manners, air, address, graces, etc., is of the utmost consequence, and will never be at rest till he has acquired them. The world is taken by the outside of things, and we must take the world as it is; you and I cannot set it right. I know at this time a man[2] of great quality and station who has not the parts of a porter, but raised himself to the station he is in singly by having a graceful figure, polite manners, and an engaging address; which by the way he

[1] In the *Égarements du Cœur et de l'Esprit* of Crébillon fils.
[2] The Maréchal Duc de Richelieu.

only acquired by habit, for he has not sense enough to get them by reflection. Parts and habits should conspire to complete you; you will have the habit of good company, and you have reflection in your power.

No. 1674

À MADAME LA MARQUISE DE MONCONSEIL

(Maty I. xli)

À Londres, ce 4 décembre V.S. **1749**

Monsieur de Nevers, et Monsieur de Nivernais, ne se démentent ni l'un ni l'autre; il ne se peut rien de plus obligeant que la lettre du dernier au premier, que vous avez eu la bonté, Madame, de m'envoyer. Evertuez-vous, je vous en supplie, pour dire de ma part à l'un et à l'autre tout ce que je devrais leur dire à cette occasion, et que vous direz bien mieux que moi.

Dans la lettre que j'ai pris la liberté d'envoyer à Monsieur de Nivernais par votre garçon, je l'ai appelé, à la mode des Papes, mon neveu, titre qui ne dégrade pas à Rome: si après cela il découvre la petite supercherie, je me flatte qu'il ne s'en offensera pas. Il faut, comme vous le dites, ménager les préjugés établis, et c'est justement là que les petites ruses sont permises pour les éluder, puisqu'on ne doit pas espérer de les détruire. Mon neveu donc n'aura l'honneur de vous faire sa cour à Paris qu'au mois de mai en un an; c'est que je veux qu'il ait tout appris avant que d'y aller; dès qu'à cet âge on a goûté les plaisirs et la dissipation de Paris, adieu toute attention sérieuse, toute application aux études un peu difficiles. Au reste, Madame, mon voyage à Paris ne dépend aucunement du sien; au contraire, nos âges ne se conviennent pas assez pour nous y trouver ensemble, et nous y serions déplacés vis-à-vis l'un de l'autre.

Au sujet des chaises pour les goutteux, j'aurai l'honneur de vous dire qu'il y en a ici de mille différentes sortes, mais je n'en ai pas vu de la sorte dont vous parlez, qui roulent moyennant une manivelle: la meilleure que j'aie vue, c'est une chaise que feu Monsieur de Broglio avait fait venir de France, et dont il fit présent à la feue reine. L'on s'y roule soi-même, par le moyen de deux roues assex grandes, une de chaque côté, qu'on tourne très facilement des deux mains; elle sert aussi fort bien dans un jardin, où le terrain est uni; mais pas où il y a des montées et des descentes. Si, à cette description, Monsieur de Nevers croit qu'une telle chaise lui conviendra, je me ferai un véritable plaisir de lui en envoyer une. Je m'en suis acheté une en dernier lieu, ayant été enrôlé, depuis un mois, dans le nombre des goutteux. L'attaque a été courte, il est vrai, mais assez vive à la main gauche; je n'en suis nullement fâché, dans l'espérance qu'elle me garantira des autres maladies, et surtout de celles de la tête. La vieillesse commence à exiger ses droits, et j'aime mieux en payer un considérable en forme de goutte, que d'être chicané par la levée de plusieurs moindres tributs, sous les noms de migraines, vertiges, maux de cœur, langueurs, etc. À propos d'incommodités, vous en avez actuellement une, dont vous ne m'avez pas fait part, et à laquelle pourtant je m'intéresse, c'est votre grossesse. Je vous supplie de la terminer par l'heureux accouchement d'un fils, car je ne veux pas que l'esprit, et les talents, qui vous distinguent de votre sexe, tombent en quenouille. Détachez en quelque petite province pour dot à Mademoiselle votre fille; mais je veux que ce soit un fils qui hérite votre empire. Puisse-t-il vous causer le moins de douleur qu'il est possible à son début dans ce monde ici, et toute la joie qu'il est possible dans ses progrès!

No. 1675

To his Son

(*Stanhope CCV*)

London, 5 December O.S. 1749

DEAR BOY,

Those who suppose that men in general act rationally because they are called rational creatures, know very little of the world; and, if they act themselves upon that supposition, will, nine times in ten, find themselves grossly mistaken. That man is *animal bipes, implume, risibile,* I entirely agree; but, for the *rationale,* I can only allow him *in actu primo* (to talk logic), and seldom *in actu secundo.* Thus the speculative cloistered pedant in his solitary cell forms systems of things as they should be, not as they are; and writes as decisively and absurdly upon war, politics, manners and characters, as that pedant talked who was so kind as to instruct Hannibal in the art of war. Such closet politicians never fail to assign the deepest motives for the most trifling actions, instead of often ascribing the greatest actions to the most trifling causes, in which they would be much seldomer mistaken. They read and write of kings, heroes, and statesmen, as never doing anything but upon the deepest principles of sound policy. But those who see and observe kings, heroes, and statesmen, discover that they have headaches, indigestions, humours and passions, just like other people; every one of which in their turns determine their wills in defiance of their reason. Had we only read in the Life of Alexander that he burnt Persepolis, it would doubtless have been accounted for from deep policy: we should have been told, that his new conquest could not have been secured without the destruction of that capital, which would have been the constant seat of cabals, con-spiracies, and revolts. But, luckily, we are informed at the same time, that this hero, this demi-god, this son and heir

1453

of Jupiter Ammon, happened to get extremely drunk with his whore, and, by way of frolic, destroyed one of the finest cities in the world.

Read men, therefore, yourself; not in books, but in nature. Adopt no systems, but study them yourself. Observe their weaknesses, their passions, their humours; of all which their understandings are, nine times in ten, the dupes. You will then know that they are to be gained, influenced or led, much oftener by little things than by great ones; and consequently you will no longer think those things little which tend to such great purposes.

Let us apply this now to the particular object of this letter; I mean, speaking in and influencing public assemblies. The nature of our constitution makes eloquence more useful and more necessary in this country than in any other in Europe. A certain degree of good-sense and knowledge is requisite for that as well as for everything else; but beyond that, the purity of diction, the elegance of style, the harmony of periods, a pleasing elocution, and a graceful action, are the things which a public speaker should attend to the most; because his audience certainly does, and understands them the best: or rather, indeed, understands little else. The late Lord Chancellor Cowper's[1] strength, as an orator, lay by no means in his reasonings, for he often hazarded very weak ones. But such was the purity and elegance of his style, such the propriety and charms of his elocution, and such the gracefulness of his action, that he never spoke without universal applause: the ears and the eyes gave him up the hearts and the understandings of the audience. On the contrary, the late Lord Townshend always spoke materially, with argument and knowledge, but never pleased. Why? His diction was not only inelegant, but frequently ungrammatical, always vulgar; his cadences false, his voice unharmonious, and his action ungraceful. Nobody heard him

[1]William Cowper, first Earl Cowper, d. 1723. He was one of the ruling Whigs during the reign of Queen Anne, and noted for his oratory.

with patience; and the young fellows used to joke upon him, and repeat his inaccuracies. The late Duke of Argyle,[1] though the weakest reasoner, was the most pleasing speaker I ever knew in my life; he charmed, he warmed, he forcibly ravished the audience, not by his matter certainly, but by his manner of delivering it. A most genteel figure, a graceful noble air, an harmonious voice, an elegancy of style, and a strength of emphasis, conspired to make him the most affecting, persuasive, and applauded speaker I ever saw. I was captivated like others, but when I came home and coolly considered what he had said, stripped of all those ornaments in which he had dressed it, I often found the matter flimsy, the arguments weak, and I was convinced of the power of those adventitious, concurring circumstances, which ignorance of mankind only calls trifling ones. Cicero in his book *de Oratore*, in order to raise the dignity of that profession which he well knew himself to be at the head of, asserts that a complete orator must be a complete everything, lawyer, philosopher, divine, etc. That would be extremely well, if it were possible, but man's life is not long enough; and I hold him to be the completest orator who speaks the best upon that subject which occurs; whose happy choice of words, whose lively imagination, whose elocution and action adorn and grace his matter, at the same time that they excite the attention and engage the passions of his audience.

You will be of the House of Commons as soon as you are of age; and you must first make a figure there, if you would make a figure, or a fortune, in your country. This you can never do without that correctness and elegancy in your own language, which you now seem to neglect, and which you have entirely to learn. Fortunately for you, it is to be learned. Care and observation will do it; but do not flatter yourself, that all the knowledge, sense, and reasoning

---

[1] John Campbell, the second and celebrated Duke (1678-1743), of whom Thomson says:
'from his rich tongue
Persuasion flows and wins the high debate.'

in the world will ever make you a popular and applauded speaker, without the ornaments and the graces of style, elocution, and action. Sense and argument, though coarsely delivered, will have their weight in a private conversation, with two or three people of sense; but in a public assembly they will have none, if naked and destitute of the advantages I have mentioned. Cardinal de Retz observes, very justly, that every numerous assembly is mob, influenced by their passions, humours, and affections, which nothing but eloquence ever did, or ever can engage. This is so important a consideration for everybody in this country, and more particularly for you, that I earnestly recommend it to your most serious care and attention. Mind your diction, in whatever language you either write or speak; contract a habit of correctness and elegance. Consider your style, even in the freest conversation, and most familiar letters. After, at least, if not before you have said a thing, reflect if you could not have said it better. Where you doubt of the propriety or elegancy of a word or a phrase, consult some good dead or living authority in that language. Use yourself to translate from various languages into English; correct those translations till they satisfy your ear, as well as your understanding. And be convinced of this truth, That the best sense and reason in the world will be as unwelcome in a public assembly, without these ornaments, as they will in public companies, without the assistance of manners and politeness. If you will please people, you must please them in their own way; and as you cannot make them what they should be, you must take them as they are. I repeat it again, they are only to be taken by *agréments*, and by what flatters their senses and their hearts. Rabelais first wrote a most excellent book, which nobody liked; then, determined to conform to the public taste,[1] he wrote *Gargantua and Pantagruel*, which everybody liked, extravagant as it was. Adieu!

[1]This was the usual legend. But as Rabelais's first books were translations of medical treatises, such as those of Hippocrates and Galen, it is hardly likely that he expected them to be popular.

No. 1676

To his Son

(*Stanhope CCVI*)

London, 9 December O.S. 1749

Dear Boy,

It is now above forty years since I have never spoken nor written one single word, without giving myself at least one moment's time to consider, whether it was a good one or a bad one, and whether I could not find out a better in its place. An unharmonious and rugged period, at this time, shocks my ears; and I, like all the rest of the world, will willingly exchange, and give up some degree of rough sense, for a good degree of pleasing sound. I will freely and truly own to you, without either vanity or false modesty, that whatever reputation I have acquired as a speaker, is more owing to my constant attention to my diction, than to my matter, which was necessarily just the same as other people's. When you come into Parliament, your reputation as a speaker will depend much more upon your words, and your periods, than upon the subject. The same matter occurs equally to everybody of common sense, upon the same question; the dressing it well, is what excites the attention and admiration of the audience.

It is in Parliament that I have set my heart upon your making a figure; it is there that I want to have you justly proud of yourself, and to make me justly proud of you. This means that you must be a good speaker there; I use the word *must*, because I know you may if you will. The vulgar, who are always mistaken, look upon a speaker and a comet with the same astonishment and admiration, taking them both for preternatural phenomena. This error dis- courages many young men from attempting that character ; and good speakers are willing to have their talent considered as something very extraordinary, if not a peculiar gift of God

to His elect. But let you and I [*sic*][1] analyse and simplify
this good speaker; let us strip him of those adventitious
plumes, with which his own pride, and the ignorance of
others have decked him, and we shall find the true definition
of him to be no more than this: A man of good common
sense, who reasons justly, and expresses himself elegantly
on that subject upon which he speaks. There is, surely, no
witchcraft in this. A man of sense, without a superior and
astonishing degree of parts, will not talk nonsense upon
any subject; nor will he, if he has the least taste or application, talk inelegantly. What then does all this mighty art
and mystery of speaking in Parliament amount to? Why,
no more than this, That the man who speaks in the House of
Commons, speaks in that House, and to four hundred
people, that opinion, upon a given subject, which he would
make no difficulty of speaking in any house in England,
round the fire, or at table, to any fourteen people whatsoever; better judges, perhaps, and severer critics of what he
says, than any fourteen gentlemen of the House of
Commons.

I have spoken frequently in Parliament, and not always
without some applause; and therefore I can assure you,
from my experience, that there is very little in it. The
elegancy of the style, and the turn of the periods, make the
chief impression upon the hearers. Give them but one or
two round and harmonious periods in a speech, which they
will retain and repeat, and they will go home as well
satisfied, as people do from an opera, humming all the way
one or two favourite tunes that have struck their ears and
were easily caught. Most people have ears, but few have
judgment; tickle those ears, and, depend upon it, you will
catch their judgments, such as they are.

Cicero, conscious that he was at the top of his profession
(for in his time Eloquence was a profession), in order to set
himself off, defines, in his Treatise *de Oratore*, an orator to

[1]Chesterfield nearly always writes this.

be such a man as never was, or never will be; and by this fallacious argument, says, that he must know every art and science whatsoever, or how shall he speak upon them? But with submission to so great an authority, my definition of an orator is extremely different from, and, I believe, much truer than his. I call that man an orator, who reasons justly, and expresses himself elegantly upon whatever subject he treats. Problems in geometry, equations in algebra, processes in chemistry, and experiments in anatomy, are never, that I have heard of, the objects of eloquence; and therefore I humbly conceive, that a man may be a very fine speaker, and yet know nothing of geometry, algebra, chemistry, or anatomy. The subjects of all Parliamentary debates, are subjects of common sense singly.

Thus I write whatever occurs to me, that I may contribute either to form or inform you. May my labour not be in vain! and it will not, if you will but have half the concern for yourself, that I have for you. Adieu!

No. 1677

TO HIS SON

(*Stanhope CCVII*)

London, 12 *December O.S.* 1749

DEAR BOY,

Lord Clarendon, in his History, says of Mr. John Hampden, *that he had a head to contrive, a tongue to persuade, and a hand to execute, any mischief.* I shall not now enter into the justness of this character of Mr. Hampden, to whose brave stand against the illegal demand of Ship-money, we owe our present liberties; but I mention it to you as the character, which, with the alteration of one single word, *good*, instead of *mischief,* I would have you aspire to, and use your utmost endeavours to deserve. The head to contrive, God must to a certain degree have given you; but it is in your own power greatly to improve it, by study, observation, and reflection. As for the *tongue to persuade*, it wholly depends upon yourself; and without it the best head will contrive to very little purpose. The hand to execute, depends likewise, in my opinion, in a great measure upon yourself. Serious reflection will always give courage in a good cause; and the courage arising from reflection is of a much superior nature to the animal and constitutional courage of a foot-soldier. The former is steady and un-shaken, where the *nodus* is *dignus vindice*; the latter is oftener improperly than properly exerted, but always brutally.

The second member of my text (to speak ecclesiastically) shall be the subject of my following discourse; *the tongue to persuade*. As judicious preachers recommend those virtues, which they think their several audiences want the most: such as truth and continence, at Court; disinterestedness, in the city; and sobriety in the country.

You must certainly, in the course of your little experience, have felt the different effects of elegant and inelegant speak-ing. Do you not suffer, when people accost you in a stammering or hesitating manner; in an untuneful voice, with false accents and cadences;[1] puzzling and blundering through solecisms, barbarisms, and vulgarisms; mis-placing even their bad words, and inverting all method? Does not this prejudice you against their matter, be it what it will? nay, even against their persons? I am sure it does me. On the other hand, Do you not feel yourself inclined, pre-possessed, nay, even engaged in favour of those who address you in the direct contrary manner? The effects of a correct and adorned style, of method and perspicuity, are

[1]It may be observed, however, that the questions of what are 'false accents and cadences' in our language, appear to have been far less settled in Lord Chester-field's time than at present. Dr. Johnson says: 'When I published the plan for my dictionary, Lord Chesterfield told me that the word *great* should be pronounced so as to rhyme to *state*, and Sir William Yonge sent me word, that it should be pronounced so as to rhyme to *seat*, and that none but an Irishman would pro-nounce it *grait*. Now here were two men of the highest rank—the one the best speaker in the House of Lords, the other the best speaker in the House of Com-mons—differing entirely.'—Boswell's *Life*, Notes of 27th March 1772.—M. But that hardly affects either accent or cadence.

incredible towards persuasion; they often supply the want of reason and argument; but when used in the support of reason and argument, they are irresistible. The French attend very much to the purity and elegancy of their style, even in common conversation; insomuch, that it is a character to say of a man, *qu'il narre bien.* Their conversations frequently turn upon the delicacies of their language, and an Academy is employed in fixing it. The *Crusca,* in Italy, has the same object; and I have met with very few Italians, who did not speak their own language correctly and elegantly. How much more necessary is it for an Englishman to do so, who is to speak it in a public assembly, where the laws and liberties of his country are the subjects of his deliberation? The tongue that would persuade, there, must not content itself with mere articulation. You know what pains Demosthenes took to correct his naturally bad elocution; you know that he declaimed by the sea-side in storms, to prepare himself for the noise of the tumultuous assemblies he was to speak to; and you can now judge of the correctness and elegancy of his style. He thought all these things of consequence, and he thought right; pray do you think so too. It is of the utmost consequence to you to be of that opinion. If you have the least defect in your elocution, take the utmost care and pains to correct it. Do not neglect your style, whatever language you speak in, or whomever you speak to, were it your footman. Seek always for the best words and the happiest expressions you can find. Do not content yourself with being barely understood; but adorn your thoughts, and dress them as you would your person; which, however well proportioned it might be, it would be very improper and indecent to exhibit naked, or even worse dressed than people of your sort are.

I have sent you, in a packet which your Leipsig acquaintance, Duval, sends to his correspondent at Rome, Lord Bolingbroke's book,[1] which he published about a year ago.

[1] *Letters on the Spirit of Patriotism, and on the Idea of a Patriot King.*

I desire that you will read it over and over again, with particular attention to the style, and to all those beauties of oratory with which it is adorned. Till I read that book, I confess I did not know all the extent and powers of the English language. Lord Bolingbroke has both a tongue and a pen to persuade; his manner of speaking in private conversation is full as elegant as his writings; whatever subject he either speaks or writes upon, he adorns with the most splendid eloquence; not a studied or laboured eloquence, but such a flowing happiness of diction, which (from care perhaps at first) is become so habitual to him, that even his most familiar conversation, if taken down in writing, would bear the press, without the least correction either as to method or style. If his conduct in the former part of his life had been equal to all his natural and acquired talents, he would most justly have merited the epithet of all-accomplished. He is himself sensible of his past errors: those violent passions, which seduced him in his youth, have now subsided by age; and take him as he is now, the character of all-accomplished is more his due than any man's I ever knew in my life.

But he has been a most mortifying instance of the violence of human passions, and of the weakness of the most improved and exalted human reason. His virtues and his vices, his reason and his passions, did not blend themselves by a gradation of tints, but formed a shining and sudden contrast. Here the darkest, there the most splendid colours; and both rendered more striking from their proximity. Impetuosity, excess, and almost extravagancy, characterized not only his passions but even his senses. His youth was distinguished by all the tumult and storm of pleasures, in which he most licentiously triumphed, disdaining all decorum. His fine imagination has often been heated and exhausted with his body, in celebrating and deifying the prostitute of the night; and his convivial joys were pushed to all the extravagancy of frantic Bacchanals. These passions were never interrupted but by a stronger—ambition. The former impaired both his constitution and his character; but the latter destroyed both his fortune and his reputation.

He has noble and generous sentiments, rather than fixed, reflected principles of good-nature and friendship; but they are more violent than lasting, and suddenly and often varied to their opposite extremes, with regard to the same persons. He receives the common attentions of civility as obligations, which he returns with interest; and resents with passion the little inadvertencies of human nature, which he repays with interest too. Even a difference of opinion upon a philosophical subject would provoke, and prove him no practical philosopher at least.

Notwithstanding the dissipation of his youth, and the tumultuous agitation of his middle age, he has an infinite fund of various and almost universal knowledge, which, from the clearest and quickest conception, and happiest memory, that ever man was blessed with, he always carries about him. It is his pocket-money, and he never has occasion to draw upon a book for any sum. He excels more particularly in history, as his historical works plainly prove. The relative political and commercial interests of every country in Europe, particularly of his own, are better known to him than perhaps to any man in it; but how steadily he has pursued the latter in his public conduct, his enemies of all parties and denominations, tell with joy.

He engaged young, and distinguished himself in business; and his penetration was almost intuition. I am old enough to have heard him speak in Parliament. And I remember, that though prejudiced against him by party, I felt all the force and charms of his eloquence. Like Belial in Milton, 'he made the worse appear the better cause.' All the internal and external advantages and talents of an orator are undoubtedly his. Figure, voice, elocution, knowledge; and above all, the purest and most florid diction, with the justest

metaphors and happiest images, had raised him to the post
of Secretary at War at four-and-twenty years old, an age
at which others are hardly thought fit for the smallest
employments.

During his long exile in France, he applied himself to
study with his characteristic ardour; and there he formed
and chiefly executed the plan of a great philosophical work.
The common bounds of human knowledge are too narrow
for his warm and aspiring imagination. He must go *extra
flammantia mœnia mundi*,[1] and explore the unknown and
unknowable regions of metaphysics, which open an unbounded field for the excursions of an ardent imagination,
where endless conjectures supply the defect of unattainable
knowledge, and too often usurp both its name and its
influence.

He has had a very handsome person, with a most engaging address in his air and manners; he has all the dignity
and good-breeding which a man of quality should or can
have, and which so few, in this country at least, really have.

He professed himself a Deist, believing in a general
Providence, but doubting of, though by no means rejecting
(as is commonly supposed) the immortality of the soul, and
a future state.

Upon the whole, of this extraordinary man, what can we
say, but—Alas! poor human nature![2]

In your destination, you will have frequent occasions to
speak in public; to princes and states abroad; to the House
of Commons, at home; judge then, whether eloquence is
necessary for you or not; not only common eloquence,
which is rather free from faults, than adorned by beauties;
but the highest, the most shining degree of eloquence. For
God's sake, have this object always in your view, and in
your thoughts. Tune your tongue early to persuasion; and

[1]Lucretius, i. 72, 73.

[2]This 'Character' of Lord Bolingbroke exists in a somewhat different and differently arranged version, among the *Characters*. This part of the letter is omitted
by Mahon and Bradshaw.

let no jarring, dissonant accents ever fall from it. Contract an habit of speaking well, upon every occasion, and neglect yourself in no one. Eloquence and good breeding, alone, with an exceeding small degree of parts and knowledge, will carry a man a great way; with your parts and knowledge, then, how far will they not carry you? Adieu.

No. 1678

To his Son

(*Stanhope CCVIII*)

London, 16 December O.S. 1749

Dear Boy,

This letter will, I hope, find you safely arrived, and well settled at Rome, after the usual distresses and accidents of a winter journey; which are very proper to teach you patience. Your stay there, I look upon as a very important period of your life; and I do believe, that you will fill it up well. I hope you will employ the mornings diligently with Mr. Harte, in acquiring weight; and the evenings in the best companies at Rome, in acquiring lustre. A formal, dull father, would recommend to you to plod out the evenings, too, at home over a book by a dim taper; but I recommend to you the evenings for your pleasures, which are as much a part of your education, and almost as necessary a one, as your morning studies. Go to whatever assemblies or *spectacles* people of fashion go to, and, when you are there, do as they do. Endeavour to outshine those who shine there the most; get the *garbo*, the *gentilezza*, the *leggiadria* of the Italians; make love to the most impertinent beauty of condition that you meet with, and be gallant with all the rest. Speak Italian, right or wrong, to everybody; and if you do but laugh at yourself first for your bad Italian, nobody else will laugh at you for it. That is the only way to speak it perfectly; which I expect you will do, because I am sure you may, before you leave Rome. View the most curious remains of antiquity with a classical spirit, and they will clear up to you many passages of the classical authors; particularly the Trajan and the Antonine Columns; where you find the warlike instruments, the dresses, and the triumphal ornaments of the Romans. Buy also the prints and explanations of all those respectable remains of Roman grandeur, and compare them with the originals. Most young travellers are contented with a general view of those things, say they are very fine, and then go about their business. I hope you will examine them in a very different way. *Approfondissez* everything you see or hear; and learn, if you can, the *why* and the *wherefore*. Inquire into the meaning and the objects of the innumerable processions, which you will see at Rome at this time. Assist at all the ceremonies, and know the reason, or at least the pretences of them; and, however absurd they may be, see and speak of them with great decency. Of all things, I beg of you not to herd with your own countrymen, but to be always either with the Romans, or with the foreign Ministers residing at Rome. You are sent abroad to see the manners and characters, and learn the languages, of foreign countries; and not to converse with English, in English; which would defeat all those ends.[1] Among your graver company, I recommend (as I have done before) the Jesuits to you; whose learning and address will both please and improve you: inform yourself, as much as you can, of the history, policy, and practice of that society, from the time of its founder, Ignatius of Loyola, who was himself a madman. If you would know their morality, you will find it fully and admirably stated in *Les Lettres d'un Provincial*, by the famous Monsieur Pascal;[2] and it is a book very well worth your reading. Few people see what they see, or hear what they hear; that is, they see

[1] He develops this in an entertaining letter-article in *The World*, 19th July 1753, No. 29.

[2] Pascal's *Letters*, eighteen in number, were published the first in 23rd January, 1656, and the last, 24th March, 1657.

and hear so inattentively and superficially, that they are very little the better for what they do see and hear. This, I dare say, neither is, nor will be your case. You will understand, reflect upon, and consequently retain what you see and hear.

You have still two years good, but no more, to form your character in the world decisively; for within two months after your arrival in England, it will be finally and irrevocably determined, one way or another, in the opinion of the public. Devote, therefore, these two years to the pursuit of perfection; which ought to be everybody's object, though in some particulars unattainable: those who strive and labour the most, will come the nearest to it. But, above all things, aim at it, in the two important arts of speaking, and pleasing; without them, all your other talents are maimed and crippled. They are the wings upon which you must soar above other people; without them you will only crawl with the dull mass of mankind. Prepossess by your air, address, and manners; persuade by your tongue; and you will easily execute what your head has contrived. I desire that you will send me very minute accounts from Rome; not of what you see, but of whom you see: of your pleasures and entertainments. Tell me what companies you frequent most, and how you are received. *Mi dica anche se la lingua Italiana va bene, e se la parla facilmente ; ma in ogni caso bisogna parlarla sempre per poter alla fine parlarla bene e pulito. Le donne l'insegnano meglio assai dei maestri. Addio caro ragazzo, si ricordi del garbo, della gentilezza, e della leggiadria ; cose tante necessarie ad un cavaliere.*

No. 1679

To his Son

(*Stanhope CCIX*)

DEAR BOY,   *London,* 19 *December O.S.* 1749

The knowledge of mankind is a very useful knowledge for everybody; a most necessary one for you, who are destined to an active public life. You will have to do with all sorts of characters; you should, therefore, know them thoroughly in order to manage them ably. This knowledge is not to be gotten systematically, you must acquire it yourself by your own observation and sagacity: I will give you such hints as I think may be useful landmarks in your intended progress.

I have often told you (and it is most true) that, with regard to mankind, we must not draw general conclusions from certain particular principles, though, in the main, true ones. We must not suppose, that because a man is a rational animal, he will, therefore, always act rationally; or, because he has such or such a predominant passion, that he will act invariably and consequentially in the pursuit of it. No; we are complicated machines; and though we have one mainspring that gives motion to the whole, we have an infinity of little wheels, which, in their turns, retard, precipitate, and sometimes stop that motion. Let us exemplify: I will suppose ambition to be (as it commonly is) the predominant passion of a minister of state, and I will suppose that minister to be an able one; will he, therefore, invariably pursue the object of that predominant passion? May I be sure that he will do so and so, because he ought? Nothing less. Sickness, or low spirits, may damp this predominant passion; humour and peevishness may triumph over it; inferior passions may at times surprise it and prevail. Is this ambitious statesman amorous? indiscreet and unguarded confidences, made in tender moments, to his wife or his mistress, may defeat all his schemes. Is he avaricious? some great lucrative object suddenly presenting itself may unravel all the work of his ambition. Is he passionate? contradiction and provocation (sometimes, it may be, too, artfully intended) may extort rash and inconsiderate expressions, or actions, destructive of his main object. Is he vain and open to flattery? an artful flattering favourite may mislead him; and even laziness may, at certain moments, make him neglect or omit

1468

the necessary steps to that height which he wants to arrive at. Seek first, then, for the predominant passion of the character which you mean to engage and influence, and address yourself to it; but without defying or despising the inferior passions; get them in your interest too, for now and then they will have their turns. In many cases you may not have it in your power to contribute to the gratification of the prevailing passion; then take the next best to your aid. There are many avenues to every man, and when you cannot get at him through the great one, try the serpentine ones, and you will arrive at last.

There are two inconsistent passions, which, however, frequently accompany each other, like man and wife; and which, like man and wife too, are commonly clogs upon each other. I mean ambition and avarice: the latter is often the true cause of the former; and then is the predominant passion. It seems to have been so in Cardinal Mazarin; who did anything, submitted to anything, and forgave anything for the sake of plunder. He loved and courted power like an usurer, because it carried profit along with it. Whoever should have formed his opinion, or taken his measures singly, from the ambitious part of Cardinal Mazarin's character, would have found himself often mistaken. Some, who had found this out, made their fortunes by letting him cheat them at play. On the contrary, Cardinal Richelieu's prevailing passion seems to have been ambition, and his immense riches only the natural consequences of that ambition gratified; and yet, I make no doubt, but that ambition has now and then its turn with the former, and avarice with the latter. Richelieu (by the way) is so strong a proof of the inconsistency of human nature, that I cannot help observing to you, that while he absolutely governed both his King and his country, and was, in a great degree, the arbiter of the fate of all Europe, he was more jealous of the great reputation of Corneille than of the power of Spain; and more flattered with being thought (what he was

1469

not) the best poet, than with being thought (what he certainly was) the greatest statesman in Europe; and affairs stood still while he was concerting the criticism upon the *Cid.* Could one think this possible if one did not know it to be true? Though men are all of one composition, the several ingredients are so differently proportioned in each individual, that no two are exactly alike; and no one at all times like himself. The ablest man will sometimes do weak things; the proudest man mean things; the honestest man ill things; and the wickedest man good ones. Study individuals then, and if you take (as you ought to do) their outlines from their prevailing passion, suspend your last finishing strokes till you have attended to and discovered the operations of their inferior passions, appetites, and humours. A man's general character may be that of the honestest man of the world: do not dispute it; you might be thought envious or ill-natured; but, at the same time, do not take this probity upon trust, to such a degree as to put your life, fortune, or reputation in his power. This honest man may happen to be your rival in power, in interest, or in love; three passions that often put honesty to most severe trials, in which it is too often cast: but first analyse this honest man yourself; and then you will be able to judge how far you may, or may not, with safety trust him.

Women are much more like each other than men; they have, in truth, but two passions, vanity and love; these are their universal characteristics. An Agrippina may sacrifice them to ambition, or a Messalina to lust, but such instances are rare; and in general, all they say and all they do tends to the gratification of their vanity or their love. He who flatters them most pleases them best; and they are most in love with him who they think is the most in love with them. No adulation is too strong for them; no assiduity too great; no simulation of passion too gross: as, on the other hand, the least word or action that can possibly be construed into a slight or contempt, is unpardonable, and never forgotten.

1470

Men are, in this respect, tender too, and will sooner forgive an injury than an insult. Some men are more captious than others; some are always wrong-headed; but every man living has such a share of vanity as to be hurt by marks of slight and contempt. Every man does not pretend to be a poet, a mathematician, or a statesman, and considered as such; but every man pretends to common sense, and to fill his place in the world with common decency; and consequently does not easily forgive those negligences, inattentions, and slights, which seem to call in question or utterly deny him both these pretensions.

Suspect, in general, those who remarkably affect any one virtue; who raise it above all others, and who, in a manner, intimate that they possess it exclusively. I say suspect them, for they are commonly impostors; but do not be sure that they are always so; for I have sometimes known saints really religious, blusterers really brave, reformers of manners really honest, and prudes really chaste. Pry into the recesses of their hearts yourself, as far as you are able, and never implicitly adopt a character upon common fame; which, though generally right as to the great outlines of characters, is always wrong in some particulars.

Be upon your guard against those, who, upon very slight acquaintance, obtrude their unasked and unmerited friendship and confidence upon you; for they probably cram you with them only for their own eating: but, at the same time, do not roughly reject them upon that general supposition. Examine further, and see whether those unexpected offers flow from a warm heart and a silly head, or from a designing head and a cold heart; for knavery and folly have often the same symptoms. In the first case there is no danger in accepting them, *valeant quantum valere possunt.* In the latter case it may be useful to seem to accept them, and artfully to turn the battery upon him who raised it.

There is an incontinency of friendship among young fellows, who are associated by their mutual pleasures only, which has, very frequently, bad consequences. A parcel of warm hearts and inexperienced heads, heated by convivial mirth, and possibly a little too much wine, vow, and really mean at the time, eternal friendship to each other, and indiscreetly pour out their whole souls in common, and without the least reserve. These confidences are as indiscreetly repealed as they were made: for new pleasures and new places soon dissolve this ill-cemented connection; and then very ill uses are made of these rash confidences. Bear your part, however, in young companies; nay, excel if you can in all the social and convivial joy and festivity that become youth. Trust them with your love-tales, if you please, but keep your serious views secret. Trust those only to some tried friend more experienced than yourself, and who, being in a different walk of life from you, is not likely to become your rival; for I would not advise you to depend so much upon the heroic virtue of mankind as to hope or believe that your competitor will ever be your friend, as to the object of that competition.

These are reserves and cautions very necessary to have, but very imprudent to show; the *volto sciolto* should accompany them.

No. 1680

To his Son

(*Stanhope CCX*)

DEAR BOY,   [*December* 1749]

Great talents and great virtues (if you should have them) will procure you the respect and the admiration of mankind; but it is the lesser talents, the *leniores virtutes*, which must procure you their love and affection. The former, unassisted and unadorned by the latter, will extort praise; but will at the same time excite both fear and envy; two sentiments absolutely incompatible with love and affection.

1472

Cæsar had all the great vices, and Cato all the great virtues that men could have. But Cæsar had the *leniores virtutes* which Cato wanted; and which made him beloved even by his enemies, and gained him the hearts of mankind in spite of their reason; while Cato was not even beloved of his friends, notwithstanding the esteem and respect which they could not refuse to his virtues; and I am apt to think that if Cæsar had wanted, and Cato possessed, those *leniores virtutes*, the former would not have attempted (at least with success), and the latter could have protected, the liberties of Rome. Mr. Addison, in his *Cato*, says of Cæsar (and I believe with truth),—

Curse on his virtues, they've undone his country.[1]

By which he means those lesser but engaging virtues of gentleness, affability, complaisance, and good-humour. The knowledge of a scholar, the courage of a hero, and the virtue of a Stoic, will be admired; but if the knowledge be accompanied with arrogance, the courage with ferocity, and the virtue with inflexible severity, the man will never be loved. The heroism of Charles XII of Sweden (if his brutal courage deserves that name) was universally admired, but the man nowhere beloved. Whereas Henry IV of France, who had full as much courage, and was much longer engaged in wars, was generally beloved upon account of his lesser and social virtues. We are all so formed, that our understandings are generally the dupes of our hearts, that is, of our passions; and the surest way to the former is through the latter, which must be engaged by the *leniores virtutes* alone, and the manner of exerting them. The insolent civility of a proud man is (for example), if possible, more shocking than his rudeness could be; because he shows you, by his manner, that he thinks it mere condescension in him; and that his goodness alone bestows upon you what you have no pretence to claim. He intimates his protection instead of his friendship, by a gracious nod instead of an usual bow; and

[1]Act IV. Sc. iv: to go on, 'Such popular humanity is treason. . . .'

rather signifies his consent that you may, than his invitation that you should, sit, walk, eat or drink with him.

The costive liberality of a purse-proud man insults the distresses it sometimes relieves; he takes care to make you feel your own misfortunes, and the difference between your situation and his; both which he insinuates to be justly merited: yours by your folly, his by his wisdom. The arrogant pedant does not communicate but promulgates his knowledge: he does not give it to you, but he inflicts it upon you; and is (if possible) more desirous to show you your own ignorance than his own learning. Such manners as these, not only in the particular instances which I have mentioned, but likewise in all others, shock and revolt that little pride and vanity which every man has in his heart, and obliterates in us the obligation for the favour conferred, by reminding us of the motive which produced, and the manner which accompanied it.

These faults point out their opposite perfections, and your own good sense will naturally suggest them to you.

But besides these lesser virtues, there are, what may be called the lesser talents or accomplishments, which are of great use to adorn and recommend all the greater; and the more so, as all people are judges of the one, and but few are of the other. Everybody feels the impression which an engaging address, an agreeable manner of speaking, and an easy politeness, makes upon them; and they prepare the way for the favourable reception of their betters. Adieu!

No. 1681

To his Son

(Stanhope CCXI)

MY DEAR FRIEND,   London, 26 December O.S. 1749

The new-year is the season in which custom seems more particularly to authorise civil and harmless lies, under the name of compliments. People reciprocally profess wishes, which they seldom form; and concern which they seldom feel. This is not the case between you and me, where truth leaves no room for compliments.

Dii tibi dent annos, de te nam cætera sumes, was said formerly to one by a man who certainly did not think it.[1] With the variation of one word only, I will, with great truth, say to you: I will make the first part conditional by changing, in the second, the *nam* into *si.* May you live as long as you are fit to live, but no longer! or, may you rather die before you cease to be fit to live than after! My true tenderness for you makes me think more of the manner than of the length of your life, and forbids me to wish it prolonged, by a single day, that should bring guilt, reproach, and shame upon you. I have not malice enough in my nature to wish that to my greatest enemy. You are the principal object of all my cares, the only object of all my hopes. I have now reason to believe that you will reward the former and answer the latter; in that case, may you live long, for you must live happy: *de te nam cætera sumes.* Conscious virtue is the only solid foundation of all happiness; for riches, power, rank, or whatever, in the common acceptation of the word, is supposed to constitute happiness, will never quiet, much less cure, the inward pangs of guilt. To that main wish I will add those of the good old nurse of Horace, in his *Epistle to Tibullus: Sapere,* you have it in a good degree already, *Et fari ut possit quæ sentiat.* Have you that? more, much more, is meant by it than common speech or mere articulation; I fear that still remains to be wished for, and I earnestly wish it you. *Gratia* and *fama* will inevitably accompany the above-mentioned qualifications. The *valetudo* is the only one that is not in your own power; Heaven alone can grant it you, and may it do so abundantly! As for the *mundus victus, non deficiente crumena,* do you deserve, and I will provide them.

[1]Ovid, *Epistles from Pontus,* ii. 1, 53. Quoted already, and again in letter of 1st Jan. 1753.

It is with the greatest pleasure that I consider the fair prospect which you have before you; you have seen, read, and learned more at your age than most young fellows have done at two or three-and-twenty. Your destination is a shining one, and leads to rank, fortune, and distinction; your education has been calculated for it; and, to do you justice, that education has not been thrown away upon you. You want but two things, which do not want conjuration, but only care, to acquire—eloquence and manners: that is, the graces of speech and the graces of behaviour. You may have them, they are as much in your power as powdering your hair is: and will you let the want of them obscure (as it certainly will do) that shining prospect which presents itself to you? I am sure you will not. They are the sharp end, the point, of the nail that you are driving, which must make way first for the larger and more solid parts to enter. Supposing your moral character as pure, and your knowledge as sound, as I really believe them both to be, you want nothing for that perfection which I have so constantly wished you, and taken so much pains to give you, but eloquence and politeness. A man who is not born with a poetical genius can never be a poet, or, at best, an extreme bad one; but every man who can speak at all can speak elegantly and correctly, if he pleases, by attending to the best authors and orators; and, indeed, I would advise those who do not speak elegantly not to speak at all; for I am sure they will get more by their silence than by their speech. As for politeness; whoever keeps good company and is not polite, must have formed a resolution, and taken some pains not to be so; otherwise he would naturally and insensibly acquire the air, the address, and the turn of those he converses with. You will, probably, in the course of this year, see as great a variety of good company, in the several capitals you will be at, as in any one year of your life; and consequently must (I should hope) catch some of their manners almost whether you will or not; but, as I dare say

you will endeavour to do it, I am convinced you will succeed, and that I shall have the pleasure of finding you, at
your return here, one of the best-bred men in Europe.

I imagine, that when you receive my letters, and come to
those parts of them which relate to eloquence and politeness,
you say, or at least think: What, will he never have done
upon these two subjects? Has he not said all he can say upon
them? Why the same thing over and over again? If you do
think or say so, it must proceed from your not yet knowing
the infinite importance of these two accomplishments;
which I cannot recommend to you too often, nor inculcate
too strongly. But if, on the contrary, you are convinced of
the utility, or rather the necessity, of these two accomplishments, and are determined to acquire them, my repeated
admonitions are only unnecessary; and I grudge no trouble
which can possibly be of the least use to you.

I flatter myself, that your stay at Rome will go a great
way towards answering all my views: I am sure it will, if
you employ your time, and your whole time, as you should.
Your first morning hours, I would have you devote to your
graver studies with Mr. Harte; the middle part of the day, I
would have employed in seeing things; and the evenings in
seeing people. You are not, I hope, of a lazy, inactive turn,
in either body or mind; and, in that case, the day is full long
enough for everything; especially at Rome, where it is not
the fashion, as it is here, and at Paris, to embezzle at least
half of it at table. But if, by accident, two or three hours are
sometimes wanting for some useful purpose, borrow them
from your sleep. Six, or at most seven hours' sleep is, for
a constancy, as much as you or anybody can want; more is
only laziness and dozing; and is, I am persuaded, both un-
wholesome and stupefying. If, by chance, your business, or
your pleasures, should keep you up till four or five o'clock
in the morning, I would advise you, however, to rise
exactly at your usual time, that you may not lose the
precious morning hours; and that the want of sleep may force

you to go to bed earlier the next night. This is what I was advised to do when very young, by a very wise man; and what, I assure you, I always did in the most dissipated part of my life. I have very often gone to bed at six in the morning, and rose, notwithstanding, at eight; by which means I got many hours in the morning, that my companions lost; and the want of sleep obliged me to keep good hours the next, or at least the third night. To this method I owe the greatest part of my reading; for, from twenty to forty, I should certainly have read very little, if I had not been up while my acquaintances were in bed. Know the true value of time; snatch, seize, and enjoy every moment of it. No idleness, no laziness, no procrastination; never put off till to-morrow what you can do to-day. That was the rule of the famous and unfortunate Pensionary De Witt, who, by strictly following it, found time, not only to do the whole business of the Republic, but to pass his evenings at assemblies and suppers, as if he had had nothing else to do or think of.

Adieu, my dear friend, for such I shall call you, and as such I shall, for the future, live with you. I disclaim all titles which imply an authority, that, I am persuaded, you will never give me occasion to exercise.

Multos, et felices, most sincerely, to Mr. Harte.

No. 1682

To the Bishop of Waterford

(*Maty III. xi*)

London, 28 *December* 1749

My Dear Lord,

This is to most people, and in most places, the season of lies, dignified and distinguished by the name of compliments; with me it is a season of truth, when I assure you that I wish you, and all who belong to you, whatever you wish for yourselves or for each other, more particularly health, in which nobody need be unhappy.

Though you would not tell me how soon and how generously you provided for Dr. Young's son,[1] he did, and with all the profession of gratitude which he owed you. I am as much obliged to you as he can be. I am glad that the young man has a good character, which you know I made a *conditio sine qua non* of my request; and I hope that my recommendation interfered with no views of your own in favour of any other person.

Lord Scarborough's picture will be finished this week, and sent to Mrs. Chenevix. I think it is very well done, and indeed ought to be by the time Barret[2] has taken to do it in; but he has taken it into his head, and I cannot say that I have discouraged him, that a great painter should also be a poet—that the same warmth of imagination equally forms both—and, consequently, when I expect him to bring me home a very good copy of a picture, he frequently brings an execrable copy of verses instead of it. The melon seeds shall go by the same opportunities of the picture and candlesticks; which I suppose will be time enough, since they are not to be sown till February.

I have not yet been able to get the workmen out of my house in town, and shall have the pleasure of their company some months longer. One would think that I liked them, for I am now full of them at Blackheath, where I am adding a gallery. *Il ne faut jamais faire les sottises à demi.* I am, my dear Lord,

Yours, etc.

[1]'I must observe here, that Lord Chesterfield never recommended any one to the ecclesiastical preferments in my gift, but Mr. Young. When he did, it was in the handsomest manner, by telling me twice in his letter, "Remember that I do not recommend, but if you approve of his character you will do a good-natured action." '—Note by the Bishop of Waterford.

[2]George Barret (1728-84), later Master-Painter to Chelsea Hospital.

1750

À Madame la Marquise de Monconseil

(*Maty I. xlii*)

À Londres, ce 1 janvier V.S. 1750

Ce jour-ci, qui est à Paris, à Versailles, et à Londres, la
fête des mensonges, est pour moi un jour de vérité, n'y
ayant rien de plus vrai ni de plus sincère que les vœux que
je fais pour votre santé, et pour votre bonheur—C'est là le
commencement d'une lettre de Rousseau,[1] que par hasard
je viens de lire dans le moment, et que j'adopte, Madame, du
fond de mon cœur, en vous écrivant ce premier jour de
notre année. Ces vœux, depuis que j'ai eu l'honneur de
vous connaître, n'ont jamais manqué ou de vérité, ou
d'ardeur; mais il me semble que cette année y a ajouté de la
vivacité, à cause de la situation dans laquelle elle vous trouve;
situation inquiétante pour vos amis, mais, ne vous en
déplaise, nullement ridicule pour vous. Quoi! faut-il donc
être toujours grosse, ou bien jamais grosse? ou bien, faut-il
un certain nombre de grossesses anniversaires fixé par la
mode? Que voulez-vous dire avec vos quarante-trois ans?
Est-ce que les lois de la nature, de pays, ou de la bienséance,
ont établi cette époque pour la stérilité? Au contraire, je
soutiens que votre grossesse actuelle est une grossesse de
bienséance et de devoir. Vous aviez trop peu travaillé pour
la société; vous lui deviez encore de votre race, et vous
recommencez à présent à vous acquitter de ce devoir. Je

[1]Jean Baptiste Rousseau (1671-1741); poet, playwright, epigrammatist. His
works were published in London in 1723.

vous en annonce encore quatre ou cinq de suite. Au reste,
puisque ni vous ni Mademoiselle votre fille ne voulez absolument pas que cet enfant soit un fils, en cas de ce malheur
envoyez-le-moi, je l'adopterai volontiers, et je me ferai
gloire même de dire qu'il est à moi. Ce sera un ouvrage de
réflexion, vous avez pris bien du temps à le composer, et je
passerai pour l'auteur d'un chef-d'œuvre; il y a des plagiaires
pour bien moins que cela.

Votre lettre, et celle de Monsieur de Nevers, ont fait tout
l'effet que je pouvais souhaiter auprès de Monsieur de
Nivernais, en faveur de votre élève; j'en ai reçu une lettre
avant-hier de Rome, dans laquelle il me marque que Monsieur et Madame de Nivernais l'ont accablé de politesses, et
qu'il y est comme enfant, même gâté, de la maison. S'il ne
mérite pas ces attentions, du moins il les reconnaît, et vous
en attribue une bonne moitié.

Faites-moi savoir, je vous en supplie, Madame, par deux
lignes de la main d'un valet, ou d'une fille de chambre,
votre heureux accouchement aussitôt qu'il arrivera, car en
vérité je m'intéresse trop à un moment si important pour
vous, pour en attendre la nouvelle, jusqu'à votre convalescence. Adieu, Madame, encore. *Molti e felici.*

No. 1684

To his Son

(Stanhope CCXII, and copy in Add. MSS. 5842. f 329.)

London, 8 *January O.S.* 1750

DEAR BOY,

I have seldom or never written to you upon the subject
of religion and morality: your own reason, I am persuaded,
has given you true notions of both; they speak best for
themselves; but, if they wanted assistance, you have Mr.
Harte at hand, both for precept and example; to your own

reason, therefore, and to Mr. Harte, shall I refer you, for the reality of both; and confine myself, in this letter, to the decency, the utility, and the necessity, of scrupulously preserving the appearances of both. When I say the appearances of religion, I do not mean that you should talk or act like a missionary, or an enthusiast, nor that you should take up a controversial cudgel against whoever attacks the sect you are of; this would be both useless and unbecoming your age; but I mean that you should by no means seem to approve, encourage, or applaud, those libertine notions, which strike at religions equally, and which are the poor threadbare topics of half-wits, and minute philosophers. Even those who are silly enough to laugh at their jokes, are still wise enough to distrust and detest their characters; for, putting moral virtues at the highest, and religion at the lowest, religion must still be allowed to be a collateral security, at least, to virtue; and every prudent man will sooner trust to two securities than to one. Whenever, therefore, you happen to be in company with those pretended *esprits forts*, or with thoughtless libertines, who laugh at all religion, to show their wit, or disclaim it, to complete their riot; let no word or look of yours intimate the least approbation; on the contrary, let a silent gravity express your dislike; but enter not into the subject, and decline such unprofitable and indecent controversies. Depend upon this truth, That every man is the worse looked upon, and the less trusted, for being thought to have no religion; in spite of all the pompous and specious epithets he may assume, of *esprit fort*, freethinker, or moral philosopher; and a wise atheist (if such a thing there is) would, for his own interest, and character in this world, pretend to some religion.

Your moral character must be not only pure, but, like Cæsar's wife, unsuspected. The least speck or blemish upon it is fatal. Nothing degrades and vilifies more, for it excites and unites detestation and contempt. There are, however, wretches in the world profligate enough to explode all notions of moral good and evil; to maintain that they are merely local, and depend entirely upon the customs and fashions of different countries: nay, there are still, if possible, more unaccountable wretches; I mean those who affect to preach and propagate such absurd and infamous notions, without believing them themselves. These are the devil's hypocrites. Avoid as much as possible the company of such people, who reflect a degree of discredit and infamy upon all who converse with them. But as you may, sometimes, by accident, fall into such company, take great care that no complaisance, no good-humour, no warmth of festal mirth, ever make you seem even to acquiesce, much less to approve or applaud, such infamous doctrines. On the other hand; do not debate, nor enter into serious argument, upon a subject so much below it: but content yourself with telling these *Apostles*, that you know they are not serious; that you have a much better opinion of them than they would have you have; and that, you are very sure, they would not practise the doctrine they preach. But put your private mark upon them, and shun them for ever afterwards.

There is nothing so delicate as your moral character, and nothing which it is your interest so much to preserve pure. Should you be suspected of injustice, malignity, perfidy, lying, etc., all the parts and knowledge in the world will never procure you esteem, friendship, or respect. A strange concurrence of circumstances has sometimes raised very bad men to high stations; but they have been raised like criminals to a pillory, where their persons and their crimes, by being more conspicuous, are only the more known, the more detested, and the more pelted and insulted. If, in any case whatsoever, affectation and ostentation are pardonable, it is in the case of morality; though, even there, I would not advise you to a pharisaical pomp of virtue. But I will recommend to you a most scrupulous tenderness for your moral character, and the utmost care not to say or do the least thing that may, ever so slightly, taint it. Show yourself, upon all occasions, the advocate, the friend, but not the bully, of Virtue. Colonel Chartres,[1] whom you have certainly heard of (who was, I believe, the most notorious blasted rascal in the world, and who had, by all sorts of crimes, amassed immense wealth), was so sensible of the disadvantage of a bad character, that I heard him once say, in his impudent profligate manner, that, though he would not give one farthing for virtue, he would give ten thousand pounds for a character; because he should get a hundred thousand by it: whereas he was so blasted that he had no longer an opportunity of cheating people. It is possible then that an honest man can neglect what a wise rogue would purchase so dear?

There is one of the vices above-mentioned, into which people of good education, and, in the main, of good principles, sometimes fall, from mistaken notions of skill, dexterity, and self-defence; I mean lying: though it is inseparably attended with more infamy and loss than any other. The prudence and necessity of often concealing the truth, insensibly seduces people to violate it. It is the only art of mean capacities, and the only refuge of mean spirits. Whereas concealing the truth, upon proper occasions, is as prudent and as innocent, as telling a lie, upon any occasion, is infamous and foolish. I will state you a case in your own department. Suppose you are employed at a foreign Court, and that the minister of that Court is absurd or impertinent enough to ask you what your instructions are, will you tell him a lie; which, as soon as found out, and found out it certainly will be, must destroy your credit, blast your character, and render you useless there? No. Will you tell him the truth then, and betray your trust? As certainly, No. But you will answer with firmness, That you are surprised at such a question; that you are persuaded he does not expect

---

[1]Francis Chartres, or Charteris (1675-1732), often lashed by Pope. The populace at his funeral caused a riot, almost tore the body out of the coffin, and cast dead dogs into the grave. Arbuthnot declared he had every vice except prodigality and hypocrisy.

an answer to it; but that, at all events, he certainly will not have one. Such an answer will give him confidence in you; he will conceive an opinion of your veracity, of which opinion you may afterwards make very honest and fair advantages. But if, in negotiations, you are looked upon as a liar, and a trickster, no confidence will be placed in you, nothing will be communicated to you, and you will be in the situation of a man who has been burnt in the cheek; and who, from that mark, cannot afterwards get an honest livelihood if he would, but must continue a thief.

Lord Bacon very justly makes a distinction between Simulation and Dissimulation, and allows the latter rather than the former; but still observes, that they are the weaker sort of politicians who have recourse to either. A man who has strength of mind, and strength of parts, wants neither of them. *Certainly* (says he) *the ablest men that ever were, have all had an openness and frankness of dealing, and a name of certainty and veracity; but then, they were like horses well-managed; for they could tell, passing well, when to stop, or turn: and at such times, when they thought the case indeed required dissimulation, if then they used it, it came to pass that the former opinion spread abroad, of their good faith and clearness of dealing, made them almost invisible.*[1]

There are people who indulge themselves in a sort of lying, which they reckon innocent, and which in one sense is so; for it hurts nobody but themselves. This sort of lying is the spurious offspring of vanity, begotten upon folly: these people deal in the marvellous; they have seen some things that never existed; they have seen other things which they never really saw, though they did exist, only because they were thought worth seeing. Has anything remarkable been said or done in any place, or in any company? they immediately present and declare themselves eye or ear witnesses of it. They have done feats themselves, un-attempted, or at least unperformed by others. They are

[1]*Essays.* 'Of Simulation and Dissimulation.'

1485

always the heroes of their own fables; and think that they gain consideration, or at least present attention, by it. Whereas, in truth, all they get is ridicule and contempt, not without a degree of distrust; for one must naturally conclude, that he who will tell any lie from idle vanity, will not scruple telling a greater for interest. Had I really seen anything so very extraordinary as to be almost incredible, I would keep it to myself, rather than, by telling it, give any one body room to doubt for one minute of my veracity. It is most certain, that the reputation of chastity is not so necessary for a woman, as that of veracity is for a man; and with reason; for it is possible for a woman to be virtuous, though not strictly chaste; but it is not possible for a man to be virtuous without strict veracity. The slips of the poor women are sometimes mere bodily frailties; but a lie in a man is a vice of the mind, and of the heart. For God's sake, be scrupulously jealous of the purity of your moral character; keep it immaculate, unblemished, unsullied; and it will be unsuspected. Defamation and calumny never attack, where there is no weak place; they magnify, but they do not create.

There is a very great difference between that purity of character, which I so earnestly recommend to you, and the stoical gravity and austerity of character, which I do by no means recommend to you. At your age, I would no more wish you to be a Cato than a Clodius. Be, and be reckoned a man of pleasure, as well as a man of business. Enjoy this happy and giddy time of your life; shine in the pleasures, and in the company of people of your own age. This is all to be done, and indeed only can be done, without the least taint to the purity of your moral character: for those mistaken young fellows, who think to shine by an impious or immoral licentiousness, shine only from their stinking, like corrupted flesh in the dark. Without this purity, you can have no dignity of character; and without dignity of character, it is impossible to rise in the world.

You must be respectable, if you will be respected. I have known people slattern away their character, without really polluting it; the consequence of which has been, that they have become innocently contemptible; their merit has been dimmed, their pretensions unregarded, and all their views defeated. Character must be kept bright, as well as clean. Content yourself with mediocrity in nothing. In purity of character, and in politeness of manners, labour to excel all, if you wish to equal many. Adieu!

No. 1685

To his Son

(*Stanhope CCXIII*)

London, 11 *January O.S.* 1750

My Dear Friend,

Yesterday I received a letter from Mr. Harte, of the 31st December N.S. which I will answer soon; and for which I desire you to return him my thanks now. He tells me two things that give me great satisfaction; one is, that there are very few English at Rome; the other is, that you frequent the best foreign companies. This last is a very good symptom; for a man of sense is never desirous to frequent those companions where he is not desirous to please, or where he finds that he displeases. It will not be expected in those companies, that at your age you should have the *garbo*, the *disinvoltura*, and the *leggiadria* of a man of five-and-twenty, who had been long used to keep the best companies; and therefore do not be discouraged, and think yourself either slighted or laughed at, because you see others, older and more used to the world, easier, more familiar, and consequently rather better received in those companies than yourself. In time your turn will come; and if you do but show an inclination, a desire to please, though you should be embarrassed, or even err in the means (which must necessarily happen to you at first), yet the will (to use a vulgar expression) will be taken for the deed; and people, instead of laughing at you, will be glad to instruct you. Good-sense can only give you the great outlines of good-breeding; but observation and usage can alone give you the delicate touches and the fine colouring. You will naturally endeavour to show the utmost respect to people of certain ranks and characters, and consequently you will show it; but the proper, the delicate manner of showing that respect, nothing but observation and time can give.

I remember, that when, with all the awkwardness and rust of Cambridge about me, I was first introduced into good company, I was frightened out of my wits. I was determined to be what I thought civil; I made fine low bows, and placed myself below everybody; but when I was spoken to, or attempted to speak myself, *obstupui, steteruntque comæ, et vox faucibus hæsit.*[1] If I saw people whisper, I was sure it was at me; and I thought myself the sole object of either the ridicule, or the censure of the whole company, who, God knows, did not trouble their heads about me. In this way I suffered, for some time, like a criminal at the bar; and should certainly have renounced all polite company for ever, if I had not been so convinced of the absolute necessity of forming my manners upon those of the best companies, that I determined to persevere, and suffer anything or everything rather than not compass that point. Insensibly it grew easier to me; and I began not to bow so ridiculously low, and to answer questions without great hesitation or stammering: if, now and then, some charitable people, seeing my embarrassment, and being *desœuvré* themselves, came and spoke to me, I considered them as angels sent to comfort me; and that gave me a little courage. I got more soon afterwards, and was intrepid enough to go up to a fine woman, and tell her that I thought it a warm day; she answered me, very civilly, that she thought so too; upon

---

[1] Virgil, *Æneid*, ii. 774.

which the conversation ceased, on my part, for some time, till she, good-naturedly resuming it, spoke to me thus: "I see your embarrassment, and I am sure that the few words you said to me cost you a great deal; but do not be discouraged for that reason, and avoid good company; we see that you desire to please, and that is the main point; you want only the manner, and you think that you want it still more than you do. You must go through your noviciate before you can profess good-breeding; and, if you will be my novice, I will present you to my acquaintance as such."

You will easily imagine how much this speech pleased me, and how awkwardly I answered it; I hemmed once or twice (for it gave me a burr in my throat) before I could tell her that I was very much obliged to her; that it was true that I had a great deal of reason to distrust my own behaviour, not being used to fine company; and that I should be proud of being her novice, and receiving her instructions. As soon as I had fumbled out this answer, she called up three or four people to her, and said: *Savez-vous* (for she was a foreigner, and I was abroad) *que j'ai entrepris ce jeune homme, et qu'il le faut rassurer? Pour moi, je crois en avoir fait la conquête, car il s'est émancipé dans le moment au point de me dire, en tremblant, qu'il faisait chaud. Il faut que vous m'aidiez à le dérouiller. Il lui faut nécessairement une passion, et s'il ne m'en juge pas digne, nous lui en chercherons quelque autre. Au reste, mon novice, n'allez pas vous encanailler avec des filles d'opéra et des comédiennes qui vous épargneront les frais et du sentiment et de la politesse, mais qui vous en coûteront bien plus à tout autre égard. Je vous le dis encore; si vous vous encanaillez vous êtes perdu, mon ami. Ces malheureuses ruineront et votre fortune, et votre santé, corromperont vos mœurs, et vous n'aurez jamais le ton de la bonne compagnie.* The company laughed at this lecture, and I was stunned with it. I did not know whether she was serious or in jest. By turns I was pleased, ashamed, encouraged, and dejected. But when I found afterwards, that both she, and those to whom she had presented me, countenanced and protected me in company, I gradually got more assurance, and began not to be ashamed of endeavouring to be civil. I copied the best manners, at first servilely, afterwards more freely, and at last I joined habit and invention.

All this will happen to you, if you persevere in the desire of pleasing, and shining as a man of the world; that part of your character is the only one about which I have at present the least doubt. I cannot entertain the least suspicion of your moral character; your learned character is out of question. Your polite character is now the only remaining object that gives me the least anxiety; and you are now in the right way of finishing it. Your constant collision with good company will, of course, smooth and polish you. I could wish that you would say, to the five or six men or women with whom you are the most acquainted, that you are sensible, that, from youth and inexperience, you must make many mistakes in good-breeding; that you beg of them to correct you, without reserve, wherever they see you fail; and that you shall take such admonitions as the strongest proofs of their friendship. Such a confession and application will be very engaging to those to whom you make them. They will tell others of them, who will be pleased with that disposition, and, in a friendly manner, tell you of any little slip or error. The Duke de Nivernais would, I am sure, be charmed, if you dropped such a thing to him; adding, that you loved to address yourself always to the best masters. Observe also, the different modes of good-breeding of several nations, and conform yourself to them respectively. Use an easy civility with the French, more ceremony with the Italians, and still more with the Germans; but let it be without embarrassment, and with ease. Bring it, by use, to be habitual to you; for, if it seems unwilling and forced, it will never please. *Omnis Aristippum decuit color, et res.* Acquire an easiness and versatility of manners, as well as of mind; and, like the chameleon, take the hue of the company you are with.

There is a sort of veteran women of condition, who, having lived always in the *grand monde*, and having possibly had some gallantries, together with the experience of five-and-twenty or thirty years, form a young fellow better than all the rules that can be given him. These women being past their bloom, are extremely flattered by the least attention from a young fellow; and they will point out to him those manners and attentions that pleased and engaged them, when they were in the pride of their youth and beauty. Wherever you go, make some of those women your friends; which a very little matter will do. Ask their advice, tell them your doubts or difficulties, as to your behaviour: but take great care not to drop one word of their experience; for experience implies age, and the suspicion of age, no woman, let her be ever so old, ever forgives.

I long for your picture, which Mr. Harte tells me is now drawing. I want to see your countenance, your air, and even your dress; the better they all three are, the better; I am not wise enough to despise any one of them. Your dress, at least, is in your own power, and I hope that you mind it to a proper degree. Yours. Adieu.

No. 1686

À Madame la Marquise de Monconseil

(*Maty I. xliii*)

À Londres, ce 18 janvier V.S. 1750

J'ai l'honneur de vous envoyer, Madame, trois ananas qui ne valent rien, premièrement parceque ce n'en est pas la saison, et ensuite parcequ'il a fallu les cueillir avant qu'ils fussent mûrs, sans quoi ils auraient été en compôte à leur arrivée à Paris. Je les envoie par un courier jusqu'à Calais, où ils seront livrés au directeur des postes, selon l'adresse que vous m'avez donnée. Comme les envies des femmes grosses se contentent plus par le nom que par le mérite des choses, j'espère que ces ananas tiendront lieu de bons, auprès de Madame la Dauphine;[1] mais le fait est qu'ils sont mauvais; la véritable saison n'est que depuis le mois de juin jusqu'à celui d'octobre.

Cette lettre, qui va par un courier, les dévancera, j'espère, assez pour vous préparer à toutes les cérémonies requises. Au moins ne croyez pas que ces ananas soient de *Babiole*, vous feriez trop de tort à mon jardinage. Les miens sont bien autre chose, mais j'ai eu ceux-ci du seul homme en Angleterre, qui les fait venir dans cette saison. Si vous me promettez d'en venir goûter à *Babiole* au mois d'août prochain, je promets de venir vous chercher à *Bagatelle* au mois de mai.

J'ai reçu la lettre du monde la plus obligeante de la part de Monsieur de Nivernais, en réponse à celle que votre élève lui a apportée de la mienne; je n'y ai pas repliqué, et cela par discrétion, puisque, fait comme il est, c'eût été lui donner la peine d'écrire encore; mais ayez la bonté d'insinuer cela auprès de Monsieur de Nevers, en même temps que vous voudrez bien l'assurer de ma parfaite reconnaissance.

Continuez, Madame, à m'honorer de vos ordres, quand je pourrai vous être bon à quelque chose, car je vous proteste que rien ne peut égaler le plaisir que j'ai à vous prouver mon attachement inviolable.

No. 1687

To his Son

(*Stanhope CCXIV*)

MY DEAR FRIEND,   *London*, 18 *January O.S.* 1750

I consider the solid part of your little edifice as so near being finished and completed, that my only remaining care

---

[1] Marie Josèphe de Saxe, mother of Louis XVI, Louis XVIII and Charles X. —M.

is about the embellishments; and that must now be your principal care too. Adorn yourself with all those graces and accomplishments, which, without solidity, are frivolous; but without which, solidity is, to a great degree, useless. Take one man, with a very moderate degree of knowledge, but with a pleasing figure, a prepossessing address, graceful in all that he says and does, polite, *liant*, and, in short, adorned with all the lesser talents; and take another man, with sound sense and profound knowledge, but without the above-mentioned advantages; the former will not only get the better of the latter, in every pursuit of every kind, but in truth there will be no sort of competition between them. But can every man acquire these advantages? I say Yes, if he please; supposing he is in a situation, and in circumstances, to frequent good company. Attention, observation, and imitation, will most infallibly do it. When you see a man, whose first *abord* strikes you, prepossesses you in his favour, and makes you entertain a good opinion of him, you do not know why: analyse that *abord*, and examine, within yourself, the several parts that compose it; and you will generally find it to be the result, the happy assemblage, of modesty unembarrassed, respect without timidity, a genteel, but unaffected attitude of body and limbs, an open, cheerful, but unsmirking countenance, and a dress, by no means negligent, and yet not foppish. Copy him, then, not servilely, but as some of the greatest masters of painting have copied others; insomuch, that their copies have been equal to the originals, both as to beauty and freedom. When you see a man, who is universally allowed to shine as an agreeable well-bred man, and a fine gentleman (as for example, the Duke de Nivernais), attend to him, watch him carefully; observe in what manner he addresses himself to his superiors, how he lives with his equals, and how he treats his inferiors. Mind his turn of conversation, in the several situations of morning visits, the table, and the evening amusements. Imitate, without mimicking him; and be

1493

his duplicate, but not his ape. You will find that he takes care never to say or do anything that can be construed into a slight, or a negligence; or that can, in any degree, mortify people's vanity and self-love; on the contrary, you will perceive that he makes people pleased with him, by making them first pleased with themselves: he shows respect, regard, esteem, and attention, where they are severally proper; he sows them with care, and he reaps them in plenty.

These amiable accomplishments are all to be acquired by use and imitation; for we are, in truth, more than half what we are, by imitation. The great point is, to choose good models, and to study them with care. People insensibly contract, not only the air, the manners, and the vices, of those with whom they commonly converse, but their virtues too, and even their way of thinking. This is so true, that I have known very plain understandings catch a certain degree of wit, by constantly conversing with those who had a great deal. Persist, therefore, in keeping the best company, and you will insensibly become like them; but if you add attention and observation, you will very soon be one of them. This inevitable contagion of company, shows you the necessity of keeping the best, and avoiding all other; for in every one, something will stick. You have hitherto, I confess, had very few opportunities of keeping polite company. Westminster school is, undoubtedly, the seat of illiberal manners and brutal behaviour. Leipsig, I suppose, is not the seat of refined and elegant manners. Venice, I believe, has done something; Rome, I hope, will do a great deal more; and Paris will, I dare say, do all that you want: always supposing, that you frequent the best companies, and in the intention of improving and forming yourself; for, without that intention, nothing will do.

I here subjoin a list of all those necessary, ornamental accomplishments (without which, no man living can either please or rise in the world) which hitherto I fear you want, and which only require your care and attention to possess.

To speak elegantly, whatever language you speak in; without which, nobody will hear you with pleasure, and, consequently, you will speak to very little purpose.

An agreeable and distinct elocution; without which nobody will hear you with patience; this everybody may acquire, who is not born with some imperfection in the organs of speech. You are not; and therefore it is wholly in your power. You need take much less pains for it than Demosthenes did.

A distinguished politeness of manners and address; which common sense, observation, good company, and imitation, will infallibly give you, if you will accept of it.

A genteel carriage, and graceful motions, with the air of a man of fashion. A good dancing master, with some care on your part, and some imitation of those who excel, will soon bring this about.

To be extremely clean in your person, and perfectly well dressed, according to the fashion, be that what it will. Your negligence of dress, while you were a schoolboy, was pardonable, but would not be so now.

Upon the whole, take it for granted, that, without these accomplishments, all you know, and all you can do, will avail you very little. Adieu!

No. 1688

To his Son

(*Stanhope CCXV*)

London, 25 January O.S. 1750

My Dear Friend,

It is so long since I have heard from you, that I suppose Rome engrosses every moment of your time; and if it engrosses it in the manner I could wish, I willingly give up my share of it. I would rather *prodesse quam conspici*. Put out your time but to good interest, and I do not desire to borrow much of it. Your studies, the respectable remains of

1495

antiquity, and your evenings' amusements, cannot, and indeed ought not, to leave you much time to write. You will probably never see Rome again; and therefore you ought to see it well now: by seeing it well, I do not mean only the buildings, statues, and paintings; though they undoubtedly deserve your attention; but I mean seeing into the constitution and government of it. But these things certainly occur to your own common sense.

How go your pleasures at Rome? Are you in fashion there; that is, do you live with the people who are? The only way of being so yourself, in time. Are you domestic enough in any considerable house to be called *le petit Stanhope?* Has any woman of fashion and good-breeding taken the trouble of abusing and laughing at you amicably to your face? Have you found a good *décrotteuse?* For these are the steps by which you must rise to politeness. I do not presume to ask if you have any attachment, because I believe you will not make me your *confident;* but this I will say eventually, that if you have one, *il faut bien payer d'attentions et de petits soins,* if you would have your sacrifice propitiously received. Women are not so much taken by beauty as men are, but prefer those men who show them the most attention.

> Would you engage the lovely fair?
>   With gentlest manners treat her;
> With tender looks and graceful air,
>   In softest accents greet her.
>
> Verse were but vain, the Muses fail,
>   Without the Graces' aid;
> The God of Verse could not prevail
>   To stop the flying maid.
>
> Attention by attentions gain,
>   And merit care by cares;
> So shall the nymph reward your pain,
>   And Venus crown your prayers.[1]

Probatum est.

[1]Verses by Lord Chesterfield himself.

A man's address and manner weighs much more with them than his beauty; and without them, the *abbati* and the *monsignori* will get the better of you. This address and manner should be exceedingly respectful, but at the same time easy and unembarrassed. Your chit-chat or *entregent* with them, neither can nor ought to be very solid; but you should take care to turn and dress up your trifles prettily, and make them every now and then convey indirectly some little piece of flattery. A fan, a ribband, or a head-dress, are great materials for gallant dissertations, to one who has got *le ton léger et aimable de la bonne compagnie.* At all events, a man had better talk too much to women than too little; they take silence for dulness, unless where they think the passion they have inspired occasions it; and in that case they adopt the notion, that

> Silence in love betrays more woe
> Than words—though ne'er so witty;
> The beggar that is dumb, we know,
> Deserves a double pity.

À propos of this subject; what progress do you make in that language in which Charles V said that he would choose to speak to his mistress?[1] Have you got all the tender diminutives in *etta*, *ina*, and *ettina*; which I presume he alluded to? You already possess, and I hope take care not to forget, that language which he reserved for his horse.[2] You are absolutely master, too, of that language in which he said he would converse with men; French. But in every language, pray attend carefully to the choice of your words and to the turn of your expression: indeed, it is a point of very great consequence. To be heard with success, you must be heard with pleasure: words are the dress of thoughts, which should no more be presented in rags, tatters, and dirt than your person should. By the way, do you mind your person and your dress sufficiently? Do you take great care of your teeth? Pray have them put in order by the best

[1]Italian.   [2]German.

operator at Rome. Are you be-laced, be-powdered, and be-feathered, as other young fellows are, and should be? At your age, *il faut du brillant, et même un peu de fracas, mais point de médiocre; il faut un air vif, aisé et noble. Avec les hommes, un maintien respectueux et en même temps respectable; avec les femmes, un caquet léger, enjoué et badin, mais toujours fort poli.*

To give you an opportunity of exerting your talents, I send you here enclosed a letter of recommendation from Monsieur Villettes to Madame de Simonetti at Milan, a woman of the first fashion and consideration there; and I shall in my next send you another from the same person to Madame Clerici at the same place. As these two ladies' houses are the resort of all the people of fashion at Milan,[1] those two recommendations will introduce you to them all. Let me know in due time if you have received these two letters, that I may have them renewed in case of accidents.

Adieu! my dear friend! study hard; divert yourself heartily: distinguish carefully between the pleasures of a man of fashion and the vices of a scoundrel: pursue the former and abhor the latter, like a man of sense.

Verses enclosed in the Letter

(Mahon, 1892 Ed. V. 417)

Wholesome Advice [to a Lady in Autumn]

Asses' milk, half a pint, take at seven or before;
Then sleep for an hour or two, and no more.
At nine stretch your arms, and oh! think, when alone
There's no pleasure in bed.—Mary, bring me my gown!
Slip on that ere you rise; let your caution be such,
Keep all cold from your breast, there's already too much;
Your pinners set right, your twitcher tied on,
Your prayers at an end, and your breakfast quite done,

---

[1] Of a shortly subsequent period, Monsieur Dutens writes: 'Il y a beaucoup de grandes maisons riches à Milan. Dans le temps que j'y étais les maisons Litta, Clerici, etc., y faisaient la première figure.'—*Mém. d'un Voyageur*, vol. i. p. 327. —M.

Retire to some author, improving and gay,
And with sense like your own, set your mind for the day.
At twelve you may walk, for at this time o' th' year,
The sun, like your wit, is as mild as 'tis clear:
But mark in the meadows the ruin of Time;
Take the hint, and let life be improved in its prime.
Return not in haste, nor of dressing take heed;
For beauty, like yours, no assistance can need.
With an appetite, thus, down to dinner you sit,
Where the chief of the feast is the flow of your wit;
Let this be indulg'd, and let laughter go round;
As it pleases your mind, to your health 'twill redound.
After dinner, two glasses at least, I approve;
Name the first to the King, and the last to your love:
Thus cheerful with wisdom, with innocence gay,
And calm with your joys gently glide through the day.
The dews of the evening most carefully shun;
Those tears of the sky for the loss of the sun.
Then in chat or at play, with a dance or a song,
Let the night, like the day, pass with pleasure along,
All cares, but of love, banish far from your mind;
And those you may end, when you please to be kind.

No. 1689

To his Son

(*Stanhope CCXVI*)

London, 5 *February O.S.* 1750

My Dear Friend,

Very few people are good economists of their fortune, and still fewer of their time; and yet of the two the latter is the most precious. I heartily wish you to be a good economist of both; and you are now of an age to begin to think seriously of these two important articles. Young people are apt to think they have so much time before them, that they may squander what they please of it, and yet have enough left; as very great fortunes have frequently seduced people to a ruinous profusion: fatal mistakes! always

1499

repented of, but always too late! Old Mr. Lowndes,[1] the famous Secretary of the Treasury in the reigns of King William, Queen Anne, and King George the First, used to say, *take care of the pence, and the pounds will take care of themselves.* To this maxim, which he not only preached but practised, his two grandsons at this time owe the very considerable fortunes that he left them.

This holds equally true as to time; and I most earnestly recommend to you the care of those minutes and quarters of hours, in the course of the day, which people think too short to deserve their attention; and yet, if summed up at the end of the year, would amount to a very considerable portion of time. For example: you are to be at such a place at twelve, by appointment; you go out at eleven to make two or three visits first; those persons are not at home; instead of sauntering away that intermediate time at a coffee-house, and possibly alone, return home, write a letter, beforehand, for the ensuing post, or take up a good book; I do not mean Descartes, Mallebranche, Locke, or Newton, by way of dipping; but some book of rational amusement; and detached pieces, as Horace, Boileau, Waller, La Bruyère, etc. This will be so much time saved, and by no means ill employed. Many people lose a great deal of time by reading, for they read frivolous and idle books; such as the absurd romances of the two last centuries, where characters that never existed are insipidly displayed, and sentiments that were never felt pompously described; the Oriental ravings and extravagances of the Arabian Nights and Mogul Tales; or the new flimsy *brochures* that now swarm in France, of Fairy Tales, *Réflexions sur le Cœur et l'Esprit, Métaphysique de l'Amour, Analyse de Beaux Sentiments;* and such sort of idle frivolous stuff, that nourishes and improves the mind just as much as whipped cream would the body. Stick to

[1]William Lowndes, who represented St. Mawes and other places. He is chiefly remarkable for his elaborate speech in the case of Ashby and White, 25th January 1704, and for his mistaken ideas as to restoring the value of the debased silver coinage in 1695.—M. See Letter to his Son of 6th November 1747.

the best established books in every language; the celebrated
poets, historians, orators or philosophers. By these
means (to use a city metaphor) you will make fifty *per cent.*
of the time of which others do not make above three or
four, or probably nothing at all.

Many people lose a great deal of their time by laziness;
they loll and yawn in a great chair, tell themselves that they
have not time to begin anything then, and that it will do as
well another time. This is a most unfortunate disposition,
and the greatest obstruction to both knowledge and business. At your age, you have no right nor claim to laziness;
I have, if I please, being *emeritus*. You are but just listed in
the world, and must be active, diligent, indefatigable. If
ever you propose commanding with dignity, you must
serve up to it with diligence. Never put off till to-morrow
what you can do to-day.

Despatch is the soul of business; and nothing contributes
more to despatch, than method. Lay down a method for
everything, and stick to it inviolably, as far as unexpected
incidents may allow. Fix one certain hour and day in the
week for your accounts, and keep them together in their
proper order; by which means they will require very little
time, and you can never be much cheated. Whatever letters
and papers you keep, docket and tie them up in their respective classes, so that you may instantly have recourse to any
one. Lay down a method also for your reading, for which
you allot a certain share of your mornings; let it be in a consistent and consecutive course, and not in that desultory and
immethodical manner, in which many people read scraps of
different authors, upon different subjects. Keep a useful and
short common-place book of what you read, to help your
memory only, and not for pedantic quotations. Never read
history without having maps, and a chronological book, or
tables, lying by you, and constantly recurred to; without
which, history is only a confused heap of facts. One
method more I recommend to you by which I have found

great benefit, even in the most dissipated part of my life; that is, to rise early, and at the same hour every morning, how late soever you may have sat up the night before. This secures you an hour or two, at least, of reading or reflection, before the common interruptions of the morning begin; and it will save your constitution, by forcing you to go to bed early, at least one night in three.

You will say, it may be, as many young people would, that all this order and method is very troublesome, only fit for dull people, and a disagreeable restraint upon the noble spirit and fire of youth. I deny it; and assert, on the contrary, that it will procure you, both more time and more taste for your pleasures; and, so far from being troublesome to you, that, after you have pursued it a month, it would be troublesome to you to lay it aside.

Business whets the appetite, and gives a taste of pleasures, as exercise does to food; and business can never be done without method; it raises the spirits for pleasures; and a *spectacle*, a ball, an assembly, will much more sensibly affect a man who has employed, than a man who has lost, the preceding part of the day; nay, I will venture to say, that a fine lady will seem to have more charms, to a man of study or business, than to a saunterer. The same listlessness runs through his whole conduct, and he is as insipid in his pleasures, as inefficient in everything else.

I hope you earn your pleasures, and consequently taste them; for, by the way, I know a great many men, who call themselves Men of Pleasure, but who, in truth, have none. They adopt other people's indiscriminately, but without any taste of their own. I have known them often inflict excesses upon themselves, because they thought them genteel; though they sat as awkwardly upon them as other people's clothes would have done. Have no pleasures but your own, and then you will shine in them. What are yours? Give me a short history of them. *Tenez-vous votre coin à table, et dans les bonnes compagnies? y brillez-vous du côté de la politesse, de l'enjouement, du badinage? Êtes-vous galant? Filez-vous le parfait amour? Est-il question de fléchir par vos soins et par vos attentions les rigueurs de quelque fière princesse?* You may safely trust me; for, though I am a severe censor of vice and folly, I am a friend and advocate for pleasures, and will contribute all in my power to yours.

There is a certain dignity to be kept up in pleasures, as well as in business. In love, a man may lose his heart with dignity; but if he loses his nose, he loses his character into the bargain. At table, a man may with decency have a distinguishing palate; but indiscriminate voraciousness degrades him to a glutton. A man may play with decency; but if he games he is disgraced. Vivacity and wit make a man shine in company; but trite jokes and loud laughter reduce him to buffoon. Every virtue, they say, has its kindred vice; every pleasure, I am sure, has its neighbouring disgrace. Mark carefully, therefore, the line that separates them, and rather stop a yard short, than step an inch beyond it.

I wish to God that you had as much pleasure in following my advice, as I have in giving it you; and you may the easier have it, as I give you none that is inconsistent with your pleasure. In all that I say to you, it is your interest alone that I consider: trust to my experience; you know you may to my affection. Adieu!

I have received no letter yet from you or Mr. Harte.

No. 1690
To his Son
(*Stanhope CCXVII*)

London, 8 *February O.S.* 1750

My Dear Friend,

You have, by this time, I hope and believe, made such a progress in the Italian language, that you can read it with ease; I mean the easy books in it: and indeed, in that, as well as in every other language, the easiest books are generally the best; for, whatever author is obscure and difficult in his own language, certainly does not think clearly. This is, in my opinion, the case of a celebrated Italian author; to whom the Italians, from the admiration they have of him, have given the epithet of *il divino*; I mean, *Dante*. Though I formerly knew Italian extremely well, I could never understand him; for which reason I had done with him, fully convinced that he was not worth the pains necessary to understand him.

The good Italian authors are, in my mind, but few; I mean authors of invention; for there are, undoubtely, very good historians, and excellent translators. The two poets worth your reading, and I was going to say, the only two, are Tasso and Ariosto. Tasso's *Gerusalemme Liberata* is altogether unquestionably a fine poem, though it has some low, and many false thoughts in it: and Boileau very justly makes it the mark of a bad taste, to compare *le clinquant du Tasse, à l'or de Virgile.*[1] The image, with which he adorns the introduction of his epic poem, is low and disgusting; it is that of a froward, sick, puking child, who is deceived into a dose of necessary physic by *du bonbon*. The verses are these:

> Così all' egro fanciul porgiamo aspersi
> Di soavil icor gli orli del vaso:
> Succhi amari ingannato intanto ei beve,
> E dall' inganno suo vita riceve.

However, the poem, with all its faults about it, may justly be called a fine one.

If fancy, imagination, invention, description, etc., constitute a poet, Ariosto is, unquestionably, a great one. His

---

[1]Satire ix. 173-176:

> *Tous les jours à la cour un sot de qualité,*
> *Peut juger de travers avec impunité;*
> *A Malherbe, à Racan, préférer Théophilé,*
> *Et le clinquant du Tasse à tout l'or de Virgile.*

Orlando, it is true, is a medley of lies and truths, sacred and profane wars, loves, enchantments, giants, mad heroes, and adventurous damsels; but then, he gives it you very fairly for what it is, and does not pretend to put it upon you for the true *épopée*, or epic poem. He says,

> Le Donne, i Cavalier, l' arme, gli amori,
> Le cortesie, l' audaci imprese, io canto.

The connections of his stories are admirable, his reflections just, his sneers and ironies incomparable, and his painting excellent. When Angelica, after having wandered over half the world alone with Orlando, pretends, notwithstanding,

> —— ch' el fior virginal cosi avea salvo,
> Come selo portò dal matern' alvo.

The author adds, very gravely,

> Forse era ver, ma non però credibile
> A chi del senso suo fosse Signore.

Astolpho's being carried to the moon, by St. John, in order to look for Orlando's lost wits, at the end of the 34th book, and the many lost things that he finds there, is a most happy extravagancy, and contains, at the same time, a great deal of sense. I would advise you to read this poem with attention. It is, also, the source of half the tales, novels, and plays that have been written since.

The *Pastor Fido* of Guarini is so celebrated, that you should read it; but in reading it, you will judge of the great propriety of the characters. A parcel of shepherds and shepherdesses, with the *true pastoral simplicity*, talk metaphysics, epigrams, *concetti*, and quibbles, by the hour, to each other.

The *Aminta del Tasso* is much more what it is intended to be, a pastoral; the shepherds, indeed, have their *concetti*, and their antitheses; but are not quite so sublime and abstracted as those in *Pastor Fido*. I think that you will like it much the best of the two.

Petrarca is, in my mind, a sing-song love-sick poet;

much admired, however, by the Italians; but an Italian, who should think no better of him than I do, would certainly say, that he deserved his *Laura* better than his *Lauro*; and that wretched quibble would be reckoned an excellent piece of Italian wit.

The Italian prose-writers (of invention I mean) which I would recommend to your acquaintance, are *Machiavelli* and *Bocaccio*; the former, for the established reputation which he has acquired, of a consummate politician (whatever my own private sentiments may be of either his politics or his morality), the latter, for his great invention, and for his natural and agreeable manner of telling his stories.

Guicciardini,[1] Bentivoglio,[2] Davila,[3] etc., are excellent historians, and deserve being read with attention. The nature of history checks, a little, the flights of Italian imaginations; which, in works of invention, are very high indeed. Translations curb them still more; and their translations of the classics are incomparable; particularly the first ten, translated in the time of Leo the Xth, and inscribed to him, under the title of the *Collana*. That original *Collana* has been lengthened since; and, if I mistake not, consists, now, of one hundred and ten volumes.

From what I have said, you will easily guess that I meant to put you upon your guard; and not to let your fancy be dazzled and your taste corrupted by the *concetti*, the quaintnesses, and false thoughts which are too much the characteristics of the Italian and Spanish authors. I think you are in no great danger, as your taste has been formed upon the best ancient models, the Greek and Latin authors of the best ages, who indulge themselves in none of the puerilities I have hinted at. I think I may say with truth, that true wit, sound taste, and good sense, are now as it were engrossed by France and England. Your old acquaintances, the

[1]Francesco Guicciardini: published his history of Italy in 20 volumes in 1534.
[2]Gui[do] Bentivoglio, Cardinal, 1579-1644.

[3]Enrico Caterina Davila, Constable of Cyprus. Published a history of the Civil Wars of France. He was murdered a year later, in 1631.

Germans, I fear, are a little below them; and your new acquaintances, the Italians, are a great deal too much above them. The former, I doubt, crawl a little; the latter, I am sure, very often fly out of sight.

I recommended to you, a good many years ago, and I believe you then read, *La Manière de Bien Penser dans les Ouvrages d'Esprit, par le Père Bouhours*; and I think it is very well worth your reading again, now that you can judge of it better. I do not know any book that contributes more to form a true taste; and you find there, into the bargain, the most celebrated passages both of the ancients and the moderns; which refresh your memory with what you have formerly read in them separately. It is followed by a book much of the same size, by the same author, entitled *Suite des Pensées Ingénieuses*.

To do justice to the best English and French authors, they have not given into that false taste; they allow no thoughts to be good that are not just and founded upon truth. The age of Louis XIV was very like the Augustan; Boileau, Molière, La Fontaine, Racine, etc., established the true and exposed the false taste. The reign of King Charles II (meritorious in no other respect) banished false taste out of England, and proscribed puns, quibbles, acrostics, etc. Since that, false wit has renewed its attacks and endeavoured to recover its lost empire, both in England and France, but without success; though I must say with more success in France than in England; Addison, Pope, and Swift having vigorously defended the rights of good sense; which is more than can be said of their contemporary French authors; who have of late had a great tendency to *le faux brillant, le rafinement, et l'entortillement*. And Lord Roscommon would be more in the right now than he was then, in saying that—

> The English bullion of one sterling line,
> Drawn to French wire, would through whole pages shine.[1]

[1] Wentworth Dillon, Earl of Roscommon, wrote in his *Essay on Translated Verse* (1684): 'The weighty bullion,' etc.

Lose no time, my dear child, I conjure you, in forming your taste, your manners, your mind, your everything; you have but two years' time to do it in; for whatever you are, to a certain degree, at twenty, you will be, more or less, all the rest of your life. May it be a long and happy one. Adieu!

No. 1691

To his Son

(Stanhope CCXVIII)

My Dear Friend,   *London, 22 February O.S.* 1750

If the Italian of your letter to Lady Chesterfield was all your own, I am very well satisfied with the progress which you have made in that language in so short a time; according to that gradation you will, in a very little time more, be master of it. Except at the French Ambassador's, I believe you hear only Italian spoken, for the Italians speak very little French, and that little generally very ill. The French are even with them, and generally speak Italian as ill; for I never knew a Frenchman in my life who could pronounce the Italian *ce ci*, or *ge gi*. Your desire of pleasing the Roman ladies will of course give you not only the desire, but the means of speaking to them elegantly in their own language. The Princess Borghese, I am told, speaks French both ill and unwillingly; and therefore you should make a merit to her of your application to her language. She is, by a kind of prescription (a longer than she would probably wish), at the head of the *beau monde* at Rome;[1] and can, consequently,

[1] A good account of the society at Rome a few years before this period is given by the President De Brosses, and another, a few years after it, by Monsieur Dutens. The former describes the Princess Borghese as 'amiable, enjouée, spirituelle, galante, et d'une figure agréable.' (*Lettres sur l'Italie*, vol. ii. p. 213, ed. 1836.) Cardinal Alexander Albani, for whom Lord Chesterfield had sent his son a letter of introduction, appears to have maintained during nearly half a century great state and hospitality, and shown especial kindness to the English. According to Dutens, 'Il disait toujours "nos bons amis, les anglais," et il m'entretenait souvent d'une idée favorite qu'il désirait fort réaliser; c'était de former une alliance entre la Cour de Londres et la Cour de Rome.'—*Mémoires*, vol. i. p. 296.—M.

establish or destroy a young fellow's fashionable character. If she declares him *amabile e leggiadro*, others will think him so, or at least, those who do not, will not dare to say so. There are in every great town some such women, whose rank, beauty, and fortune have conspired to place them at the head of the fashion. They have generally been gallant, but within certain decent bounds. Their gallantries have taught both them and their admirers good-breeding, without which they could keep up no dignity; but would be vilified by those very gallantries which put them in vogue. It is with these women, as with ministers and favourites at Court; they decide upon fashion and characters, as these do on fortunes and preferments. Pay particular court, therefore, wherever you are, to these female sovereigns of the *beau monde*; their recommendation is a passport through all the realms of politeness. But then, remember that they require minute, officious attentions. You should, if possible, guess at and anticipate all their little fancies and inclinations; make yourself familiarly and domestically useful to them, by offering yourself for all their little commissions, and assisting in doing the honours of their houses, and entering with seeming unction into all their little grievances, bustles, views; for they are always busy. If you are once *ben ficcato* at the Palazzo Borghese, you will soon be in fashion at Rome; and being in fashion will soon fashion you; for that is what you must now think of very seriously.

I am sorry that there is no good dancing-master at Rome, to form your exterior air and carriage, which, I doubt, are not yet the genteelest in the world; but you may, and I hope you will, in the mean time, observe the air and carriage of those who are reckoned to have the best, and form your own upon them. Ease, gracefulness, and dignity, compose the air and address of a man of fashion, which is as unlike the affected attitudes and motions of a *petit maître*, as it is to the awkward, negligent, clumsy, and slouching manner of a booby.

I am extremely pleased with the account Mr. Harte has given me of the allotment of your time at Rome. Those five hours every morning which you employ in serious studies with Mr. Harte are laid out with great interest, and will make you rich all the rest of your life. I do not look upon the subsequent morning hours, which you pass with your *cicerone*, to be ill-disposed of; there is a kind of connexion between them; and your evening diversions in good company are, in their way, as useful and necessary. This is the way for you to have both weight and lustre in the world; and this is the object which I always had in view in your education.

Adieu, my friend! Go on and prosper.

Mr. Grevenkop has just received Mr. Harte's letter of the 19th N.S.

No. 1692

À MADAME LA MARQUISE DE MONCONSEIL
(*Maty I. xliv*)

À Londres, ce **8** *mars V.S.* 1750

Je vous ai fait quartier, Madame, depuis quelque temps, mais, soit que vous m'en teniez compte, ou soit que vous m'en blâmiez, je n'y entre pour rien, également exempt de mérite, ou de crime. J'ai été accablé de migraines, et excédé d'affaires; d'affaires de famille j'entends, et de détails qui demandaient un arrangement, auquel je ne suis ni naturellement trop porté, ni trop propre. Mes migraines m'ont quitté, et je vous envoie les prémices d'une tête qui n'est pas encore bien rétablie; ils auront apparemment quelque goût du terroir; mais les sacrifices ont toujours été reçus plus ou moins favorablement, selon les moyens et les intentions de ceux qui les faisaient, et point sur le pied de leur valeur intrinsèque. Recevez donc, Madame, mes offrandes, quelque médiocres qu'elles soient en elles-mêmes, comme celles d'un cœur qui vous est tout dévoué.

1510

Je suis charmé d'apprendre que les ananas aient si bien réussi; mais assurément il ne leur fallait pas moins que l'envie d'une femme grosse, pour les faire trouver bons, et le goût que Madame la Dauphine y a trouvé, me paraît une preuve incontestable de sa grossesse; dans cette supposition, vous pourrez peut-être avoir sauvé à la France un Duc de Bourgogne, et je serai trop heureux d'avoir pu contribuer au mérite que vous en aurez.

J'ai parlé à —— au sujet des plans et des manuscrits de feu son oncle, mais il n'a pas voulu se prêter à la moindre communication de ces papiers. C'est un jeune homme élevé au métier des armes, entêté du mérite supérieur de son oncle, et qui croit posséder exclusivement, dans ces paperasses, des trésors immenses et uniques.

Nous avons eu ici ce matin un second tremblement de terre, plus vif encore que celui d'aujourd'hui il y a un mois. Toutes les maisons de Londres en ont été ébranlées, et quelques cheminées sont tombées; c'était à cinq heures et demie ce matin. J'étais profondément endormi, mais la force de la secousse m'a réveillé en sursaut, et j'ai cru voir le moment où je serais écrasé. L'avez-vous senti chez vous, ou avons-nous joui privativement de ce phénomène? En tout cas, j'espère qu'il ne vous aura pas effrayée dans votre situation présente; vos ouvrages méritent bien d'être portés au dernier point de perfection.

Je doute fort si j'aurai le plaisir de vous faire ma cour cette année; ce ne sera pas au moins, comme vous jugez bien, la volonté qui manquera, mais c'est que j'envisage bien des circonstances peu favorables à ce voyage. Je tâcherai pourtant de les écarter, s'il m'est possible, n'y ayant rien que je souhaite plus ardemment que le plaisir de vous assurer encore une fois en personne de la vérité de mes sentiments, et de l'attachement inviolable avec lequel je serai toujours, etc.

No. 1693

To his Son

(Stanhope CCXIX)

London, 8 *March O.S.* 1750

Young as you are, I hope you are in haste to live; by living, I mean living with lustre and honour to yourself, with utility to society, doing what may deserve to be written, or writing what may deserve to be read; I should wish both. Those who consider life in that light will not idly lavish one moment. The present moments are the only ones we are sure of, and as such the most valuable; but yours are doubly so at your age, for the credit, the dignity, the comfort, and the pleasure of all your future moments depend upon the use you make of your present ones.

I am extremely satisfied with your present manner of employing your time; but will you always employ it as well? I am far from meaning always in the same way, but I mean as well in proportion in the variation of age and circumstances. You now study five hours every morning; I neither suppose that you will, nor desire that you should, do so for the rest of your life. Both business and pleasure will justify and equally break in upon those hours; but then, will you always employ the leisure they leave you in useful studies? If you have but an hour, will you improve that hour, instead of idling it away? While you have such a friend and monitor with you as Mr. Harte, I am sure you will; but, suppose that business and situations should, in six or seven months, call Mr. Harte away from you, tell me truly, what may I expect and depend upon from you when left to yourself? May I be sure that you will employ some part of every day in adding something to that stock of knowledge which he will have left you? May I hope that you will allot one hour in the week to the care of your own affairs, to keep them in that order and method which every prudent man does?

But, above all, may I be convinced that your pleasures, whatever they may be, will be confined within the circle of good company and people of fashion? Those pleasures I recommend to you; I will promote them, I will pay for them; but I will neither pay for, nor suffer, the unbecoming, disgraceful, and degrading pleasures (they cannot be called pleasures) of low and profligate company. I confess, the pleasures of high life are not always strictly philosophical; and I believe a Stoic would blame my indulgence; but I am yet no Stoic, though turned of five-and-fifty, and I am apt to think that you are rather less so at eighteen. The pleasures of the table among people of the first fashion may indeed sometimes, by accident, run into excesses; but they will never sink into a continual course of gluttony and drunkenness. The gallantry of high life, though not strictly justifiable, carries, at least, no external marks of infamy about it. Neither the heart nor the constitution is corrupted by it; neither nose nor character lost by it; manners, possibly, improved. Play, in good company, is only play, and not gaming, not deep, and consequently not dangerous, nor dishonourable. It is only the inter-acts of other amusements.

This, I am sure, is not talking to you like an old man, though it is talking to you like an old friend. These are not hard conditions to ask of you. I am certain you have sense enough to know how reasonable they are on my part, how advantageous they are on yours; but have you resolution enough to perform them? Can you withstand the examples and the invitations of the profligate, and their infamous missionaries? For I have known many a young fellow seduced by a *mauvaise honte*, that made him ashamed to refuse. These are resolutions which you must form, and steadily execute for yourself, whenever you lose the friendly care and assistance of your *Mentor*. In the mean time, make a greedy use of him; exhaust him, if you can, of all his knowledge; and get the prophet's mantle from him, before he is taken away himself.

IV. X

You seem to like Rome. How do you go on there? Are you got into the inside of that extraordinary government? Has your Abbate Foggini[1] discovered many of those mysteries to you? Have you made an acquaintance with some eminent Jesuits? I know no people in the world more instructive. You would do very well to take one or two such sort of people home with you to dinner every day; it would be only a little *minestra* and *macaroni* the more; and a three or four hours' conversation *de suite* produces a thousand useful informations, which short meetings and snatches at third places do not admit of; and many of those gentlemen are by no means unwilling to dine *gratis*. Whenever you meet with a man eminent in any way, feed him, and feed upon him at the same time; it will not only improve you, but give you a reputation of knowledge, and of loving it in others.

I have been lately informed of an Italian book, which I believe may be of use to you, and which, I dare say, you may get at Rome; written by one Alberti, about fourscore or a hundred years ago, a thick quarto. It is a classical description of Italy; from whence, I am assured, that Mr. Addison, to save himself trouble, has taken most of his remarks and classical references.[2] I am told that it is an excellent book for a traveller in Italy.

What Italian books have you read, or are you reading? Ariosto I hope is one of them. Pray apply yourself diligently to Italian; it is so easy a language, that speaking it constantly, and reading it often, must, in six months more, make you perfectly master of it; in which case you will never forget it; for we only forget those things of which we know but little.

[1]Pietro Foggini (1713-1783): he became second librarian in the Vatican, and a member of the Pontifical Academy of History.

[2]Addison's *Remarks on Several Parts of Italy*. Macaulay: 'They abound with classical quotations happily introduced, but his quotations, with scarcely a single exception, are taken from Latin verse....'—*Essay on Addison*. Alberti's book, *Discrizione di tutta l'Italia*, was published in 1550. Addison claimed originality, either of origin or treatment, for his allusions. Sterne had much of Macaulay's idea of Addison's originality, but expresses it in terms unsuitable for reading aloud in the family circle.

But, above all things, to all that you learn, to all that you say, and to all that you do, remember to join *the Graces*. All is imperfect without them; with them, everything is at least tolerable. Nothing could hurt me more than to find you unattended by them. How cruelly should I be shocked, if, at our first meeting, you should present yourself to me without them! Invoke then, and sacrifice to them every moment; they are always kind, where they are assiduously courted. For God's sake, aim at perfection in everything; *Nil actum reputans si quid superesset agendum.* Adieu. Yours, most tenderly.

No. 1694

TO HIS SON

(Stanhope CCXX)

London, 19 *March O.S.* 1750

MY DEAR FRIEND,

I acknowledge your last letter of the 24th February N.S. In return for your earthquake, I can tell you that we have had, here, more than our share of earthquakes, for we had two very strong ones in eight-and-twenty days. They really do too much honour to our cold climate; in your warm one, they are compensated by favours from the sun, which we do not enjoy.

I did not think that the present Pope[1] was a sort of man to build seven modern little chapels at the expense of so respectable a piece of antiquity as the *Coliseum*. However, let his Holiness's taste of *virtù* be ever so bad, pray get somebody to present you to him, before you leave Rome; and without hesitation kiss his slipper, or whatever else the *étiquette* of that Court requires. I would have you see all

---

[1]Prospero Lambertini, Benedict XIV, who reigned from 1740 to 1758. Even Voltaire owns that he was 'aimé de la Chrétienté pour la douceur et la gaieté de son caractère.'—*Siècle de Louis XV*, ch. xxxvi. His chief works, *De Synodo Diœcesano*, and *De Canonizatione Sanctorum*, are still read as standard works.

those ceremonies; and I presume that you are, by this time, ready enough at Italian to understand and answer *il Santo Padre* in that language. I hope, too, that you have acquired address, and usage enough of the world, to be presented to anybody, without embarrassment or disapprobation. If that is not yet quite perfect, as I cannot suppose it is entirely, custom will improve it daily, and habit at last complete it. I have for some time told you, that the great difficulties are pretty well conquered. You have acquired knowledge, which is the *principium et fons*; but you have now a variety of lesser things to attend to, which collectively make one great and important object. You easily guess that I mean the Graces, the air, address, politeness, and, in short, the whole *tournure* and *agréments* of a man of fashion; so many little things conspire to form that *tournure*, that though separately they seem too insignificant to mention, yet aggregately they are too material, for me (who think for you down to the very lowest things) to omit. For instance: do you use yourself to carve, eat, and drink genteely, and with ease? Do you take care to walk, sit, stand, and present yourself gracefully? Are you sufficiently upon your guard against awkward attitudes, and illiberal, ill-bred, and disgusting habits; such as scratching yourself, putting your fingers in your mouth, nose, and ears? Tricks always acquired at schools, often too much neglected afterwards; but, however, extremely ill-bred and nauseous. For I do not conceive that any man has a right to exhibit, in company, any one excrement, more than another. Do you dress well, and think a little of the *brillant* in your person? That too is necessary, because it is *prévenant*. Do you aim at easy, engaging, but at the same time civil or respectful manners, according to the company you are in? These, and a thousand other things, which you will observe in people of fashion, better than I can describe them, are absolutely necessary for every man; but still more for you, than for almost any man living. The showish, the shining, the engaging parts of the char-

1516

acter of a fine gentleman, should (considering your destination) be the principal objects of your present attention.

When you return here, I am apt to think that you will
find something better to do, than to run to Mr. Osborne's
at Gray's Inn, to pick up scarce books. Buy good books,
and read them; the best books are the commonest, and the
last editions are always the best, if the editors are not blockheads; for they may profit of the former. But take care not
to understand editions and title-pages too well. It always
smells of pedantry, and not always of learning. What
curious books I have, they are indeed but few, shall be at
your service. I have some of the old Collana, and the
Macchiavel of 1550. Beware of the *bibliomanie*.

In the midst of either your studies or your pleasures,
pray never lose view of the object of your destination; I
mean the political affairs of Europe. Follow them politically,
chronologically, and geographically, through the newspapers, and trace up the facts which you meet with there to
their sources; as for example: consult the treaties of *Neustadt*
and *Abo*, with regard to the disputes, which you read of
every day in the public papers, between Russia and Sweden.
For the affairs of Italy, which are reported to be the objects
of present negotiations, recur to the Quadruple Alliance of
the year 1718, and follow them down through their several
variations to the Treaty of Aix-la-Chapelle, 1748; in which
(by the bye) you will find the very different tenures by
which the Infant Don Philip, your namesake, holds Parma
and Placentia. Consult, also, the Emperor Charles the
Sixth's Act of Cession of the kingdoms of Naples and
Sicily, in 1736. The succession to the kingdoms of Naples
and Sicily being a point, which, upon the death of the
present King of Spain, is likely to occasion some disputes,
do not lose the thread of these matters; which is carried on
with great ease, but, if once broken, is resumed with
difficulty.

Pray tell Mr. Harte that I have sent his packet to Baron

Firmian, by Count Einsiedlen, who is gone from hence this day for Germany, and passes through Vienna in his way to Italy, where he is in hopes of crossing upon you somewhere or other. Adieu, my friend!

Χαριτες, Χαριτες

No. 1695

TO LORD HUNTINGDON

(*Steuart 3*)

London, 26 March O.S. 1750

WELCOME MY DEAR LORD,

Welcome, my dear Lord, to Caen, and may half a dozen of the blithest Marquises there make you amends for the loss of Berenice. In this victory over yourself you have excelled Titus, who was not near so young when *Invitus Invitam dimisit*, and you are so likely to equal him in all other respects, that for the sake of mankind, I could almost wish you ill enough to wish you his power.

Your notion of our parties is so just that one would think you must have been concerned with them all, to know them so well; but yet as things are circumstanced here, it will be impossible for you not to adopt to a certain degree some one. In business one must have connections, and party forms those connections; the difference is that a fool embraces with zeal the errors of his party, a knave, the guilt, but a man of sense and virtue the general principle only, and therefore he adopts that party whose general principle he knows to be right.[1] The natural rights and liberty of mankind are the true objects of Whiggism, for which reason your own good sense and virtue made you adopt that party in spite of all the prejudices of a Westminster and Oxford education, but not without seeing the knavery, or

---

[1] If there are two parties, a man ought to adhere to that which he dislikes least. . . .
Most men enter into a party rashly . . . etc.—Halifax, *Political Maxims*.

the folly of most of the individuals, who either bubbled or bribed, often act directly contrary to the right principles which they profess. Cicero reckons *Idem sentire de Republica* one of the strongest bonds of friendship, but I fear that now *Idem sentire de re privata* is the strongest, if not the only cement of our political connections. Besides, the present extraordinary and disjointed state of things here (which by the way cannot last very long as it is) makes a man of fashion's first setting out in the busy world very difficult and delicate. It is upon his first setting out, that his subsequent character, and figure in a great measure depend, and I am therefore extremely glad that you have no thoughts of returning here at this time. Travel on, my dear Lord, for a couple of years more at least, and add to your own great natural and acquired talents, the languages, the characters, and the manners of those several nations of Europe with whom you may probably hereafter have a great deal to do. See with your own eyes, which is much better than reading, their constitutions, their maxims, and their manner of government. As for their histories, do not be discouraged by that imperfect memory which you complain of, read them and I will answer for your remembering whatever you ought to remember. Memory is only attention, and you will, I am sure, give attention wherever it is due. Let compilers and commentators stuff their empty heads with trifling and uninteresting facts and dates; you will distinguish which are worth retaining, those you will attend to, and those you will retain.

How long do you propose staying at Caen? Were I impertinent enough to advise, you would stay till Michaelmas next, by which time you will be so much master of the language and the exercises, that Paris, where I would wish you to pass all the next winter, would have nothing left to do but give the last finishing touches to both. While you are at Paris, I would wish you to give one hour every day to an Italian master, that you might have some knowledge of that language before you go into that country, where it is almost the only one that is spoke. If from Paris in the month of May 1751 you allot the remainder of the summer for the Provinces in your way to Italy, you may cross the Alps at a very proper season, the beginning of September, free from the heats or the snows. Can you, my dear Lord, forgive an old fellow this impertinent didactical sort of letter, which could only become him to a son of his own? Believe but one truth, and you will. I love you as well. I interest myself as tenderly in whatever concerns you, and shall be while I live with the truest esteem and affection, my dear Lord, Your most faithful humble servant,

CHESTERFIELD.

Postscript.—Lady Chesterfield charges me with her compliments and thanks to you.

No. 1696

TO HIS SON

(*Stanhope CCXXI*)

London, 29 *March O.S.* 1750

MY DEAR FRIEND,

You are now, I suppose, at Naples, in a new scene of *virtù*, examining all the curiosities of Herculaneum,[1] watching the eruptions of Mount Vesuvius, and surveying the magnificent churches and public buildings by which Naples is distinguished. You have a Court there into the bargain, which, I hope, you frequent and attend to. Polite manners, a versatility of mind, a complaisance even to enemies, and the *volto sciolto*, with the *pensieri stretti*, are only to be learned at Courts; and must be well learned by whoever would either shine or thrive in them. Though they do not change the nature, they smooth and soften the manners of

---

[1]Pompeii was not excavated until 1763, though discoveries began to be made in 1748.

mankind. Vigilance, dexterity, and flexibility supply the place of natural force; and it is the ablest mind, not the strongest body, that prevails there. Monsieur and Madame Fogliani will, I am sure, show you all the politeness of Courts; for I know no better bred people than they are. Domesticate yourself there while you stay at Naples, and lay aside the English coldness and formality. You have also a letter to Comte Mahony, whose house I hope you frequent, as it is the resort of the best company. His sister, Madame Bulkeley, is now here, and had I known of your going so soon to Naples, I would have got you, *ex abundanti*, a letter from her to her brother. The conversation of the moderns in the evening, is full as necessary for you, as that of the ancients in the morning.

You would do well, while you are at Naples, to read some very short history of that kingdom. It has had great variety of masters, and has occasioned many wars; the general history of which will enable you to ask many proper questions, and to receive useful informations in return. Inquire into the manner and form of that government; for constitution it has none, being an absolute one; but the most absolute governments have certain customs and forms, which are more or less observed by their respective tyrants. In China it is the fashion of the Emperors, absolute as they are, to govern with justice and equity; as in the other Oriental monarchies it is the custom to govern with violence and cruelty. The King of France, as absolute in fact, as any of them, is by custom only more gentle; for I know of no constitutional bar to his will. England is now the only monarchy in the world that can properly be said to have a constitution; for the people's rights and liberties are secured by laws. I cannot reckon Sweden and Poland to be monarchies, those two Kings having little more to say than the Doge of Venice. I do not presume to say anything of the constitution of the Empire to you, who are *jurisperitorum Germanicorum facile princeps.*

When you write to me, which, by the way, you do pretty seldom, tell me rather whom you see, than what you see. Inform me of your evening transactions and acquaintances; where, and how you pass your evenings; what English people you meet with, and a hint of their characters; what people of learning you have made acquaintance with; and, if you will trust me with so important an affair, what *belle passion* inflames you. I interest myself most in what personally concerns you most; and this is a very critical year in your life. To talk like a virtuoso, your canvas is, I think, a good one, and *Raphael Harte* has drawn the outlines admirably; nothing is now wanting but the colouring of Titian, and the Graces, the *morbidezza*, of Guido; but that is a great deal. You must get them soon, or you will never get them at all. *Per la lingua Italiana sono sicuro ch' ella n' è adesso professore, a segno tale ch' io non ardisca dirle altra cosa in quella lingua se non—Addio.*

No. 1697

To SOLOMON DAYROLLES, ESQ.

(*Maty II. lvi*)

London, 30 March O.S. 1750

DEAR DAYROLLES,

Your signs of life came very seasonally to convince me, that the concern you were in at leaving your *dear country*[1] had not put an end to it. I happened to relate very properly the agonies I saw you in at leaving England, in company, where a lady seemed to think that she was the cause of them. She inquired minutely into the degree and nature of them; spoke of them with tenderness and compassion, though she confessed a quarrel with you for three days before you went away, which had broke off all com-

[1]Mr. Dayrolles had been in England on leave of absence between July 1749 and March 1750. The lady is possibly Christabella Peterson, whom he married on 9th July, 1751.

munication between you. To this I answered like your godfather, that to part with her would have been sufficient cause for your grief; but to part with her offended and incensed, more than justified the despair I observed in you. I obliged her at last to confess, that she wished she had seen you the day before you went. Make your most of these informations in your next letter to her.

You found Holland just as you left it, that is to say, in the same state of insolvency and confusion. I fear it will be soon worse, if my suspicions are founded; for I have good reason to suspect, that your rulers are wild enough to think of engaging in a new war. It is now beginning in the North; and, though publicly it was discouraged, privately it is encouraged, not only in Holland, but *elsewhere.* The Czarina will, I am convinced, soon strike the first blow. The Court of Vienna hopes that the King of Prussia will strike the second, and give them a pretence to the third. If France does not interpose, the King of Prussia is demolished. If France does, it can only be by way of diversion, in falling upon the Queen of Hungary; and that will necessarily be in Flanders, which, it is *hoped* and believed, will force the Maritime Powers to take a part. Bentinck, now at Vienna, could tell us more of this, if he pleased.

I have not heard one word about Mr. Harte,[1] which makes me believe that I shall not. He shall be no loser, however, and other people no gainers, by the refusal.

Mr. Durand brought me a letter from my Baron, full of complaints of his health. Make him my compliments, and tell him that he shall hear from me soon.

On Thursday sevennight the Parliament rises; and the Tuesday following his Majesty sets out for Hanover. The Regency is at last settled, and the Duke not to be one.

Adieu, mon cher enfant; soyez persuadé que je vous aimerai toujours.

---

[1]Lord Chesterfield had lately applied to obtain for Mr. Harte a prebend of Windsor.—M.

No. 1698

To Solomon Dayrolles, Esq.

(Maty II. lvii)

London, 14 *April O.S.* 1750

Dear Dayrolles,

I could not refuse this recommendation of a *virtuosa* to a *virtuoso*. The girl is a real prodigy; but sometimes a prodigy without a puff will not do. Your hearing her once, and your puffing her afterwards, is all that she desires. The great point is to get the Princess of Orange to hear her, which she thinks will *make her fortune*. Even the great Handel has deigned to recommend her there; so that a word from your Honour will be sufficient. Adieu!

Yours faithfully.

No. 1699

À Madame la Marquise de Monconseil

(Maty I. xlv)

À Londres, ce 19 *avril V.S.* 1750

Me voici hors d'inquiétude, Madame, puisque vous voilà hors d'affaires. Vous vous étiez trop longtemps désaccoutumée d'un métier, qui demande de l'habitude pour être facile, et je vous avoue que je craignais pour vous, plus que je ne pouvais, ou que je ne voulais vous dire. Si vous comptez de continuer la fabrique des enfants, n'y mettez plus, s'il vous plaît, un si long intervalle, mais faites-les tout de suite, et surtout ayez à l'avenir un peu plus d'attention au genre masculin. Il semble que vous ne peuplez que pour les Amazones; mais je veux absolument, pour l'honneur de mon sexe, que vous nous donniez un fils qui vous ressemble. Au reste, Mademoiselle la première, dont les vœux ont été exaucés en dépit des miens, par l'arrivée de Mademoiselle la seconde, a tort, et elle regrettera, avec le temps, le succès de ses vœux, car je me trompe fort si Mademoiselle la seconde ne sera pas Mademoiselle Benjamin; au lieu qu'un frère ne l'aurait éclipsée que pour un temps, et son interposition entre elle et vous aurait bientôt fini pour l'armée ou les affaires.

Vous me reprochez mon malheur, comme s'il y avait de ma faute; cela n'est pas généreux, Madame, et je ne vous y reconnais point. Il m'est assez sensible de ne pouvoir pas avoir le bonheur de vous faire ma cour cette année, sans que vous y ajoutiez la mortification d'en soupçonner ma volonté. Pour m'en dédommager un peu, je vous enverrai un ambassadeur extraordinaire, muni de mes pleins pouvoirs, auquel je vous prie d'ajouter foi en tout ce qu'il vous dira de ma part. C'est votre élève, qui sera à Paris vers la St. Michel, établi à l'académie de La Guérinière. J'espère que son dernier séjour à Rome l'aura un peu formé, mais en tout cas je compte sur Paris, c'est-à-dire sur vous; s'il est gauche ou impoli, je vous supplie de ne lui rien passer, mais de lui en parler très sérieusement, et de temps en temps lui lâcher des traits de ridicule, qui font souvent plus d'effet sur les jeunes gens, que les remonstrances sérieuses. Je lui ai déjà fait savoir qu'il vous appartient en propre, que je vous ai transporté tous mes droits sur lui, et que son crédit et sa faveur auprès de moi dépendront uniquement des rélations que j'en recevrai de votre part. C'est un esclavage bien doux et bien utile que je lui destine; et s'il a le bon sens qu'on m'assure qu'il a, il le trouvera tel, et aura pour vous les sentiments de considération, d'estime, d'amitié, et de respect avec lesquels je vous donne actuellement le bon soir.

No. 1700

To his Son

(*Stanhope CCXXII*)

My Dear Friend,   *London, 26 April O.S.* 1750

As your journey to Paris approaches, and as that period will, one way or another, be of infinite consequence to you, my letters will henceforwards be principally calculated for that meridian. You will be left there to your own discretion, instead of Mr. Harte's; and you will allow me, I am sure, to distrust a little the discretion of eighteen. You will find in the Academy a number of young fellows much less discreet than yourself. These will all be your acquaintances; but look about you first and inquire into their respective characters, before you form any connections among them; and *cæteris paribus*, single out those of the most considerable rank and family. Show them a distinguishing attention; by which means you will get into their respective houses, and keep the best company. All those French young fellows are excessively *étourdis*; be upon your guard against scrapes and quarrels; have no corporal pleasantries with them, no *jeux de main*, no *coups de chambrière*, which frequently bring on quarrels. Be as lively as they, if you please, but at the same time be a little wiser than they. As to letters, you will find most of them ignorant; do not reproach them with that ignorance, nor make them feel your superiority. It is not their fault they are all bred up for the army; but, on the other hand, do not allow their ignorance and idleness to break in upon those morning hours which you may be able to allot to your serious studies. No breakfastings with them, which consume a great deal of time; but tell them (not magisterially and sententiously) that you will read two or three hours in the morning, and that for the rest of the day you are very much at their service. Though, by the way, I hope you will keep wiser company in the evenings.

I must insist upon your never going to what is called the English coffee-house at Paris, which is the resort of all the scrub English, and also of the fugitive and attainted Scotch and Irish: party quarrels and drunken squabbles are very frequent there; and I do not know a more degrading place in all Paris. Coffee-houses and taverns are by no means creditable at Paris. Be cautiously upon your guard against the infinite number of fine-dressed and fine-spoken *chevaliers d'industrie* and *aventuriers*, which swarm at Paris, and keep everybody civilly at arm's length, of whose real character or rank you are not previously informed. Monsieur le Comte or Monsieur le Chevalier in a handsome laced coat, *et très bien mis*, accosts you at the play, or some other public place; he conceives at first sight an infinite regard for you, he sees that you are a stranger of the first distinction, he offers you his services, and wishes nothing more ardently than to contribute, as far as may be in his little power, to procure you *les agréments de Paris*. He is acquainted with some ladies of condition, *qui préfèrent une petite société agréable, et des petits soupers aimables d'honnêtes gens, au tumulte et à la dissipation de Paris*; and he will, with the greatest pleasure imaginable, have the honour of introducing you to these ladies of quality. Well, if you were to accept of this kind offer, and go with him, you would find, *au troisième*, a handsome painted poxed strumpet, in a tarnished silver or gold second-hand robe, playing a sham party at cards for *livres* with three or four sharpers, well-dressed enough, and dignified by the titles of Marquis, Comte, and Chevalier. The lady receives you in the most polite and gracious manner, and with all those *compliments de routine* which every French woman has equally. Though she loves retirement and shuns *le grand monde*, yet she confesses herself obliged to the Marquis for having procured her so inestimable, so accomplished an acquaintance as yourself; but her concern is how to amuse you, for she never suffers play at her house for above a *livre*; if you can amuse yourself with that low play till supper, *à la bonne heure*. Accordingly you sit down to that little play, at which the good company take care that you shall win fifteen or sixteen *livres*, which gives them an opportunity of celebrating both your good luck and your good play. Supper comes up, and a good one it is, upon the strength of your being to pay for it. *La Marquise en fait les honneurs au mieux*, talks sentiments, *mœurs, et morale*; interlarded with *enjouement*, and accompanied with some oblique ogles, which bid you not despair in time. After supper, *pharaon, lansquenet*, or *quinze* happen accidentally to be mentioned; the Chevalier proposes playing at one of them for half-an-hour, the Marquise exclaims against it, and vows she will not suffer it, but is at last prevailed upon, by being assured *que ce ne sera que pour des riens*. Then the wished-for moment is come, the operation begins; you are cheated, at best, of all the money in your pocket, and if you stay late, very probably robbed of your watch and snuff-box; possibly murdered for greater security. This, I can assure you, is not an exaggerated, but a literal description of what happens every day to some raw and inexperienced stranger at Paris. Remember to receive all these civil gentlemen, who take such a fancy to you at first sight, very coldly, and take care always to be previously engaged, whatever party they propose to you.

You may happen sometimes, in very great and good companies, to meet with some dexterous gentlemen, who may be very desirous, and also very sure, to win your money if they can but engage you to play with them. Therefore, lay it down as an invariable rule never to play with men, but only with women of fashion, at low play, or with women and men mixed. But at the same time, whenever you are asked to play deeper than you would, do not refuse it gravely and sententiously, alleging the folly of staking what would be very inconvenient for one to lose, against what one does not want to win; but parry those invitations ludicrously, *et en badinant*. Say that if you were sure to lose

1528

you might possibly play, but that as you may as well win, you dread *l'embarras des richesses* ever since you have seen what an incumbrance they were to poor Harlequin, and that therefore you are determined never to venture the winning above two louis a-day: this sort of light trifling way of declining invitations to vice and folly, is more becoming your age, and at the same time more effectual than grave philosophical refusals. A young fellow who seems to have no will of his own, and who does everything that is asked of him, is called a very good-natured, but at the same time is thought a very silly, young fellow. Act wisely, upon solid principles and from true motives, but keep them to yourself, and never talk sententiously. When you are invited to drink, say you wish you could, but that so little makes you both drunk and sick, *que le jeu ne vaut pas la chandelle*.

Pray show great attention, and make your court to Monsieur de la Guérinière;[1] he is well with Prince Charles,[2] and many people of the first distinction at Paris; his commendations will raise your character there, not to mention that his favour will be of use to you in the Academy itself. For the reasons which I mentioned to you in my last, I would have you be *interne* in the Academy for the first six months; but after that, I promise you that you shall have lodgings of your own *dans un hôtel garni*, if in the meantime I hear well of you, and that you frequent, and are esteemed in, the best French companies. You want nothing now, thank God, but exterior advantages, that last polish, that *tournure du monde*, and those Graces which are so necessary to adorn and give efficacy to the most solid merit. They are only to be acquired in the best companies, and better in the best French companies than in any other. You will not want opportunities, for I shall send you letters that will establish

[1]François Robichon, Sieur de la Guérinière (d. 1751); 'l'un des hommes les plus habiles que la France ait produits dans l'art de soigner et de dresser les chevaux.' He published two works on that subject.

[2]Perhaps Prince Charles of Lorraine, brother-in-law of Maria Theresa.—M.

you in the most distinguished companies, not only of the *beau monde*, but of the *beaux esprits* too. Dedicate, therefore, I beg of you, that whole year to your own advantage and final improvement, and do not be diverted from those objects by idle dissipations, low seduction, or bad example. After that year, do whatever you please; I will interfere no longer in your conduct. For I am sure both you and I shall be safe then. Adieu.

No. 1701

To Solomon Dayrolles, Esq.

(*Mahon III. 376*)

London, 27 *April O.S.* 1750

Dear Dayrolles,

I am two letters in your debt; but as I knew that you were rambling, I did not know where to tender the payment.

By this time it is probable that you are re-established at the Hague. Had an unhappy foreigner been obliged to pass as many days at Plymouth as you passed at Calais, how admirably he would have diverted himself, and how politely he would have been received! Whereas, I dare say, you passed your time very well at Calais, in case you were not too much an Englishman to think so.

It is very true, that, after a series of difficulties, which, I believe, were never made before upon so trifling an occasion, Mr. Harte has at last got a prebend of Windsor. I am most extremely glad of it; for, that debt being now paid, I owe no man living anything. As it is necessary that he should come over here to take possession of his stall, I have directed him to bring the boy to Paris, and to fix him in La Guérinière's academy there, *pour le dégourdir, le dégraisser et le décrotter.* Some proper steps have been already taken towards that at Rome. . . .

When he arrives at Paris, I will send him a letter of recommendation *à Son Excellence Madame de Berkenroodt*; *valeat quantum*. In all events, it will be a good house for him to frequent. *Vous y mettrez du vôtre aussi, s'il vous plaît*, by writing a word or two in his favour to the lady, or her husband, or both. Pray buy me six dozen of pints of the Cape wine you mention, and have it carefully packed up, and directed *à Madame la Marquise de Monconseil, dans la rue de Verneuil, Faubourg St. Germain, à Paris*, and then send it with a note to *Messieurs Testas Père et Fils, à Amsterdam*, recommending to their care to forward it to her. Draw upon me for what more you shall disburse, than the twopence of mine now in your hands.

Comte Obdam's sale, I suppose, draws near, at which pray buy me such bustoes and vases as you shall find are universally allowed to be both antique and fine, at such rates as you shall think reasonable; in the whole, you may go as far as two hundred pounds, if the objects are curious and worth it.

Shall you not be surprised, if, at your return here, you find a *pendant* for your Rubens, full as large, and by a still greater master? I have reason to believe that will be the case, and then I shall undoubtedly have two of the most capital pictures in England of those two great masters. For the *virtuosi* here now unanimously confess that all the Rubenses in England must strike to mine.

I believe, as you say, that you found things in the United Provinces just as you left them, a great deal talked of, and nothing done. However, they would do well to consider, that, in their situation, not to advance is to go backwards. You may depend upon it, that, whatever you may have heard said to the contrary, war was the original design, and the Prussian bearskin was again scantled out upon paper; but the strong declarations, and indeed preparations, of France on one hand, and the apprehensions which Russia, on the other, had just reasons to entertain of the Turk, have respectively obliged *certain powers* to put water in their wine; and I now verily believe that the North will clear up, and settle for some time in peace.

Lord Harrington is arrived here from Ireland; bonfires were made and a thousand insults offered him at his departure.

Pray, make my compliments to my Baron, to whom I owe a letter; which I have not paid for mere want of specie. Is he got to his own house again? Surely it has undergone lustrations enough to be sufficiently purified for his reception. *La Belle Cécile se sauvera bientôt ou bien séchera sur pied pour l'amour de Monsieur le Capitaine.* Everything here is just as you left it. I am, and ever shall be so, with regard to you; *c'est tout dire; bon soir, mon enfant.*

No. 1702

To his Son

(*Stanhope CCXXIII*)

London, 30 April O.S. 1750

MY DEAR FRIEND,

Mr. Harte, who in all his letters gives you some dash of panegyric, told me in his last a thing that pleases me extremely; which was, that at Rome you had constantly preferred the established Italian assemblies, to the English conventicles set up against them by dissenting English ladies. That shows sense, and that you know what you are sent abroad for. It is of much more consequence to know the *mores multorum hominum* than the *urbes*. Pray continue this judicious conduct wherever you go, especially at Paris, where, instead of thirty, you will find above three hundred English herding together, and conversing with no one French body.

The life of *les milords anglais* is regularly, or if you will, irregularly, this. As soon as they rise, which is very late, they breakfast together, to the utter loss of two good morn-

1532

ing hours. Then they go by coachfuls to the Palais, the Invalides, and Notre Dame; from thence to the English coffee-house, where they make up their tavern party for dinner. From dinner, where they drink quick, they adjourn in clusters to the play, where they crowd up the stage, drest up in very fine clothes, very ill made by a Scotch or Irish tailor. From the play to the tavern again, where they get very drunk, and where they either quarrel among themselves, or sally forth, commit some riot in the streets, and are taken up by the watch. Those who do not speak French before they go, are sure to learn none there. Their tender vows are addressed to their Irish laundress, unless by chance some itinerant English-woman, eloped from her husband, or her creditors, defrauds her of them. Thus, they return home, more petulant, but not more informed, than when they left it; and show, as they think, their improvement, by affectedly both speaking and dressing in broken French.

Hunc tu Romane *caveto.*

Connect yourself, while you are in France, entirely with the French; improve yourself with the old, divert yourself with the young; conform cheerfully to their customs, even to their little follies, but not to their vices. Do not, however, remonstrate or preach against them, for remonstrances do not suit with your age. In French companies in general, you will not find much learning, therefore take care not to brandish yours in their faces. People hate those who make them feel their own inferiority. Conceal all your learning carefully, and reserve it for the company of *les Gens d'Église,* or *les Gens de Robe*; and even then let them rather extort it from you than find you over-willing to draw it. You are then thought, from that seeming unwillingness, to have still more knowledge than it may be you really have, and with the additional merit of modesty into the bargain. A man who talks of, or even hints at, his *bonnes fortunes,* is seldom believed, or if believed, much blamed; whereas a

1533

man who conceals with care is often supposed to have more than he has, and his reputation of discretion gets him others. It is just so with a man of learning; if he affects to show it, it is questioned, and he is reckoned only superficial; but if afterwards it appears that he really has it, he is pronounced a pedant. Real merit of any kind, *ubi est non potest diu celari*; it will be discovered, and nothing can depreciate it, but a man's exhibiting it himself. It may not always be rewarded as it ought; but it will always be known. You will in general find the women of the *beau monde* at Paris more instructed than the men, who are bred up singly for the army, and thrown into it at twelve or thirteen years old; but then that sort of education, which makes them ignorant of books, gives them a great knowledge of the world, an easy address, and polite manners.

Fashion is more tyrannical at Paris than in any other place in the world; it governs even more absolutely than their King, which is saying a great deal. The least revolt against it is punished by proscription. You must observe, and conform to all the *minuties* of it, if you will be in fashion there yourself; and if you are not in fashion, you are nobody. Get therefore, at all events, into the company of those men and women *qui donnent le ton*; and though at first you should be admitted upon that shining theatre only as a *persona muta*, persist, persevere, and you will soon have a part given you. Take great care never to tell in one company what you see or hear in another, much less to divert the present company at the expense of the last; but let discretion and secrecy be known parts of your character. They will carry you much farther, and much safer, than more shining talents. Be upon your guard against quarrels at Paris; honour is extremely nice there, though the asserting of it is exceedingly penal. Therefore *point de mauvaises plais-anteries, point de jeux de main, et point de raillerie piquante*.

Paris is the place in the world where, if you please, you may the best unite the *utile* and the *dulce*. Even your

1534

pleasures will be your improvements, if you take them with the people of the place, and in high life. From what you have hitherto done everywhere else, I have just reason to believe, that you will do everything you ought at Paris. Remember that it is your decisive moment; whatever you do there will be known to thousands here, and your character there, whatever it is, will get before you hither. You will meet with it at London. May you and I both have reason to rejoice at that meeting! Adieu.

No. 1703

TO HIS SON

(*Stanhope CCXXIV*)

London, 8 *May O.S.* 1750

MY DEAR FRIEND,

At your age the love of pleasures is extremely natural, and the enjoyment of them not unbecoming; but the danger, at your age, is mistaking the object, and setting out wrong in the pursuit. The character of a man of pleasure dazzles young eyes; they do not see their way to it distinctly, and fall into vice and profligacy. I remember a strong instance of this a great many years ago. A young fellow, determined to shine as a man of pleasure, was at the play, called the *Libertine Destroyed,* a translation of *le Festin de Pierre* of Molière's.[1] He was so struck with what he thought the fine character of the Libertine, that he swore he would be the *Libertine Destroyed.* Some friends asked him, whether he had not better content himself with being only the libertine, without being *destroyed?* to which he answered with great warmth, "No, for that being destroyed was the perfection

---

[1] No play of that name is traceable; it is probably Shadwell's *The Libertine,* 1675, popularly supposed to be from *Le Festin de Pierre*; it is a free adaptation of that play, of Rosimond's *Le Nouveau Festin de Pierre,* and, more significantly, perhaps, J.-B. La Rose's *L'Athée Foudroyé.* Shadwell refers to the Spanish *L'Atiesto Fulminato* of Tirso de Molina. See some plays of Shadwell edited by D. M. Walmsley, 1930.

of the whole." This, extravagant as it seems in this light, is really the case of many an unfortunate young fellow, who, captivated by the name of pleasures, rushes indiscriminately, and without taste, into them all, and is finally *destroyed*. I am not stoically advising, nor parsonically preaching to you, to be a stoic at your age; far from it; I am pointing out to you the paths to pleasures, and am endeavouring only to quicken and heighten them for you. Enjoy pleasures, but let them be your own, and then you will taste them: but adopt none; trust to nature for genuine ones. The pleasures that you would feel, you must earn; the man who gives himself up to all, feels none sensibly. Sardanapalus, I am convinced, never in his life felt any. Those only who join serious occupations with pleasures, feel either as they should do. Alcibiades, though addicted to the most shameful excesses, gave some time to philosophy and some to business. Julius Cæsar joined business with pleasure so properly, that they mutually assisted each other; and, though he was the husband of all the wives at Rome, he found time to be one of the best scholars, almost the best orator, and absolutely the best general there. An uninterrupted life of pleasures is as insipid as contemptible. Some hours given every day to serious business, must whet both the mind and the senses, to enjoy those of pleasure. A surfeited glutton, an emaciated sot, and an enervated rotten whoremaster never enjoy the pleasures to which they devote themselves; they are only so many human sacrifices to false gods. The pleasures of low life are all of this mistaken, merely sensual, and disgraceful nature; whereas those of high life, and in good company (though possibly in themselves not more moral), are more delicate, more refined, less dangerous, and less disgraceful; and, in the common course of things, not reckoned disgraceful at all. In short, pleasure must not, nay, cannot, be the business of a man of sense and character; but it may be, and is, his relief, his reward. It is particularly so with regard to the women, who have the utmost contempt for those

1536

men, that, having no character nor consideration with their
own sex, frivolously pass their whole time in *ruelles*, and at
toilettes. They look upon them as their lumber, and remove
them whenever they can get better furniture. Women
choose their favourites more by the ear than by any other
of their senses, or even their understandings. The man
whom they hear the most commended by the men, will
always be the best received by them. Such a conquest
flatters their vanity, and vanity is their universal, if not their
strongest, passion. A distinguished shining character is irresistible with them; they crowd to, nay, they even quarrel
for, the danger, in hopes of the triumph. Though by the
way (to use a vulgar expression), she who conquers, only
catches a tartar, and becomes the slave of her captive. *Mais
c'est là leur affaire*. Divide your time between useful occupations and elegant pleasures. The morning seems to belong
to study, business, or serious conversations with men of
learning and figure; not that I exclude an occasional hour at
a *toilette*. From sitting down to dinner, the proper business
of the day is pleasure, unless real business, which must never
be postponed for pleasure, happens accidentally to interfere.
In good company, the pleasures of the table are always
carried to a certain point of delicacy and gratification, but
never to excess and riot. Plays, operas, balls, suppers, gay
conversations in polite and cheerful companies, properly
conclude the evenings; not to mention the tender looks that
you may direct, and the sighs that you may offer, upon these
several occasions, to some propitious or unpropitious
female deity; whose character and manners will neither disgrace nor corrupt yours. This is the life of a man of real
sense and pleasure; and by this distribution of your time,
and choice of your pleasures, you will be equally qualified
for the busy, or the *beau monde*. You see I am not rigid,
and do not require that you and I should be of the same
age. What I say to you, therefore, should have the more
weight, as coming from a friend, not a father. But, low com-

pany, and their low vices, their indecent riots, and profligacy, I never will bear, nor forgive.

I have lately received two volumes of Treatises, in German and Latin, from Hawkins, with your orders, under
your own hand, to take care of them for you, which orders
I shall most dutifully and punctually obey; and they wait
for you in my library, together with your great collection
of rare books, which your Mamma sent me upon removing
from her old house.

I hope you not only keep up, but improve in your
German, for it will be of great use to you when you come
into business, and the more so, as you will be almost the
only Englishman who can either speak or understand it.
Pray speak it constantly to all Germans, wherever you meet
them, and you will meet multitudes of them at Paris. Is
Italian now become easy and familiar to you? Can you
speak it with the same fluency that you can speak German?
You cannot conceive what an advantage it will give you, in
negotiations, to possess Italian, German, and French, perfectly, so as to understand all the force and *finesse* of those
three languages. If two men of equal talents negotiate together, he who best understands the language in which the
negotiation is carried on, will infallibly get the better of the
other. The signification and force of one single word is
often of great consequence in a treaty, and even in a letter.

Remember the *Graces*, for without them *ogni fatica è vana*.
Adieu.

No. 1704

TO LORD HUNTINGDON

(*Steuart 4*)

MY DEAR LORD,   *London, 16 May O.S.* 1750
I most gladly and gratefully accept the flattering appellation with which you honour me in your last letter; I
wish I deserved it better, I was going to say even, literally,

if my more than paternal affection for you had not checked
that wish. It was glorious enough for the Scipio family to
have adopted Æmilianus.

I am very glad that my thoughts concerning your future
motions coincided so perfectly with your own, and I am
therefore sure that I was right. Paris (as you will make
it) is now the place of all Europe, the properest for you.
Your edifice is so solidly founded, and so strongly built,
that you have nothing now to think of but the ornaments;
and as mankind is made, they are the striking, and consequently not inconsiderable parts of the whole. The Found-
ling Hospital is as strong, and undoubtedly a much more
useful building than the Banqueting House; but the outside
of the latter universally prevails, over the inside of the
former. The French politeness, compliments, phrases, etc.,
are but poor embellishments, when unsupported by parts
and knowledge, but when they adorn a merit like yours, in
my mind they give perfection. It is in this view that I send
an old schoolfellow of yours, my boy, to the Academy at
Paris next October. He has a great stock both of ancient
and modern learning, but a very small one yet, of manners,
and of that useful knowledge, the knowledge of the world.
Let me most earnestly recommend him, my dear Lord, to
your countenance, favour, and if he deserves it, friendship.
Consider him as one absolutely belonging to you, and
whose character you may establish in the world, by the
force of your own. I have pointed you out to him as his
patron and his model; if he comes but near the one, he will
be worthy of the other; and in the tenderest wishes that I
can form for him, I cannot think of a better, than that he
may be reckoned *a friend of Lord Huntingdon's*. Miss Pitt,[1]
the Maid of Honour to the late Queen, will be at Paris with
Madame de Mirepoix,[2] the French Ambassadress, about the

[1]Ann, daughter of Robert Pitt of Boconnock and Harriet Villiers; Maid of
Honour to Queen Caroline and Privy Purse to the Princess Dowager of Wales.

[2]Anne-Marguérite-Gabrielle de Beauveau-Craon (1707-?1790), m. 1, 1721,
Prince de Lixin; 2, 1739, Marquis de Mirepoix.

time that you will get there; you are acquainted with her, and she will, I am sure, with great pleasure, bring you acquainted with the best company at Paris; but, however, I would recommend to you to get as many letters as you can from the people of fashion at Caen to their friends and relations at Paris. Such introductions are useful to those few travellers, who like you go to Paris to see the French and not the English.

Is there another Berenice to be dismissed when you leave Caen or several? The more, the more easily they are parted with.

Lady Chesterfield, and Camden House, charge me with their compliments and thanks to you. Accept my sincerest wishes for everything that you wish yourself.

Your faithful friend and servant.

No. 1705

To his Son

(Stanhope CCXXV)

London, 17 May O.S. 1750

My Dear Friend,

Your apprenticeship is near out, and you are soon to set up for yourself; that approaching moment is a critical one for you, and an anxious one for me. A tradesman who would succeed in his way must begin by establishing a character of integrity and good manners; without the former, nobody will go to his shop at all; without the latter, nobody will go there twice. This rule does not exclude the fair arts of trade. He may sell his goods at the best price he can within certain bounds. He may avail himself of the humour, the whims, and the fantastical tastes of his customers; but what he warrants to be good must be really so, what he seriously asserts must be true, or his first fraudulent profits will soon end in a bankruptcy. It is the same in higher life, and in the great business of the world. A man who does not solidly establish and really deserve a character of truth, probity, good manners, and good morals, at his first setting out in the world, may impose and shine like a meteor for a very short time, but will very soon vanish, and be extinguished with contempt. People easily pardon, in young men, the common irregularities of the senses; but they do not forgive the least vice of the heart. The heart never grows better by age; I fear rather worse, always harder. A young liar will be an old one, and a young knave will only be a greater knave as he grows older. But should a bad young heart, accompanied with a good head (which, by the way, very seldom is the case), really reform in a more advanced age from a consciousness of its folly, as well as of its guilt, such a conversion would only be thought prudential and political, but never sincere. I hope in God, and I verily believe, that you want no moral virtue. But the possession of all the moral virtues, *in actu primo*, as the logicians call it, is not sufficient; you must have them in *actu secundo* too; nay, that is not sufficient neither; you must have the reputation of them also. Your character in the world must be built upon that solid foundation, or it will soon fall, and upon your own head. You cannot, therefore, be too careful, too nice, too scrupulous, in establishing this character at first, upon which your whole depends. Let no conversation, no example, no fashion, no *bon mot*, no silly desire of seeming to be above, what most knaves and many fools call prejudices, ever tempt you to avow, excuse, extenuate, or laugh at the least breach of morality; but show upon all occasions, and take all occasions to show, a detestation and abhorrence of it. There, though young, you ought to be strict; and there only, while young, it becomes you to be strict and severe. But there, too, spare the persons while you lash the crimes. All this relates, as you easily judge, to the vices of the heart, such as lying, fraud, envy, malice, detraction, etc.; and I do not extend it to the little frailties of youth, flowing from high spirits and warm blood. It would ill become you, at your age, to declaim against them, and sententiously censure a gallantry, an accidental excess of the table, a frolic, an inadvertency; no, keep as free from them yourself as you can, but say nothing against them in others. They certainly mend by time, often by reason; and a man's worldly character is not affected by them, provided it be pure in all other respects.

To come now to a point of much less, but yet of very great consequence, at your first setting out. Be extremely upon your guard against vanity, the common failing of inexperienced youth; but particularly against that kind of vanity that dubs a man a coxcomb; a character which, once acquired, is more indelible than that of the priesthood. It is not to be imagined by how many different ways vanity defeats its own purposes. One man decides peremptorily upon every subject, betrays his ignorance upon many, and shows a disgusting presumption upon the rest. Another desires to appear successful among the women; he hints at the encouragement he has received from those of the most distinguished rank and beauty, and intimates a particular connection with some one; if it is true, it is ungenerous; if false, it is infamous; but in either case he destroys the reputation he wants to get. Some flatter their vanity by little extraneous objects which have not the least relation to themselves; such as being descended from, related to, or acquainted with, people of distinguished merit, and eminent characters. They talk perpetually of their grandfather such-a-one, their uncle such-a-one, and their intimate friend Mr. such-a-one, with whom, possibly, they are hardly acquainted. But admitting it all to be as they would have it, what then? Have they the more merit for these accidents? Certainly not. On the contrary, their taking up adventitious, proves their want of intrinsic merit; a rich man never borrows. Take this rule for granted, as a never-failing one;

that you must never seem to affect the character in which you have a mind to shine. Modesty is the only sure bait when you angle for praise. The affectation of courage will make even a brave man pass only for a bully; as the affectation of wit will make a man of parts pass for a coxcomb. By this modesty I do not mean timidity and awkward bashfulness. On the contrary, be inwardly firm and steady, know your own value, whatever it may be, and act upon that principle; but take great care to let nobody discover that you do know your own value. Whatever real merit you have other people will discover; and people always magnify their own discoveries, as they lessen those of others.

For God's sake, revolve all these things seriously in your thoughts before you launch out alone into the ocean of Paris. Recollect the observations that you have yourself made upon mankind, compare and connect them with my instructions, and then act systematically and consequentially from them; not *au jour la journée.* Lay your little plan now, which you will hereafter extend and improve by your own observations, and by the advice of those who can never mean to mislead you; I mean Mr. Harte and myself.

No. 1706

To his Son

(*Stanhope CCXXVI*)

London, 24 *May O.S.* 1750

My Dear Friend,

I received yesterday your letter of the 7th N.S. from Naples, to which place I find you have travelled classically, critically, and *da virtuoso.* You did right, for whatever is worth seeing at all, is worth seeing well, and better than most people see it. It is a poor and frivolous excuse, when anything curious is talked of that one has seen, to say, *I saw it, but really I did not much mind it.* Why did they go to see it, if they would not mind it?—or why would they not mind it when they saw it? Now you are at Naples, you pass part of your time there, *en honnête homme, da garbato cavaliere,* in the Court, and the best companies. I am told that strangers are received with the utmost hospitality at Prince ——'s, *que lui il fait bonne chère, et que Madame la Princesse donne chère entière; mais que sa chair est plus que hazardée ou mortifiée même;* which in plain English means, that she is not only tender, but rotten. If this be true, as I am pretty sure it is, one may say to her in a literal sense, *juvenumque prodis, publica cura.*

Mr. Harte informs me that you are clothed in sumptuous apparel; a young fellow should be so, especially abroad, where fine clothes are so generally the fashion. Next to their being fine, they should be well made, and worn easily; for a man is only the less genteel for a fine coat, if in wearing it he shows a regard for it, and is not as easy in it as if it were a plain one.

I thank you for your drawing, which I am impatient to see, and which I shall hang up in a new gallery that I am building at Blackheath,[1] and very fond of; but I am still more impatient for another copy, which I wonder I have not yet received—I mean the copy of your countenance. I believe, were that a whole length, it would still fall a good deal short of the dimensions of the drawing after Dominichino, which you say is about eight feet high; and I take you, as well as myself, to be of the family of the *Piccolomini.* Mr. Bathurst tells me that he thinks you rather taller than I am; if so, you may very possibly get up to five feet eight inches, which I would not compound for, though I would wish you five feet ten. In truth, what do I not wish you that has a tendency to perfection? I say a tendency only, for absolute perfection is not in human nature, so that it

[1]He built a gallery at the house at Blackheath, which had been left him by his brother.

would be idle to wish it; but I am very willing to compound for your coming nearer to perfection than the generality of your contemporaries; without a compliment to you, I think you bid fair for that. Mr. Harte affirms (and, if it were consistent with his character, would I believe swear) that you have no vices of the heart; you have undoubtedly a stock both of ancient and modern learning, which, I will venture to say, nobody of your age has, and which must now daily increase, do what you will. What then do you want towards that practical degree of perfection which I wish you? Nothing but the knowledge, the turn, and the manners of the world; I mean the *beau monde*. These it is impossible that you can yet have quite right; they are not given, they must be learned. But then, on the other hand, it is impossible not to acquire them, if one has a mind to them; for they are acquired insensibly, by keeping good company, if one has but the least attention to their characters and manners. Every man becomes, to a certain degree, what the people he generally converses with are. He catches their air, their manners, and even their way of thinking. If he observes with attention he will catch them soon, but if he does not, he will at long run contract them insensibly. I know nothing in the world but poetry that is not to be acquired by application and care. The sum total of this is a very comfortable one for you, as it plainly amounts to this, in your favour—that you now want nothing but what even your pleasures, if they are liberal ones, will teach you. I congratulate both you and myself, upon your being in such a situation, that, excepting your exercises, nothing is now wanting but pleasures to complete you. Take them, but (as I am sure you will) with people of the first fashion, wherever you are, and the business is done; your exercises at Paris, which I am sure you will attend to, will supple and fashion your body; and the company you will keep there will, with some degree of observation on your part, soon give you their air, address, manners—in short, *le ton de la bonne com-*

pagnie. Let not those considerations, however, make you vain—they are only between you and me; but as they are very comfortable ones, they may justly give you a manly assurance, a firmness, a steadiness, without which a man can neither be well bred, or in any light appear to advantage, or really what he is. They may justly remove all timidity, awkward bashfulness, low diffidence of one's self, and mean abject complaisance to every or any body's opinion. La Bruyère says very truly, *on ne vaut dans ce monde, que ce que l'on veut valoir*: it is a right principle to proceed upon in the world, taking care only to guard against the appearances and outward symptoms of vanity. Your whole then, you see, turns upon the company you keep for the future. I have laid you in variety of the best at Paris, where, at your arrival, you will find a cargo of letters, to very different sorts of people, as *beaux esprits, savants, et belles dames.* These, if you will frequent them, will form you, not only by their examples, but by their advice and admonitions in private, as I have desired them to do; and consequently add to what you have, the only one thing now needful.

Pray tell me what Italian books you have read, and whether that language is now become familiar to you. Read Ariosto and Tasso through, and then you will have read all the Italian poets, who, in my opinion, are worth reading. In all events, when you get to Paris, take a good Italian master to read Italian with you three times a week; not only to keep what you have already, which you would otherwise forget, but also to perfect you in the rest. It is a great pleasure, as well as a great advantage to be able to speak to people of all nations, and well in their own language. Aim at perfection in everything, though in most things it is un-attainable; however, they who aim at it, and persevere, will come much nearer it, than those whose laziness and des-pondency makes them give it up as unattainable. *Magnis tamen excidit ausis*[1] is a degree of praise which will always

[1]Ovid, *Metamorphoses*, ii. 328. Quoted again, Letter of 17th September 1757.

attend a noble and shining temerity, and a much better sign in a young fellow, than *serpere humi, tutus nimium timidusque procellæ.*[1] For men, as well as women,

———— born to be controlled,
Stoop to the forward and the bold.[2]

A man sets out in the world with real timidity and diffidence, has not an equal chance in it; he will be discouraged, put by, or trampled upon. But, to succeed, a man, especially a young one, should have inward firmness, steadiness, and intrepidity; with exterior modesty and *seeming* diffidence. He must modestly, but resolutely, assert his own rights and privileges. *Suaviter in modo,* but *fortiter in re.* He should have an apparent frankness, and openness, but with inward caution and closeness. All these things will come to you by frequenting and observing good company. And by good company, I mean that sort of company, which is called good company by everybody of that place. When all this is over, we shall meet; and then we will talk over, *tête à tête,* the various little finishing strokes, which conversation and acquaintance occasionally suggest, and which cannot be methodically written.

Tell Mr. Harte that I have received his two letters of the 2nd and 8th N.S. which, as soon as I have received a third, I will answer. Adieu, my dear! I find you will do.

[1]Horace, *Ars Poetica,* i. 28.

[2]From Waller's *Of Love.* See letter of 19th Oct. 1748. He quotes them again in letter of 1st Nov. 1750.

No. 1707

To Solomon Dayrolles, Esq.

(*Maty II. lix*)

London, 25 May O.S. 1750

Dear Dayrolles,

I find your journey through Flanders has been, like every man's journey through the world, some good and some bad; but, upon the whole, it is as well as being at the Hague. By what you observed, it is evident that the Court of Vienna will not lay out a shilling upon the Barrier Towns, but throw that burthen, as they do every other, upon the Maritime Powers; saying, that they get nothing by Flanders, but that it is our business to take care of it. I am an Austrian in my politics, and would support that House, if I could; but then I would be theii ally, not their bubble; their friend, but not their victim.

With your leave, Sir, it is none of Boden's trumpery that is to hang over against the Rubens, but a Holy Family, the masterpiece of Titian; for which the late Regent had agreed to give forty thousand livres to the Chapter at Rheims.[1] It was accordingly sent him; but when it arrived at Paris he was dead and gone, not to the Holy family, I believe. His son, the present Duke of Orleans, chose rather to return the picture than the money; the Chapter was obliged to take it back, and there it has remained ever since. I accidentally heard of this, and that the Chapter was special poor; upon which I determined to try what I could do, and I have succeeded. As this picture was brought from Italy by the famous Cardinal de Lorraine, after he had been at the Council of Trent, and given by him to the Cathedral of Rheims, of which he was Archbishop, he gave them at the same time his own picture, a whole length, done by Titian;

[1]See *Journal de-Marais,* ii., June, 1723. The Regent was so excited by his discovery that he deserted his new mistress, Mlle. Houel, to come to Paris to see the picture, a huge canvas 14 feet in length.

which I have likewise got; they are both arrived at Paris, and I expect them here very soon. This, you will allow, is no trumpery, and I have now done with pictures; I am brimful, and not ill filled.

Comte Obdam's *virtù* will, I think, for the reason you give, go very cheap; few people in Holland understanding those things, or even thinking that they do. I would not give sixpence for his bronzes, nor a shilling for his books; but for some of his antique marbles, I would give reasonably. Those which, upon the face of the catalogue, I should choose, are the following ones:

297. *Hermes* (Buste) *juvenis Romani cum lorica et sago, in marmore. Ant.*

298. *Bacchus, cum corona hederacea. Ant.*

302. *Caput juvenis Romani, supra basin. Ant.*

305. *Statua cum anaglyphis, sacrificium in honorem Priapi efformantibus. Ant.*

There are also in the appendix two bustos, one of Homer, the other of Apollo, by Girardon; which, if they go extremely cheap, as possibly they may, I should be glad of them; by extremely cheap, I mean about ten pounds a-piece. For the four antiques above-marked, *l'un portant l'autre*; if they are fine, I would go as far as five and twenty pounds a-piece. But should these which I have mentioned have great faults, and others which I have not mentioned have great beauties, I refer to your decision, who are upon the place, and have *un coup d'œil vif et pénétrant*.

You will see Hop at the Hague next week; it is sooner than he proposed to go, but he is ordered, which gives him some apprehensions. You will also see the famous Madame de Boccage,[1] who sets out from hence with her husband, and Abbé Guasco *de l'Académie des Inscriptions*, next Tuesday. She has translated Milton into French verse, and gave

[1]Marie-Anne Lepage, wife of Fiquet du Boccage, 1710-1802. Her poems were numerous, and some were much admired; among them were a translation of Milton's *Paradise Lost*, and of Pope's *Temple of Fame* (see Letter of the 1st November), and the *Colombiade*, an epic in ten books, on the discovery of America. She published an account of her travels in England, Holland and Italy.

a tragedy last winter at Paris, called *les Amazones*. She has good parts, *n'affiche pas le bel esprit*. Pray, give them *un petit dîner*, and let them know that I did them justice with you; they stay but a few days at the Hague, so cannot be very troublesome to you. But I possibly shall, if I lengthen this letter; so, *bon soir*.

No. 1708

To his Son

(*Stanhope CCXXVII*)

London, 5 June O.S. 1750

MY DEAR FRIEND,

I have received your picture, which I have long waited for with impatience; I wanted to see your countenance, from whence I am very apt, as I believe most people are, to form some general opinion of the mind. If the painter has taken you, as well as he has done Mr. Harte (for his picture is by far the most like I ever saw in my life), I draw good conclusions from your countenance, which has both spirit and *finesse* in it. In bulk you are pretty well increased since I saw you; if your height is not increased in proportion, I desire that you will make haste to complete it. Seriously, I believe that your exercises at Paris will make you shoot up to a good size; your legs, by all accounts, seem to promise it. Dancing excepted, the wholesome part is the best part of those academical exercises. *Ils dégraissent leur homme.* *À propos* of exercises; I have prepared everything for your reception at Monsieur de la Guérinière's, and your room, etc., will be ready at your arrival. I am sure you must be sensible how much better it will be for you to be *interne* in the Academy, for the first six or seven months at least, than to be *en hôtel garni*, at some distance from it, and obliged to go to it every morning, let the weather be what it will, not to mention the loss of time too; besides, by living and boarding in the Academy, you will make an acquaintance

1550

with half the young fellows of fashion at Paris; and in a very little while be looked upon as one of them in all French companies; an advantage that has never yet happened to any one Englishman that I have known. I am sure you do not suppose that the difference of the expense, which is but a trifle, has any weight with me in this resolution. You have the French language so perfectly, and you will acquire the French *tournure* so soon, that I do not know anybody likely to pass his time so well at Paris as yourself. Our young countrymen have generally too little French, and too bad address, either to present themselves, or be well received in the best French companies; and, as a proof of it, there is no one instance of an Englishman's having ever been suspected of a gallantry with a French woman of condition, though every French woman of condition is more than suspected of having a gallantry. But they take up with the disgraceful and dangerous commerce of prostitutes, actresses, dancing-women, and that sort of trash; though, if they had common address, better achievements would be extremely easy. *Un arrangement*, which is in plain English a gallantry, is, at Paris, as necessary a part of a woman of fashion's establishment, as her house, table, coach, etc. A young fellow must therefore be a very awkward one to be reduced to, or of a very singular taste, to prefer drabs and danger to a commerce (in the course of the world not disgraceful) with a woman of health, education, and rank. Nothing sinks a young man into low company, both of women and men, so surely as timidity, and diffidence of himself. If he thinks that he shall not, he may depend upon it, he will not please. But with proper endeavours to please, and a degree of persuasion that he shall, it is almost certain that he will. How many people does one meet with everywhere, who with very moderate parts, and very little knowledge, push themselves pretty far, singly by being sanguine, enterprising and persevering? They will take no denial from man or woman; difficulties do not discourage them; repulsed twice or thrice, they rally, they charge again, and nine times in ten prevail at last. The same means will much sooner, and more certainly, attain the same ends, with your parts and knowledge. You have a fund to be sanguine upon, and good forces to rally. In business (talents supposed) nothing is more effectual, or successful, than a good, though concealed, opinion of one's self, a firm resolution, and an unwearied perseverance. None but madmen attempt impossibilities; and whatever is possible, is one way or another to be brought about. If one method fails, try another, and suit your methods to the characters you have to do with.

At the treaty of the Pyrenees, which Cardinal Mazarin and Don Louis de Haro concluded, *dans l'Isle des Faisans*, the latter carried some very important points by his constant and cool perseverance.[1] The Cardinal had all the Italian vivacity and impatience; Don Louis all the Spanish phlegm and tenaciousness. The point which the Cardinal had most at heart was, to hinder the re-establishment of the Prince of Condé, his implacable enemy; but he was in haste to conclude, and impatient to return to Court; where absence is always dangerous. Don Louis observed this, and never failed at every conference to bring the affair of the Prince of Condé upon the *tapis*. The Cardinal for some time refused even to treat upon it; Don Louis, with the same *sang froid* as constantly persisted, till he at last prevailed; contrary to the intentions and the interest both of the Cardinal and of his Court. Sense must distinguish between what is impossible, and what is only difficult; and spirit and perseverance will get the better of the latter. Every man is to be had one way or another, and every woman almost any way.

I must not omit one thing, which is previously necessary to this, and indeed to everything else; which is attention, a

[1]The conference began on 13th Aug. 1659, and ended on 7th November. The Isle des Faisans is a tiny island in the Bidassoa. The secret despatches of Cardinal Mazarin during his conferences with Don Louis de Haro were published in two volumes at Amsterdam in 1693.

flexibility of attention; never to be wholly engrossed by any past or future object, but instantly directed to the present one, be it what it will. An absent man can make but few observations; and those will be disjointed and imperfect ones, as half the circumstances must necessarily escape him. He can pursue nothing steadily, because his absences make him lose his way. They are very disagreeable, and hardly to be tolerated in old age; but in youth, they cannot be forgiven. If you find that you have the least tendency to them, pray watch yourself very carefully, and you may prevent them now; but if you let them grow into a habit, you will find it very difficult to cure them hereafter; and a worse distemper I do not know.

I heard with great satisfaction the other day, from one who has been lately at Rome, that nobody was better received in the best companies than yourself. The same thing, I dare say, will happen to you at Paris; where they are particularly kind to all strangers, who will be civil to them, and show a desire of pleasing. But they must be flattered a little, not only by words, but by a seeming preference given to their country, their manners, and their customs; which is but a very small price to pay for a very good reception. Were I in Africa, I would pay it to a negro for his good-will. Adieu.

No. 1709

TO HIS SON

(*Stanhope CCXXVIII*)

London, 11 *June O.S.* 1750

MY DEAR FRIEND,

The President Montesquieu (whom you will be acquainted with at Paris) after having laid down, in his book *de l'Esprit des Lois*, the nature and principles of the three different kinds of government, viz. the democratical, the

monarchical, and the despotic, treats of the education necessary for each respective form. His chapter upon the education proper for the monarchical I thought worth transcribing, and sending to you. You will observe that the monarchy which he has in his eye is France.[1]

. . . .

Though our government differs considerably from the
French, inasmuch as we have fixed laws, and constitutional
barriers, for the security of our liberties and properties; yet
the President's observations hold pretty near as true in
England as in France. Though monarchies may differ a
good deal, kings differ very little. Those who are absolute
desire to continue so, and those who are not, endeavour to
become so; hence, the same maxims and manners almost in
all Courts; voluptuousness and profusion encouraged, the
one to sink the people into indolence, the other into poverty,
consequently into dependency. The Court is called the
world here, as well as at Paris; and nothing more is meant,
by saying that a man knows the world, than that he knows
Courts. In all Courts you must expect to meet with connections without friendship, enmities without hatred,
honour without virtue, appearances saved, and realities
sacrificed; good manners, with bad morals; and all vice and
virtue so disguised, that whoever has only reasoned upon
both, would know neither, when he first met them at Court.
It is well that you should know the map of that country,
that when you come to travel in it, you may do it with
greater safety.

From all this, you will of yourself draw this obvious conclusion, That you are in truth but now going to the great
and important school, the world; to which Westminster and
Leipsig were only the little preparatory schools, as Mary-le-

[1]Lord Chesterfield here transcribes the second chapter of the fourth book of
the *Esprit des Lois*. It appears needless to reprint so long a passage from so
popular and well-known a work—M. It is, however, included in Sir Charles
Strachey's edition, ii. 61 *seq*.

bone, Windsor, etc., are to them. What you have already acquired, will only place you in the second form of this new school instead of the first. But if you intend, as I suppose you do, to get into the shell, you have very different things to learn from Latin and Greek; and which require much more sagacity and attention, than those two dead languages; the language of pure and simple nature, the language of nature variously modified, and corrupted by passions, prejudices, and habits; the language of simulation, and dissimulation; very hard, but very necessary to decipher. Homer has not half so many, nor so difficult dialects, as the great book of the school you are now going to. Observe therefore progressively and with the greatest attention, what the best scholars in the form immediately above you do, and so on, till you get into the shell yourself. Adieu.

Pray tell Mr. Harte that I have received his letter of the 27th May N.S. and that I advised him never to take the English news-writers literally, who never yet inserted any one thing quite right. I have both his patent and his Mandamus,[1] in both which he is Walter,[2] let the newspapers call him what they please.

No. 1710

À MADAME DU BOCCAGE

(*Maty I. lxxxv*)

À Londres, ce 14 *juin V.S.* 1750

Parlons naturellement, Madame. Convenez avec moi que votre mérite, et la réputation que vous vous êtes acquise, vous seront partout des recommandations suffisantes, et vous procureront en tout pays l'accueil que vous avez

[1] As Prebendary of Windsor; an appointment which Lord Chesterfield had at this time, not without difficulty, obtained for Mr. Harte.—See letter to Dayrolles of 27th April 1750.—M.

[2] See note to letter of 4th Oct. 1746. There was apparently some mistake in the newspaper announcements.

trouvé en Hollande. Je n'ai pas prétendu vous recommander à M. Dayrolles; je vous ai simplement annoncée. J'ai été votre nouvelliste, et j'ai mis seulement dans ma feuille volante que Madame du Boccage se disposait à partir de Londres pour la Haye. Voilà tout ce qu'il faut à de certaines gens.

En quatre jours de séjour en Hollande, vous vous en êtes fait les mêmes idées, qu'un séjour de plus de quatre ans m'en avaient données, et vous me les rappelez toutes en quatre lignes. Il est si vrai que les hommes y sont tardifs, que je ne me souviens pas d'y en avoir vu, qui fussent ce qu'en tout autre pays on appellerait jeunes. Mais si vous y croyez les femmes aussi tranquilles que les eaux de leurs canaux, et aussi propres que leurs maisons, les deux tiers des maris n'en conviendraient pas, et vous diraient, à l'oreille s'entend, que ce n'est qu'à l'extérieur. Chez elles ce sont des *Amazones*,[1] et les maris les malheureux captifs, destinés à perpétuer la *gunarchie*. Aussi peuplent-ils infiniment, et du plus grand sérieux du monde. Ils envisagent la fabrique des enfants comme un article nécessaire à leur commerce, et s'en acquittent en bons citoyens.

L'épithète d'immobile, que vous donnez à mon ami L——, est des plus justes. Le bon homme semble avoir seulement le soin et non la propriété de ses tableaux. Il les montre avec une indifférence si stoïque, qu'il me rappelle certains messieurs noirs en Turquie qui ont un soin immobile des plus beaux originaux du monde. Il est vrai que je lui envie un bon nombre de ses tableaux, et je crois pouvoir le faire, sans donner la moindre atteinte au dixième commandement, qui suppose sans doute que les gens jouissent de ce qu'il ne faut pas que les autres convoitent. Je trouve ce cas de conscience des plus clairs, et sûrement des plus commodes; car il va loin, je ne sais si les vingt-quatre[2] y ont pensé.

Rassurez-vous, Madame, sur les avances que la singu-

[1]Referring to her new tragedy.　　[2]The Doctors of Sorbonne.—M.

larité de mon Baron vous aura obligée de faire pour voir un
tel original. Sa réputation depuis longtemps constatée met
toutes les autres réputations en sûreté. Depuis plus de
quinze ans, il a renoncé publiquement et solemnellement à
celui des cinq sens, qui seul met les réputations en danger;[1]
et observé sa renonciation avec un scrupule, qui devrait faire
rougir tous les rois de la terre. Je m'attends tous les jours
à votre portrait, et suis bien sûr qu'il m'en fera part: je
promets de vous en envoyer copie. S'il ne ressemble pas
bien, du moins il ne sera pas flatté: mon Baron n'est nullement adulateur. Au reste, Madame, ne laissez pas séduire
votre goût par le sien; ne vous prêtez pas à la simplicité, ou
plutôt à la fadeur, de la tragédie grecque, que nous faisons
semblant d'admirer pour paraître savants, mais qui nous
ennuie fort. Excitez toujours, comme il vous convient de le
faire, des passions plus délicates, plus douces que celles de
l'horreur et de la crainte; et ne nous donnez pas des *chorus*
de gens inconnus, pour développer, Dieu sait par quel
moyen, ce que les plus intéressés de la pièce semblent
ignorer. Vous ne m'êtes pas suspecte; et vos *Amazones*, avec
leur simplicité, me sont garantes du contraire.

Qu'il me serait glorieux, si mon buste méritait la place
que vous lui offrez! Mais qu'il me serait humiliant, si l'on
vous obligeait de faire les preuves de votre nouveau venu!
Croyez-moi, Madame, ne nous commettons ni l'un ni l'autre;
allons au plus sûr. Je vous enverrai deux bustes, qui non
seulement méritent mais exigent une place dans votre jardin,
tant ils se sont trouvés bien dans votre cabinet, je veux dire
Milton et Pope; ils n'y craindront pas la compagnie, quelque
bonne qu'elle soit; d'ailleurs, ils ont déjà leurs preuves et
leurs patentes contresignées de votre propre main: dès qu'ils
seront faits, je vous les enverrai.

Nous ne nous flattons pas que vous regrettiez un peu
l'Angleterre, mais nous espérons de n'être pas bannis de

---

[1] The sense of feeling. Baron de Kreuningen had, it appears, a morbid dread of
the plague.—M.

votre souvenir. Nous prétendons que nos regrets de votre départ nous donnent de certains droits. En vérité, Madame, vous vous êtes fait dans ce pays-ci autant d'amis et de serviteurs, que vous y avez fait de connaissances; dans un sens je prétends au haut bout dans cette compagnie, mais c'est uniquement par le respect et l'attachement, avec lesquels j'ai l'honneur d'être, très parfaitement,

Votre très humble et obéissant serviteur.

Madame de Chesterfield me charge de ses compliments pour vous et pour Monsieur du Boccage; permettez que j'y ajoute les miens pour lui.

No. 1711

To Solomon Dayrolles, Esq.

(*Mahon III. 384*)

DEAR DAYROLLES,   *London, 19 June O.S.* 1750

I must say, as most fools do, *who would have thought it?* My fine Titian has turned out an execrable bad copy. By good luck, the condition of the obligation was such, that, if certain good judges at Paris should declare it either a copy, or essentially damaged, the Chapter of Rheims was to take it back again, I paying the carriage. This has happened; and the best painters in Paris pronounced it not only a copy, but a damned one; so that I am only in for the carriage back. The Chapter must have been more fools than knaves in the affair; for, had they known it to be a copy, they might have known, at the same time, that it would be returned them; by which they would get nothing but the discrediting of their picture for ever.

I have received a letter from Madame du Boccage, containing a panegyric of his Majesty's Resident at the Hague. *Il est très aimable, très poli, il est au mieux avec tout ce qu'il y a de meilleur ici, et il fait très bonne chère. Faire bonne chère,* you know, always sums up a French panegyric. She says, that by your means she received a thousand civilities at the Hague. She did so here, notwithstanding that Madame de Mirepoix and she had a quarrel, in which they both contrived, as all ladies when they quarrel do, to be both extremely in the wrong.

I do not know whether my friend Abbé Guasco's judgment in *virtù* will be of any great service to us at Comte Obdam's, and I would sooner trust to your own *coup d'œil, qui est mordieu vif et perçant!*

I am very much *par voies, et par chemins,* between London and Blackheath, but much more at the latter, which is now in great beauty. The shell of my gallery is finished, which, by three bow-windows, gives me three different, and the finest, prospects in the world. I have already two or three of your Cantelupe melons, which are admirable; I have covered those, which are not yet ripe, with frames of oiled paper, which I am assured will do much better than glasses.

I am glad that Hop is better than he thinks himself, for he received his orders to go to Hanover, with some uneasiness, knowing that Bentinck was to be there also, in his way from Vienna. When Bentinck returns to the Hague, some new scene or other will open. He must be either Cæsar or nobody. I rather expect to see him soon the latter; combining all the circumstances that you and I know.

The Prince of Wales's last child[1] was at last christened the day before yesterday, after having been kept at least a fortnight longer than it should have been out of a state of salvation, by the jumble of the two Secretaries of State, whose reciprocal despatches carried, nor brought, nothing decisive. Our English Atlas[2] has carried our part of the globe with him to Woburn, *ou il s'ébaudit, et se délecte.* Adieu.

[1] Prince Frederick William (30th May 1750; 29th Dec. 1765).

[2] The Duke of Bedford. At the same period Mr. Pelham makes the same complaint of his Grace's love of ease. 'With him it is all jollity, boyishness, and vanity; he persuades himself that riding post from London to Woburn and back again once in a week or fortnight is doing a great deal of business.' (To the Duke of Newcastle, 25th July 1750. Coxe's Pelham.)—M.

No. 1712

À MADAME LA MARQUISE DE MONCONSEIL

(Maty I. xlvi)

À Londres, ce 28 juin V.S. 1750

Prenez garde, Madame, on vous fâchera exprès, tant votre colère est flatteuse, et votre vengeance douce; mais quoique vous soyez désabusée du motif de votre colère, exécutez pourtant votre vengeance, dont vous aurez bientôt l'occasion, puisque votre élève vous fera sa cour au mois d'octobre prochain. Pardonnez-moi à présent un détail ennuyant sur un sujet, auquel je prends un si tendre intérêt. J'ai donc fait mes arrangements avec Monsieur de la Guérinière pour le recevoir interne dans son académie; son gouverneur l'y établira, et puis le quittera, pour s'en retourner ici. J'ai cru qu'à son âge, et sans gouverneur, il était plus sûr de le mettre dans l'académie, que de le laisser en hôtel garni; et d'ailleurs, qu'à l'académie il fera connaissance avec vos jeunes français, et sera plus à l'abri des jeunes anglais, contre lesquels je suis extrêmement sur mes gardes. J'adresserai son gouverneur à l'Abbé Sallier, pour concerter avec lui, avant qu'il le quitte, les maîtres qu'il lui faudra pour la géométrie, l'astronomie, et la philosophie. Je suis persuadé que l'Abbé Sallier voudra bien lui indiquer des sujets convenables. Comme il est accoutumé, depuis plus d'un an, d'avoir assez de liberté, dont par parenthèse il n'a jamais abusé, je ne compte pas l'enfermer dans l'académie, et j'ai fait dire à Monsieur de la Guérinière qu'après que les exercices du matin seront finis, il doit lui permettre d'aller où il voudra, c'est-à-dire dans des certaines bornes. Voilà donc tout arrangé par rapport au savoir, et aux exercices; mais il reste un article bien intéressant, je veux dire les mœurs, les manières, la politesse, le ton du beau monde; c'est à quoi, si vous le voulez bien, vous pouvez plus contribuer que personne, et j'ose vous en supplier. Prenez avec lui un certain ton d'autorité, parlez-lui ouvertement, s'il est nécessaire, sur sa conduite, et ne lui passez point la moindre chose. S'il est gauche, s'il a mauvais air, s'il est impoli, moquez-vous de lui, et tournez-le en ridicule; sur ces articles-là, c'est souvent le moyen le plus efficace avec les jeunes gens. Permettez-lui d'être votre galopin chez vous; traitez-le sans façon, et ayez la bonté de me dire tout naturellement ce que vous en pensez. Après les soins que j'ai eu de son éducation, indépendamment de ma tendresse pour lui, je me fais une affaire, je me pique même de sa réussite dans le monde. Ce n'est pas pour vous faire un fade compliment, mais c'est très véritablement que je vous proteste, que je crois que sa réussite dans le monde dépendra plus de vous que de tout autre chose. Je le recommande donc, Madame, à ces sentiments d'amitié dont vous m'avez toujours honoré, et dont vous ne pouvez pas me donner une preuve plus sensible, que par vos bontés à cet autre moi-même.

No. 1713

To his Son

(Stanhope CCXXIX)

London, 9 July O.S. 1750

My Dear Friend,

I should not deserve that appellation in return from you, if I did not freely and explicitly inform you of every corrigible defect, which I may either hear of, suspect, or at any time discover in you. Those who in the common course of the world will call themselves your friends; or whom, according to the common notions of friendship, you may possibly think such, will never tell you of your faults, still less of your weaknesses. But on the contrary, more desirous to make you their friend, than to prove themselves yours, they will flatter both, and, in truth, not be sorry for either. Interiorly, most people enjoy the inferiority of their best friends. The useful and essential part of friendship, to you, is reserved singly for Mr. Harte and myself; our relations to you stand pure, and unsuspected of all private views. In whatever we say to you, we can have no interest but yours. We can have no competition, no jealousy, no secret envy or malignity. We are therefore authorised to represent, advise, and remonstrate; and your reason must tell you that you ought to attend to, and believe us.

I am credibly informed, that there is still a considerable hitch or hobble in your enunciation; and that when you speak fast, you sometimes speak unintelligibly. I have formerly and frequently laid my thoughts before you so fully upon this subject, that I can say nothing new upon it now. I must therefore only repeat, that your whole depends upon it. Your trade is to speak well both in public and in private. The manner of your speaking is full as important as the matter, as more people have ears to be tickled, than understandings to judge. Be your productions ever so good, they will be of no use, if you stifle and strangle them in their birth. The best compositions of Corelli,[1] if ill executed and played out of tune, instead of touching, as they do when well performed, would only excite the indignation of the hearers, when murdered by an unskilled performer. But to murder your own productions, and that *coram populo*, is a *Medean cruelty*, which Horace absolutely forbids. Remember of what importance Demosthenes, and one of the Gracchi, thought *enunciation*; read what stress Cicero, and Quintilian lay upon it; even the herb-women at Athens were correct judges of it. Oratory with all its graces, that of enunciation in particular, is full as necessary in our government, as it ever was in Greece or Rome. No man can make a fortune or a figure in this country, without speaking, and speaking well, in public. If you will persuade,

[1]The celebrated composer and violin-player, Arcangello Corelli (1653-1713). Very popular at the time, and who has, of course, maintained his reputation. Tickell wrote of Addison that his lines were 'sweet as Corelli, and as Virgil strong.'

you must first please; and if you will please, you must tune your voice to harmony, you must articulate every syllable distinctly, your emphases and cadences must be strongly and properly marked; and the whole together must be graceful and engaging; if you do not speak in that manner, you had much better not speak at all. All the learning you have, or ever can have, is not worth one groat without it. It may be a comfort, and an amusement to you in your closet, but can be of no use to you in the world. Let me conjure you therefore, to make this your only object, till you have absolutely conquered it, for that is in your power; think of nothing else, read and speak for nothing else.

Read aloud, though alone, and read articulately and distinctly, as if you were reading in public, and on the most important occasion. Recite pieces of eloquence, declaim scenes of tragedies to Mr. Harte, as if he were a numerous audience. If there is any particular consonant which you have a difficulty in articulating, as I think you had with the *R*, utter it millions and millions of times, till you have uttered it right. Never speak quick, till you have first learned to speak well. In short, lay aside every book and every thought that does not directly tend to this great object, absolutely decisive of your future fortune and figure.

The next thing necessary in your destination, is writing correctly, elegantly, and in a good hand too; in which three particulars, I am sorry to tell you, that you hitherto fail. Your handwriting is a very bad one, and would make a scurvy figure in an office book of letters, or even in a lady's pocket-book. But that fault is easily cured by care, since every man who has the use of his eyes and of his right hand

Can write whatever hand he pleases.

As to the correctness and elegancy of your writing, attention to grammar does the one, and to the best authors the other. In your letter to me of the 27th of June N.S. you

omitted the date [name?] of the place, so that I only con-
jectured from the contents that you were at Rome.

Thus I have, with the truth and freedom of the tenderest
affection, told you all your defects, at least all that I know
or have heard of. Thank God they are all very curable, they
must be cured, and I am sure you will cure them. That
once done, nothing remains for you to acquire, or for me to
wish, but the turn, the manners, the address, and the Graces
of the polite world; which experience, observation, and good
company will insensibly give you. Few people at your age
have read, seen, and known so much as you have, and consequently few are so near as yourself to what I call perfection, by which I only mean, being very near as well as the
best. Far, therefore, from being discouraged by what you
still want, what you already have should encourage you to
attempt, and convince you that by attempting you will inevitably obtain it. The difficulties which you have sur-
mounted were much greater than any you have now to
encounter. Till very lately your way has been only through
thorns and briars; the few that now remain are mixed with
roses. Pleasure is now the principal remaining part of your
education. It will soften and polish your manners; it will
make you pursue and at last overtake the Graces. Pleasure
is necessarily reciprocal; no one feels who does not at the
same time give it. To be pleased, one must please. What
pleases you in others, will in general please them in you.
Paris is indisputably the seat of the Graces; they will even
court you, if you are not too coy. Frequent and observe
the best companies there, and you will soon be naturalized
among them; you will soon find how particularly attentive
they are to the correctness and elegancy of their language,
and to the graces of their enunciation; they would even call
the understanding of a man in question, who should neglect,
or not know the infinite advantages arising from them.
Narrer, réciter, déclamer bien, are serious studies among
them, and well deserve to be so everywhere. The conversa-

tions, even among the women, frequently turn upon the elegancies, and minutest delicacies of the French language. An *enjouement*, a gallant turn prevails in all their companies, to women, with whom they neither are, nor pretend to be, in love; but should you (as may very possibly happen) fall really in love there, with some women of fashion and sense (for I do not suppose you capable of falling in love with a strumpet) and that your rival, without half your parts or knowledge, should get the better of you, merely by dint of manners, *enjouement, badinage*, etc., how would you regret not having sufficiently attended to those accomplishments which you despised as superficial and trifling, but which you would then find of real consequence in the course of the world! And men, as well as women, are taken by these external graces. Shut up your books then now as a business, and open them only as a pleasure; but let the great book of the world be your serious study; read it over and over, get it by heart, adopt its style, and make it your own.

When I cast up your account as it now stands, I rejoice to see the balance so much in your favour; and that the items *per contra* are so few, and of such a nature that they may be very easily cancelled. By way of debtor and creditor, it stands thus:

Creditor. By French.	Debtor. To English.
German.	Enunciation.
Italian.	Manners.
Latin.	
Greek.	
Logic.	
Ethics.	
History.	
Jus-- ⎰Naturæ.⎱ Gentium. Publicum.	

This, my dear friend, is a very true account, and a very encouraging one for you. A man who owes so little, can clear it off in a very little time, and if he is a prudent man will; whereas a man, who by long negligence owes a great deal, despairs of ever being able to pay; and therefore never looks into his accounts at all.

When you go to Genoa, pray observe carefully all the *environs* of it, and view them with somebody who can tell you all the situations and operations of the Austrian army, during that famous siege, if it deserves to be called one; for in reality the town never was besieged, nor had the Austrians any one thing necessary for a siege. If Marquis Centurioni, who was last winter in England, should happen to be there, go to him with my compliments, and he will show you all imaginable civilities.

I could have sent you some letters to Florence, but that I knew Mr. Mann[1] would be of more use to you than all of them. Pray make him my compliments. Cultivate your Italian, while you are at Florence, where it is spoken in its utmost purity, but ill-pronounced.

Pray save me the seed of some of the best melons you eat, and put it up dry in paper. You need not send it me; but Mr. Harte will bring it in his pocket when he comes over. I should likewise be glad of some cuttings of the best figs, especially *il fico gentile*, and the Maltese; but as this is not the season for them, Mr. Mann will, I dare say, undertake that commission, and send them to me at the proper time by Leghorn.

Adieu. Endeavour to please others, and divert yourself as much as ever you can, *en honnête et galant homme.*

P.S. I send you the enclosed to deliver to Lord Rochford,[2] upon your arrival at Turin.

[1]Afterwards Sir Horace Mann. From 1740 till his death in 1786 British Envoy at Florence; the correspondent of Walpole.

[2]William Henry, fourth Earl of Rochford (1717-1781), of the family of Nassau de Zulenstein, was sent in 1749 as Envoy Extraordinary to the King of Sardinia. In 1766, he was appointed Ambassador at Paris, and in 1768 Secretary of State.

No. 1714

À Madame du Boccage

(*Maty I. lxxxvi*)

À Londres, ce 25 juillet V.S. 1750

Vous avez paré le coup, que j'allais vous porter. Au moment que je reçois la vôtre, je prenais la plume pour vous attaquer; je la prends à présent pour vous remercier d'une lettre, dont les agréments et les détails intéressants, non seulement calment ma colère, mais excitent ma plus vive reconnaissance. En conscience vous nous devez réparation du mauvais tour que vous nous avez joué. Vous n'êtes venue ici que pour nous donner des regrets de votre départ; vous nous flattiez d'un plus long séjour; mais dès que vous avez senti que votre coup était fait, vous vous êtes sauvée. Nous vous condamnons donc à de grosses amendes épistolaires, d'autant plus justes qu'elles ne sont que proportionnées à vos moyens. Au reste ce n'était pas seulement à l'Angleterre que vous en vouliez, mais aux puissances maritimes; puisque Dayrolles, qui est ici depuis huit jours, m'assure qu'en regrets sur votre départ la Hollande fait cause commune avec nous; mais elle démêlera cette affaire comme il lui plaira; pour moi, en véritable allié, je ne pense qu'à mon intérêt particulier.

On dit que Cléopâtre[1] n'a pas réussi. La pièce manque sans doute de conduite; j'ai peine à croire que l'auteur d'Aristomène et de Denis le Tyran ait fait une mauvaise pièce sur un si beau sujet. Il a sûrement du feu, du génie, de la verve; mais n'importe, il aura manqué à quelque règle de théâtre; il est proscrit. Vous vous êtes forgé des chaînes poétiques bien rudes, sous le poids desquelles tout bon auteur doit gémir, et souhaiter de les briser; au lieu qu'un auteur sans feu, comme au amant sans vigueur, chérit ses chaînes; l'un devient régulier, et l'autre respectueux, par impuissance.

[1]A tragedy by Marmontel.

Rome sauvée[1] ne réussira peut-être pas non plus. Voltaire veut se faire des règles nouvelles, et la mode, chez vous encore plus qu'ici, décide des ouvrages des poètes comme de ceux des marchands. Je suis sûr pourtant que son Cicéron ne ressemblera guère à celui de Crébillon, qui dans le plus bel endroit de sa vie est un imbécile. Enfin, quoiqu'en dise votre public, tout ce que Voltaire fait me charme. Toujours les plus beaux vers du monde, et des pensées brillantes et justes; je n'en demande pas davantage; *non paucis offendar maculis*.[2]

Sur l'échantillon que Madame de Graffigny a donné de la délicatesse de son esprit dans ses Lettres Péruviennes, j'augure bien de sa comédie,[3] quoique ces comédies tragiques et larmoyantes ne soient pas de mon goût. Qu'on me donne les choses pour ce qu'elles sont; j'aime à rire et à pleurer dans les formes; il y a pourtant quelque chose à dire en leur faveur. Horace permet à la comédie de s'élever de temps en temps;[4] et l'intérêt, les sentiments et les situations touchantes ne sont pas bornés aux rois et aux héros. La vie ordinaire les fournit.

J'ai lu les soi-disantes lettres de Ninon de l'Enclos,[5] et me suis douté qu'on avait emprunté un nom si célèbre, pour faire passer un ouvrage médiocre. Il n'a pas ce caractère marqué, qui aurait distingué les lettres de cette célèbre catin. Le second volume, comme vous le dites, vaut mieux, encore ne vaut-il guère. J'ai l'honneur d'être avec un respectueux attachement,

Madame, votre, etc.

---

[1] By Voltaire, first acted at Sceaux with the Duchesse du Maine.

[2]

Non ego paucis
Offendar maculis, quas aut incuria fudit,
Aut humana parum cavit natura.
HORACE.

[3] *Cénie.* See Letter to his Son, 20th Feb. 1752.

[4]

Interdum tamen, et vocem Comœdia tollit.
Ars Poetica.

[5] She died in 1706. Some of her letters had been published with those of Saint-Evremond early in the century.

No. 1715

À MADAME LA MARQUISE DE MONCONSEIL

(*Maty I. xlvii*)

À Londres, ce 25 juillet V.S. 1750

Permettez-moi, Madame, d'entamer une petite controverse avec vous sur l'affaire en question; mais pas pourtant dans l'esprit ordinaire des controverses, où les deux parties débutent dans la ferme résolution de ne pas se laisser persuader; pour moi mon esprit est ouvert à la conviction, j'ai seulement quelques doutes à vous proposer. Si votre élève est interne chez La Guérinière, il y trouvera assez mauvaise compagnie, qui l'engageront à leurs parties de jeu, de cabaret, et de filles; la chose est très possible; mais aussi en y allant, tous les matins, comme externe, pour apprendre ses exercices, n'est-il pas exposé aux mêmes dangers? N'y trouvera-t-il pas les mêmes personnes? et ces mêmes personnes, par les raisons que vous donnez, ne formeront-elles pas de liaisons avec lui, et ne le fréquenteront-elles pas quoiqu'il soit en pension ailleurs? Monsieur de la Guérinière n'aura-t-il pas aussi un peu l'œil sur sa conduite, et surtout sur les liaisons qu'il y formerait? En pension, je le croirais beaucoup plus exposé aux incursions des barbares ses compatriotes, et débauche pour débauche, je préférerais la française à l'anglaise; d'ailleurs, j'ai tout lieu de croire qu'il déteste foncièrement le jeu, et le vin; pour le reste, il a jusqu'ici eu des égards, et pour sa santé, et pour la bienséance. On ne peut pas s'attendre qu'à son âge, il veuille, ou même qu'il puisse, toujours vivre avec des gens d'un âge plus avancé, et d'un certain caractère; les jeunes gens se cherchent, se trouvent, et où en trouvera-t-il de meilleurs qu'à l'académie? S'il doit y aller tous les matins faire ses exercices, ne seront-ils pas souvent négligés? Un matin froid, pluvieux, sombre, est décourageant; on congédie le carrosse, un ami entre à déjeuner, adieu les exercices de cette matinée. J'ai dit; toute réflexion faite, ai-je tort? Si vous me dites encore que je l'ai, j'en conviendrai. Il est vrai que si l'on pouvait trouver à le mettre en une pension, où le maître et la maîtresse de la maison fussent des gens d'une certaine tournure, que le mari eût de l'esprit, du savoir, des manières, et la femme un peu le ton de la passablement bonne compagnie, je comprends bien qu'il pourrait y être mieux qu'à l'académie; mais où trouver une telle pension? Des gens de cette sorte n'ont garde de s'embarrasser d'un jeune étourdi de dix-huit ans; le mari craindrait pour sa femme, si elle était jeune; et si elle était vieille, elle craindrait pour ses filles. Enfin j'attends vos ordres, et vos idées ultérieures, avant que de prendre finalement mon parti.

1716

To Edward Eliot

(*MSS. of the Earl of St. Germans*)

London, 31 *July*, 1750

Sir,

I am extremely glad to hear that Mr. Harte has got the living; you know that I thought Lord Chancellor too well-bred to dispute with the Prince of Wales. I was in hopes that Mr. Harte would have been here by Michaelmas, but by his last letter I find he will not be here so soon, for he says that he is determined not to pass the Alps till the heats are entirely over, and therefore does not propose being at Paris till the end of October at soonest. His last letter was from Sienna, where he had a diarrhœa, and his pupil a return of the same illness which he had last year in Carniola. These accidents may possibly delay their journey to Paris still longer, so that I believe an application to the Arch-bishop will be necessary. I hope his Grace will not be less civil than the Bishop of Exeter has been. It is a thing very seldom refused. I fancy soon after Harte returns he will in a lawful way humm Mademoiselle Ravaud, and doubtless he will make a very great husband. As for the lady's powers, I do not question them. My compliments to all at Gosfield; and be persuaded yourself of the truth and esteem with which I am, etc.

No. 1717

To his Son

(*Stanhope CCXXX*)

London, 6 August O.S. 1750

My Dear Friend,

Since your letter from Sienna, which gave me a very imperfect account both of your illness and your recovery, I have not received one word either from you or Mr. Harte. I impute this to the carelessness of the post singly; and the great distance between us, at present, exposes our letters to those accidents. But when you come to Paris, from whence the letters arrive here very regularly, I shall insist upon your writing to me constantly once a week; and that upon the same day, for instance, every Thursday, that I may know by what mail to expect your letter. I shall also require you to be more minute in your account of yourself than you have hitherto been, or that I have required; because of the informations which I have received from time to time from Mr. Harte. At Paris you will be out of your time, and must set up for yourself; it is then that I shall be very solicitous to know how you carry on your business. While Mr. Harte was your partner, the care was his share, and the profit yours. But at Paris, if you will have the latter, you must take the former along with it. It will be quite a new world to you, very different from the little world that you have hitherto seen; and you will have much more to do in it. You must keep your little accounts constantly every morning, if you would not have them run into confusion, and swell to a bulk that would frighten you from ever looking into them at all. You must allow some time for learning what you do not know, and some for keeping what you do know; and you must leave a great deal of time for your pleasures, which (I repeat it again) are now become the most necessary part of your education. It is by conversations, dinners, suppers, entertainments, etc., in the best companies, that you must be formed for the world. *Les manières, les agréments, les grâces,* cannot be learned by theory; they are only to be got by use among those who have them; and they are now the main object of your life, as they are the necessary steps to your fortune. A man of the best parts, and the greatest learning, if he does not know the world by his own experience and observation, will be very absurd, and consequently very unwelcome in company. He may say very good things; but they will probably be so ill-timed, misplaced, or improperly addressed, that he had much better hold his tongue. Full of his own matter, and uninformed of, or inattentive to, the particular circumstances and situations of the company, he vents it indiscriminately; he puts some people out of countenance, he shocks others, and frightens all, who dread what may come out next. The most general rule that I can give you for the world, and which your experience will convince you of the truth of, is: Never to give the tone to the company, but to take it from them; and to labour more to put them in conceit with themselves, than to make them admire you. Those whom you can make like themselves better, will, I promise you, like you very well.

A system-monger, who, without knowing anything of the world by experience, has formed a system of it in his dusty cell, lays it down, for example, that (from the general nature of mankind) flattery is pleasing. He will therefore flatter; but how? Why, indiscriminately. And instead of repairing and heightening the piece judiciously, with soft colours, and a delicate pencil; with a coarse brush, and a great deal of whitewash, he daubs and besmears the piece he means to adorn. His flattery offends even his patron, and is almost too gross for his mistress. A man of the world knows the force of flattery as well as he does; but then he knows how, when, and where to give it; he proportions his dose to the constitution of the patient. He flatters by application, by inference, by comparison, by hint, and seldom directly. In the course of the world there is the same difference, in every thing, between system and practice.

I long to have you in Paris, which is to be your great school; you will be then in a manner within reach of me.

Tell me, are you perfectly recovered, or do you still find any remaining complaint upon your lungs? Your diet should be cooling, and at the same time nourishing. Milks of all kinds are proper for you; wines of all kinds bad. A great deal of gentle, and no violent, exercise, is good for you. Adieu! *Gratia, fama, valetudo contingat abunde.*

No. 1718
À Madame la Marquise de Monconseil
(*Maty I. xlviii*)

À Londres, ce 9 août V.S. 1750

Que vous dirai-je, Madame? Votre amitié, vos soins, vos attentions, sont uniques; on n'est accoutumé à rien de pareil, le moyen donc d'y répondre! Mettez-vous seulement, pour un moment, dans ma situation vis-à-vis de vous, et soyez persuadé que tout ce que votre cœur vous dirait en pareil cas, et il vous dit toujours tout ce qu'il faut, est précisément ce que je pense, ce que je sens, mais ce que je ne prétends pas vous dire.

Faute de trouver un meilleur parti, nous convenons donc de l'académie, pour les raisons que je vous ai données, et que l'Abbé Sallier paraît approuver. Votre élève, si je ne m'y trompe, a plus besoin d'être décrotté, par la compagnie de vos jeunes gaillards, que d'être retenu, et je crains plutôt sa trop grande application aux études, que sa trop grande dissipation dans le monde. Ce qui lui manque le plus, c'est cet air, cette tournure, ces manières, ce monde, qui sont nécessaires pour un jeune homme; d'ailleurs, il a de l'ambition, et se pique, et se plaît à être dans les bonnes compagnies, de façon que j'ose répondre qu'il ne formera des liaisons qu'avec les meilleurs sujets de l'académie. Je reconnais bien l'Abbé Sallier dans la lettre qu'il vous écrit; j'y trouve le bon sens, le bon cœur, et les sentiments, qui lui ont acquis depuis longtemps l'estime, et l'amitié de tous les honnêtes gens, qui ont le bonheur de le connaître. Ayez la bonté, Madame, de lui dire de ma part, tout ce que la plus vive reconnaissance devrait dire; je tâcherai de la lui témoigner moi-même bientôt en droiture.

Vous aurez bientôt à Paris, Mylady Hervey, son fils, sa fille, son gendre, et *tutti quanti.* Elle a voulu absolument vous porter quelque chose de ma part, et en effet elle vous porte une petite tabatière, mais ne croyez pas que ce soit en forme de présent. Pour vous tranquilliser sur ce sujet, je vous déclare, que la tabatière ne me coute que deux louis, et que je vous l'envoie, simplement pour vous montrer à quel point nous imitons bien la porcelaine de Dresde, et pour moins que le quart du prix.

Vous serez fâchée, je crois, d'apprendre que Monsieur le Duc de Richmond[1] vient de mourir d'une fièvre continue; son âge, et sa force, lui promettaient encore bien des années. Le Maréchal de Coigny, dont l'âge ne promettait pas tout-à-fait la même chose, s'est bien mieux tiré de sa dernière maladie, dont j'ai en vérité un joie sensible; il jouit même de la vie, selon Monsieur de Matignon, qui a assuré Milord Bolingbroke, qu'il est même rajeuni, et plus gai que jamais: c'est bien un aimable Antée.

[1]Charles Lennox, second Duke of Richmond.

No. 1719

À MADAME LA MARQUISE DE MONCONSEIL

(Maty I. xlix)

À Londres, ce 16 août V.S. 1750

Connaissant comme vous le faites, Madame, mes sentiments, et mon zèle pour tout ce qui vous touche, vous
jugerez bien du chagrin que me cause l'impuissance où je
me trouve d'exécuter les ordres, dont vous m'avez honoré
en dernier lieu. J'ai envisagé l'affaire, au premier abord,
comme difficile, mais à présent je sais qu'elle est impossible.
J'ai sondé le gué, et quoique je ne suis nullement en liaison
avec les ministres j'en ai parlé à un, qui m'a dit très naturellement que cela ne pouvait se faire. Vous savez, me dit-il,
l'esprit de rébellion qui est enraciné dans ces gens-la;[1] leur
foi et la foi punique c'est la même; la clémence ne les gagne
pas, les serments qu'il font au gouvernement ne les tiennent
point; vous n'ignorez pas non plus que les deux tiers de
ceux qui étaient dans la dernière rébellion, étaient des gens
qui avaient été dans l'avant-dernière, et qui ne jouissaient
de leurs vies, et de leurs biens, qu'en vertu de l'indulgence
et du pardon du feu roi. Plusieurs même avaient des
charges, pour lesquelles ils avaient prêté serment de fidélité,
qui ne les retint pourtant pas, que le tocsin de la rébellion
fût sonné. Le nom même de ———, ajouta-t-il, car je fus
obligé de lui dire le nom, implique rébellion de père en fils;
vous saviez tout cela aussi bien que moi, et les menées
secrètes de ces messieurs, pendant que vous étiez dans les
affaires; jugez donc s'il convient, ou à la sûreté, ou à la
dignité du Gouvernement, d'en être une seconde fois la
dupe? Je me trouvai, Madame, dans la nécessité de convenir
de la vérité de tout ce qu'il me disait, puisqu'il n'ignorait
pas que je savais que tout ce qu'il me disait était très vrai.
Je vous dirai, de plus, que tous ces rebelles fugitifs chez vous

[1]The exiled Jacobites.

et ailleurs, prennent date seulement de la rébellion publique, se flattant que le Gouvernement ignore leurs cabales, et leurs secrètes menées du depuis; au lieu que, tout au contraire, il en est parfaitement informé. Il voit les deux tiers de leurs lettres; ils se trahissent les uns les autres, et j'ai eu souvent entre mes mains, en même temps, les lettres du même homme, les unes pour tâcher de faire sa paix avec le Gouvernement, et les autres au Prétendant, pour l'assurer que ce n'était qu'une reconciliation simulée, pour être plus en état de le servir. Malgré tout cela, je suis fâché de ne pouvoir pas être utile à une personne, à qui vous vous intéressez.

J'ai écrit, et en vérité du fond de mon cœur, une lettre de remerciements à l'Abbé Sallier, que j'aime, et que je respecte.

No. 1720

To Lord Huntingdon

(Steuart 5)

London, 3 September O.S. 1750

My Dear Lord,

My inclinations would lead me to write to you much oftener, but my discretion ought (it may be) to hinder me from writing to you so often. Forgot by and forgetting both the polite and the political world, my letters can neither give you amusement nor information. They can only tell you how much I love, honour and esteem you, and you know that already. You make me very happy, my dear Lord, in the friendship and protection which you promise me for my boy. If he deserves them they will be the greatest advantages that I could procure him, and if he does not, of which no man living can judge better than yourself, do not throw them away upon him. But in the meantime look upon him eventually as your dependent, your client, your creature, for those are my instructions to him. He will be

1576

in La Guérinière's Academy at Paris about the end of
October, or the beginning of November next, which I
think is much about the time that you propose being there.
Paris is now a properer sphere for you to move in than
Caen, as you have gone through the necessary gradations
to the best companies which are only to be found in the
great capitals. I hope that your distrust of your own
memory as to facts and dates does not discourage you from
the study of history, chronology and geography; the only
study (I will venture to say it) that can be of use to you
these thirty years. Shut up your classical and philosophical
books, which are merely ornamental, and of which you are
already more than sufficiently master, and lay them by, till
either a disgust of business, or a satiety of the world, makes
you open them again in your own closet, as a decent, an
elegant, and a comfortable refuge. History, chronology, or
geography, unconnected with each other, or not extended
beyond the bounds of one country, are severally difficult,
and indeed useless to retain. But when supported by each
other, and combined with those of other countries, their
relations help, nay force the memory. By history I mean
modern history only, and by modern history I mean almost
only that of the last three hundred years. Remoter history
deserves only a general knowledge, and indeed a general
notion, and that too a very doubtful one, is all that can be
had of it. I would give myself very little trouble about
the history of England before the reign of Henry IV, that
of France before the reign of Louis XI, that of Spain
before the reign of Ferdinand the Catholic, and that of the
Empire before Maximilian, the grandfather of Charles V.
But from those periods to the present one, my attention
would increase and my inquiries grow more minute. That
knowledge is all that your great natural and acquired
talents want to enable you to make that figure in business,
and in Parliament, which you ought to, and I am sure will
make. The transition from business to pleasure is natural

and proper; they should be joined, they whet each other, the one is better done, and the other better tasted, by the alternative. What, then, is become of that corner of your heart which the late Berenice enjoyed? Has it not got a new lodger? a prudent lover, and such I think you will be, if such a one can be, will only let out part of his heart and always keep a share of it for his own, and his friend's use. He takes a lodger, not a tenant. If Caen has not furnished you with a good lodger, Paris certainly will; with this difference only, that a Bill of Health may be previously more necessary at Paris than at Caen.

I have sauntered away good part of this summer at Blackheath, in those amusements of gardening, and idle reading, which my former youth and spirits would have despised, but which now stand in the stead of pleasures with me. The different stages of life fortunately bring with them different ways of thinking, and upon the whole such a proportion of good and bad, that none of them are either to be envied or pitied by the others. Adieu, my dear Lord, be convinced of those sentiments of friendship and esteem with which I shall ever be your most faithful humble servant.

No. 1721

To Lord Huntingdon

(*Steuart 6*)

London, 16 September O.S. 1750

My Dear Lord,

The bearer of this is Mr. Wingfield,[1] eldest son to Lord Powerscourt of Ireland, a very worthy man and my very good friend. He was bred first at the University of Dublin, and afterwards at that of Cambridge, and is said to have a good share of all learning. He is now going to the Academy

[1]Edward Wingfield (1729-1764) who succeeded his father as Viscount Powerscourt in 1751.

at Caen for a year or two, and desires to be under your protection while you continue there; in which I am sure he shows judgment. He told me that he heard that I was well with you, and therefore desired me to give him a letter to you. I was too much flattered with the reason of his request to have refused him any one thing, in consequence of it. I told him that I was extremely well with you, and would have told him so, had I even thought the contrary; this letter followed, of course. You will, I am sure, my dear Lord, excuse my impertinence, which at worst will lead you into no great trouble, as Mr. Wingfield would equally have been in the Academy with you. I am not personally acquainted with him, so can say nothing more to you about him.

I hope you think of leaving Caen soon, and going to Paris for the winter. A metropolis is now the only proper scene for you, for I will venture to prophesy that no theatre can be too great, for the part that you are able to act.

No. 1722

To Lord Huntingdon

(*Steuart 7*)

Bath, 24 September O.S. 1750

My Dear Lord,

You will have found before this time, to your cost, that I had received and acknowledged your letter of July the 5th N.S. This is to acknowledge your last of the 20th Sept. N.S., which was obliged to follow me to Bath, where I have now been three days, and where I shall stay six weeks at least. Indigestions, the common cause of many distempers, had brought on my old and disagreeable vertiginous complaints, which these waters constantly remove for a time, without radically curing them.

The many conveniences that will attend your going to

Paris with the Marquis de Blangy are in my opinion as many good reasons for your delaying your journey there till he goes; he may, if he pleases, save you from those gross impositions, by which the tradesmen of Paris particularly distinguish our countrymen; and he has, doubtless, many acquaintances there to whom he will introduce you. I only want to have you introduced into one good French society, and I am sure you will soon be invited to many others. I will in a very few days send you a couple of letters to two Paris ladies, not beauties I confess, but of good sense, I mean good female sense. The one is Madame du Boccage, a lady of Normandy, whom you have certainly heard of upon account of her translation of Milton, and her Tragedy of the Amazons. The other is Madame de Monconseil, at whose house you will meet good company, as to men, but few women, because of the reputation *trop hasardée* of her mother. As for my men acquaintance, they are most of them dead, or dispersed in the Provinces. But I am in no sort of pain about your being in the very best French companies, for you have a mind to it, which few or none of our countrymen have, and you have all the means of pleasing there, which still fewer of our countrymen have. The French (no matter from what motive, probably vanity) are desirous to see, and to be seen by, strangers of merit, who are desirous to see, and be seen, by them; which I am sure will be your case. It will be impossible for you to avoid entirely the English who swarm at Paris, nor would I advise you to repulse them all; but your main object will I am sure be, to get the acquaintance, and study the characters, and manners of the best French companies. You know too well the use of travelling to live in England all the while you are abroad, as most of our English do.

The verses of the Cordelier, which I forgot to thank you for in my former letter, were very pretty ones; the author seems to have a *much* stronger vocation to the mysteries of the Pagan than of the Christian system. But the Cordeliers

1580

have long been famous for their Priapeian zeal and devotion. I should pity those poor enthusiasts you have lately seen at La Trappe, if I did not know that enthusiasm carries along with it, not only its comforts but its joys. It is the source of a thousand ills to society, but of a thousand pleasures to the enthusiasts themselves. What strange notions must those distempered brains have formed, of an all-wise and omnipotent Being, to suppose that he placed us here, to be a burden to ourselves, and at least useless, if not prejudicial to society. But whoever has lived much in the world and read much of it, will wonder at none of those absurdities and extravagancies, which the mind of man intimidated by fear, invited by interest, or perverted by vanity, is capable of entertaining very seriously, and even with warmth and acrimony. Witness, most of the systems of philosophy, and most sects of religion.

I am very angry at you, my dear Lord, for telling me of your verses to Lord Stormont, and not sending them me at the same time. You have excited an impatience in me which will make me think the quickest return of the post from Caen very tedious. I expect them by the next. They cannot be better than I expect from the poet, but they may be worse, and yet very good ones.

Give me leave, with my usual freedom, to recommend two very silly things to you while you are at Paris, I mean dancing and a dancing master; for though I agree with Cicero that *Nemo sobrius saltat*, yet as the world is not *sobrius*, and as you are in it, you must, and particularly at your age, conform to it. You will sometimes be under a necessity of dancing, and then you had better do it well than ill. *Gervilliers le Cadet* is the master I recommend to you; being very sure that he gives the best air, and most graceful carriage, ornaments that are by no means to be despised by people of your age and rank. In that silly exercise, as in much more material things, a bad master is worse than none.

I am extremely concerned to hear of your late indisposition, *let it have been what it will.* If it was the result of pleasure, I hope it will make you more careful at Paris, where the danger is much greater. If it was an unacquired complaint, and constitutional, pray have great attention to it in your regimen and manner of living. At your age, I squandered away a great deal of health, in the notion that my stock of it was inexhaustible, which I now find too late, it was not. May yours, my dear Lord, with all the other good things, that the good nurse wishes, and you already possess, last long.

Your most faithful humble servant.

No. 1723

À MADAME DU BOCCAGE

(*Maty I. lxxxix*)

À Londres, ce 25 septembre V.S. 1750

Rassurez-vous, Madame; je vous recommande un anglais, mais ne croyez pas que j'aie l'intention de vous charger de tous mes compatriotes. Je les connais trop pour abuser jusqu'à ce point de l'amitié dont vous m'honorez; mais celui-ci est une exception dont vous conviendrez et dont vous me saurez gré. C'est le Comte de Huntingdon, que j'ai l'honneur de vous présenter; jeune seigneur que le mérite et les talents distinguent encore plus que sa naissance; quoiqu'il soit un des plus anciens pairs de Angleterre, de la famille illustre des Hastings descendant en droite ligne de ce Milord Hastings, qui joue un rôle si considérable dans la tragédie de *Jane Shore*, que vous avez sûrement lue, écrite par Rowe, l'auteur de la *Belle Pénitente*.

Pour revenir à mon homme, il réunit à un génie politique une érudition profonde; et son cœur ne le cède en rien à son esprit. Enfin pour tout dire, il est digne d'avoir les entrées chez vous, sans quoi je me serais bien donné de garde d'y avoir été son introducteur. Il a été un an et demi à l'académie de Caen; votre mérite par conséquent ne pouvait lui être inconnu. Il a exigé de mon amitié cette recommandation; et j'ai été bien flatté de pouvoir lui en donner une preuve si essentielle, et de vous réitérer les assurances du véritable attachement, avec lequel j'ai l'honneur d'être, etc.

No. 1724

À MADAME LA MARQUISE DE MONCONSEIL

(Maty I. l)

À Londres, ce 25 septembre V.S. 1750

En dépit de mes promesses, Madame, de ne vous point endosser mes compatriotes, en voici un que je prends la liberté de vous recommander. Au reste, ne craignez rien, ne vous en fâchez pas d'abord, et j'ose dire que vous m'en saurez gré après. C'est Monsieur le Comte de Huntingdon, un des premiers pairs d'Angleterre, et dont la famille est célèbre dans les plus anciennes chroniques. Son mérite et ses talents égalent au moins sa naissance; une érudition profonde le distingue de toute notre jeune noblesse; enfin, il ne lui manque, pour la perfection, que ce qu'il trouvera chez vous, mieux que partout ailleurs, c'est-à-dire *du monde*. J'ose ajouter un autre mérite qu'il aura, je me flatte, auprès de vous, c'est celui d'être particulièrement de mes amis. Il me regarde comme son père, et je le considère comme mon fils adoptif: je vous supplie donc, Madame, très instamment de vouloir bien le protéger, l'encourager, et même le conseiller. Il a trop de discernement pour ne pas connaître d'abord tout le prix de votre amitié et trop de sentiments pour jamais l'oublier; et pour tout dire, il sera bientôt à votre égard, ce qu'est à présent son père adoptif, et
Votre très fidèle serviteur.

No. 1725

To Lord Huntingdon

(*Steuart 8*)

Bath, 29 September O.S. 1750

My Dear Lord,

I send you here enclosed the two letters that I promised you in my last; and I thank you for the opportunity you have given me of obliging, as I am sure I shall, two people whom I am very desirous to oblige. For they have both of them much more sense and discernment than is necessary to make them know the value of the acquaintance I procure them. The letter to Monsieur du Boccage is equally addressed to Madame, but I direct it to him that he may not, as sometimes he does, think himself neglected in comparison of Madame. He is a man of good plain sense and good nature, desirous to oblige, and loving to have his house the resort of people of parts. Madame, both as a woman and as poetess, relishes a little flattery, and I am sure that nobody can season it better for her than yourself. Mrs. Pitt, your old acquaintance, will, I believe, be at Paris when you arrive there, and I recommend to you to address yourself to her immediately, as she can, and I dare say will, with pleasure introduce you into the best companies. My young relation will not be at Paris till near Christmas, but as he has several letters of recommendation from acquaintances that he has made in Italy, and from other persons here, he may possibly be of some use to you after his arrival, and I am very sure will be both proud and happy if he can.

The tender part which I take, my dear Lord, in everything that relates to you, has, I fear, often made me impertinent already, and will, I believe, often make me so again, but I am sure that in consideration of my zeal, you will forgive the indiscreet effects of it. This means that I am going to advise again, and so I am. It just now occurs to me, that very few people in Italy speak tolerable French, and most of them none at all. This is a great disadvantage and drawback to such foreigners as go there, without a certain stock of Italian; I would, therefore, recommend to you to have an Italian master, for an hour every morning, while you stay at Paris, to teach you that language grammatically, which will enable you to speak it very soon after you are in Italy. Besides the disagreeable situation that a man is in who neither speaks nor understands the language spoken by the rest of the company; it is certain that no man can appear what he really is, much less to any advantage, when his thoughts are cramped and checked for want of proper words and expressions. This Italian master, and Monsieur Gervilliers, the dancing master, whom I again venture to recommend to you, are the only masters you can have time for at Paris, and the only masters you can want, being yourself master of everything else. As for mistresses, I do not presume to stint you, the more the better, provided they are such as neither endanger your health nor your character, and Paris abounds with such, as well as with their opposites. Singing, dancing, and theatrical girls with *id genus omne* are vilifying and dangerous, though much the fashion. You will not, I am sure, see better and approve of them, and yet follow worse. Forgive, my dear Lord, all these freedoms in your most sincere friend and faithful servant.

No. 1726

À Madame du Boccage

(*Maty I. lxxxvii*)

À Londres, ce 30 septembre V.S. 1750

Vous nous enlevez donc, Madame, toute cette force et cette énergie de notre langue, dont nous nous piquons; vous y ajoutez les grâces de la vôtre, et vous insultez aux anglais, même en anglais. Cela n'est pas honnête; vous auriez dû

vous contenter d'écrire et de parler mieux que personne
votre propre langue, et nous laisser jouir exclusivement de
la nôtre. Vous prétendiez que je répondisse en anglais; je
m'en donnerai bien de garde. Les crimes de lèse-grammaire
sont pardonnables dans une langue étrangère, mais non dans
la sienne propre, et j'aimerais mieux paraître criminel à tous
les yeux du monde qu'aux vôtres. Raillerie à part, Madame,
la lettre dont vous m'avez honoré, est presque sans faute.
Elle vous a coûté bien du temps et de la peine, dites-vous,
mais aussi il y a des anglais qui se disent lettrés, et qui
n'écrivent pas si bien. Je dois me justifier de n'y avoir pas
répondu plûtôt; la raison n'en est que trop valable. Depuis
plus de deux mois, j'ai été accablé de vertiges et de migraines,
au point de ne pouvoir ni lire ni écrire. Des palliatifs les
ont adoucis, et je pars dans trois jours pour Bath,[1] dans
l'espérance d'y trouver ma guérison. L'espérance est autant
de gagné dans les maux de langueur. La faculté prononce
que ce n'est qu'indigestion (maladie du bon ton, effet ordinaire de la belle gourmandise) et m'a condamné à votre
régime de rôti et de bouilli, à l'exclusion de tout ragoût.
Ainsi je ferais une pitoyable figure à Paris aux quatrième et
cinquième services, à la mode aujourd'hui, ou vos héros
gourmands se disputent le prix à force d'estomac, comme
les héros se disputaient la victoire aux jeux Olympiques, à
force de bras, de jambes, et d'adresse.

On m'assure que Voltaire s'est établi pour toujours à
Berlin; expliquez-moi les motifs d'une telle émigration.
Académicien, Historiographe de France, Gentilhomme ordinaire du Roi, et d'ailleurs riche, renonce-t-il à la France
pour jouir des agréments et de la délicatesse Germanique?
Je ne le comprends pas; s'il est vrai qu'il ait tout de bon
dit adieu à la France, il vous donnera bientôt des pièces bien
hardies. La Bastille a jusqu'ici fort gêné et ses vers et sa
prose.

[1]This does not tally with his remarks to Lord Huntingdon. Perhaps this letter
should be dated the 20th. But it makes no matter.

Je n'ai pas encore reçu le paquet, que vous avez bien voulu m'envoyer. Le monde littéraire de France m'est tout aussi inconnu, depuis six mois, que celui de la lune: nous destinez-vous bientôt quelque chose de votre façon, pour me consoler de l'inaction, dans laquelle mon esprit languit faute d'aliment? Je ne compte pas votre charmante épître sur Vauxhall et Ranelagh, comme un ouvrage pour vous; c'est un délassement pour un talent comme le vôtre, en attendant quelque ouvrage plus considérable. L'Essai de Pope sur la Critique serait un objet digne de votre attention, en cas que vous voulussiez traduire, mais je vous conseille fort de travailler d'invention, et de finir la nouvelle tragédie, que vous avez ébauchée. Vous êtes du petit nombre de ceux, auxquels la paresse n'est pas permise.

Adieu, Madame; en vérité ma misérable tête, peu digne de vous entretenir quand elle est au mieux, l'est à présent moins que jamais; mais pardonnez à l'esprit, en faveur des sentiments du cœur, avec lesquels je serai éternellement,

Madame, etc.

No. 1727

À MADAME DU BOCCAGE

(Maty I. xci)

À Londres, ce 13 octobre V.S. 1750

MADAME,

Nous avons tous deux eu du bonheur; j'ai reçu votre lettre du 6 octobre N.S. et vous n'en avez pas reçu une très longue de ma part, écrite dix ou douze jours avant. La poste semble se connaître en lettres, et ne livrer que celles qui en valent la peine. Dans cette lettre perdue j'avais accusé la réception du gros paquet de livres, que vous avez eu la bonté de m'envoyer, sur lesquels, j'avais hasardé mes sentiments; dans celle-ci je vous remercie du paquet, que Monsieur Hotham[1] m'a donné de votre part. Le porteur ne m'a

---

[1]Chesterfield's nephew, Sir Charles Hotham.

pas moins plû que le paquet; il s'est bien formé en France, je l'ai trouvé bien aimable, ou s'il ne l'est pas, il me l'a paru parcequ'il a parlé, beaucoup de vous, Madame, précisément comme j'en pensais, et une conformité de sentiments prévient extrêmement.

Je suis charmé de *Cénie*, malgré l'aversion que j'ai pour les comédies tragiques ou larmoyantes. Cette pièce, quoique touchante, n'est pas tragique. Les situations en sont intéressantes, mais pas affreuses; les sentiments sont vrais, c'est la nature, on s'y retrouve; et ce ne sont pas ces beaux sentiments de caillettes, qu'on n'a jamais sentis. Une autre chose, qui me la recommande, est qu'elle n'est pas en vers, et par conséquent sent moins le brodequin. Je ne puis vous pardonner vos comédies en vers, je suis choqué d'entendre le pagnoteries de Frontin et de Lisette, et les grossières naïvetés de Lubin dans les plux beaux vers du monde. Pour la tragédie je la livre aux poètes; à bien des égards elle ne peut être naturelle, et les vers lui donnent une dignité, qui lui est absolument nécessaire; mais dans la comédie, qui doit être une représentation naturelle de la vie ordinaire, il est monstrueux d'y faire parler les gens en vers bien rimés. Mais dit-on, d'après Horace, la comédie élève de temps en temps sa voix: je le veux bien à un certain point de prose soutenue, et convenable au caractère et au sujet; mais tel, qui doit parler comme on parle, ne s'élève point jusqu'à parler comme on n'a jamais parlé. Un de nos célèbres auteurs comiques l'a essayé. C'est le Chevalier Etherege, qui a fait deux comédies excellentes, intitulés, *She would if she could*, et *The Man of Mode, or Sir Fopling Flutter*; et dans une troisième intitulée *Love in a Tub*, il a écrit les grands rôles en vers rimés:[1] mais le public s'est soulevé contre cette insulte faite au sens commun, et en vengeur équitable il a condamné la pièce pour toujours.

Nous ne méritons pas l'honneur, que vous nous faites de traduire nos pièces et nos romans. Votre théâtre est trop juste

[1] *Love in a Tub* was Etherege's first play.

et trop châtié pour souffrir la plupart de nos pièces, qui poussent non seulement la liberté, mais la licence, au-delà des bornes de la décence et de la vraisemblance. Je ne crois pas que nous en ayons six de présentables chez vous dans l'état où elles sont. Il faudrait nécessairement les refondre. Si Prévôt traduit notre Clarice,[1] il doit l'abréger d'une bonne moitié; il y a un furieux superflu, et en même temps un intérêt touchant, et des situations intéressantes. Celui qui l'a écrite, qui est aussi l'auteur de *Pamela*, est un libraire, qui manque de savoir et de style, mais qui connaît le cœur. Des sept volumes il en faudrait faire trois.

Mille grâces au reste à la bonne compagnie, que vous me nommez. Que j'aurais été aise d'avoir prévenu ce souvenir par ma présence! Madame Bulkeley est très aimable, et digne de la place qu'elle occupait à ce souper.

Je fais réflexion, peut-être un peu trop tard, que si ma dernière lettre vous est enfin parvenue, et que celle-ci la suive de près, je vous aurai causé une indigestion littéraire, et que par régime vous serez obligée de ne me plus écrire crainte des suites. Je finirai donc brusquement, et sans vous dire à quel point je suis, etc.

P.S. Le Maréchal de Saxe n'étant à présent d'aucune secte, il ne s'embarrassera guère où son corps reposera.[2] Les vers en auront également leur part soit sous la protection de St. Pierre, soit sous celle de Luther ou de Calvin: mais sa gloire est en sûreté, nous en sommes malheureusement les garants, nous y rendons justice. Les préjugés de nation et de secte vous permettront-ils d'en faire autant en France?

[1] Richardson's *Clarissa*.

[2] Maréchal de Saxe, being a Protestant, an objection was made to his being interred, like Turenne, at St. Denis. But a superb monument was erected to him at Strasburg. He was the natural son of Frederick Augustus II of Poland.

No. 1728

TO LORD HUNTINGDON

(*Steuart 9*)

Bath, 20 *October O.S.* 1750

MY DEAR LORD,

The observation of Rabelais, let him have taken it from whom he pleases, I take to be a very just one, and the weaker sex can certainly bear repetition better than the stronger. As you wish me that degree of female fortitude, to undergo the repeated assurances of your friendship, let me tell you that I have it in that respect, beyond any lady in the world; I am even more than a Messalina, for she could be tired though not satiated; I can be neither. Therefore, throwing off all female modesty, and avowing all female desires, I invite you to repetition, it cannot be too frequent. I promise to receive it with the strongest sense of gratitude and delight. I was set out for this place, when Mr. Cunningham left your letter at my house in town; disorders in my stomach had produced others in my head, and obliged me to have recourse to these waters, which always patch me up but without curing me radically. When I retuin to London I hope to have the pleasure of seeing Mr. Cunningham, who must have merit since you esteem him, after six months' acquaintance, for your discernment does not require six days to discover merit. The ordinary people have a superstition about knives, they will neither give nor receive them, ingeniously supposing that they cut love; I am not exceedingly superstitious, but were I so, I should in this case lay it aside, and defy the best-tempered knife at Caen or in Christendom to give the least wound to my friendship for you, and I will be vain enough to add, or to yours for me. I most thankfully accept, and shall most carefully preserve the knife you have sent me, as a mark of your friendship, and not as fatal to it. Lady Chesterfield charges me

1590

with a thousand compliments, and thanks to you, for your
present to her, which she values, as she ought to do upon
its own account, but much more upon yours. I hope you
have received my two last letters of, I do not recollect what
dates, but in the last of the two I sent you inclosed two
letters for two ladies at Paris, which I hope will prove of
use to you. You will also find Mrs. Pitt[1] there, who can,
and I dare say will, be of more use to you, by way of introducing you into French company than all the letters of
recommendation in the world. She is in a manner domestic
in all the best houses at Paris, particularly at Madame de
Mirepoix's. You will, you should, and you may, employ
most of your hours there in pleasures; but you will, I am
sure, too, reserve some for serious occupations; permit me,
therefore, my dear Lord, with my usual and possibly indiscreet freedom, to recommend to you modern history for
the employment of those reserved hours. The new edition
of *Les Mémoires de Sully*,[2] in three quarto volumes, deserves
your attention better than any book that I know of that
kind, as it will give you the truest, and the clearest notion
of the most interesting period of the French history, and a
general one, of the co-temporary history of Europe. There
is another book, but a much smaller lately come out at Paris,
which I will venture to recommend to lie constantly upon
your table. I mean *L'Histoire Chronologique de la France, par
le Président Hénault*. It is not drily chronological nor con-

[1]Penelope Atkins, a famous beauty, wife of George Pitt, of Strathfieldsaye,
afterwards Lord Rivers.

[2]The *Œconomies Royales* as written by Maximilien de Bethune, Duc de Sully
(1559-1641), and as printed in 1638, adopt throughout the cumbrous fiction of
the second person—the Secretaries of Sully recounting to their master, under his
dictation, all that he has seen and done! In 1745, the Abbé de l'Écluse undertook
the revision of these Memoirs, and by judiciously restoring the first person and
omitting some of the *longueurs*—

'We've not so good a word but have the thing'

—has made them one of the most agreeable historical works to be found in any
language. The edition referred to by Lord Chesterfield is that of 1747 with
London on the title page, but really printed in Paris. Since, and by reason of
that publication, says Sismondi, 'la réputation de Sully a grandi de nouveau.'—
Hist. des Français, vol. xxiii. p. 478.—M.

fined to France alone. It is short, but clear and enlivened by some very pretty and just reflections. I am sure I need not suggest to you that to make the reading of history useful, and even to retain it, it must always be accompanied by chronological tables and maps, which are justly called by somebody or other the two eyes of history. The House of Lords must be your end, history one and the chief of your means; the others you have already; the *sapere* and the *fari* are your own, and that all the other parts of Horace's wish may long and inseparably attend you, is the most ardent wish of, my dear Lord, your most sincere friend and faithful servant

CHESTERFIELD.

Postscript.—I lay aside the ceremony of an *enveloppe* to my letters, that you may not pay a great deal more for them than they are worth.

No. 1729

TO HIS SON

(Stanhope CCXXXI)

London, 22 October O.S. 1750

MY DEAR FRIEND,

This letter will, I am persuaded, find you, and I hope safely, arrived at Montpellier; from whence I trust that Mr. Harte's indisposition will, by being totally removed, allow you to get to Paris before Christmas. You will there find two people, who, though both English, I recommend in the strongest manner possible to your attention, and advise you to form the most intimate connections with them both, in their different ways. The one is a man whom you already know something of, but not near enough; it is the Earl of Huntingdon; who, next to you, is the truest object of my affection and esteem, and who (I am proud to say it) calls me and considers me as his adopted father. His parts are as quick as his knowledge is extensive; and if quality were worth putting into account, where every other item is so much more valuable, his is the first almost in this country: the figure he will make soon after he returns to it will, if I am not more mistaken than ever I was in my life, equal his birth and my hopes. Such a connection will be of infinite advantage to you; and I can assure you that he is extremely disposed to form it upon my account; and will, I hope and believe, desire to improve and cement it upon your own.

In our Parliamentary government, connections are absolutely necessary; and, if prudently formed, and ably maintained, the success of them is infallible. There are two sorts of connections, which I would always advise you to have in view. The first I will call equal ones; by which I mean those where the two connecting parties reciprocally find their account, from pretty near an equal degree of parts and abilities. In those, there must be a freer communication; each must see that the other is able, and be convinced that he is willing to be of use to him. Honour must be the principle of such connections; and there must be a mutual dependence, that present and separate interest shall not be able to break them. There must be a joint system of action; and in case of different opinions, each must recede a little, in order at last to form an unanimous one. Such, I hope, will be your connection with Lord Huntingdon. You will both come into Parliament at the same time; and if you have an equal share of abilities and application, you and he, with other young people, whom you will naturally associate, may form a band which will be respected by any administration, and make a figure in the public. The other sort of connections I call unequal ones; that is, where the parts are all on one side, and the rank and fortune on the other. Here, the advantage is all on one side; but that advantage must be ably and artfully concealed. Complaisance, an engaging manner, and a patient toleration of certain airs of superiority, must cement them. The weaker party must be taken by the heart, his head giving no hold; and he must be governed by being made to believe that he governs. These people, skilfully led, give great weight to their leader. I have formerly pointed out to you a couple that I take to be proper objects for your skill; and you will meet with many more, for they are very rife.

The other person, whom I recommend to you, is a woman; not as a woman, for that is not immediately my business; besides, I fear she is turned of fifty. It is Lady Hervey, whom I directed you to call upon at Dijon; but who, to my great joy, because to your great advantage, passes all this winter at Paris. She has been bred all her life at Courts; of which she has acquired all the easy good-breeding, and politeness, without the frivolousness. She has all the reading that a woman should have; and more than any woman need have; for she understands Latin perfectly well, though she wisely conceals it. As she will look upon you as her son, I desire that you will look upon her as my delegate; trust, consult, and apply to her without reserve. No woman ever had, more than she has, *le ton de la parfaitement bonne compagnie, les manières engageantes, et le je ne sais quoi qui plaît.* Desire her to reprove and correct any, and every, the least error and inaccuracy in your manners, air, address, etc. No woman in Europe can do it so well; none will do it more willingly, or in a more proper and obliging way. In such a case she will not put you out of countenance, by telling you of it in company; but either intimate it by some sign, or wait for an opportunity when you are alone together. She is also in the best French company, where she will not only introduce, but *puff* you, if I may use so low a word. And I can assure you, that it is no little help in the *beau monde*, to be puffed there by a fashionable woman. I send you the enclosed billet to carry her, only as a certificate of the identity of your person, which I take it for granted she could not know again.

You would be so much surprised to receive a whole letter from me, without any mention of the exterior ornaments necessary for a gentleman, as manners, elocution, air, address, graces, etc., that to comply with your expectations, I will touch upon them; and tell you, that, when you come to England, I will show you some people whom I do not care to name, raised to the highest stations, simply by those exterior and adventitious ornaments; whose parts would never have entitled them to the smallest office in the excise. Are they then necessary, or worth acquiring, or not? You will see many instances of this kind at Paris, particularly a glaring one, of a person raised to the highest posts and dignities in France, as well as to be absolute sovereign of the *beau monde*, singly by the graces of his person and address; by woman's chit chat, accompanied with important gestures; by an imposing air, and pleasing *abord*.[1] Nay, by these helps he even passes for a wit, though he hath certainly no uncommon share of it. I will not name him, because it would be very imprudent in you to do it. A young fellow, at his first entrance into the *beau monde* must not offend the king *de facto* there. It is very often more necessary to conceal contempt than resentment, the former being never forgiven, but the latter sometimes forgot.

There is a small quarto book, entitled *Histoire Chronologique de la France*, lately published by Le Président Hénault;[2] a man of parts and learning, with whom you will probably get acquainted with at Paris. I desire that it may always lie upon your table, for your recourse as often as you read history. The chronology, though chiefly relative to the history of France, is not singly confined to it; but the most interesting events of all the rest of Europe are also inserted, and many of them adorned by short, pretty, and

[1]The Maréchal de Richelieu, as before.

[2]Le Président Hénault is well known by the chronology which Lord Chesterfield mentions. In 1765, Horace Walpole describes him as follows at a supper at Madame du Deffand's. 'The President is very near deaf and much nearer superannuated. He sits by the table; the mistress of the house, who formerly was his, inquires after every dish on the table, is told who has eaten of which, and then bawls the bills of fare of every individual into the President's ears.' To the Hon. H. Conway, 6th Oct. 1765.—M.

just reflections. The new edition of *les Mémoires de Sully*, in three quarto volumes, is also extremely well worth your reading, as it will give you a clearer and truer notion of one of the most interesting periods of the French history, than you can yet have formed, from all the other books you may have read upon the subject. That prince, I mean Henry the Fourth, had all the accomplishments and virtues of a Hero and of a King; and almost of a man. The last are the more rarely seen; may you possess them all! Adieu!

Pray make my compliments to Mr. Harte, and let him know that I have this moment received his letter of the 12th N.S. from Antibes. It requires no immediate answer; I shall therefore delay mine till I have another from him. Give him the enclosed, which I have received from Mr. Eliot.

No. 1730

To his Son

(*Stanhope CCXXXII*)

London, 1 November O.S. 1750

MY DEAR FRIEND,

I hope this letter will not find you still at Montpellier, but rather be sent after you from thence to Paris, where I am persuaded that Mr. Harte could find as good advice for his leg as at Montpellier, if not better; but if he is of a different opinion, I am sure you ought to stay there as long as he desires.

While you are in France, I could wish that the hours you allot for historical amusement should be entirely devoted to the history of France. One always reads history to most advantage in that country to which it is relative; not only books, but persons being ever at hand to solve the doubts and clear up difficulties. I do by no means advise you to throw away your time in ransacking, like a dull antiquarian,

1596

the minute and unimportant parts of remote and fabulous times. Let blockheads read what blockheads wrote. A general notion of the history of France, from the conquest of that country by the Franks, to the reign of Louis XI, is sufficient for use, consequently sufficient for you. There are, however, in those remote times, some remarkable eras that deserve more particular attention; I mean those in which some notable alterations happened in the constitution and form of government. As for example, the settlement of Clovis in Gaul, and the form of government which he then established; for, by the way, that form of government differed in this particular from all the other Gothic governments, that the people, neither collectively nor by representatives, had any share in it. It was a mixture of monarchy and aristocracy; and what were called the States-General of France consisted only of the nobility and clergy till the time of Philip le Bel, in the very beginning of the fourteenth century; who first called the people to those assemblies, by no means for the good of the people, who were only amused by this pretended honour, but, in truth, to check the nobility and clergy, and induce them to grant the money he wanted for his profusion; this was a scheme of Enguerrand de Marigny, his Minister, who governed both him and his kingdom to such a degree, as to be called the coadjutor and governor of the kingdom. Charles Martel laid aside these assemblies, and governed by open force. Pepin restored them, and attached them to him, and with them the nation; by which means he deposed Childeric, and mounted the throne. This is a second period worth your attention. The third race of Kings, which begins with Hugues Capet, is a third period. A judicious reader of history will save himself a great deal of time and trouble, by attending with care only to those interesting periods of history which furnish remarkable events and make eras; going slightly over the common run of events. Some people read history as others read the *Pilgrim's Progress*; giving equal attention to, and indiscriminately loading their memories with every part alike. But I would have you read it in a different manner: take the shortest general history you can find of every country, and mark down in that history the most important periods; such as conquests, changes of kings, and alterations of the form of government, and then have recourse to more extensive histories or particular treatises relative to these great points. Consider them well, trace up their causes, and follow their consequences. For instance, there is a most excellent though very short history of France by Le Gendre. Read that with attention, and you will know enough of the general history; but when you find there such remarkable periods as are above mentioned, consult Mézeray and other the best and minutest historians, as well as political treatises upon those subjects. In later times, Memoirs, from those of Philip de Commines down to the innumerable ones in the reign of Louis XIV, have been of great use, and thrown great light upon particular parts of history.

Conversation in France, if you have the address and dexterity to turn it upon useful subjects, will exceedingly improve your historical knowledge; for people there, however classically ignorant they may be, think it a shame to be ignorant of the history of their own country; they read that if they read nothing else, and having often read nothing else, are proud of having read that, and talk of it willingly; even the women are well instructed in that sort of reading. I am far from meaning by this that you should always be talking wisely, in company, of books, history, and matters of knowledge. There are many companies which you will and ought to keep, where such conversations would be misplaced and ill-timed; your own good sense must distinguish the company and the time. You must trifle with triflers, and be serious only with the serious; but dance to those who pipe. *Cur in theatrum Cato severe venisti?* was justly said to an old man; how much more so would it be to one of your age? From the moment that you are dressed and go out, pocket all your knowledge with your watch, and never pull it out in company unless desired; the producing of the one un-asked, implies that you are weary of the company; and the producing of the other unrequired will make the company weary of you. Company is a republic[1] too jealous of its liberties to suffer a dictator even for a quarter of an hour; and yet in that, as in all republics, there are some few who really govern, but then it is by seeming to disclaim, instead of attempting to usurp the power; that is the occasion in which manners, dexterity, address, and the undefinable *je ne sais quoi* triumph; if properly exerted their conquest is sure, and the more lasting for not being perceived. Remember that this is not only your first and greatest, but ought to be almost your only object while you are in France.

I know that many of your countrymen are apt to call the freedom and vivacity of the French, petulancy and ill-breeding; but should you think so, I desire upon many accounts that you will not say so. I admit that it may be so, in some instances of *petits maîtres étourdis*, and in some young people unbroken to the world; but I can assure you, that you will find it much otherwise with people of a certain rank and age, upon whose model you will do very well to form yourself. We call their steady assurance impudence. Why? Only because what we call modesty is awkward bashfulness, and *mauvaise honte*. For my part, I see no impudence, but, on the contrary, infinite utility and advan-tage, in presenting one's self with the same coolness and un-concern, in any and every company; till one can do that, I am very sure that one can never present one's self well. Whatever is done under concern and embarrassment must be ill-done; and, till a man is absolutely easy and uncon-cerned in every company, he will never be thought to have kept good, nor be very welcome in it. A steady assurance,

[1]"One evening, in a circle of wits, Goldsmith found fault with me for talking of Johnson as entitled to the honour of unquestionable superiority. "Sir," said he, "you are for making a monarchy of what should be a republic.""—Boswell's *Life of Johnson*. (Bradshaw.)

with seeming modesty, is possibly the most useful qualifica-
tion that a man can have in every part of life. A man would
certainly not make a very considerable fortune and figure in
the world, whose modesty and timidity should often, as
bashfulness always does, put him in the deplorable and
lamentable situation of the pious Æneas, when, *obstupuit,
steteruntque comæ, et vox faucibus hæsit.* Fortune (as well as
women),

——— born to be controlled,
Stoops to the forward and the bold.

Assurance and intrepidity, under the white banner of seeming modesty, clear the way for merit, that would otherwise
be discouraged by difficulties in its journey; whereas bare-
faced impudence is the noisy and blustering harbinger of a
worthless and senseless usurper.

You will think that I shall never have done recommending to you these exterior worldly accomplishments, and
you will think right, for I never shall; they are of too great
consequence to you for me to be indifferent or negligent
about them—the shining part of your future figure and
fortune depends now wholly upon them. These are the
acquisitions which must give efficacy and success to those
you have already made. To have it said and believed that
you are the most learned man in England, would be no
more than was said and believed of Dr. Bentley;[1] but to
have it said at the same time that you are also the best bred,
most polite, and agreeable man in the kingdom, would be
such a happy composition of a character, as I never yet knew
any one man deserve, and which I will endeavour, as well as
ardently wish, that you may. Absolute perfection is, I well
know, unattainable; but I know, too, that a man of parts
may be unweariedly aiming at and arrive pretty near it.
Try, labour, persevere. Adieu.

[1]Chesterfield, perhaps following Boyle, regarded Bentley as something of a
pedant. See his amusing *Dialogue of the Dead* between Bentley and Horace.
Miscellaneous Pieces.

No. 1731

À MADAME LA MARQUISE DE MONCONSEIL

(Maty I. li)

À Bath, ce 1 novembre V.S. 1750

Tenez-moi compte, Madame, d'un silence que j'ai gardé longtemps par la force de mon esprit, en dépit des mouvements de mon cœur, qui en murmurait souvent, et qui à tous moments voulait vous dire deux mots. Voici le cas; vers la fin de l'automne, mes vertiges, mes migraines, et enfin tout ce qui peut désoler une tête, s'unirent pour accabler la mienne; il ne lui en fallait sûrement pas tant. Sur ces entrefaites, cette tête, qui sait bien le respect qu'elle doit à la vôtre, et qui, même quand elle est au mieux, soutient fort mal ce vis-à-vis, prit sagement le parti de se cacher, en attendant mieux. Ce mieux est à la fin venu; j'ai porté cette tête ici, sa ressource ordinaire, je l'ai rétablie tellement quellement à force de boire, ces eaux s'entend. La voici donc qui revient, et qui se présente derechef très respectueusement à la vôtre, c'est-à-dire que je suis beaucoup mieux, et en état de vous réitérer les assurances des sentiments d'estime et d'amitié, qui sont à l'épreuve de tous les maux du monde.

Vous avez donc trouvé le moyen, comme je n'en doutais point, de garder Madame d'Hervey tout l'hiver à Paris: vous avez raison, elle aussi. Ses lettres sont autant d'éloges de la France, et des français, au point même de nous être injurieuses. Elle a souvent le plaisir de vous voir, cela seul me suffirait pour en dire autant, ou davantage. Au reste, je ne souhaite pas d'être si souvent le sujet de vos conversations, puisque, quelque prévenues que vous soyez toutes les deux en ma faveur, vous me connaissez toutes les deux trop bien, pour qu'il n'entre point bien des *mais* dans ces conversations; au lieu que j'aimerais mieux que chacune parlât de moi séparément à des gens qui ne me connaissent pas, et alors chacune pourrait, et je me flatte bien qu'elle le voudrait, mentir impunément à mon avantage.

Votre élève est actuellement en France, rôdant en Languedoc, Provence, Dauphiné, etc. Il aura l'honneur de vous faire sa cour avant Noël. Il cherche les grâces à Paris; je lui ai mandé où il les trouverait; si vous croyez que je m'y suis trompé, ayez la bonté, Madame, de lui indiquer leur demeure, au moins j'en ai agi de bonne foi avec lui.

J'apprends de Berlin que Voltaire a dit un adieu perpétuel à la France, et s'est établi dans le nouveau séjour des Muses, sous l'Auguste, et en même temps le Mécène, du Nord; mais il faut avouer aussi, qu'il a montré plus que de l'art poétique dans le marché qu'il a fait avec ce Prince; car il a la Clef d'or de Chambellan, l'Ordre de l'Amitié, cinq mille écus d'entrée, et autant de rente viagère, dont deux mille, en cas de sa mort, sont substitués sur sa nièce. Ces conditions sentent plus une des montagnes du Pérou, que celle du Parnasse.[1] Il y a déjà joué son Cicéron par appel, comme d'abus, du tribunal poétique de la France à celui de Berlin, et votre arrêt y a été cassé; mais vous avez tant de beaux esprits à Paris, que vous ne vous ressentirez pas de la perte de celui-ci. Les dames même vous en dédommagent. La comédie pathétique de Madame de Graffigny est excellente dans ce goût-là,[2] et le Milton de Madame du Boccage a, je vous en assure, beaucoup de mérite.[3] Elle l'a beaucoup abrégé, mais avec jugement; et sa traduction du *Temple de la Renommée* de Pope est d'une exactitude étonnante. Bon soir, Madame.

[1] 'Savez-vous, Monsieur, ce qui me prouve le plus la supériorité du vôtre [esprit] et ce qui fait que je vous trouve un grand philosophe? c'est que vous êtes devenu riche.' Madame du Deffand to Voltaire, 28th October 1759.

[2] She was the authoress of *Cénie*.

[3] This moderate praise, even to Madame du Boccage's friend, sufficiently disproves the sarcasm of Horace Walpole, who says of her translation of Milton that 'my Lord Chesterfield prefers the copy to the original!' (To Sir H. Mann, 2nd April 1750.)—M.

No. 1732
À Madame la Marquise de Monconseil
(*Maty I. lii*)

À Bath, ce 5 *novembre V.S.* 1750

Nos dernières lettres se sont croisées, Madame. J'ai reçu la vôtre deux jours après avoir envoyé la mienne; de façon que ma justification trottait en même temps que mon accusation. Celle-ci ne sera donc qu'un remerciement de l'attention que vous avez bien voulu faire à mon silence, qui ne méritait pas vos regrets, ou vos reproches.

Ce lien de notre commerce, cet enfant enfin, l'objet qui a donné lieu aux termes qui pourraient être suspects aux curieux qui ouvriraient nos lettres, aura bientôt l'honneur de vous faire sa cour. Il aura bien plus besoin de votre secours, qu'il n'en aurait eu, s'il eût été l'objet d'un soupçon bien fondé; une telle naissance aurait rendu une bonne moitié de mes soins inutiles. Suppléez, Madame, à ce défaut par les vôtres, et rendez-le au moins digne d'une naissance, qui l'aurait rendu plus digne de vos soins. Vous le pouvez, vous qui êtes capable de donner à l'amitié ce que les autres ne savent donner qu'à des sentiments plus vifs. Réellement je compte sur vous uniquement, pour faire la fortune de cet *être* que je vous remets; les autres lui feront des politesses, m'en diront du bien, mais se soucieront très peu au fond du reste. Il en serait précisément où il en est actuellement, et à cet âge c'est reculer que de ne pas avancer: mais je suis bien sûr que vous en agirez d'une toute autre façon. Vous lui direz ses défauts avec cette autorité, qui accompagne toujours la justesse de votre critique, et la manière avec laquelle vous la ferez. Il faut nécessairement qu'il soit gauche, et embarrassé. L'allemagne ne donne pas les grâces, et l'italie ne les donne guère plus. Ce n'est que dans les bonnes compagnies à Paris qu'on les peut acquérir: permettez-lui donc, non seulement, mais ordonnez-lui de fréquenter votre maison les soirées, c'est-à-dire quand il n'y sera pas de trop, et pour vous en soulager quelquefois, fourrez-le dans d'autres compagnies; ce sera une contrainte bien douce, et bien avantageuse pour lui. Il a sûrement un très grand fond de savoir; je ne sais s'il a de l'esprit, mais je sais bien que s'il en a, vous mettrez le comble à son caractère en lui donnant les manières, et les grâces, qui ornent les meilleurs caractères, et qui expient en quelque façon les fautes des plus mauvais. Dans le train ordinaire du monde, combien de gens ne voyons-nous pas, qui ne se sauvent qu'en faveur de leurs manières, et d'autres qui, avec un mérite très solide, ne se font pas jour, faute de ces manières! On a beau savoir, c'est le je ne sais quoi, qui le fait valoir; il n'y a que les sauvages qui portent les pierres précieuses brutes.

Adieu, Madame, je pars d'ici en trois jours; et ce sera de Londres que vous aurez les premières nouvelles de votre très humble serviteur.

No. 1733

To his Son

(Stanhope CCXXXIII)

London, 8 November O.S. 1750

My Dear Friend,

Before you get to Paris, where you will soon be left to your own discretion, if you have any, it is necessary that we should understand one another thoroughly; which is the most probable way of preventing disputes. Money, the cause of much mischief in the world, is the cause of most quarrels between fathers and sons; the former commonly thinking that they cannot give too little, and the latter that they cannot have enough; both equally in the wrong. You must do me the justice to acknowledge, that I have hitherto neither stinted nor grudged any expense that could be of use or real pleasure to you; and I can assure you, by the way, that you have travelled at a much more considerable expense than I did myself; but I never so much as thought of that while Mr. Harte was at the head of your finances, being very sure that the sums granted were scrupulously applied to the uses for which they were intended. But the case will soon be altered, and you will be your own receiver and treasurer. However, I promise you that we will not quarrel singly upon the *quantum*, which shall be cheerfully and freely granted; the application and appropriation of it will be the material point, which I am now going to clear up, and finally settle with you. I will fix, or even name, no settled allowance, though I well know in your own mind what would be the proper one; but I will first try your drafts, by which I can in a good degree judge of your conduct. This only I tell you in general, that, if the channels through which my money is to go are the proper ones, the source shall not be scanty; but should it deviate into dirty, muddy and obscure ones (which, by the bye, it cannot do for a week without my knowing it), I give you fair and timely notice that the source will instantly be dry. Mr. Harte, in establishing you at Paris, will point out to you those proper channels; he will leave you there upon the foot of a man of fashion, and I will continue you upon the same. You will have your coach, your valet de chambre, your own footman, and a valet de place—which, by the way, is one servant more than I had. I would have you well dressed, by which I mean, dressed as the generality of people of fashion are—that is, not to be taken notice of, for being either more or less fine than other people; it is by being well dressed, not finely dressed, that a gentleman should be distinguished. You must frequent *les spectacles*, which expense I shall willingly supply. You must play, *à des petits jeux de commerce*, in mixed companies; that article is trifling; I shall pay it cheerfully. All the other articles of pocket-money are very inconsiderable at Paris, in comparison of what they are here; the silly custom of giving money wherever one dines or sups, and the expensive importunity of subscriptions, not being yet introduced there. Having thus reckoned up all the decent expenses of a gentleman, which, I will most readily defray, I come now to those which I will neither bear nor supply. The first of these is gaming, which, though I have not the least reason to suspect you of, I think is necessary eventually to assure you, that no consideration in the world shall ever make me pay your play-debts; should you ever urge to me that your honour is pawned, I shall most immovably answer you, that it was your honour, not mine, that was pawned, and that your creditor might e'en take the pawn for the debt.

Low company and low pleasures are always much more costly than liberal and elegant ones. The disgraceful riots of a tavern are much more expensive, as well as dishonourable, than the (sometimes pardonable) excesses in good company. I must absolutely hear of no tavern scrapes and squabbles.

I come now to another and very material point; I mean women; and I will not address myself to you upon this subject, either in a religious, a moral, or a parental style. I will even lay aside my age, remember yours, and speak to you, as one man of pleasure, if he had parts too, would speak to another. I will, by no means, pay for whores, and their never-failing consequences, surgeons; nor will I, upon any account, keep singers, dancers, actresses, and *id genus omne*; and, independently of the expense, I must tell you, that such connections would give me, and all sensible people, the utmost contempt for your parts and address; a young fellow must have as little sense as address, to venture, or more properly to sacrifice his health, and ruin his fortune, with such sort of creatures; in such a place as Paris especially, where gallantry is both the profession and the practice of every woman of fashion. To speak plainly; I will not forgive your understanding claps and poxes; nor will your constitution forgive them you. These distempers, as well as their cures, fall nine times in ten upon the lungs. This argument, I am sure, ought to have weight with you; for I protest to you, that if you meet with any such accident, I would not give one year's purchase for your life. Lastly, there is another sort of expense that I will not allow, only because it is a silly one; I mean the fooling away your money in baubles at toyshops. Have one handsome snuff-box (if you take snuff) and one handsome sword; but then no more very pretty and very useless things.

By what goes before, you will easily perceive that I mean to allow you whatever is necessary, not only for the figure, but for the pleasures of a gentleman, and not to supply the profusion of a rake. This, you must confess, does not savour of either the severity or parsimony of old age. I consider this agreement between us as a subsidiary treaty on my part for services to be performed on yours. I promise you, that I will be as punctual in the payment of subsidies as England has been during the last war; but then I give you notice at the same time, that I require a much more scrupulous execution of the treaty on your part than we met with on that of our Allies; or else that payment will be stopped. I hope that all I have now said was absolutely unnecessary, and that sentiments more worthy and more noble than pecuniary ones, would of themselves have pointed out to you the conduct I recommend; but, in all events, I resolved to be once for all explicit with you, that in the worst that can happen, you may not plead ignorance, and complain that I had not sufficiently explained to you my intentions.

Having mentioned the word rake, I must say a word or two more on that subject, because young people too frequently, and always fatally, are apt to mistake that character for that of a man of pleasure; whereas, there are not in the world two characters more different. A rake is a composition of all the lowest, most ignoble, degrading, and shameful vices; they all conspire to disgrace his character and to ruin his fortune; while wine and the pox contend which shall soonest and most effectually destroy his constitution. A dissolute, flagitious footman or porter makes full as good a rake as a man of the first quality. By the bye, let me tell you that in the wildest part of my youth I never was a rake, but, on the contrary, always detested and despised the character.

A man of pleasure, though not always so scrupulous as he should be, and as one day he will wish he had been, refines at least his pleasures by taste, accompanies them with decency, and enjoys them with dignity. Few men can be men of pleasure, every man may be a rake. Remember that I shall know everything you say or do at Paris, as exactly as if, by the force of magic, I could follow you everywhere, like a sylph or a gnome, invisible myself. Seneca says, very prettily, that one should ask nothing of God, but what one should be willing that men should know; nor of men, but what one should be willing that God should know; I advise you to say or do nothing at Paris, but what you would be willing that I should know. I hope, nay I believe, that will be the case. Sense, I dare say, you do not want; instruction, I am sure, you have never wanted; experience, you are daily gaining; all which together must inevitably (I should think) make you both *respectable et aimable*, the perfection of a human character. In that case nothing shall be wanting on my part, and you shall solidly experience all the extent and tenderness of my affection for you; but dread the reverse of both! Adieu.

P.S. When you get to Paris, after you have been to wait on Lord Albemarle,[1] go to see Mr. Yorke,[2] whom I have

---

[1] William Anne Keppel, second Earl of Albemarle (1702-1754), 'the spendthrift Earl,' died as Ambassador at Paris, 22nd December 1754. A sketch of his character and fortunes is given by Lord Chesterfield in his letter of 27th May 1752. He commanded the first line of Cumberland's army at Culloden.

[2] Joseph, third son of Lord Chancellor Hardwicke, was at this time Secretary of Embassy at Paris, but became, in 1751, Envoy at the Hague. He was created Lord Dover in 1788, and died without issue in 1792.—M.

particular reasons for desiring that you should be well with, as I shall hereafter explain to you. Let him know that my orders, and your own inclinations, conspired to make you desire his friendship and protection.

No. 1734

To his Son

(Stanhope CCXXXIV)

[*November* 1750]

MY DEAR FRIEND,

I have sent you so many preparatory letters for Paris, that this, which will meet you there, shall only be a summary of them all.

You have hitherto had more liberty than anybody of your age ever had; and I must do you the justice to own, that you have made a better use of it than most people of your age would have done; but then, though you had not a jailer, you had a friend with you. At Paris, you will not only be unconfined, but unassisted. Your own good sense must be your only guide; I have great confidence in it, and am convinced that I shall receive just such accounts of your conduct at Paris as I could wish; for I tell you beforehand, that I shall be most minutely informed of all that you do, and almost of all that you say there. Enjoy the pleasures of youth, you cannot do better; but refine and dignify them like a man of parts; let them raise and not sink, let them adorn and not vilify, your character; let them, in short, be the pleasures of a gentleman, and taken with your equals at least, but rather with your superiors, and those chiefly French.

Inquire into the characters of the several Academicians before you form a connection with any of them; and be most upon your guard against those who make the most court to you.

You cannot study much in the Academy; but you may

study usefully there, if you are an economist of your time, and bestow only upon good books those quarters and halves of hours, which occur to everybody in the course of almost every day; and which, at the year's end, amount to a very considerable sum of time. Let Greek, without fail, share some part of every day: I do not mean the Greek poets, the catches of Anacreon, or the tender complaints of Theocritus, or even the porter-like language of Homer's heroes; of whom all smatterers in Greek know a little, quote often, and talk of always; but I mean Plato, Aristoteles, Demosthenes, and Thucydides, whom none but adepts know. It is Greek that must distinguish you in the learned world, Latin alone will not. And Greek must be sought to be retained, for it never occurs like Latin. When you read history, or other books of amusement, let every language you are master of have its turn; so that you may not only retain, but improve in, every one. I also desire that you will converse in German and Italian with all the Germans and the Italians with whom you converse at all. This will be a very agreeable and flattering thing to them, and a very useful one to you.

Pray apply yourself diligently to your exercises; for though the doing them well is not supremely meritorious, the doing them ill is illiberal, vulgar, and ridiculous.

I recommend theatrical representations to you, which are excellent at Paris. The tragedies of Corneille and Racine, and the comedies of Molière, well attended to, are admirable lessons, both for the heart and the head. There is not, nor ever was, any theatre comparable to the French. If the music of the French operas does not please your Italian ear, the words of them, at least, are sense and poetry, which is much more than I can say of any Italian opera that I ever read or heard of in my life.

I send you the enclosed letter of recommendation to Marquis Matignon, which I would have you deliver to him as soon as you can; you will, I am sure, feel the good effects of his warm friendship for me and Lord Bolingbroke, who has also wrote to him upon your subject. By that, and by the other letters which I have sent you, you will be at once so thoroughly introduced into the best French company, that you must take some pains if you will keep bad; but that is what I do not suspect you of. You have, I am sure, too much right ambition to prefer low and disgraceful company to that of your superiors both in rank and age. Your character, and consequently your fortune, absolutely depends upon the company you keep, and the turn you take at Paris. I do not, in the least, mean a grave turn; on the contrary, a gay, a sprightly, but, at the same time, an elegant and liberal one.

Keep carefully out of all scrapes and quarrels. They lower a character extremely, and are particularly dangerous in France, where a man is dishonoured by not resenting an affront, and utterly ruined by resenting it. The young Frenchmen are hasty, giddy, and petulant; extremely national and *avantageux*. Forbear from any national jokes or reflections, which are always improper, and commonly unjust. The colder northern nations generally look upon France as a whistling, singing, dancing, frivolous nation; this notion is very far from being a true one, though many *petits maîtres* by their behaviour seem to justify it; but those very *petits maîtres*, when mellowed by age and experience, very often turn out very able men. The number of great generals and statesmen, as well as excellent authors, that France has produced is an undeniable proof that it is not that frivolous, unthinking, empty nation that northern prejudices suppose it. Seem to like and approve of everything at first, and I promise you that you will like and approve of many things afterwards.

I expect that you will write to me constantly once every week, which I desire may be every Thursday; and that your letters may inform me of your personal transactions; not of what you see, but of whom you see, and what you do.

Be your own monitor, now that you will have no other. As to enunciation, I must repeat it to you again and again, that there is no one thing so necessary; all other talents, without that, are absolutely useless, except in your own closet.

It sounds ridiculously to bid you study with your dancing-master; and yet I do. The bodily carriage and graces are of infinite consequence to everybody, and more particularly to you.

Adieu for this time, my dear child. Yours tenderly.

No. 1735

To his Son

(*Stanhope CCXXXV*)

London, 12 *November O.S.* 1750

My Dear Friend,

You will possibly think that this letter turns upon strange, little trifling objects; and you will think right, if you consider them separately; but if you take them aggregately, you will be convinced that, as parts, which conspire to form that whole, called the exterior of a man of fashion, they are of importance. I shall not dwell now upon those personal graces, that liberal air, and that engaging address, which I have so often recommended to you; but descend still lower, to your dress, cleanliness, and care of your person.

When you come to Paris, you must take care to be extremely well dressed, that is, as the fashionable people are. This does by no means consist in the finery, but in the taste, fitness, and manner of wearing your clothes; a fine suit ill-made, and slatternly or stiffly worn, far from adorning, only exposes the awkwardness of the wearer. Get the best French tailor to make your clothes, whatever they are, in the fashion, and to fit you, and then wear them; button them or unbutton them, as the genteelest people you see do.

Let your man learn of the best *friseur* to do your hair well, for that is a very material part of your dress. Take care to have your stockings well gartered up, and your shoes well buckled; for nothing gives a more slovenly air to a man than ill-dressed legs. In your person you must be accurately clean; and your teeth, hands, and nails should be superlatively so. A dirty mouth has real ill consequences to the owner, for it infallibly causes the decay, as well as the intolerable pain of the teeth; and it is very offensive to his acquaintance, for it will most inevitably stink. I insist therefore that you wash your teeth the first thing that you do every morning, with a soft sponge and warm water, for four or five minutes, and then wash your mouth five or six times. *Mouton*, whom I desire you will send for upon your arrival at Paris, will give you an opiate, and a liquor to be used sometimes. Nothing looks more ordinary, vulgar, and illiberal, than dirty hands, and ugly, uneven and ragged nails. I do not suspect you of that shocking, awkward trick of biting yours; but that is not enough; you must keep the ends of them smooth and clean, not tipped with black, as the ordinary people's always are. The ends of your nails should be small segments of circles, which, by a very little care in the cutting, they are very easily brought to; every time that you wipe your hands, rub the skin round your nails backwards, that it may not grow up and shorten your nails too much. The cleanliness of the rest of your person, which by the way will conduce greatly to your health, I refer from time to time to the bagnio. My mentioning these particulars arises (I freely own) from some suspicion that the hints are not unnecessary; for when you were a schoolboy, you were slovenly and dirty above your fellows. I must add another caution, which is, that upon no account whatever you put your fingers, as too many people are apt to, in your nose or ears. It is the most shocking, nasty, vulgar rudeness that can be offered to company; it disgusts one, it turns one's stomach; and, for my own part, I would much rather know that a man's fingers were actually in his breech, than see them in his nose. Wash your ears well every morning, and blow your nose in your handkerchief whenever you have occasion; but, by the way, without looking at it afterwards.

There should be in the least, as well as in the greatest parts of a gentleman, *les manières nobles*. Sense will teach you some, observation others; attend carefully to the manners, the diction, the motions, of people of the first fashion, and form your own upon them. On the other hand, observe a little those of the vulgar, in order to avoid them; for though the things which they say or do may be the same, the manner is always totally different; and in that, and nothing else, consists the characteristic of a man of fashion. The lowest peasant speaks, moves, dresses, eats, and drinks, as much as a man of the first fashion; but does them all quite differently; so that by doing and saying most things in a manner opposite to that of the vulgar, you have a great chance of doing and saying them right. There are gradations in awkwardness and vulgarism, as there are in everything else. *Les manières de robe*, though not quite right, are still better than les *manières bourgeoises*; and these, though bad, are still better than *les manières de campagne*. But the language, the air, the dress, and the manners of the Court, are the only true standard *des manières nobles, et d'un honnête homme. Ex pede Herculem* is an old and true saying, and very applicable to our present subject; for a man of parts, who has been bred at Courts, and used to keep the best company, will distinguish himself, and is to be known from the vulgar, by every word, attitude, gesture, and even look. I cannot leave these seeming *minuties*, without repeating to you the necessity of your carving well, which is an article, little as it is, that is useful twice every day of one's life; and the doing it ill is very troublesome to one's self, and very disagreeable, often ridiculous, to others.

Having said all this, I cannot help reflecting what a formal

dull fellow, or a cloistered pedant, would say, if they were
to see this letter; they would look upon it with the utmost
contempt, and say that surely a father might find much
better topics for advice to a son. I would admit it, if I had
given you, or that you were capable of receiving no better;
but if sufficient pains have been taken to form your heart
and improve your mind, and, as I hope, not without success,
I will tell those solid gentlemen, that all these trifling things,
as they think them, collectively form that pleasing *je ne sais
quoi*, that *ensemble*, which they are utter strangers to, both
in themselves and others. The word *aimable* is not known
in their language, or the thing in their manners. Great usage
of the world, great attention, and a great desire of pleasing,
can alone give it; and it is no trifle. It is from old people's
looking upon these things as trifles, or not thinking of them
at all, that so many young people are so awkward and so
ill-bred. Their parents, often careless and unmindful of
them, give them only the common run of education, as
school, university, and then travelling, without examining,
and very often without being able to judge if they did examine, what progress they make in any one of these stages.
Then they carelessly comfort themselves, and say, that their
sons will do like other people's sons; and so they do, that is,
commonly very ill. They correct none of the childish, nasty
tricks, which they get at school; nor the illiberal manners
which they contract at the university; nor the frivolous and
superficial pertness, which is commonly all that they acquire
by their travels. As they do not tell them of these things,
nobody else can; so they go on in the practice of them,
without ever hearing, or knowing, that they are unbecoming, indecent, and shocking. For, as I have often formerly
observed to you, nobody but a father can take the liberty
to reprove a young fellow grown up, for those kind of
inaccuracies and improprieties of behaviour. The most intimate friendship, unassisted by the paternal superiority,
will not authorise it. I may truly say, therefore, that you

are happy in having me for a sincere, friendly, and quick-sighted monitor. Nothing will escape me; I shall pry for your defects, in order to correct them, as curiously as I shall seek for your perfections, in order to applaud and reward them; with this difference only, that I shall publicly mention the latter, and never hint at the former, but in a letter to, or a *tête-à-tête* with you. I will never put you out of counten-ance before company, and I hope you will never give me reason to be out of countenance for you, as any one of the above-mentioned defects would make me. *Prætor non curat de minimis* was a maxim in the Roman law, for causes only of a certain value were tried by him; but there were inferior jurisdictions, that took cognizance of the smallest. Now I shall try you, not only as a Prætor in the greatest, but as Censor in lesser, and as the lowest magistrate in the least cases.

I have this moment received Mr. Harte's letter of the 1st November, New Style; by which I am very glad to find that he thinks of moving towards Paris, the end of this month, which looks as if his leg were better; besides, in my opinion, you both of you only lose time at Montpellier; he would find better advice, and you better company, at Paris. In the meantime, I hope you go into the best company there is at Montpellier, and there always is some at the Intendant's or the Commandant's. You will have had full time to have learned *les petites chansons Languedociennes*, which are ex-ceedingly pretty ones, both words and tunes. I remember, when I was in those parts, I was surprised at the difference which I found between the people on one side, and those on the other side of the Rhone. The *Provencaux* were, in general, surly, ill-bred, ugly, and swarthy: the Langue-dociens the very reverse; a cheerful, well-bred, handsome people. Adieu! Yours most affectionately.

P.S. Upon reflection, I direct this letter to Paris; I think you must have left Montpellier before it could arrive there.

No. 1736

To Lord Huntingdon

(*Steuart 10*)

London, 15 November O.S. 1750

My Dear Lord,

I owe you what I can never pay you in value, though I can in number, two letters. My journey from Bath hindered me from acknowledging your former, and the frivolous hurry which every man after having been two months out of London finds himself in at his return to it delayed my acknowledging the latter. But I have still something to thank you for, and very heartily too. I think myself obliged to any man living who gives me pleasure, but when that pleasure has the stamp of confidence and friendship upon it, it is at least doubled. I would not commend your verses to you if I thought it possible that you could suspect flattery, or even common civility to have any share in the commendation; but a copy of verses upon a woman in the warmth of a young passion is by no means an object for your vanity, or my adulation. You are as much above making bad verses as you are above valuing yourself upon making good ones. One sees that love made these verses, and love is the best muse, where love is concerned. You have not stolen from your model, but you have thought like him, and I will add, better. Whoever was the subject of them, and whatever passed between you and that subject has not the least relation to your moral character; let dulness, age, or bigotry say what they will about it; but for my part, I have met with no one body absurd enough to suppose that you left England a spotless virgin, or to expect, if you had, that you would have returned such to it. Desires are natural to youth and warm blood, and the gratification of them is neither disgraceful nor criminal, unless procured by crimes. I have had the pleasure since my return from Bath to see your friend, Mr. Cunningham, who seems to me to be a very pretty fellow; though in this case I own I am a very partial judge, from your commendation of him, and from his manner of speaking of you; either of which would have biased me in his favour. I question whether this letter will find you still at Caen, and I am full as willing that it should be sent after you to Paris, where I want you to be. I am sure that you will like it, and I am as sure that Paris will like you. You will not live there as most of our countrymen do, who herd together, pass their evenings at a coffee house, and their nights at the tavern or the bawdy-house, and then complain of the difficulty of getting into French company, which they never once try to do. Wherever you knock, I am sure it will be opened unto you, and you know the true intention and use of travelling too well to neglect being acquainted with the manners and characters of the people of the several countries where you go. Let me recommend to you, my dear Lord, to frequent the Foreign Ministers residing at Paris, which is to some degree, travelling in several countries at once; besides that, when you leave Paris, they will give you letters of recommendation to their respective Courts. I will not in concluding this letter, pretend to tell you, what I know I cannot express, how faithfully and affectionately I am, my dear Lord, yours.

No. 1737
To his Son
(*Stanhope CCXXXVI*)

London, 19 November O.S. 1750

MY DEAR FRIEND,

I was very glad to find, by your letter of the 12th N.S. that you had informed yourself so well of the state of the French marine at Toulon, and of the commerce at Marseilles; they are objects that deserve the inquiry and attention of every man, who intends to be concerned in public affairs. The French are now wisely attentive to both; their commerce is incredibly increased within these last thirty years; they have beaten us out of great part of our Levant trade; their East-India trade has greatly affected ours; and, in the West Indies, their Martinico establishment supplies, not only France itself, but in the greatest part of Europe, with sugars; whereas our islands, as Jamaica, Barbados, and the Leeward, have now no other market for theirs but England. New France, or Canada, has also greatly lessened our fur and skin trade. It is true (as you say) that we have no treaty of commerce subsisting (I do not say *with Marseilles*) but with France. There was a treaty of commerce made, between England and France, immediately after the treaty of Utrecht; but the whole treaty was conditional, and to depend upon the Parliament's enacting certain things, which were stipulated in two of the articles; the Parliament, after a very famous debate, would not do it; so the treaty fell to the ground; however, the outlines of that treaty are, by mutual and tacit consent, the general rules of our commerce with France. It is true, too, that our commodities, which go to France, must go in our bottoms; the French having imitated, in many respects, our famous Act of Navigation, as it is commonly called. This Act was made in the year 1652, in the Parliament held by Oliver Cromwell. It forbids all foreign ships to bring into England any merchandise or commodities whatsoever, that were not of the growth and produce of that country to which those ships belonged, under penalty of the forfeiture of such ships. This Act was particularly levelled at the Dutch; who were, at that time, the carriers of almost all Europe, and got immensely by freight. Upon this principle, of the advantages arising from freight, there is a provision in the same Act, that even the growth and produce of our own colonies in America shall not be carried from thence to any other country in Europe, without first touching in England; but this clause has lately been repealed, in the instances of some perishable commodities, such as rice, etc., which are allowed to be carried directly from our American colonies to other countries. The Act also provides, that two-thirds, I think, of those who navigate the said ships shall be British subjects. There is an excellent, and little book, written by the famous Monsieur Huet,[1] Évêque d'Avranches, *Sur le Commerce des Anciens*, which is very well worth your reading, and very soon read. It will give you a clear notion of the rise and progress of commerce. There are many other books which take up the history of commerce where Monsieur d'Avranches leaves it, and bring it down to these times: I advise you to read some of them with care; commerce being a very essential part of political knowledge in every country, but more particularly in this, which owes all its riches and power to it.

I come now to another part of your letter, which is the orthography, if I may call bad spelling *orthography*. You spell induce, *enduce*; and grandeur, you spell grand*ure*; two faults, of which few of my house-maids would have been guilty. I must tell you, that orthography, in the true sense of the word, is so absolutely necessary for a man of letters, or a gentleman, that one false spelling may fix a ridicule upon him for the rest of his life; and I know a man of quality, who never recovered the ridicule of having spelled *wholesome* without the *w*.

Reading with care will secure everybody from false spelling; for books are always well spelled, according to the orthography of the times. Some words are indeed doubtful, being spelled differently by different authors of equal authority, but those are few; and in those cases every man has his option, because he may plead his authority either way; but where there is but one right way, as in the two words above-mentioned, it is unpardonable and ridiculous for a gentleman to miss it: even a woman of a tolerable

[1]See Letter of 30th August, 1748.

education would despise, and laugh at a lover, who should send her an ill-spelled *billet-doux*. I fear, and suspect, that you have taken it into your head, in most cases, that the matter is all, and the manner little or nothing. If you have, undeceive yourself, and be convinced that, in everything, the manner is full as important as the matter. If you speak the sense of an angel, in bad words, and with a disagreeable utterance, nobody will hear you twice, who can help it. If you write epistles as well as Cicero, but in a very bad hand, and very ill-spelled, whoever receives, will laugh at them; and if you had the figure of Adonis, with an awkward air and motions, it will disgust instead of pleasing. Study manner therefore in everything, if you would be anything. My principal inquiries of my friends at Paris concerning you, will be relative to your manner of doing whatever you do. I shall not inquire whether you understand Demosthenes, Tacitus, or the *jus publicum imperii*; but I shall inquire whether your utterance is pleasing, your style not only pure but elegant, your manners noble and easy, your air and address engaging; in short, whether you are a gentleman, a man of fashion, and fit to keep good company or not; for, till I am satisfied in these particulars, you and I must by no means meet; I could not possibly stand it. It is in your power to become all this at Paris, if you please. Consult with Lady Hervey and Madame Monconseil upon all these matters, and they will speak to you, and advise you freely. Tell them, that *bisogna compatire ancora*, that you are utterly new in the world, that you are desirous to form yourself, that you beg they will reprove, advise, and correct you, that you know that none can do it so well, and that you will implicitly follow their directions. This, together with your careful observation of the manners of the best company, will really form you.

Abbé Guasco,[1] a friend of mine, will come to you as soon

[1]Octavien de Guasco, a native of Pignerol, in 1712 became a Canon of Tournay, and a Member of the *Académie des Inscriptions*, to which he contributed several

as he knows of your arrival at Paris; he is well received in the best companies there, and will introduce you to them. He will be desirous to do you any service he can; he is active and curious, and can give you information upon most things. He is a sort of *complaisant* of the President Montesquieu, to whom you have a letter.

I imagine that this letter will not wait for you very long at Paris, where I reckon you will be in about a fortnight. Adieu!

No. 1738

À MADAME DU BOCCAGE

(Maty I. xc)

À Londres, ce 26 novembre V.S. 1750

MADAME,

Il n'y a que six jours, que j'ai reçu la lettre et le paquet, que vous avez bien voulu m'envoyer; agréez mes remerciements de l'un et de l'autre.

Les procès, que vous m'envoyez à décider, vous les portez (pour parler en terme de palais) *coram non judice*, et si je prétendais en juger, on appellerait avec raison de ma sentence: n'importe, tout le monde juge; souvent ceux qui en sont les moins capables sont les plus décisifs, ainsi je vous envoie mes arrêts, que vous ferez biffer des registres, quand il vous plaira.

In primis, je décide sans balancer, que le Cardinal de Richelieu est l'auteur de son propre Testament; et que le plaidoyer de Voltaire ne prouve rien contre. L'ouvrage est marqué au coin d'un Ministre d'État, et d'un Ecclésiastique.

J'ai plus de difficulté à décider le procès actuellement litipendant entre votre Roi et le clergé. Les lettres contre le clergé sont bien écrites, ainsi que les réponses; mais sans

interesting essays. His *Dissertations historiques, politiques et littéraires* were published in 1756, and his *De l'usage des Statues chez les Anciens* in 1768. He was also the author of an *Histoire du Pape Clement V*, and the translator of Cantemir into Italian—but these works have remained unpublished.

prononcer, je suis pour le roi, et je considère le clergé de toutes les religions comme un corps, qui a des intérêts et des vues distinctes de ceux du reste du genre humain. Les rois les plus despotiques n'en veulent qu'aux corps et aux biens des hommes; mais tout clergé, depuis le Grand Lama du Thibet jusqu'à sa Sainteté à Rome, et l'Archevêque de Cantorbery à Londres, prétend au despotisme sur les esprits; despotisme d'autant plus dangereux qu'étant une fois établi, il entraîne tout le reste. Le corps et les biens ne sont plus que des guenilles; ces messieurs ont votre salut exclusivement entre leur mains; et que ne fait-on pas pour l'obtenir? Sept ou huit siècles de suite du règne du clergé, et de l'ignorance, l'ont assez démontré.

Mais cette affaire du clergé paraît avoir cédé la place chez vous à celle des États de Bretagne, qui a l'avantage de la nouveauté. Ce n'est pas peu dans tout pays, et moins en France qu'en tout autre. Vous sentez bien que comme anglais et parlementaire, je dois être le très humble serviteur des États, ainsi je me tais sur cet article, de peur d'être recusé comme juge partial. Le cheval appela autrefois l'homme à son secours contre le cerf; l'homme le monta, le secourut, le subjugua, et en resta le maître. Les hommes appelèrent aussi les rois à leur secours l'un contre l'autre. Heureusement les chevaux ignorent encore leur force, et les sujets leurs droits natuiels; s'ils les savaient qu'il y aurait de cavaliers désarçonnés et des rois détrônés! Un reste d'ignorance sur ces matières peut-être est les mieux.

Je suis pour la force de l'éducation, convenant en même temps que le naturel entre pour quelque chose en ce que nous sommes. L'éducation ne donne pas sûrement de l'esprit à ceux à qui la nature a refusé le sens commun; mais l'éducation décide de la tournure de cette portion d'esprit qu'on a; et de même du cœur, qui n'est pas fait à la vérité, mais en grand partie façonné, par l'éducation. C'est par elle sans doute que les bouchers, les bourreaux, et les inquisiteurs, sont moins compatissants et plus sanguinaires

que les autres hommes. Pour ce qui est de ces beaux sentiments d'affection naturelle, qui brillent dans les romans,
dans les tragédies, et même à présent dans vos comédies
larmoyantes, rien n'est plus fou: un père, une mère, un
mari, une femme, des enfants, qui ne se sont jamais vus, se
connaissent réciproquement par un certain saisissement, un
frisson, un tout ce qu'il vous plaira, que leur cause ce sentiment naturel à la vue de l'objet. Si un tel sentiment existait,
quelles découvertes, et par conséquent quel désordre, ne
causerait-il pas à Paris et à Londres! Quel nombre de
citoyens changeraient de père, et verseraient de ces belles
larmes d'attendrissement, en découvrant leurs véritables
papas dans les palais de Versailles et de St. James, ou peut-
être dans le régiment des gardes!

Voilà mes sentiments sur la bibliothèque que vous m'avez
fournie, et qui m'a beaucoup amusé. Je vous dirai là-dessus
très véritablement, ce que les épîtres dédicatoires disent
presque toujours sans vérité, que si je crains votre goût, je
compte en même temps sur votre indulgence.

Madame de Chesterfield, qui vous fait mille compliments,
est occupée à lire les livres, que vous m'avez envoyés, dont
j'ai fait trois portions, pour elle, pour Milady Allen, et pour
Madame Cleland. Je voudrais pouvoir vous envoyer quelque chose d'ici pour vous amuser; mais il ne paraît rien qui
le mérite. Les Muses sont si occupées chez vous, qu'elles
n'ont pas le loisir de nous faire visite; et vous savez qu'Apol-
lon ne fréquente guère, surtout dans cette saison, le
cinquante troisième degré de latitude septentrionale.

1739

To Edward Eliot

(*MSS. of the Earl of St. Germans*)

Sir,   *London,* 29 *November* 1750

I delayed acknowledging the favour of your letter till
I could inform you with some degree of precision when

Mr. Harte would be in England; which till yesterday I have
not been able to do. I reckon now that he will be at Paris
about the 21st of next month O.S. And supposing him to
stay there, as probably he will, a fortnight, he may very
well be here in London on the 8th, 9th, or at farthest 10th
of January O.S. His Windsor installation may I suppose
be dispatched in three or four days, so that about the 15th
he may set out for the living which you were so kind as to
procure him, and save all his distances. I think you may
depend upon the certainty of this calculation, and prepare
for him with the bishop of the diocese whatever may be
necessary for his institution and induction. I believe that
very few things could have given either you or me more
pleasure than the opportunities we have both had of showing the truth of our regard to one who so well deserves it,
and of procuring him a comfortable welcome at his return
to his own country. I am now too old and too insignificant
to hope to be of any farther use to him, though while I live
I will endeavour it; but it is a comfort to me to reflect that
he has in you a friend, who will most probably be as able,
as now willing, to serve him. I am with the greatest truth
and esteem, etc.

No. 1740

À Madame la Marquise de Monconseil

(*Maty I. liii*)

À Londres, ce 7 décembre V.S. 1750

Que vos accusations d'esprit, d'habileté, et de netteté
seraient flatteuses, Madame, si elles étaient fondées! En ce
cas-là, je passerais volontiers condamnation, et je ne m'en
défendrais point, de peur d'être absous; mais ce sont les
menaces que vous me faites, en conséquence de mes crimes
supposés, qui m'allarment. Vous voulez changer le style et
le ton de vos lettres—au nom de Dieu n'y changez rien!

nous y perdrions trop tous les deux. N'allez pas prendre l'esprit à la mode, mais contentez-vous de celui que vous avez, et dont je vous assure que la mode ne passera jamais. Les carats sont, il est vrai, à la mode, c'est qu'ils ne coûtent pas beaucoup, et on les met en mille figures fantastiques, mais ils n'ont pu bannir la mode des bons gros diamants, que leur valeur intrinsèque a soutenus jusqu'ici, et soutiendra toujours: mais en tout cas, si vous voulez changer votre esprit, pour prendre celui de la nouvelle fabrique, je vous demande en grâce de vouloir bien donner votre vieux à votre élève. S'il en a lui-même, il se contentera bien du vôtre, et s'il n'en a pas, laissez aux autres le soin de lui en donner du leur; vous y perdriez vos peines, et il ne vous en tiendrait pas compte.

Vous avez bien raison de dire qu'il faut être ce qu'on est; cela est si vrai que, quelque chose que l'on fasse, on le sera toujours au fond, la matière restera toujours la même. On en peut varier la façon, et y donner quelques nouveaux contours; mais, on a beau faire, si c'est du plomb, ce ne sera que du plomb; vouloir lui donner le brillant de l'or, c'est lui donner un ridicule, cette lourde matière n'en est pas susceptible. Pour les manières extérieures, le liant, la politesse, je crois qu'on les peut acquérir par l'usage; pourvu qu'il y ait un certain fond de sens commun, puisqu'on les voit si souvent couvrir, et même quelquefois orner, de petits esprits, et de grands défauts: au moins vous menerez votre élève aux bonnes écoles pour les apprendre. Introduit par vous, il faut qu'il soit une bête des plus indociles, s'il ne les apprend pas. Je compte qu'en quinze jours d'ici il aura l'honneur de vous faire sa cour, étant actuellement sur la route de Provence à Paris.

Il y a deux ans que je tâche d'avoir de ces gros chiens d'Irlande, dont la race y est devenue extrêmement rare, par l'extinction de leurs ennemis les loups. On m'en envoya deux il y a six mois, que je destinais pour Monsieur le Prince du Conti, mais je découvris qu'il y avait un mélange de

1626

Danois, qui les avait épaissis, de sorte que je les renvoyai. J'en attends bientôt des véritables, que j'aurai l'honneur d'envoyer d'abord à son Altesse; en attendant, je vous prie d'envoyer vos ordres à quelqu'un à Calais pour les recevoir, et faites-moi savoir à qui je les y dois adresser. Je serai toujours charmé de pouvoir être bon à quelque chose à un Prince de ce mérite.

No. 1741

À Madame du Boccage

(*Maty I. lxxxviii*)

[*Décembre* 1750]

Madame,

M. Stanhope mon parent, dont j'ai eu l'honneur de vous entretenir en Angleterre, a celui de vous porter cette lettre à Paris. Je ne sais s'il est digne de vous être présenté; mais je sais que chaque fois qu'il aura l'honneur de vous voir, il en deviendra plus présentable. Si l'esprit se communiquait comme la petite vérole, je lui procure une belle occasion d'en prendre, et de la meilleure sorte: mais il est très sûr qu'on prend insensiblement le ton et les manières de ceux qu'on fréquente. C'est pourquoi je vous supplie, Madame, souffrez qu'il vous fasse de temps en temps sa cour comme ami de votre maison, aux heures qu'il vous sera le moins incommode: il y a des examples, qui valent mieux que tous les préceptes du monde, et des conseils meilleurs que des ordres. Il connaît déjà, et respecte, comme tout le monde, votre réputation; mais sans compliment vous valez encore mieux, ce qu'il saura bien à mesure qu'il aura l'honneur de vous connaître personnellement. Je vous demande en grâce, Madame, point de façons, point d'indulgence à son égard; mais prenez avec lui ce ton d'autorité, auquel l'amitié, dont vous m'honorez, est le moindre de vos droits. Ne lui passez rien, ordonnez souverainement; et, n'en déplaise au

Président,[1] j'ose répondre que son obéissance à un tel despotisme n'aura pas la crainte, mais le choix, pour principe.

Me pardonnez-vous cette liberté? Oui, Madame, je connais trop vos sentiments pour en douter: vous savez aussi ceux, avec lesquels j'ai l'honneur d'être,

Madame, etc.

No. 1742

To his Son

(*Stanhope CCXXXVII*)

Mon Cher Ami,   *À Londres, ce 24 décembre V.S.* 1750

Vous voilà à la fin Parisien, et il faut s'adresser à un Parisien en français. Vous voudrez bien aussi me répondre de même, puisque je serai bien aise de voir à quel point vous possedez l'élégance, la délicatesse, et l'orthographe de cette langue, qui est devenue, pour ainsi dire, la langue universelle de l'Europe. On m'assure que vous la parlez fort bien, mais il y a bien et bien. Et tel passera pour la bien parler hors de Paris, qui passerait lui-même pour Gaulois à Paris. Dans ce pays des modes, le langage même a la sienne, et qui change presque aussi souvent que celle des habits.

L'affecté, le précieux, le néologique, y sont trop à la mode d'aujourd'hui. Connaissez-les, remarquez-les, et parlez-les même, à la bonne heure, mais ne vous en laissez pas infecter. L'esprit aussi a sa mode, et actuellement à Paris, c'est la mode d'en avoir, en dépit même de Minerve; tout le monde court après l'esprit, qui par parenthèse ne se laisse jamais attraper; s'il ne se présente pas, on a beau courir. Mais malheureusement pour ceux qui courent après, ils attrapent quelque chose qu'ils prennent pour de l'esprit, et qu'ils donnent pour tel. C'est tout au plus la bonne fortune d'Ixion, c'est une vapeur qu'ils embrassent, au lieu de la déesse qu'ils poursuivent. De cette erreur résultent ces

[1]Montesquieu, who in his *Esprit des Lois*, alleges that fear is the main principle of every despotic government.—M.

beaux sentiments qu'on n'a jamais senti, ces pensées fausses que la nature n'a jamais produite, et ces expressions entortillées et obscures, que non seulement on n'entend point, mais qu'on ne peut pas même déchiffrer ni deviner. C'est de tous ces ingrédients que sont composés les deux tiers des nouveaux livres français qui paraissent. C'est la nouvelle cuisine du Parnasse, où l'alambic travaille au lieu du pot et de la broche, et où les quintessences et les extraits dominent. N.B. Le sel Attique en est banni.

Il vous faudra bien de temps en temps manger de cette nouvelle cuisine. Mais ne vous y laissez pas corrompre le goût. Et quand vous voudrez donner à manger à votre tour, étudiez la bonne vieille cuisine du temps de Louis Quatorze. Il y avait alors des chefs admirables, comme Corneille, Boileau, Racine, et La Fontaine. Tout ce qu'ils apprétaient était simple, sain, et solide. Sans métaphore, ne vous laissez pas éblouir par le faux brillant, le recherché, les antithèses à la mode; mais servez-vous de votre propre bon sens, et appelez les anciens à votre secours, pour vous en garantir. D'un autre côté, ne vous moquez pas de ceux, qui s'y sont laissés séduire; vous êtes encore trop jeune pour faire le critique, et pour vous ériger en vengeur sévère du bon sens lésé. Seulement ne vous laissez pas pervertir, mais ne songez pas à convertir les autres. Laissez-les jouir tranquillement de leurs erreurs dans le goût, comme dans la religion. Le goût en France a depuis un siècle et demi, eu bien du haut et du bas, aussi bien que la France même. Le bon goût commença seulement à se faire jour, sous le règne, je ne dis pas de Louis Treize, mais du Cardinal de Richelieu, et fut encore épuré sous celui de Louis Quatorze, grand Roi au moins, s'il n'était pas grand homme. Corneille était le restaurateur du vrai, et le fondateur du théâtre français; se ressentant toujours un peu des *Concetti* des italiens et des *Agudeze* des espagnols; témoin les épigrammes qu'il fait débiter à Chimène[1] dans tout l'excès de sa douleur.

[1]In *Le Cid.*

Mais avant son temps, les troubadours, et les romanciers
étaient autant de fous, qui trouvaient des sots pour les
admirer. Vers la fin du règne du Cardinal de Richeleiu, et
au commencement de celui de Louis Quatorze, l'Hôtel de
Rambouillet était le Temple du Goût, mais d'un goût pas
encore tout à fait épuré. C'était plustôt un laboratoire
d'esprit, où l'on donnait la torture au bon sens, pour en
tirer une essence subtile. Voiture[1] y travaillait, et suait même
à grosses gouttes pour faire de l'esprit. Mais enfin Boileau
et Molière fixèrent le goût du vrai; en dépit des Scudéry et
des Calprenèdes, &c. Ils déconfirent et mirent en fuite les
Artamènes, les Jubas, les Oroondates, et tous ces héros de
romans, qui valaient pourtant chacun seul une armée. Ces
fous cherchèrent dans les bibliothèques un asile qu'on leur
refusa; et ils n'en trouvèrent que dans quelques ruelles. Je
vous conseille pourtant de lire un tome de Cléopâtre et un
de Clélie, sans quoi il vous sera impossible de vous former
une idée de ces extravagances; mais Dieu vous garde d'aller
jusqu'au douzième.

Le goût resta pur et vrai pendant presque tout le règne
de Louis Quatorze, et jusqu'à ce qu'un très beau génie y
donna (mais sans le vouloir) quelque atteinte. C'était Monsieur de Fontenelle,[2] qui avec tout l'esprit du monde, et un
grand savoir, sacrifiait peut-être un peu trop aux grâces,
dont il était le nourrisson, et l'élève favori. Admiré avec
raison, on voulut l'imiter; mais malheureusement pour le
siècle, l'auteur des Pastorales, de l'Histoire des Oracles, et
du Théâtre Français, trouva moins d'imitateurs, que le
Chevalier d'Her ne trouva de singes. Contrefait depuis par
mille auteurs, il n'a pas été imité que je sache par un seul.

[1]Vincent Voiture (1598-1648) was the son of a wine-merchant of Amiens.
Protected by the Comte d'Avaux and Cardinal de la Valette, guided by his talent,
he made one of the group at the Hôtel de Rambouillet. His literary output consisted of letters, and some minor verse. He had the art of pleasing to the last
degree.

[2]Bernard le Bouyer de Fontenelle (1657-1757). This great artist's *Entretien
sur la Pluralité des Mondes* has recently been translated into English. His *Éloges*
are masterpieces; his *Dialogues des Morts* models in their kind.

A l'heure qu'il est, l'empire du vrai goût ne me paraît pas trop bien affermi en France; il subsiste à la vérité, mais il est déchiré par des partis; il y a le parti des petits maîtres, celui des caillettes, celui des fades auteurs dont les ouvrages sont, *verba et voces et præterea nihil,* et enfin un parti nombreux et fort à la mode, d'auteurs qui débitent dans un galimatias métaphysique leurs faux raffinements, sur les mouvements et les sentiments *de l'âme, du cœur, et de l'esprit.*

Ne vous en laissez pas imposer par la mode; ni par des cliques que vous pourrez fréquenter; mais essayez toutes ces différentes espèces, avant que de les recevoir en paiement au coin du bon sens et de la raison; et soyez bien persuadé que *rien n'est beau que le vrai.*[1] Tout brillant qui ne résulte pas de la solidité et de la justesse de la pensée, n'est qu'un faux brillant. Le mot italien sur le diamant est bien vrai à cet égard, *quanto piu sodezza, tanto piu splendore.*

Tout ceci n'empêche pas que vous ne deviez vous conformer extérieurement aux modes et aux tons des différentes compagnies où vous vous trouverez. Parlez épigrammes avec les petits maîtres, sentiments faux avec les caillettes, et galimatias avec les beaux esprits par état. À la bonne heure; à votre âge, ce n'est pas à vous à donner le ton à la compagnie, mais au contraire à le prendre. Examinez bien pourtant, et pesez tout cela en vous-même; distinguez bien le faux du vrai, et ne prenez pas *le clinquant du Tasse pour l'or de Virgile.*

Vous trouverez en même temps, à Paris, des auteurs et des compagnies très solides. Vous n'entendrez point des fadaises, du précieux, du guindé, chez Madame de Monconseil, ni aux hôtels de Matignon et de Coigny, où elle vous présentera; le Prèsident Montesquieu ne vous parlera pas *pointes.* Son livre de l'Esprit des Lois, écrit en langue vulgaire, vous plaira, et vous instruira également.

Fréquentez le théâtre quand on y jouera les pièces de

---

[1]An allusion to the line of Boileau in his *Épître au Marquis de Seignelay,*
'Rien n'est beau que le vrai; le vrai seul est aimable.'

Corneille, de Racine, et de Molière, où il n'y a que du naturel et du vrai. Je ne prétends pas par là donner l'exclusion à plusieurs pièces modernes qui sont admirables, et en dernier lieu, Cénie, pièce pleine de sentiments, mais de sentiments vrais, naturels, et dans lesquels on se réconnaît. Voulez-vous connaître les caractères du jour, lisez les ouvrages de Crébillon le fils, et de Marivaux. Le premier est un peintre excellent; le second a beaucoup étudié et connaît bien le cœur, peut-être même un peu trop. *Les Égarements du Cœur et de l'Esprit* par Crébillon est un livre excellent dans ce genre; les caractères y sont bien marqués; il vous amusera infiniment, et ne vous sera pas inutile. *L'Histoire Japonais de Tanzaï, et de Neadarné,* du même auteur, est une aimable extravagance, et parsemée de réflexions très justes; enfin vous trouverez bien à Paris de quoi vous former un goût sûr et juste, pourvu que vous ne preniez pas le change.

Comme je vous laisse sur votre bonne foi à Paris sans surveillant, je me flatte que vous n'abuserez pas de ma confiance. Je ne demande pas que vous soyez Capucin; bien au contraire, je vous recommande les plaisirs, mais j'exige que ce soient les plaisirs d'un honnête homme. Ces plaisirs là donnent du brillant au caractère d'un jeune homme; mais la débauche avilit et dégrade. J'aurai des relations très vraies et détaillées de votre conduite, et selon ces relations je serai plus, ou moins, ou point du tout, à vous. Adieu!

P.S. Ecrivez-moi sans faute une fois la semaine, et répondez à celle-ci en français. Faufilez-vous tant que vous le pourrez chez les ministres étrangers. C'est voyager en différents endroits sans changer de place. Parlez italien à tous les italiens, et allemand à tous les allemands que vous trouverez, pour entretenir ces deux langues.

Je vous souhaite, mon cher, autant de nouvelles années que vous mériterez, et pas une de plus. Mais puissiez-vous en mériter un grand nombre!

No. 1743
To the Duke of Dorset[1]
(Hist. MSS. Comm. Stopford Sackville MSS. vii 169)

[*Dec.* 1750?]

I endeavoured yesterday to have the honour of making my compliments to your Grace upon your return to a situation which I suppose you liked, and in which I am sure you were liked. . . . Your Grace is well enough acquainted with your present and my former subjects to imagine all the industry and vigour of their solicitations. I have within this fortnight received a hundred, in the intention that I should trouble you with them, which I have fairly told them that I will not do. But . . . your Grace will, I am sure, forgive me if I most earnestly apply to you in favour of one or two people who, in my opinion, have just claims to whatever I can do to serve them, and that I believe your Grace will allow to be the case of a Lord Lieutenant's pages.

Mr. Mason, nephew to Lord Molesworth, was one of mine. I had an opportunity of doing well for him by making him a cornet in his uncle's regiment. I only mean therefore by this . . . to recommend him to your general protection.

Richard Bailey, a gentleman of an extreme good Derbyshire family, was another of my pages, and a very pretty young fellow. I made him a lieutenant in an additional company in Otway's, which being soon broke, he was soon reduced to half-pay. . . . I at last obtained leave for him to *buy* a lieutenancy in Lee's, where he is at present. I only recommend him to your Grace as a plant of mine which, at

[1] Lionel Cranfield Sackville (1688-1765), first Duke, succeeded his father as seventh Earl in 1706, created Duke in 1720. Viceroy of Ireland for the second time, 1750-1755.

1633

a proper time, I hope you will transplant into some better place.

But I come now to a most humble and earnest request to your Grace, the case being extremely compassionate. It is in favour of William Heathcote, my third page, now a half-pay lieutenant. He is a younger brother of a Derbyshire gentleman of a very good family and a tolerable estate, but encumbered with nine or ten brothers and sisters, insomuch that I do not believe his share comes to ten pounds. I made him a lieutenant in one of the new raised companies, which were soon after broke. . . . While he was in commission he applied himself extremely to his business, was very sober and diligent, without being dull. And I will answer for him that he will not make your Grace either ashamed or repent of any favour you may be pleased to show him.

Isaac Bickerstaffe,[1] whose family was known to your Grace at Dublin, and particularly to Mr. Bayle, was my fourth page. He is now a second lieutenant, and I beg leave only to recommend him to your general protection.

Your Grace will further forgive my sending you the enclosed letter from Capt. Cane, who was a gentleman-usher to Lady Chesterfield, and is really a very pretty fellow. . . . I only trouble your Grace with his letter to give me an opportunity of doing justice to his character, which I really think is the best I know in all Ireland of people of this rank.

By the number of names I have mentioned, your Grace may probably at first think my requests very numerous, and consequently very impertinent, but I must beg that you will observe that in truth they are reducible to one single one . . . and your favour to him will be laying the greatest obligation upon your Grace's most humble and obedient servant.

[1]Author of *Love in a Village* (d. 1812).

No. 1744
À Madame la Marquise de Monconseil
(*Maty I. liv*)

[*Décembre* 1750]

Voici à la fin, Madame, votre futur élève, que j'ai l'honneur de vous présenter: j'ignore pourtant assez quel présent je vous fais, je sais seulement que, quelqu'il puisse être actuellement, il ne tiendra qu'à vous de le rendre bien présentable à l'avenir. Il y a de certains exemples qui sont plus instructifs que tous les préceptes du monde. Comme vous avez pris la résolution de ne pas faire des garçons vous-même, adoptez pour quelque temps au moins, je vous en supplie, celui-ci; l'adoption est cent fois plus importante que la façon, qui n'est à ce qu'on dit que fortuite. Je n'ai pas des vues ambitieuses pour votre élève; je ne demande pas qu'il gagne des provinces, je souhaite seulement qu'il gagne des cœurs, qu'il soit poli, aimable, et qu'il ait les sentiments et les manières d'un honnête homme, c'est-à-dire, que vous l'adoptiez, et que je puisse l'appeler le petit Stanhope. Très sérieusement, Madame, point de ménagements, point de politesses de votre part, mais prenez avec lui ce ton d'autorité, auquel l'amitié dont vous m'honorez est le moindre de vos droits: gouvernez-le despotiquement, un tel esclavage lui sera aussi utile qu'agréable.

No. 1745
To Lord Huntingdon
(*Steuart 11*)

My Dear Lord,   *London*, 31 *December O.S.* 1750

I delayed discharging my letter to you till I could take better aim at you than your last gave me reason to think I could. I now take it for granted that you are fixed at Paris, and this is levelled at you there.

You need not have given yourself any trouble to procure

a recommendation to Lord Albemarle, and to tell you the plain truth it was below Lord Huntingdon to have any recommendation to any English Minister abroad. I should have sent you one to Lord Albemarle if I had thought it either useful or proper for you. All that one of your rank has to do with regard to the British Ministers residing at foreign Courts, is to make them the first visit upon your arrival, and then it is their duty, and if they have common sense, it will be their inclination, to do you all the service they can. Therefore, when you go on farther, as to Turin, where Lord Rochford resides; Florence, where Mr. Mann resides; and so on, only make them the first visit, and all the rest follows. As for other letters of recommendation to the natives of the several places that you go to, always get as many as you can; but then let them be from people of the first fashion to others of the same sort, for otherwise they will rather embarrass than help you. I would advise you for that reason to cultivate the Foreign Ministers residing at the places where you are, and they will give you the proper recommendations to their best acquaintances at their own Courts. As for instance, at Paris get acquainted with the Pope's Nuncio, the Venetian Ambassador, the Neapolitan, Florentine, and Genoese Ministers, who will all be proud of giving you letters when you leave it. There is another advantage too in this, which is, that by frequenting those gentlemen, you in some measure learn the manners and the views of their respective countries; for they all talk more or less in pursuance of those views. Lord Albemarle will immediately present you to the King and the Royal Family, and when you are once thus made free of that Court, I would recommend to you to go there often, which few English do. But by going there you put yourself in the way of the best company, you are invited to dinner by the Ministers, and you daily make new acquaintances. Moreover, it will be of use to you to distinguish yourself from the common herd of English who infest Paris and disgrace

1636

their own country. Mr. Cunningham tells me that you propose keeping house at Paris; permit me, my dear Lord, to say a word or two upon that subject with my usual freedom. If you once keep what can be called a table it will lead you into an incredible, and I will add an unnecessary expense. Because you will be obliged in that case to entertain in your turn those who have entertained you. Whereas a table is not in the least expected from a traveller, a young man, *et un garçon*. You will find the life of Paris sufficiently expensive without that addition. And, though I would by no means advise you to refuse yourself any pleasure or utility, upon account of the expense, I should [be] extremely sorry that you should run in debt one shilling for anything unnecessary. Estates in land I know by experience fall infinitely shorter of the rental than anybody unacquainted with them could imagine; and provided you indulge yourself in everything that can be really either useful or pleasant to you abroad, I could wish that you returned home rather before than behind hand. Debt is a heavy clog upon any man who would make a figure in the world. Courts presume, and competitors triumph upon it. I just now reflect (and blush as I reflect) how impertinently didactic this letter is. Pardon, nay, I am sure you will pardon it; you want advice so little, that you are willing to hear it, and able to judge of it; and experience can sometimes hang out useful lights, for much better parts to steer by; it is in that view only, my dear Lord, that I send you my paper lanthorn, dim as it may be, to glimmer at least before you, in the dark windings you are now to go through. I shall go on till you rebuke me, happy if I can once in my life, be of any use to you, and sure that my errors can never mislead your judgment.

My young relation and your old schoolfellow will by this time have made his court to you at Paris, and I beg that you will tell me without the least reserve what you think of him, for I cannot know him myself not having seen him since he was a mere boy. Whatever he is, you can make him better, and it is your interest to do so, for I have made him your own. I shall bring him into the next Parliament, there to follow implicitly your orders, which by that time you will be here to give him. You will have, I dare say, much better dependents, but the more dependents you have the better, numbers always giving more weight than sometimes they deserve. *A propos* of this, give me leave to hint to you, though I would by no means wish you to herd with the English in general, that it may be of great use to you, to form certain connections with such young Englishmen abroad as are likely to make some figure in the world, either from their parts, their rank or their fortune. For between you and I whatever connection you form, you must govern though they must not think so. The Marquis of Rockingham, whose father is lately dead, has a very great estate and great interest in Yorkshire, two circumstances that will give him weight let his parts be what they will, and I do not know what they are; as such he is worth your laying hold on, and you may certainly get him. I have only mentioned him, as an instance of the sort of people whom it may be worth your while to cultivate at present in order to govern hereafter.

I hope to receive some verses upon some other *Princess* at Paris. I do not look upon the change of Sovereigns of that sort to be disloyalty; their power should, I think, be consular, for one year only, and then it never does much mischief. Adieu, my dear Lord, forgive all this prating of an old fellow, in favour of an old friend, who is with the sincerest affection your most faithful humble servant.

Postscript.—I direct this letter to Lord Albemarle's not knowing where else to direct; pray send me your directions for my next. Compliments upon the New Year are too much profaned for me to make you any. Judge for yourself what I wish you in that respect.

1638

No. 1746

VARIOUS ENCLOSURES IN LETTERS TO HIS SON
Dates undetermined
(*Stanhope CCCCXXXV*)

MAXIMS OF CARDINAL DE RETZ

1. Il y a souvent de la folie à conjurer; mais il n'y a rien de pareil pour faire les gens sages dans la suite: au moins pour quelque temps. Comme le péril dans ces sortes d'affaires dure même après les occasions, l'on est prudent et circonspect dans les moments qui les suivent.

2. Un esprit médiocre, et susceptible par conséquent d'injustes défiances, est de tous les caractères celui qui est le plus opposé à un bon chef de parti; dont la qualité la plus souvent et la plus indispensablement nécessaire, est de supprimer en beaucoup d'occasions, et de cacher en toutes, les soupçons même les plus légitimes.

3. Rien n'anime et n'appuye plus un mouvement, que le ridicule de celui contre lequel on le fait.

4. Le secret n'est pas si rare qu'on le croit, entre des gens qui sont accoutumés à se mêler des grandes affaires.

5. Descendre jusqu'aux petits est le plus sûr moyen de s'égaler aux grands.

6. La mode qui a du pouvoir en toutes choses, ne l'a si sensiblement en aucune, qu'à être bien ou mal à la Cour; il y a des temps où la disgrâce est une manière de feu qui purifie toutes les mauvaises qualités, et qui illumine toutes les bonnes; il y a des temps où il ne sied pas bien à un honnête homme d'être disgracié.

7. La souffrance aux personnes d'un grand rang, tient lieu d'une grande vertu.

8. Il y a une espèce de galimatias que la pratique fait connaître quelquefois, mais que la spéculation ne fait jamais entendre.

9. Toutes les puissances ne peuvent rien contre la réputation d'un homme qui se la conserve dans son corps.

10. On est aussi souvent dupe par la défiance que par la confiance.

11. L'extrémité du mal n'est jamais à son période, que quand ceux qui commandent ont perdu la honte; parce que c'est justement le moment dans lequel ceux qui obéissent perdent le respect; et c'est dans ce même moment que l'on revient de la léthargie: mais par des convulsions.

12. Il y a un voile qui doit toujours couvrir tout ce que l'on peut dire, et tout ce que l'on peut croire, du droit des peuples et de celui des rois, qui ne s'accordent jamais si bien ensemble que dans le silence.

13. Il y a des conjonctures dans lesquelles on ne peut plus faire que des fautes; mais la fortune ne met jamais les hommes dans cet état, qui est de tous le plus malheureux, et personne n'y tombe que ceux qui s'y précipitent par leur faute.

14. Il sied plus mal à un Ministre de dire des sottises, que d'en faire.

15. Les avis que l'on donne à un Ministre passent pour des crimes, toutes les fois qu'on ne le lui est point agréable.

16. Auprès des princes, il est aussi dangereux, et presque aussi criminel, de pouvoir le bien que de vouloir le mal.

17. Il est bien plus naturel à la peur de consulter que de décider.

18. Cette circonstance paraît ridicule; mais elle est fondée. À Paris, dans les émotions populaires, les plus échauffés ne veulent pas, ce qu'ils appellent, *se désheurer*.

19. La flexibilité est de toutes les qualités la plus nécessaire pour le maniement des grandes affaires.

20. On a plus de peine dans les partis, de vivre avec ceux qui en sont, que d'agir contre ceux qui y sont opposés.

21. Les plus grands dangers ont leurs charmes, pour peu que l'on aperçoive de gloire dans la perspective des mauvais succès; les médiocres dangers n'ont que des horreurs, quand la perte de la réputation est attachée à la mauvaise fortune.

1640

22. Les extrêmes sont toujours fâcheux. Mais ce sont des moyens sages quand ils sont nécessaires: ce qu'ils ont de consolant c'est qu'ils ne sont jamais médiocres, et qu'ils sont décisifs quand ils sont bon.

23. Il y a des conjonctures où la prudence même ordonne de ne consulter que le chapitre des accidents.

24. Il n'y a rien dans le monde qui n'ait son moment décisif; et le chef-d'œuvre de la bonne conduite, est de connaître et de prendre ce moment.

25. L'abomination joint au ridicule fait le plus dangereux et le plus irrémédiable de tous les composés.

26. Les gens faibles ne plient jamais quand ils le doivent.

27. Rien ne touche et n'émeut tant les peuples, et même les compagnies, qui tiennent beaucoup du peuple, que la variété des spectacles.

28. Les exemples du passé touchent sans comparaison plus les hommes, que ceux de leur siècle; nous nous accoutumons à tout ce que nous voyons; et peut-être que le Consulat du Cheval de Caligula ne nous aurait pas tant surpris, que nous nous l'imaginons.

29. Les hommes faibles se laissent aller ordinairement au plus grand bruit.

30. Il ne faut jamais contester ce qu'on ne croit pas pouvoir obtenir.

31. Le moment où l'on reçoit les plus heureuses nouvelles, est justement celui où il faut redoubler son attention pour les petites.

32. Le pouvoir dans les peuples est fâcheux, en ce qu'il nous rend responsables de ce qu'ils font malgré nous.

33. L'une des plus grandes incommodités des guerres civiles, est, qu'il faut encore plus d'application à ce que l'on ne doit pas dire à ses amis, qu'à ce que l'on doit faire contre ses ennemis.

34. Il n'y a point de qualité qui dépare tant un grand homme, que de n'être pas juste à prendre le moment décisif de la réputation. L'on ne le manque presque jamais que

pour mieux prendre celui de la fortune; c'est en quoi l'on se trompe, pour l'ordinaire, doublement.

35. La vue la plus commune dans les imprudences c'est celle que l'on a de la possibilité des resources.

36. Toute compagnie est peuple; ainsi tout y dépend des instants.

37. Tout ce qui paraît hasardeux, et qui pourtant ne l'est pas, est presque toujours sage.

38. Les gens irrésolus prennent toujours, avec facilité, les ouvertures qui les mènent à deux chemins, et qui par conséquent ne les pressent pas d'opter.

39. Il n'y a point de petits pas dans les grandes affaires.

40. Il y a des temps où certaines gens ont toujours raison.

41. Rien ne persuade tant les gens qui ont peu de sens que ce qu'ils n'entendent pas.

42. Il n'est pas sage de faire, dans les factions, où l'on n'est que sur la défensive, ce qui n'est pas pressé. Mais l'inquiétude des subalternes est la chose la plus incommode dans ces rencontres; ils croient que dès qu'on n'agit pas, on est perdu.

43. Les chefs dans les factions n'en sont les maîtres, qu'autant qu'ils savent prévenir ou apaiser les murmures.

44. Quand la frayeur est venue à un certain point, elle produit les mêmes effets que la témérité.

45. Il est aussi nécessaire de choisir les mots dans les grandes affaires, qu'il est superflu de les choisir dans les petites.

46. Rien n'est plus rare ni plus difficile aux Ministres qu'un certain ménagement dans le calme qui suit immédiatement les grandes tempêtes, parce que la flatterie y redouble, et que la défiance n'y est pas éteinte.

47. Il ne faut pas nous choquer si fort des fautes des ceux qui sont nos amis, que nous en donnions de l'avantage à ceux contre lesquels nous agissons.

48. Le talent d'insinuer est plus utile que celui de per-

suader, parce que l'on peut insinuer à tout le monde, et que l'on ne persuade presque jamais personne.

49. Dans les matières qui ne sont pas favorables par elles-mêmes, toutes changment qui n'et pas nécessaire est pernicieux, parce qu'il est odieux.

50. Il faut faire voir à ceux qui ne sont naturellement faibles toutes sortes d'abîmes: parce que c'est le vrai moyen de les obliger de se jeter dans le premier chemin qu'on leur ouvre.

51. L'on doit hasarder le possible toutes les fois que l'on se sent en état de profiter même du manquement de succès.

52. Les hommes irrésolus se déterminent difficilement pour les moyens, quoique même ils soient déterminés pour la fin.

53. C'est presque jeu sûr avec les hommes fourbes, de leur faire croire que l'on veut tromper ceux que l'on veut servir.

54. L'un des plus grands embarras que l'on ait avec les Princes, c'est que l'on est souvent obligé, par la considération de leur propre service, de leur donner des conseils dont on ne peut pas leur dire les véritables raisons.

55. Quand on se trouve obligé de faire un discours que l'on prévoit ne devoir pas agréer, l'on ne peut lui donner trop d'apparence de sincérité: parce que c'est l'unique moyen de l'adoucir.

56. On ne doit jamais se jouer avec la faveur: on ne la peut trop embrasser quand elle est véritable; on ne le peut trop éloigner quand elle est fausse.

57. Il y a de l'inconvénient à s'engager sur des suppositions de ce que l'on croit impossible; et pourtant il n'y a rien de si commun.

58. La plupart des hommes examinent moins les raisons de ce qu'on leur propose contre leur sentiment, que celles qui peuvent obliger celui qui les propose de s'en servir.

59. Tout ce qui est vuide dans les temps de faction et d'intrigue passe pour mystérieux dans les esprits de ceux qui ne sont pas accoutumés aux grandes affaires.

60. Il n'est jamais permis à un inférieur de s'égaler en paroles à celui à qui il doit du respect, quoiqu'il s'y égale dans l'action.

61. Tout homme que la fortune seule, par quelque accident, a fait homme public, devient presque toujours avec un peu de temps un particulier ridicule.

62. La plus grande imperfection des hommes est la complaisance, qu'ils trouvent, à se persuader que les autres ne sont point exempts des défauts qu'ils se reconnaissent à eux-mêmes.

63. Il n'y a que l'expérience qui puisse apprendre aux hommes à ne pas préférer ce qui les pique dans le présent à ce qui les doit toucher bien plus essentiellement dans l'avenir.

64. Il faut s'appliquer, avec soin, dans les grandes affaires encore plus que dans les autres, à se défendre du goût qu'on trouve pour la plaisanterie.

65. On ne peut assez peser les moindres mots dans les grandes affaires.

66. Il n'y a que la continuation du bonheur qui fixe la plupart des amitiés.

67. Quinconque assemble le peuple, l'émeut.

I have taken the trouble of extracting and collecting for your use, the foregoing political Maxims of the Cardinal de Retz, in his *Memoirs*. They are not aphorisms of his invention, but the true and just observations of his own experience in the course of great business. My own experience attests the truth of them all. Read them over with attention as here above, and then read with the same attention, and *tout de suite*, the *Memoirs*; where you will find the facts and characters from whence those observations are drawn, or to which they are applied; and they will reciprocally help to fix each other in your mind. I hardly know any book so necessary for a young man to read and remember. You will there find how great business is really carried on; very differently from what people, who have never been concerned in it, imagine. You will there see what Courts and courtiers really are, and observe that they are neither so good as they should be, nor so bad as they are thought by most people. The Court poet, and the sullen cloistered pedant, are equally mistaken in their notions, or at least in the accounts they give us of them. You will observe the coolness in general, the perfidy in some cases, and the truth in a very few, of Court friendships. This will teach you the prudence of a general distrust; and the imprudence of making no exception to that rule upon good and tried grounds. You will see the utility of good-breeding towards one's greatest enemies; and the high imprudence and folly of either insulting or injurious expressions. You will find in the Cardinal's own character, a strange, but by no means an uncommon mixture, of high and low, good and bad, parts and indiscretion. In the character of Monsieur le Duc d'Orléans, you may observe the model of weakness, irresolution, and fear, though with very good parts. In short, you will, in every page of that book, see that strange inconsistent creature, Man, just as he is. If you would know that period of history (and it is well worth knowing) correctly, after you have read the Cardinal's *Memoirs*, you should read those of Joly, and of Madame de Motteville; both which throw great light upon the first. By all those accounts put together, it appears that Anne of Austria (with great submission to a crowned head do I say it) was a bitch. She had spirit and courage without parts, devotion without common morality, and lewdness without tenderness either to justify or to dignify it. Her two sons were no more Louis the Thirteenth's than they were mine; and, if Buckingham had stayed a little longer, she would probably have had another by him.

Cardinal Mazarin was a great knave, but no great man; much more cunning than able; scandalously false, and dirtily greedy. As for his enemy, Cardinal de Retz, I can truly call him a man of great parts, but I cannot call him a great man. He never was so much so as in his retirement. The ladies had then a great, and have always had some share in State affairs in France; the spring and the streams of their politics have always been, and always will be, the interest of their present lover, or their resentment against a discarded and perfidious one. Money is their great object, of which they are extremely greedy, if it coincides with their arrangement with the lover for the time being; but true glory and public good never enter into their heads. They are always governed by the man they love, and they always govern the man who loves them. He or she who loves the most is always governed by him or her who loves the least. Madame de Montbazon governed Monsieur de Beaufort, who was fond of her; whereas she was only proud of his rank and popularity. The *Drudi* for the time being always governed Madame and Mademoiselle de Chevreuse, and steered their politics. Madame de Longueville governed her brother the Prince de Conti, who was in love with her; but Marsillac, with whom she was in love, governed her. In all female politics, the head is certainly not the part that takes the lead; the true and secret spring lies lower and deeper. La Palatine, whom the Cardinal celebrates as the ablest and most sensible woman he ever met with, and who seems to have acted more systematically and consequentially than any of them, starts aside, however, and deviates from her plan whenever the interests or the inclinations of La Vieuville, her lover, required it. I will add (though with great submission to a late friend of yours at Paris) that no woman ever yet either reasoned or acted long together consequentially; but some little thing, some love, some resentment, some present momentary interest, some supposed slight or some humour, always breaks in upon, and oversets their most prudent resolutions and schemes.

Axioms in Trade

(*Stanhope CCCCXXXVIII*)

(DRAWN UP BY LORD CHESTERFIELD FOR HIS SON)

To sell, upon the whole, more than you buy.

To buy your materials as cheap, and to sell your manufactures as dear as you can.

To ease the manufactures, as much as possible, of all taxes and burthens.

To lay small or no duties upon your own manufactures exported, and to lay high duties upon all foreign manufactures imported.

To lay small or no duties upon foreign materials that are necessary for your own manufactures; but to lay very high duties upon, or rather totally prohibit, the exportation of such of your own materials as are necessary for the manufacture of other countries, as wool, fuller's earth, etc.

To keep the interest of money low, that people may place their money in trade.

Not to imagine (as people commonly do) that it is either prudent or possible to prohibit the exportation of your gold or silver, whether coined or uncoined. For, if the balance of trade be against you, that is, if you buy more than you sell, you must necessarily make up that difference in money; and your bullion, or your coin, which are in effect the same thing, must and will be exported in spite of all laws. But if you sell more than you buy, then foreigners must do the same by you, and make up their deficiency in bullion or coin. Gold and silver are but merchandise, as well as cloth or linen; and that nation that buys the least and sells the most, must always have the most money.

A free trade is always carried on with more advantage to the public than an exclusive one by a company. But the particular circumstances of some trades may sometimes require a joint stock and exclusive privileges.

1647

All monopolies are destructive to trade.

To get as much as possible, the advantages of manufacturing and freight.

To contrive to undersell other nations in foreign markets.

1751

London, 3 *January O.S.* 1751

My Dear Friend,

By your letter of the 5th N.S. I find that your *début* at Paris has been a good one; you are entered into good company, and I dare say you will not sink into bad. Frequent the houses where you have been once invited, and have none of that shyness which makes most of our countrymen strangers where they might be intimate and domestic if they pleased. Wherever you have a general invitation to sup when you please, profit of it with decency, and go every now and then. Lord Albemarle will, I am sure, be extremely kind to you; but his house is only a dinner house, and, as I am informed, frequented by no French people. Should he happen to employ you in his bureau, which I much doubt, you must write a better hand than your common one, or you will get no credit by your manuscripts; for your hand is at present an illiberal one; it is neither a hand of business nor of a gentleman, but the hand of a schoolboy writing his exercise, which he hopes will never be read.

Madame de Monconseil gives me a favourable account of you, and so do Marquis de Matignon and Madame du Boccage; they all say that you desire to please, and consequently promise me that you will; and they judge right; for whoever really desires to please, and has (as you have now) the means of learning how, certainly will please; and that is the great

1649

point of life; it makes all other things easy. Whenever you are with Madame de Monconseil, Madame du Boccage, or other women of fashion, with whom you are tolerably free, say frankly and naturally: *Je n'ai point d'usage du monde, j'y suis encore bien neuf, je souhaiterais ardemment de plaire, mais je ne sais guère comment m'y prendre; ayez la bonté, Madame, de me faire part de votre secret de plaire à tout le monde. J'en ferai ma fortune, et il vous en restera pourtant toujours plus qu'il ne vous en faut.* When, in consequence of this request, they shall tell you of any little error, awkwardness, or impropriety, you should not only feel but express the warmest acknowledgment. Though nature should suffer, and she will at first hearing them, tell them *Que la critique la plus sévère, est à votre égard la preuve la plus marquée de leur amitié.* Madame du Boccage tells me particularly to inform you, *Qu'il me fera toujours plaisir et honneur de me venir voir; il est vrai qu'à son âge le plaisir de causer est froid, mais je tâcherai de lui faire connaissance avec des jeunes gens, etc.* Make use of this invitation, and as you live in a manner next door to her, step in and out there frequently. Monsieur du Boccage will go with you, he tells me, with great pleasure, to the plays, and point out to you whatever deserves your knowing there. This is worth your acceptance too; he has a very good taste. I have not yet heard from Lady Hervey upon your subject, but as you inform me that you have already supped with her once, I look upon you as adopted by her; consult her in all your little matters; tell her any difficulties that may occur to you; ask her what you should do or say in such cases; she has *l'usage du monde en perfection,* and will help you to acquire it. Madame de Berkenrode *est pétrie de grâces,* and your quotation is very applicable to her. You may be there, I dare say, as often as you please, and I would advise you to sup there once a week.

You say, very justly, that as Mr. Harte is leaving you, you shall want advice more than ever; you shall never want mine; and as you have already had so much of it, I must rather

repeat than add to what I have already given you; but that
I will do, and add to it occasionally, as circumstances may
require. At present, I shall only remind you of your two
great objects, which you should always attend to: they are
Parliament and foreign affairs. With regard to the former,
you can do nothing, while abroad, but attend carefully to
the purity, correctness, and elegancy of your diction, the
clearness and gracefulness of your utterance, in whatever
language you speak. As for the Parliamentary knowledge,
I will take care of that, when you come home. With regard
to foreign affairs, everything you do abroad may and ought
to tend that way. Your reading should be chiefly historical;
I do not mean of remote, dark, and fabulous history, still
less of gimcrack natural history of fossils, minerals, plants,
etc., but I mean the useful, political, and constitutional
history of Europe, for these last three centuries and a half.
The other thing necessary for your foreign object, and not
less necessary than either ancient or modern knowledge, is
a great knowledge of the world, manners, politeness, address, and *le ton de la bonne compagnie*. In that view, keeping
a great deal of good company is the principal part to which
you are now to attend. It seems ridiculous to tell you, but
it is most certainly true, that your dancing-master is at this
time the man in all Europe of the greatest importance to
you. You must dance well, in order to sit, stand, and walk
well; and you must do all these well, in order to please.
What with your exercises, some reading, and a great deal of
company, your day is, I confess, extremely taken up; but
the day, if well employed, is long enough for everything;
and I am sure you will not slattern away one moment of it
in inaction. At your age people have strong and active
spirits, alacrity and vivacity in all they do; are *impigri*, indefatigable, and quick. The difference is, that a young
fellow of parts exerts all those happy dispositions in the
pursuit of proper objects; endeavours to excel in the solid,
and in the showish parts of life; whereas a silly puppy, or a

dull rogue, throws away all his youth and spirits upon trifles, when he is serious, or upon disgraceful vices, while he aims at pleasures. This, I am sure, will not be your case; your good sense and your good conduct hitherto are your guarantees with me for the future. Continue only at Paris as you have begun, and your stay there will make you, what I have always wished you to be; as near perfection as our nature permits.

Adieu, my dear; remember to write to me once a week, not as to a father, but without reserve as to a friend.

No. 1748

À Madame la Marquise de Monconseil

(Maty I. lv)

À Londres, ce 7 janvier V.S. 1751

Je suis charmé, Madame, que vous soyez si contente de notre enfant, comme vous voulez bien l'appeler; pour moi je suis content, dès que vous croyez qu'il est du bois dont on en fait. Paris, sous vos auspices et vos ordres, fera le reste. Je ne vous dirai pas ce qu'il m'a écrit sur votre sujet; votre panégyrique n'y est pas tout à fait si bien tourné que celui de Pline, mais il me paraît partir plus du cœur. Il est pénétré de vos bontés, et je vois qu'il en connaît tout le prix, car il me recommande instamment de vous supplier de vouloir bien lui dire naturellement jusqu'à ses moindres défauts. Vous me demandez, si je compte de le laisser à Paris sur sa bonne foi; je vous réponds qu'oui, et je vous en donnerai mes raisons. Son gouverneur, auquel je puis me fier, m'assure qu'il n'y a pas le moindre risque. Cela étant, nous voilà en quelque façon à l'abri des grands écueils de la jeunesse; et pour le reste, je crois qu'il est bon qu'un jeune homme s'accoutume de bonne heure à se tirer d'affaire, et à ne pas s'appuyer sur un autre: d'ailleurs, je n'ai jamais vu qu'un gouverneur facilitât à son élève l'entrée dans les

1652

bonnes compagnies; mais, au contraire, j'ai souvent vu qu'ils la leur fermaient. En effet, on tolère bien un jeune homme dans des compagnies, où on ne le souffrirait pas s'il était toujours accompagné d'un gouverneur sérieux, et rebarbatif. De plus, j'ai tant de surveillants sur lui à Paris, qu'il est impossible que j'ignore sa conduite quinze jours de suite, et il sait fort bien qu'au premier faux pas, je le ferai revenir.

No. 1749

To his Son

(*Stanhope CCCCXLI*)

[*January* 1751]

Your riding, fencing, and dancing, constantly, at the Academy, will, I hope, lengthen you out a little; therefore, pray take a great deal of those exercises; for I would very fain have you be, at least, five feet eight inches high, as Mr. Harte once wrote me word that he hoped you would. Mr. Pelham likewise told me, that you speak German and French as fluently and correctly as a Saxon or a Parisian. I am very glad of both; take care not to forget the former; there is no danger of your forgetting the latter. As I both thank and applaud you for having, hitherto, employed yourself so well abroad, I must again repeat to you, that the manner in which you shall now employ it, at Paris, will be finally decisive of your fortune, figure, and character in the world, and consequently of my esteem and kindness. Eight or nine months determine the whole; which whole is very nearly complete. It consists in this only; to retain and increase the learning you have already acquired; to add to it the still more useful knowledge of the world; and to adorn both, with the manners, the address, the air, and the graces of a man of fashion. Without the last, I will say of your youth and your knowledge what Horace says to Venus—

Parum comis sine te Juventas,
Mercuriusque.[1]

[1]*Odes*, I. 30.

The two great subjects of conversation now at Paris are, the dispute between the Crown and the Clergy, and between the Crown and the States of Brittany; inform yourself thoroughly of both; which will let you into the most material parts of the French history and constitution. There are four letters printed, and very well written, against the pretended rights and immunities of the Clergy; to which there is an answer, very well written too, in defence of those immunities. Read them both with attention; and also all representations, memorials, and whatever shall appear, for or against the claims of the States of Brittany. I dare say that ninety-nine in a hundred of the English at Paris do not give themselves the trouble of inquiring into those disputes, but content themselves with saying that there is a confounded bustle and rout between the King and the Priests, and between the King and the States of Brittany, but that, for their parts, they do not trouble their heads about them; fight dog, fight bear; but, with submission to them, these are objects worthy the attention and inquiries of a man of sense and business.

Adieu, my dear child! Yours tenderly.

No. 1750

To ——— [1]

(Mahon, V. 450)

À Londres, ce 10 janvier V.S. 1751

MONSIEUR,

La Renommée ne passe pas pour être véridique; elle grossit les objets tant en bien qu'en mal; elle prend des forces à mesure qu'elle fait du chemin; enfin elle a cent bouches, et où trouvera-t-on cent bouches qui disent la vérité? C'est pourtant à ces défauts que je suis redevable

---

[1](From the MS. in the British Museum. *Egerton Miscell. MS. Letters*, vol. iv. p. 153.) It does not appear to whom the letter was addressed: possibly Voltaire, Crébillon fils, or Fontenelle.

des préjugés que vous paraissez avoir en ma faveur; et ne pardonne-t-on pas volontiers aux défauts dont on profite? On les chérit même au fond du cœur en dépit de l'esprit. Pour moi je jouis de ces préjugés flatteurs qui m'ont procuré une marque si distinguée de votre estime que l'est le recueil de vos ouvrages que Monsieur Monet m'a donné de votre part il y a quelque temps. J'en avais déjà vu quelques-uns qui m'avaient donné l'envie et l'impatience de voir les autres, et ces autres ont autorisé et fixé tous les sentiments que les premiers avaient fait naître. Je ne vous les détaillerai pas, Monsieur, vous les méritez trop bien pour souhaiter de les entendre, et même pour n'en pas souffrir. Je vous ménagerai donc à cet égard. Mais en même temps vous devez bien sentir que le principe même de ce ménagement est encore une raison de plus pour toute l'estime et la considération avec lesquelles j'ai l'honneur d'être.

No. 1751

À Madame du Boccage

(*Maty I. xcii*)

À Londres, ce 14 *janvier V.S.* 1751

En vérité, Madame, ma reconnaissance égale votre bonté, c'est tout dire en deux mots. Deux feuilles de compliments n'en marqueraient pas si bien l'étendue; aussi mon jeune voyageur sent comme il le doit, les attentions dont vous l'avez comblé. Il se fait gloire d'avoir reçu vos ordres au sujet d'un maître à danser; il se considère comme votre fils adoptif; il fait même allusion à je ne sais qui dans la fable, dont les Muses se chargèrent du soin de l'éducation. Il est sûrement en bonne école; s'il n'en profite pas, ce sera sa faute, puisque vous daignez l'instruire par vos conseils, et par vos exemples. Non seulement il n'a pas l'usage du beau monde, mais je crains qu'il n'ait l'usage du monde allemand et italien, ayant passé plus de quatre ans dans ces deux pays; et comme les bons maîtres préfèrent d'enseigner à ceux qui n'ont jamais appris, plutôt qu'à ceux qui ont eu de mauvais principes, il se pourrait que la raideur allemande et la pantalonnade italienne retarderaient les progrés du bel usage. Vous taxez, Madame, votre pays de frivolité, le nôtre en a tout autant; a différence n'est que dans la façon; la frivolité anglaise est sérieuse, et la frivolité française enjouée. Sosie (dans *l'Amphitryon*[1]) préfère un vice commode à une bruyante vertu; et moi le frivole aimable au frivole ennuyeux. Il n'est à présent question ni de l'un, ni de l'autre ici; notre Parnasse, devenu stérile, ne produit rien de bon ni de mauvais; nos pâtissiers mêmes s'en plaignent, obligés de payer plus cher du bon papier, qui n'est pas gâté. Le papier, que vous me faites espérer de m'envoyer quand il paraîtra, ne le sera pas, du moins si les personnes que vous me nommez l'ont employé. Les lettres de Mesdames de la Fayette, de Coulanges, etc., excitent également ma curiosité; ce sont des noms qu'on est accoutumé de respecter.

J'ai ouï lire à M. de Fontenelle, quand j'etais dernièrement à Paris, deux de ses six comédies philosophiques,[2] dont vous m'annoncez la publication: elles étaient pleines de sentiment et de délicatesse, mais il y manquait un peu du levain comique. J'ose parler ainsi d'un moderne, mais non de Terence, quoiqu'entre vous et moi, je le pense. J'ai l'honneur d'être, etc.

[1]Molière. Act i. Scene 4.
  J'aime mieux un vice commode
  Qu'une fatigante vertu;
but it is Mercury who says it.

[2]Fontenelle's comedies include *Le Tyran, Le Testament, Henriette, Lysianasse.*

No. 1752

To his Son

(*Stanhope CCXXXIX*)

London, 14 January O.S. 1751

My Dear Friend,

Among the many good things Mr. Harte has told me of you, two in particular gave me great pleasure. The first, that you are exceedingly careful and jealous of the dignity of your character; that is the sure and solid foundation upon which you must both stand and rise. A man's moral character is a more delicate thing than a woman's reputation of chastity. A slip or two may possibly be forgiven her, and her character may be clarified by subsequent and continued good conduct; but a man's moral character once tainted, is irreparably destroyed. The second was, that you had acquired a most correct and extensive knowledge of foreign affairs, such as the history, the treaties, and the forms of government of the several countries of Europe. This sort of knowledge, little attended to here, will make you not only useful, but necessary, in your future destination, and carry you very far. He added, that you wanted from hence some books relative to our laws and constitution, our colonies, and our commerce; of which you know less than of those of any other part of Europe. I will send you what short books I can find of that sort, to give you a general notion of those things; but you cannot have time to go into their depths at present, you cannot now engage with new folios; you and I will refer the constitutional part of this country to our meeting here, when we will enter seriously into it, and read the necessary books together. In the mean time, go on in the course you are in of foreign matters; converse with ministers and others of every country, watch the transactions of every Court, and endeavour to trace them up to their source. This, with your physics, your geometry, and your exercises, will be all that you can possibly have time for at Paris; for you must allow a great deal for company and pleasures; it is they that must give you those manners, that address, that *tournure* of the *beau monde*, which will qualify you for your future destination. You must first please, in order to get the confidence, and consequently the secrets, of the Courts and ministers for whom and with whom you negotiate.

I will send you by the first opportunity, a short book written by Lord Bolingbroke, under the name of Sir John Oldcastle, containing remarks upon the History of England; which will give you a clear general notion of our constitution, and which will serve you, at the same time (like all Lord Bolingbroke's works), for a model of eloquence and style.[1] I will also send you Sir Josiah Child's[2] little book upon trade, which may properly be called the Commercial Grammar. He lays down the true principles of commerce, and his conclusions from them are generally very just.

Since you turn your thoughts a little towards trade and commerce, which I am very glad you do, I will recommend a French book to you, that you will easily get at Paris, and which I take to be the best book in the world of that kind; I mean the *Dictionnaire de Commerce de Savary*, in three volumes in folio; where you will find everything that relates to trade, commerce, specie, exchange, etc., most clearly stated; and not only relative to France, but to the whole world. You will easily suppose, that I do not advise you to read such a book *tout de suite*; but I only mean that you should have it at hand to have recourse to occasionally.

With this great stock of both useful and ornamental knowledge, which you have already acquired, and which, by your application and industry, you are daily increasing, you will lay such a solid foundation of future figure and for-

---

[1] Chesterfield refers to 'Remarks on the History of England, from the Minutes of Humphrey Oldcastle,' which appeared in *The Craftsman* from September 1730 to May 1731. They were much admired by Lord Chatham.

[2] Sir Josiah Child (1630-1699); *Essay on Trade*, etc. Child's Bank is famous.

tune, that, if you complete it by all the accomplishments of manners, graces, etc., I know nothing which you may not aim at, and, in time, hope for. Your great point at present at Paris, to which all other considerations must give way, is to become entirely a man of fashion; to be well-bred without ceremony, easy without negligence, steady and intrepid with modesty, genteel without affectation, insinuating without meanness, cheerful without being noisy, frank without indiscretion, and secret without any mysteriousness; to know the proper time and place for whatever you say or do, and to do it with an air of *condition*; all this is not so soon nor so easily learned as people imagine, but requires observation and time. The world is an immense folio, which demands a great deal of time and attention to be read and understood as it ought to be; you have not yet read above four or five pages of it; and you will have but barely time to dip now and then in other less important books.

Lord Albemarle has (I know) wrote to a friend of his here that you do not frequent him so much as he expected and desired; that he fears somebody or other has given you wrong impressions of him; and that I may possibly think, from your being seldom at his house, that he has been wanting in his attentions to you. I told the person who told me this, that, on the contrary, you seemed, by your letters to me, to be extremely pleased with Lord Albemarle's behaviour to you; but that you were obliged to give up dining abroad, during your course of experimental philosophy. I guessed the true reason, which I believe was, that, as no French people frequent his house, you rather chose to dine at other places; where you were likely to meet with better company than your countrymen; and you were in the right of it. However, I would have you show no shyness to Lord Albemarle, but go to him, and dine with him oftener than it may be you would wish; for the sake of having him speak well of you here when he returns. He is a good deal in fashion here, and his *puffing* you (to use an awkward expression) before your return here, will be of great use to you afterwards. People in general take characters, as they do most things, upon trust, rather than be at the trouble of examining them themselves; and the decisions of four or five fashionable people, in every place, are final, more particularly with regard to characters, which all can hear, and but few judge of. Do not mention the least of this to any mortal, and take care that Lord Albemarle do not suspect that you know anything of the matter.

Lord Huntingdon and Lord Stormont[1] are, I hear, arrived at Paris; you have, doubtless, seen them. Lord Stormont is well spoken of here. However, in your connections, if you form any with them, show rather a preference to Lord Huntingdon, for reasons which you will easily guess.

Mr. Harte goes this week to Cornwall, to take possession of his living. He has been installed at Windsor. He will return hither in about a month, when your literary correspondence with him will be regularly carried on. Your mutual concern at parting was a good sign for both.

I have this moment received good accounts of you from Paris. Go on, *vous êtes en bon train*. Adieu!

No. 1753

To his Son

(Stanhope CCXL)

London, 21 January O.S. 1751

My Dear Friend,

In all my letters from Paris, I have the pleasure of finding, among many other good things, your docility mentioned with emphasis. This is the sure way of improving in those things, which you only want. It is true, they are little;

[1]David Murray (1727-1796) succeeded, in 1748, as seventh Viscount Stormont. He afterwards filled various public offices, as Ambassador to Paris and Secretary of State; on the death of his uncle, in 1792, he became the second Earl of Mansfield. At this time he was *attaché* to the Embassy in Paris.

but it is as true, too, that they are necessary things. As they are mere matters of usage and mode, it is no disgrace for anybody of your age to be ignorant of them; and the most compendious way of learning them is, fairly to avow your ignorance, and to consult those who, from long usage and experience, know them best. Good sense, and good nature, suggest civility in general; but, in good breeding, there are a thousand little delicacies, which are established only by custom; and it is these little elegancies of manners which distinguish a courtier and a man of fashion from the vulgar. I am assured, by different people, that your air is already much improved; and one of my correspondents makes you the true French compliment of saying, *J'ose vous promettre qu'il sera bientôt comme un de nous autres.* However unbecoming this speech may be in the mouth of a Frenchman, I am very glad that they think it applicable to you; for I would have you not only adopt, but rival, the best manners and usages of the place you are at, be they what they will; that is the versatility of manners, which is so useful in the course of the world. Choose your models well at Paris, and then rival them in their own way. There are fashionable words, phrases, and even gestures at Paris, which are called *du bon ton*; not to mention *certaines petites politesses et attentions, qui ne sont rien en elles-mêmes,* which fashion has rendered necessary. Make yourself master of all these things, and to such a degree as to make the French say, *qu'on dirait que c'est un Français*; and when hereafter you shall be at other Courts, do the same thing there, and conform to the fashionable manners and usage of the place; that is what the French themselves are not apt to do; wherever they go, they retain their own manners, as thinking them the best; but granting them to be so, they are still in the wrong not to conform to those of the place. One would desire to please, wherever one is; and nothing is more innocently flattering, than an approbation and an imitation of the people one converses with.

I hope your colleges with Marcel[1] go on prosperously. In those ridiculous, though, at the same time, really important lectures, pray attend; and desire your professor also to attend more particularly to the chapter of the arms. It is they that decide a man's being genteel or otherwise, more than any other part of the body. A twist, or stiffness in the wrist, will make any man in Europe look awkward. The next thing to be attended to, is your coming into a room, and presenting yourself to a company. This gives the first impression; and the first impression is often a lasting one. Therefore, pray desire Professor Marcel to make you come in and go out of his room frequently, and in the supposition of different companies being there, such as ministers, women, mixed companies, etc. Those who present themselves well have a certain dignity in their air, which, without the least seeming mixture of pride, at once engages, and is respected.

I should not so often repeat, nor so long dwell upon such trifles, with anybody that had less solid and valuable knowledge than you have. Frivolous people attend to those things *par préférence*; they know nothing else; my fear with you is, that, from knowing better things, you should despise these too much, and think them of much less consequence than they really are; for they are of a great deal, and more especially to you.

Pleasing, and governing women, may in time be of great service to you. They often please and govern others. *À propos*: are you in love with Madame de Berkenrode still, or has some other taken her place in your affections? I take it for granted, that *quæ te cumque domat Venus, non erubescendis adurit ignibus. Un arrangement honnête sied bien à un galant homme.* In that case, I recommend you to the utmost discretion, and the profoundest silence. Bragging of,

---

[1]The most celebrated dancing-master of his day. He once exclaimed, in a transport of enthusiasm, real or pretended, *Que de choses dans un menuet!* On another occasion he said to one of his English pupils, *Monsieur, on saute dans les autres pays; on ne danse qu'à Paris!*—M.

hinting at, intimating, or even affectedly disclaiming and denying such an *arrangement*, will equally discredit you among men and women. An unaffected silence upon that subject is the only true medium.

In your commerce with women, and indeed with men too, *une certaine douceur* is particularly engaging; it is that which constitutes that character, which the French talk of so much, and so justly value; I mean *l'aimable*. This *douceur* is not so easily described as felt. It is the compound result of different things: a complaisance, a flexibility, but not a servility of manners; an air of softness in the countenance, gesture and expression; equally whether you concur or differ with the person you converse with. Observe those carefully, who have that *douceur*, which charms you and others; and your own good sense will soon enable you to discover the different ingredients of which it is composed. You must be more particularly attentive to this *douceur*, whenever you are obliged to refuse what is asked of you, or to say what in itself cannot be very agreeable to those to whom you say it. It is then necessary the gilding of a disagreeable pill. *L'aimable* consists in a thousand of these little things aggregately. It is the *suaviter in modo*, which I have so often recommended to you. The *respectable*, Mr. Harte assures me, you do not want, and I believe him. Study then carefully, and acquire perfectly the *aimable*, and you will have everything.

Abbé Guasco, who is another of your panegyrists, writes me word, that he has taken you to dinner at Marquis de St. Germain's;[1] where you will be welcome as often as you please, and the oftener the better. Profit of that, upon the principle of travelling in different countries without changing places. He says too, that he will take you to the Parliament, when any remarkable cause is to be tried. That is very well; go through the several chambers of the Parliament, and see and hear what they are doing; join practice

[1]Ambassador from Turin at the Court of France.

and observation to your theoretical knowledge of their rights and privileges. No Englishman has the least notion of them.

I need not recommend you to go to the bottom of the constitutional and political knowledge of countries; for Mr. Harte tells me, that you have a peculiar turn that way, and have informed yourself most correctly of them.

I must now put some queries to you, as to a *juris publici peritus*, which I am sure you can answer me, and which I own I cannot answer myself; they are upon a subject now much talked of.

1st, Are there any particular forms requisite for the election of a King of the Romans, different from those which are necessary for the election of an Emperor?

2ndly, Is not a king of the Romans as legally elected by the votes of a majority of the Electors, as by two-thirds, or by the unanimity of the Electors?

3rdly, Is there any particular law or constitution of the empire that distinguishes, either in matter or in form, the election of a King of the Romans from that of an Emperor? And is not the Golden Bull of Charles the Fourth equally the rule for both?

4thly, Were there not, at a meeting of a certain number of the Electors (I have forgotten when), some rules and limitations agreed upon concerning the election of a King of the Romans? and were those restrictions legal, and did they obtain the force of law?

How happy am I, my dear child, that I can apply to you for knowledge, and with a certainty of being rightly informed! It is knowledge, more than quick, flashy parts, that makes a man of business. A man who is master of his matter will, with inferior parts, be too hard in Parliament, and indeed anywhere else, for a man of better parts, who knows his subject superficially: and if to his knowledge he joins eloquence and elocution, he must necessarily soon be at the head of that assembly; but without those two, no knowledge is sufficient.

Lord Huntingdon writes me word he has seen you, and that you have renewed your old school acquaintance. Tell me fairly your opinion of him, and of his friend Lord Stormont; and also of the other English people of fashion you meet with. I promise you inviolable secrecy on my part. You and I must now write to each other as friends, and without the least reserve; there will for the future be a thousand things in my letters, which I would not have any mortal living but yourself to see or know. Those you will easily distinguish, and neither show nor repeat; and I will do the same by you.

To come to another subject, for I have a pleasure in talking over every subject with you: How deep are you in Italian? Do you understand Ariosto, Tasso, Boccaccio, and Machiavelli? If you do, you know enough of it, and may know all the rest, by reading, when you have time. Little or no business is written in Italian letters that may in time come in your way, and to speak Italian tolerably, to those very few Italians who speak no French, give yourself no farther trouble about that language, till you happen to have full leisure to perfect yourself in it. It is not the same with regard to German; your speaking and writing that well, will particularly distinguish you from every other man in England; and is, moreover, of great use to any one who is, as probably you will be, employed in the Empire. Therefore, pray cultivate it sedulously, by writing four or five lines of German every day, and by speaking it to every German you meet with.

You have now got a footing in a great many good houses at Paris, in which I advise you to make yourself domestic. This is to be done by a certain easiness of carriage, and a decent familiarity. Not by way of putting yourself upon the frivolous footing of being *sans conséquence*, but by doing in some degree, the honours of the house and table, calling yourself *en badinant, le galopin d'ici*, saying to the master or mistress, *ceci est de mon département, je m'en charge, avouez que je m'en acquitte à merveille.* That sort of *badinage* has something engaging and *liant* in it, and begets that decent familiarity, which it is both agreeable and useful to establish in good houses and with people of fashion. Mere formal visits, dinners and suppers, upon formal invitations, are not the thing; they add to no connection nor information; but it is the easy, careless ingress and egress, at all hours, that forms the pleasing and profitable commerce of life.

The post is so negligent, that I lose some letters from Paris entirely, and receive others much later than I should. To this I ascribe my having received no letter from you for above a fortnight, which, to my impatience, seems a long time. I expect to hear from you once a week. Mr. Harte is gone to Cornwall, and will be back in about three weeks. I have a packet of books to send by the first opportunity, which, I believe, will be Mr. Yorke's return to Paris. The Greek books come from Mr. Harte, and the English ones from your humble servant.

Read Lord Bolingbroke's with great attention, as well to the style as to the matter. I wish you could form yourself such a style in every language. Style is the dress of thoughts, and a well-dressed thought, like a well-dressed man, appears to great advantage. Yours. Adieu.

No. 1754

À Madame la Marquise de Monconseil

(*Maty I. lvi*)

À Londres, ce 21 *janvier V.S.* 1751

C'est un témoignage bien flatteur pour votre fils adoptif, que vous ne vous repentiez pas, Madame, de son adoption; pour lui, je vois qu'il en connaît tout le prix; il s'en fait tant d'honneur, que je le soupçonne de vouloir renoncer à mon nom, pour prendre le vôtre selon les anciennes règles de l'adoption. Pour moi j'y consens, c'est à

vous à être sur vos gardes là-dessus. Je trouve qu'il a raison
de ne vous pas reconnaître en titre de Gouvernante, les idées
d'âge et de mauvaise humeur étant inséparablement attachés
à ce caractère; au lieu que les pouvoirs que donne à une
mère d'adoption un esprit et un caractère comme le vôtre,
sont bien plus étendus, et plus respectés même, que ceux de
la nature. On y obéit avec plaisir, et par conséquent avec
fruit. Je lui ai écrit aujourd'hui[1] sur le mot à l'oreille que
vous m'avez dit hier; mais d'une façon qu'il est impossible
qu'il vous en soupçonne le moins du monde. Je lui conseille,
entre autres choses, une politesse et des attentions univer-
selles pour tout le monde, sans faire le moindre semblant
de savoir qu'il en manque. Je m'étends là-dessus, et je lui
recommande de vous consulter. Ayez donc la bonté,
Madame, de lui inculquer cette politesse générale, que doit
avoir tout honnête homme; car je suis sûr que ce que vous
lui direz fera plus d'impression sur son esprit, que tout ce
que je pourrais lui dire, et il a raison. L'usage du monde ne
s'acquiert pas dans un jour, il est vrai, il y faut même du
temps, mais au moins il s'acquiert bien plutôt quand il est
accompagné de conseils tels que les vôtres. Les bonnes
maisons, où vous l'avez placé, lui donneront nécessairement
les usages, et les manières du beau monde. Du côté du
savoir, le témoignage que vous m'avez envoyé de notre
Abbé Sallier lui est bien glorieux; je joins mes vœux aux
siens, ou, pour mieux dire, ce serait le comble des miens, de
le voir penser comme vous. Je vous supplie, Madame, de
dire à notre Abbé de ma part, tout ce que je devrais lui dire
moi-même, sur ses attentions, sa politesse, son amitié: il en
aura plus de plaisir, et j'en aurai plus d'honneur, que si je
lui faisais payer le port d'une lettre pour le lui dire beaucoup
moins bien.

[1]See Letter to his Son, 21st Jan. 1751.

No. 1755

To his Son

(*Stanhope CCXLI*)

London, 28 January O.S. 1751

My Dear Friend,

A bill for ninety pounds sterling, was brought me, the other day, said to be drawn upon me by you; I scrupled paying it at first, not upon the account of the sum, but because you had sent me no letter of advice, which is always done in those transactions; and still more, because I did not perceive that you had signed it. The person who presented it desired me to look again, and that I should discover your name at the bottom; accordingly I looked again, and with the help of my magnifying glass, did perceive, that what I had first taken only for somebody's mark was, in truth, your name written in the worst and smallest hand I ever saw in my life. I cannot write quite so ill, but it was something like this:

philip Stanhope.

However, I paid it at a venture; though I would almost rather lose the money, than that signature should be yours. All gentlemen, and all men of business, write their names always in the same way, that their signatures may be so well known as not to be easily counterfeited; and they generally sign in a larger character than their common hand; whereas your name was in a less, and a worse hand than your common writing. This suggested to me the various accidents which may very probably happen to you while you write so ill.

For instance, if you were to write in such a character to the Secretary's office, your letter would immediately be sent to the decipherer, as containing matters of the utmost secrecy, not fit to be trusted to the common character. If you

were to write to an antiquarian, he (knowing you to be a
man of learning) would certainly try it by the Runic, Celtic,
or Sclavonian alphabet; never suspecting it to be a modern
character. And, if you were to send a *poulet* to a fine woman,
in such a hand, she would think that it really came from the
poulaillier, which, by the bye, is the etymology of the word,
poulet; for Henry the Fourth of France used to send *billets-
doux* to his mistresses, by his *poulaillier*, under pretence of
sending them chickens; which gave the name of *poulets* to
those short, but expressive, manuscripts.

I have often told you, that every man who has the use of
his eyes and of his hand, can write whatever hand he pleases;
and it is plain that you can, since you write both the Greek
and German characters, which you never learned of a writing-master, extremely well, though your common hand,
which you learned of a master, is an exceeding bad and
illiberal one, equally unfit for business or common use. I
do not desire that you should write the laboured, stiff character of a writing master; a man of business must write
quick and well, and that depends singly upon use. I would
therefore advise you to get some very good writing-master
at Paris, and apply to it for a month only, which will be
sufficient; for, upon my word, the writing of a genteel plain
hand of business is of much more importance than you
think. You will say, it may be, that when you write so very
ill, it is because you are in a hurry? a man of sense may be
in haste, but can never be in a hurry, because he knows, that
whatever he does in a hurry he must necessarily do very ill.
He may be in haste to dispatch an affair, but he will take
care not to let that haste hinder his doing it well. Little
minds are in a hurry, when the object proves (as it commonly does) too big for them; they run, they hare, they
puzzle, confound, and perplex, themselves; they want to do
everything at once, and never do it at all.[1] But a man of
sense takes the time necessary for doing the thing he is

[1]This sounds like the Duke of Newcastle.

about well: and his haste to dispatch a business, only appears by the continuity of his application to it: he pursues it with a cool steadiness, and finishes it before he begins any other. I own your time is much taken up, and you have a great many different things to do; but remember, that you had much better do half of them well, and leave the other half undone, than do them all indifferently. Moreover, the few seconds that are saved in the course of the day, by writing ill instead of well, do not amount to an object of time, by any means equivalent to the disgrace or ridicule of writing the scrawl of a common whore. Consider, that if your very bad writing could furnish me with matter of ridicule, what will it not do to others, who do not view you in the same light that I do. There was a Pope, I think it was Pope Chigi,[1] who was justly ridiculed for his attention to little things, and his inability in great ones; and therefore called *maximus in minimis*, and *minimus in maximis*. Why? Because he attended to little things, when he had great ones to do. At this particular period of your life, and at the place you are now in, you have only little things to do; and you should make it habitual to you to do them well, that they may require no attention from you when you have, as I hope you will have, greater things to mind. Make a good handwriting familiar to you now, that you may hereafter have nothing but your matter to think of, when you have occasion to write to kings and ministers. Dance, dress, and present yourself habitually well now, that you may have none of those little things to think of hereafter, and which will be all necessary to be done well occasionally, when you will have greater things to do.

As I am eternally thinking of everything that can be relative to you, one thing has occurred to me which I think necessary to mention, in order to prevent the difficulties which it might otherwise lay you under; it is this—as you get more acquaintances at Paris, it will be impossible for you

---

[1] Alexander VII. See Letter, 10th August 1749.

to frequent your first acquaintances so much as you did while you had no others. As for example, at your first *début* I suppose you were chiefly at Madame Monconseil's, Lady Hervey's, and Madame Du Boccage's. Now that you have got so many other houses, you cannot be at theirs so often as you used; but pray take care not to give them the least reason to think that you neglect or despise them for the sake of new and more dignified and shining acquaintances, which would be ungrateful and imprudent on your part, and never forgiven on theirs. Call upon them often, though you do not stay with them so long as formerly; tell them that you are sorry you are obliged to go away, but that you have such and such engagements, with which good-breeding obliges you to comply; and insinuate that you would rather stay with them. In short, take care to make as many personal friends, and as few personal enemies as possible. I do not mean by personal friends, intimate and confidential friends, of which no man can hope to have half a dozen in the whole course of his life; but I mean friends in the common acceptation of the word, that is, people who speak well of you, and who would rather do you good that harm, consistently with their own interest and no farther. Upon the whole, I recommend to you again and again *les grâces*. Adorned by them, you may, in a manner, do what you please; it will be approved of; without them your best qualities will lose half their efficacy. Endeavour to be fashionable among the French, which will soon make you fashionable here. Monsieur de Matignon already calls you *le petit français*. If you can get that name generally at Paris it will put you *à la mode*. Adieu! my dear child.

No. 1756

To his Son

(*Stanhope CCXLII*)

London, 4 February O.S. 1751

My Dear Friend,

The accounts which I receive of you from Paris grow every day more and more satisfactory. Lord Albemarle has wrote a sort of panegyric of you, which has been seen by many people here, and which will be a very useful forerunner for you. Being in fashion is an important point for anybody anywhere, but it would be a very great one for you to be established in the fashion here before you return. Your business would be half done by it, as I am sure you would not give people reason to change their favourable presentiments of you. The good that is said of you will not, I am convinced, make you a coxcomb; and, on the other hand, the being thought still to want some little accomplishments will, I am persuaded, not mortify you, but only animate you to acquire them; I will, therefore, give you both fairly in the following extract of a letter which I lately received from an impartial and discerning friend.

'J'ose vous assurer que Monsieur Stanhope réussira. Il a un grand fond de savoir, et une mémoire prodigieuse, sans faire parade de l'un ou de l'autre. Il cherche à plaire, et il plaira. Il a de la physionomie; sa figure est jolie quoique petite. Il n'a rien de gauche quoiqu'il n'ait pas encore toutes les grâces requises, que Marcel et les femmes lui donneront bientôt. Enfin il ne lui manque que ce qui devait nécessairement lui manquer à son âge; je veux dire, les usages, et une certaine délicatesse dans les manières, qui ne s'acquièrent que par le temps et la bonne compagnie. Avec son esprit, il les prendra bientôt, il y a déjà fait des progrès, et il fréquente les compagnies les plus propres à les lui donner.'

By this extract, which I can assure you is a faithful one, you and I have both the satisfaction of knowing how much you have and how little you want. Let what you have, give you (if possible) rather more *seeming* modesty, but at the same time more interior firmness and assurance; and let what you want, which you see is very attainable, redouble your attention and endeavours to acquire it. You have, in truth, but that one thing to apply to it, and a very pleasing application it is, since it is through pleasures that you must arrive at it. Company, suppers, balls, *spectacles*, which show you the models upon which you should form yourself, and all the little usages, customs, and delicacies which you must adopt, and make habitual to you, are now your only schools and universities; in which young fellows and fine women will give you the best lectures.

Monsieur du Boccage is another of your panegyrists; and he tells me that Madame du Boccage *à pris avec vous le ton de mie et de bonne*; and that you like it very well. You are in the right of it; it is the way of improving; endeavour to be upon that footing with every woman you converse with; excepting where there may be a tender point of connection; a point which I have nothing to do with; but if such a one there is, I hope she has not *de mauvais ni de vilains bras*, which I agree with you in thinking a very disagreeable thing.

I have sent you, by the opportunity of Pollock the courier, who was once my servant, two little parcels of Greek and English books; and shall send you two more by Mr. Yorke; but I accompany them with this caution; that, as you have not much time to read, you should employ it in reading what is most necessary; and that is, indisputably, modern historical, geographical, chronological, and political knowledge; the present constitution, maxims, force, riches, trade, commerce, characters, parties, and cabals of the several Courts of Europe. Many who are reckoned good scholars, though they know pretty accurately the govern-

ments of Athens and Rome, are totally ignorant of the constitution of any one country now in Europe, even of their
own. Read just Latin and Greek enough to keep up your
classical learning, which will be an ornament to you while
young and a comfort to you when old. But the true, useful
knowledge, and especially for you, is the modern knowledge above-mentioned. It is that which must qualify you
both for domestic and foreign business, and it is to that,
therefore, that you should principally direct your attention;
and I know, with great pleasure, that you do so. I would
not thus commend you to yourself, if I thought commendations would have upon you those ill-effects which they frequently have upon weak minds. I think you are much above
being a vain coxcomb, overrating your own merit, and in-
sulating others with the superabundance of it. On the contrary, I am convinced, that the consciousness of merit
makes a man of sense more modest, though more firm. A
man who displays his own merit is a coxcomb, and a man
who does not know it is a fool. A man of sense knows it,
exerts it, avails himself of it, but never boasts of it; and
always *seems* rather to under than overvalue it, though, in
truth, he sets the right value upon it. It is a very true
maxim of La Bruyère's (an author well worth your studying)
qu'on ne vaut dans ce monde, que ce que l'on veut valoir. A
man who is really diffident, timid, and bashful, be his merit
what it will, never can push himself in the world; his des-
pondency throws him into inaction; and the forward, the
bustling, and the petulant will always get the better of him.
The manner makes the whole difference. What would be
impudence in one man, is only a proper and decent assurance in another. A man of sense, and of knowledge of the
world, will assert his own rights and pursue his own objects
as steadily and intrepidly as the most impudent man living,
and commonly more so; but then he has art enough to
give an outward air of modesty to all he does. This engages
and prevails, whilst the very same things shock and fail,

from the overbearing or impudent manner only of doing them. I repeat my maxim, *suaviter in modo sed fortiter in re.* Would you know the characters, modes, and manners of the latter end of the last age, which are very like those of the present, read La Bruyère. But would you know man, independently of modes, read La Rochefoucauld, who, I am afraid, paints him very exactly.

Give the enclosed to Abbé Guasco, of whom you make good use, to go about with you and see things. Between you and me, he has more knowledge than parts. *Mais un habile homme sait tirer parti de tout*; and everybody is good for something. President Montesquieu is, in every sense, a most useful acquaintance. He has parts joined to great reading and knowledge of the world. *Puisez dans cette source tant que vous pourrez.*

Adieu! May the Graces attend you; for without them *ogni fatica è vana.* If they do not come to you willingly, ravish them, and force them to accompany all you think, all you say, and all you do.

No. 1757

À Madame la Marquise de Monconseil

(Maty I. lvii)

À Londres, ce 7 février V.S. 1751

Vous voulez absolument que votre élève ait du fond; je le veux bien, et je le crois même; mais si ce fond n'est pas orné par les manières, la politesse, les attentions, et toutes ces petites grâces extérieures, qui sont si aimables, et si nécessaires, il devient assez inutile, et ne rendra guère au propriétaire.

On se fait respecter et estimer par un fond de mérite, et d'érudition; mais cela ne suffit pas, il faut plaire, et on ne plaît que par les agréments et les grâces. C'est le langage que je lui tiens dans toutes mes lettres; il me paraît en sentir tout le vrai, il a tous les jours devant les yeux le meilleur

modèle, car je crois qu'il ne manque guère un jour de vous
voir, et si à la fin, avec tout cela, il ne se forme point, même
malgré lui, il faut qu'il joue d'un furieux malheur. Dites-
moi naturellement, Madame, je vous en prie, lui trouvez-
vous du mieux à cet égard depuis qu'il est à Paris? Se fait-il
peu à peu? Marcel lui a-t-il donné un peu meilleur air? et
commence-t-il à prendre la couleur de ces bonnes compagnies, qui ont bien voulu le recevoir et le tolérer? S'il a
gagné du terrain, il avancera toujours; mais s'il en est encore
précisément là où il en était à son arrivée à Paris, j'en déses-
pérerai, nonobstant tous vos soins. Il a une telle confiance
en vous, que tout ce que vous lui direz fera cent fois plus
d'effet sur lui que toutes mes leçons; cela va presque à
l'adoration, et vous jugez bien que j'encourage cette disposition. N'y allez donc plus si doucement, et ne lui passez
pas la moindre chose. Par rapport à la petite confidence qu'il
vous a faite au sujet de sa dépense, je vous dirai que je lui
avais donnée carte blanche sur cet article, avec ordre de ne
me pas ménager, en tout se qui serait nécessaire, ou même
décent; mais puisqu'il aime mieux savoir à quoi s'en tenir,
et que vous êtes aussi de son avis, pour l'accoutumer à une
sorte de règle dans sa dépense, je le veux bien, à condition
que vous fixiez la somme nécessaire, par mois. Par exemple,
voulez-vous mille, quinze cents, ou deux mille francs par
mois? D'un côté, je ne voudrais pas lui fournir pour une
dépense inutile et frivole; et de l'autre, je ne voudrais pas
qu'il manquât d'argent pour faire une dépense honorable:
si vous fixez, par exemple, sa dépense en gros à quinze cents
livres par mois, je n'entends pas, entre nous, qu'en cas de
besoin il n'aille pas au delà; car je ne veux point, par une
épargne déplacée, le priver d'aucun des avantages réels qui
accompagnent une certaine dépense honnête: ayez la bonté
donc, Madame, de me dire la somme que vous jugez à
propos que je lui nomme, bien entendu toujours, que nous
ne nous brouillerons pas sur un petit excédent de temps en
temps.

1676

La lettre de l'Abbé de la Ville est assurément bien flatteuse pour moi; je l'ai aimé quoiqu'ennemi, et comme tel, je l'ai estimé assez pour le craindre; mais depuis qu'il nous a été permis d'être bons amis, j'ai conservé pour lui les mêmes sentiments, épurés de cet alliage, qu'y met toujours la crainte.[1] Faites-lui, je vous en supplie, Madame, mille compliments de ma part quand vous le verrez. J'espère que dans le pays d'où il date sa lettre, son mérite et ses talents sont aussi bien recompensés, qu'ils y doivent être connus: pour finir, demandez vous-même ce que je vous dois être, et soyez persuadée, Madame, que je le suis.

No. 1758

TO HIS SON

(Stanhope CCXLIII)

London, 11 *February O.S.* 1751

MY DEAR FRIEND,

When you go to the play, which I hope you do often, for it is a very instructive amusement, you must certainly have observed the very different effects which the several parts have upon you, according as they are well or ill acted. The very best tragedy of Corneille's, if well spoken and acted, interests, engages, agitates, and affects your passions. Love, terror, and pity, alternately possess you. But if ill spoken and acted, it would only excite your indignation or your laughter. Why? It is still Corneille's; it is the same sense, the same matter, whether well or ill acted. It is then merely the manner of speaking and acting that makes this great difference in the effects. Apply this to yourself, and conclude from it, that if you would either please in a private company, or persuade in a public assembly, air, looks, gestures, graces, enunciation, proper accents, just emphasis,

[1]It will be remembered that the Abbé de la Ville was French Envoy at the Hague during Chesterfield's mission there in 1745.

and tuneful cadences, are full as necessary as the matter itself. Let awkward, ungraceful, inelegant, and dull fellows say what they will in behalf of their solid matter and strong reasonings, and let them despise all those graces and ornaments, which engage the senses and captivate the heart; they will find (though they will possibly wonder why) that their rough unpolished matter, and their unadorned, coarse, but strong arguments, will neither please nor persuade, but, on the contrary, will tire out attention and excite disgust. We are so made, we love to be pleased better than to be informed; information is, in a certain degree, mortifying, as it implies our previous ignorance; it must be sweetened to be palatable.

To bring this directly to you; know that no man can make a figure in this country, but by Parliament. Your fate depends upon your success there as a speaker; and, take my word for it, that success depends much more upon manner than matter. Mr. Pitt, and Mr. Murray, the Solicitor-General,[1] uncle to Lord Stormont, are, beyond comparison, the best speakers; why? Only because they are the best orators. They alone can inflame or quiet the House; they alone are so attended to, in that numerous and noisy assembly, that you might hear a pin fall while either of them is speaking. Is it that their matter is better, or their arguments stronger, than other people's? Does the House expect extraordinary informations from them? Not in the least; but the House expects pleasure from them, and therefore attends; finds it, and therefore approves. Mr. Pitt, particularly, has very little Parliamentary knowledge; his matter is generally flimsy, and his arguments often weak: but his eloquence is superior, his action graceful, his enunciation just and harmonious; his periods are well turned, and every

---

[1] William Murray (1705-1793): Solicitor-General, 1742; Chief Justice with the title of Baron Mansfield, 1756; Earl of Mansfield, 1776. In the Gordon Riots in London in 1780 his house in Bloomsbury Square, with his valuable library, was burnt.

1678

word he makes use of is the very best, and the most expressive that can be used in that place. This, and not his matter, made him Paymaster, in spite of both King and ministers. From this, draw the obvious conclusion. The same thing holds full as true in conversation, where even trifles, elegantly expressed, well looked, and accompanied with graceful action, will ever please, beyond all the home-spun, unadorned sense in the world. Reflect, on one side, how you feel within yourself, while you are forced to suffer the tedious, muddy, and ill-turned narration of some awkward fellow, even though the fact may be interesting; and on the other hand, with what pleasure you attend to the relation of a much less interesting matter, when elegantly expressed, genteely turned, and gracefully delivered. By attending carefully to all these *agréments* in your daily conversation, they will become habitual to you, before you come into Parliament; and you will have nothing then to do but to raise them a little when you come there. I would wish you to be so attentive to this object, that I would not have you speak to your footman but in the very best words that the subject admits of, be the language which it will. Think of your words, and of their arrangement, before you speak; choose the most elegant, and place them in the best order. Consult your own ear, to avoid cacophony; and what is very near as bad, monotony. Think also of your gesture and looks, when you are speaking even upon the most trifling subjects. The same things differently expressed, looked, and delivered, cease to be the same things. The most passionate lover in the world cannot make a stronger declaration of love than the *Bourgeois Gentilhomme* does in this happy form of words, *Mourir d'amour me font belle Marquise vos beaux yeux.*[1] I defy anybody to say more; and yet I would advise nobody to say that; and I would recommend to you rather to smother and conceal your passion entirely than to reveal it in these words. Seriously, this

[1]M. Jourdain is taught five ways in which to declare his love, but Chesterfield has invented a sixth. See Act II. vi.

holds in everything, as well as in that ludicrous instance. The French, to do them justice, attend very minutely to the purity, the correctness and the elegancy of their style, in conversation, and in their letters. *Bien narrer* is an object of their study; and though they sometimes carry it to affectation, they never sink into inelegancy, which is much the worse extreme of the two. Observe them, and form your French style upon theirs; for elegancy in one language will reproduce itself in all. I knew a young man, who being just elected a member of Parliament, was laughed at for being discovered, through the keyhole of his chamber door, speaking to himself in the glass, and forming his looks and gestures. I could not join in that laugh, but on the contrary, thought him much wiser than those who laughed at him; for he knew the importance of those little graces in a public assembly, and they did not. Your little person (which I am told by the way is not ill-turned), whether in a laced coat, or a blanket, is specifically the same; but yet, I believe, you choose to wear the former; and you are in the right, for the sake of pleasing more. The worst-bred man in Europe, if a lady let fall her fan, would certainly take it up and give it to her; the best-bred man in Europe could do no more. The difference, however, would be considerable; the latter would please by doing it gracefully; the former would be laughed at for doing it awkwardly. I repeat it, and repeat it again, and shall never cease repeating it to you, air, manners, graces, style, elegancy, and all those ornaments, must now be the only objects of your attention; it is now, or never, that you must acquire them. Postpone, therefore, all other considerations; make them now your serious study; you have not one moment to lose. The solid and the ornamental united are undoubtedly best; but were I reduced to make an option, I should, without hesitation, choose the latter.

I hope you assiduously frequent Marcel, and carry graces from him; nobody had more to spare than he had formerly. Have you learned to carve? for it is ridiculous not to carve well. A man who tells you gravely that he cannot carve, may as well tell you that he cannot blow his nose; it is both as necessary and as easy.

Make my compliments to Lord Huntingdon, whom I love and honour extremely, as I dare say you do; I will write to him soon, though I believe he has hardly time to read a letter; and my letters to those I love are, as you know by experience, not very short ones; this is one proof of it, and this would have been longer, if the paper had been so. Good night then, my dear child.

No. 1759

À Madame la Marquise de Monconseil

(*Maty I. lviii*)

Londres, ce 25 février V.S. 1751

Il n'y a que vous au monde qui sachiez combiner les vrais et solides devoirs, avec tous les agréments de l'amitié; les autres sacrifient, trop souvent, par des mouvements d'amour propre, les premiers aux derniers, ils suppriment ce qu'ils devraient dire, pour ne pas dire ce qui déplaira, quelque nécessaire qu'il soit qu'on le sache. Vous, Madame, au contraire, vous vous acquittez des vrais devoirs de l'amitié, en découvrant la vérité, quelque désagréable qu'elle puisse être, plutôt que de laisser ignorer un mal, auquel peut-être on peut trouver du remède à présent, mais qui, en peu de temps, pourrait devenir incurable. Il y a, dans le portrait que vous m'avez envoyé, et qui, je suis bien sûr, est fort ressemblant, des traits qui me choquent infiniment, et qui défigurent tout à fait l'assemblage, malgré d'autres bons traits qui s'y trouvent. Je crains même qu'il ne soit bien difficile de corriger l'original, puisque jusqu'ici vous y avez perdu vos peines, et que, depuis trois ans, j'y ai travaillé sans relâche, et comme il paraît sans succès. Je lui envoie encore par cette poste une lettre, mais des plus fortes, sur ce sujet:

et pour ne vous pas commettre avec lui, et le refroidir à
votre égard, ce qui serait perdre l'unique remède que j'espère,
je lui dis qu'en même temps que je reçus, de votre part, une
lettre qui lui était très favorable, j'en reçus une autre d'un
de mes amis à Paris, sur son sujet, d'une nature bien dif-
férente, dont je fais semblant de lui envoyer l'extrait; après
cela je lui fais son portrait, sur les mémoires que vous m'avez
fournis, et je finis par des remontrances les plus fortes, qu'il
n'aura garde, je crois, de vous montrer. Pour le dépayser
encore plus, et pour vous mettre en état de lui parler encore
plus fortement sur ces matières, je lui dis que je vous ai
envoyé en même temps copie de ce portrait, pour que vous
me disiez véritablement s'il lui ressemble ou non. Ayez donc
la bonté, Madame, de lui dire que vous avez reçu une telle
lettre de ma part, et que vous vous trouvez extrêmement
embarrassée sur ce que vous me devez répondre; que vous
voyez bien que je suis outré même du soupçon que ce portrait lui ressemble: que serait-ce donc si vous alliez constater
cette ressemblance? Ceci lui donnera l'alarme bien chaude,
et en même temps vous fournira une occasion, non suspecte,
de lui dire les choses du monde les plus fortes, sous prétexte
de ménagements pour lui vis-à-vis de moi. En effet, il est
perdu s'il ne se corrige pas foncièrement de ces mauvaises
manières, de cette pente à désapprouver tout, et de ce pen-
chant à disputer avec aigreur et empire. Qu'il ait de l'esprit,
qu'il ait du bon si vous le voulez, c'est un bon fond; mais
aussi vous savez mieux que moi que c'est un fond qui rap-
portera bien peu, s'il n'est pas cultivé par les bonnes
manières, la douceur, les grâces, les agréments, enfin par
tout ce qui vous distingue. Il est encore jeune, il est vrai;
mais aussi, depuis un an et demi, il a fréquenté tout ce qu'il
y avait de meilleure compagnie en Italie, et même, depuis
qu'il est à Paris, il aurait dû s'être formé considérablement,
vu les bonnes compagnies qu'il a fréquentées depuis plus de
deux mois, pour ne rien dire de vos préceptes, et de votre
exemple. Avec tout cela, vous m'avouez, et je suis sûr que

vous mettez tout au mieux, que les progrès sont bien lents;
c'est-à-dire qu'il n'en a point fait du tout. Ceci me fait
presque désesperer, et je n'attends de remède, si tant est que
j'en attende, que de votre part. Sur votre sujet, il pense au
moins comme il doit, et cela étant, il doit naturellement souhaiter de penser comme vous sur tous les autres sujets. Pour
vous mettre aussi encore mieux avec lui, s'il est possible, je
lui ai mandé que c'était simplement à votre sollicitation, que
je m'étais à la fin porté à fixer la somme qu'il devait dépenser
par mois, et qu'il avait si souvent souhaité; que je trouvais
quinze cents francs par mois une somme très raisonnable,
mais que pourtant nous ne nous brouillerions pas, s'il
prenait, en cas de besoin, jusqu'à deux mille; bien entendu
toujours, comme vous me l'avez conseillé, qu'il ne prit pas
pour cela un ton de supériorité ou de mépris pour ceux qui
n'en auraient point tant. Moyennant toutes ces circonstances, vous n'avez rien à craindre en ne le pas ménageant;
dites-lui librement ces vérités, de votre part il écoutera
patiemment et avec attention: sa fortune est absolument
entre vos mains; s'il se corrige, ce ne sera que par vous.
Indépendamment de toute tendresse personnelle, il a été si
longtemps l'objet de mes soins, et je me suis tant flatté d'en
faire quelque chose de bon, qu'il me serait très chagrinant
d'échouer près du port; et ce serait précisément le cas si,
avec un fond d'esprit naturel, et beaucoup d'acquis, il lui
manquait les manières si nécessaires pour les faire valoir.

Pardonnez-moi, Madame, ces détails, pardonnez-moi la
peine que je vous donne. Je sais que vous me le pardonnez,
puisque je sais que votre amitié n'a point de bornes; ma
reconnaissance n'en aura point non plus, et ne finira qu'avec
mes jours.

No. 1760

To his Son

(*Stanhope CCXLIV*)

My Dear Friend,   *London, 28 February O.S.* 1751
     This epigram in Martial,

> Non amo te, Sabidi, nec possum dicere quare,
> Hoc tantum possum dicere, non amo te;[1]

has puzzled a great many people; who cannot conceive how
it is possible not to love anybody, and yet not to know the
reason why. I think I conceive Martial's meaning very
clearly, though the nature of epigram, which is to be short,
would not allow him to explain it more fully; and I take it
to be this, 'O Sabidis, you are a very worthy deserving man;
you have a thousand good qualities, you have a great deal
of learning; I esteem, I respect, but for the soul of me I
cannot love you, though I cannot particularly say why.
You are not *aimable*; you have not those engaging manners,
those pleasing attentions, those graces, and that address,
which are absolutely necessary to please, though impossible
to define. I cannot say it is this or that particular thing that
hinders me from loving you, it is the whole together; and
upon the whole you are not agreeable.' How often have I,
in the course of my life, found myself in this situation, with
regard to many of my acquaintance, whom I have honoured
and respected without being able to love? I did not know
why, because, when one is young, one does not take the
trouble, nor allow oneself the time, to analyse one's sentiments, and to trace them up to their source. But subsequent
observation and reflection have taught me why. There is a
man, whose moral character, deep learning, and superior
parts, I acknowledge, admire, and respect; but whom it is

[1]Martial, *Epigrammatum*, i. 33. 'Ad Sabidium.' Tom Brown 'of facetious
memory' (1663-1704) is supposed to have written his well-known lines, 'I do not
like thee, Dr. Fell,' from this epigram.

impossible for me to love, that I am almost in a fever whenever I am in his company. His figure (without being deformed) seems made to disgrace or ridicule the common structure of the human body. His legs and arms are never in the position which, according to the situation of his body, they ought to be in; but constantly employed in committing acts of hostility upon the Graces. He throws anywhere, but down his throat, whatever he means to drink; and only mangles what he means to carve. Inattentive to all the regards of social life, he mistimes or misplaces everything. He disputes with heat, and indiscriminately; mindless of the rank, character and situation of the several gradations of familiarity or respect; he is exactly the same to his superiors, his equals, and his inferiors; and therefore, by a necessary consequence, absurd to two of the three. Is it possible to love such a man? No. The utmost I can do for him, is to consider him a respectable Hottentot.[1]

I remember that when I came from Cambridge, I had acquired among the pedants of an illiberal seminary a sauciness of literature, a turn to satire and contempt, and a strong tendency to argumentation and contradiction. But I had been but a very little in the world, before I found that this would by no means do; and I immediately adopted the opposite character; I concealed what learning I had; I applauded often without approving; and I yielded commonly, without conviction. *Sauviter in modo* was my Law and my Prophets; and if I pleased (between you and me), it was much more owing to that than to any superior knowledge or merit of my own.

À propos, the word *pleasing* puts one in mind of Lady Hervey: pray tell her, that I declare her responsible to me for your pleasing; that I consider her as a pleasing Falstaff, who not only pleases herself, but is the cause of pleasing in others; that I know she can make anything of anybody; and

[1]This character used to be supposed to be meant for Dr. Johnson; 'I have no doubt that it was,' Boswell said. It is now universally agreed to be meant for Lyttelton.

that, as your governess, if she does not make you please, it must be only because she will not, and not because she cannot. I hope you are, *du bois dont on en fait*; and if so, she is so good a sculptor, that I am sure she can give you whatever form she pleases. A versatility of manners is as necessary in social, as a versatility of parts is in political life. One must often yield, in order to prevail: one must humble oneself, to be exalted; one must, like St. Paul, become all things to all men, to gain some; and (by the way) men are taken by the same means, *mutatis mutandis*, that women are gained; by gentleness, insinuation, and submission; and these lines of Mr. Dryden's will hold to a minister as well as to a mistress.

> The prostrate lover, when he lowest lies,
> But stoops to conquer, and but kneels to rise.[1]

In the course of the world, the qualifications of the chameleon are often necessary; nay, they must be carried a little farther, and exerted a little sooner; for you should, to a certain degree, take the hue of either the man or the woman that you want, and wish to be upon terms with. *À propos*, Have you yet found out at Paris any friendly and hospitable Madame de Lursay,[2] *qui veut bien se charger du soin de vous éduquer?* And have you had any occasion of representing to her, *qu'elle faisait donc des nœuds?* But I ask your pardon, Sir, for the abruptness of the question, and acknowledge that I am meddling with matters that are out of my department. However, in matters of less importance I desire to be *de vos secrets le fidèle dépositaire*. Trust me with the general turn and colour of your amusements at Paris. Is it *le fracas du grand monde, comédies, bals, opéras, cour, etc.?* Or is it *des petites sociétés moins bruyantes mais pas pour cela moins agréables?* Where are you the most *établi?* Where are you *le petit Stanhope? Voyez-vous encore jour à quelque arrangement honnête?* Have you made any acquaintance among the young Frenchmen who ride at your Academy;

[1] *Amphytrion*, Act iii.   [2] See Letter of 26th Nov. 1749.

and who are they? Send me this sort of chit-chat in your letters, which, by the bye, I wish you would honour me with somewhat oftener. If you frequent any of the myriads of polite Englishmen who infest Paris, who are they? Have you finished with Abbé Nollet,[1] and are you *au fait* of all the properties and effects of *air?* Were I inclined to quibble, I would say, that the effects of air, at least, are best to be learned of Marcel. If you have quite done with l'Abbé Nollet, ask my friend l'Abbé Sallier[2] to recommend to you some meagre philomath, to teach you a little geometry and astronomy; not enough to absorb your attention, and puzzle your intellects, but only enough, not to be grossly ignorant of either. I have of late been a sort of an *astronome malgré moi*, by bringing last Monday, into the House of Lords, a bill for reforming our present Calendar, and taking the New Style. Upon which occasion I was obliged to talk some astronomical jargon, of which I did not understand one word, but got it by heart, and spoke it by rote from a master. I wished that I had known a little more of it myself; and so much I would have you know. But the great and necessary knowledge of all is, to know yourself and others: this knowledge requires great attention and long experience; exert the former, and may you have the latter! Adieu.

P.S. I have this moment received your letters of the 27th February, and the 2nd March N.S. The seal shall be done as soon as possible. I am glad that you are employed in Lord Albemarle's bureau; it will teach you, at least the mechanical part of that business, such as folding, entering, and docketing letters; for you must not imagine that you are into the *fin fin* of the correspondence, nor indeed is it fit that you should at your age. However, use yourself to secrecy as to the letters you either read or write, that in

[1]Jean Antoine Nollet (1700-1770) was lecturer on experimental philosophy to the Duke of Savoy, and afterwards Professor of physics in Paris. He was in his day famous as an electrician, and a member of many European literary societies.

[2]Claude Sallier (1685-1761) was an active and distinguished member of the *Académie des Inscriptions*, and became in 1729 member of the *Académie Française*.

time you may be trusted with *secret, very secret, separate, apart,* etc. I am sorry that this business interferes with your riding; I hope it is but seldom; but I insist upon its not interfering with your dancing-master, who is at this time the most useful and necessary of all the masters you have or can have.

No. 1761

To Lord Huntingdon

(*Steuart 12*)

London, 3 March O.S. 1751

My Dear Lord,
I have spared you a great while; your time, I knew, was much better employed at Paris than in reading my letters, and my time has been engrossed, though not near so agreeably employed as it would have been in writing to you, by preparing a Bill which I brought into the House of Lords last week, for correcting the inconvenient and disgraceful errors of our present calendar, and for establishing the Gregorian Calendar, or New Style. But you shall not escape me, and you must sometimes bear with longer and duller letters from me than those which I believe you often receive at Paris, by a more pleasing and quicker conveyance than the post. I have heard much of you and from different hands; and what I have heard was exactly what I was very sure I should hear. You have found that it is not difficult for a Lord Huntingdon to get into what companies he pleases, and I am very sure that my Lord Huntingdon will always choose the best. I am informed that there are as many competitors for the vacant throne of the Princess of Granville, as there were for Alexander's. And your heart, like his empire, I believe, may be extensive enough to provide for them all. Indeed, I hope so, for a heart is much easier under a republican government than under a monarchical one. I have heard that you intend to push your

travels very far, and that, not content with going all over Europe, you propose visiting Greece, and Egypt. Upon this occasion, my dear Lord, you will forgive me again if I assume the privilege of an old advising friend. The several countries and Courts of Europe, their characters, their constitutions, their politics and their manners, are very proper objects of your observation and attention, and will require all the time that you can well spare abroad. But the wild arabs in Egypt and the ignorant slaves of Greece are infinitely below your notice, and unworthy of the time they would take up. The broken pyramids and ruined temples of those desolated countries are below your attention, except in copper plates, where they are to be seen with full as much advantage, and with much less time, trouble and danger. It is extremely probable that before you have finished your European travels, the situation of affairs in England may require your return to it. There are certain favourable moments for a man of your sort to begin the world with, which ought not to be lost, and it would give me the greatest concern if those moments should happen while you were at Grand Cairo. While you are in Europe you are à portée to judge yourself, and to be informed by your friends of those opportunities, and in the mean time you are qualifying yourself more and more every day to improve them. May I go on with my impertinent advice? You seem to say that I may. I would wish you then to stay at Paris till the end of August next, and then to make the best of your way to Rome, there to stay seven or eight months, and afterwards to bestow as much time in the whole, upon Naples, Milan, Turin, Venice, etc. Great capitals are properer objects for you than a great variety of places; take buildings and curiosities in your way, but go very little out of your way for them. From Italy, Germany will deserve one year of your time, I mean the principal courts of it, as Vienna, Berlin, and Dresden. Flanders and the United Provinces may in three months finish your course. This is the plan which it may be I too officiously offer you; but I offer it you sincerely as the best that occurs to me. My young traveller is proud of the countenance you show him at Paris. I have pointed you out to him as his model and his patron, and he seems convinced that nothing can be more for his credit or his interest, than to be like and to belong to you.

Indeed, my dear Lord, I have the greatest satisfaction in knowing that you have already in a great degree acquired, and are in a way of acquiring in the greatest, the only one thing you wanted, for that perfection which Lucretius ascribes to Memmius, *Omnibus ornatum—excellere rebus.* I mean the turn, the manners and the fashion of good company.

Your most faithful friend and servant.

No. 1762

To his Son

(*Stanhope CCXLV*)

[*March* 1751]

My Dear Friend,

I mentioned to you, some time ago, a sentence, which I would most earnestly wish you always to retain in your thoughts and observe in your conduct. It is *suaviter in modo, fortiter in re.* I do not know any one rule so unexceptionally useful and necessary in every part of life. I shall therefore take it for my text to-day; and as old men love preaching, and I have some right to preach to you, I here present you with my sermon upon these words. To proceed then regularly and *pulpitically*; I will first show you, my beloved, the necessary connection of the two members of my text, *suaviter in modo, fortiter in re.* In the next place, I shall set forth the advantages and utility resulting from a strict observance of the precept contained in my text; and conclude with an application of the whole. The *suaviter in modo* alone would degenerate and sink into a mean, timid complaisance, and passiveness, if not supported and digni-fied by the *fortiter in re*; which would also run into impetu-osity and brutality if not tempered and softened by the *suaviter in modo*; however, they are seldom united. The warm choleric man with strong animal spirits despises the *suaviter in modo*, and thinks to carry all before him by the *fortiter in re*. He may, possibly, by great accidents, now and then succeed, when he has only weak and timid people to deal with; but his general fate will be to shock, offend, be hated, and fail. On the other hand, the cunning, crafty man, thinks to gain all ends by the *suaviter in modo* only: *he be-comes all things to all men*; he seems to have no opinion of his own, and servilely adopts the present opinion of the present person; he insinuates himself only into the esteem of fools, but is soon detected, and surely despised by every-body else. The wise man (who differs as much from the cunning as from the choleric man) alone joins the *suaviter in modo* with the *fortiter in re*.

Now to the advantages arising from the strict observance of this precept. If you are in authority, and have a right to command, your commands delivered *suaviter in modo* will be willingly, cheerfully, and consequently well obeyed; whereas, if given only *fortiter*, that is brutally, they will rather, as Tacitus says, be interpreted than executed. For my own part, if I bid my footman bring me a glass of wine in a rough, insulting manner, I should expect that in obey-ing me he would contrive to spill some of it upon me; and I am sure I should deserve it. A cool, steady resolution should show, that where you have a right to command you will be obeyed; but, at the same time, a gentleness in the manner of enforcing that obedience should make it a cheer-ful one, and soften, as much as possible, the mortifying consciousness of inferiority. If you are to ask a favour, or even to solicit your due, you must do it *suaviter in modo*, or you will give those who have a mind to refuse you either, a pretence to do it by resenting the manner; but, on the other hand, you must, by a steady perseverance and decent tenaciousness, show the *fortiter in re.* The right motives are seldom the true ones of men's actions, especially of kings, ministers, and people in high stations; who often give to importunity, and fear what they would refuse to justice or to merit. By the *suaviter in modo* engage their hearts, if you can; at least, prevent the pretence of offence; but take care to show enough of the *fortiter in re* to extort from their love of ease, or their fear, what you might in vain hope for from their justice or good-nature. People in high life are hardened to the wants and distresses of mankind as surgeons are to their bodily pains; they see and hear of them all day long, and even of so many simulated ones, that they do not know which are real and which not. Other sentiments are therefore to be applied to than those of mere justice and humanity; their favour must be captivated by the *suaviter in modo*; their love of ease disturbed by un-wearied importunity, or their fears wrought upon by a decent intimation of implacable, cool resentment; this is the true *fortiter in re.* This precept is the only way I know in the world of being loved without being despised, and feared without being hated. It constitutes the dignity of character, which every wise man must endeavour to establish.

Now to apply what has been said, and so conclude.

If you find that you have a hastiness in your temper, which unguardedly breaks out into indiscreet sallies or rough expressions, to either your superiors, your equals, or your inferiors, watch it narrowly, check it carefully, and call the *suaviter in modo* to your assistance; at the first impulse of passion be silent till you can be soft. Labour even to get the command of your countenance so well, that those emotions may not be read in it; a most unspeakable advantage in business. On the other hand, let no complaisance, no gentle-ness of temper, no weak desire of pleasing on your part, no wheedling, coaxing, nor flattery, on other people's, make you recede one jot from any point that reason and prudence have bid you pursue; but return to the charge, persist, persevere, and you will find most things attainable that are possible. A yielding, timid meekness is always abused and insulted by the unjust and the unfeeling; but when sustained by the *fortiter in re*, is always respected, commonly successful. In your friendships and connections, as well as in your enmities, this rule is particularly useful; let your firmness and vigour preserve and invite attachments to you; but, at the same time, let your manner hinder the enemies of your friends and dependents from becoming yours; let your enemies be disarmed by the gentleness of your manner, but let them feel at the same time the steadiness of your just resentment; for there is great difference between bearing malice, which is always ungenerous, and a resolute self-defence, which is always prudent and justifiable. In negotiations with foreign Ministers, remember the *fortiter in re*; give up no point, accept of no expedient, till the utmost necessity reduces you to it, and even then dispute the ground inch by inch; but then, while you are contending with the minister *fortiter in re*, remember to gain the man by the *suaviter in modo*. If you engage his heart, you have a fair chance for imposing upon his understanding, and determining his will. Tell him in a frank and gallant manner that your ministerial wrangles do not lessen your personal regard for his merit; but that, on the contrary, his zeal and ability in the service of his master increase it; and that of all things you desire to make a good friend of so good a servant. By these means you may and will very often be a gainer; you never can be a loser. Some people cannot gain upon themselves to be easy and civil to those who are either their rivals, competitors, or opposers, though, independently of those accidental circumstances, they would like and esteem them. They betray a shyness and an awkwardness in company with them, and catch at any little thing to expose them; and so, from temporary and only occasional opponents, make them their personal enemies. This is exceedingly weak and detrimental, as indeed is all humour in business; which can only be carried on successfully by unadulterated good policy and right reasoning. In such situations I would be more particularly and *noblement* civil, easy, and frank, with the man whose designs I traversed; this is commonly called generosity and magnanimity, but is, in truth, good sense and policy.

The manner is often as important as the matter, sometimes more so; a favour may make an enemy, and an injury may make a friend, according to the different manner in which they are severally done. The countenance, the address, the words, the enunciation, the Graces, add great efficacy to the *suaviter in modo*, and great dignity to the *fortiter in re*; and consequently they deserve the utmost attention.

From what has been said I conclude with this observation: that gentleness of manners, with firmness of mind, is a short but full description of human perfection, on this side of religious and moral duties; that you may be seriously convinced of this truth, and show it in your life and conversation, is the most sincere and ardent wish of

Yours.

No. 1763

To his Son

(*Stanhope CCXLVI*)

London, 11 *March O.S.* 1751

My Dear Friend,

I received by the last post a letter from Abbé Guasco, in which he joins his representations to those of Lord Albemarle, against you remaining any longer in your very bad lodgings at the Academy; and, as I do not find that any advantage can arise to you from being *interne* in an Academy, which is full as far from the riding-house, and from all your other masters, as your lodgings will probably be, I agree to your removing to an *hôtel garni*; the Abbé will help you to find one, as I desire him by the enclosed, which you will give him. I must, however, annex one condition to your going into private lodgings, which is an absolute exclusion of English breakfasts and suppers at them; the former consume the whole morning, and the latter employ the evenings very ill, in senseless toasting *à l'Anglaise* in their infernal claret. You will be sure to go to the riding-house as often as possible, that is, whenever your new business at Lord Albemarle's does not hinder you. But at all events, I insist upon your never missing Marcel, who is at present of more consequence to you than all the *bureaux* in Europe; for this is the time for you to acquire *tous ces petits riens*, which, though in arithmetical account, added to one another *ad infinitum*, they would amount to nothing, in the account of the world amount to a great and important sum. *Les agréments et les grâces*, without which you will never be anything, are absolutely made up of all those *riens*, which are more easily felt than described. By the way, you may take your lodgings for one whole year certain, by which means you may get them much cheaper; for though I intend to see you here in less than a year, it will be but for a little time, and you will return to Paris again, where I intend you shall stay till the end of April twelvemonth, 1752; at which time, provided you have got all *la politesse, les manières, les attentions, et les grâces du beau monde*, I shall place you in some business suitable to your destination.

I have received, at last, your present of the cartoon from Dominichino, by Blanchet. It is very finely done; it is pity that he did not take in all the figures of the original. I will hang it up, where it shall be your own again some time or other.

Mr. Harte is returned in perfect health from Cornwall, and has taken possession of his prebendal house at Windsor, which is a very pretty one. As I dare say you will always feel, I hope you will always express, the strongest sentiments of gratitude and friendship for him. Write to him frequently, and attend to the letters you receive from him. He shall be with us at Blackheath, alias *Babiole*, all the time that I propose you shall be there, which I believe will be the month of August next.

Having thus mentioned to you the probable time of our meeting, I will prepare you a little for it. Hatred, jealousy, or envy, make most people attentive to discover the least defects of those they do not love; they rejoice at every new discovery they make of that kind, and take care to publish it. I thank God, I do not know what those three ungenerous passions are, having never felt them in my own breast; but love has just the same effect upon me, except that I conceal, instead of publishing, the defects which my attention makes me discover in those I love. I curiously pry into them; I analyse them; and, wishing either to find them perfect or to make them so, nothing escapes me, and I soon discover every the least gradation towards, or from, that perfection. You must therefore expect the most critical *examen* that ever anybody underwent; I shall discover your least, as well as your greatest defects, and I shall very freely tell you of them, *Non quod odio habeam, sed quod amem.* But I shall tell them you *tête-à-tête*, and as *Micio*, not as *Demea*;[1] and I will tell them to nobody else. I think it but fair to inform you beforehand, where I suspect that my criticisms are likely to fall; and that is more upon the outward, than upon the inward man; I neither suspect your heart nor your head; but, to be plain with you, I have a strange distrust of your air, your address, your manners, your *tournure*, and particularly of your *enunciation* and elegancy of style. These will be all put to the trial; for while you are with me, you must do the honours of my house and table; the least inaccuracy or inelegancy will not escape me; as you will find

[1]In the *Adelphi* of Terence.

by *a look* at the time, and by a remonstrance afterwards when we are alone You will see a great deal of company of all sorts at *Babiole*, and particularly foreigners. Make therefore, in the mean time, all these exterior and ornamental qualifications your peculiar care, and disappoint all my imaginary schemes of criticism. Some authors have criticised their own works first, in hopes of hindering others from doing it afterwards; but then they do it themselves with so much tenderness and partiality for their own production, that not only the production itself, but the preventive criticism, is criticised. I am not one of those authors; but on the contrary, my severity increases with my fondness for my work; and if you will but effectually correct all the faults I shall find, I will insure you from all subsequent criticisms from other quarters.

Are you got a little into the interior, into the constitution of things at Paris? Have you seen what you have seen thoroughly? For, by the way, few people see what they see, or hear what they hear. For example: if you go to *les Invalides*, do you content yourself with seeing the building, the hall where three or four hundred cripples dine, and the galleries where they lie; or you inform yourself of the numbers, the conditions of their admission, their allowance, the value and nature of the fund by which the whole is supported? This latter I call *seeing*, the former is only *staring*. Many people take the opportunity of *les vacances*, to go and see the empty rooms, where the several chambers of the Parliament did sit; which rooms are exceedingly like all other large rooms; when you go there, let it be when they are full; see and hear what is doing in them; learn their respective constitutions, jurisdictions, objects, and methods of proceeding; hear some causes tried in every one of the different chambers. *Approfondissez les choses.*

I am glad to hear that you are so well at Marquis de St. Germain's, of whom I hear a very good character. How are you with the other foreign ministers at Paris? Do you frequent the Dutch Ambassador or Ambassadress? Have you any footing at the Nuncio's or at the Imperial and Spanish Ambassador's? It is useful. Be more particular in your letters to me, as to your manner of passing your time, and the company you keep. Where do you dine and sup oftenest? whose house is most your home? Adieu. *Les grâces, les grâces!*

No. 1764

To his Son

(Stanhope CCXLVII)

London, 18 *March O.S.* 1751

MY DEAR FRIEND,

I acquainted you in a former letter that I had brought a bill into the House of Lords, for correcting and reforming our present calendar, which is the Julian, and for adopting the Gregorian. I will now give you a more particular account of that affair, from which reflections will naturally occur to you that I hope may be useful, and which I fear you have not made. It was notorious, that the Julian calendar was erroneous, and had overcharged the solar year with eleven days. Pope Gregory XIII corrected this error; his reformed calendar was immediately received by all the Catholic Powers of Europe, and afterwards adopted by all the Protestant ones, except Russia, Sweden, and England. It was not, in my opinion, very honourable for England to remain in a gross and avowed error, especially in such company; the inconvenience of it was likewise felt by all those who had foreign correspondences, whether political or mercantile. I determined, therefore, to attempt the reformation; I consulted the best lawyers, and the most skilful astronomers, and we cooked up a bill for that purpose. But then my difficulty began; I was to bring in this bill, which was necessarily composed of law jargon and

1698

astronomical calculations, to both which I am an utter stranger. However, it was absolutely necessary to make the House of Lords think that I knew something of the matter, and also to make them believe that they knew something of it themselves, which they do not. For my own part, I could just as soon have talked Celtic or Sclavonian to them as astronomy, and they would have understood me full as well; so I resolved to do better than speak to the purpose, and to please instead of informing them. I gave them, therefore, only an historical account of calendars, from the Egyptian down to the Gregorian, amusing them now and then with little episodes; but I was particularly attentive to the choice of my words, to the harmony and roundness of my periods, to my elocution, to my action. This succeeded, and ever will succeed; they thought I informed, because I pleased them; and many of them said, that I had made the whole very clear to them, when, God knows, I had not even attempted it. Lord Macclesfield, who had the greatest share in forming the bill, and who is one of the greatest mathematicians and astronomers in Europe,[1] spoke afterwards with infinite knowledge, and all the clearness that so intricate a matter would admit of; but as his words, his periods, and his utterance were not near so good as mine, the preference was most unanimously, though most unjustly, given to me. This will ever be the case; every numerous assembly is *mob*, let the individuals who compose it be what they will. Mere reason and good sense is never to be talked to a mob; their passions, their sentiments, their senses, and their seeming interests, are alone to be applied to. Understanding they have collectively none; but they have ears and eyes, which must be flattered and seduced; and this can only be done by eloquence, tuneful periods, graceful action, and all the various parts of oratory.

[1] George Parker, second Earl of Macclesfield (1697-1764). In November 1751 he was unanimously elected President of the Royal Society. He built a private observatory at Sherburn Castle, Oxfordshire.

When you come into the House of Commons, if you imagine that speaking plain and unadorned sense and reason will do your business, you will find yourself most grossly mistaken. As a speaker, you will be ranked only according to your eloquence, and by no means according to your matter; everybody knows the matter almost alike, but few can adorn it. I was early convinced of the importance and powers of eloquence, and from that moment I applied myself to it. I resolved not to utter one word, even in common conversation, that should not be the most expressive and the most elegant that the language could supply me with for that purpose; by which means I have acquired such a certain degree of habitual eloquence, that I must now really take some pains, if I would express myself very inelegantly. I want to inculcate this known truth into you, which you seem by no means to be convinced of yet—that ornaments are at present your only objects. Your sole business now is to shine, not to weigh. Weight without lustre is lead. You had better talk trifles elegantly, to the most trifling woman, than coarse inelegant sense to the most solid man. You had better return a dropped fan genteely, than give a thousand pounds awkwardly; and you had better refuse a favour gracefully, than grant it clumsily. Manner is all in everything; it is by manner only that you can please, and consequently rise. All your Greek will never advance you from Secretary to Envoy, or from Envoy to Ambassador; but your address, your manner, your air, if good, very probably may. Marcel can be of much more use to you than Aristotle. I would, upon my word, much rather that you had Lord Bolingbroke's style and eloquence, in speaking and writing, than all the learning of the Academy of Sciences, the Royal Society, and the two Universities united.

Having mentioned Lord Bolingbroke's style, which is, undoubtedly, infinitely superior to anybody's, I would have you read his works, which you have, over and over again, with particular attention to his style. Transcribe, imitate,

1700

emulate it, if possible; that would be of real use to you in the House of Commons, in negotiations, in conversation; with that, you may justly hope to please, to persuade, to seduce, to impose; and you will fail in those articles, in proportion as you fall short of it. Upon the whole, lay aside, during your year's residence at Paris, all thoughts of all that dull fellows call solid, and exert your utmost care to acquire what people of fashion call shining. *Prenez l'éclat et le brillant d'un galant homme.*

Among the commonly-called little things to which you do not attend, your handwriting is one, which is indeed shamefully bad, and illiberal; it is neither the hand of a man of business, nor of a gentleman, but of a truant schoolboy; as soon, therefore, as you have done with Abbé Nollet, pray get an excellent writing-master, since you think that you cannot teach yourself to write what hand you please; and let him teach you to write a genteel, legible, liberal hand, and quick, not the hand of a *procureur*, or a writing-master, but that sort of hand in which the first *Commis* in foreign bureaux commonly write; for I tell you truly, that were I Lord Albemarle, nothing should remain in my bureau written in your present hand. From hand to arms the transition is natural;—is the carriage and motion of your arms so too? The motion of the arms is the most material part of a man's air, especially in dancing; the feet are not near so material. If a man dances well from the waist upwards, wears his hat well, and moves his head properly, he dances well. Do the women say that you dress well? for that is necessary, too, for a young fellow. Have you *un goût vif,* or a passion for anybody? I do not ask for whom; an Iphigenia would both give you the desire, and teach you the means to please.

In a fortnight or three weeks you will see Sir Charles Hotham at Paris, in his way to Toulouse, where he is to stay a year or two. Pray be very civil to him, but do not carry him into company, except presenting him to Lord

Albemarle; for, as he is not to stay at Paris above a week, we do not desire that he should taste of that dissipation: you may show him a play and an opera. Adieu, my dear child!

No. 1765

To his Son

(*Stanhope CCXLVIII*)

London, 25 March O.S. 1751

My Dear Friend,

What a happy period of your life is this! Pleasure is now, and ought to be, your business. While you were younger, dry rules, and unconnected words, were the unpleasant objects of your labours. When you grow older, the anxiety, the vexations, the disappointments, inseparable from public business, will require the greatest share of your time and attention; your pleasures may, indeed, conduce to your business, and your business will quicken your pleasures; but still your time must, at least, be divided; whereas now it is wholly your own, and cannot be so well employed as in the pleasures of a gentleman. The world is now the only book you want, and almost the only one you ought to read; that necessary book can only be read in company, in public places, at meals, and in *ruelles*. You must be in the pleasures, in order to learn the manners of good company. In premeditated, or in formal business, people conceal, or at least endeavour to conceal, their characters; whereas pleasures discover them, and the heart breaks out through the guard of the understanding. Those are often propitious moments for skilful negotiators to improve. In your destination particularly, the able conduct of pleasures is of infinite use; to keep a good table, and to do the honours of it gracefully, and *sur le ton de la bonne compagnie*, is absolutely necessary for a foreign minister. There is a certain light chit-chat, useful to keep off improper and too serious subjects, which is only to be learned in the pleasures of good company. In truth, it may be trifling; but trifling as it is, a man of parts, and experience of the world, will give an agreeable turn to it. *L'art de badiner agréablement* is by no means to be despised.

An engaging address, and turn to gallantry, is often of very great service to foreign ministers. Women have, directly, or indirectly, a good deal to say in most Courts. The late Lord Strafford[1] governed, for a considerable time, the Court of Berlin, and made his own fortune, by being well with Madame de Wartemberg, the first King of Prussia's mistress. I could name many other instances of that kind. That sort of agreeable *caquet de femmes*, the necessary forerunner of closer conferences, is only to be got by frequenting women of the first fashion, *et qui donnent le ton*. Let every other book then give way to this great and necessary book, the World; of which there are so many various readings, that it requires a great deal of time and attention to understand it well: contrary to all other books, you must not stay at home, but go abroad to read it; and, when you seek it abroad, you will not find it in booksellers' shops and stalls, but in Courts, in *hôtels*, at entertainments, balls, assemblies, spectacles, etc. Put yourself upon the foot of an easy, domestic, but polite familiarity and intimacy, in the several French houses to which you have been introduced. Cultivate them, frequent them, and show a desire of becoming *enfant de la maison*. Get acquainted as much as you can with *les gens de cour*; and observe, carefully, how politely they can differ, and how civilly they can hate; how easy and idle they can seem in the multiplicity of their business; and how they can lay hold of the proper moments to carry it on, in the midst of their pleasures. Courts, alone, teach versatility and politeness; for there is no living there without

[1] Thomas Wentworth, Lord Raby (1672-1739), first Earl of Strafford of the second creation. He was Ambassador Extraordinary at Berlin during the reign of Queen Anne, and was impeached for his share in the Treaty of Utrecht. He built Wentworth House, near Sheffield. See *Wentworth Papers*, Cartwright Ed. 1883.

them. Lord Albemarle has, I hear, and am very glad of it, put you into the hands of Messieurs de Bissy.[1] Profit by that, and beg of them to let you attend them in all the companies of Versailles and Paris. One of them, at least, will naturally carry you to Madame de la Vallières, unless she is discarded by this time, and Gelliot[2] retaken. Tell them frankly, *que vous cherchez à vous former, que vous êtes en main de maîtres, s'ils veulent bien s'en donner la peine.* Your profession has this agreeable peculiarity in it, which is, that it is connected with, and promoted by pleasures; and it is the only one in which a thorough knowledge of the world, polite manners, and an engaging address, are absolutely necessary. If a lawyer knows his law, a parson his divinity, and a *financier* his calculations, each may make a figure and a fortune in his profession, without great knowledge of the world, and without the manners of gentlemen. But your profession throws you into all the intrigues, and cabals, as well as pleasures, of Courts; in those windings and labyrinths, a knowledge of the world, a discernment of characters, a suppleness and versatility of mind, and an elegancy of manners, must be your clue; you must know how to soothe and lull the monsters that guard, and how to address and gain the fair that keep, the golden fleece. These are the arts and the accomplishments absolutely necessary for a foreign minister; in which it must be owned, to our shame, that most other nations out-do the English; and, *cæteris paribus*, a French minister will get the better of an English one, at any third Court in Europe. The French have something more *liant*, more insinuating and engaging in their manner, than we have. An English minister shall have resided seven years at a Court, without having made any one personal connection there, or without being intimate and domestic in any one house. He is always the English minister, and never naturalised. He receives his orders, demands an audience, writes

[1]See d'Alembert to Mme du Deffand, 16th Feb. 1753.
[2]Probably Pierre Jélyot, the opera singer.

an account of it to his Court, and his business is done. A French minister, on the contrary, has not been six weeks at a Court, without having, by a thousand little attentions, insinuated himself into some degree of favour with the Prince, his wife, his mistress, his favourite, and his minister. He has established himself upon a familiar and domestic footing, in a dozen of the best houses of the place, where he has accustomed the people to be not only easy, but unguarded before him; he makes himself at home there, and they think him so. By these means he knows the interior of those Courts, and can almost write prophecies to his own, from the knowledge he has of the characters, the humours, the abilities, or the weaknesses, of the actors. The Cardinal d'Ossat was looked upon at Rome as an Italian, and not as a French Cardinal; and Monsieur d'Avaux,[1] wherever he went, was never considered as a foreign minister, but as a native, and a personal friend. Mere plain truth, sense, and knowledge, will by no means do alone in Courts; art and ornaments must come to their assistance. Humours must be flattered; the *mollia tempora* must be studied and known; confidence, acquired by seeming frankness, and profited of by silent skill. And, above all, you must gain and engage the heart, to betray the understanding to you. *Hæ tibi erunt artes.*

The death of the Prince of Wales,[2] who was more beloved for his affability and good-nature, than esteemed for his steadiness and conduct, has given concern to many, and apprehensions to all. The great difference of the ages of the King and Prince George, presents the prospect of a minority; a disagreeable prospect for any nation! But it is to be hoped, and is most probable, that the King, who is now perfectly recovered of his late indisposition, may live to see his grandson of age.[3] He is, seriously, a most hopeful

[1]Jean Antoine, Comte d'Avaux, was the plenipotentiary of France at the Conferences of Nimeguen, and afterwards Ambassador in Holland until the war in 1688. His *Lettres et Négociations* were published at the Hague in 1710.—M.

[2]Frederick, Prince of Wales, died 20th March 1751.

[3]George III was twenty-two when he succeeded in 1760.

1705

boy; gentle and good-natured, with good sound sense. This event has made all sorts of people here historians, as well as politicians. Our histories are rummaged for all the particular circumstances of the six minorities we have had since the conquest, viz. those of Henry III, Edward III, Richard II, Henry VI, Edward V, and Edward VI; and the reasonings, the speculations, the conjectures, and the predictions, you will easily imagine, must be innumerable and endless, in this nation, where every porter is a consummate politician. Doctor Swift says, very humorously, "Every man knows that he understands religion and politics, though he never learned them; but many people are conscious they do not understand many other sciences, from having never learned them." Adieu!

No. 1766
To his Son
(*Stanhope CCXLIX*)

London, 7 April O.S. 1751

My Dear Friend,

Here you have altogether, the pocket-books, the compasses, and the patterns. When your three Graces have made their option, you need only send me, in a letter, small pieces of the three mohairs they fix upon. If I can find no way of sending them safely, and directly to Paris, I will contrive to have them left with Madame Morel, at Calais; who, being Madame Monconseil's agent there, may find means of furthering them to your three ladies, who all belong to your friend Madame Monconseil. Two of the three, I am told, are handsome; Madame Polignac, I can swear, is not so; but, however, as the world goes, two out of three is a very good composition.

You will also find in the packet a compass ring, set round with little diamonds, which I advise you to make a present of to Abbé Guasco, who has been useful to you, and will continue to be so; as it is a mere bauble, you must add to the value of it by your manner of giving it him. Show it him first, and, when he commends it, as probably he will, tell him that it is at his service, *et que comme il est toujours par voie et par chemins, il est absolument nécessaire qu'il ait une boussole.* All those little gallantries depend entirely upon the manner of doing them; as, in truth, what does not? The greatest favours may be done so awkwardly and bunglingly as to offend; and disagreeable things may be done so agreeably as almost to oblige. Endeavour to acquire this great secret; it exists, it is to be found, and is worth a great deal more than the grand secret of the alchemists would be if it were, as it is not, to be found. This is only to be learned in Courts, where clashing views, jarring opinions, and cordial hatreds, are softened, and kept within decent bounds, by politeness and manners. Frequent, observe, and learn Courts. Are you free of that of St. Cloud?[1] Are you often at Versailles? Insinuate and wriggle yourself into favour at those places. L'Abbé de la Ville, my old friend[2], will help you at the latter; your three ladies may establish you in the former. The good-breeding *de la ville et de la cour* are different; but, without deciding which is intrinsically the best, that of the Court is, without doubt, the most necessary for you, who are to live, to grow, and to rise in Courts. In two years' time, which will be as soon as you are fit for it, I hope to be able to plant you in the soil of a *young Court*[3] here; where, if you have all the address, the suppleness, and versatility of a good courtier, you will have a great chance of thriving and flourishing. Young favour is easily acquired, if the proper means are employed; and when acquired, it is

[1]St. Cloud was the seat of the Duke of Orléans.

[2]Jean Ignace de la Ville (*c.* 1690-1774) had been preceptor to the children of the Marquis de Fénelon during his embassy at the Hague, and in 1744 was appointed successor to the Marquis in his diplomatic post, although with the inferior rank of envoy. A few months before his death the post of *directeur des affaires étrangères* was created for him, and he was made bishop *in partibus*. He was also distinguished in literature, and was elected in 1746 a member of the French Academy.—M.

[3]Lord Chesterfield here alludes to the household of the Princess Dowager of Wales, and of her son, afterwards King George III.—M.

warm, if not durable; and the warm moments must be snatched and improved. *Quitte pour ce qui en peut arriver après.* Do not mention this view of mine for you, to any mortal; but learn to keep your own secrets, which, by the way, very few people can do.

If your course of experimental philosophy with Abbé Nollet is over, I would have you apply to Abbé Sallier for a master to give you a general notion of astronomy and geometry; of both which you may know as much as I desire you should, in six months' time. I only desire that you should have a clear notion of the present planetary system, and the history of all the former systems. Fontenelle's *Pluralité des Mondes* will almost teach you all you need know upon that subject. As for geometry, the first seven books of Euclid will be a sufficient portion of it for you. It is right to have a general notion of those abstruse sciences, so as not to appear quite ignorant of them, when they happen, as sometimes they do, to be the topics of conversation; but a deep knowledge of them requires too much time, and engrosses the mind too much. I repeat it again and again to you, Let the great book of the world be your principal study. *Nocturna versate manu, versate diurna;* which may be rendered thus in English: Turn over *men by day, and women by night.* I mean only the best editions.

Whatever may be said at Paris of my speech upon the Bill for the reformation of the present calendar, or whatever applause it may have met with here, the whole, I can assure you, is owing to the words and to the delivery, but by no means to the matter; which, as I told you in a former letter, I was not master of. I mention this again, to show you the importance of well-chosen words, harmonious periods, and good delivery; for, between you and me, Lord Macclesfield's speech was, in truth, worth a thousand of mine. It will soon be printed, and I will send it you. It is very instructive. You say, that you wish to speak but half as well as I did; you may easily speak full as well as ever I did; if you will but give the same attention to the same objects that I did at your age, and for many years afterwards; I mean correctness, purity and elegance of style, harmony of periods, and gracefulness of delivery. Read over and over again the third book of the Cicero *de Oratore*, in which he particularly treats of the ornamental parts of oratory; they are indeed properly oratory, for all the rest depends only upon common sense, and some knowledge of the subjects you speak upon. But if you would please, persuade, and prevail in speaking, it must be by the ornamental parts of oratory. Make them, therefore, habitual to you; and resolve never to say the most common things even to your footman, but in the best words you can find, and with the best utterance. This, with *les manières, la tournure, et les usages du beau monde*, are the only two things you want; fortunately they are both in your power; may you have them both! Adieu!

No. 1767

To Lord Huntingdon

(Steuart 13)

London, 8 *April O.S.* 1751

My Dear Lord,

In my last letter to you I took the liberty of representing freely against a design, which I was informed that you entertained of going into Greece, Egypt, etc., and I foretold that some situations might possibly exist in England, from which you ought not to be so remote. Like most prophets whose predictions seem to be in any degree verified, I happened to be more prophetic than I thought myself, and in a very different sense from what I meant; to be plain, I meant the death of the King, who I then thought in a bad state of health, and little thought that his son would die before him. But that has happened, and it is upon the present situation of affairs, flowing from that unexpected event, that I now trouble you, as your faithful and affectionate friend and servant. The young Prince whom I will now call the Prince of Wales, the warrant being signed for the Patent to create him such, is but thirteen years old; his immediate establishment as Prince of Wales will be but a narrow one, but is to increase with his years. I do by no means think it worth your while to come over here now in order to be of that first establishment, could it be brought about; the two next years of what I will call your education abroad being in my opinion much better employed in other countries than they could be in your own about the person of a child. But, on the other hand, that child, who will in two years be adolescent, and possibly King, ought not then to be a stranger to your name, your person, and, above all, to your abilities. You must be acquainted with and about him, before he has taken all his habits and most of his early impressions. Should the King die, as there is too much reason to fear he may while his grandson is a minor, the scene will be too great and delicate a one for you to be long absent from. A Regency is eventually to be settled by Act of Parliament, and I believe this Session. But the *minor* has *an Uncle* who will be of that Regency as *Uncles* have formerly been. Your ancestor, Lord Hastings,[1] was a firm friend to a minor King, and suffered for it; avert both the omens, but his successor, Lord Huntingdon, must not be absent in such an important exigency. I have already spoke to the Ministers upon your subject, and shown them the fitness, or rather the necessity of your being placed about the person of the Prince of Wales, when his establishment shall be extended; they seem to agree with me; but, however, though when the case happens I will exert my utmost endeavours for that purpose, the solicitations of a private and insignificant person as I am, will be of very little use, if you are not *à portée* to

---

[1]William, Lord Hastings, charged with high treason by the Duke of Gloucester (Richard III), and beheaded 13th June 1483. The Duke of Cumberland was thought by some to be aspiring to the throne.

enforce them by your presence. From these principles then, my dear Lord, I draw this plan for you, by way of conclusion. To go to Italy in September next, and to come out of Italy the September following, and to employ that year till September 1753 in Germany, Flanders and Holland, and then return to England, and distinguish yourself in the scene of business. Leave pyramids, temples, sculpture and paintings to minds much below yours. *Tu regere Imperio populos Romane memento.* Should anything happen in the meantime, that in my opinion would require your return sooner, which I do not think will, I will send you the earliest and truest account of it, and you will judge upon the state of the case whether my opinion is right or wrong. Whatever it may be you shall always have it, for, be persuaded, my dear Lord, that I have nothing more at heart than to help you as far as I can to make that figure in the world, which all circumstances conspire to enable you to make. You must look upon this letter, which goes by a safe hand, to be the foundation, and key to my future letters to you upon these subjects. For in those that go by the common post I must be less explicit than I have been in this. Adieu, my dear Lord, forgive this freedom in consideration of the friendship and attachment that produce it.
Yours most faithfully.

No. 1768

À Madame la Marquise de Monconseil

(Maty I. lix)

À Londres, ce 11 avril V.S. 1751

Ne vous en déplaise, Madame, il ne paraît pas que j'aie pris la mouche trop fort, puisque vous convenez, en même temps, que mes mercuriales ont fait quelque effet. Avec le peuple, et les gens de l'âge de votre élève, qui sont très peuple, il faut charger les objets un peu au delà du vrai, et je vous avoue que j'avais fait une *caricatura* du portrait que vous m'aviez envoyé, pour qu'il vit ses défauts au microscope. Je continue actuellement de prêcher sur les textes que vous m'avez fournis. J'espère que je ne prêche pas aussi inutilement que font la plupart des prédicateurs. Vous pouvez juger, et me dire mieux que personne, si je prêche avec fruit. Se forme-t-il aux usages, prend-t-il le ton, les manières, les attentions, les grâces? Dites-moi, je vous en supplie, Madame, s'il fréquente les bonnes compagnies, si les liaisons qu'il a formées avec des gens de son âge sont bonnes, et quelles maisons il hante le plus. Je ne vous fais point d'excuses de toutes ces questions impertinentes: ce serait trop tard, et vous y êtes accoutumée.

Dans notre tragédie anglaise de *Caton*, quelqu'un demande à Caton, si César ne rougit pas de faire telle et telle chose; Caton repond,

César rougir! n'a-t-il pas vu Pharsale?[1]

Faites en l'application à votre très humble serviteur.

Comme vous me flattez de temps en temps, en me reprochant mon silence, dont vous devriez plutôt me savoir gré, je vous préviendrai cette fois ici, en vous rendant compte de ce qui m'a empêché jusqu'à présent, de répondre à la dernière lettre dont vous m'avez honoré; c'est que n'ayant plus à faire avec les corps terrestres, je me suis amusé avec les corps célestes, et je me suis si bien familiarisé avec les planètes, que, si vous le vouliez, je suis en état de vous donner un supplément à la *Pluralité des Mondes*. Ne croyez pas, au reste, que je préférasse ce commerce avec les planètes au vôtre; rien moins: au contraire, c'était pour établir, par acte de parlement, votre style dans ce pays ici. J'avais remarqué, depuis longtemps que vous datiez vos lettres onze jours plûtôt que moi, et que je les recevais avant même que le jour de leur date fut venu ici. J'étais persuadé que vous deviez avoir raison; je le dis à des astronomes, qui m'assur-

[1]"Caesar ashamed! has he not seen Pharsalia?"
Addison's *Cato* (IV. iv).

èrent qu'oui, et que si je m'en informais du soleil ou de la lune, ils ne vous désavoueraient point; que même un Pape avait été de votre avis, il y a près de deux cents ans,[1] et avait introduit ce qu'on appelle le nouveau style. Comme bon Protestant je ne voulais avoir rien à faire avec un Pape, mais c'était votre style, qui est bien le meilleur que je connaisse, que je voulais adopter. Il m'a fallu pourtant, pour satisfaire au public, qui n'a pas l'honneur de vous connaître comme moi, le payer de quelques arguments astronomiques. De là je suis devenu astronome, et c'est un plaisir que de m'entendre parler d'années tropiques, d'années luni-solaires, intercalaires, etc.; mais enfin voilà votre style établi ici. Voyez par là comment le public ignore presque toujours les véritables causes des évènements; car il ne vous soupçonne pas d'entrer pour quelque chose dans celui-ci.

No. 1769

To his Son

(Stanhope CLL)

À Londres, ce 15 avril V.S. 1751

Mon CHER AMI,

Comment vont les grâces, les manières, les agréments, et tous ces petits riens si nécessaires pour rendre un homme aimable? Les prenez-vous? y faites vous des progrès? Le grand secret c'est l'art de plaire, et c'est un art qu'il ne tient qu'à un chacun d'acquérir, supposant un certain fond de sens commun. Un tel vous plaît par tel endroit; examinez pourquoi, faites comme lui, et vous plairez par le même endroit aux autres. Pour plaire aux femmes, il faut être considéré des hommes. Et pour plaire aux hommes, il faut savoir plaire aux femmes. Les femmes, dont la vanité est sans contredit la passion dominante, la trouvent flattée par les attentions d'un homme qui est généralement estimé parmi

[1] 1582 was the date of the reformation of the Calendar by Gregory XIII.

les hommes. Quand il est marqué à ce coin, elles lui donnent le cours, c'est-à-dire, la mode. De l'autre côté, un homme sera estimable parmi les hommes, sans pourtant être aimable, si les femmes n'y ont pas mis la dernière main. Il est aussi nécessaire que les deux sexes travaillent à sa perfection qu'à son être; portez aux femmes le mérite de votre sexe, vous en rapporterez la douceur, les agréments, et les grâces du leur, et les hommes qui vous estimaient seulement auparavant, vous aimeront après. Les femmes sont les véritables raffineuses de l'or masculin; elles n'y ajoutent pas du poids il est vrai, mais elles y donnent l'éclat et le brillant. À propos, on m'assure que Madame de Blot,[1] sans avoir des traits, est jolie comme un cœur, et que nonobstant cela, elle s'en est tenue jusqu'ici scrupuleusement à son mari, quoiqu'il y ait déjà plus d'un an qu'elle est mariée. Elle n'y pense pas; il faut décrotter cette femme-là. Décrottez-vous donc tous les deux réciproquement. Force, assiduités, attentions, regards tendres, et déclarations passionnées de votre côté, produiront au moins quelque velléité du sien. Et quand une fois la velléité y est, les œuvres ne sont pas loin.

Comme je vous tiens pour le premier *juris-peritus* et politique de tout le corps Germanique, je suppose que vous aurez lu la lettre du Roi du Prusse à l'Electeur de Mayence, au sujet de l'élection d'un Roi des Romains, et de l'autre côté, une pièce, intitulée, *Représentation impartiale de ce qui est juste à l'égard de l'élection d'un Roi des Romains*, etc. La première est très bien écrite, mais pas fondée sur les lois et les usages de l'Empire; la seconde est très mal écrite, au moins en français, mais fondée. Je crois qu'elle aura été écrite par quelque allemand qui s'était mis dans l'esprit qu'il entendait le français. Je suis persuadé pourtant que l'élégance et la délicatesse de la lettre du Roi de Prusse en im-

---

[1]Marie-Cécile-Pauline d'Ennery, who married in 1749 Gilbert de Chavigny, Baron de Blot. She was a lady-in-waiting to the Duchess of Orléans. See a note to the letter of H. Walpole, vol. v. p. 391, ed. 1840. Madame du Deffand says of her: 'Sa figure, son maintien en imposent; elle a beaucoup d'admirateurs.' (To H. Walpole, 17th April 1774.)—M.

poseront aux deux tiers du public en dépit de la solidité et de la vérité de l'autre pièce. Telle est la force de l'élégance et de la délicatesse.

Je souhaiterais que vous eussiez la bonté de me détailler un peu plus particulièrement vos allures à Paris. Où est-ce par exemple que vous dinez tous les vendredis, avec cet aimable et respectable vieillard Fontenelle? Quelle est la maison qui est pour ainsi dire votre domicile? Car on en a toujours une où l'on est plus établi, et plus à son aise qu'ailleurs. Qui sont les jeunes français avec lesquels vous êtes le plus lié? Fréquentez-vous l'hôtel d'Hollande; et vous êtes-vous fourré encore dans celui du Comte de Caunitz?[1] Monsieur de Pignatelli, a-t-il l'honneur d'être du nombre de vos serviteurs? Et le Nonce du Pape vous a-t-il compris dans son Jubilé? Dites-moi aussi naturellement comment vous êtes avec Milord Huntingdon; le voyez-vous souvent? Le cultivez-vous? Répondez spécifiquement à toutes ces questions dans votre première lettre.

On me dit que le livre de Duclos[2] n'est pas à la mode à Paris, et qu'on le critique furieusement; c'est apparemment parce qu'on l'entend, et ce n'est plus la mode d'être intelligible. Je respecte infiniment la mode, mais je respecte bien plus ce livre, que je trouve en même temps vrai, solide, et brillant. Il y a même des épigrammes, que veut-on de plus?

Le Chevalier Hotham sera parti (je compte) de Paris pour son séjour de Toulouse. J'espère qu'il y prendra des manières, au moins en a-t-il bien besoin. Il est gauche, il est taciturne, et n'a pas le moindre *entregent:* qualités pourtant très nécessaires pour se distinguer ou dans les affaires, ou dans le beau monde. Au vrai, ces deux choses sont si liées, qu'un homme ne figurera jamais dans les affaires qui

[1]Afterwards Prince, and Prime Minister to Maria Theresa; but at this period her Ambassador at Paris.—M.

[2]Charles Pileau Duclos (*c.* 1705-1772), a novelist and satirical writer, succeeded Voltaire as historiographer of France. The book referred to was *Considérations sur les Mœurs du XVIIIme Siècle,* a satire on the French nation at that time. He also wrote *Voyages en Italie,* and *Mémoires secrets sur les règnes de Louis XIV et Louis XV.*

ne sait pas briller aussi dans le beau monde. Et pour réussir parfaitement bien dans l'un ou dans l'autre, il faut être *in utrumque paratus*. Puissiez-vous l'être, mon cher ami; et sur ce, nous vous donnons le bon soir.

P.S. Lord and Lady Blessington, with their son, Lord Mountjoy, will be at Paris next week, in their way to the south of France. I send you a little packet of books by them. Pray go to wait upon them as soon as you hear of their arrival, and show them all the attentions you can.[1]

No. 1770

To his Son

(*Stanhope CCLI*)

London, 22 *April O.S.* 1751

My Dear Friend,

I apply to you now as to the greatest *virtuoso* of this, or perhaps any other age; one whose superior judgment and distinguishing eye hindered the King of Poland from buying a bad picture at Venice, and whose decisions in the realms of *virtù* are final and without appeal. Now to the point: I have had a catalogue sent me, *d'une vente à l'amiable de tableaux des plus grands maîtres appartenants au Sieur Araignon Apéren, valet-de-chambre de la Reine, sur le quai de la Mégisserie au coin de l'Arche Marion*. There I observe two large pictures of Titian, as described in the enclosed page of the catalogue, No. 18, which I should be glad to purchase upon two conditions: the first is, that they be undoubted originals of Titian in good preservation; and the other, that they come cheap. To ascertain the first (but without disparaging your skill), I wish you would get some undoubted connoisseurs to examine them carefully; and if,

---

[1] William Stewart, Viscount Mountjoy, was in 1745 promoted to the title of Earl of Blessington, on the recommendation of Lord Chesterfield, when Lord-Lieutenant of Ireland. His only son, Lord Mountjoy, died in early youth at Paris, and at his own death, in 1769, his titles became extinct.—M.

upon such critical examination, they should be unanimously allowed to be undisputed originals of Titian, and well preserved, then comes the second point, the price; I will not go above two hundred pounds sterling for the two together; but as much less as you can get them for. I acknowledge that two hundred pounds seems to be a very small sum for two undoubted Titians of that size; but, on the other hand, as large Italian pictures are now out of fashion at Paris, where fashion decides of everything, and as these pictures are too large for common rooms, they may, possibly, come within the price above limited. I leave the whole of this transaction (the price excepted, that I will not exceed) to your consummate skill and prudence, with proper advice joined to them. Should you happen to buy them for that price, carry them to your own lodgings, and get a frame made to the second, which I observe has none, exactly the same with the other frame, and have the old one new gilt; and then get them carefully packed up, and sent me by Rouen.

I hear much of your conversing with *les beaux esprits* at Paris; I am very glad of it; it gives a degree of reputation, especially at Paris; and their conversation is generally instructive, though sometimes affected. It must be owned, that the polite conversation of the men and women of fashion at Paris, though not always very deep, is much less futile and frivolous than ours here. It turns at least upon some subject, something of taste, some point of history, criticism, and even philosophy, which, though probably not quite so solid as Mr. Locke's, is however better, and more becoming rational beings, than our frivolous dissertations upon the weather or upon whist. Monsieur Duclos observes, and I think very justly, *qu'il y a à présent en France une fermentation universelle de la raison qui tend à se développer.* Whereas, I am sorry to say, that here that fermentation seems to have been over some years ago, the spirit evaporated, and only the dregs left. Moreover *les beaux esprits* at Paris are com-

monly well-bred, which ours very frequently are not; with
the former your manners will be formed; with the latter,
wit must generally be compounded for at the expense of
manners. Are you acquainted with Marivaux, who has certainly studied, and is well acquainted with the heart; but
who refines so much upon its *plis et replis*, and describes
them so affectedly, that he often is unintelligible to his
readers, and sometimes so I dare say to himself. Do you
know *Crébillon le fils?* He is a fine painter, and a pleasing
writer; his characters are admirable and his reflections just.
Frequent these people, and be glad, but not proud, of frequenting them; never boast of it as a proof of your own
merit, nor insult, in a manner, other companies, by telling
them affectedly what you, Montesquieu, and Fontenelle were
talking of the other day; as I have known many people do
here, with regard to Pope and Swift, who had never been
twice in company with either; nor carry into other companies the tone of those meetings of *beaux esprits*. Talk
literature, taste, philosophy, etc., with them, *à la bonne
heure*; but then with the same ease, and more *enjouement*,
talk *pompons*, *moires*, etc., with Madame de Blot, if she
requires it. Almost every subject in the world has its proper
time and place; in which no one is above or below discussion. The point is, to talk well upon the subject you talk
upon; and the most trifling, frivolous subjects will still give
a man of parts an opportunity of showing them. *L'usage
du grand monde* can alone teach that. This was the distinguishing characteristic of Alcibiades, and a happy one it
was; that he could occasionally, and with so much ease,
adopt the most different, and even the most opposite habits
and manners, that each seemed natural to him. Prepare
yourself for the great world, as the *athletæ* used to do for
their exercises; oil (if I may use that expression) your mind
and your manners, to give them the necessary suppleness
and flexibility; strength alone will not do, as young people
are too apt to think.

1718

How do your exercises go on? Can you manage a pretty vigorous *sauteur* between the pillars? Are you got into stirrups yet? *Faites-vous assaut aux armes?* But above all, what does Marcel say of you? Is he satisfied? Pray be more particular in your accounts of yourself; for, though I have frequent accounts of you from others, I desire to have your own too. Adieu!

Yours truly and tenderly.

No. 1771

To his Son

(*Stanhope CCLII*)

London, 2 *May O.S.* 1751

My Dear Friend,

Two accounts, which I have very lately received of you, from two good judges, have put me into great spirits: and they have given me reasonable hopes, that you will soon acquire all that I believe you want; I mean the air, the address, the graces, and the manners of a man of fashion. As these two pictures of you are very unlike that which I received, and sent you some months ago, I will name the two painters: the first is an old friend and acquaintance of mine, Monsieur D'Aillon. His picture, is, I hope, like you; for it is a very good one. Monsieur Tollot's is still a better; and so advantageous a one, that I will not send you a copy of it, for fear of making you too vain. So far I will tell you, that there was only one *but* in either of their accounts; and it was this: I gave D'Aillon the question, ordinary and extraordinary, upon the important article of Manners; and extorted this from him: *Mais, si vous voulez, il lui manque encore ce dernier beau vernis qui relève les couleurs, et qui donne l'éclat à la pièce. Comptez qu'il l'aura, il a trop d'esprit pour n'en pas connaître tout le prix, et je me trompe bien, ou plus d'une personne travaille à le lui donner.* Monsieur Tollot

1719

says, *Il ne lui manque absolument pour être tout ce que vous souhaitez qu'il soit, que ces petits riens, ces grâces de détail, cette aisance aimable, que l'usage du grand monde peut seul lui donner. À cet égard on m'assure qu'il est en de bonnes mains; je ne sais si on ne veut pas dire par là dans de beaux bras.* Without entering into a nice discussion of the last question, I congratulate you and myself upon your being so near that point which I so anxiously wish you may arrive at. I am sure, that all your attention and endeavours will be exerted; and, if exerted, they will succeed. Mr. Tollot says that you are inclined to be fat; but I hope you will decline it as much as you can; not by taking anything corrosive to make you lean, but by taking as little as you can of those things that would make you fat. Drink no chocolate, take your coffee without cream; you cannot possibly avoid suppers at Paris, unless you avoid company too, which I would by no means have you do; but eat as little at supper as you can, and make even an allowance for that little at your dinners. Take, occasionally, a double dose of riding and fencing; and now that the summer is come, walk a good deal in the Tuileries; it is a real inconveniency to anybody to be fat, and besides it is ungraceful for a young fellow. *A propos*, I had like to have forgot to tell you that I charged Tollot to attend particularly to your utterance and diction—two points of the utmost importance. To the first he says, *Il ne s'énonce pas mal, mais il serait à souhaiter qu'il le fît encore mieux; et il s'exprime avec plus de feu que d'élégance. L'usage de la bonne compagnie mettra aussi ordre à tout cela.* These, I allow, are all little things separately; but, aggregately, they make a most important and great article in the account of a gentleman. In the House of Commons you can never make a figure, without elegancy of style and gracefulness of utterance; and you can never succeed as a courtier at your own Court, or as a minister at any other, without those innumerable *petits riens dans les manières, et dans les attentions.* Mr. Yorke is by this time at Paris; make your court to him, but not so as to disgust in the least Lord Albemarle, who may possibly dislike your considering Mr. Yorke as the man of business, and him as only *pour orner la scène*. Whatever your opinion may be upon *that point*, take care not to let it appear; but be well with them both, by showing no public preference to either.

Though I must necessarily fall into repetitions, by treating the same subject so often, I cannot help recommending to you again the utmost attention to your air and address. Apply yourself now to Marcel's lectures, as diligently as you did formerly to Professor Mascow's; desire him to teach you every genteel attitude, that the human body can be put into; let him make you go in and out of his room frequently, and present yourself to him, as if he were by turns different persons; such as a minister, a lady, a superior, an equal, an inferior, etc. Learn to sit genteely in different companies; to loll genteely, and with good manners, in those companies where you are authorised to be free; and to sit up respectfully where the same freedom is not allowable. Learn even to compose your countenance occasionally to the respectful, the cheerful, and the insinuating. Take particular care that the motions of your hands and arms be easy and graceful, for the genteelness of a man consists more in them than in anything else, especially in his dancing. Desire some women to tell you of any little awkwardness that they observe in your carriage; they are the best judges of those things, and if they are satisfied, the men will be so too. Think now only of the decorations. Are you acquainted with Madame Geoffrain,[1] who has a great deal of wit, and who, I am informed, receives only the very best company in her house?

[1]Marie Thérèse Rodet (1699-1779) married at the age of fifteen M. Geoffrin. 'On a prétendu,' says M. de Laporte, 'que c'était cet homme bon et simple qui lisant toujours le même volume s'apercevait seulement de temps à autre que l'auteur se répétait un peu!' Madame Geoffrin was of a very different character; she collected around her one of the most brilliant literary circles of her day, and held what her enemies called *le Bureau d'Esprit*. Horace Walpole says of her: 'I think she has one of the best understandings I ever met, and more knowledge of the world.' (To Lady Hervey, 3rd Oct. 1765.)—M.

≫≫ 1751 ≪≪

Do you know Madame Dupin, who, I remember, had beauty, and I hear has wit and reading?[1] I could wish you to converse only with those who, either from their rank, their merit, or their beauty, require constant attention; for a young man can never improve in company where he thinks he may neglect himself. A new bow must be constantly kept bent; when it grows older, and has taken the right turn, it may now and then be relaxed.

I have this moment paid your draft of 89*l.* 15*s.*; it was signed in a very good hand; which proves that a good hand may be written without the assistance of magic. Nothing provokes me much more, than to hear people indolently say that they cannot do what is in everybody's power to do, if it be but in their will. Adieu!

No. 1772

To his Son

(Stanhope CCLIII)

London, 6 May O.S. 1751

MY DEAR FRIEND,

The best authors are always the severest critics of their own works; they revise, correct, file, and polish them, till they think they have brought them to perfection. Considering you as my work, I do not look upon myself as a bad author, and am therefore a severe critic. I examine narrowly into the least inaccuracy or inelegancy, in order to correct, not to expose them, and that the work may be perfect at last. You are, I know, exceedingly improved in your air, address, and manners, since you have been at Paris; but still there is, I believe, room for farther improvement, before

[1]Louise-Marie-Madeleine (de Fontaine), 1707-1799, wife of Claude Dupin, *fermier général*, had a considerable taste for literature. Fontenelle and Marivaux, and many other distinguished men of letters, used to meet at her table both at Paris and at Chenonceaux. An account of her life at the latter is given in Rousseau's *Confessions*; and he adds, 'j'y devins gras comme un moine.'

1722

you come to that perfection which I have set my heart upon seeing you arrive at; and till that moment I must continue filing and polishing. In a letter that I received by last post, from a friend of yours at Paris, there was this paragraph: *Sans flatterie, j'ai l'honneur de vous assurer que Monsieur Stanhope réussit ici au delà de ce qu'on attendrait d'une personne de son âge; il voit très bonne compagnie, et ce petit ton, qu'on regardait d'abord comme un peu décidé et un peu brusque, n'est rien moins que cela, parcequ'il est l'effet de la franchise, accompagnée de la politesse et de la déférence. Il s'étudie à plaire, et il y réussit. Madame de Puisieux[1] en parlait l'autre jour avec complaisance et intérêt: vous en serez content à tous égards.* This is extremely well, and I rejoice at it; one little circumstance only may, and I hope will, be altered for the better. Take pains to undeceive those who thought that *petit ton un peu décidé et un peu brusque;* as it is not meant so, let it not appear so. Compose your countenance to an air of gentleness and *douceur,* use some expressions of diffidence of your own opinion, and deference to other people's; such as *s'il m'est permis de le dire—je croirais—ne serait-ce pas plutôt comme cela? Au moins j'ai tout lieu de me défier de moi-même;* such mitigating, engaging words do by no means weaken your argument; but, on the contrary, make it more powerful, by making it more pleasing. If it is a quick and hasty manner of speaking that people mistake *pour décidé et brusque,* prevent their mistakes for the future, by speaking more deliberately, and taking a softer tone of voice; as in this case you are free from the guilt, be free from the suspicion too. Mankind, as I have often told you, is more governed by appearances, than by realities; and, with regard to opinion, one had better be really rough and hard, with the appearance of gentleness and softness, than just the reverse. Few people have penetration enough to discover, attention enough to observe, or even concern enough to examine, beyond the exterior; they take their notions from

[1]Charlotte-Félicité le Tellier-Louvuis-de-Rebenac. The Marquis de Puyzieulx was still Minister of Foreign Affairs.

the surface, and go no deeper; they commend, as the gentlest and best-natured man in the world, that man who has the most engaging exterior manner, though possibly they have been but once in his company. An air, a tone of voice, a composure of countenance to mildness and softness, which are all easily acquired, do the business; and without farther examination, and possibly with the contrary qualities, that man is reckoned the gentlest, the modestest, and the best-natured man alive. Happy the man who, with a certain fund of parts and knowledge, gets acquainted with the world early enough to make it his bubble, at an age when most people are the bubbles of the world! for that is the common case of youth. They grow wiser, when it is too late; and ashamed and vexed at having been bubbles so long, too often turn knaves at last. Do not therefore trust to appearances and outside yourself, but pay other people with them; because you may be sure that nine in ten of mankind do, and ever will, trust to them. This is by no means a criminal or blameable simulation, if not used with an ill intention. I am by no means blameable in desiring to have other people's good word, good will, and affection, if I do not mean to abuse them. Your heart, I know, is good, your sense is sound, and your knowledge extensive. What then remains for you to do? Nothing but to adorn those fundamental qualifications, with such engaging and captivating manners, softness, and gentleness, as will endear you to those who are able to judge of your real merit, and which always stand in the stead of merit with those who are not. I do not mean by this to recommend to you *le fade doucereux*, the insipid softness of a gentle fool; no, assert your own opinion, oppose other people's when wrong; but let your manner, your air, your terms, and your tone of voice, be soft and gentle, and that easily and naturally, not affectedly. Use palliatives when you contradict; such as, *I may be mistaken, I am not sure, but I believe, I should rather think, etc.* Finish any argument or dispute with some little good-natured pleasantry, to show that you are neither hurt your self, nor meant to hurt your antagonist; for an argument kept up a good while often occasions a temporary alienation on each side. Pray observe particularly, in those French people who are distinguished by that character, *cette douceur de mœurs et de manières*, which they talk of so much, and value so justly; see in what it consists; in mere trifles, and most easy to be acquired, where the heart is really good. Imitate, copy it, till it becomes habitual and easy to you. Without a compliment to you, I take it to be the only thing you now want; nothing will sooner give it you than a real passion, or, at least, *un goût vif*, for some woman of fashion; and, as I suppose that you have either the one or the other by this time, you are consequently in the best school. Besides this, if you were to say to Lady Hervey, Madame Monconseil, or such others as you look upon to be your friends, *On dit que j'ai un certain petit ton trop décidé et trop brusque, l'intention pourtant n'y est pas; corrigez-moi, je vous en supplie, et châtiez-moi même publiquement quand vous me trouverez sur le fait. Ne me passez rien, poussez votre critique jusqu'à l'excès; un juge aussi éclairé est en droit d'être sévère, et je vous promets que le coupable tâchera de se corriger.*

   Yesterday I had two of your acquaintances to dine with me, Baron B. and his companion Monsieur S. I cannot say of the former, *qu'il est pétri de grâces*; and I would rather advise him to go and settle quietly at home, than to think of improving himself by farther travels. *Ce n'est pas le bois dont on en fait.* His companion is much better, though he has a strong *tocco di tedesco.* They both spoke well of you, and so far I liked them both. Comment vont nos affaires avec l'aimable petite Blot? Se prête-t-elle à vos fleurettes, êtes-vous censé être sur les rangs? Madame Dupin est-elle votre Madame de Lursay, et fait-elle quelquefois des nœuds? Seriez-vous son Meilcour?[1] Elle a, dit-on, de la douceur, de l'esprit, des manières; il y a à apprendre dans un tel ap-

[1]Also in Crébillon.

prentissage. A woman like her, who has always pleased, and often been pleased, can best teach the art of pleasing— that art without which *ogni fatica è vana*. Marcel's lectures are no small part of that art; they are the engaging forerunner of all other accomplishments. Dress is also an article not to be neglected, and I hope you do not neglect it; it helps in the *premier abord*, which is often decisive. By dress, I mean your clothes being well made, fitting you, in the fashion and not above it; your hair well done, and a general cleanliness and spruceness in your person. I hope you take infinite care of your teeth; the consequences of neglecting the mouth are serious, not only to oneself but to others. In short, my dear child, neglect nothing; a little more will complete the whole. Adieu! I have not heard from you these three weeks, which I think a great while.

No. 1773

To his Son

(*Stanhope CCLIV*)

London, 10 May O.S. 1751

MY DEAR FRIEND,

I received yesterday, at the same time, your letters of the 4th and the 11th N.S., and being much more careful of my commissions than you are of yours, I do not delay one moment sending you my final instructions concerning the pictures. The man you allow to be a Titian, and in good preservation; the woman is an indifferent and a damaged picture; but, as I want them for furniture for a particular room, companions are necessary; and therefore I am willing to take the woman, for better for worse, upon account of the man; and if she is not too much damaged, I can have her tolerably repaired, as many a fine woman is, by a skilful hand here; but then I expect the lady should be, in a manner, thrown into the bargain with the man; and in this state of affairs, the woman being worth little or nothing, I will not go above fourscore *louis* for the two together.

As for the Rembrandt you mention, though it is very cheap if good, I do not care for it. I love *la belle nature*; Rembrandt paints caricaturas. Now for your own commissions, which you seem to have forgotten. You mention nothing of the patterns which you received by Monsieur Tollot, though I told you in a former letter, which you must have had before the date of your last, that I should stay till I received the patterns pitched upon by your ladies; for as to the instructions which you sent me in Madame Monconseil's hand, I could find no mohairs in London that exactly answered that description. I shall, therefore, wait till you send me (which you may easily do in a letter) the patterns chosen by your three Graces.

I would, by all means, have you go now and then, for two or three days, to Maréchal Coigny's,[1] at Orli; it is but a proper civility to that family, which has been particularly civil to you; and, moreover, I would have you familiarise yourself with, and learn the interior and domestic manners of, people of that rank and fashion. I also desire that you will frequent Versailles and St. Cloud, at both which Courts you have been received with distinction. Profit by that distinction, and familiarise yourself at both. Great Courts are the seats of true good-breeding; you are to live at Courts, lose no time in learning them. Go and stay sometimes at Versailles for three or four days, where you will be domestic in the best families, by means of your friend Madame de Puisieux, and mine, L'Abbé de la Ville. Go to the King's and the Dauphin's levées, and distinguish yourself from the rest of your countrymen, who, I dare say, never go there when they can help it. Though the young Frenchmen of fashion may not be worth forming intimate connections

[1] François de Franquetot, duc de Coigny distinguished himself by his victories over the Imperial forces at Parma and at Guastella in 1734. He was raised to the rank of Maréchal in 1735, and to a Dukedom in 1747, and died in 1759.

with, they are well worth making acquaintance of; and I do not see how you can avoid it, frequenting so many good French houses as you do, where, to be sure, many of them come. Be cautious how you contract friendships, but be desirous, and even industrious, to obtain an universal acquaintance. Be easy, and even forward, in making new acquaintances; that is the only way of knowing manners and characters in general, which is at present your great object. You are *enfant de famille* in three ministers' houses; but I wish you had a footing, at least, in thirteen; and that I should think you might easily bring about by that common chain which, to a certain degree, connects those you do not with those you do know. For instance, I suppose that neither Lord Albemarle nor Marquis de St. Germain would make the least difficulty to present you to Comte Caunitz, the Nuncio, etc. *Il faut être rompu au monde*, which can only be done by an extensive, various, and almost universal acquaintance.

When you have got your emaciated Philomath, I desire that his triangles, rhomboids, etc., may not keep you one moment out of the good company you would otherwise be in. Swallow all your learning in the morning, but digest it in company in the evenings. The reading of ten new characters is more your business now than the reading of twenty old books; showish and shining people always get the better of all others, though ever so solid. If you would be a great man in the world when you are old, shine and be showish in it while you are young; know everybody and endeavour to please everybody—I mean exteriorly, for fundamentally it is impossible. Try to engage the heart of every woman, and the affections of almost every man, you meet with. Madame Monconseil assures me that you are most surprisingly improved in your airs, manners, and address; go on, my dear child, and never think that you are come to a sufficient degree of perfection; *nil actum reputans si quid superesset agendum*; and in those shining parts of

1728

the character of a gentleman, there is always something remaining to be acquired. Modes and manners vary in different places, and at different times; you must keep pace with them, know them, and adopt them, wherever you find them. The great usage of the world, the knowledge of characters, the *brillant d'un galant homme*, is all that you now want. Study Marcel and the *beau monde* with great application, but read Homer and Horace only when you have nothing else to do. Pray who is *la belle Madame de Case*, whom I know you frequent? I like the epithet given her very well; if she deserves it, she deserves your attention too. A man of fashion should be gallant to a fine woman, though he does not make love to her, or may be otherwise engaged. *On lui doit des politesses, on fait l'éloge de ses charmes, et il n'en est ni plus ni moins pour cela*: it pleases, it flatters; you get their good word, and you lose nothing by it. These *gentillesses* should be accompanied, as indeed everything else should, with *un air, un ton de douceur et de politesse. Les grâces* must be of the party, or it will never do; and they are so easily had, that it is astonishing to me everybody has them not; they are sooner gained than any woman of common reputation and decency. Pursue them but with care and attention, and you are sure to enjoy them at last; without them, I am sure, you will never enjoy anybody else. You observe, truly, that Sir Charles Hotham is *gauche*; it is to be hoped that will mend with keeping company, and is yet pardonable in him, as just come from school. But reflect what you would think of a man, who had been any time in the world, and yet should be so awkward. For God's sake, therefore, now, think of nothing but shining, and even distinguishing yourself in the most polite Courts, by your air, your address, your manners, your politeness, your *douceur*, your graces. With these advantages (and not without them), take my word for it, you will get the better of all rivals, in business as well as in *ruelles*. Adieu!

1729

※※ 1751 ※※

Send me your patterns by the next post, and also your instructions to Grevenkop, about the seal, which you seem to have forgotten.

No. 1774

To his Son

(*Stanhope CCLV*)

London, 16 May O.S. 1751

My Dear Friend,

In about three months from this day we shall probably meet. I look upon that moment as a young woman does upon her wedding-day; I expect the greatest pleasure, and yet cannot help fearing some little mixture of pain. My reason bids me doubt a little of what my imagination makes me expect. In some articles I am very sure that my most sanguine wishes will not be disappointed; and those are the most material ones. In others, I feel something or other which I can better feel than describe. However, I will attempt it. I fear the want of that amiable and engaging *je ne sais quoi*, which, as some philosophers have, unintelligibly enough, said of the soul, is all in all, and all in every part; it should shed its influence over every word and action. I fear the want of that air and first *abord* which suddenly lays hold of the heart, one does not know distinctly how or why. I fear an inaccuracy, or at least inelegancy, of diction, which will wrong and lower the best and justest matter. And lastly, I fear an ungraceful if not an unpleasant utterance, which would disgrace and vilify the whole. Should these fears be at present founded, yet the objects of them are (thank God) of such a nature that you may, if you please, between this and our meeting, remove every one of them. All these engaging and endearing accomplishments are mechanical, and to be acquired by care and observation as easily as turning or any mechanical trade. A common country fellow taken from the plough, and enlisted in an

1730

old corps, soon lays aside his shambling gait, his slouching air, his clumsy and awkward motions, and acquires the martial air, the regular motions, and the whole exercise of the corps, and particularly of his right and left hand man. How so? Not from his parts, which were just the same before as after he was enlisted; but either from a commendable ambition of being like, and equal to, those he is to live with, or else from the fear of being punished for not being so. If then both or either of these motives change such a fellow in about six months' time, to such a degree as that he is not to be known again, how much stronger should both these motives be with you, to acquire, in the utmost perfection, the whole exercise of the people of fashion with whom you are to live all your life? Ambition should make you resolve to be at least their equal in that exercise, as well as the fear of punishment, which most inevitably will attend the want of it. By that exercise I mean the air, the manners, the graces, and the style of people of fashion. A friend of yours, in a letter I received from him by the last post, after some other commendations of you, says: *Il est étonnant, que pensant, avec tant de solidité qu'il fait, et ayant le goût aussi sûr, et aussi délicat, qu'il s'exprime avec si peu d'élégance et de délicatesse. Il néglige même totalement le choix des mots et la tournure des phrases.* This I should not be so much surprised or concerned at, if it related only to the English language; which hitherto you have had no opportunity of studying, and but few of speaking, at least to those who could correct your inaccuracies. But if you do not express yourself elegantly and delicately in French and German (both which languages I know you possess perfectly and speak eternally), it can be only from an unpardonable inattention to what you most erroneously think a little object, though in truth it is one of the most important of your life. Solidity and delicacy of thought must be given us; it cannot be acquired, though it may be improved; but elegancy and delicacy of expression may be acquired by whoever will take the necessary care and pains. I am sure you love me so well, that you would be very sorry, when we meet, that I should be either disappointed or mortified; and I love you so well, that I assure you I should be both if I should find you want any of those exterior accomplishments which are the indispensably necessary steps to that figure and fortune which I so earnestly wish you may one day make in the world.

I hope you do not neglect your exercises of riding, fencing, and dancing, but particularly the latter; for they all concur to *dégourdir* and to give a certain air. To ride well is not only a proper and graceful accomplishment for a gentleman, but may also save you many a fall hereafter; to fence well may possibly save your life; and to dance well is absolutely necessary in order to sit, stand, and walk well. To tell you the truth, my friend, I have some little suspicion that you now and then neglect or omit your exercises for more serious studies. But now *non est his locus*; everything has its time; and this is yours for your exercises; for when you return to Paris, I only propose your continuing your dancing, which you shall two years longer, if you happen to be where there is a good dancing-master. Here, I will see you take some lessons with your old master Desnoyers, who is our Marcel.

What says Madame Dupin to you? I am told she is very handsome still; I know she was so some few years ago. She has good parts, reading, manners, and delicacy; such an *arrangement* would be both creditable and advantageous to you. She will expect to meet with all the good-breeding and delicacy that she brings; and, as she is past the glare and *éclat* of youth, may be the more willing to listen to your story, if you tell it well. For an attachment, I should prefer her to *la petite Blot*; and, for a mere gallantry, I should prefer *la petite Blot* to her; so that they are consistent, *et l'une n'empêche pas l'autre*. Adieu! Remember *la douceur et les grâces*.

1732

No. 1775

To Lord Huntingdon

(*Steuart 14*)

London, 18 *May O.S.* 1751

My Dear Lord,

By your consulting me about your future motions, I will suppose that you have forgiven me the liberty I took of representing against some of your intended ones; I will therefore proceed with my usual parental freedom, which I assure you, my dear Lord, flows from more than common parental affection. To begin with your affairs here. I have spoke very explicitly to the Duke of Newcastle and Lord Chancellor, with relation to your being placed about the Prince of Wales upon the first extension of his establishment, which in case the King lives so long will not be made in less than two or three years. I will not, I believe I need not tell you what I said upon that subject. They told me that what I said confirmed what common fame had already told them; that they were convinced of the expediency of what I proposed, and would do their utmost to bring it about. I answered the Duke of Newcastle that I wanted something more explicit than those general Ministerial assurances, and I asked him whether he would empower me to tell you in his name that you might depend upon his hearty and sincere endeavours, when the case of the extension of the Prince of Wales's establishment should exist; he answered that I not only might, but that he desired that I would. So far then this matter, which I believe I have more at heart than you have, rests well. However, in order to secure it the better, I could wish that you would write the Duke of Newcastle a letter of compliment and thanks for what he has empowered me to tell you. He is full of little vanity, and your flattering it in that manner will fix him.

Now let me attend you to Spain. Far from having the

least objection to your going there, I entirely approve of it; the general character and manners of that nation differ more from those of the rest of Europe than any other two European nations differ from each other. There are many very fine and curious remains of Gothic and Moorish antiquity. Few travellers go there, which is another reason why I approve of your going; and you will be there as much within call of events as you would be at Rome or Naples. But since you will take the uncommon trouble of going to Spain, in my mind you had better give the next winter to it, and see it thoroughly. This therefore is the route that I would propose to you. To go to Bayonne at the latter end of next September, from thence through Navarre to Madrid, and there to stay three months at least; from Madrid to go through New Castile and Andalusia to Seville, from Seville to Gibraltar, through Granada, Valencia and Catalonia to Barcelona; and from Barcelona, if you do not dislike the sea, to go on board some ship that you will always find there, and sail to Genoa or Leghorn, so as to be in Italy by April next; and to leave Italy the April following for Germany, Flanders, Holland, etc. I will send you very good letters of recommendation for Spain, and you will do well to get others from the Spanish Ambassador now residing at Paris, and to the French Minister residing at Madrid. The advantage of knowing something of the language of the place one goes to is so great, and the Spanish language is so very easy, that I will suggest to you to take a Spanish master during the remainder of your stay at Paris. For with your quickness and application, you will in three months' time get Spanish enough not to be at a loss in your way to Madrid nor in company, when you get there. I hope you will prolong your stay at Paris, as much as you can consistently with this scheme; you are there I know in the best companies, much better than you can find in the provinces, which therefore you need but run through. Three weeks between Paris and Bayonne will give you time to see

1734

all that is worth your seeing in your way, as Toulouse, Bordeaux, etc. So that you may very well enjoy Paris, and whoever you enjoy in it, till the first of September.

In my opinion you could not do too much for Madame de Berkenrode, and possibly that may be her opinion too, and I hope she has put you to that trial in other instances besides the Ball. When I wore her chains, which I did about seven years ago in Holland, she was infinitely agreeable. I hope your servitude has been better rewarded than mine was.

I like the blunt good sense and observations of Duclos in his *Considérations sur les Mœurs du Siècle.* The manner might have been more genteel, but it may be the matter would have been weakened by it. A common case among the very genteel and polite French authors. He says very truly, and I see you agree with him, *qu'il y une fermentation de raison en France qui tend à se developper;* it is certain that the French in general think more, wish and endeavour to know more, than they use to do. Knowledge is in fashion, and the fashion in France is as absolute as the King. All the women sip some knowledge, though few drink deep of it; but still that little makes them, in my opinion, much more agreeable company than ours, who are either very silent or very trivial.

Your servant and client, Mr. Stanhope, tells me that he is very happy in your friendship and protection. I hope he will continue to deserve them, and to know the weight and lustre they will give him. His success in the world is now the only object I have in it, since yours is out of all doubt. Adieu, my dear Lord; I am with the tenderest attachment your most faithful servant.

No. 1776

À Madame du Boccage

(*Maty I. xciii*)

À Londres, ce 20 mai V.S. 1751

Pourquoi m'écrire à présent, ou pourquoi ne m'avoir pas écrit plutôt, direz-vous? Un moment, Madame; pourquoi, s'il vous plaît, m'avoir envoyé ce receuil de lettres, où Monsieur de la Rochefoucauld, Mesdames de la Fayette et de Coulanges, font une si mince figure vis-à-vis de Madame de Sévigné, et pourquoi accompagnez-vous ce recueil d'une lettre, qui valait bien la meilleure des siennes? Bien d'autres que moi se trouveraient embarrassés; répondrai-je? Gardez-vous en bien, dit mon amour-propre; faites plutôt une impolitesse qu'une sottise; voyez les débris du naufrage de tous ces beaux esprits, voulez-vous échouer sur le même écueil? Ne pouvant répondre à ce raisonnement, j'ai pris le parti de ne pas répondre à votre charmante lettre; voilà la véritable cause de mon silence, mais la conscience reprend quelquefois ses droits en dépit de l'amour-propre. À la fin j'envisageai ce que je vous devais, et je me reprochai le crime de ne pas tâcher au moins de m'acquitter; c'est une dette, il est vrai, que je manque de moyens de payer, mais la bonne foi exige qu'on donne ce qu'on peut à ses créanciers, ne serait-ce qu'un sou par livre sterling. En effet, Madame, le moyen de vous payer le plaisir que vous m'avez procuré, non seulement par les livres que vous m'avez envoyés, mais encore plus par les lettres dont vous m'avez honoré? Enfin, je crois avoir trouvé un expédient pour m'acquitter; c'est de vous envoyer quatre ambassadeurs, pour vous faire amende honorable en mon nom, quoique, par parenthèse, leurs noms valent mille fois mieux que le mien. C'est Shakespeare, Milton, Dryden, et Pope, l'honneur de notre nation; qui, s'ils vous connaissaient, se feraient honneur d'être placés chez vous. Vous les y trouverez à votre retour en Normandie; ils partent la semaine prochaine pour Dieppe. Ayez quelque bonté pour Dryden, jaloux de la préférence que vous avez donnée à Milton et à Pope. Vous ferez à Shakespeare tel accueil que vous jugerez à propos, vu que quelquefois il mérite le meilleur, et quelquefois le plus mauvais. Il ne paraît rien ici dans le genre littéraire, digne de votre attention. Deux ou trois pièces de théâtre ont été sifflées, ou tolérées par compassion pour leurs auteurs, qu'on savait avoir grand faim; les autres se sont épuisés en dissertations politiques sur le ministère, à la mode du pays. Il en est autrement chez vous, où, comme remarque Duclos, il y a une fermentation d'esprit, qui se développe tous les jours. À propos de Duclos, j'aime son dernier livre,[1] quoique je sache qu'on le critique à Paris. Il a bien étudié les caractères, et bien exposé les préjugés: il dit des vérités avec force, peut-être n'a-t-il pas cette élégance travaillée de style, ni cette politesse de phrases tant à la mode à présent; mais son livre n'en est pas moins bon.

Vauxhall et Ranelagh ont repris les deux premiers jours de cette année qui aient senti l'été; j'ai été à l'un et à l'autre, sans y trouver les mêmes agréments qu'il y a deux ans. Au contraire, ils n'ont fait que réveiller le souvenir du mauvais tour que vous nous avez joué. Recommencez par voie de réparation: plutôt que de ne pas paraître du tout, paraissez comme vous avez déjà fait, pour disparaître. C'est une de ces fautes, que plus vous les ferez plus on vous la pardonnera. Que je serais heureux de pouvoir encore vous réitérer à Blackheath, qui, par parenthèse, est fini, les assurances de respect, avec lesquels j'ai l'honneur d'être,

Madame, etc.

[1] Again *Considèrations sur les Mœurs du Siècle.*

No. 1777

To his Son

(*Stanhope CCLVI*)

London, 23 May O.S. 1751

My Dear Friend,

I have this moment received your letter of the 25th N.S., and being rather somewhat more attentive to my commissions than you are to yours, return you this immediate answer to the question you ask me about the two pictures. I will not give one livre more than what I told you in my last, having no sort of occasion for them, and not knowing very well where to put them if I had them.

I wait with impatience for your final orders about the mohairs; the mercer persecuting me every day, for three pieces which I thought pretty, and which I have kept by me, eventually to secure them, in case your ladies should pitch upon them.

What do you mean by your *Si j'osais?* qu'est ce qui vous empêche d'oser? On ose toujours quand il y a espérance de succès; et on ne perd rien à oser, quand même il n'y en a pas. Un honnête homme sait oser, et quand il faut oser il ouvre la tranchée par des travaux, des soins, et des attentions; s'il n'en est pas délogé d'abord il avance toujours à l'attaque de la place même. Après de certaines approches le succès est infaillible, et il n'y a que les nigauds qui en doutent, ou qui ne le tentent point. Serait-ce le caractère respectable de Madame de la Vallière, qui vous empêche d'oser, ou serait-ce la vertu farouche de Madame Dupin qui vous retient? La sagesse invincible de la belle Madame Case vous décourage-t-elle plus que sa beauté ne vous invite? Mais fi donc. Soyez convaincu que la femme la plus sage se trouve flattée, bien loin d'être offensée, par une déclaration d'amour, faite avec politesse et agrément. Il se peut bien qu'elle ne s'y prêtera point, c'est-à-dire si elle a un goût ou une passion pour quelque autre; mais en tout cas elle ne vous en saura pas mauvais gré; de façon qu'il n'est pas question d'oser dès qu'il n'y a pas de danger. Mais si elle s'y prête, si elle écoute, et qu'elle vous permet de redoubler votre déclaration, comptez qu'elle se moquera bien de vous si vous n'osez pas tout le reste. Je vous conseille de débuter plutôt par Madame Dupin, qui a encore de la beauté plus qu'il n'en faut pour un jeune drôle comme vous; elle a aussi du monde, de l'esprit de la délicatesse; son âge ne lui laisse pas absolument le choix de ses amants et je vous réponds qu'elle ne rejetterait pas les offres de vos très humbles services. Distinguez-la donc par vos attentions, et des regards tendres; et prenez les occasions favorables de lui dire à l'oreille que vous voudriez bien que l'amitié et l'estime fussent les seuls motifs de vos égards pour elle, mais que des sentiments bien plus tendres en sont les véritables sources. Que vous souffriez bien en les lui déclarant, mais que vous souffriez encore plus en les lui cachant.

Je sens bien qu'en lui disant cela pour la première fois vous aurez l'air assez sot, et assez penaud, et que vous le direz fort mal. Tant mieux, elle attribuera votre désordre à l'excès de votre amour, au lieu de l'attribuer à la véritable cause, votre peu d'usage du monde, surtout dans ces matières. En pareil cas l'amour propre est le fidèle ami de l'amant. Ne craignez donc rien, soyez galant homme: parlez bien, et on écoutera. Si on ne vous écoute pas la première parlez une seconde, une troisième, une quatrième fois; si la place n'est pas déjà prise, soyez sûr qu'à la longue elle est prenable.

I am very glad you are going to Orli, and from thence to St. Cloud; go to both, and to Versailles also, often. It is that interior, domestic familiarity with people of fashion that alone can give you *l'usage du monde, et les manières aisées.* It is only with women one loves, or men one respects, that the desire of pleasing exerts itself; and without the desire of pleasing, no man living can please. Let that desire be the spring of all your words and actions. That happy talent, the art of pleasing, which so few do, though almost all might, possess, is worth all your learning and knowledge put together. The latter can never raise you high without the former; but the former may carry you, as it has carried thousands, a great way without the latter.

I am glad that you dance so well as to be reckoned by Marcel among his best scholars; go on, and dance better still. Dancing well is pleasing *pro tanto*, and makes a part of that necessary *whole*, which is composed of a thousand parts, many of them of *les infiniment petits quoiqu'infiniment nécessaires*.

I shall never have done upon this subject, which is indispensably necessary towards your making any figure or fortune in the world; both which I have set my heart upon, and for both which you now absolutely want no one thing but the art of pleasing; and I must not conceal from you that you have still a good way to go before you arrive at it. You still want a thousand of those little attentions that imply a desire of pleasing; you want a *douceur* of air and expression that engages; you want an elegancy and delicacy of expression, necessary to adorn the best sense and most solid matter; in short, you still want a great deal of the *brillant* and the *poli*. Get them at any rate; sacrifice hecatombs of books to them; seek for them in company, and renounce your closet till you have got them. I never received the letter you refer to, if ever you wrote it. Adieu, *et bon soir, Monseigneur!*

No. 1778

À MADAME LA MARQUISE DE MONCONSEIL

(*Maty I. lx*)

À Londres, ce 23 mai 1751

Votre principe est excellent, Madame, de répondre promptement quand on peut répondre agréablement, et la pratique vous en est facile; mais ce n'est pas la même chose avec les autres, qui voudraient seulement quelquefois ce que vous pouvez toujours. Il s'ensuit que vous répondrez toujours promptement, et par choix; moi rarement, et par devoir. Votre seconde lettre, qui m'est parvenue hier, avant que j'eusse répondu à la première, me met à présent dans le cas de ce devoir.

Que je vous envie votre séjour à —— dont je connais par expérience tous les agréments! si j'étais aussi jeune que l'aimable maître de ce charmant séjour, je prendrais la poste, et je viendrais vous y surprendre. Madame d'Hervey, qui vient de jouir de cette société, m'en a écrit des merveilles; merveilles s'entend qui ne m'ont pas émerveillé, connaissant comme je faisais la plupart des acteurs, et surtout le rôle que vous y jouez. Mais hélas! je suis dans le pitoyable cas de sentir toute la force des tentations, sans avoir la force d'y succomber; car, au fond, ce n'est que faiblesse de ne s'y pas prêter. Les plaisirs ne sont que trop clairsemés; la raison nous dit de les saisir, ce n'est que la faiblesse ou la paresse qui nous en détourne. Je parle des plaisirs et des tentations des honnêtes gens, et non des crimes, comme vous jugez bien. Au défaut des plaisirs, qui m'ont abandonné, et auxquels je ne pense plus à moins d'en procurer s'il m'était possible aux autres, je vais la semaine prochaine prendre, a leur place, les petits amusements de *Babiole*, c'est-à-dire m'y promener, chipoter beaucoup dans mon petit jardin, et y soigner mes ananas, et mes melons: c'est que dans ces deux articles, je prétends briller. Passez-moi la mauvaise plaisanterie, et je vous dirai que les ménagianas, les scaligérianas, et tous ces sortes d'anas, n'approchent point de mes ananas. Pour mes melons, ils sont archimelons; à force d'art et de soins, je brave notre climat, et je fais venir des melons si délicieux, que s'il y avait moyen de vous servir comme on sert l'empereur de la lune, à coup d'arbalète, je vous en décocherais de temps en temps jusqu'à *Bagatelle*, qui feraient rougir votre meilleur climat.

À propos de plantes, écorce tant qu'il vous plaira, Madame, à laquelle vous dites que j'attache trop de prix, sachez au moins que, sans l'écorce, l'arbre dépérit, et perd, non seulement de sa beauté, mais de sa valeur intrinsèque. Il en est de même d'un homme, avec tout le savoir du monde, s'il n'a pas le désir, l'art, les moyens de plaire; on ne le recherche point, mais au contraire, on est bien fâché de le trouver. Vous ne voulez pas, dites-vous, qu'on balance entre le choix d'un mérite solide, et des agréments frivoles; mais pourquoi faut-il opter? Le mérite solide doit-il nécessairement donner l'exclusion aux agréments; je ne le crois pas, mais bien au contraire, je crois qu'il manque quelques chose à la tête d'un homme, quelques talents, et quelques connaissances qu'il ait d'ailleurs, s'il ne connaît pas la nécessité de posséder ces grâces et ces agréments, qu'on appelle frivoles, mais qui pourtant ne sont rien moins. On les peut acquérir si l'on veut; ce sont des choses purement mécaniques, qui dépendent uniquement de l'observation, et de l'imitation. Je veux absolument que notre garçon les ait; je menace, je flatte, je fulmine, j'amadoue tour à tour. Je le fais venir ici au mois d'août prochain, pour en faire l'analyse, la révision, et les corrections moi-même; mais dans un mois je vous le renvoye, pour faire, s'il est possible, les progrès qui lui restent à faire. Quelque éloigné qu'il soit encore du but, il n'avancerait pas d'un pouce ici. Dans les maux chroniques, c'est la continuation des remèdes qui fait l'effet; et dans son mal, qui me paraît opiniâtre, Paris et vos soins sont les seuls remèdes auxquels j'ai de la confiance. Je proteste que la première fois que je le verrai, s'il est gauche, s'il se présente mal, s'il a mauvais air, et mauvaises manières, il me donnera la fièvre. La maussaderie des gens auxquels je ne prends point d'intérêt me la donne bien; en pareil cas il me la donnerait avec transport au cerveau.

Avouez que vous m'avez joué un mauvais tour, en montrant ma précédente à Fontenelle; ce n'est pas que je craigne sa critique plus que la vôtre, mais c'est que la sienne a le champ libre, et la vôtre est retenue par l'amitié. Tout vieux qu'il est, il sera clairvoyant; jeune comme vous êtes, vous serez aveugle. Le bandeau de l'amitié, que je préfère à présent à celui de l'amour, me garantira bien de tout ce que j'aurais bien lieu de craindre de votre jugement; vous portez ce bandeau plus serré, et moi j'en profite plus que tout autre; ne le levez donc à mon égard, que pour mieux envisager les sentiments, avec lesquels je vous donne le bon soir.

No. 1779
To his Son
(*Stanhope CCLVII*)

Greenwich, 6 June O.S. 1751

My Dear Friend,

Solicitious and anxious as I have ever been to form your heart, your mind, and your manners, and to bring you as near perfection as the imperfection of our natures will allow, I have exhausted, in the course of our correspondence, all that my own mind could suggest, and have borrowed from others whatever I thought could be useful to you; but this has necessarily been interruptedly, and by snatches. It is now time, and you are of an age to review, and to weigh in your own mind, all that you have heard, and all that you have read, upon these subjects; and to form your own character, your conduct, and your manners, for the rest of your life, allowing for such improvements as a further knowledge of the world will naturally give you. In this view, I would recommend to you to read, with the greatest attention, such books as treat particularly of those subjects, reflecting seriously upon them, and then comparing the speculation with the practice. For example, if you read in the morning some of La Rochefoucauld's maxims, consider them, examine them well, and compare them with the real characters you meet with in the evening. Read La Bruyère in the morning, and see in the evening whether his pictures are like. Study the heart and the mind of man, and begin with your own. Meditation and reflection must lay the foundation of that knowledge; but experience and practice must, and alone can, complete it. Books, it is true, point out the operations of the mind, the sentiments of the heart, the influence of the passions— and so far they are of previous use; but without subsequent practice, experience, and observation, they are as ineffectual, and would even lead you into as many errors, in fact, as a map would do, if you were to take your notions of the towns and provinces from their delineations in it. A man would reap very little benefit by his travels, if he made them only in his closet upon a map of the whole world. Next to the two books that I have already mentioned, I do not know a better for you to read, and seriously reflect upon, than *Avis d'une mère à un fils; par la Marquise de Lambert.*[1] She was a woman of a superior understanding and knowledge of the world, had always kept the best company, was solicitous that her son should make a figure and a fortune in the world, and knew better than anybody how to point out the means. It is very short, and will take you much less time to read than you ought to employ in reflecting upon it after you have read it. Her son was in the army; she wished he might rise there; but she well knew that, in order to rise, he must first please. She says to him, therefore, *à l'égard de ceux dont vous dépendez, le premier mérite est de plaire.* And, in another place, *Dans les emplois subalternes vous ne vous soutenez que par les agréments. Les maîtres sont comme les maîtresses; quelque service que vous leur ayez rendu, ils cessent de vous aimer quand vous cessez de leur plaire.* This, I can assure you, is at least as true in Courts as in camps, and possibly more so. If to your merit and knowledge you add the art of pleasing, you may very probably come in time to

[1]The volume which Lord Chesterfield mentions appeared in 1727, and the collected works of the Marquise de Lambert were published in 1748, and again in 1813. She died in 1733, at a very advanced age, *après une vie toujours infirme et une vieillesse fort souffrante*, adds M. Auger.—M.

be Secretary of State; but, take my word for it, twice your merit and knowledge, without the art of pleasing, would, at most, raise you to the *important post* of Resident at Hamburgh or Ratisbon.[1] I need not tell you now, for I often have, and your own discernment must have told you, of what numberless little ingredients that art of pleasing is compounded, and how the want of the least of them lowers the whole; but the principal ingredient is, undoubtedly, *la douceur dans les manières*; nothing will give you this more than keeping company with your superiors. Madame Lambert tells her son, *que vos liaisons soient avec des personnes au-dessus de vous, par là vous vous accoutumez au respect et à la politesse; avec ses égaux on se néglige, l'esprit s'assoupit.* She advises him, too, to frequent those people, and to see their inside; *il est bon d'approcher les hommes, de les voir à découvert, et avec leur mérite de tous les jours.* A happy expression! It was for this reason that I have so often advised you to establish and domesticate yourself, wherever you can, in good houses of people above you, that you may see their *everyday* character, manners, habits, etc. One must see people undressed to judge truly of their shape; when they are dressed to go abroad, their clothes are contrived to conceal, or at least palliate, the defects of it— as full-bottomed wigs were contrived for the Duke of Burgundy,[2] to conceal his hump-back. Happy those who have no faults to disguise, nor weaknesses to conceal! There are few, if any such; but unhappy those who know so little of the world as to judge by outward appearances! Courts are the best keys to characters; there every passion is busy, every art exerted, every character analysed; jealousy, ever watchful, not only discovers, but exposes, the mysteries of the trade, so that even bystanders, *y apprennent à deviner.* There, too, the great art of pleasing is practised, taught, and

[1] Both these appointments were afterwards held by Philip Stanhope.

[2] Louis, the eldest grandson of Louis XIV, and the pupil of Fénelon: he died in the prime of life, to the great grief of the nation, in 1712.—M.

1745

learned, with all its graces and delicacies. It is the first thing needful there; it is the absolutely necessary harbinger of merit and talents, let them be ever so great. There is no advancing a step without it. Let misanthropes and would-be philosophers declaim as much as they please against the vices, the simulation, and the dissimulation of Courts; those invectives are always the result of ignorance, ill-humour, or envy. Let them show me a cottage,[1] where there are not the same vices of which they accuse Courts; with this difference only, that in a cottage they appear in their native deformity, and that in Courts, manners and good-breeding make them less shocking, and blunt their edge. No, be convinced that the good-breeding, the *tournure, la douceur dans les manières,* which alone are to be acquired at Courts, are not the showish trifles only which some people call or think them; they are a solid good; they prevent a great deal of real mischief; they create, adorn, and strengthen friendships; they keep hatred within bounds; they promote good-humour and good-will in families, where the want of good-breeding and gentleness of manners is commonly the original cause of discord. Get then, before it is too late, an habit of these *mitiores virtutes;* practise them upon every the least occasion, that they may be easy and familiar to you upon the greatest; for they lose a great degree of their merit if they seem laboured, and only called in upon extraordinary occasions. I tell you truly, this is now the only doubtful part of your character with me; and it is for that reason that I dwell upon it so much, and inculcate it so often. I shall soon see whether this doubt of mine is founded; or rather, I hope I shall soon see that it is not.

This moment I receive your letter of the 9th N.S. I am sorry to find that you have had, though ever so slight, a return of your Carniolan[2] disorder; and I hope your con-

---

[1] See Letter, 10th May 1748.

[2] Meaning the lung-trouble he suffered from at Carniola. See Letter of 17th Oct. 1749 and of 4th Aug. 1752.

clusion will prove a true one, and this will be the last. I will send the mohairs by the first opportunity. As for the pictures, I am already so full, that I am resolved not to buy one more, unless by great accident I should meet with something surprisingly good, and as surprisingly cheap.

I should have thought that Lord Huntingdon, at his age, and with his parts and address, need not have been reduced to keep an opera whore, in such a place as Paris, where so many women of fashion generously serve as volunteers. I am still more sorry that he is in love with her, for that will take him out of good company, and sink him into bad— such as fiddlers, pipers, and *id genus omne*: most unedifying and unbecoming company for a man of fashion!

Lady Chesterfield makes you a thousand compliments. Adieu, my dear child;

No. 1780

To his Son

(*Stanhope CCLVIII*)

Greenwich, 10 *June O.S.* 1751

MY DEAR FRIEND,
Your ladies were so slow in giving their specific orders, that the mohairs, of which you at last sent me the patterns, were all sold. However, to prevent farther delays (for ladies are apt to be very impatient, when at last they know their own minds), I have taken the quantities desired of three mohairs which come nearest to the description you sent me some time ago in Madame Monconseil's own hand, and I will send them to Calais by the first opportunity. In giving *la petite Blot* her piece, you have a fine occasion of saying fine things, if so inclined.

Lady Hervey, who is your puff and panegyrist, writes me word, that she saw you lately dance at a ball, and that you dance very genteelly. I am extremely glad to hear it;

1747

for (by the maxim that *omne majus continet in se minus*), if you dance genteelly, I presume you walk, sit, and stand genteelly too; things which are much more easy, though much more necessary, than dancing well. I have known very many genteel people who could not dance well; but I never knew anybody dance very well who was not genteel in other things. You will probably often have occasion to stand in circles, at the levées of princes and ministers, when it is very necessary *de payer de sa personne, et d'être bien planté*, with your feet not too near nor too distant from each other. More people stand and walk, than sit, genteely. Awkward ill-bred people, being ashamed, commonly sit bolt upright and stiff; others, too negligent and easy, *se vautrent dans leur fauteuil*, which is ungraceful and ill-bred, unless where the familiarity is extreme; but a man of fashion makes himself easy, and appears so, by leaning gracefully, instead of lolling supinely; and by varying those easy attitudes, instead of that stiff immobility of a bashful booby. You cannot conceive, nor can I express, how advantageous a good air, genteel motions, and engaging address are, not only among women, but among men, and even in the course of business; they fascinate the affections, they steal a preference, they play about the heart till they engage it. I know a man, and so do you, who, without a grain of merit, knowledge, or talents, has raised himself millions of degrees above his level, singly by a good air and engaging manners; insomuch, that the very prince who raised him so high, calls him *mon aimable vaurien:*[1] but of this do not open your lips, *pour cause*. I give you this secret, as the strongest proof imaginable of the efficacy of air, address, *tournure, et tous ces petits riens*.

Your other puff and panegyrist, Mr. Harte, is gone to Windsor, in his way to Cornwall, in order to be back soon

[1]This allusion (see letter of 22nd October 1750) seems to point to the Maréchal Duc de Richelieu. Once, it is said, Louis XV, by a slight variation of phrase, instead of *mon aimable vaurien*, called him to his face *le plus grand vaurien de France*. *Sire*, replied the Maréchal, with a low bow, *Votre majesté s'oublie!*—M.

enough to meet you here; I really believe he is as impatient for that moment as I am, *et c'est tout dire*; but, however, notwithstanding my impatience, if by chance you should then be in a situation, that leaving Paris would cost your heart too many pangs, I allow you to put off your journey, and to tell me, as Festus did Paul, *at a more convenient season I will speak to thee.* You see by this that I eventually sacrifice my sentiments to yours, and this is a very uncommon object of paternal complaisance. Provided always, and be it understood (as they say in acts of parliament), that *quæ te cumque domat Venus, non erubescendis adurit ignibus.* If your heart will let you come, bring with you only your valet-de-chambre, Christian, and your own footman; not your valet-de-place, whom you may dismiss for the time, as also your coach; but you had best keep on your lodgings, the intermediate expense of which will be but inconsiderable, and you will want them to leave your books and baggage in. Bring only the clothes you travel in, one suit of black, for the mourning for the Prince will not be quite out by that time, and one suit of your fine clothes, two or three of your laced shirts, and the rest plain ones; of other things, as bags, feathers, etc., as you think proper. Bring no books, unless two or three for your amusement upon the road; for we must apply singly to English, in which you are certainly no *puriste*, and I will supply you sufficiently with the proper English authors. I shall probably keep you here till about the middle of October, and certainly not longer; it being absolutely necessary for you to pass the next winter at Paris; so that, should any fine eyes shed tears for your departure, you may dry them by the promise of your return in two months.

Have you got a master for geometry? If the weather is very hot, you may leave your riding at the *manège* till you return to Paris, unless you think the exercise does you more good than the heat can do you harm; but I desire you will not leave off Marcel for one moment; your fencing likewise, if you have a mind, may subside for the summer; but you will do well to resume it in the winter, and to be *adroit* at it, but by no means for offence, only for defence in case of necessity. Good night! Yours!

P.S. I forgot to give you one commission when you come here; which is, not to fail bringing the *grâces* along with you.

No. 1781

To the Bishop of Waterford

(*Maty III. ix*)

My Dear Lord,   *Blackheath* 1751

I am very glad to hear of your safe arrival upon Irish ground, after your distresses upon the Irish seas; escapes always make people either much bolder or more timid than they were before; yours, I hope, will have the former of these effects, and encourage you rather to visit your friends in England.

I have been a country gentleman a great while, for me, that is; for I have now been a fortnight together at Blackheath, and stay three or four days longer. The *furor hortensis* has seized me, and my acre of ground here affords me more pleasure than kingdoms do to kings; for my object is not to extend, but to enrich it. My gardener calls me, and I must obey. Be as well and as cheerful as you can; and believe me most faithfully and truly   Yours.

No. 1782

To his Son

(*Stanhope CCLIX*)

My Dear Friend,   *Greenwich,* 13 *June O.S.* 1751

Les *bienséances* are a most necessary part of the knowledge of the world. They consist in the relations of persons,
1750

things, time, and place; good sense points them out, good company perfects them (supposing always an attention and a desire to please), and good policy recommends them.

Were you to converse with a king, you ought to be as easy and unembarrassed as with your own valet-de-chambre; but yet every look, word, and action, should imply the utmost respect. What would be proper and well-bred with others, much your superiors, would be absurd and ill-bred with one so very much so. You must wait till you are spoken to; you must receive, not give, the subject of conversation; and you must even take care that the given subject of such conversation does not lead you into any impropriety. The art would be to carry it, if possible, to some indirect flattery; such as commending those virtues in some other person, in which that prince either thinks he does, or at least would be thought by others to excel. Almost the same precautions are necessary to be used with ministers, generals, etc., who expect to be treated with very near the same respect as their masters, and commonly deserve it better. There is, however, this difference, that one may begin the conversation with them, if on their side it should happen to drop, provided one does not carry it to any subject, upon which it is improper either for them to speak or be spoken to. In these two cases, certain attitudes and actions would be extremely absurd, because too easy, and consequently disrespectful. As for instance, if you were to put your arms across in your bosom, twirl your snuffbox, trample with your feet, scratch your head, etc., it would be shockingly ill-bred in that company; and, indeed, not extremely well-bred in any other. The great difficulty in those cases, though a very surmountable one by attention and custom, is to join perfect inward ease with perfect outward respect.

In mixed companies with your equals (for in mixed companies all people are to a certain degree equal) greater ease and liberty are allowed; but they too have their bounds within *bienséance*. This is a social respect necessary; you may start your own subject of conversation with modesty, taking great care, however, *de ne jamais parler de cordes dans la maison d'un pendu.* Your words, gestures, and attitudes, have a greater degree of latitude, though by no means an unbounded one. You may have your hands in your pockets, take snuff, sit, stand, or occasionally walk, as you like; but I believe you would not think it very *bienséant* to whistle, put on your hat, loosen your garters or your buckles, lie down upon a couch, or go to bed and welter in an easy chair. These are negligences and freedoms which one can only take when quite alone; they are injurious to superiors, shocking and offensive to equals, brutal and insulting to inferiors. That easiness of carriage and behaviour, which is exceedingly engaging, widely differs from negligence and inattention, and by no means implies that one may do whatever one pleases; it only means that one is not to be stiff, formal, embarrassed, disconcerted, and ashamed, like country bumpkins, and people who have never been in good company; but it requires great attention to, and a scrupulous observation of *les bienséances*; whatever one ought to do, is to be done with ease and unconcern; whatever is improper must not be done at all. In mixed companies also, different ages and sexes are to be differently addressed. You would not talk of your pleasures to men of a certain age, gravity, and dignity; they justly expect from young people a degree of deference and regard. You should be full as easy with them as with people of your own years; but your manner must be different; more respect must be implied; and it is not amiss to insinuate, that from them you expect to learn. It flatters and comforts age, for not being able to take a part in the joy and titter of youth. To women you should always address yourself with great outward respect and attention, whatever you feel inwardly; their sex is by long prescription entitled to it; and it is among the duties of *bienséance*; at the same time that respect is very properly and very agreeably mixed with a degree of *enjouement*, if you have it; but then, that *badinage* must either directly or indirectly tend to their praise, and even not be liable to a malicious construction to their disadvantage. But here too great attention must be had to the difference of age, rank, and situation. A *maréchale* of fifty must not be played with like a young coquette of fifteen; respect and *serious enjouement*, if I may couple those two words, must be used with the former, and mere *badinage, ʒesté même d'un peu de polissonnerie*, is pardonable with the latter.

Another important point of *les bienséances*, seldom enough attended to, is, not to run your own present humour and disposition indiscriminately against everybody; but to observe, conform to, and adopt theirs. For example, if you happened to be in high good-humour and a flow of spirits, would you go and sing a *pont-neuf*,[1] or cut a caper, to la Maréchale de Coigny, the Pope's Nuncio, or Abbé Sallier, or to any person of natural gravity and melancholy, or who at that time should be in grief? I believe not; as, on the other hand, I suppose, that if you were in low spirits, or real grief, you would not choose to bewail your situation with *la petite Blot*. If you cannot command your present humour and disposition, single out those to converse with who happen to be in the humour the nearest to your own.

Loud laughter is extremely inconsistent with *les bienséances*, as it is only the illiberal and noisy testimony of the joy of the mob at some very silly thing. A gentleman is often seen, but very seldom heard, to laugh. Nothing is more contrary to *les bienséances* than horse play, or *jeux de main* of any kind whatever, and has often very serious, sometimes very fatal consequences. Romping, struggling, throwing things at one another's head, are the becoming pleasantries of the mob, but degrade a gentleman; *giuoco di mano, giuoco de villano*, is a very true saying, among the few true sayings of the Italians.

[1] A Ballad.

Peremptoriness and decision in young people is *contraire aux bienséances*; they should seldom seem to assert, and always use some softening, mitigating expression; such as, *s'il m'est permis de le dire; je croirais plutôt; si j'ose m'expliquer*, which softens the manner, without giving up, or even weakening the thing. People of more age and experience expect, and are entitled to, that degree of deference.

There is a *bienséance* also with regard to people of the lowest degree; a gentleman observes it with his footman, even with the beggar in the street. He considers them as objects of compassion, not of insult; he speaks to neither *d'un ton brusque*, but corrects the one coolly, and refuses the other with humanity. There is no one occasion in the world, in which *le ton brusque* is becoming a gentleman. In short, *les bienséances* are another word for *manners*, and extend to every part of life. They are propriety; the graces should attend in order to complete them. The graces enable us to do, genteely and pleasingly, what *les bienséances* require to be done at all. The latter are an obligation upon every man; the former are an infinite advantage and ornament to any man. May you unite both!

Though you dance well, do not think that you dance well enough, and consequently not endeavour to dance still better. And though you should be told that you are genteel, still aim at being genteeler. If Marcel should, do not you be satisfied. Go on; court the graces all your life-time. You will find no better friends at Court; they will speak in your favour, to the hearts of princes, ministers, and mistresses.

Now that all tumultuous passions and quick sensations have subsided with me, and that I have no tormenting cares nor boisterous pleasures to agitate me, my greatest joy is to consider the fair prospect you have before you, and to hope and believe you will enjoy it. You are already in the world, at an age when others have hardly heard of it. Your character is hitherto not only unblemished in its moral part,

1754

but even unsullied by any low, dirty, and ungentlemanlike vice, and will, I hope, continue so. Your knowledge is sound, extensive, and avowed, especially in everything relative to your destination. With such materials to begin, what then is wanting? Not fortune, as you have found by experience. You have had, and shall have, fortune sufficient to assist your merit and your industry; and, if I can help it, you never shall have enough to make you negligent of either. You have too *mens sana in corpore sano*—the greatest blessing of all. All therefore that you want is as much in your power to acquire, as to eat your breakfast when set before you. It is only that knowledge of the world, that elegancy of manners, that universal politeness, and those graces, which keeping good company, and seeing variety of places and characters, must inevitably, with the least attention on your part, give you. Your foreign destination leads to the greatest things, and your parliamentary situation will facilitate your progress. Consider then this pleasing prospect as attentively for yourself, as I consider it for you. Labour on your part to realise it, as I will on mine to assist and enable you to do it. *Nullum numen abest, si sit prudentia.*

Adieu, my dear child! I count the days till I have the pleasure of seeing you. I shall soon count the hours, and at last the minutes, with increasing impatience.

P.S.—The mohairs are this day gone from hence for Calais, recommended to the care of Madame Morel, and directed, as desired, to the Comptroller-General. The three pieces come to six hundred and eighty French livres.

No. 1783

To his Son

(*Stanhope CCLX*)

My Dear Friend,   *Greenwich, 20 June O.S.* 1751

So very few people, especially young travellers, see what they see, or hear what they hear, that though I really

believe it may be unnecessary with you, yet there can be no
harm in reminding you, from time to time, to see what you
see, and to hear what you hear; that is, to see and hear as
you should do. Frivolous, futile people, who make at least
three parts in four of mankind, only desire to see and hear
what their frivolous and futile præcursors have seen and
heard—as St. Peter's, the Pope, and High Mass, at Rome;
Notre Dame, Versailles, the French King, and the French
comedy, in France. A man of parts sees and hears very differently from these gentlemen, and a great deal more. He
examines and informs himself thoroughly of everything he
sees or hears, and, more particularly, as it is relative to his
own profession or destination. Your destination is political;
the object, therefore, of your inquiries and observations
should be the political interior of things; the forms of
government, laws, regulations, customs, trade, manufactures, etc., of the several nations of Europe. This knowledge
is much better acquired by conversation, with sensible and
well-informed people, than by books—the best of which,
upon these subjects, are always imperfect. For example,
there are "Present States of France," as there are of England;
but they are always defective, being published by people
uninformed, who only copy one another. They are, however, worth looking into, because they point out objects for
inquiry, which otherwise might possibly never have occurred to one's mind; but an hour's conversation with a
sensible *Président* or *Conseiller* will let you more into the
true state of the Parliament of Paris than all the books in
France. In the same manner, the *Almanach Militaire* is
worth your having; but two or three conversations with
officers will inform you much better of their military regulations. People have, commonly, a partiality for their own
professions, love to talk of them, and are even flattered by
being consulted upon the subject; when, therefore, you are
with any of those military gentlemen (and you can hardly
be in any company without some) ask them military ques-

tions. Inquire into their methods of discipline, quartering, and clothing their men; inform yourself of their pay, their perquisites, *leurs montres, leurs étapes, etc.* Do the same as to the *marine*, and make yourself particularly master of that *détail*, which has, and always will have, a great relation to the affairs of England; and, in proportion as you get good information, make minutes of them in writing.

The regulations of trade and commerce in France are excellent, as appears but too plainly for us, by the great increase of both, within these thirty years; for, not to mention their extensive commerce in both the East and West Indies, they have got the whole trade of the Levant from us; and now supply all the foreign markets with their sugars, to the ruin almost of our sugar colonies, as Jamaica, Barbados, and the Leeward Islands. Get, therefore, what information you can of these matters also.

Inquire too into their Church matters; for which the present disputes between the Court and the Clergy give you fair and frequent opportunities. Know the particular rights of the Gallican Church, in opposition to the pretensions of the See of Rome. I need not recommend ecclesiastical history to you, since I hear you study *Dupin*[1] very assiduously.

You cannot imagine how much this solid and useful knowledge of other countries will distinguish you in your own (where, to say the truth, it is very little known or cultivated) besides the great use it is of in all foreign negotiations; not to mention, that it enables a man to shine in all companies. When kings and princes have any knowledge, it is of this sort, and more particularly; therefore it is the usual topic of their levée conversations, in which it will qualify you to bear a considerable part; it brings you more acquainted with them; and they are pleased to have people talk to them on a subject in which they think to shine.

[1] Louis Ellies Dupin (1657-1719) was Professor of Philosophy at the Collège Royal. His *Bibliothèque*, or Universal History of Ecclesiastical Writers, some 61 volumes, met with the disapproval of Bossuet. Chesterfield's allusion, of course, is to the Madame Dupin mentioned in the former letters.

There is a sort of chit-chat, or *small-talk*, which is the general run of conversation at Courts, and in most mixed companies. It is a sort of middling conversation, neither silly nor edifying; but, however, very necessary for you to be master of. It turns upon the public events of Europe, and then is at its best; very often upon the number, the goodness, or badness, the discipline, or the clothing of the troops of different princes; sometimes upon the families, the marriages, the relations of princes, and considerable people; and, sometimes, *sur la bonne chère*, the magnificence of public entertainments, balls, masquerades, etc. I would wish you to be able to talk upon all these things better, and with more knowledge, than other people; insomuch that, upon those occasions, you should be applied to, and that people should say, *I dare say, Mr. Stanhope can tell us.*

Second-rate knowledge, and middling talents, carry a man farther at Courts, and in the busy part of the world, than superior knowledge and shining parts. Tacitus very justly accounts for a man's having always kept in favour, and enjoyed the best employments, under the tyrannical reigns of three or four of the very worst emperors, by saying that it was not *propter aliquam eximiam artem, sed quia par negotiis neque supra erat.*[1] Discretion is the great article; all those things are to be learned, and only learned by keeping a great deal of the best company. Frequent those good houses where you have already a footing, and wriggle yourself somehow or other into every other. Haunt the Courts particularly, in order to get that *routine.*

This moment I receive yours of the 18th N.S. You will have had some time ago my final answers concerning the pictures; and, by my last, an account that the mohairs were gone to Madame Morel at Calais, with the proper directions. I am sorry that your two sons-in-law, the Princes Borghese,[2]

[1]Tacitus, *Annals,* vi. 39.

[2]The name of 'sons-in-law' to these young princes was a pleasantry of Lord Chesterfield, founded on the acquaintance of Mr. Stanhope with their mother at Rome.—M.

1758

are such boobies; however, as they have the honour of being so nearly related to you, I will show them what civilities I can.

I confess you have not time for long absences from Paris at present, because of your various masters, all which I would have you apply to closely while you are now in that capital; but when you return thither, after the visit you intend me the honour of, I do not propose your having any master at all, except Marcel once or twice a week. And then the Courts will, I hope, be no longer strange countries to you; for I would have you run down frequently to Versailles and St. Cloud for three or four days at a time. You know the Abbé de la Ville, who will present you to others, so that you will soon be *faufilé* with the rest of the Court. Court is the soil in which you are to grow and flourish; you ought to be well acquainted with the nature of it; like all other soil, it is in some places deeper, in others lighter, but always capable of great improvement by cultivation and experience.

You say that you want some hints for a letter to Lady Chesterfield; more use and knowledge of the world will teach you occasionally to write and talk genteelly, *sur des riens*, which I can tell you is a very useful part of worldly knowledge; for, in some companies, it would be imprudent to talk upon anything else, and with very many people it is impossible to talk of anything else; they would not understand you. Adieu!

No. 1784

To his Son

(Stanhope CCLXI)

My Dear Friend,   *London, 24 June, O.S.* 1751

Air, address, manners, and graces, are of such infinite advantage to whoever has them, and so peculiarly and essentially necessary for you, that now, as the time of our meeting draws near, I tremble for fear I should not find you possessed of them; and, to tell you the truth, I doubt you are not yet sufficiently convinced of their importance. There is, for instance, your intimate friend, Mr. Hayes,[1] who, with great merit, deep knowledge, and a thousand good qualities, will never make a figure in the world while he lives. Why? Merely for want of those external and showish accomplishments which he began the world too late to acquire; and which, with his studious and philosophical turn, I believe he thinks are not worth his attention. He may very probably make a figure in the republic of letters; but he had ten thousand times better make a figure as a man of the world and of business in the republic of the United Provinces, which, take my word for it, he never will.

As I open myself, without the least reserve, whenever I think that my doing so can be of any use to you, I will give you a short account of myself when I first came into the world, which was at the age you are of now, so that (by the way) you have got the start of me in that important article by two or three years at least. At nineteen, I left the University of Cambridge, where I was an absolute pedant; when I talked my best, I quoted Horace; when I aimed at being facetious, I quoted Martial; and when I had a mind to be a fine gentleman, I talked Ovid. I was convinced that none but the ancients had common sense; that the classics contained everything that was either necessary, useful, or ornamental to men; and I was not without thoughts of wearing the *toga virilis* of the Romans, instead of the vulgar and illiberal dress of the moderns. With these excellent notions, I went first to the Hague, where, by the help of several letters of recommendation, I was soon introduced into all the best company, and where I very soon discovered that I was totally mistaken in almost every one notion I had entertained. Fortunately I had a strong desire to please (the mixed result of good-nature, and a vanity by no means

[1]See Letter of 8th July 1751.

1760

blameable), and was sensible that I had nothing but the desire. I therefore resolved, if possible, to acquire the means too. I studied attentively and minutely the dress, the air, the manner, the address, and the turn of conversation of all those whom I found to be the people in fashion, and most generally allowed to please. I imitated them as well as I could; if I heard that one man was reckoned remarkably genteel, I carefully watched his dress, motions, and attitudes, and formed my own upon them. When I heard of another whose conversation was agreeable and engaging, I listened and attended to the turn of it. I addressed myself, though *de très mauvaise grâce*, to all the most fashionable fine ladies; confessed and laughed with them at my own awkwardness and rawness, recommending myself as an object for them to try their skill in forming.

By these means, and with a passionate desire of pleasing everybody, I came by degrees to please some; and I can assure you, that what little figure I have made in the world, has been much more owing to that passionate desire I had of pleasing universally, than to any intrinsic merit or sound knowledge I might ever have been master of. My passion for pleasing was so strong (and I am very glad it was so), that I own to you fairly, I wished to make every woman I saw in love with me, and every man I met with admire me. Without this passion for the object, I should never have been so attentive to the means; and I own I cannot conceive how it is possible for any man of good-nature and good sense to be without this passion. Does not good-nature incline us to please all those we converse with, of whatever rank or station they may be? And does not good sense and common observation show of what infinite use it is to please? Oh! but one may please by the good qualities of the heart, and the knowledge of the head, without that fashionable air, address, and manner, which is mere tinsel. I deny it. A man may be esteemed and respected, but I defy him to please without them. Moreover, at your age, I would not have contented myself with barely pleasing; I wanted to shine and to distinguish myself in the world as a man of fashion and gallantry, as well as business. And that ambition or vanity, call it what you please, was a right one; it hurt nobody, and made me exert whatever talents I had. It is the spring of a thousand right and good things.

I was talking you over the other day with one very much your friend, and who has often been with you, both at Paris and in Italy. Among the innumerable questions which you may be sure I asked him concerning you, I happened to mention your dress (for, to say the truth, it was the only thing of which I thought him a competent judge), upon which he said that you dressed tolerably well at Paris; but that in Italy you dressed so ill, that he used to joke with you upon it, and even to tear your clothes. Now, I must tell you, that at your age it is as ridiculous not to be very well dressed, as at my age it would be if I were to wear a white feather and red-heeled shoes. Dress is one of the various ingredients that contribute to the art of pleasing; it pleases the eyes at least, and more especially of women. Address yourself to the senses if you would please; dazzle the eyes, soothe and flatter the ears of mankind; engage their heart, and let their reason do its worst against you. *Suaviter in modo* is the great secret. Whenever you find yourself engaged insensibly in favour of anybody of no superior merit or distinguished talent, examine and see what it is that has made those impressions upon you: you will find it to be that *douceur*, that gentleness of manners, that air and address, which I have so often recommended to you; and from thence draw this obvious conclusion, that what pleases you in them will please others in you; for we are all made of the same clay, though some of the lumps are a little finer, and some a little coarser; but, in general, the surest way to judge of others is to examine and analyse oneself thoroughly. When we meet, I will assist you in that analysis, in which every man wants some assistance against his own self-love. Adieu!

1762

No. 1785

TO HIS SON

(*Stanhope CCLXII*)

Greenwich, 30 *June O.S.* 1751

MY DEAR FRIEND,

Pray give the enclosed to our friend the Abbé;[1] it is to congratulate him upon his *canonicat,* which I am really very glad of, and I hope it will fatten him up to Boileau's *Chanoine;* at present he is as meagre as an apostle or a prophet. By the way, has he ever introduced you to la Duchesse d'Aiguillon?[2] If he has not, make him present you; and if he has, frequent her, and make her many compliments from me. She has uncommon sense and knowledge for a woman, and her house is the resort of one set of *les beaux esprits.* It is a satisfaction and a sort of credit to be acquainted with those gentlemen, and it puts a young fellow in fashion. *A propos des beaux esprits,* have you *les entrées* at Lady Sandwich's,[3] who, old as she was, when I saw her last, had the strongest parts of any woman I ever knew in my life? If you are not acquainted with her, either the Duchess d'Aiguillon or Lady Hervey can, and I dare say will, introduce you. I can assure you it is very well worth your while, both upon her own account, and for the sake of the people of wit and learning who frequent her. In such companies there is always something to be learned, as well as manners; the conversation turns upon something above trifles: some point of literature, criticism, history, etc., is discussed with ingenuity and good manners; for I must do the French people of learning justice; they are not bears, as most of ours are; they are gentlemen.

[1]Guasco.

[2]This was probably the Duchess Dowager, Anne Charlotte de Crussol de Florensac, surnamed at Court *la bonne Duchesse d'Aiguillon.* She translated Pope's *Eloisa to Abelard,* and also one of Ossian's poems, into French.

[3]Elizabeth, daughter of John Wilmot, Earl of Rochester, and widow of Edward Montague, third Earl of Sandwich. She died at Paris in 1757.—M.

Our Abbé writes me word that you were gone to Compiègne; I am glad of it; other Courts must form you for your own. He tells me too that you have left off riding at the *manège*; I have no objection to that, it takes up a great deal of the morning; and if you have got a genteel and firm seat on horseback, it is enough for you, now that tilts and tournaments are laid aside. I suppose you have hunted at Compiègne. The King's hunting there, I am told, is a fine sight. The French manner of hunting is gentleman-like; ours is only for bumpkins and boobies. The poor beasts here are pursued and run down by much greater beasts than themselves; and the true British fox-hunter is most undoubtedly a species appropriated and peculiar to this country, which no other part of the globe produces.[1]

I hope you apply the time you have saved from the riding-house to useful more than to learned purposes; for I can assure you, they are very different things. I would have you allow but one hour a day for Greek; and that more to keep what you have than to increase it; by Greek, I mean useful Greek books, such as Demosthenes, Thucydides, etc., and not the poets, with whom you are already enough acquainted. Your Latin will take care of itself. Whatever more time you have for reading, pray bestow it upon those books which are immediately relative to your destination; such as modern history in the modern languages; memoirs, anecdotes, letters, negotiations, etc. Collect also, if you can, authentically, the present state of all the Courts and countries in Europe, the characters of the kings and princes, their wives, their ministers and their whores, their several views, connections and interests; the state of their *finances*, their military force, their trade, manufactures, and commerce. That is the useful, the necessary knowledge for you,

[1]Mr. Ernst quotes:

He thought at heart, like courtly Chesterfield,
Who, after a long chase through hills, dales, bushes,
And what not, though he rode beyond all price,
Ask'd next day, 'if men ever hunted twice?'

Don Juan, xix. 35.

and indeed for every gentleman. But with all this, remember that living books are much better than dead ones; and throw away no time (for it is thrown away) with the latter, which you can employ well with the former; for books must now be only your amusement, but by no means your business. I had much rather that you were passionately in love with some determined coquette of condition (who would lead you a dance, fashion, supple, and polish you), than that you knew all Plato and Aristotle by heart; an hour at Versailles, Compiègne, or St. Cloud, is now worth more to you than three hours in your closet with the best books that ever were written.

I hear the dispute between the Court and the Clergy is made up amicably; both parties have yielded something; the King being afraid of losing more of his soul, and the Clergy more of their revenue. Those gentlemen are very skilful in making the most of the vices, and the weaknesses of the laity. I hope you have read and informed yourself fully of everything relative to that affair; it is a very important question, in which the priesthood of every country in Europe is highly concerned. If you would be thoroughly convinced that their tithes are of divine institution, and their property the property of God Himself, not to be touched by any power on earth, read Frà-Paolo *De beneficiis*, an excellent and short book; for which, and some other treatises against the Court of Rome, he was stilettoed; which made him say afterwards, upon seeing an anonymous book written against him, by order of the Pope, *Conosco bene lo stile Romano.*

The Parliament of Paris, and the States of Languedoc, will, I believe, hardly scramble off; having only reason and justice, but no terrors on their side.[1] Those are political

[1] 'Au mois de mai 1751, un nouvel édit porta création de deux millions de rentes viagères sur l'Hôtel de Ville et de 900,000 livres de rentes héréditaires sur la ferme des postes; le tout estimé équivaloir à un emprunt de cinquante millions. Le parlement (de Paris) se crut obligé à faire des réprésentations nouvelles. . . . Les États de Languedoc se plaignirent très hautement.'—Sismondi, *Histoire des Français*, vol. xxix. p. 18.—M.

and constitutional questions that well deserve your attention and inquiries; I hope you are thoroughly master of them. It is also worth your while to collect and keep all the pieces written upon those subjects.

I hope you have been thanked by your ladies, at least, if not paid in money, for the mohairs which I sent by a courier to Paris some time ago, instead of sending them to Madame Morel at Calais, as I told you I should. Do they like them, and do they like you the better for getting them? *La petite Blot devrait au moins payer de sa personne.* As for Madame de Polignac, I believe you will very willingly hold her excused from personal payment.

Before you return to England, pray go again to Orli for two or three days, and also to St. Cloud, in order to secure a good reception there at your return. Ask the Marquis de Matignon, too, if he has any orders for you in England, or any letters or packets for Lord Bolingbroke. Adieu! Go on and prosper.

No. 1786
To his Son
(*Stanhope CCLXIII*)

Greenwich, 8 *July* O.S. 1751

My Dear Friend,
The last mail brought me your letter of the 3rd July N.S. I am glad that you are so well with Colonel Yorke as to be let into secret correspondences. Lord Albemarle's reserve to you is, I believe, more owing to his secretary than to himself; for you seem to be much in favour with him; and possibly, too, *he has no very secret letters* to communicate. However, take care not to discover the least dissatisfaction upon this score; make the proper acknowledgments to Colonel Yorke for what he does show you; but let neither Lord Albemarle nor his people perceive the least coldness on your part upon account of what they do not show you.

1766

It is very often necessary not to manifest all one feels. Make
your court to, and connect yourself as much as possible
with Colonel Yorke; he may be of great use to you hereafter; and when you take leave, not only offer to bring over
any letters or packets by way of security, but even ask, as a
favour, to be the carrier of a letter from him to his father the
Chancellor. *A propos* of your coming here: I confess that I
am weakly impatient for it, and think a few days worth
getting; I would, therefore, instead of the 25th of next
month N.S. which was the day that some time ago I appointed for your leaving Paris, have you set out on Friday
the 20th of August N.S.; in consequence of which you will
be at Calais some time on the Sunday following, and probably at Dover within four-and-twenty hours afterwards. If
you land in the morning, you may in a post-chaise get to
Sittingborne that day; if you come on shore in the evening,
you can only get to Canterbury, where you will be better
lodged than at Dover. I will not have you travel in the night,
nor fatigue and overheat yourself, by running on four-score
miles the moment you land. You will come straight to
Blackheath, where I shall be ready to meet you, and which
is directly upon the Dover road to London; and we will go
to town together, after you have rested yourself a day or two
here. All the other directions, which I gave you in my former letter, hold still the same. But, notwithstanding this
regulation, should you have any particular reason for leaving
Paris two or three days sooner or later than the above-
mentioned, *vous êtes le maître*. Make all your *arrangements*
at Paris for about a six weeks' stay in England, at farthest.

I had a letter the other day from Lord Huntingdon, of
which one-half at least was your panegyric; it was extremely
welcome to me from so good an hand. Cultivate that friendship; it will do you honour, and give you strength. Connections in our mixed parliamentary government are of
great use.

I send you here enclosed the particular price of each of

the mohairs, but I do not suppose that you will receive a shilling for any one of them. However, if any of your ladies should take an odd fancy to pay, the shortest way, in the course of business, is for you to keep the money, and to take so much less from Sir John Lambert[1] in your next draft upon him.

I am very sorry to hear that Lady Hervey is ill. Paris does not seem to agree with her; she used to have great health here. *À propos* of her; remember, when you are with me, not to mention her but when you and I are quite alone, for reasons which I will tell you when we meet; but this is only between you and me, and I desire that you will not so much as hint it to her, or anybody else.

If old Curzay[2] goes to the Valley of Jehosaphat, I cannot help it; it will be an ease to our friend Madame Monconseil, who I believe maintains her, and a little will not satisfy her in any way.

Remember to bring your mother some little presents; they need not be of value, but only marks of your affection and duty for one who has always been tenderly fond of you. You may bring Lady Chesterfield a little Martin snuff-box of about five louis; and you need bring over no other presents, you and I not wanting *les petits présents pour entretenir l'amitié.*

Since I wrote what goes before, I have talked you over minutely with Lord Albemarle, who told me that he could very sincerely commend you upon every article but one; but upon that one you were often joked, both by him and others. I desired to know what that was; he laughed, and told me it was the article of dress, in which you were exceedingly negligent. Though he laughed, I can assure you

---

[1]A Banker at Paris.

[2]Madame de Curzay was the mother of Madame de Monconseil. A satirical sketch of both is given by Madame du Deffand: 'Je pretendais qu'on avait dans sa cuillère le portrait de Madame de Cursay, et de Madame de Monconseil, de la première en se regardant dans le large, et de la seconde en la prenant de l'autre sens!' (Lettre à H. Walpole, du 23 mars 1777.)—M.

that it is no laughing matter for you; and you will possibly be surprised when I assert (but, upon my word, it is literally true) that to be very well dressed is of much more importance to you, than all the Greek you know will be of these thirty years. Remember, the world is now your only business, and you must adopt its customs and manners, be they silly, or be they not. To neglect your dress, is an affront to all the women you keep company with, as it implies that you do not think them worth that attention which everybody else does; they mind dress, and you will never please them if you neglect yours; and if you do not please the women, you will not please half the men you otherwise might. It is the women who put a young fellow in fashion, even with the men. A young fellow ought to have a certain fund of coquetry, which should make him try all the means of pleasing, as much as any coquette in Europe can do. Old as I am, and little thinking of women, God knows, I am very far from being negligent of my dress; and why?— from conformity to custom; and out of decency to men, who expect that degree of complaisance. I do not, indeed, wear feathers and red heels, which would ill-suit my age; but I take care to have my clothes well made, my wig well combed and powdered, my linen and person extremely clean. I even allow my footmen forty shillings a year extraordinary, that they may be spruce and clean. Your figure especially, which from its stature cannot be very majestic and interesting, should be the more attended to in point of dress; as it cannot be *imposante*, it should be *gentille, aimable, bien mise*. It will not admit of negligence and carelessness.

I believe Mr. Hayes thinks you have slighted him a little of late, since you have got into so much other company. I do not, by any means, blame you for not frequenting his house so much as you did at first, before you had got into so many other houses, more entertaining and more instructing than his; on the contrary, you do very well; however, as he was extremely civil to you, take care to be so to him, and make up in manner what you omit in matter. See him, dine with him before you come away, and ask his commands for England.

Your triangular seal is done, and I have given it to an English gentleman, who sets out in a week for Paris, and who will deliver it to Sir John Lambert for you.

I cannot conclude this letter without returning again to the showish, the ornamental, the shining parts of your character; which, if you neglect, upon my word you will render the solid ones absolutely useless; nay, such is the present turn of the world, that some valuable qualities are even ridiculous, if not accompanied by the genteeler accomplishments. Plainness, simplicity, and Quakerism, either in dress or manners, will by no means do; they must both be laced and embroidered; speaking or writing sense, without elegancy and turn, will be very little persuasive; and the best figure in the world, without air and address, will be very ineffectual. Some pedants may have told you, that sound sense and learning stand in need of no ornaments; and, to support that assertion, elegantly quote the vulgar proverb, that *good wine needs no bush*; but surely the little experience you have already had of the world, must have convinced you that the contrary of that assertion is true. All those accomplishments are now in your power; think of them, and of them only. I hope you frequent La Foire St. Laurent,[1] which I see is now open; you will improve more by going there with your mistress, than by staying at home and reading Euclid with your geometry master. Adieu, *Divertisse₹-vous, il n'y a rien de tel.*

[1] The *Foire St. Laurent* was held every summer at Paris, near the Church of St. Laurent. As at our own Mayfair and Bartholomew Fair, plays were acted: Le Sage contributed many pieces.

No. 1787
To his Son
(*Stanhope CCLXIV*)

Greenwich, 15 *July O.S.* 1751

My Dear Friend,

As this is the last, or the last letter but one, that I think I shall write before I have the pleasure of seeing you here, it may not be amiss to prepare you a little for our interview, and for the time we shall pass together. Before kings and princes meet, ministers on each side adjust the important points of precedence, arm-chairs,[1] right hand and left, etc., so that they know previously what they are to expect, what they have to trust to; and it is right they should; for they commonly envy or hate, but most certainly distrust each other. We shall meet upon very different terms; we want no such preliminaries; you know my tenderness, I know your affection. My only object, therefore, is to make your short stay with me as useful as I can to you; and yours, I hope, is to co-operate with me. Whether, by making it wholesome, I shall make it pleasant to you, I am not sure. Emetics and cathartics I shall not administer, because I am sure you do not want them; but for alteratives you must expect a great many; and I can tell you, that I have a number of *nostrums*, which I shall communicate to nobody but yourself. To speak without a metaphor, I shall endeavour to assist your youth with all the experience that I have purchased, at the price of seven-and-fifty years. In order to this, frequent reproofs, corrections, and admonitions will be

[1] These questions of arm-chairs in visits of ceremony were at this period frequently and warmly debated, especially in the Germanic empire. The Memoirs of the Margravine of Bareith give an account of several such, as, for instance, at Frankfort in 1741: 'Comme il n'y avait point d'exemple qu'une fille de roi et une impératrice se fussent trouvées ensemble, je ne savais point les prétensions que je devais exercer.' She held a conference with two Prussian ministers of state on this most important subject. 'Ils furent d'avis l'un et l'autre que je ne pouvais prétendre le fauteuil, mais que cependant ils insisteraient pour me le faire obtenir!' —*Mem.* vol. ii. p. 344.—M.

necessary; but then, I promise you, that they shall be in a gentle, friendly, and secret manner; they shall not put you out of countenance in company, nor out of humour when we are alone. I do not expect, that, at nineteen, you should have that knowledge of the world, those manners, that dexterity, which few people have at nine-and-twenty. But I will endeavour to give them you; and I am sure you will endeavour to learn them, as far as your youth, my experience, and the time we shall pass together will allow. You may have many inaccuracies (and to be sure you have, for who has not at your age?), which few people will tell you of, and some nobody can tell you of but myself. You may possibly have others too, which eyes less interested, and less vigilant than mine, do not discover; all those you shall hear of, from one whose tenderness for you will excite his curiosity, and sharpen his penetration. The smallest inattention, or error in manners, the minutest inelegancy of diction, the least awkwardness in your dress and carriage, will not escape my observation, nor pass without amicable correction. Two of the most intimate friends in the world can freely tell each other their faults, and even their crimes; but cannot possibly tell each other of certain little weaknesses, awkwardness, and blindnesses of self-love; to authorize that unreserved freedom, the relation between us is absolutely necessary. For example, I had a very worthy friend, with whom I was intimate enough to tell him his faults; he had but few; I told him of them, he took it kindly of me, and corrected them. But then, he had some weaknesses that I could never tell him of directly, and which he was so little sensible of himself, that hints of them were lost upon him. He had a scrag neck, of about a yard long; notwithstanding which, bags being in fashion, truly he would wear one to his wig, and did so; but never behind him, for, upon every motion of his head, his bag came forwards over one shoulder or the other. He took it into his head too, that he must, occasionally, dance minuets, because other people did; and he did so, not only extremely ill, but so awkward, so disjointed, so slim, so meagre, was his figure, that, had he danced as well as ever Marcel did, it would have been ridiculous in him to have danced at all. I hinted these things to him as plainly as friendship would allow, and to no purpose; but to have told him the whole, so as to cure him, I must have been his father, which, thank God, I am not. As fathers commonly go, it is seldom a misfortune to be fatherless; and, considering the general run of sons, as seldom a misfortune to be childless. You and I form, I believe, an exception to that rule; for, I am persuaded, that we would neither of us change our relation, were it in our power. You will, I both hope and believe, be not only the comfort, but the pride of my age; and, I am sure, I will be the support, the friend, the guide of your youth. Trust me without reserve; I will advise you without private interest, or secret envy. Mr. Harte will do so too; but still there may be some little things proper for you to know, and necessary for you to correct, which even his friendship would not let him tell you of so freely as I should; and some of which he may possibly not be so good a judge of as I am, not having lived so much in the great world.

One principal topic of our conversation will be, not only the purity, but the elegancy of the English language, in both which you are very deficient. Another will be the constitution of this country, which I believe you know less of than of most other countries in Europe. Manners, attentions, and address will also be the frequent subjects of our lectures; and whatever I know of that important and necessary art, the art of pleasing, I will unreservedly communicate to you. Dress too (which, as things are, I can logically prove requires some attention) will not always escape our notice. Thus, my lectures will be more various, and in some respects more useful than Professor Mascow's; and therefore, I can tell you, that I expect to be paid for them; but, as possibly you would not care to part with your ready money, and as I do not think that it would be quite handsome in me to accept it, I will compound for the payment, and take it in attention and practice.

Pray remember to part with all your friends, acquaintances, and mistresses (if you have any) at Paris, in such a manner as may make them not only willing, but impatient to see you there again. Assure them of your desire of returning to them; and do it in a manner that they may think you in earnest, that is, *avec onction et une espèce d'attendrissement*. All people say pretty nearly the same things upon those occasions; it is the manner only that makes the difference, and that difference is great.

Avoid, however, as much as you can charging yourself with commissions in your return from hence to Paris; I know by experience that they are exceedingly troublesome, commonly expensive, and very seldom satisfactory at last to the persons who give them; some you cannot refuse, to people to whom you are obliged, and would oblige in your turn; but as to common fiddle-faddle commissions, you may excuse yourself from them with truth, by saying that you are to return to Paris through Flanders, and see all those great towns; which I intend you shall do, and stay a week or ten days at Brussels.

Adieu! A good journey to you, if this is my last; if not, I can repeat again what I shall wish constantly.[1]

No. 1788

To Solomon Dayrolles, Esq.

(*Maty II. lxi*)

DEAR DAYROLLES,   *London, 31 July O.S.* 1751

I most heartily wish you and Mrs. Dayrolles joy,[2] and I believe you have had it. May it continue long! I came to

[1]Philip Stanhope stayed in England until 15th November, and then returned to Paris as *attaché* to Lord Albemarle's embassy.

[2]Dayrolles m. on 4th July, Christabella, daughter of Col. Peterson.

town this morning on purpose to make my compliments to you both, but you were gone to shady groves. I hope you will take those of Greenwich in their turn, and the sooner the better.

En ceci
La femme est comprise aussi.

Lady Chesterfield would have come, to have waited upon Mrs. Dayrolles, but was prevented by a great cold. Adieu!

No. 1789

À Madame la Marquise de Monconseil

(*Maty I. lxi*)

À Blackheath, ce 1 août V.S. 1751

J'ai doublement regretté votre silence, Madame, n'en sachant que trop la cause, dont votre élève m'avait instruit, et, je lui rends justice, avec tout l'intérêt que la plus vive reconnaissance de vos bontés devait lui donner. Il m'avait appris la maladie de Madame votre mère,[1] par conséquent vos justes alarmes: je vous assurerais aussi des miennes, si je ne vous en croyais pas très persuadée. Les liens du sang ne sont pas toujours les liens de l'amitié: mais l'amitié fondée sur un mérite, une estime, une confiance réciproques, devient plus vive, et plus tendre, quand elle est resserrée par les liens du sang. C'était bien votre cas, et comme vous sentez plus délicatement que toute autre tout ce que vous devez sentir, j'ai bien jugé de votre douleur, avant que d'en avoir été informé par vous-même, par la dernière lettre dont vous m'avez honoré; c'est ce qui m'a empêché de vous écrire plutôt. Vous étiez trop occupée pour un commerce ordinaire, et je trouve qu'il n'y a rien de plus frivole, de plus importun, et même de plus impertinent, que des lettres con-solatoires, quand les chagrins sont réels. Elles ne se trouvent

[1]Madame de Curzay.—See letter to his son of 8th July.

placées, à mon avis, qu'entre deux personnes, dont l'une veut faire parade de son esprit, et l'autre de sa douleur. Me prouvera-t-on que je ne dois pas m'affliger des malheurs ou de la mort d'une personne que j'aime? Qui me prouverait cela prouverait trop, et même je n'y gagnerais rien; car alors, par une conséquence nécessaire, je ne dois pas prendre part à leur plaisir, leur santé, et leur bonheur. Qui est insensible à l'un, le sera à l'autre; c'est sur le principe opposé, que je partage actuellement avec vous la joie que vous ressentez de la convalescence, je ne dis pas d'une mère, mais d'une amie si chère. Ayez aussi la bonté, Madame, de l'en assurer de ma part, avec mes très humbles respects.

J'attends votre élève ici en huit jours, mais comme il n'est votre élève que de huit mois, je m'attends à trouver encore l'édition assez imparfaite, et c'est pour l'examiner, la revoir, et la corriger, que je le fais venir pour six semaines, ou deux mois, tout au plus. A cet âge, il y a ordinairement de certains défauts, dont la correction est uniquement du ressort de l'autorité; la simple amitié peut plus facilement reprocher un crime qu'une faiblesse. *Vous êtes criminel,* se dit fort bien, d'une certaine façon, d'ami à ami; mais, *vous êtes gauche, impoli, maussade, ou fat,* ne se dit, et ne se peut dire, que par une autorité décidée d'un côté, à une dépendance reconnue de l'autre; tant la vanité de l'esprit est plus sensible que la vertu du cœur. Du côté du cœur, je me flatte, car on m'en assure, que je n'aurai pas beaucoup à faire; mais quant à l'extérieur, aux manières, aux attentions, et quelques millions de certains petits riens, qui par leur nombre deviennent objet, je crains que j'aurai bien de la besogne. L'accueil que votre protection et vos soins lui ont procuré à Paris, lui aura fait accroire, ou bien qu'il n'y avait rien à changer pour le mieux, ou du moins qu'il n'était point nécessaire. C'est de quoi je le désabuserai parfaitement dans nos entretiens ensemble, en cas que vous nous en donniez le loisir; car, vu le ton sur lequel il est monté dans ses lettres sur votre sujet, et que c'est un ton dont je prends facilement l'unisson, vous avez toute la mine d'être le principal objet de ces entretiens.

Depuis trois mois, je suis presque toujours ici, où j'ai plus joui de ma nouvelle galerie que de mon jardin, ou des charmantes promenades voisines, tant le temps a été mauvais. Cet été a si bien contrefait l'hiver, que, sans le secours du calendrier, on s'y serait trompé. Le peu de fruit que j'ai n'a point de goût, mais heureusement mes ananas, qui, à ce qu'on dit, rassemblent les goûts de tous les fruits, ont bravé le froid, moyennant un bon feu qu'ils tiennent chez eux. Malgré cela, quelques livres, et quelques amis, font couler le temps assez doucement, et c'est tout ce que je demande; je ne prétends plus en jouir.

Je vois souvent notre ami Bolingbroke, mais je le vois avec bien du chagrin. Une humeur à la joue, qu'il a eue depuis longtemps, s'est dernièrement déclarée cancéreuse, et fait de grands progrès depuis peu.[1] Jusqu'ici cela ne lui a pas causé de douleur, et c'est tout ce qu'il demande, car pour le reste, il a pris son parti. En vérité un esprit comme le sien, si fort au-dessus du commun, méritait bien que la nature eût aussi fait un effort en sa faveur, du côté du corps, et lui eût donné une santé et une durée extraordinaires.

No. 1790

To Major Irwine (at Dublin)

(In the possession of Mrs. Reynolds-Peyton)

Sir,   *Blackheath,* 1 *September* 1751

Should you ever be miserable enough to want my assistance, or I unexpectedly happy enough to be able to give you any, your commands will want no preamble to introduce, nor excuses to attend them. My friendship and esteem for you will sufficiently incline, though your situation will not sufficiently enable, me to serve you. Lord

[1]He died on 15th December.

Albemarle is too good a courtier, and I too bad a one, for us to have met more than once, since his return to England. I have twice endeavoured to see him, but to no purpose, since you desired me to speak to him; but I will persevere till I do; not that I think I can be of any use to you there, but that you may not think that I would omit the least possible occasion of being so. If Lord George Sackville is sincerely in your interest, your affair will certainly do, as he has not only a great deal to say with his father, but as he is the Duke of Cumberland's military man of confidence in Ireland. I heartily wish that you could get to be Lieutenant-Colonel to your father's regiment, because with that rank, at your age, the rest would do itself. And if you can get the consent of the Government, I would advise you not to haggle with Pearce about the price, but to make him a *pont d'or* to go out upon.

My young man has been with me here this fortnight, and in most respects I am very well satisfied with him; his knowledge is sound and extensive, and, by all that I have yet observed, his heart is what I could wish it. But for his air and manners, Paris has still a great deal left to do. He stoops excessively, which I have known *some very pretty* fellows do; though he dances very well; and as to manners, the easy and genteel turn *d'un honnête homme* is yet very much wanting. I shall carry him with me in a fortnight to Bath for the season, where I shall rub him till his re-exportation to Paris, which will be the first week in November, for near a year more. I hardly flatter myself with the hopes of seeing you at Bath this season; nor indeed would I advise you to leave Ireland till your affair is decided one way or another. The observation, *que les absents ont toujours tort*, is in general true; and in your case, would be particularly true with regard to a certain General whom I know.

I am extremely obliged to you for your kindness to your Lieutenant Heathcote, in which I think I have some share, though I hope and believe that he deserves it personally.

1778

I will end this abruptly, rather than employ the common words to assure you of the uncommon esteem and friendship with which I am

Your most faithful humble servant.

P.S.—Pray make my compliments to the Primate,[1] and to the house of Clements.

No. 1791

TO LORD HUNTINGDON

(Steuart 15)

MY DEAR LORD,   *London,* 16 *September O.S.* 1751

People commonly pay in some way or other for their partialities, and you shall pay a shilling for yours to me; it is I am sure to some partial expressions of yours that I singly owe the distinction of Monsieur Duclos's present, and letter, and the enclosed acknowledgment to him for both I must desire you to pay for, and deliver to him, not knowing how to direct it myself. I really value him as a man, and admire him as an author. He thinks strongly and with freedom; his mind is not enslaved with his body, and I think I see in his last book a sturdy honesty, which I prefer to the fashionable *gentillesses* which the French complain so much of the want of. They say that he is obscure; I do not think him so, and I believe he is only thought so, because he is so much deeper than those superficial authors to which they are of late so much accustomed, and whose studied phrases only skim the surface.

The opinion you give me in your former letter of the French authors whom you have been reading in your *retirement* flatters and confirms mine, which I am now proud of saying has long been exactly the same. If we consider the age of Lewis the Fourteenth impartially, and free from that classical enthusiasm which we adopt so early, and conse-

[1] Dr. George Stone, Archbishop of Armagh from 1746 to 1765. Chesterfield had been instrumental in his elevation.

quently cherish so long, we shall find it in no respect (except the epic) inferior to the Augustan age, and in the dramatic infinitely superior.

I set out to-morrow morning for Bath, not so much for the recovery as for the preservation of my health, which I will willingly compound to have neither better nor worse than it is at present. I wish it better, but with my constitution and at my age, cannot expect that it will; but the fear that it may be worse is much better grounded, and that fear carries me to Bath. This advantage you receive from it, that being in the hurry to-day, which every man is in who is to take a journey to-morrow, my letter will be shorter and consequently less tedious, may be less impertinent too than usual. Adieu then for this time, my dear Lord, and believe me with the most inviolable attachment, yours

Postscript.—Forgive me this word; remember your favourite *Titus.*

No. 1792

To Solomon Dayrolles, Esq.

(Mahon III. 435)

Dear Dayrolles, Bath, 5 October O.S. 1751

I am heartily glad to find that you nicked your passage to Holland so well, for a day or two later it would have been a bad one; I mean for Madame Dayrolles, *car pour vous, vous avez le pied marin,* and moreover are Minister to the Master of the Seas.

I have been here now just three weeks, though I have drank these waters but a fortnight, upon account of a most confounded cold, which I got at my first arrival. However I find *du mieux,* as Rodrigue happily expresses himself in his gazettes,[1] and I expect a thorough vamp, before I leave this place, which I shall do just time enough to exhibit a brown suit with a very rich gold button, at the birthday.[2]

[1]Of Cologne. [2]30th October O.S.

1780

The Bentinck faction rules without rivals at your Court
at the Hague; I wish them joy of the profit they may make
of their administration, but in conscience I cannot congratulate them upon the honour they acquire by it. Every
common newspaper shows that there is no government at
all; the people even are convinced of it, and do not think of
obeying it; a thing that never happens in any country,
except where the people know themselves to be stronger
than the Government; in that case the Government is never
respected, and consequently useless.

I am astonished at Slingelandt's being displeased, that I
did not answer, or rather reply to, his letter, for mine was an
answer to his. He tells me an anecdote, a fact which I dare
say is a very true one; well, what answer is to be made to it?
None that I know of, unless I had laid hold of that opportunity to have kept up a regular correspondence with him,
and to say the truth, my literary correspondence is already
more extensive than my eyes, my head, or my laziness, will
admit of.

I am glad of the accounts you give me of my Baron and
Duncan, both of whom I love; and pray tell them so. I will
write to the former soon, though this is not a place from
whence I can write him a letter to his mind. Here I neither
inquire, nor know anything of the busy world. I hardly
read a newspaper. Thank God, I am safe and quiet on shore;
and as I do not intend to put to sea again, why should I study
navigation any more? I read here a great deal, but then it is
partly for my own amusement, and partly for the improvement of my little friend, who is with me. In that way he
labours most willingly, and is even for more of it than I
desire to give him. But what I labour at most, and find the
most difficulty in, is, to give him *les manières, la politesse, et
la tournure,* of a man of fashion. He thinks knowledge is all;
there I differ from him, and endeavour to convince him that,
without manners and address, it is very useless. However,
I gain ground, and he is already very different from what

you saw him. He makes his compliments to you and Madame Dayrolles. Pray make mine to her too; and tell her that, time out of mind, there has always been, *un vieux Dayrolles, et un jeune Dayrolles*, and that, as you cannot now claim the latter appellation, it is incumbent upon her to make us a *jeune Dayrolles, dans la fabrique duquel je la prie très instamment de mettre beaucoup du sien.*

Before you leave the Hague, pray remember to beg or steal for me some melon-seed of the largest and best Cantelupes. The older it is the better. *Adieu, mon cher enfant.*

I am, with the truest affection,

Yours.

No. 1793

À Madame la Marquise de Monconseil

(*Maty I. lxii*)

À Bath, ce 7 octobre V.S. 1751

J'ai attendu le retour de votre élève, et ambassadeur, pour faire de ma réponse à votre dernière une lettre de récréance pour lui. Il est vrai que j'ai attendu bien plus longtemps que je ne comptais, ma santé m'ayant obligé d'avoir recours aux eaux de Bath, qui l'ont rétablie, autant que mon chétif tempérament gâté le leur a permis. La joie que j'ai sentie de la convalescence de Madame votre mère, n'a pas nui à la mienne; car elle était très sincère, et il n'y a rien de plus sain que la joie, surtout pour moi, quand vous y avez tant de part.

Je vous l'avouerai, votre petit ambassadeur à son premier abord me frappa furieusement, non par les grâces qui l'accompagnaient, mais par son air, et ses manières. Je ne comprends pas encore où il les avait pêchés. Je m'appliquai d'abord à le décrotter, et je crois que vous trouverez que je n'y ai pas mal réussi, quoique je convienne qu'il lui reste encore bien du chemin à faire, pour être ce que nous voudrions qu'il fût. Il se tient mieux, il se présente mieux, il ne frétille plus tant des pieds, et il s'est corrigé de plusieurs de ces manières gracieuses qu'il avait apprises à l'école, et qu'il avait cultivées depuis, sous les soins des ours, qu'il avait eu le malheur de rencontrer dans ses voyages. Ce qui me donne de l'espérance, c'est qu'il sent à présent ce qui lui manque, et qu'il me demande instamment de vous supplier de vouloir le revoir, et le corriger de ses moindres défauts, pour en faire, s'il se peut, une édition parfaite. Je souscris volontiers à sa requête, et je vous conjure de ne lui rien passer; non seulement il prendra en bonne part les réprimandes ou le ridicule que vous lui donnerez, mais il vous en saura gré. Il pense sur votre sujet comme il doit, et par conséquent il est convaincu que vous ne pouvez penser que juste sur le sien. Si après cela, malgré tous nos soins, le beau vernis lui manque, il n'y a d'autre parti à prendre qui de le placer chez Martin![1] Il aura l'honneur de vous présenter de ma part deux babioles de porcelaine de la manufacture d'ici; ayez la bonté, Madame, de les accepter, non pas comme un présent, car ils ne prétendent pas l'être, mais comme une redevance. Le Saint Père accepte bien une jument, que le Roi de Naples lui envoye tous les ans, quoique le bon homme n'en ait que faire, ou, en cas de besoin, en trouverait d'aussi bonnes chez lui; mais c'est qu'il la regarde comme une marque de la fidélité, et de la soumission de ce monarque au Saint Siège; et pourtant soyez persuadée que le Roi des Deux Siciles n'est pas plus zélé Papiste, que je ne vous suis attaché.

Voulez-vous laisser retourner Madame d'Hervey ou non, ou est-ce qu'elle ne veut pas s'en retourner? Par ses lettres, je la soupçonne d'un arrangement avec notre Maréchal; il n'y est question que de lui, elle est à tous moments à—— et pour mieux cacher son jeu, elle affiche des sentiments d'amitié et d'attachement pour la Maréchale; enfin, si

[1]The inventor of a beautiful varnish at Paris.—M.

1783

quelque chose manque à cet arrangement, ce n'est sûrement pas la bonne volonté. Je languis doublement pour son retour, car si elle ne revient pas, à qui parlerai-je de vous, quand votre élève sera parti? et il faut pourtant que j'en parle, fut-ce aux roseaux.

No. 1794

To Solomon Dayrolles, Esq.

(Mahon III. 439)

London, 28 October O.S. 1751

DEAR DAYROLLES,

I arrived here but last night from Bath, which journey delayed till now my answer to your last. I have brought with me from Bath a stock of health, which, with my economy, will, I think, last me for a year, and I pretend now to no more. Formerly I was foolish enough to think of no more than *au jour la journée*; and now I am wise enough to expect no more than *de l'an à l'année*.

I am very glad that all was so quiet in Holland, upon an event so little expected as the death of the Prince of Orange. Various conjectures and deep political refinements will be made upon the probable consequences of it; you shall have mine for nothing. *Or sus donc.* In my mind, the whole will depend upon the conduct of the *Gouvernante*.[1] If that be moderate, gentle, and economical, this event will secure and fix the Stadtholder-form of government more effectually than the life of the Prince of Orange could have done. A minority is not a time for enterprises, nor for the extension of power; and the people the most jealous of their liberties are lulled by the very name of it into a security, if no imprudent step be taken to rouse their fears and awaken their jealousies. In the mean time, those who, having had the greatest share in the former Republican Government, were

[1]The Princess Dowager of Orange.

the most uneasy at the alteration of it, if not provoked, will not disturb, and will insensibly grow used, and to some degree reconciled, to the present form, if gently and moderately administered. Many or most of these will be dead, by the time that the young Stadtholder comes to be of age; and the growing generation, who will be of age with him, will have seen, nor known no other kind of government, and will naturally look up to a young prince. As for the herd of the people, a minor is always the object of their compassion, and consequently of their love. In these circumstances, her Royal Highness may, if she pleases, fix and settle her son's future government upon a more solid foundation than his father could have done. But if, on the contrary, spirit, which always means heat and fury, should be the word, and the active and busy administration of your Catherines and Marys of Medicis, your Annes of Austria, etc., should prove the model of your *Gouvernante*, that conduct which very near destroyed them in an absolute government, will ruin her and her family irretrievably in a free one.

Now I have shot my bolt, to another point. I send you inclosed the best supplement I can think of to your valedictory letter; by which, as you will find, I leave the preceding paragraph entire as it was, and add to it, as by way of recollection, the exclamation relative to the present state of affairs. If you should think it too rhetorical and declamatory, you may easily whittle it down to more simplicity; but as those pieces are always known to be laboured and studied, if flourishes are proper anywhere, I think they are so upon those formal occasions. But in all events, I insist upon your having the whole looked over and corrected by Chais, or some other person more used to write and to correct than I am. *A propos*, you will soon have occasion to deliver it, for the Duke of Newcastle told me this morning that Mr. Yorke would go to the Hague in a few days; and that, in a few days after his arrival there, you would receive your orders to go to Brussels.

Creighton gave me your melon-seed, for which I thank you.

. . . .

Creighton tells me, moreover, that Mrs. Dayrolles eats but little, and is sick after eating that little. Pray, with my compliments to her, ask her from me, what she takes to be the cause of that disorder.

I have no news to send you from hence; I have been too few hours in town to know any, and am moreover too indifferent to ask for any.

By a little *brochure*, which my Baron has sent me, and which I take to be written under, at least, the inspection of the King of Prussia, it appears to me that some changes are intended to be made in the form of government of Sweden. If so, that may produce some northern squabbles, though I think they will be carried on rather by the pen than the sword. For I see very many good reasons why both Russia and the King of Prussia should rather scold than fight. But if they should come to blows, I foretell that Russia will have the better on't.

Pray make my compliments to my Baron; and tell him that I will soon send him a long and uninteresting letter: my waters, my journey, and my unsettled state for these last two months have hindered me from doing it sooner. This is already too long, so good night to you.   Yours.

No. 1795
À M. le Baron de Kreuningen[1]
(*Mahon III. 442*)

À Londres, ce 3 novembre V.S. 1751

Me voici, mon cher Baron, dans mon quartier d'hiver, revenu de Bath, radoubé, me portant bien, et s'il est possible, plus que jamais votre fidèle ami et serviteur.

---

[1] P. A. de Huybert, Baron van Kruiningen (1693-1780), referred to by Chesterfield as 'my Baron,' was sheriff of Muiden from 1717-39. His daughter married Robert Trevor.

Votre dernière feuille Sibylline que j'ai soigneusement
gardé du vent, accompagnait deux petites brochures dont
l'une fait faire des réflexions; je veux dire celle sur les
affaires de la Suède. Je la crois écrite par les ordres, si non
de la main, du Roi de Prusse. Il parait vouloir sonder le
gué pour voir jusqu'où les États de Suède pourraient faire
quelque changement dans la forme présente de leur
gouvernement, sans que la Reine ou quelque autre puissance
en put prendre l'alarme, ou même le prétendre. Car en
vérité c'est trop ridicule de dire qu'un État indépendant ne
peut pas changer la forme de son gouvernement quand il le
juge à propos. Et s'il ne le peut pas, il ne faut plus l'appeler
un royaume libre, mais une province conquise par cette
puissance qui est en droit de lui imposer une telle loi.
L'autre brochure, c'est-à-dire, la lettre de Monsieur D'Agen,
est une pièce fausse et scandaleuse.

. . . .

L'évènement imprévu de la mort du Prince d'Orange doit
bien exercer les politiques chez vous; et il est sûr que vous
êtes dans une espèce de crise. Si votre gouvernement suit
des conseils doux et modérés, voici l'occasion de rétablir vos
finances, et de remettre l'ordre. Mais si au contraire votre
Gouvernante (comme je ne l'espère pas) se prête à la
fougue, aux emportements, aux fureurs, enfin aux proscriptions de certaines cervelles brûlées que je connais chez vous,
je ne dirai pas les suites que j'en crains; elles ne sont que trop
claires. Mais comme elle a réellement beaucoup de bon sens,
et comme elle a été assez longtemps chez vous pour connaître le génie de la république, je suis persuadé qu'elle se
conduira fort sagement. *Mon patron*[1] dont vous jouissez à
présent, mais pour peu de temps, vous aura dit tout ce qui
se passe ici, mieux que je ne le pourrais faire. Il est au fait de
tout, il hante les grands, et il est le fidèle dépositaire de tous
leurs secrets. Il va s'escrimer en politique à Bruxelles contre
Monsieur le Marquis de Botta d'Adorno,[2] et vous n'avez

[1]A friendly nickname for Mr. Dayrolles.   [2]Now Imperial Minister at Brussels.

qu'à lui dire quelle barrière et quel tarif vous souhaitez, et il vous les donnera. Que-dites vous de sa femme? N'est-elle pas belle? Elle l'est sûrement et indépendamment de la comparaison d'une moitié à l'autre. Mon dit patron n'a pu vous porter un autre paquet de mauvais livres que je vous avais destiné, n'ayant plus de place dans son équipage, mais je n'attends qu'une occasion favorable de vous l'envoyer, enrichi et augmenté même de quelques autres, qui ont paru depuis. Au reste, ne vous attendez pas à l'esprit; nous n'en avons plus ici, le sens commun devient même assez rare. Chaque pays a son époque d'esprit, et de bon goût; la France a eu la sienne, nous avons eu la nôtre, nous dégringolons tous deux, que sait-on si quelque jour l'Allemagne n'aura pas aussi la sienne?

Un de mes amis, homme d'esprit, pour ce temps-ci, s'entend, a traduit, ou pour mieux dire a imité, la pièce de *Cénie* de Madame de Graffigny. Il en a fait comme de raison une tragédie, et il a substitué à la place de la suivante, qui y jouait un rôle trop important, un nouveau caractère plus convenable, et plus lié au sujet. Enfin, selon moi, il a très judicieusement corrigé tous les défauts de l'original. Il ne l'a pas encore donné au théâtre, mais dès qu'elle sera imprimée je vous l'enverrai.

Votre santé, mon cher Baron, comment va-t-elle? Il me semble que votre Tronchin fait plus le philosophe que le médecin. Pour moi j'aime un *médecin tant mieux*, et qui me donne des remèdes pour me rendre encore mieux. Car pour les consolations philosophiques, elles ne tiennent point contre les maux réels. Je ne connais que deux sortes de maux: le mal physique, et le mal moral: tout le reste n'est que dans l'imagination; que je sois seulement exempt de ces deux et alors

Tristitiam et metus
Tradam protervis in Mare Creticum
Portare ventis.[1]

Adieu, mon cher Baron. Adieu!

1788 [1]Horace, *Odes*, I. 26.

No. 1796

À Madame du Boccage

(*Maty I. xciv*)

MADAME,　　　　　*À Londres, ce 7 novembre V.S.* 1751

Mon pupille s'en retourne à Paris, pour vous faire sa cour; permettez qu'il vous porte mon hommage. Je ne vous offre pas cette lettre en payement de celle dont vous m'avez honoré. Que Voltaire réponde, s'il le peut, à de telles lettres que votre dernière; il me suffit d'en connaître le prix. Vous m'y parlez, Madame, de mon buste; oui, faites-le parler comme vous faites parler les quatre que j'ai eu l'honneur de vous envoyer, et il passera à Dieppe par le premier bon vent. A ce titre-là ces illustres morts me feraient un accueil gracieux; à l'exception de Pope, que malheureusement m'a trop bien connu pour prendre le change, mais qui comme ami peut-être ne me trahirait pas. Voici pourtant ce que je trouverais encore mieux: promettez de me faire parler moi-même, comme vous les avez fait parler, c'est-à-dire, comme vous parlez vous-même, et vous me verrez un beau matin, non en buste, mais en personne dans la rue de la Sourdière;[1] acceptez plutôt ce dernier parti, il ne vous coûterait guères, et j'y gagnerais infiniment.

Nous n'avons plus d'esprit ici, ou nous en sommes tous pleins, comme *le Menteur*[2] de vérités, car il n'en sort point. Notre Parnasse n'a point depuis longtemps produit des fleurs, mais bien des chardons et des épines, que certains animaux qui s'ébaudissent au bas de cette montagne, dévorent avec avidité; je n'ai garde de vous en envoyer. Un homme de ma connaissance, qui n'est pas mauvais poète,[3] travaille actuellement à une traduction de *Cénie*, ou

[1]The house of Madame du Boccage at Paris.

[2]An allusion to the two lines in Corneille's *Le Menteur:*
　　　　'Vous avez tout le corps bien plein de vérités,
　　　　Il n'en sort jamais une.'

[3]The Rev. Philip Francis, known as the translator of Horace and as the father of Sir Philip.—M.　See Note on p. 1836.

plutôt à une imitation: il en fait, comme de raison une tragédie; il substitue à la place de la suivante un caractère plus intéressant, et plus lié avec le principal sujet. Je trouve ces changements judicieux; et parce qu'il m'en a montré, j'augure très bien du reste: quand il paraîtra, j'aurai l'honneur de vous l'envoyer.

J'apprends que Duclos va donner un nouveau roman. J'en suis bien aise, il écrit avec force, et est dégagé de préjugés plus même qu'il n'ose l'avouer. Ayez la bonté d'assurer Monsieur du Boccage que je l'estime et que je l'honore infiniment; j'espère que la goutte l'a quitté. Je ne finirais point, si je vous détaillais ce que Mesdames de Chesterfield, Cleland, Montagu, et Milady Allen voudraient que je vous disse de leur part, encore moins si je vous exprimais les sentiments d'admiration et de respect, avec lesquels j'ai l'honneur d'être.

Madame, etc.

No. 1797

TO SOLOMON DAYROLLES, ESQ.

(Mahon III. 446)

DEAR DAYROLLES,   *London, 15 November O.S.* 1751

I have received yours of the 19th N.S. for which this is only an acknowledgment, but no equivalent. All the news of yesterday, such as speech, addresses, etc., you will have authentically from the office; and I have nothing to add to it, but that Lord Coventry,[1] who moved the address in our House, did it well enough, though agitated at the same time, by the two strong passions of fear and love, Miss Gunning[2]

[1] George William, sixth Earl of Coventry.

[2] "The two Miss Gunnings are twenty times more the subject of conversation than the two brothers (Pelham) or Lord Granville. These are two Irish girls of no fortune, who are declared the handsomest women alive. I think their being two so handsome and such perfect figures is their chief excellence, for singly I have seen much handsomer women than either; however, they can't walk in the Park or go to Vauxhall but such crowds follow that they are generally driven away.' (H. Walpole to Mann, 18th June 1751.)—M.

being seated on one side of him, and the House on the other.
Her mother told Lord Granville, who sat next to her, that
she was glad for her daughter's sake, that my Lord had got
so well through it, for that the poor girl was ready to faint
away. That affair is now within a few days of its crisis, but
whether that will be marriage or settlement is undecided;
most people think the latter, for my part I rather believe the
former.

Sans vanité, as people commonly say, when they say a
vain thing, I am of my Baron's opinion, and think it would
not be the worse for *la Gouvernante*, if she pursued the
measures which I mentioned in my last. I would not give
her just the advice which Lord Clarendon was accused of
having given King Charles II at his restoration, not to mind
his friends, but to gain his enemies. But I would advise her
to think rather more of gaining over reasonable enemies
than of gratifying unreasonable friends; she is extremely ill
at this Court, and Lord Holderness complains much of the
reception she gave him. It is apprehended here that she will
not continue in the hands we wish; were that the worst I
should see no great harm in it, for I know them to be too
rough and too heavy for the present delicate situation of her
affairs. She should not think of governing by a faction,
which they are, and a very small one too, of which I take
Sacrelier to be the head and the poor Greffier to be the tail.
But she should consult indiscriminately the ablest and the
most respectable people of the several provinces upon the
single principle of the public good, and without adopting
their provincial piques and prejudices. She should take off
all proscriptions, and mitigate all that military stuff of
councils of war with unlimited powers down to the mere
necessary discipline of an army. Private and public economy
should be her great objects; and if she would act firmly upon
such principles she would not want our advice, but I believe would do a great deal better without it. I would not
desire a finer part to act than she has; and, were I in her case,

1791

I would undertake to fix the present form of government upon a more solid foundation than it has been upon since the time of William I. She has parts enough to do all this, if passion did not interfere; for she has undoubtedly the best parts of the whole.

Lord Holderness's baggage is not yet arrived, consequently I have not yet received my Baron's bill of fare, but by a little specimen of it, which he sent me lately in a specimen of a letter, I believe I shall not be able to furnish him with some of the rarities that he desires; for he composes these bills of fare upon the advertisements in the newspapers, and the pastry cooks have been beforehand with him at this season of minced pies. He is now pastorally inclined, and has wrote to me for some particular pastorals, which to this hour I am very sure no gentlemen ever heard of or read.

My boy set out this morning for Paris, improved a good deal, in my mind, *du côté des manières*. Lord Albemarle has promised to employ him in his *bureau* as much as if he were *Secrétaire de Légation*, and if he does, it will be just as well as if he were, the salary excepted, which I do not much mind. But whether this promise will be verified or not, *considering some things which you and I know*, is not so certain. In all events, he has time enough before him; and, if Paris will not do, some other place, some time or other, will. Make my compliments to Madame Dayrolles, and tell her that declining to answer my questions is a full answer to them.[1]

Adieu. Yours.

[1]'Mrs. Dayrolles does not choose to send your Lordship an answer to your question. At first she imagined the pains in her stomach proceeded from eating raw apples, but now she is glad there is no forbidden fruit in the case.' (Mr. Dayrolles to Lord Chesterfield, 19th November N.S. 1731. Original MS.)—M.